VOLUME
4

PERSPECTIVES
AND REALITIES

REPORT
OF THE ROYAL COMMISSION
ON ABORIGINAL PEOPLES

Canadian Cataloguing in Publication Data

Canada. Royal Commission on Aboriginal Peoples.
Report of the Royal Commission on Aboriginal Peoples.

Issued also in French under the title:
Rapport de la Commission royale sur les peuples autochtones.

Contents:
v. 1. Looking forward, looking back –
v. 2. Restructuring the relationship –
v. 3. Gathering strength –
v. 4. Perspectives and realities –
v. 5. Renewal: a twenty-year commitment
ISBN 0-660-16413-2 (V. 1);
ISBN 0-660-16414-0 (V. 2);
ISBN 0-660-16415-9 (V. 3);
ISBN 0-660-16416-7 (V. 4);
ISBN 0-660-16417-5 (V. 5).
Cat. no. Z1-1991/1-1E (V. 1);
Cat. no. Z1-1991/1-2E (V. 2);
Cat. no. Z1-1991/1-3E (V. 3);
Cat. no. Z1-1991/1-4E (V. 4);
Cat. no. Z1-1991/1-5E (V. 5).

1. Native peoples – Canada.
2. Native peoples – Canada – Social conditions.
3. Native peoples – Canada – Economic conditions.
4. Native peoples – Canada – Politics and government.
I. Title.

E78.C2R46 1996   971'.00497   C96-980078-9

Available in Canada through
your local bookseller
or by mail from
Canada Communication Group – Publishing
Ottawa, Canada K1A 0S9

Cat. no. Z1-1991/1-4E
ISBN 0-660-16416-7

Cover: Jane Ash-Poitras, "Buffalo Hierophany", 1992, mixed media,
105.5 cm x 75.5 cm, framed.
Endpapers: Mireille Siouï, "Dans la maison d'Handiaouich, la petite tortue",
intaglio, watercolour on paper, 50 x 32.5 centimetres.
Both, collection of the Indian Art Centre, Department of Indian Affairs
and Northern Development. Photographer, Lawrence Cook.
Photograph facing page 1: Fred Cattroll.
Photograph of Louis Riel facing page 199: National Archives of Canada, Neg. no. C6688.

Canada	Groupe
Communication	Communication
Group	Canada
Publishing	Édition

VOLUME

4

PERSPECTIVES
AND REALITIES

CONTENTS

5 ◼ Métis Perspectives   199

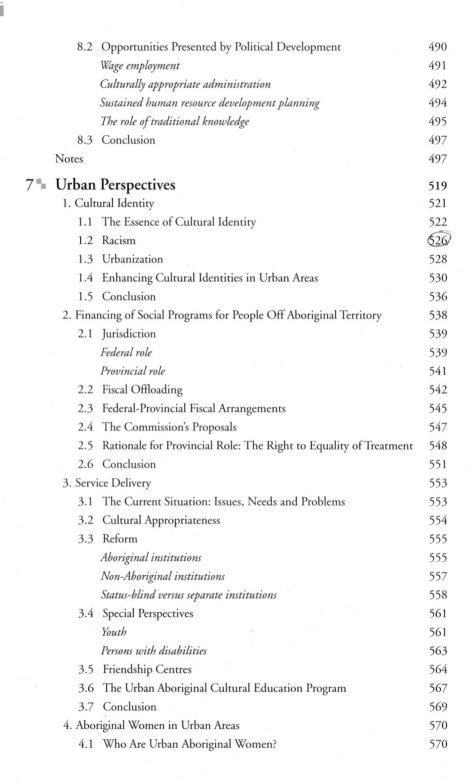

A Note About Sources

Among the sources referred to in this report, readers will find mention of testimony given at the Commission's public hearings; briefs and submissions to the Commission; submissions from groups and organizations funded through the Intervener Participation Program; research studies conducted under the auspices of the Commission's research program; reports on the national round tables on Aboriginal issues organized by the Commission; and commentaries, special reports and research studies published by the Commission during its mandate. After the Commission completes its work, this information will be available in various forms from a number of sources.

This report, the published commentaries and special reports, published research studies, round table reports, and other publications released during the Commission's mandate will be available in Canada through local booksellers or by mail from

> Canada Communication Group – Publishing
> Ottawa, Ontario
> K1A 0S9

A CD-ROM will be published following this report. It will contain the report, transcripts of the Commission's hearings and round tables, overviews of the four rounds of hearings, previously published research studies, the round table reports, and the Commission's special reports and commentaries, together with a resource guide for educators. The CD-ROM will be available in libraries across the country through the government's depository services program and for purchase from

> Canada Communication Group – Publishing
> Ottawa, Ontario
> K1A 0S9

Briefs and submissions to the Commission, as well as research studies not published in book or CD-ROM form, will be housed in the National Archives of Canada after the Commission completes its work.

A Note About Terminology

The Commission uses the term *Aboriginal people* to refer to the indigenous inhabitants of Canada when we want to refer in a general manner to Inuit and to First Nations and Métis people, without regard to their separate origins and identities.

The term *Aboriginal peoples* refers to organic political and cultural entities that stem historically from the original peoples of North America, not to collections of individuals united by so-called 'racial' characteristics. The term includes the Indian, Inuit and Métis peoples of Canada (see section 35(2) of the *Constitution Act, 1982*).

Aboriginal people (in the singular) means the individuals belonging to the political and cultural entities known as Aboriginal peoples.

The term *Aboriginal nations* overlaps with the term Aboriginal peoples but also has a more specific usage. The Commission's use of the term nation is discussed in some detail in Volume 2, Chapter 3, where it is defined as a sizeable body of Aboriginal people with a shared sense of national identity that constitutes the predominant population in a certain territory or collection of territories.

The Commission distinguishes between local communities and nations. We use terms such as *a First Nation community* and *a Métis community* to refer to a relatively small group of Aboriginal people residing in a single locality and forming part of a larger Aboriginal nation or people. Despite the name, a First Nation community would not normally constitute an Aboriginal nation in the sense just defined. Rather, most (but not all) Aboriginal nations are composed of a number of communities.

Our use of the term *Métis* is consistent with our conception of Aboriginal peoples as described above. We refer to Métis as distinct Aboriginal peoples whose early ancestors were of mixed heritage (First Nations, or Inuit in the case of the Labrador Métis, and European) and who associate themselves with a culture that is distinctly Métis. The more specific term *Métis Nation* is used to refer to Métis people who identify themselves as a nation with historical roots in the Canadian west. Our use of the terms Métis and Métis Nation is discussed in some detail in Chapter 5 of this volume.

Following accepted practice and as a general rule, the term *Inuit* replaces the term *Eskimo*. As well, the term *First Nation* replaces the term *Indian*. However, where the subject under discussion is a specific historical or contemporary nation, we use the name of that nation (for example, Mi'kmaq, Dene, Mohawk). Often more than one spelling is considered acceptable for these nations. We try to use the name preferred by particular nations or communities, many of which now use their traditional names. Where necessary, we add the more familiar or generic name in parentheses – for example, Siksika (Blackfoot).

Terms such as Eskimo and Indian continue to be used in at least three contexts:

1. where such terms are used in quotations from other sources;
2. where Indian or Eskimo is the term used in legislation or policy and hence in discussions concerning such legislation or policy (for example, the *Indian Act*, the Eskimo Loan Fund); and
3. where the term continues to be used to describe different categories of persons in statistical tables and related discussions, usually involving data from Statistics Canada or the Department of Indian Affairs and Northern Development (for example, status Indians, registered Indians).

1

INTRODUCTION

We have something they do not know about – we have our teachings, our value systems, our attitudes, our clan systems and on and
on and on....Let's educate them.

Right now, they think they do not want to know about us. They
look at us in a mystical way. They think we worship smoke. They think
we are in a dream world. They fund us so they can continue to look
at us as unreal. They educated us to a point where we almost forgot
who we are. Now it is time we educate them, people to people.

We are different. We have a different perspective on life and all
creation. We have many wonderful things to share. We have different and wonderful teachings to share that are simple to live by, reasonable, sensible, for the good of all within the community, full of
respect. These have remained a mystery to mankind until now.

Merle Assance-Beedie
Orillia, Ontario
14 May 1993

ONE OF THE KEYS to understanding the goals and aspirations of Aboriginal peoples in Canada is recognizing their diversity. Aboriginal people do not constitute a monolithic entity, speaking with one voice through one designated leader.
The term is broad, embracing a variety of cultural traditions and social experience. There are differences not only between First Nations, Inuit and Métis
people but also among First Nations.

Beyond the cultural distinctions, Aboriginal people of the various nations
have differing experiences of life in this country. There are those born and
raised in remote or isolated communities, living according to the traditions of
their forebears. Others live in the heart of Canada's largest cities, surrounded by

a multitude of cultural influences. Our hearings showed that Aboriginal youth have different priorities from those of Aboriginal elders and Aboriginal women. The fact that priorities differ does not necessarily mean there is conflict among these groups. Rather, each experience of life in Canada gives rise to a different set of issues and concerns, problems and solutions.

Our mandate was written with this diversity in mind. Our terms of reference instruct us to look at the position and role of Aboriginal women under existing social conditions and legal arrangements and in the future; the position and role of Aboriginal elders; the situation of Aboriginal youth; the constitutional and legal position of Métis people and First Nations people living off-reserve; and the difficulties specific to Aboriginal people who live in the North. Our task was also to study and make concrete recommendations to improve the quality of life for Aboriginal people living in cities.

In this volume, our goal is to give voice to the diversity of Aboriginal peoples and the diversity of the Aboriginal experience in Canada. We do this by highlighting their various perspectives and by showing how the issues identified in our mandate appear from these perspectives.

By 'perspective' we mean the way individuals see themselves in relation to the world around them and the issues that come to matter to those individuals. A perspective provides a particular insight into the relative importance of things, shaped by experience. It is a world view and, as such, transcends single, specific issues. A perspective provides the framework through which an individual approaches all issues.

The perspectives we identify come from careful listening to the many people who spoke to us. The distinct voices that emerge are those of Aboriginal women, elders, youth, Métis people, people living in the North, and Aboriginal people living in urban areas. The careful reader will realize that, even within these perspectives, there is diversity of opinion. Groups are made up of individuals, and individuals do not always agree. Where there is a range of opinion, we try to provide the spectrum. Our task here is to answer these questions: What matters most to this group? Why does it matter? And what should be done to address these concerns?

We are not simply regrouping issues and recommendations from preceding volumes. Our intent is to provide another dimension to the issues. Where appropriate, we direct readers to other chapters or volumes for a more detailed discussion of specific issues. In all chapters in this volume, the major themes arise from what was said at the hearings, what emerged from the briefs we received from groups and individuals across the country, and what our research program revealed. Where appropriate, we offer recommendations.

1. WOMEN'S PERSPECTIVES

We have been told by Aboriginal people that all things – creation, life – begin with women. All the issues mentioned in our terms of reference have a fundamental impact on women, and women are involved in all the perspectives identified here. We place their perspective at the beginning of this volume.

The concerns of Aboriginal women are an integral part of our approach to every area of our mandate and thus can be found throughout our report and other Commission documents. Here we focus specifically on issues of importance raised by Aboriginal women and the problems and the solutions they identified. The need for healing is a recurring theme for Aboriginal women. Healing will bring about the full inclusion of Aboriginal women in all areas of Aboriginal society. For many Aboriginal women and, indeed, for many Aboriginal people, healing is a necessary first step in rebuilding their nations.

2. Elders' Perspectives

The elders represent another way of seeing the world. Their perspective and their understanding of Canada have much to contribute to discussions of future relationships in this country.

Elders in Aboriginal communities are those recognized and respected for knowing, living and teaching the traditional knowledge. They see the world through the eyes of the ancestors and interpret the contemporary world through lessons passed down through generations. Their wisdom is transferred to young people who seek their teachings. The elders are a living bridge between the past and the present. They also provide a vision for the future, a vision grounded in tradition and informed by the experience of living on the land, safeguarding and disseminating knowledge gained over centuries.

Elders have much to contribute in the quest for self-determination and a better relationship among all Canadians. They are educators in the broadest sense of the word. In all areas of our mandate – from health to education, from justice to lands and resources – there is a place for the elders.

The elders are willing to share if we are willing to listen. We hope to do justice to their words.

3. Youth Perspectives

Aboriginal youth are in the unique position of coping with the legacies of a colonial past while keeping a hopeful eye on the future – their future.

More than half of all Aboriginal people in Canada are under the age of 25. Our recommendations are forward-looking, often intended for the long term. It is youth who will take the necessary steps to renew the relationship between Canada's Aboriginal and non-Aboriginal people. At present, their circumstances give cause for concern – too many youth are dropping out of school, attempting and committing suicide, abusing substances. These youth must struggle to find a place for themselves as Aboriginal people in the modern world. Some have been victims of physical, sexual or psychological abuse; all have experienced the effects of systemic racism. We have been told of instances where the youth of a community have tried to take the initiative, only to find themselves excluded in the development of decisions that directly affect their lives.

But youth have demonstrated incredible resilience in the face of these obstacles. They have sustained their hope and their drive to ensure a better future for themselves and their communities.

More and more young people are gaining a strong sense of pride as Aboriginal people. They want to learn their peoples' traditional values, beliefs and practices and to have a say in their future. They tell us that programs and initiatives developed for them without their input have not worked and never will. Aboriginal youth are looking for empowerment, and in many ways, they are beginning to empower themselves.

4. Métis Perspectives

There are profound and persistent misunderstandings about Métis people, mis-understandings that extend to both the identity of Métis people and their rights as Aboriginal people. In some cases, they have even been subject to misunder-standing or rejection by other Aboriginal people.

We believe that in presenting Métis perspectives we can contribute to greater public awareness and understanding of Métis people and their aspirations. Their life experience in Canada, politically and socially, is markedly different from that of First Nations and Inuit. Their rights, ignored and abused for gen-erations, are in urgent need of recognition and restoration.

As one of the Aboriginal peoples of Canada, Métis people want to be rec-ognized as having their own unique cultural and political traditions. They are seek-ing nation-to-nation relationships with Canada. As with other Aboriginal peoples, land and self-determination are central issues. Métis people are seeking to build their own institutions and organizations based on the foundation of their culture.

5. Northern Perspectives

The North is a unique area of Canada – not just geographically but politically and socially as well – as a region where Aboriginal people often constitute a majority. Across the North, Aboriginal people make up a large enough propor-tion of the population to exert a strong political influence.

Apart from a few scattered wage employment centres, Aboriginal ways of earning a living, of making decisions and of using the environment have influ-enced the non-Aboriginal people who have come to the North. Together, Aboriginal and non-Aboriginal northerners have developed distinctive forms of governance based on Aboriginal and European traditions. They face distinct eco-nomic and environmental challenges. In our chapter on the North, we explain what is different about northern Canada and offer some recommendations concerning the challenges unique to northern Aboriginal peoples.

We address specific issues of concern to Inuit. All their communities are in the North, yet Inuit also live beyond Canadian borders. They are part of a larger circumpolar population, with relations in Russia, Alaska and Greenland. They are people of the North, an area that has shaped their culture and perspective.

In some instances, Inuit share the same struggles confronting all Aboriginal peoples in Canada. But their historical relationship with Canada is different from that of First Nations and Métis peoples, giving rise to their own unique issues. Too often policies developed to meet the needs of other Aboriginal peoples have been applied to Inuit, sometimes with devastating consequences. Inuit are involved in major political developments in northern Canada, such as the creation of the new territory of Nunavut in the eastern Northwest Territories, Nunavik in northern Quebec, and the implementation of self-government for the Inuvialuit in the western Arctic. Inuit wish to move forward without losing sight of the past, of their history, language and culture.

For some, the North is merely a matter of geography. We have found that it is also a distinct social, political and cultural terrain.

6. Urban Perspectives

The migration of Aboriginal people to urban centres is a relatively recent phenomenon. Today, about half of all Aboriginal people live in cities or towns. The urbanization of Aboriginal people raises significant policy issues. Yet the issues of rural, band-based First Nations have dominated the public debate and allocation of financial resources since the beginning of relations between Aboriginal and non-Aboriginal governments.

Some urban Aboriginal people feel caught between two worlds. They are physically and socially removed from their Aboriginal communities and unrecognized in their urban neighbourhoods. The issues confronting urban Aboriginal people – governance, access to culturally appropriate services, cultural identity and intercultural relationships – have been woefully neglected by Canadian governments and Aboriginal authorities in the past.

Many Aboriginal people in urban areas want to live in a way that allows them to understand and express their culture. In the chapter on urban perspectives, we focus on the most pressing issues facing urban Aboriginal people and offer recommendations to address these concerns.

We hope this volume will give non-Aboriginal readers an appreciation and understanding of the diversity of Aboriginal perspectives and experience in Canada. We want to make it clear why we are a royal commission on Aboriginal 'peoples', not Aboriginal 'people'. Recognizing this plurality is the first step toward understanding who Aboriginal peoples are and what their visions are for the future.

We hope Aboriginal readers will see something of themselves reflected in these pages, that they will hear echoes of the voices of brothers and sisters, grandmothers and grandfathers, and, equally important, that voices will emerge that they had not heard before, voices of those who have travelled different paths.

Aboriginal people told the Commission that all of us – Aboriginal and non-Aboriginal – can learn from one another. We must bridge the gap between peoples of different nations and different traditions, using the building blocks of understanding, empathy and respect. With this volume, we hope to create a foundation of understanding upon which to renew that relationship.

2

WOMEN'S PERSPECTIVES

> Our people will not heal and rise toward becoming self governing and strong people both in spirit and vision until the women rise and give direction and support to our leaders. That time is now, the women are now actively participating in insuring the empowerment of their people. Life is a daily struggle as women, as mothers, as sisters, as aunties and grandmothers. We are responsible for the children of today and those of tomorrow. It is with pure kindness and our respect for life that allows us to gladly take up this responsibility to nurture the children, to teach of what we know, from what we have learned through trial and error.[1]

WITH THESE WORDS, Nongom Ikkwe, an Aboriginal women's organization in Manitoba, opened its submission to the Commission. It was a message we heard in many different ways from Aboriginal women across the country.

Our terms of reference directed us to examine the position and role of Aboriginal women at present and in the future. The perspectives of First Nations, Inuit and Métis women concerning the various elements of the Commission's mandate are reflected throughout our report. But the best way to present the concerns of Aboriginal women is to let them speak directly in their own words. Where appropriate, we make recommendations to address these concerns.

The experience of Aboriginal women was described to us in compelling detail. In their words we saw their sadness, desperation, anger and pain, but we also saw their strength, courage, wisdom and hope. Throughout history, Aboriginal women have made many adjustments to cope with the circumstances facing them, and they continue to do so today.

Women were highly respected in many traditional Aboriginal societies; their thoughts and views were sought before decisions affecting the community were made.

> The historical relationships and responsibilities of women in Iroquois/Mohawk society are quite significant, particularly within traditional political culture. During the formation of the Five Nations Confederacy, a woman was the first person to accept the Peacemaker's message of peace and unity. This woman was given the name Jikonsahseh, the 'Mother of Nations', by the Peacemaker, who explained that all women would have an important role in this peace.[2]

This is not to say that Aboriginal women enjoyed prominent roles in all pre-contact societies. For example, we note that decisions among Inuit concerned mainly hunting and fishing. Leadership was organized but not institutionalized. Decisions were most often made by consensus, with one individual (usually a man) putting the group decision into action.[3]

With the onset of colonization, the position and role of Aboriginal women were undermined by imported ideas and values that displaced and devalued them:

> Before colonization, Aboriginal peoples had social and political organizations with distinct social classes, which ranged from simpler structures to highly complex systems of social order, social control in governments. Every individual filled a particular role and had a specific purpose within the community; life unfolded with much harmony. Since European contact, our traditions, dignity and self-respect have been systematically taken away from us.
>
> Joyce Courchene
> Indigenous Women's Collective of Manitoba
> Winnipeg, Manitoba, 3 June 1993*

The imposition of the *Indian Act* over the last 120 years, for example, is viewed by many First Nations women as immensely destructive. Residential schools and relocations subjected Aboriginal communities to such drastic changes in their way of life that their culture suffered immeasurable damage. In Volume 1, particularly Chapters 8 to 13, we examined these areas of federal policy and action. In this volume, we focus on their impact on Aboriginal women.

We begin with a brief demographic overview. Of the total Aboriginal population of 811,400, an estimated 51 per cent (414,100) are women.[4] As of 1991, women outnumbered men in each of the Aboriginal groups except Inuit.

---

* Transcripts of the Commission's hearings are cited with the speaker's name and affiliation, if any, and the location and date of the hearing. See *A Note About Sources* at the beginning of this volume for information about transcripts and other Commission publications.

The female-to-male ratio is higher among Aboriginal people than in the general population of Canada (96.1 versus 97.7 males per 100 females – see Table 2.1). Over time the ratio will become higher for females; that is, Aboriginal women will represent an even greater share of the Aboriginal population and, by the year 2016, even Inuit women will outnumber Inuit men. The reason Inuit men outnumbered Inuit women in the past, particularly in the older age groups, is not well understood. It may have to do with differential mortality patterns experienced by the population at an earlier point in history.

One of the more dramatic demographic changes anticipated in the next 25 years is that Aboriginal women's share of the population, both in the labour force age group and in the older age group (65+), will increase. In particular, the share of Aboriginal women aged 65 and over will more than double by 2016, rising from 1.7 per cent of the Aboriginal population to 3.9 per cent, while the share of men in that age group will reach only 2.8 per cent (Table 2.1).

In 1991, the life expectancy of Aboriginal women (75 years) was seven years longer than that of their male counterparts (67.9 years) but still lagged behind other Canadian women by nearly six years. As shown in Table 2.1, Aboriginal women give birth to more children on average than non-Aboriginal women. Depending on the Aboriginal group, the number of births per woman ranges from 2.1 to 3.4 compared to 1.7 among all Canadian women.

In terms of their geographic distribution, there are fewer First Nations women than men residing on reserves. In non-reserve areas, particularly urban areas, Aboriginal women outnumber men.

Generally, Aboriginal women are better educated than Aboriginal men – for example, more acquire at least some post-secondary schooling (Table 2.2). The proportion of Aboriginal women who obtain a post-secondary degree or certificate, however, is not very different from the proportion of men, perhaps in part because more women have to leave school for family or other reasons.

Even though Aboriginal women tend to be better educated than men, they are no more likely to find jobs (Table 2.3). Their participation rate in the labour force is much lower than Aboriginal men's – 53.4 per cent versus 72.4 per cent. Although there is a smaller percentage of women 15 years and older seeking work, those that do participate in the labour force fare better than men. Their unemployment rate is 21.1 per cent, compared to 27.6 per cent for men. In addition, the percentage of those who are self-employed is half that of Aboriginal men and well below that of all Canadian women. It is not surprising, then, to find that the average annual income of Aboriginal women is about $11,900, compared to $17,400 for Aboriginal men. Aboriginal women are far behind their non-Aboriginal counterparts, for whom the average annual income is about $17,600.

The occupations of Aboriginal women help to explain their low incomes, with nearly 28 per cent in clerical occupations and 26 per cent in the service

Text continues on page 17.

TABLE 2.1
Comparison of Demographic Characteristics, 1991 and 2016

	Total Canadian		Total Aboriginal[1]		Registered NAI		Non-Registered NAI		Métis		Inuit	
Population, 1991	26,999,040		720,600		438,000		112,600		139,400		37,800	
Males per 100 Females	97.7		96.1		96.2		93.4		96.0		104.2	
Age Groups	F	M	F	M	F	M	F	M	F	M	F	M
(% of population, 1991)												
0-14 years	10.3	10.8	18.0	18.5	17.0	17.5	20.6	20.9	18.5	18.8	19.4	22.5
15-64 years	33.9	34.1	31.3	29.0	32.0	29.9	29.7	26.2	31.1	28.8	28.5	27.3
65+ years	6.2	4.7	1.7	1.5	1.9	1.7	1.4	1.2	1.4	1.4	1.1	1.2
Projected Population, 2016[2]	37,119,800		1,093,400		665,600		178,400		199,400		60,300	
Males per 100 Females	98.2		95.5		94.6		97.7		96.2		97.3	
Age Groups	F	M	F	M	F	M	F	M	F	M	F	M
(% of population, 2016)												
0-14 years	8.2	8.6	11.9	12.5	10.4	10.9	17.2	18.1	11.2	10.4	14.9	15.5
15-64 years	33.4	33.9	35.3	33.6	36.6	34.8	30.4	30.0	36.0	35.3	33.2	32.1
65+ years	8.9	7.0	3.9	2.8	4.3	2.9	3.0	2.3	3.7	3.4	2.6	1.8
Life Expectancy at Birth, 1991 (years)	80.9	74.6	75.0	67.9	74.0	66.9	77.9	71.4	76.9	70.4	68.8	57.6

TABLE 2.1 (continued)
Comparison of Demographic Characteristics, 1991 and 2016

	Total Canadian		Total Aboriginal[1]		Registered NAI		Non-Registered NAI		Métis		Inuit	
	F	M	F	M	F	M	F	M	F	M	F	M
Fertility Rate, 1991 (births/woman)[3]	1.7	—	—	—	2.9	—	2.1	—	2.5	—	3.4	—
Location												
(% of population, 1991)												
On-reserve[4]	—	—	47.4	52.6	47.4	52.6	—	—	—	—	—	—
Off-reserve	—	—	52.9	47.1	55.9	44.1	51.7	48.3	51.0	49.0	50.3	49.7
Urban off-reserve	—	—	54.0	46.0	56.1	43.9	52.4	47.6	52.0	48.0	65.2	44.8
Rural off-reserve	—	—	50.6	49.4	55.1	44.9	50.5	49.5	49.2	50.8	48.9	51.1

Notes:

— = not available or not applicable.

NAI = North American Indian.

1. Data based on the adjusted Aboriginal identity population for 1991.

2. Aboriginal population projections for 2016 based on current trends in fertility, mortality and migration.

3. Fertility rate for Aboriginal women aged 15-49 not available.

4. Data not shown for the very small number of non-registered North American Indians, Métis and Inuit who lived on Indian reserves or in settlements in 1991.

Source: Statistics Canada, 1991 Aboriginal Peoples Survey, custom tabulations; Statistics Canada, 1991 Census, catalogue numbers 93-324, 93-326, 93-328 and 93-329; Statistics Canada, 1991 Census, Summary Table, unpublished; Mary Jane Norris, Don Kerr and François Nault, "Projections of the Aboriginal Identity Population in Canada, 1991-2016", research study prepared by Statistics Canada for RCAP (February 1995).

TABLE 2.2
Comparison of Educational Characteristics, 1991

	Total Canadian		Total Aboriginal[4]		Registered NAI		Non-Registered NAI		Métis		Inuit	
	F	M	F	M	F	M	F	M	F	M	F	M
Highest Level of Education												
(% of population aged 15-64)[1]												
Less than grade 9	11.7	11.8	24.9	25.9	28.4	29.4	11.4	13.4	18.2	20.1	48.8	44.2
High school, no certificate	23.0	22.5	31.7	32.5	31.9	33.4	30.6	31.9	32.4	34.2	21.3	18.9
High school certificate	21.9	20.5	12.4	13.3	10.9	10.8	18.1	20.2	13.7	16.1	8.2	9.2
Other non-university[2]	24.8	23.6	22.3	21.8	20.9	20.4	27.5	24.3	24.5	23.2	18.7	25.1
University, no degree	7.9	7.8	5.4	3.9	5.5	4	6.5	5.3	5.4	3.3	—	—
University degree	10.7	13.8	2.9	2.3	2.1	1.6	5.4	4.7	3.7	2.8	—	—
Population that Quit High School	—	—	92,960	83,820	57,515	50,700	11,275	10,050	18,490	17,705	6,190	5,845
(% of population aged 15-49)												
Returned	—	—	28.1	17.9	27.2	17.7	34.6	19.6	33.1	20.8	11.7	10.0
Took equivalency upgrading	—	—	14.4	13.1	15.4	13.5	11.4	13.3	11.9	10.8	17.6	17.5
Major Field of Post-Secondary Study[3]												
(% of population aged 15+)												
Education, recreation, counselling	15.8	5.4	15.3	6.4	16.5	7.4	12.2	5.3	15.2	5.3	20.4	5.2
Fine and applied arts	8.0	3.4	7.8	3.0	6.4	3.0	10.0	2.7	10.1	3.6	-	-
Humanities	7.0	5.2	3.7	2.7	3.6	2.5	4.9	4.0	2.6	2.3	-	-
Social sciences	8.8	8.3	12.5	10.4	13.5	11.2	12.3	9.5	11.4	10.2	-	5.8

TABLE 2.2 (continued)
Comparison of Educational Characteristics, 1991

Major Field of Post-Secondary Study[3]	Total Canadian		Total Aboriginal[4]		Registered NAI		Non-Registered NAI		Métis		Inuit	
	F	M	F	M	F	M	F	M	F	M	F	M
(% of population aged 15+)												
Commerce/management/administration	29.7	15.6	30.9	10.0	30.1	10.8	29.6	9.8	31.6	9.5	41.9	6.9
Agricultural/biological science technology	4.5	4.9	5.7	4.3	4.6	4.7	8.0	3.7	6.3	4.2	6.0	-
Engineering/applied sciences	0.7	6.7	-	1.3	-	1.3	-	1.8	-	1.3	-	-
Engineering/applied science technology/trades	3.5	41.6	6.2	57.1	5.9	54.2	7.8	59.6	6.3	58.0	7.6	70.5
Health science and technology	19.5	4.2	16.6	3.1	18.5	3.3	14.3	2.2	14.5	3.7	12.9	-
Math/physical sciences	2.1	4.3	0.4	1.0	-	0.8	-	1.1	0.9	0.9	-	-

Notes:

— = not available or not applicable.

- = numbers too small to show because of sampling reliability.

NAI = North American Indian.

1. Population no longer attending school.

2. Includes those with and without a non-university post-secondary certificate/diploma.

3. Columns may not add to 100% because of rounding errors and/or suppression of small numbers.

4. Table based on unadjusted data from the Aboriginal Peoples Survey, 1991.

Source: Statistics Canada, 1991 Aboriginal Peoples Survey, custom tabulations; Statistics Canada, 1991 Census, catalogue numbers 93-324, 93-326, 93-328 and 93-329; Statistics Canada, 1991 Census, Summary Table, unpublished; Mary Jane Norris, Don Kerr and François Nault, "Projections of the Aboriginal Identity Population in Canada, 1991-2016", research study prepared by Statistics Canada for RCAP (February 1995).

TABLE 2.3
Comparison of Economic Characteristics, 1991

	Total Canadian		Total Aboriginal[1]		Registered NAI		Non-Registered NAI		Métis		Inuit	
	F	M	F	M	F	M	F	M	F	M	F	M
Labour Force Status												
(% of population aged 15+)[1]												
Unemployment rate	10.2	10.1	21.1	27.6	22.9	32.3	19.1	17.8	16.9	25.5	25.5	25.8
Participation rate	59.9	76.4	53.4	72.4	48.7	67.5	61.7	82.3	59.4	78.6	56.8	70.1
Self-employed	2.9	6.8	1.7	3.6	1.2	2.3	2.9	4.2	2.0	6.0	1.9	4.6
Lack of child care reported as a barrier to employment	—		16.4	4.2	—		—		—		—	
Total Income												
(% of population aged 15+)												
Less than $10,000	36.0	19.7	60.3	47.1	63.1	52.4	53.1	34.9	52.9	42.2	67.8	46.5
$10,000-$19,999	29.5	19.6	23.8	21.6	22.8	22.5	24.5	19.3	27.7	20.1	17.4	22.3
$20,000+	34.5	60.7	15.9	31.3	14.2	25.1	22.2	46.1	16.4	37.7	14.8	31.2
Average total annual income ($)	17,577	30,205	11,897	17,392	11,056	14,968	14,326	22,924	12,598	19,763	11,576	18,381

Notes:

— = not available or not applicable.

NAI = North American Indian.

1. Unemployment and participation rates relate to the Aboriginal population aged 15+ that is out of school.

2. Table based on unadjusted data from the Aboriginal Peoples Survey, 1991.

Source: Statistics Canada, 1991 Aboriginal Peoples Survey, custom tabulations; Statistics Canada, 1991 Census, catalogue numbers 93-324, 93-326, 93-328 and 93-329; Statistics Canada, 1991 Census, Summary Table, unpublished; Mary Jane Norris, Don Kerr and François Nault, "Projections of the Aboriginal Identity Population in Canada, 1991-2016", research study prepared by Statistics Canada for RCAP (February 1995).

TABLE 2.4
Comparison of Occupational Distribution, 1991

	Aboriginal Population[1]		Non-Aboriginal Population[1]	
	Male	Female	Male	Female
	%	%	%	%
Management/administration	6.9	7.6	14.0	10.3
Natural science/engineering/maths	2.5	0.7	5.9	1.8
Social sciences	2.2	7.1	1.6	3.0
Religion	0.2	—	0.3	0.1
Teaching	1.6	6.1	2.9	6.3
Medicine and health	0.8	6.1	2.0	9.1
Arts and literature	1.8	1.5	1.7	1.7
Clerical	5.8	27.9	7.1	31.7
Sales	4.5	5.9	9.1	9.5
Service	11.3	25.6	10.1	15.8
Farming and related	3.7	1.3	4.4	2.1
Fishing/trapping	3.0	0.7	0.5	0.1
Forestry and logging	4.2	0.3	0.9	0.1
Mining and related	1.3	—	0.8	0.0
Processing	3.8	2.0	3.9	1.7
Machinery	2.6	0.3	3.2	0.3
Production/fabrication	6.3	1.8	8.8	3.2
Construction	20.3	0.7	10.3	0.4
Transportation/equipment	6.4	1.3	5.9	0.7
Materials handling	3.1	0.7	2.2	0.8
Other crafts	1.1	0.8	1.5	0.6
Other	6.8	1.5	2.9	0.9

Notes:
— = not available or not applicable.
1. Percentage of the Aboriginal and non-Aboriginal populations aged 15+ in the experienced labour force employed in the occupations listed.

Source: Statistics Canada, 1991 Aboriginal Peoples Survey, custom tabulations; Statistics Canada, 1991 Census, catalogue numbers 93-324, 93-326, 93-328 and 93-329; Statistics Canada, 1991 Census, Summary Table, unpublished; Mary Jane Norris, Don Kerr and François Nault, "Projections of the Aboriginal Identity Population in Canada, 1991-2016", research study prepared by Statistics Canada for RCAP (February 1995).

TABLE 2.5
Receipt of Financial Assistance for Education Purposes, 1991

	Total Canadian		Total Aboriginal[2]		Registered N$_{AI}$		Non-Registered N$_{AI}$		Métis		Inuit	
	F	M	F	M	F	M	F	M	F	M	F	M
Financial Assistance	—	—	14,519	9,250	9,755	4,920	2,565	1,920	3,095	2,215	325	260
(% of total)												
Applied/received	—	—	54.7	57.2	65.2	65.8	26.3	23.3	45.5	42.4	-	-
Applied/did not receive	—	—	7.3	10.9	5.6	9.7	13.4	14.2	9.0	8.0	-	-
Never applied	—	—	32.6	30.4	24.3	20.7	56.3	57.0	38.0	47.1	34.0	57.9
Source of Assistance	—	—	8,495	4,725	6,360	3,235	680	450	1,410	940	175	-
(% of population receiving assistance for post-secondary education)[1]												
DI$_{AND}$/band funding	—	—	61.7	54.6	80.6	78.8	-	-	8.0	-	-	-
Grant/bursary/scholarship	—	—	9.7	14.6	5.4	6.7	25.8	34.5	23.5	31.8	-	-
Student loan	—	—	19.7	21.9	7.9	9.8	63.3	40.3	52.0	50.4	-	-
Other	—	—	19.9	22.8	16.1	14.0	23.2	35.2	33.1	47.4	-	-

Notes:

— = not available or not applicable.

- = numbers too small to show because of sampling reliability.

N$_{AI}$ = North American Indian.

1. May not add to 100%, as individuals may have had more than one source of financial assistance.

2. Table based on unadjusted data from the Aboriginal Peoples Survey, 1991.

Source: Statistics Canada, 1991 Aboriginal Peoples Survey, custom tabulations; Statistics Canada, 1991 Census, catalogue numbers 93-324, 93-326, 93-328 and 93-329; Statistics Canada, 1991 Census, Summary Table, unpublished; Mary Jane Norris, Don Kerr and François Nault, "Projections of the Aboriginal Identity Population in Canada, 1991-2016", research study prepared by Statistics Canada for R$_{CAP}$ (February 1995).

industry (see Table 2.4). On the brighter side, proportionately more Aboriginal women than men hold management or administrative jobs (7.6 per cent versus 6.9 per cent). They also lead in teaching (6.1 per cent versus 1.6 per cent) and in medicine and health-related occupations (6.1 per cent versus 0.8 per cent). In some of these occupations, however, Aboriginal women tend to work in para-professional positions.

It is clear that Aboriginal women engage in skills upgrading. More women than men returned to high school or to equivalency upgrading – 42.5 per cent versus 31 per cent (Table 2.2). Furthermore, of those having completed post-secondary school, nearly three times as many Aboriginal women as men completed schooling in management or administration, and their proportion was on a par with that of Canadian women (30 per cent each, as shown in Table 2.4). Aboriginal women are seeking and receiving financial assistance for schooling in almost the same proportions as men. For status Indians, the main source of funding is the department of Indian affairs or the band, while for other Aboriginal groups it is student loans and other sources (Table 2.5).

Aboriginal women lag behind men and well behind Canadian women as a whole on many social and economic indicators, but statistics do not reveal why. Women themselves provide a deeper understanding of the barriers that have been placed in their path, barriers that must be recognized, acknowledged and removed before real progress can be made. We believe that by going through the process of acknowledging the harm caused by these barriers, individuals, families, communities, nations and governments will be able to work together to eliminate them.

We have stated our belief that the time has come to resolve a fundamental contradiction at the heart of Canada, to restore Aboriginal nations to a place of honour in our shared history, and to recognize their continuing presence as collectives participating in Canadian life. Before Aboriginal and non-Aboriginal people can get on with the work of reconciliation, we must deal with the wounds of the past. Aboriginal women told us about the healing that must occur, and we saw in community after community the leadership being demonstrated by Aboriginal women. When we review the historical position and role of Aboriginal women, we begin to see how certain patterns of exclusion became entrenched. Yet we also see a source of the strength Aboriginal women retain to this day – a commitment and conviction to embrace and pass on their Aboriginal heritage.

1. HISTORICAL POSITION AND ROLE OF ABORIGINAL WOMEN: A BRIEF OVERVIEW

There was, in pre-contact times, a vibrant richness, diversity and complexity to Aboriginal culture and social organization (see Volume 1, Chapter 3). Aboriginal societies in North America evolved over thousands of years, interacting with their respective physical and social environments. These centuries of separate development led to belief systems, cultures and forms of social organization that differed substantially from European patterns.

The position and role of Aboriginal women varied among the diverse nations. Some historical literature suggests that Aboriginal women were either ignored or seen as having roles ancillary to those of men. These records are problematic because they were generally written by non-Aboriginal men – fur traders, explorers, missionaries and the like. Regrettably, the views of Aboriginal women were often not recorded.[5] What was observed by European settlers was the power Aboriginal women enjoyed in the areas of family life and marriage, politics and decision making, and the ceremonial life of their people. It has been noted that the Jesuits, steeped in a culture of patriarchy, complained about the lack of male control over Aboriginal women and set out to change that relationship.[6]

A conversation between Skonaganleh:rá (Sylvia Maracle) and Osennontion (Marlyn Kane) reveals their understanding of Aboriginal women's roles and responsibilities and provides some insight into what happened to change things:

> *S.* In our community, the woman was defined as nourisher, and the man, protector, and as protector, he had the role of helper. He only reacted: she acted. She was responsible for the establishment of all the norms – whether they were political, economic, social or spiritual....

> *O.* She did not have to compete with her partner in the running of the home and the caring of the family. She had her specific responsibilities to creation which were different, but certainly no less important, than his. In fact, if anything, with the gifts given her, woman was perhaps *more* important....

> *S.* Woman has had a traditional role as Centre, maintaining the fire – the fire which is at the centre of our beliefs. She is the Keeper of the Culture. She has been able to play that role even in a home divided....She has maintained her role despite intermarriage which caused her to be cut off from her roots, both legislatively and sometimes physically....Her home is divided as a result of....I don't know how many more ways you can divide her house and she'll continue to maintain that fire – *but she will!*

> *O.* In addition to all the responsibilities already talked about, perhaps the most daunting for woman, is her responsibility for the men – how they conduct themselves, how they behave, how they treat her. She has to remind them of *their* responsibilities and she has to know when and how to correct them when they stray from those. At the beginning, when the 'others' first came here, we held our rightful positions in our societies, and held the respect due us by the men, because that's the way things were then, when we were following our ways. At that

time, the European woman was considered an appendage to her husband, his possession. Contact with that...and the imposition of his ways on our people, resulted in our being assimilated into those ways. We forgot our women's responsibilities and the men forgot theirs.[7]

These views are supported by Winona Stevenson, who suggests that "the deconstruction of our colonization will shed considerable light on why our communities are so troubled today and why Aboriginal women are at the bottom of Canada's socio-economic ladder....[O]ur re-education will serve to bring more people home, to encourage our youth and lost ones to safely reconnect with their pasts and communities." She concludes, "Once our beliefs become founded on more secure bases, individual confidence, self-esteem and pride will grow."[8]

During our public hearings, Aboriginal women spoke of a time when these systems and forms of social organization were strong:

> We believe that true Aboriginal government must reflect the values which our pre-contact governments were based upon. We point out that, according to traditional teachings, the lodge is divided equally between women and men, and that every member has equal if different rights and responsibilities within the lodge. Historically, the lodge was a political as well as a spiritual centre of our societies. In the context of political theory, there was no division between church and state. The lodge governed our relationship with each other, with other nations, and with the Creator and all of Creation.
>
> Marilyn Fontaine
> Aboriginal Women's Unity Coalition
> Winnipeg, Manitoba, 23 April 1992

Inuit women remembered what it was like:

> When I was a young girl, people used to work together, together in communities. My father at that time, he was the Chief Elder and he was responsible for the communities and for their well-being...in regard to hunting, hunting caribou, fishing and helping older people. Right now it is very difficult. A different life that we are facing today. [translation]
>
> Elder Silpa Edmunds
> Winnipeg, Manitoba
> 21 April 1992

There is agreement that women were traditionally responsible for decisions about children, food preparation and the running of the camp. While clear divisions of labour along gender lines existed, women's and men's work was equally valued. If a woman was a sloppy sewer, her husband might freeze; a man who was a poor hunter would have a hungry family. Everyone in the camp worked hard and everyone had a specific role based on their age, gender and capabilities.

Martha Flaherty, President
Pauktuutit (Inuit Women's Association of Canada)
Ottawa, Ontario, 2 November 1993

Until 40 years ago, most Inuit lived among extended families in small camps. Hunting, fishing and gathering provided food for the family, and furs were exchanged for tea and other goods. During the 1950s and early '60s, Inuit were obliged, for the first time, to send their children to school.[9] The population in newly established settlements grew as families left the camps to join their children.[10] One Inuit woman recalls how life changed for her and her family:

> The details of our stories may be different, but a lot of the experiences are the same. My mother talks about how it was for people on the land – I talk more about the people who are the adults in the community right now....When I got into school, everything changed for me all at once. My parents didn't have a say any more in the way my life went. When I came in off the land, the people with any type of authority were Qallunaat [non-Aboriginal]. The teachers were Qallunaat, the principals were Qallunaat, the nurses were Qallunaat, the RCMP were Qallunaat, the administrators were Qallunaat....They acted like our parents but they weren't our parents. It seemed to us at the time that the administrators...and whoever else was in authority were talking above our heads, talking about our welfare and not letting us have a say about it. They treated us like we belonged to them, not to our parents. We didn't have a say and our parents and grandparents didn't have a say....They taught us a new culture, a different culture from our own, they taught us that we have to live like the white people. We had to become like the white people.[11]

A research study conducted for Pauktuutit describes what happened when Inuit families moved to the settlements and draws a connection between the breakdown of traditional sex roles and the rise of spousal assault as a social problem:

> [Inuit] females seemed to adapt more easily to the new life. Today they are more likely than men to complete their high school education, to obtain and hold jobs – and less likely to develop problems with alcohol, drugs and crime. Now the roles in a wage-employment consumer economy are reversed, and the women, especially the younger women, are more likely to be the major providers for their families. This may constitute the central, underlying reason for the alarming rates of spousal assault that plague northern communities: men feel threatened by their loss of status and identity, by the

increased power and identity of women – to restore their sense of balance of power, men hit the women.[12]

As we have shown throughout this report, Aboriginal people see evidence of profound injustice in many aspects of government policy. Aboriginal women told us that the damaging effects of these policies are still at work today.

2. REVERSING A PATTERN OF EXCLUSION – WOMEN'S PRIORITIES FOR CHANGE

Aboriginal women appearing before the Commission represented every facet of society. We observed that many are active in social, cultural, economic and political matters. Some hold prominent positions in regional, national and international Aboriginal political organizations, economic development corporations, educational institutions, student organizations, health care agencies and women's organizations. Many are employed as directors of friendship centres and cultural centres, as teachers, managers of businesses and social workers, as counsellors at women's shelters, in treatment centres, child care centres and seniors' facilities, as directors of band and tribal council portfolios, and as community health representatives. They are First Nations, Inuit and Métis women living in urban and rural communities. They come from all age groups.

It is clear that despite such diverse cultural backgrounds and places of residence, there are many commonalities among Aboriginal women, the greatest of which is an overriding concern for the well-being of themselves, their children, extended families, communities and nations. Their common vision is of a future in which the values of kindness, honesty, sharing and respect are a part of everyday life.

It is also clear that the women who appeared before us are determined to effect change in their current life situations. They told us that their priorities for change are

1. the *Indian Act* and the impact of the Bill C-31 amendments;
2. health and social services that are culturally appropriate, with a priority focus on healing;
3. the vulnerability of women and children to violence; and
4. accountability and fairness in self-government.

3. ABORIGINAL WOMEN AND INDIAN POLICY: EVOLUTION AND IMPACT

The *Indian Act* and the 1985 amendments in Bill C-31 were recurring topics in presentations by Aboriginal women to the Commission. The policies they embody were cited as particularly damaging to Aboriginal peoples and to the role of women in Aboriginal communities. Many feel that the obstacles confronting them today have their roots in these policies.

We presented a detailed analysis of the evolution of government policy, as implemented through the *Indian Act*, and its impact on the social and political cohesion of First Nations in Volume 1, Chapter 9. Here we examine the development of federal legislation to show how certain sexist notions evolved into fundamental principles underlying Indian policy. Readers are encouraged to turn to the earlier chapter for a more in-depth analysis of the development of Indian policy and the *Indian Act*.

> I shall always be Native no matter where on the face of this earth, let alone this continent, I live. All I ask for myself and other Native women is to be granted the respect we have lost over the document entitled the *Indian Act*.
>
> Pauline Lewis
> Eskasoni, Nova Scotia, 6 May 1992

> It is necessary to begin by recalling that for a century, as a result of the enactment of the *Indian Act*, which purely and simply legalized discrimination, an Aboriginal woman who married a non-Aboriginal was driven out of her community, cut off from her family and deprived of her status and some of the rights pertaining thereto. [translation]
>
> Philo Desterres
> Quebec Native Women's Association
> Montreal, Quebec, 21 May 1993

The subjective sense of belonging implied by membership in an Aboriginal nation is well expressed in the following passage from *The Road*, an analysis of the evolution of tribal self-government in the United States:

> Indian tribes are a common mental experience and natural fact for most Indians. Birth into a family, a territory, a spiritual world, and a race is a fact, but it is less significant than the mental experience that tribal people share. The essence of this mental experience is a world view – a warm, deep and lasting communal bond among all things in nature in a common vision of their proper relationship. This consciousness cements a collective culture that has proved resilient in modern society. Among members of the community it assumes the form of an interpersonal spiritual communion which has never been and may never be destroyed by outside forces. It continues to be the center of the tribal circle – the foundation of the whispering ideology of tribalism in this land.[13]

Membership was thus a function of the sense of belonging, the "common mental experience", and was determined by each nation on the basis of age-old principles derived from its own traditions of recognition, acceptance and kinship. In some cases, membership was confined largely to those who were born or married into the Aboriginal nation in question. In others, such as that of the Haudenosaunee, wholesale adoptions of entire groups of people were permitted. In all cases, questions of membership were for the Aboriginal nation itself to decide. There was no externally imposed definition of who could identify with and belong to a particular people or nation.

Canadian law changed all that, beginning in the historical period of displacement and assimilation. Many of the laws from this period are still operative.

Many Aboriginal people told the Commission that government policies and legislation designed to undermine their collective sense of identity have chipped away at their right to be self-governing, self-determining peoples. From this perspective, following the end of the historical stage we have described as contact and co-operation, Aboriginal peoples have been distinctly disadvantaged. If we accept this – and in the face of irrefutable evidence, we do – then Aboriginal women must be considered doubly disadvantaged.

The colonial and post-Confederation legislation applied to Aboriginal people finds its conceptual origins in Victorian ideas of race and patriarchy. Its effect has been increasingly to marginalize women in Aboriginal society and to diminish their social and political roles in community life. For example, after 1876 and the passage of the *Indian Act*, Indian women were denied the right to vote in band elections or to participate in reserve land-surrender decisions, and, where their husbands died without leaving a will, they were required to be 'of good moral character' in order to receive any of their husband's property.

An Indian woman could not even control her own cultural identity because it came to depend increasingly on the identity of her husband. A woman who married a man without Indian status lost her own status. Despite having been born into an Indian community, upon 'marrying out' she was no longer considered an Indian in the eyes of the government or the law. The children of such a marriage would not be recognized as Indian either. But a non-Indian woman who married a man with Indian status immediately became an Indian, as did any children of that marriage. A double standard was at work.

The issue of identity under the *Indian Act* has been and continues to be a source of personal pain and frustration for Indian women. Through its restrictive and sexist definition of 'Indian' and the selective application of the involuntary enfranchisement provisions, the *Indian Act* has created a legal fiction as to cultural identity. This has profoundly affected the rights of women of Indian ancestry, denying these rights entirely in the case of the thousands of women and their descendants who were subject, against their will, to loss of status and enfranchisement and to subsequent removal from their home communities because they married men without Indian status. Categories of aboriginality have been created through Canadian law as though Aboriginal identity and the rights that go with that identity could be chopped and channelled into ever more specific compartments or, in some cases, excised completely.

Thus, aboriginality has been broken down for purposes of colonial and later federal policy into the categories of Métis, Inuit and Indian, with the latter further broken down into status and non-status Indians. Even within the status category, there are 'new status' and 'old status' Indians, on-reserve and off-reserve status Indians, subsection 6(1) status Indians and subsection 6(2) status Indians, and on and on. Each new category brings with it different rights and risks. These categories have little to do with culture, upbringing or identity and everything to do with administration, bureaucracy and an apparently continuing federal policy of assimilation that persists to this day.

The *Indian Act* was conceived and implemented in part as an overt attack on Indian nationhood and individual identity, a conscious and sustained attempt by non-Aboriginal missionaries, politicians and bureaucrats – albeit at times well intentioned – to impose rules to determine who is and is not 'Indian'. A woman's view of herself as an Indian and the views of Indian nations about the identity of their citizens were not factors in the equation.

In these and many other ways, the *Indian Act* undermined Aboriginal rights, Aboriginal identity and Aboriginal culture. It created divisions within peoples and communities that fester to this day. The grand chief of the Assembly of First Nations, Ovide Mercredi, described the legacy of the act thus:

> What is especially hurtful about the *Indian Act* is that while we did not make it, nor have we ever consented to it, it has served to divide our peoples. We sometimes buy into *Indian Act* definitions and categories in our own assessment of people and politics. This is part of the legacy of colonialism. When Parliament tried to correct its mistakes in 1985, it exacerbated them instead. What else could be expected of a law imposed on us by the federal government?[14]

For many Aboriginal women, the *Indian Act* is a monument to the history of discriminatory federal policy. Thus, to understand the present situation of women under the *Indian Act*, it is helpful to look at how that policy developed and how Victorian notions were transformed into fundamental policy principles that continue to affect the lives of First Nations women today.

3.1 Policy Development and its Impact on First Nations Women

The first 100 years: 1850-1950

> Historically the *Indian Act* has thoroughly brainwashed us. Since 1869 Indian women already were legislated as to who she should be.

Six times the *Indian Act* changed on Indian women. But each time she lost a little bit of her rights as an Indian.

Nellie Carlson
Indian Rights for Indian Women
Edmonton, Alberta, 11 June 1992

The earliest laws dealing directly and explicitly with Indian people date from the middle of the nineteenth century and were enacted as part of the reserve policy of imperial and colonial governments to protect reserve lands from encroachment by non-Indian settlers. Once protected lands had been set aside for exclusive Indian use and occupation, it became necessary to define who was Indian.

The first statutory definition of 'Indian' is found in *An Act for the better protection of the Lands and Property of the Indians in Lower Canada*, passed in 1850. The definition is quite inclusive. It includes all those of Indian blood and their descendants, non-Indians who have married Indians living on the designated lands, and even persons adopted in infancy by Indians.[15] Within one year, this definition became more restrictive as a result of amending legislation that denied non-Indian men who married Indian women the right to acquire Indian status, but Indian status could still be gained by non-Indian women who married Indian men.

The descendants of all intermarriages who actually resided on a reserve would nonetheless still be considered Indians irrespective of the status of one of the spouses, since they would fall within that part of the definition of Indian that referred to Indian blood.[16] However, it is obvious that the same rule did not apply to men and women in mixed marriages as it had under the earlier legislation. For the first time, Indian status began to be associated with the male line of descent.

The concept of enfranchisement was introduced in 1857 through *An Act to encourage the gradual Civilization of the Indian Tribes in the Province, and to amend the Laws respecting Indians*.[17] The act applied to both Upper and Lower Canada, and its operating premise was that by removing the legal distinctions between Indians and non-Indians through enfranchisement and by facilitating the acquisition of individual property by Indians, it would be possible in time to absorb Indians fully into colonial society. An enfranchised Indian was, in effect, actually renouncing Indian status and the right to live on protected reserve land in order to join non-Aboriginal colonial society. The modern department of Indian affairs describes the nature and effect of the *Gradual Civilization Act* as follows:

> [The act]...contained property and monetary inducements to encourage Indians to leave tribal societies and seek enfranchisement. An enfranchised person could receive land and a sum of money equal to the principal of the annuities and other yearly revenues received by the band. The intent of this legislation was that enfranchised Indians

would continue to reside in the Native community but would have the same rights as non-Indian citizens.[18]

The act applied only to adult male Indians. Under section 3 of the act, to be enfranchised an Indian had to be male, over age 21, able to read and write either English or French, reasonably well educated, free of debt, and of good moral character as determined by a commission of examiners. The right to exercise the franchise depended upon meeting the requirements in federal and provincial legislation in terms of property ownership. Thus, there was no automatic right to vote. Indians were given a three-year qualifying period to acquire these attributes.

Women were not to be enfranchised independently. Yet if an Indian man was enfranchised, his wife and children were automatically enfranchised along with him, regardless of their wishes; willingly or not, they lost their Indian status. From a woman's perspective, this act perpetuated the notion of a wife and children as the husband's property, his chattels. Unlike her husband, the enfranchised woman did not receive a share of reserve lands, because by this time, in keeping with prevailing Victorian notions, maleness and the right to possess and live on reserve lands were becoming fixtures of Indian policy.

If an enfranchised man died, for example, his children of lineal descent were given precedence to inherit the estate and to live on his land. His wife would inherit the estate and land allotted to him if and only if there were no children of lineal descent. She would then have the right to use it only until her re-marriage or death, at which point it would revert to Crown ownership.

In the pre-Confederation period, concepts were introduced that were foreign to Aboriginal communities and that, wittingly or unwittingly, undermined Aboriginal cultural values. In many cases, the legislation displaced the natural, community-based and self-identification approach to determining membership – which included descent, marriage, residency, adoption and simple voluntary association with a particular group – and thus disrupted complex and interrelated social, economic and kinship structures. Patrilineal descent of the type embodied in the *Gradual Civilization Act*, for example, was the least common principle of descent in Aboriginal societies, but through these laws, it became predominant.[19] From this perspective, the *Gradual Civilization Act* was an exercise in government control in deciding who was and was not an Indian.

At Confederation, the secretary of state became the superintendent general of Indian affairs and, in 1868, acquired control over Indian lands and funds through federal legislation. The definition of 'Indian' was finalized on a patrilineal model, excluding non-Indian men who married Indian women but including non-Indian women who married Indian men.[20]

The first important piece of post-Confederation legislation, the *Gradual Enfranchisement Act*, was passed in 1869.[21] This act went further than previous legislation in its 'civilizing' and assimilative purposes and in marginalizing Indian women: for the first time, Indian women were accorded fewer legal rights than Indian men in their home communities. The prevailing Victorian social and political norms were now extended to include reserve communities.[22] For example, Indian women were denied the right to vote in band elections; voting was now restricted to adult men, as it was in Canadian society generally. As well, a new provision was added to the provisions carried over from the *Gradual Civilization Act.* Now a woman who married an Indian man from another band lost membership in her home community, as did her children, and she became a member of her husband's band.

In the eyes of Aboriginal women, the most damaging aspects of this legislation were the new provisions that penalized women who married non-Indian men. Under the earlier *Gradual Civilization Act,* there had been no penalty for such a marriage beyond the fact that the non-Indian husband did not gain Indian status upon marriage. Under this new legislation, by contrast, the Indian wife was legally stripped of her recognized Indian identity, and she and the children of the marriage lost the rights that flowed from Indian status. They were no longer entitled to treaty payments, for example, unless the band council agreed to continue them. No similarly disadvantageous provisions applied to Indian men who married non-Indian women. Aside from the inherent unfairness of this policy, there were other potentially damaging consequences for women. A woman could be compelled to leave the reserve – her home community – since her non-Indian husband could be summarily ejected by the superintendent general.

From the perspective of the twentieth century, one may well wonder how such a policy could make its way into federal legislation. The official explanation at the time focused on concerns about control over reserve lands and the need to prevent non-Indian men from gaining access to them. Thus, in 1869 the secretary of state wrote to the Mohawks of Kahnawake regarding the marrying out provisions of the new legislation, stressing that the goal was "preventing men not of Indian Blood having by marrying Indian women either through their Wives or Children any pretext for Settling on Indian lands".[23]

The *Gradual Enfranchisement Act* permitted reserves to be subdivided into lots; the superintendent general could then issue 'location tickets' allocating specific lots to individual Indian men or women.[24] In the earlier *Gradual Civilization Act,* the fear had been that non-Indian men might gain control over Indian lands; hence the need to exclude them from Indian status and reserve residency rights. In the *Gradual Enfranchisement Act,* that same rationale was extended to justify the exclusion of women from their own communities. Moreover, given the social values of the day, it also seems to have been assumed that Indian women who married non-Indians would be protected by them and would acquire property rights under Canadian law through their non-Indian spouse, thus rendering unnecessary the protection that came from Indian status and the property rights they might have as members of an Indian community on protected reserve lands.

In the relatively short period between the 1850 Lower Canada legislation and the 1869 *Gradual Enfranchisement Act*, it seems apparent that Indian women were singled out for discriminatory treatment under a policy that made their identity as Indian people increasingly dependent on the identity of their husbands. They were subject to rules that applied only to them as women and that can be summarized as follows: they could not vote in band elections; if they married an Indian man from another band, they lost membership in their home communities; if they married out by wedding a non-Indian man, they lost Indian status, membership in their home communities, and the right to transmit Indian status to the children of that marriage; if they married an Indian man who became enfranchised, they lost status, membership, treaty payments and related rights and the right to inherit the enfranchised husband's lands when he died. Despite strong objections, these discriminatory provisions were carried forward into the first *Indian Act* in 1876.[25]

1876: The first *Indian Act*

In its 100 sections, the 1876 *Indian Act* consolidated and expanded previous Indian legislation, carrying forward the provisions that put Indian women at a disadvantage compared to Indian men. Commenting on these provisions, historian J.R. Miller highlights the irony of the official justification that these measures were necessary to protect Indian lands and social structures:

> The *Indian Act*'s tracing of Indian descent and identity through the father was the unthinking application of European patrilineal assumptions by a patriarchal society; but it accorded ill with those Indian societies, such as the Iroquoian, in which identity and authority flowed through the female side of the family. All these attempts at cultural remodelling also illustrate how the first step on the path of protection seemed always to lead to the depths of coercion.[26]

As we will see, a large share of the effects of this coercion was borne by Indian women.

The *Indian Act* went through a number of changes as amendments were introduced and adopted over the years, usually in response to unanticipated administrative problems or to strengthen the assimilative thrust of federal Indian policy. Although most of the provisions that discriminated against women were simply carried forward from earlier legislation, additional measures of the same nature were also adopted. Thus, in 1884, an amendment permitted the wife of an Indian man who held reserve land by location ticket to receive one-third of her husband's estate, if he died without a will. But the amendment stated that the widow might receive it only if she were living with him at the time of death and was "of good moral character" as determined by federal authorities.[27] This amendment applied standards to women that were not applied to men, standards that were, moreover, ambiguous and that could be interpreted arbitrarily by officials outside Indian communities.

Amendments in 1920 increased the power of the superintendent general at the expense of the band council. Until this time, councils had the authority to decide whether an Indian woman who married out would continue to receive treaty annuity payments and band money distributions, or whether she would get a lump sum settlement. Many bands allowed these women to continue receiving payments and distributions so they could retain some link to the home community. The 1920 amendments removed this power from the band and lodged it in the hands of the superintendent general of Indian affairs.[28] The official rationale for this provision was set out in a letter from Deputy Superintendent General Duncan Campbell Scott:

> When an Indian woman marries outside the band, whether a non-treaty Indian or a white man, it is in the interest of the Department, and in her interest as well, to sever her connection wholly with the reserve and the Indian mode of life, and the purpose of this section was to enable us to commute her financial interests. The words "with the consent of the band" have in many cases been effectual in preventing this severance....The amendment makes in the same direction as the proposed Enfranchisement Clauses, that is it takes away the power from unprogressive bands of preventing their members from advancing to full citizenship.[29]

Importantly, in that same set of amendments were new enfranchisement provisions that allowed the governor in council, on the recommendation of the superintendent general, forcibly to enfranchise any Indian, male or female, if found to be "fit for enfranchisement", along with his or her children.[30]

The 1951 amendments to the *Indian Act*

The *Indian Act* was completely revised in 1951. A number of provisions were introduced that would affect Indian women. The provisions dealing with status, membership and enfranchisement were significantly modified in a way that further disadvantaged women and their children. The status provisions became vastly more elaborate and spelled out in great detail who was and was not entitled to be registered as an Indian for federal government purposes.

The mention of Indian blood, a feature of the definition of 'Indian' since 1876, was replaced by the notion of registration, with a strong emphasis on the male line of descent.[31] The new rules dealt with acquisition and loss of Indian status, referring to persons who were "entitled to be registered" as "Indian". Only they would be recognized as Indian by federal authorities. The result was that many people of Indian ancestry and culture who had been involuntarily enfranchised, who had been deleted from treaty or band lists accidentally or intentionally, or who simply did not qualify for status under the old rules were no longer eligible for registration under the new rules.

The effect was to introduce new ironies and injustices in the status system, many of which worked against Indian women and their descendants. A good example of the illogicality and injustice of the new system is provided by the so-called 'double mother' rule, first introduced at this time. Section 12 (1)(a)(iv) of the revised act stated that a child lost Indian status at age 21 if his or her mother and grand-mother had obtained status only through marriage to a man with Indian status. The logic seemed to be that after two generations in which non-Indian women had married into an Indian community, any children of the second generation marriage should be removed on the basis of their mixed culture and blood quantum.

Aside from the obvious assimilative purpose of the new rule, a specific problem arose in the case of women of Indian ancestry who did not have Indian status under Canadian law but who were nonetheless Indian by birth, culture and membership in an Indian community. The Mohawk community at Akwesasne, where the Canada-United States border bisects the reserve, provides the best example of how the double mother rule could bring about a manifest wrong. At Akwesasne, Mohawk persons from the American side would not be considered Indians by Canadian authorities. If two generations of Mohawk women from the American side had married Mohawk men from the Canadian side, the double mother rule would apply to remove Indian status from the third-generation children when they turned 21. It did not matter that such a child might be wholly Mohawk in ancestry, culture and language and never have lived anywhere else but on the Canadian side of the reserve. Canadian authorities would strip such a person of Indian status at 21 and deny him or her the legal right to continue living as an Indian person in that part of the reserve community under the control of Indian affairs officials.

The marrying out provisions that had caused such distress to Indian women, their families and communities were repeated in the now infamous subsection 12(1)(b) and were actually strengthened in the new act by connecting them to the concept of involuntary enfranchisement via subsection 108(2). Henceforth, an Indian woman who married out would not only lose Indian status, she could also be enfranchised against her will as of the date of her marriage. These provisions are seen by Indian women as having been particularly discriminatory and ultimately highly damaging to them.

Such a woman lost any claim to Indian status – under the new rules, upon marriage she was not entitled to registration. Like generations of women before her who had married out, loss of status meant loss of the right under Canadian law to hold land on the reserve and loss of status for any children of the marriage. With the loss of status and membership came the forced sale or disposal of any reserve lands she may have held. Adding forced enfranchisement to loss of status meant that she was also struck off the band list and was no longer entitled to distributions of band moneys.

Before these new provisions were introduced in 1951, women who had lost their Indian status through marrying out had often been able to retain their links to their communities. Some Indian agencies would issue an informal identity card known as a 'red ticket' identifying such women as entitled to share in band treaty moneys and, in many cases, to continue to live on the reserve.[32] Because they were no longer legally Indians but remained members of the reserve community by virtue of band practice and their red tickets, the precise status in law of such women was unclear to Indian affairs officials and the general Canadian public. With forced enfranchisement upon marrying out, there could no longer be doubt in anyone's mind that they were not Indian and, moreover, not part of any Indian community.

Nonetheless, Indian women who had married out before the 1951 changes were permitted to keep their red ticket status if they did not accept a lump sum settlement in exchange for their treaty payments. However, an amendment to the *Indian Act* in 1956 stopped this practice. After 1956, 'red ticket' women were paid a lump sum of 10 times the average annual amount of all payments paid over the preceding 10 years. These women were put in the same unfavourable position as Indian women who married out after the 1951 revision.[33]

The children of mixed marriages were not mentioned in the 1951 legislation. Despite the lack of legal authority for it, enfranchisement was forced on them too, under subsection 108(2). To correct this injustice, in 1956 Indian status was restored to these children. But the 1956 *Indian Act* amendments also allowed the governor in council "by order [to] declare that all or any of her children are enfranchised as of the date of the marriage or any such other date as the order may specify".[34] While there do not appear to be any common or consistent criteria regarding how the discretion of the governor in council was to be exercised, the usual practice was that off-reserve children were enfranchised but children living on-reserve were allowed to keep their status.

None of these provisions applied to Indian men. They could not be enfranchised against their will after 1951 except through a stringent judicial inquiry procedure as prescribed in the revised *Indian Act*. This difference in treatment created a huge imbalance between the number of enfranchised men and the number of involuntarily enfranchised women. Between 1955 and 1975 (when forced enfranchisement of women stopped), 1,576 men became enfranchised (along with 1,090 wives and children), while 8,537 women (as well as 1,974 of their children) were forcibly enfranchised and lost their status. From 1965 to 1975, only five per cent of enfranchisements were voluntary; 95 per cent were involuntary, and the great majority of these involved women.[35]

Post-1951 to pre-1985: Growing awareness, growing tension

Between 1951 and 1985, equality and civil rights movements were a prominent feature of the socio-political landscape in North America. Aboriginal voices were being raised, and there was growing awareness of the concerns of Aboriginal people, including the concerns of Indian women. The governments of the day were making some effort to consult Aboriginal people about issues affecting them, but there was little change in the *Indian Act* until the early 1980s.

The status provisions of the *Indian Act* and the exclusion of women who married out were of great concern to the Aboriginal women's groups that sprang up during this period. In 1970, the Royal Commission on the Status of Women tabled its final report. The commission was particularly concerned that the "special kind of discrimination under the terms of the *Indian Act*....the loss of Indian status, or enfranchisement, implies that rights and privileges given to a member of a band...will be denied to that person....Enfranchisement or deletion of the name of an Indian from the Indian Registry is much more frequent for women than for men". The commission recommended that the act be amended "to allow an Indian woman upon marriage to a non-Indian to (a) retain her Indian status and (b) transmit her Indian status to her children".[36]

Two important court cases challenged this inequality head on. Jeannette Corbiere Lavell, an Ojibwa woman and member of the Wikwemikong band on Manitoulin Island in Ontario, had married a non-Indian in 1970. She was living in Toronto when she brought the action in 1971, charging that subsection 12(1)(b) violated the equality clause in the 1960 *Canadian Bill of Rights* on the grounds of discrimination by reason of sex. She lost her case at trial, the judge taking the position that this was an issue that Indians ought to resolve for themselves by pressuring Parliament for an amendment to the *Indian Act* if they agreed that this was necessary.[37] Lavell later won her case on appeal.[38] However, this decision was revisited when another case was brought forward by Yvonne Bedard.

Yvonne Bedard, from the Six Nations Reserve in southern Ontario, lost her status when she married out in 1964. She separated from her husband in 1970 and returned to the reserve with her two children to live in a house inherited from her mother. In order to live in her family home, Bedard found she had to obtain band council permission to reside on-reserve, as she was no longer a status Indian and therefore no longer legally entitled to inherit property on the reserve. Nor were her children. She was given a year to dispose of the property and later obtained an extension, but when it expired, the band council decided she must leave the reserve. Fearing eviction, Bedard brought legal action against the band. Her case was argued on the same grounds as the *Lavell* case, and she won by virtue of the legal precedent of that case. In the decision, the judge noted that the entire *Indian Act* might be inoperative because it violated the Bill of Rights.[39]

Ultimately, these two cases were joined and appealed to the Supreme Court of Canada. A decision was brought down in August 1973. The *Indian Act* marrying out provisions were upheld by the slimmest margin, and Lavell and Bedard lost.[40]

New awareness and new tensions were born of these unsuccessful legal challenges. The tensions stemmed from the perception that women's rights were pitted against Aboriginal rights (as in Bedard's challenge to the authority of the band council). There was also concern from band councils and some Aboriginal leaders that reinstatement of non-status and enfranchised women and children would severely strain their already limited financial resources, since it would mean providing housing and social services if they chose to return to reserve communities. In the face of a history of federal assimilation policy and in the absence of guarantees of additional funds for these purposes, many reserve communities feared they would simply inherit the consequences of this aspect of the failure of federal Indian policy. This concern foreshadowed what occurred with the adoption of Bill C-31 in 1985, when thousands of Indian women and their children and descendants regained Indian status and band membership.

Significantly, both Lavell and Bedard pursued their cases without any support – moral or otherwise – from their communities, band councils, or Indian political organizations. On the contrary, they were actively opposed, not only by the government of Canada but also by their own communities.[41]

3.2 Bill C-31

The 1982 amendment of the constitution, incorporating the *Canadian Charter of Rights and Freedoms*, included the provision, in section 15, that "every individual is equal before and under the law and has the right to the equal protection and benefit of the law without discrimination based on race, national or ethnic origin, colour, religion, sex, age, or mental or physical disability". Section 15 of the Charter came into effect on 17 April 1985. The Charter accomplished overnight what the *Canadian Bill of Rights* and the *Canadian Human Rights Act*[42] had been unable to do – motivating the government to eliminate provisions of the *Indian Act* that had been criticized for discriminating against Indian women. Some influence was also exerted by the case of *Lovelace* v. *Canada*, in which Canada's treatment of Indian women under the *Indian Act* was strongly criticized by the United Nations Human Rights Committee.[43]

Bill C-31 provisions

This led to the passage of Bill C-31 in 1985. The bill amended various sections of the *Indian Act*, in particular the status and band membership provisions. While Indian status would continue to be determined by the federal government, status was restored to those who lost it under subsection 12(1)(b) and other similarly discriminatory sections of the status and membership provisions. The general rule was that in future Indian status would be granted to those with at least one parent with status. The concept of enfranchisement, voluntary or otherwise, was totally abolished, and those who lost status through enfranchisement had their status restored. First-generation children of restored persons were granted first-time status. Band membership was guaranteed for some classes of persons restored to status or admitted to status for the first time. Not all were guaranteed automatic band membership, however.

Legal status as an Indian and band membership were formally separated in the act, with the former remaining under federal control.[44] A band may now take control of its own membership from the department of Indian affairs by following the procedures set out in Bill C-31. Once a band has taken control of its membership, persons may be added to or deleted from the list of members according to the rules established by the band in a membership code. In short, the department of Indian affairs will no longer maintain the membership list for that particular band and will no longer have a say in how band membership decisions are made.

These procedures in Bill C-31 call for a band membership code that respects the rights of people reinstated to Indian status or who have first-time Indian status under circumstances that give them 'acquired rights' to band membership before the band took control of its membership. A band membership code must be adopted by a vote of the band electors, which in theory includes non-resident (off-reserve) members. This is unlike the case of band council elections which, under sections 74 to 79 of the *Indian Act*, are restricted to resident band members.[45] Bands also received authority under Bill C-31, subject to certain conditions, to pass by-laws determining residency rights on the reserve.

The amendments concerning restoration of Indian status and band control of membership would be a source of conflict when it came time to implement Bill C-31. There was concern that some bands might reject persons who had acquired or re-acquired Indian status through Bill C-31, whether because of sex discrimination or because of concerns that resources needed to accommodate new members might not be forthcoming from the federal government. To forestall this possibility, subsection 10(4) of the 1985 *Indian Act* included a provision that prohibited First Nations from excluding certain classes of persons from their membership lists.

Thus, when they took control of their membership lists from the department of Indian affairs upon the adoption of a membership code, bands were required to include as part of their initial band membership, among others, all persons who had an acquired right to be on the list supplied by the federal government. The provision was designed not only to protect newly reinstated women and their children but also to protect women who had acquired status on marriage to a status Indian before the 1985 amendments.

The impact of Bill C-31

The impact of Bill C-31 was enormous and profound. In 1989, the Department of Indian Affairs and Northern Development began a study to determine its effects. The study was developed and conducted in consultation with three national Aboriginal organizations – the Assembly of First Nations, through its chiefs committee on citizenship, the Native Women's Association of Canada and the Native Council of Canada (now the Congress of Aboriginal Peoples).[46]

The department of Indian affairs had seriously underestimated the number of persons likely to seek reinstatement. More than 21,000 applications, representing 38,000 individuals, were received in the first six months after enactment. A backlog of applications took five years to clear. By June 1990, 75,761 applications had been made, representing 133,134 persons. The status Indian population grew by 19 per cent in five years because of Bill C-31 alone and, when natural growth was included, by a total of 33 per cent.[47]

The report summarizing the results of the study describes the registration process, noting that responsibility for determining whether an individual is eligible for registration as a status Indian rests with the registrar, who applies the criteria outlined in section 6 of the Indian Act. The process includes searches of departmental records on the individual and/or the individual's family. If the required information cannot be located in the register, a more detailed and time-consuming search of pre-1951 records is undertaken.[48]

The documentation required to prove eligibility for Indian status and the slow pace of approval were criticized. In some instances, the existence of people had not been recorded on paper, and it became necessary to seek sworn affidavits as evidence of family relationships and declarations from elders as verification of past band affiliation. In addition, the process was particularly difficult for individuals raised by adoptive parents. Adoptees of Indian descent experienced problems because of the confidentiality of provincial adoption records. Problems also arose for status Indian women with children born out of wedlock, who had to prove that the father was a status Indian before the children could be registered.[49]

> Our children, if they are born outside the framework of a union recognized by the [Indian Act], are also victims of discrimination. When their father is Aboriginal, he must sign a declaration or, under [Bill] C-31, our child will be considered to have been born of a non-Indian father. [translation]
>
> Philo Desterres
> Quebec Native Women's Association
> Montreal, Quebec, 27 May 1993

> They developed...such complex systems for re-registration. There are some things the average Canadian citizen cannot understand and doesn't have to confront, which are still aberrations, which are disguised in the way people are re-registered or even how the status is

to be transmitted from one person to another, except it is necessary to understand the situation of the women who fought for it. It was that or nothing. [translation]

Michèle Rouleau
Quebec Native Women's Association
Montreal, Quebec, 27 May 1993

Of the applications received by mid-1990, 55 per cent (73,554) of all individuals seeking registration had been approved, 16 per cent (21,397) were disallowed, 8 per cent were active files, 9 per cent were inactive files, and 12 per cent were classified as "other completions". Of the 8 per cent classified as active, the majority were those requiring additional information from the applicant. Of the 16 per cent disallowed, three-quarters were denied registration under subsection 6(2), which provides that individuals seeking registration must establish that one parent is entitled to registration under subsection 6(1).[50]

As of 30 June 1995, Bill C-31 had added 95,429 persons to the status Indian population in Canada, more than half of them (57.2 per cent, 54,589) female.[51] The enormous increase in the status Indian population did not result in an equal increase in the population of reserve communities. This is largely because most persons restored to Indian status or with first-time status under Bill C-31 still live off-reserve.[52] Through its survey of 2,000 registrants, the study found that 32 per cent of those individuals currently living off-reserve would like to live on a reserve. To a second survey question asking registrants living off-reserve if they might return to a reserve or Crown land at some time in the future, 52 per cent replied in the affirmative and another 15 per cent were uncertain.[53]

Although most Bill C-31 registrants continue to live off-reserve, it is not always by choice, since it has been difficult for some of them to get reserve residency rights even when they are band members (an issue discussed later in this chapter). Some bands experienced significant population increases from Bill C-31 registrants while others had none. The average band increased in size by 19 per cent, although 80 per cent of the bands had fewer than 15 Bill C-31 registrants living on-reserve. (It is estimated that 4,600 of the Bill C-31 registrants lived on reserve in 1984 and that 2,700 more had moved to a reserve between 1985 and 1990.[54])

Clearly, the full impact of Bill C-31 on reserve communities has yet to be felt. Some band leaders and community members are concerned about the possibility of crowding and disruption and have been resistant to inclusion of new band members in their communities. Services that could be affected by a population increase include housing, health and post-secondary education.

Indian women have their own concerns about Bill C-31. Women make up the majority of people reinstated under the bill, and fully three-quarters of those whose Indian status was restored – as opposed to those who gained status for the first time – are women.[55] Despite its avowed intent of bringing about sexual equality in the status and membership provisions of the *Indian Act*, Bill C-31 is nonetheless seen by many Aboriginal women as a continuation of the sexist policies of the past.

3.3 The *Indian Act* and Bill C-31: Areas of Concern to First Nations Women

There are strong concerns among Aboriginal people that, in eliminating the major forms of discrimination in the original *Indian Act*, new ones have been created. For example, as noted in the Bill C-31 study summary report, "bands that control their own membership under the Act may now restrict eligibility for some of the rights and benefits that used to be automatic with status".[56] Moreover, sex discrimination, supposedly wiped out by the 1985 amendments, remains. Thus, for example, in some families Indian women who lost status through marrying out before 1985 can pass Indian status on to their children but not to their children's children. However, their brothers, who may also have married out before 1985, can pass on status to their children for at least one more generation, even though the children of the sister and the brother all have one status Indian parent and one non-Indian parent. Such anomalies result from the fact that the Bill C-31 amendments build on past status and membership policies and provisions. They are, in this respect, somewhat reminiscent of the 1951 revisions in which the notion of 'entitlement to registration as an Indian' replaced that of 'Indian blood', but without breaking with past practices.

These past practices favour descent through the male line, as imposed during the Victorian era. Although Canada no longer subscribes to these values, the legacy of discrimination continues to be felt by First Nations communities:

> I married a non-Aboriginal person and was discriminated against....In 1985 the act was amended and so I regained my status, along with a number of other women. And yet the discrimination continued. This is an act which has lasted 125 years, and it is difficult to change something that old because it becomes part of people's lives. It became a habit, a tradition for our Aboriginal people to discriminate against these women. Today we are still suffering this discrimination even though the law has been amended. We speak of discrimination because I returned to my community....When the time came to apply for housing for the reinstated women, they were always told there was no land. Many excuses were given: "we have no money", "the band councils have no money"....In my community I had to fight for six years in order to meet with the chiefs....There are people

who cannot return to their communities for the reasons I have given you because the bands do not accept them.... [translation]

Mèrilda St. Onge
Women of the Montagnais Nation
Sept-Îles, Quebec, 19 November 1992

What the Aboriginal leaders are unfortunately applying today, I am not saying all leaders, is the policy of exclusion. In the first years of implementation of Bill C-31, from 1985 to 1987, the approach of some band councils was simply to try to make some rules that would not accept the re-registered women....I think this was extremely regrettable and the government bears a large part of the guilt...it is obvious that there was very strong opposition to the return of people to the communities because the people have no more houses, the people have no more room....There is a terrible lack of space so the issue of re-registration is strongly linked to the issue of land. [translation]

Michèle Rouleau
Quebec Native Women's Association
Montreal, Quebec, 27 May 1993

The testimony of many First Nations women before the Commission points to their determination to fight against discrimination and policies of exclusion:

In short, an epic struggle which has left its mark has contributed to our understanding of the obstacles, in particular the strength of the prejudices and ravages caused by the *Indian Act*, but which has above all helped to strengthen the determination of the Aboriginal women to fight discrimination wherever it is found, beginning with the discrimination that operates at the grassroots in the communities. [translation]

Philo Desterres
Quebec Native Women's Association
Montreal, Quebec, 27 May 1993

In the next few pages we examine the major areas that concern Indian women in the current version of the *Indian Act*. In some cases, women are not the only ones affected. However, because the majority of people restored to Indian status under the 1985 amendments were women, they feel the impact more profoundly and encounter these obstacles more often than do Aboriginal men.

Indian status under section 6

Though I regained my status under Bill C-31, my children were denied status. The children of my male cousin, who traces his descent from our common grandmother through the male line, have full status. I am challenging this inequality in another court case, pending in British Columbia.[57]

Sharon McIvor
Native Women's Association of Canada
Toronto, Ontario, 26 June 1992

First Nations women told the Commission that Bill C-31 has created a situation where, over time, their descendants may be stripped of their Indian status and rights in some circumstances in which Indian men and their descendants would be unaffected. The discrepancy arises out of the categories used to designate Indian status under Bill C-31.

The bill created two main categories of status Indians. Under subsection 6(1), legal status is assigned to all those who had status before 17 April 1985, all persons who are members of any new bands created since 17 April 1985 (none have been created), and all individuals who lost status through the discriminatory sections of the *Indian Act*. More specifically, these classes of persons are as follows:

- section 6(1)(a): this is a grandfather clause granting Indian status to persons entitled to it under the pre-1985 version of the *Indian Act;*
- section 6(1)(b): persons entitled to status as a member of a band declared by the governor in council to exist after Bill C-31 came into force (there are none: the class is therefore empty[58]);
- section 6(1)(c): persons regaining status under Bill C-31 who lost or were denied status because of
    - the double mother rule (former section 12(1)(a)(iv));
    - marriage out (that is, to a non-Indian) (former section 12(1)(b));
    - illegitimate children of an Indian mother and non-Indian father (former section 12(2));
    - involuntary enfranchisement upon marriage to a non-Indian, including any children involuntarily enfranchised because of the involuntary enfranchisement of the mother (former subsection 12(1)(a)(iii) and 109(2));
- section 6(1)(d): persons 'voluntarily' enfranchised upon application by the Indian man, including the Indian wife and children enfranchised along with him (former subsection 12(1)(1)(iii) and 109(1));
- section 6(1)(e): persons enfranchised because of other enfranchisement provisions, that is, residency outside Canada for more than five years (former section 13 between 1927 and 1951) and upon obtaining higher education or professional standing (former section 111 between 1867 and 1920); and
- section 6(1)(f): children whose parents are both entitled to be registered under any of the preceding subsections of section 6.

Subsection 6(2) covers people with only one parent who is or was a status Indian under any part of section 6(1). It must be stressed that the one-parent rule in subsection 6(2) applies only if that parent is entitled to status under sub-section 6(1). Thus, if an individual has one parent covered by subsection 6(2) and one who is non-Indian, the individual is not entitled to status. The children or other descendants of Indian women who lost status under the discriminatory provisions described earlier will generally gain status under subsection 6(2), not subsection 6(1), since the reason their mothers lost status in the first place was that their fathers did not have Indian status when their parents were married.

As discussed earlier, the rules are complex and difficult to apply, particularly in cases where applicants may not have the required documentary proof of their ancestry. This can be a problem in some areas where written records are lacking and where oral traditions are still strong. It is also a problem where Indian children were adopted by non-Indian parents and the records are covered by the *Privacy Act* or withheld because of the confidentiality of provincial adoption records.[59]

Moreover, and more alarmingly for future generations of First Nations people, the consequences of falling within subsection 6(1) or subsection 6(2) are felt by the woman's children and grandchildren. For these descendants, the way their parents and grandparents acquired status will be important determinants of whether they will have Indian status and, if they do, whether and to what extent they will be able to pass it on to their children. The effects of the 6(1) and 6(2) designation are felt most acutely in the third generation (see Figure 2.1).

Comparing examples 3 and 5, it is clear in the situation of marriage to a non-Indian that the children of a 6(1) parent and a 6(2) parent have different rights under the amended *Indian Act*. Where the parent marries out, the child in example 3 will still have Indian status, while the child in example 5 will not. Yet each will have one parent with Indian status and one without. When one recalls that the children of women who lost status under the discriminatory pro-visions of the earlier versions of the *Indian Act* will have gained their own status through subsection 6(2), it is clear that they will be at a relative disadvantage.

A woman who gained status under subsection 6(2) will see the impact immediately if she marries out: her children will not have Indian status. All other factors being equal, this rule creates a situation in which the descendants of a woman who married out before 1985 will have fewer Indian rights than those of her brother who married out at the same time, despite the fact that their degree of Indian ancestry is the same.

An example helps illustrate the inequality that results from these rules. The following is taken from the *Report of the Aboriginal Justice Inquiry of Manitoba* (which recommended that this form of discrimination cease):

> John and Joan, a brother and sister, were both registered Indians. Joan married a Métis man before 1985 so she lost her Indian status under section 12(1)(b) of the former Act. John married a white woman before 1985 and she automatically became a status Indian. Both John

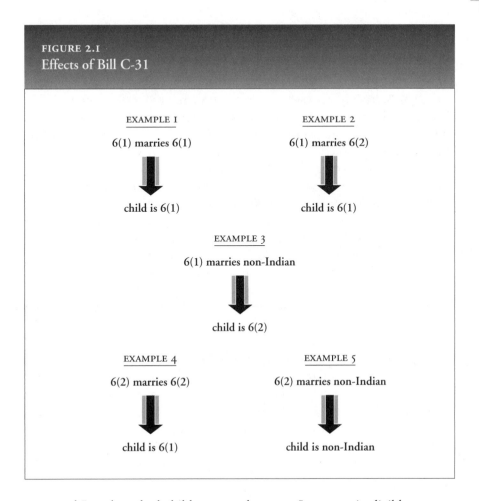

FIGURE 2.1
Effects of Bill C-31

EXAMPLE 1

6(1) marries 6(1)

child is 6(1)

EXAMPLE 2

6(1) marries 6(2)

child is 6(1)

EXAMPLE 3

6(1) marries non-Indian

child is 6(2)

EXAMPLE 4

6(2) marries 6(2)

child is 6(1)

EXAMPLE 5

6(2) marries non-Indian

child is non-Indian

and Joan have had children over the years. Joan now is eligible to regain her status under section 6(1)(c) and her children will qualify under section 6(2). They are treated as having only one eligible parent, their mother, although both parents are Aboriginal. John's children gained status at birth as both parents were Indians legally, even though only one was an Aboriginal person.

Joan's children can pass on status to their offspring only if they also marry registered Indians. If they marry unregistered Aboriginal people or non-Aboriginal people, then no status will pass to their children. All John's grandchildren will be status Indians, regardless of who his children marry. Thus, entitlement to registration for the second generation has nothing to do with racial or cultural characteristics. The Act has eliminated the discrimination faced by those who lost status, but has passed it on to the next generation.[60]

The establishment of categories for Indian status was a concoction of the federal government, and instead of devising a bill that would truly repair the situation, it created a 'paper blood system' that denied thousands of individuals the opportunity to claim or reclaim their heritage. The national Aboriginal organizations had certainly not suggested such a system, nor did they consent to it. Their position was that as many individuals as possible should be registered covering at least three generations. In fact, the Assembly of First Nations and the Native Women's Association of Canada issued a joint news release on 22 June 1984 reaffirming their position: "The federal government must remedy the injustice created to people of Indian ancestry by repealing sections of the *Indian Act* that deny Indian status to Indians and reinstate all generations who lost status as a result of discriminatory laws enacted by the Parliament of Canada."[61]

In 1985, the Assembly of First Nations made a presentation to the House of Commons standing committee on Indian affairs stating that "there must be full reinstatement of all our citizens who have lost status or whose status has never been recognized....[W]e cannot accept new provisions which will discriminate among different generations of our citizens, procedurally or otherwise, who have been affected by the discriminatory provisions".[62] Despite these concerns, the amendments requested by the Native Women's Association of Canada and the Assembly of First Nations were not included in Bill C-31.

The categorization of Indian status under Bill C-31 has implications for the entire Aboriginal population in coming generations. At present rates of marriage outside the 6(1) and 6(2) categories, status Indians will begin to disappear from the Indian register if the rules are not changed (see Volume 1, Chapter 2). One report on the problem supports this conclusion in the strongest of terms, noting that Bill C-31 "is the gateway to a world in which some Indians are more equal than others" because the 6(1)/6(2) distinction creates "two classes of Indians: *full* Indians...and *half* Indians". Moreover, the report concludes, "In the long run these rules will lead to the extinction of First Nations".[63]

> My mother married a non-Native person, and before Bill C-31 she lost her birthright, her inherent right, and her nationality right as a Native person. She, like many women who lost their status for one reason or another, regained her status through Bill C-31. This bill also allowed her children to be recognized as status, but this is where it ends....As it stands now, I am a status person under section 6(2) of Bill C-31. My two girls are not Native through the government's eyes. They have one-quarter Native blood. Do I tell my daughters that they are not Native because their governments say it's so? No. And I don't think so, and neither should the government.
>
> Corrine Chappell
> Charlottetown, Prince Edward Island
> 5 May 1992

It was very confusing. I don't want my children to be confused as to who they are. I married a man [who regained status under] Bill C-31. And, first of all, I told my children they were Métis and all of a sudden they can be Treaty. And I decided to leave that up to them, what they want to do. It was very confusing and...I want them to know who they are.

Pat Harper
Metis Women of Manitoba
Winnipeg, Manitoba, 22 April 1992

The Commission believes that the solution to this problem lies in the process of nation building. We set forth a number of recommendations to this end in our chapter on governance (Volume 2, Chapter 3).

The impact of band membership codes

I thought by applying and receiving my [*Indian Act* status under Bill C-31] I would have the same benefits as other status Indians. [But] I don't have equal rights and, in fact, I have less identity than before....I can't have a home on the reserve....The reserves at present could possibly house us, the Bill C-31 minority Aboriginal people, but refuse to....I will probably have a resting place when the time comes, but why should I accept to be buried on reserve land after I die, when I could also enjoy sharing all the services that are being kept away from me today....

[The problem is] coming from...Chief and Council. I know they are really against Bill C-31s. They have, I guess, no use for [us].

Florence Boucher
Lac La Biche, Alberta
9 June 1992

Before 1985, Indian status and band membership were practically synonymous: all band members were status Indians, and almost all status Indians were members of particular bands (those that were not were on a 'general list' of Indians). The department of Indian affairs maintained both the general list and the band lists. The 1985 amendments gave bands the authority to take control of their membership lists and determine who was and was not a band member. For the first time, Indian status and band membership were separated.

Strict rules were put in place to protect existing band members and those who acquired the right to band membership through section 6. A woman's ability to be recognized as a band member and to be treated in the same manner as other First Nations people is a significant issue. This is particularly true for women with Indian status gained under Bill C-31.

Under the 1985 amendments, bands can adopt a membership code if a simple majority of "electors of the band" agree to it in a vote called for that purpose.[64] Adoption of a membership code means that the band, not the department of Indian affairs, will maintain the membership list according to its own rules as set out in the membership code. Under the *Indian Act*, electors of the band are all band members over the age of 18,[65] whether they live on- or off-reserve. By December 1995, about 240 bands had adopted membership codes and 370 had not.

The 1985 amendments to the *Indian Act* contain apparently conflicting provisions. On one hand, First Nations can assume control of membership. This implies a form of self-government in which it is bands alone that decide their membership. On the other hand, under section 10, certain categories of persons acquired the right to have their names placed on band lists maintained by the department of Indian affairs before these lists were transferred to the bands and as soon as the amendments were passed into law. Under normal circumstances, persons whose names were placed on departmentally maintained band lists would automatically become band members, irrespective of the wishes of the bands concerned. This flies in the face of band control of membership, since the department of Indian affairs would still be making decisions about band membership, this time by restoring Indian status and band membership to those eligible under Bill C-31.

The primary intent of section 10 is to give bands control of their membership, with a secondary goal being to protect the acquired rights to membership of Bill C-31 registrants. In other words, the theory seemed to be that these persons ought not to be deprived of band membership arbitrarily by bands that may not have wished to include them as band members. Acquired rights did prevent bands from subsequently adopting band membership codes that excluded persons with these rights. Persons with these acquired rights of band membership would, in principle, have the right to vote on all band matters on which the general membership can vote.[66] This would include band membership codes. However, for reasons discussed below, this did not always happen, and band membership decisions were sometimes taken without the participation of those with acquired rights of membership.

The protection of acquired rights to band membership was established in two phases. In the first phase, which lasted roughly two years from the adoption of Bill C-31, until 28 June 1987, the following categories of Bill C-31 registrants under subsection 6(1) were automatically entitled to have their names placed on departmental band lists of the bands with which they were associated: 6(1)(a), (b), (c) and, under (f), those children born after Bill C-31 became law in 1985, both of whose parents are or were entitled to registration as a member of that band. Thus, their acquired rights were vested immediately and were in this sense absolute – the department of Indian affairs was required by law to place their names on the band lists it maintained before handing over responsibility for those lists to the bands that asked for it.

In the second phase, registrants in the other categories of Bill C-31 were required to wait until 29 June 1987 before their rights to band membership became vested. In this sense, their acquired rights were conditional. If by that date the band with which they were associated had not adopted a band membership code – so that the band lists remained with the department of Indian affairs – they acquired the right to have their names entered on the lists. These categories of persons were as follows under section 6: 6(1)(d), (e) and the balance of those falling under (f), along with those eligible under 6(2).

These provisions were minimum rules. Bands could go beyond them, but they were required by law to meet these standards. These standards apply to the 370 bands that did not pass their own membership codes. Anyone who met these criteria was placed on a membership list. Of the 240 bands that did adopt membership codes, 81 per cent did so in the four weeks preceding the 29 June 1987 deadline.[67]

Acquired rights translate only into the right to be part of the initial band population for purposes of deciding on a band membership code. There is nothing to prevent these codes from subsequently being amended to exclude individuals on grounds other than the rights that they acquired before the membership code came into force. In other words, if a band decided to narrow the definition of membership by excluding individuals on grounds other than those related to acquired rights, they could do so. The fact that this might also affect certain members who had acquired rights as well would make no difference; they could be excluded. Moreover, even where Bill C-31 registrants remained on band-controlled membership lists, some bands passed residency by-laws, the effect of which was to prevent Bill C-31 band members from returning to the reserve community. New Bill C-31 band members, most of whom still live off-reserve, often cannot participate in band decisions made through band councils because they cannot meet the residency requirement under the *Indian Act* for voting on these decisions, or because the band operates according to custom and has similar residency requirements.[68] The department of Indian affairs has been frank in acknowledging the shortcomings of the acquired rights provisions:

> The amended Act allows a band that can obtain a majority vote of its eligible electors to control its own membership and, accordingly, 232 bands now [in 1990] control their own membership lists. In these cases, the Department adds the name of the person to the Indian Register, but cannot add them to the band list, nor ensure they are able to reside on reserve or participate in community decisions.[69]

In addition, because the number of people applying for restoration of Indian status was much higher than had been predicted by the department, and because restoration is a complicated and time-consuming process involving proof of descent, status decisions were sometimes delayed. In fact, in many cases it took years to get a decision. Given that most band membership codes were adopted in the first two years after passage of Bill C-31, and given that it took five years to clear up the backlog of Bill C-31 status applications, it is clear that in the interval between individuals applying for and being granted Indian status, many bands went ahead and adopted membership codes without the participation of the very people whose interests were most likely to be affected by the provisions of membership codes.

Because of delays in processing applications, it seems apparent in retrospect that bands that wished to adopt membership codes were not always aware of who their potential new members might be. By the same token, since there was no requirement that the band membership codes be published, it seems equally clear that many Bill C-31 applicants were unaware that the bands with which they were affiliated and that they might have re-joined were going ahead with codes that could exclude them. As a result, Bill C-31 registrants with an acquired right to have their names placed on band lists maintained by the department have been restored to Indian status but have found that the department no longer maintains their band's list and that they have been excluded from membership under a membership code adopted without their participation or knowledge.

Thus, in the survey of Bill C-31 registrants, the department found that only 15 per cent of registrants had been able to participate in the process by which a band membership code was adopted. These problems, coupled with the impact of the *Indian Act* rules requiring reserve residency as a precondition for voting, compelled the department of Indian affairs to conclude that "[g]enerally, only regular band members were involved in developing and voting on these rules".[70]

Membership codes still do not have to be published, so even today Bill C-31 registrants are often unaware of decisions being taken by the bands with which they are associated.[71] The department of Indian affairs has refused to intervene, on the grounds that these are issues between the individuals and bands concerned. Many Bill C-31 cases are now before the courts, involving First Nations women and their descendants who are often no further ahead than when they first applied for reinstatement, having to rely on costly litigation to obtain the band membership that they believed these amendments had given them.[72]

In the same way, a number of bands have gone to court to prevent people who acquired or regained status under Bill C-31 from acquiring band membership. The bands have argued that their right to control their own membership is an Aboriginal or treaty right protected under the *Constitution Act, 1982* that enables them to ignore the requirement in Bill C-31 to reinstate the persons who acquired rights to band membership during the first phase. In the *Sawridge Band* case, however, the trial judge found this argument to be without foundation, ruling that subsection 35(4) operates in the section 35 context to prevent bands from discriminating against Indian women in their membership decisions. He also found that whatever power bands may have had to determine their membership was extinguished before the advent of section 35: "no aboriginal right either to discriminate against aboriginal women, or to control membership at large, ever survived to enjoy the protection of subsection 35(1)".[73]

As mentioned, 240 bands representing nearly 40 per cent of the status Indian population had adopted band membership codes by December 1995. Band membership codes are based on one of four principles of descent. According to Clatworthy and Smith, among the 236 bands that had adopted codes by 1992, the breakdown was as follows:[74]

- The one-parent rule – used by 90 bands across the country – holds that an individual is eligible for membership if one parent is a band member.
- Under the two-parent rule, used by 67 bands, both parents must be band members.
- Another 49 bands follow the rules set out in subsections 6(1) and 6(2) of the *Indian Act*. This, of course, is the same rule used by bands without a membership code, except that in the latter case the department of Indian affairs enforces it, not the band.
- The fourth and final type of membership rule is based on blood quantum and is the method chosen by 30 bands. A blood quantum rule sets a criterion for membership based on the number of Indian ancestors in an individual's family history. Blood quantum codes measure a person's quantum by adding the quantum of each parent and dividing by two. An individual with one parent of 100 per cent Indian blood and one parent with no Aboriginal blood is considered to be 50 per cent Indian. Similarly, if both parents are considered 50 per cent Indian, the child is considered 50 per cent Indian. A typical blood quantum criterion for band membership is 50 per cent, although there are codes where the quantum is set either above or below this level.

While ostensibly supportive of self-government, membership codes have the potential to undermine it in the future. An issue arises that is of concern not only to women. For example, the one-parent membership rule is more inclusive than the *Indian Act* rules – thereby enlarging the potential band membership under codes based on this rule – but the same cannot be said for blood quantum and two-parent rules. The two-parent rule in particular has the potential to reduce band size drastically, first through restricting the initial band population and then by penalizing the children of those who marry out.

It is clear that at current rates of marrying out, some band populations will decline quickly in the coming years.[75] Self-government seems to imply a larger rather than a smaller population if critical mass and economies of scale are to be maintained. Although a smaller group is more likely to include people who are also status Indians under federal rules and thereby entitled to all the benefits available to Indian persons, such a group appears less likely to be able to develop the infrastructure of a modern government without bringing in additional members. This may be a recipe for continuing dependency.

Another problem is that the appeal mechanisms recommended by the new *Indian Act* rules do not need to be established by the bands that have adopted membership codes.[76] Thus, persons refused membership must go to court to challenge membership decisions. While the acquired rights provisions are supposed to ensure that no one is denied membership unfairly, some Aboriginal women told the Commission that such practices do exist. They would like to see band membership codes reviewed and, if necessary, revised to ensure fairness and the protection of acquired rights. There was also a general call for some sort of appeal mechanism, such as a separate and impartial appeal tribunal. Appeal mechanisms are discussed in our chapter on governance (Volume 2, Chapter 3).

Ultimately, any policy that creates distinctions within a group can create divisions in that group. The amended act establishes a series of distinctions around which disputes can develop: subsection 6(1) versus subsection 6(2), members versus non-members, and Indian versus non-Indian. Even more damaging, these categories have the potential to become the basis for social divisions within First Nations communities. Divisions within a group can be accentuated, and tensions heightened, when resources are scarce.

For example, initially the non-Indian spouses of status Indian band members will have a lesser status in the band community. After one generation, however, they will be joined by the non-Indian children of 6(2) status Indians who have married non-Indians. After two generations, these non-Indian children will reach adulthood and may marry each other or other 6(2) status Indians. In either case, their children will not be Indians under the *Indian Act.* Thus, within a couple of generations, Indian band communities will have sizeable populations of non-Indians who, under current federal funding formulae – based on the number of status Indians in a given band – will begin to put strains on federally funded services. Moreover, these people will also be ineligible for federal programs available to status Indians, such as uninsured health benefits and post-secondary education. An underclass will thus have been created in First Nations communities.[77]

In the same way, one- and two-parent band membership codes may also lead to divisions within communities. For example, under a two-parent code, in 50 years band members may well be outnumbered by non-members in a community. Since only band members will have voting rights, however, they will be in a position to control political life and the allocation of benefits such as housing. At the other end of the spectrum may be bands with one-parent membership codes in which the band membership is large but increasingly composed of non-Indians as a result of the way the 6(1) and 6(2) distinctions work in the case of out-marriage. Funding based on the number of status Indians will not be able to keep pace with community needs. Although all band members, whether status Indian or not, will be able to vote and to decide on the allocation of vital resources, band members who are status Indians and who 'count' for purposes of funding may grow to resent those who are not but who nonetheless take part in the benefits of band membership. These are hypothetical projections based on existing rules. This is not the future we have in mind.

The right to live on-reserve

> I think it's a trick when they reinstate the people...they were promising too much of everything, the housing and the land. But we don't have land. I don't have land. I got a house, [but] it belongs to my husband....But whenever I go on the reserve I won't have land. I have to go and chop a tree and look around and sit on that stump, see if there is any room where I can live, put my house.
>
> Samaria Reynolds
> Indigenous Women's Collective
> Winnipeg, Manitoba, 29 April 1992

The right to live on a reserve is an emotional as well as a political issue. For many Bill C-31 registrants, the reserve is an important source of personal identity: it is part of their traditional homeland, their community. The department of Indian affairs survey supports this observation. It found that, of the 2,000 Bill C-31 registrants whose views were canvassed, almost two-thirds reported that they applied for Indian status for reasons of identity or because of the culture and sense of belonging that it implied.[78]

Most people whose Indian status was restored through Bill C-31 (as opposed to those who gained Indian status for the first time) were compelled in one way or another to leave their home communities; hence the attempt in Bill C-31 to repair, at least partially, the injustice done to them and their descendants. However, current reserve residents also leave their home communities for a number of reasons – to pursue post-secondary educational opportunities, for health care, to acquire marketable skills they cannot acquire on the reserve. As we point out in our chapter on Aboriginal people in urban areas (Chapter 7, later in this volume), Aboriginal women also leave their communities to escape physical and sexual abuse. Others leave because they feel that their needs are not being taken seriously and that they have no control over issues that directly affect them. But many leave with the intention of coming back and with the expectation of having a place to live when they return.

Reserve residency is not an absolute right for people with Indian status or even for those who belong to a particular band, whether the membership list is maintained by the department or by the band. In fact, subject to a number of ambiguously worded limitations and guidelines, the authority to decide on-reserve residency matters rests with the band council under subsection 81(1) of the *Indian Act* – a power provided in the 1985 amendments.

Unfortunately, the *Indian Act*, in most respects, is not very helpful in determining what rights, if any, an adult member of a band has to live on a reserve. For example, one might have assumed that, to protect the acquired membership rights of Bill C-31 registrants, residency rights would be part of the acquired rights that bands would be obliged to take into account in their by-laws. They are not, however. As a result, many Bill C-31 registrants who might otherwise wish to return to their reserve communities continue to live off-reserve.

In addition, many women object to being affiliated automatically with the bands that Indian affairs records show they were connected to in the past through their fathers or husbands. In this regard, Indian affairs acknowledges that "[r]egistrants would much prefer to be affiliated with a band closer to their domicile or to a band with which the mother or wife in a marriage is affiliated".[79]

Indian women have concerns about the right of their children to live on reserves. Children have special rights with regard to residence. The *Indian Act* provides in section 18.1 that children may reside on reserve lands if they are dependants of, or in the custody of, a band member who is himself or herself resident on-reserve. This provision was part of the Bill C-31 amendments. The most common situations would be cases of adoption, court-ordered custody and foster children. Because the conditional acquired rights described earlier and referred to in subsection 11(2) have been avoided by the many bands that passed membership codes before 29 June 1987, and because band membership codes may exclude children who might otherwise have been included on band membership lists under the new membership codes, situations can arise where the natural children of band members may not themselves be band members. For example, under a blood quantum test, an Indian man and his non-Indian wife would both be band members, but their child (being only 50 per cent 'Indian') might not be. However, the children will be allowed to live on-reserve because of section 18.1 as long as they are dependants. This provision would seem to constrain the authority of bands to exclude from reserve residency minor children who are not band members.

Many Indian women believe that further analysis is called for. They would like to see a review of residency by-laws to ensure that they do not unfairly affect a particular group, especially as relating to Bill C-31 people. Women would also like the relationship between residency by-laws and band membership codes examined to ensure that the two do not operate jointly to exclude people in ways they would not do individually.

Land-holding system on reserves

Many, though not all, Indian bands operate under a 'certificate of possession' system. Aboriginal women told the Commission that the regulations for issuing certificates of possession are a limiting feature of the *Indian Act* because of sexual discrimination.

The certificate of possession (CP) system is set out in section 20 of the *Indian Act*. Under it, an Indian is not 'lawfully' in possession of reserve land without an allotment by the band council as approved by the minister. A CP is therefore evi-

dence of the right to possess reserve land and to occupy that land. But this right
can be terminated if an individual ceases to be a band member. Section 25 provides that when an Indian ceases to be entitled to reside on a reserve, he or she
has six months to give the right of possession to another band member (or the
band). After that, the land automatically reverts to the band. Extensions can be
granted, and the act allows for compensation for improvements.

This system can create a curious situation in which a band member without a CP can be expelled from the reserve by the band, but one with a CP cannot
be expelled because the certificate carries with it the right to occupy the land.
However, under section 25, any individual can lose the right to reside on a reserve
upon loss of Indian status or band membership. We have already seen that
some individuals might have problems obtaining membership in a band even
though they have obtained Indian status. This has ramifications for descendants,
because the children of people stripped of membership or status will not be able
to inherit, possess or even reside on reserve land. Most notably, this includes non-
Indian spouses of Indian persons married after 1985 as well as spouses of Bill
C-31 women and, potentially, their children. This affects Indian women and
their families disproportionately.

There is no prohibition against women owning property through a certificate of possession. But the cumulative effect of a history of legislation that has
excluded women and denied them property and inheritance rights, together with
the sexist language embedded in the legislation before the 1985 amendments,
has created a perception that women are not entitled to hold a CP. In a brief to
the Commission, the B.C. Native Women's Society stated:

> In the past, the Department of Indian Affairs has followed the prac-
> tice of issuing Certificates of Possession solely to the oldest male
> member of the family. This tradition has been carried over from
> European notions of land holding and succession and it has resulted
> in the dismantling of many Aboriginal systems. For example, before
> contact, in many matrilineal systems, women held elevated positions
> of power and prestige superior to those of their husbands.
> Furthermore, the descendence of those rights and power continued
> through the female, not male, lineage....After contact, Aboriginal
> women not only lost their formal positions of power and prestige they
> formerly held but the new system may have caused them to lose their
> right to live with their children in their own community.[80]

A further complicating factor is the division of property when a marriage
fails. Marriage and the division of marriage assets upon marriage breakdown are
governed by provincial law, but the *Indian Act* is paramount on reserves. A court
cannot order the division of on-reserve property on the same basis as it can with
other property. Likewise, no court can order that one party shall have exclusive

possession of the matrimonial home. Indian women on-reserve, therefore, are seriously disadvantaged. In 1986, a precedent-setting decision was made on this point. In the case of *Derrickson* v. *Derrickson*, the court held that a woman cannot apply for possession of the matrimonial home unless the certificate of possession is solely in her name. The most she can hope for is an award of compensation to replace her half-interest in the house.[81]

This is seen as extremely unfair, because land and housing are in short supply on many reserves. Also, in an abusive situation, such a ruling could force a woman away from her support network of community, friends and family. The B.C. Native Women's Society has suggested that courts should view the issue as one of federal and provincial jurisdiction rather than one about "whether the application of Euro-Canadian rules and values relating to family and property are appropriate".[82]

In principle, many Indian women want the presumption of equitable interest in reserve lands of married (or equivalent) spouses reflected in legislation. Some possibilities were put forth, such as introducing new legislation, amending the *Indian Act*, or referentially incorporating provincial laws on this matter. Any such amendments or legislation would have to recognize and respect Indian custom marriages. Rather than amending the *Indian Act*, which would involve much energy, effort and resources, another approach would address the concerns of Aboriginal women and serve the ultimate goal.

In our vision of self-government, nations are made up of thousands of individuals – who should not be categorized as status or non-status, 6(1) or 6(2). All should be equal citizens of strong, healthy nations. The most offensive parts of the *Indian Act* cannot be changed overnight, but in re-establishing their concept of nationhood, Aboriginal people can overcome the many divisions that have arisen over the years as a result of federal policies. Many Aboriginal women who appeared before us spoke in eloquent terms about this important task.

In Volume 2, Chapter 3, we argued that in the reconstruction and recognition of Aboriginal nations, the intrusive, sex-biased and outdated elements of the Indian Act can be eliminated. The three-stage recognition procedure we recommend includes

- organizing for recognition (including the enumeration of potential citizens);
- preparing the nation's constitution and seeking endorsement; and
- getting recognition under the proposed Aboriginal Nations Recognition and Government Act.

One of the most important tasks in the first stage will be enumerating potential populations of citizens. At this early stage in the recognition process, the errors and injustices of past federal Indian policy should be corrected by identifying candidates for citizenship in the Aboriginal nation. Candidates should include not only those persons who are now members of the communities concerned but also those persons who wish to be members of the nation and can trace their descent from or otherwise show a current or historical social, political or family connection to that nation. Financial resources to meet the needs of all citizens of a nation will be a matter for treaty negotiation between Aboriginal nations and the federal and provincial governments.

As nations are rebuilt, it is envisioned that their citizenship codes will embrace all individuals who have ties to the nation but who, for reasons highlighted here, have been excluded in the past. These new citizenship provisions will eliminate concerns about the effects of Bill C-31 in creating categories of 'full Indians' and 'half Indians'. Rather than imposing restrictive band membership codes that may result in the destruction of communities over time,[83] Aboriginal nations, renewed and strengthened in the ways we have proposed, would implement a citizenship code that fosters inclusion and nurtures nation building.

The role of Aboriginal women in nation building cannot be underestimated and must not be ignored. As we have observed, many Aboriginal women play a special role in articulating visions of nationhood founded on the best of past traditions and culture. These visions must guide the present leadership if Aboriginal nationhood within a renewed Canadian federation is to become a living, vibrant and egalitarian reality.

RECOMMENDATION

The Commission recommends that

Participation in 4.2.1
Nation Building
The government of Canada provide funding to Aboriginal women's organizations, including urban-based groups, to
  (a) improve their research capacity and facilitate their participation in all stages of discussion leading to the design and development of self-government processes; and
  (b) enable them to participate fully in all aspects of nation building, including developing criteria for citizenship and related appeal processes.

4. HEALTH AND SOCIAL SERVICES: A PRIORITY ON HEALING

I find that there are so many changes that our people have undergone, so many adaptations that we have had to make to survive. There are many deep-rooted emotional problems that do not get addressed – the problems we see day to day in the high number of suicides, death by misadventure, violent deaths, high jail populations, alcohol and drug abuse and just so many throw-away people that we have.

Mavis Henry
Pauquachin Band
Esquimalt, British Columbia, 21 May 1992

Aboriginal women involved in health and social services, in both staff and volunteer capacities, have articulated what they see going on around them and identified what is needed. They are keenly aware of the difficulties encountered daily as Aboriginal people try to achieve a basic standard of health and social services:

Health is a matter of people's lives and if we as Aboriginal people want self-determination, we have to look at how we are going to recover from past and current diseases and illnesses so that we can build a healthy and sound nation.

Marlene Poitras
Edmonton, Alberta
11 June 1992

Every Canadian is aware of the fact that all people carry the experiences of the past into their present lives. For the majority, it's the basis of progress. For the Métis, the past is a collection of bitter memories which, in many cases, results in people internalizing our problems, losing our sense of dignity and self-esteem and sliding downhill into despair, which is dealt with through alcohol and drugs. Far too often the outcome is to recreate our own misery and pass it on to the next generation. Invariably, alcoholism and substance abuse is the spark that ignites family violence, child abuse, crime and all sorts of disorders within our homes and communities. The effects are felt outside the walls of our homes. It has an impact within our schools, our churches, our community administrations, our economic development efforts and everything that touches our lives.

Sandra DeLaronde
President, Metis Women of Manitoba
Winnipeg, Manitoba, 3 June 1993

The failure of governments to provide Métis people with sufficient resources to deal with social issues is a sign of the indifference of public policy, Sandra DeLaronde concluded.

The Aboriginal Women's Canadian Labour Force (AWCLF) assists women who encounter difficulties in the workplace. Through personal and collective experiences "as Aboriginal women trying to survive and get ahead in the context of a deeply entrenched, hostile Canadian work environment", the AWCLF identified a number of issues confronting Aboriginal women, including racism and sexism:

> We see a lot of evidence...where Aboriginal women have played a leadership role in the development of institutions which will eventually be rolled into self-government, such as child welfare, the court worker program, to name two of the more prominent kinds of developments....
>
> However, despite their many contributions and developing roles as leaders, Aboriginal women continue to face special challenges....high unemployment, very low income, high rates of conflict with the law, poor health and a high incidence of suicide and teenage pregnancies....Aboriginal women also have to deal with issues such as abuse, negative stereotyping and limited participation in decision-making positions.
>
> Jeri Von Ramin
> Aboriginal Women's Canadian Labour Force
> Winnipeg, Manitoba, 23 April 1992

Aboriginal women also reported problems related to a lack of Aboriginal staff in agencies and turnover in that staff:

> Every year we have different nurses...different doctors coming in. This is really hard on the people....The alcohol and drug problems causing family problems, spousal assault and abuse, child neglect, all of these things have happened and I lived them....I've seen women and men suffering. I've seen children suffering because of alcohol abuse and I've seen elders suffering. I know that our people are doing all they can to help in these areas, trying to get training so that they can try to help lower the number of people suffering....
>
> Mary Teya
> Community Health Representative
> Fort McPherson, Northwest Territories, 7 May 1992

Despite the problems, Aboriginal women are providing leadership and facilitating change. Nancy van Heest described the role of Urban Images, an organization serving First Nations people in the urban setting:

> Initially, Urban Images worked to help women literally get off the streets, out of a life of prostitution or substance abuse, and to assist persons who wanted to get off social assistance....In the eight years the program ran, there were approximately 500-plus Aboriginal women in attendance with 376 graduating. In 1993, after self-evaluation...Urban Images changed its program focus to the Aboriginal family and now we

have men in our classroom. The rationale for this shift of focus is that family systems is a more effective method. Previously the program was aimed at helping only the individual prepare for employment. There was no recognition of the importance of working with the whole family....We know that it is a waste of money to simply use a narrow pre-employment program....Unless the students empower themselves to successfully address their personal issues and future problems, these same problems will return and destroy them.

Nancy van Heest
Urban Images for First Nations
Vancouver, British Columbia, 2 June 1993

In our chapter on health and healing (Volume 3, Chapter 3), we cited testimony and research showing that Aboriginal people suffer disproportionately from social and emotional ill health. Reduced life expectancy and poor physical health are two major consequences, but another less tangible consequence is the undermining of collective self-esteem. In testimony and consultation, Aboriginal people shared insights about directions for change and progress toward wellness and well-being. In some places, they are already putting those insights into practice. For instance, we heard that in many communities Aboriginal women are providing leadership in facilitating healing processes and other initiatives:

As far as I am concerned, they are the strength of our communities. They always have been. As men, we may deny that because our egos get in the way. But, the fact is that in my tribe, the women were the voice of our community a hundred years ago.

Phil Hall
Alderman, District of Chilliwack
Victoria, British Columbia, 22 May 1992

Our roles and responsibilities have been altered. Women have had to take more responsibility, not only for the family but for the community, with very little support by leaders, by people who make decisions; and many times, as women we are left out of the decision-making processes.

Lillian Sanderson
La Ronge Native Women's Council
La Ronge, Saskatchewan, 28 May 1992

The inequalities in health and well-being between Aboriginal and non-Aboriginal people extend from physical ill health to social, emotional and community ill health. When we examine patterns and dynamics over time, we conclude that no matter what the disease or social dysfunction, it is likely to be more severe among Aboriginal people. Aboriginal concepts of health and healing take the view that all elements of life and living are interdependent. From this perspective, the Canadian system of health care is deficient because it does not address the full range of causes of ill health, nor does it encourage whole health and well-being. Certain approaches have been tried in the past and have met with limited success because they were unable to account for the underlying imbalance in relations between Aboriginal peoples and the institutions and systems of the dominant society.

Aboriginal people have told us that the past can be forgiven but it cannot be forgotten. It infuses the present and gives shape to institutions, attitudes and practices that are hostile to the aspirations of Aboriginal people to assume their rightful place in a renewed Canadian federation. Aboriginal people have also said that only by facing up to the fundamental contradictions of colonialism can true healing and reconciliation take place:

> In our communities right now we need a lot of healing. There is a lot of hurt...it is hurt because of the way we, as a people, have been treated for the past 500 years. Those issues have to come out and they have to be discussed. We have to be healed so that we are no longer classed as second-class citizens. We are the Aboriginal people of this land, and we must be respected for that.
>
> Rosa Wright
> Fort Simpson, Northwest Territories
> 26 May 1992

Aboriginal women are profoundly aware of the need for healing, not just of the body, but of the mind, spirit and environment. Overall wellness is the ultimate goal. Aboriginal women spoke about healing as an essential component in all areas of Aboriginal life:

> If improving the material living conditions of Aboriginal people is to be realized, then the all-around development of men and women as part of a comprehensive process must be accompanied by deeply entrenched cultural values, social relations, education and wellness so that they may achieve fulfilment as distinct personalities in accordance with their possibilities and capabilities.
>
> Marlene Buffalo
> Samson Band
> Hobbema, Alberta, 10 June 1992

> We knew we had to look back to see where we've been and we had to take a real honest, hard look at where we are now to see the reality of what we're living in right now. And we had to look ahead to see what a healthy community must be like.
>
> Alma Brooks
> Wabanoag Medicine Lodge
> Kingsclear, New Brunswick, 19 May 1992

Our real goal, however, is to end all forms of violence and abuse in our communities. This will only happen when the conditions which exacerbate violence are dealt with – alcohol and drug abuse, the devaluation of women and girls, poverty and dependence, overcrowded housing and economic instability. We also need our communities to be places which provide opportunities for personal healing and growth, and our lands, economies and institutions to be Inuit controlled.

Martha Flaherty
President, Pauktuutit
Ottawa, Ontario, 2 November 1993

Aboriginal women were also clear about the types of initiatives they wish to see in their communities. They focused on initiatives that are holistic and include principles of equality and respect for self and family:

Modern medicine now knows that self-esteem is an important part of a healthy human being. By feeling good about yourself – by knowing that you have value, that your life means something – you will have confidence to lead a healthy life. More importantly, you will have the ability to add something to your family and community....We believe that education is one of the priorities in community development. It is our firm belief that the quality of education and training is crucial to improving the standard of living for our young people....We believe strongly that anything less will result in a continuation of the band-aid approach which perpetuates the tragedy of the status quo.

Violet Mundy
Community Health, Ucluelet Tribe
Port Alberni, British Columbia, 20 May 1993

Little information has been collected systematically about the number of Aboriginal professionals involved in health and healing services, although under-representation of Aboriginal people among health and social service professionals is acknowledged to be significant and widespread. The dearth of information reflects the low priority that has generally been accorded to the development of Aboriginal human resources in Canada, and the absence of this vital information is an obstacle to planning.

In Volume 3, Chapter 3, we set out a number of recommendations to address the complex issues surrounding Aboriginal health and social services. We were told that Aboriginal people believe the capacity to exercise responsibility resides in all beings in the natural world and that when all parts of the whole are fulfilling their responsibilities, the result is balance, harmony and holistic health

– a healthy mind, body and spirit. Holistic solutions to long-standing dilemmas are being developed in diverse forms and in widely scattered locations, drawing on Aboriginal traditions of knowledge and a realistic assessment of current conditions. These initiatives mobilize the inner strength of individuals and communities, and Aboriginal people are increasingly pressing federal, provincial, territorial and municipal governments and service agencies to move aside and create political and organizational space for Aboriginal initiatives.

In Volume 3, Chapter 3, we proposed a significant shift in the locus of control of personal and community services, away from centralized, bureaucratic regulation and toward Aboriginal community control. We also endorsed the development of distinct institutions mandated by Aboriginal governments and accountable to Aboriginal people. We proposed that the new directions for Aboriginal health and healing systems be based on four guidelines for action:

- equity of health and social welfare outcomes;
- holism in the diagnosis of problems, their treatment and prevention;
- Aboriginal authority over health systems and, where feasible, community control over services; and
- diversity in the design of systems and services.

We also proposed four practical strategies for the reconstruction of health and healing systems in Aboriginal nations and communities, strategies that are preconditions for the health and social well-being of Aboriginal people no matter which governments are in charge:

- the development of a system of Aboriginal healing centres and healing lodges under Aboriginal control as the principle units of holistic and culture-based health and wellness services;
- the development of Aboriginal human resources adequate to the new system, its values and assumptions;
- the full and active support of mainstream health and social service authorities and providers in meeting the health and healing goals of Aboriginal people; and
- the implementation of an infrastructure development program to address the most immediate health threats in Aboriginal communities, including the provision of clean water, basic sanitation facilities and safe housing.

The participation of Aboriginal women in these initiatives should be viewed by Aboriginal governments as not only desirable but imperative. As we have shown, women are providing leadership in many community-based projects, and they are often in the front line of service provision. The importance that Aboriginal women attach to healing cannot be overstated, and their role in achieving wellness needs to be acknowledged and incorporated in all aspects of the design, development and implementation of health and social services.

RECOMMENDATION

The Commission recommends that

Participation in
Health Institutions

4.2.2

Aboriginal governments and organizations provide for the full and fair participation of Aboriginal women in the governing bodies of all Aboriginal health and healing institutions.

In our chapter on health and healing, we set forth other recommendations relevant to Aboriginal women. For example, we called upon the government of Canada to fund national Aboriginal organizations, including women's organizations, to prepare a comprehensive, co-ordinated plan for human resource development in health and healing that builds on regional and local knowledge and initiatives.

Concerning certain existing initiatives – the Community Health Representative Program, the National Native Alcohol and Drug Abuse Program and the Indian and Inuit Health Careers Program – we recommended that Canadian governments and national Aboriginal organizations, including national Aboriginal women's organizations, examine how to expand and improve these programs so that they become cornerstones of the more holistic and integrative approaches needed to address the health and social needs of Aboriginal people.

In Chapter 7 of this volume, we discuss migration patterns and the urban experience of many Aboriginal women, particularly in relation to housing and social services. In acknowledgement of the critical role and responsibility Aboriginal women have assumed in urban areas, we recommend in that chapter that urban service agencies seek direction and guidance from Aboriginal women in formulating policy, programs and services respecting Aboriginal women. We also recommend that non-Aboriginal individuals and organizations whose work or responsibilities affect Aboriginal women's lives receive comprehensive information and education on the specific condition and needs of urban Aboriginal women.

In further discussion on health matters, Aboriginal women also spoke to us about the importance of the environment. In the far north, for example, we heard that poor sanitation is a serious problem:

> This is preventable, but in a lot of cases [there are] inadequate sewage lagoons, disposable solid wastes, inadequate clean, running water....There is evidence that certain Baffin communities are con-

taminated with PCBs....This recognized contamination of the sea mammals affects the staple diet of many of the Inuit who eat the traditional Native foods. Concerns have been raised that PCBs can be transferred to the milk of breast-feeding mothers.

Ineaq Korgak
Executive Assistant, Baffin Regional Health Board
Iqaluit, Northwest Territories, 26 May 1992

On the west coast, where many Aboriginal people depend upon healthy fish stocks, we heard that

the human and environmental crisis is exacerbated by other factors that are ignored, or inadequately dealt with by regulations: wood fibre 'lost' and damaging habitat through smothering, oxygen depletion...leakage of toxic leachates from solids and sludges in landfills into soil and air; 'spills' of processed chemicals....We, the Tseshaht Nation, have taken the steps towards joint management to protect our resources....Our nation relies heavily on the land and sea as the Creator put it here for us all to share.

Lisa Gallic
Tseshaht Band
Port Alberni, British Columbia, 20 May 1992

In other parts of the country, we heard further representations from Aboriginal women, for example, about the effects of uranium mining:

The Baker Lake Concerned Citizens Committee speaks for the average person in Baker Lake, people who have nothing to gain and everything to lose if uranium mining goes ahead. If anything happened to the caribou, we Inuit would have nothing left but welfare. So our clean environment means everything to us. If people don't understand that, then they won't understand how determined we are to protect our environment and our culture.

Joan Scottie
Baker Lake Concerned Citizens Committee
Rankin Inlet, Northwest Territories, 19 November 1992

We also heard about environmental protection in general:

We believe that there needs to be the inclusion of environmental protection to ensure a future for all children. It must identify the rights of the earth and our responsibilities to protect the earth. Continued unrestrained development threatens us all. Aboriginal people and all Canadians need constitutional protection from more mega-project dams, clear-cut logging, mining and environmentally dangerous industries. Rather than holding out the individual or the collective to be sacred, the basic premise must be that the earth should be held sacred.

Marilyn Fontaine
Aboriginal Women's Unity Coalition
Winnipeg, Manitoba, 23 April 1992

Concerns related to the environment were raised by Aboriginal women throughout our hearings; for more detailed analysis and recommendations, see Volume 4, Chapter 6 dealing with the north; Volume 3, Chapter 3 on health and healing; and Volume 2, Chapter 4 on lands and resources.

5. THE NEED FOR PLACES OF REFUGE

In 1969, the YWCA operated a residence for status Indian women in downtown Toronto. It was called simply 'Y Place' and was funded by the Department of Indian Affairs and Northern Development. By 1973, Aboriginal women had become involved in the administration of the residence and renamed it Anduhyaun, Ojibwa for 'our home'.

Twenty years later, Anduhyaun is still in operation, providing Aboriginal women and their children with a culturally based supportive environment and the resources to work on a variety of problems, including abusive relationships, family and marital breakdown, legal and financial difficulties, and alcohol and drug abuse. Staff at Anduhyaun help Aboriginal women get housing, medical services, further education, skills development and employment. They also operate a food bank.[84]

In describing their work, managing director Catherine Brooks noted that many Aboriginal women who become residents of Anduhyaun are accompanied by their children, who have also been exposed to or experienced violence. She spoke about other experiences Aboriginal women go through such as discrimination in housing and employment.

In 1986, Anduhyaun began to work on the development of a second-stage supportive housing program (first-stage housing is the shelter operation). The purpose of the second-stage program is to support women making changes in their lives by addressing issues underlying substance abuse and assisting them in formulating and attaining their goals:

> Whether her goals are to become an effective parent or reunite her family or acquire education or skills for...employment that is meaningful to her, Anduhyaun's purpose is to support her in achieving her goals.

Catherine Brooks
Managing Director, Anduhyaun
Toronto, Ontario, 26 June 1992

In their written brief, Anduhyaun relayed their belief that the underlying cause of violence is the sense of lack of control experienced by Aboriginal people. The answer, they believe, is self-determination in every facet of community life, which means "seeing our situation as it is, then developing and controlling the community responsive resources to change our lives in positive directions".[85]

Along with the need for an increased emphasis on culturally appropriate health and social services, we were struck by the many interventions that disclosed the vulnerability of Aboriginal women and children. We heard testimony from individual women who have survived violence. We also heard from Aboriginal women's organizations whose representatives described the current difficulties and special challenges that Aboriginal women face. But, of equal importance, we heard about the goals Aboriginal women are pursuing in the firm belief that "they will lead to positive, healthy changes in their lives and those of their children as well as those of their community as a whole".[86]

In Volume 3, we examined family and community violence. We highlighted the fact that violence is a complex, multi-faceted and widespread social problem in many Aboriginal communities. Since it was raised by so many Aboriginal women during our hearings, we raise the issue again here. We believe it is important to let their voices express their feelings of vulnerability and to convey what they are doing about it.

Some Aboriginal women spoke to us during private sessions because they feared repercussions from their disclosure. At one private session organized by an Aboriginal women's association in June 1993, 30 Aboriginal women spoke about incidents of sexual abuse and violence in their lives. One woman told us:

> In my community, I've been ostracized, blacklisted. I'm a graduate of university and have spoken out against practices of band employees who use their power and authority...have pressed charges of battery against my husband and found that there is a band by-law that says anyone who is separated, who is not an original member, is taken off the band list. This applies to widows, women who've been abused, etc. Since then, I've been physically and verbally assaulted....We want to have our own centres, and we can't wait for band councils to decide when the community is going to go into healing...so much of the sickness is in our families...and our own people discriminate against us in the most hurtful ways. [I was] scared to come here today...it gets lonely, fighting that battle and not knowing who is going to be the oppressor, because they're one of us.

At other locations women spoke more generally about the issue, often on behalf of other Aboriginal women in their community:

> During the workshop that we had in my community, the people identified many of the problems. They didn't blame anyone. They took full responsibility for the reality of life in their community and I was very proud of them. It took a lot of courage for them to do that. But they

talked about family violence...sexual abuse...a very high percentage of alcohol and drug abuse and use. But they saw that the alcohol and the drugs were – had become – a mechanism of survival, to survive the pain and the sense of helplessness and powerlessness, the fact that no one listens to them, no one validates their frustration. No voice.

> Alma Brooks
> Wabanoag Medicine Lodge
> Kingsclear, New Brunswick, 19 May 1992

Aboriginal women also spoke about the initiatives they have begun in their communities to deal with family violence:

I had no interest in women's issues. I also did not like the idea of being in close association with many women. I had seven biological sisters and I had trouble getting along with them. So I said...'I don't know if I really want to work with many women'....Three months later I find myself hired at the Manitoba Committee on Wife Abuse as a liaison worker. I quickly contacted a few Aboriginal women...and formed an ad hoc Aboriginal women's committee. We were bewildered, hurt and perplexed when the non-Native women criticized and scoffed at our organizing. We carried on in spite of this and slowly worked on our dream of services for abused Aboriginal women.

> Virginia Miracle
> Ikwe Widdjiitiwin
> Winnipeg, Manitoba, 23 April 1992

And so Ikwe Widdjiitiwin, which means 'women helping one another', was established. According to Darlene Hall (then executive director), the 20-bed short-term crisis shelter for abused women and children in Winnipeg opened its doors on 22 December 1989. Since opening, they have had more than 350 women and 1,000 children in residence. Their philosophy can be summarized thus:

Solutions towards the end of family violence can be realized by utilizing the holistic integrated approach of the traditional four directions of empowerment: mental, by respect; physical, by sharing; emotional, by caring; and spiritual, by hope.

> Darlene Hall
> Executive Director, Ikwe Widdjiitiwin
> Winnipeg, Manitoba, 23 April 1992

In Iqaluit, Northwest Territories, we heard that the Baffin Region Aggvik Society provided safe haven for 100 families in 1987-88 and 303 families in 1991-92:

Women's voices have often not been heard because of the reluctance to share family issues publicly. Women have always been responsible for family relationships. Family relationships are the basis of Inuit culture. Therefore, women must have a voice in how the culture is developed. They must be encouraged to talk about these issues, since they are essential to a healthy culture and lifestyle.

Leetia James Aivik
Vice-Chair, Baffin Regional Women's Shelter
Iqaluit, Northwest Territories, 26 May 1992

Some estimates suggest that violence occurs in 80 per cent of Aboriginal families.[87] As we pointed out in *Choosing Life: A Special Report on Suicide Among Aboriginal People*, the statistical evidence shows that rates of suicide among Aboriginal people are significantly higher than among Canadians generally and that the gap is greatest among the young. Adolescents and young adults are in the category of greatest risk. Most disturbing of all, we identified a strong possibility that if the rate remains high, the number of suicides will rise in the next 10 to 15 years as the youth population grows.[88]

Aboriginal women, as the givers of life, custodians of culture and language, and caretakers of children, want to ensure that the violence stops. And despite obstacles encountered in both Aboriginal and non-Aboriginal society, First Nations, Inuit and Métis women continue to demonstrate a powerful determination to change their situation and to work co-operatively with others:

> As women we do have responsibilities. We are the keepers of our culture and we are the teachers of our children. I would just like to say that for our men that we don't want to walk behind you. We want to walk beside you. We want to heal with you and we want to help you make those decisions that are needing to be made for the future of our people and that we walk together.

Lillian Sanderson
La Ronge Native Women's Council
La Ronge, Saskatchewan, 28 May 1992

As the views of Aboriginal women attest, it is vitally important to work on relationships among Aboriginal people in their communities.

> When relationships turn sour, what is the healthy thing to do? We apologize, don't we. That is pretty basic, but very fundamental to the process of change in a relationship....When you say, 'I'm sorry', you begin again on another positive note....The first round of these hearings...the Anishnabe communities expressed their deepest hurts over and over. At this point, we need to hear 'I'm sorry'....We need to hear this from the intellectuals of this country, the educators, the religious organizations, the health professionals, doctors, nurses, social workers, police et cetera, et cetera. Until we get this response, we cannot move forward towards healing....

> We...have homework to do ourselves on our relationships in our communities....Let's work towards healing our relationships there too.
>
> Merle Assance-Beedie
> Barrie and Area Native Advisory Circle
> Orillia, Ontario, 13 May 1993

In our discussion of the family in Volume 3, Chapter 2, we pointed out that although not all Aboriginal communities are suffering from high levels of family and communal violence, the frequency of violent behaviour directed at Aboriginal women and children is alarming. Issues of family violence are also addressed in our special report, *Bridging the Cultural Divide: A Report on Aboriginal People and Criminal Justice in Canada*, in which we discuss the need to ensure the safety of Aboriginal women and children in Aboriginal justice systems.[89] We believe that a system that cannot protect women and children is a system that fails.

That report highlighted two case studies that feature a strong role for women, a role that has helped them ensure that developments in this area do not further victimize women and children. One option we proposed was that a body be located at the nation level to review criminal justice initiatives specifically as they relate to issues of family violence. This function could be fulfilled by Aboriginal women's groups active in the nation or, where such groups are not in place, Aboriginal nations could establish women's groups to review and approve such programs before implementation. Aboriginal society is not free from the sexism that exists in the rest of Canadian society, and unless this reality is acknowledged and concrete steps are taken to address it through the justice system, women and children will remain at risk.

In considering the concept of distinct Aboriginal justice systems, we addressed the needs of women and children. We concluded that women must be consulted and participate in the development of such systems. We concluded also that the *Canadian Charter of Rights and Freedoms* applies to Aboriginal governments, so that individuals subject to the laws or actions of such governments enjoy the protection of its provisions.

As we concluded in *Bridging the Cultural Divide*, the provisions of the Charter, particularly section 25, operating in conjunction with Aboriginal charters, means that Aboriginal nations have a wide measure of flexibility to design justice systems more reflective of their own cultures, customs and traditions. (For a complete discussion of issues surrounding the *Canadian Charter of Rights and Freedoms*, see Volume 2, Chapter 3.)

Until the fundamental restructuring of relationships between Aboriginal and non-Aboriginal governments takes place, we believe it is necessary to establish transitional measures. In *Bridging the Cultural Divide*, one of the transitional mechanisms we recommend is the establishment by legislation of an Aboriginal justice council. This body would determine which Aboriginal initiatives would be funded and what the level of funding would be. It would be broadly representative of First Nations, Inuit and Métis peoples, Aboriginal people from urban areas, and women and youth. Among other functions, it would undertake research. We also identified a number of issues that call for the kind of research best performed by Aboriginal legal scholars and practitioners in conjunction with members of their nations. We have in mind, for example, the development of Aboriginal charters of rights and adjudication processes.

We also recommended that the government of Canada convene an intergovernmental conference of federal, provincial and territorial ministers of justice and attorneys general, solicitors general, ministers of correctional services and ministers responsible for Aboriginal affairs to address the issues raised and recommendations made in *Bridging the Cultural Divide*. Representatives of Aboriginal nations, communities and organizations should also be invited to attend, including those who work directly in the development and implementation of Aboriginal healing and restorative justice projects. We therefore see strong participation by Aboriginal women.

Other initiatives must also occur. In Volume 3, Chapter 2, we discussed family violence as it was described to the Commission by Aboriginal women, men, people with disabilities, youth and elders. We discussed the various barriers to change and provided some guidance to solutions advanced by people in the communities. We also set out some ground rules for action suggested by those who spoke to us:

- Do not stereotype all Aboriginal people as violent.
- Make sure that assistance is readily available to those at risk.
- Do not make social or cultural excuses for violent actions.
- Attend to the safety and human rights of the vulnerable.
- Do not imagine that family violence can be addressed as a single problem.
- Root out the inequality and racism that feed violence in its many forms.

In that chapter, we recommended that Aboriginal leaders take a firm public stance in support of the right of women, children, seniors, persons with disabilities and all other vulnerable members of the community to be free from violence and that they endorse a policy of zero tolerance of violations of the physical, emotional or economic security of all Aboriginal persons. The importance of seeing and hearing Aboriginal leaders speak out against violence cannot be overstated. Aboriginal women expect their leaders to take a strong stand on this issue and to be role models for others.

We also recommended that Aboriginal governments adopt the principle of including women, youth, elders and persons with disabilities in governing councils and decision-making bodies, the modes of representation and participation of these persons being those that they find most congenial.

We also believe that reinstatement of community standards where they have been eroded is essential to securing a safe environment for women, children, seniors and persons with disabilities. In Volume 3, Chapter 2, we recommended that Aboriginal leaders and agencies serving vulnerable people encourage communities, with the full participation of women, to design and put into action codes of behaviour aimed at engaging all citizens in the creation and maintenance of safe communities and neighbourhoods.

Peace and harmony can be restored to families in part by stopping family violence. Other concerns with respect to the position and role of Aboriginal women remain to be addressed, however.

6. The Rise of Aboriginal Women's Organizations

During the period 1951-1970, Aboriginal people became more aware of their legal rights and as a result organized to address their concerns. Aboriginal women's organizations came into being and took on a range of issues, including the development of women in leadership roles and the resolution of health and social problems in their communities. This was a far cry from the first organizations started in 1937 by the Indian affairs department with the stated goal of assisting Indian women "to acquire sound and approved practices for greater home efficiency".[90]

First instituted and promoted by the department during the Depression, Indian homemakers' associations formed on reserves across Canada between 1930 and 1960. In the 1960s, most of these groups underwent a transformation from clubs focusing on home economics to clubs involved in public affairs, tackling issues such as housing standards, living conditions, Aboriginal rights and women's rights. The Indian Homemakers' Association of British Columbia was formed in 1965 to amalgamate clubs throughout the province.[91] Incorporated in 1969, it has the distinction of being the country's oldest provincial Aboriginal women's organization in operation today. Other associations, chapters and locals regrouping Aboriginal women were established across Canada, on reserves, in rural communities and in urban centres.[92]

The idea of a national body to represent Aboriginal women emerged at a 1970 international conference of Aboriginal women in Albuquerque, New Mexico, and in March 1971 the first National Native Women's Conference was held in Canada. In August 1974, the Native Women's Association of Canada (NWAC) convened its first annual assembly in Thunder Bay, Ontario. Until the early 1980s, NWAC would speak on behalf of First Nations, Inuit and Métis women.

In 1984, because of major differences in language, culture, and circumstances, Inuit women felt a need to create their own organization – Pauktuutit. Its mandate is to foster a greater awareness of the needs of Inuit women and to encourage their participation in community, regional and national concerns in relation to social, cultural and economic development.[93]

In 1992, the Métis National Council of Women was incorporated as a federation of six independent provincial and territorial Métis women's organizations: British Columbia, Alberta, Northwest Territories, Saskatchewan, Manitoba and Ontario.

Although stated differently, the goals and objectives of each Aboriginal women's organization are similar: improving the quality of life for Aboriginal women and their children by achieving equal participation in the social, economic, cultural and political life not only of their communities but of Canadian society as a whole.

Throughout the 1970s and '80s, the discriminatory provisions in the *Indian Act* were a central focus of concern. Women such as Yvonne Bedard, Jeannette Corbiere-Lavell, Mary Two Axe Early and Sandra Lovelace instituted legal proceedings challenging the loss of Indian status and rights. Aboriginal women wanted to see major changes in their lives and communities, and they were determined to take action locally, regionally, nationally and internationally:

> In 1981, Sandra Lovelace took her case to the United Nations Human Rights Committee. It held that Canada was in contravention of article 27 of the *International Covenant on Civil and Political Rights*. The committee ruled that the cultural rights guaranteed by article 27 of the Covenant were denied because she was forced to be separate from her community. Only after this decision did the Canadian government try to correct the situation, finally enacting Bill C-31 in 1985....This could not have happened if it were not for the Aboriginal women speaking out.
>
> Kathy Martin
> The Pas, Manitoba
> 20 May 1992

Although the discriminatory provisions of the *Indian Act* were important, a wide range of other concerns captured the attention of Aboriginal women's organizations. They were also placing increased emphasis on their participation in the decision-making processes of other national Aboriginal organizations.

Discussions on the patriation of the constitution had been occurring for a number of years, but it was not until 1981 that representatives of three national Aboriginal groups – the Assembly of First Nations (AFN), the Inuit Committee on National Issues (ICNI, predecessor of Inuit Tapirisat), and the Native Council of Canada (NCC) – became more involved.[94] A first ministers conference, convened in November 1981, produced a political accord on constitutional reform supported by the federal government and nine provinces. This accord had one glaring omission: Aboriginal rights. The Aboriginal Rights Coalition, led by NCC, ICNI, NWAC, the Dene Nation, the Council for Yukon Indians, the Nisga'a Tribal Council and the National Association of Friendship

Centres, initiated a series of public protests. With the support of Canadian women concerned about sexual equality and a support network of Canadian church organizations through Project North, they were able to have Aboriginal and treaty rights – albeit qualified as 'existing' Aboriginal and treaty rights – recognized in section 35 (1) of the *Constitution Act, 1982*.

During the first ministers conferences held between 1983 and 1987, NWAC continued to be involved in meetings of AFN's constitutional working group and the Native Council of Canada's constitutional process. During the 1983 first ministers conference, NWAC was instrumental in gaining a further amendment to section 35 of the act: "Notwithstanding any other provision of this Act, the aboriginal and treaty rights referred to in subsection (1) are guaranteed equally to male and female persons".

NWAC was not a formal participant in these conferences, however. It did not have its own seat at the table, nor was it given equitable funding. During the constitutional talks in 1992, NWAC launched a court case to gain equal participation and funding. In March 1992, the Native Women's Association of Canada put forward legal arguments that the Charter rights of Aboriginal women had been infringed by the government of Canada. After losing in the Federal Court, Trial Division,[95] NWAC was heard in the Federal Court of Appeal in June 1992. On August 28 of that year, the Federal Court of Appeal ruled unanimously in favour of NWAC. Speaking on behalf of the court, Justice Mahoney found that by funding the participation of the Assembly of First Nations, the Métis National Council, the Native Council of Canada and Inuit Tapirisat of Canada in the constitutional process and excluding the equal participation of NWAC,

> the Canadian Government has accorded the advocates of male dominated aboriginal self-governments a preferred position in the exercise of an expressive activity....It has thereby taken action which has had the effect of restricting the freedom of expression of Aboriginal women in a manner offensive to paragraph 2(b) and section 28 of the Charter.[96]

The federal government appealed this decision to the Supreme Court of Canada. The decision was overturned on 27 October 1994. Speaking for the court, Justice Sopinka said:

> The four Aboriginal groups invited to discuss possible constitutional amendments are all bona fide national representatives of Aboriginal people in Canada and, based on the facts in this case, there was no requirement under s. 2(b) of the Charter to also extend an invitation and funding directly to the respondents....I have concluded that the arguments of the respondents with respect to s. 15 must also fail. The lack of an evidentiary basis for the arguments with

respect to ss. 2(b) and 28 is equally applicable to any arguments advanced under s. 15(1) of the Charter in this case.[97]

Although NWAC ultimately lost the case, it made the point that Aboriginal women want a say in the decisions that will affect their future. At the July 1993 intergovernmental conference of federal, provincial and territorial ministers responsible for Aboriginal affairs, held in Inuvik, Northwest Territories, the Native Women's Association of Canada was officially invited to participate. NWAC also had its own seat at a similar conference in Toronto in February 1994.

7. THE NEED FOR FAIRNESS AND ACCOUNTABILITY

Aboriginal women and their organizations point out that active participation by everyone, men and women, is needed to eliminate obstacles and clear the path to a better future for Aboriginal peoples.

> We must never stop demonstrating forcefully our solidarity with the major Aboriginal demands which, fundamentally, concern the right to life and to dignity. But at the same time, we must not confuse solidarity with a false superficial unanimity that excludes all thinking and debate. On the contrary, it is important to stimulate thinking and discussion if we, as women and men on an equal footing, are to succeed in defining our future together. That is the best demonstration of solidarity that we can give. [translation]
>
> Michèle Rouleau
> Quebec Native Women's Association
> Montreal, Quebec, 27 May 1993

Our public hearings and the reports submitted in the context of the Commission's Intervener Participation Program demonstrated that these organizations are fulfilling a major role in raising awareness and understanding of the needs, issues and aspirations of Aboriginal women among other Aboriginal people and organizations, governments and the general public. Through their own research, project and program development, advocacy and other activities, Aboriginal women are making substantial contributions to effect change. This work must continue and be supported.

Aboriginal women continue to feel the need for separate organizations, circles, networks and other forums in which to pursue issues of particular concern to them and to fulfil their aspirations. Governments and other organizations should recognize, respect and include them in all areas of decision making. Earlier in this chapter, we recommended that the government of Canada provide funding to the national organizations representing Aboriginal women to support their capacity to conduct research and participate in all stages of the self-government process.

Throughout our hearings, when Aboriginal women referred to issues of fairness and accountability, it was generally in the context of self-government. These views were forceful, holistic and visionary:

I see self-government as being necessary to preserve our philosophical uniqueness. I do not want to see merely a European western model of government that is run by Indians. Rather, I want an Indian government that operates in accordance with traditional principles and customs, one that rests on a spiritual base and emphasizes group, not individual rights. I understand very well that self-government implies certain essential requisites, such as an adequate land base and economic self-sufficiency.

Marlene Buffalo
Samson Band
Hobbema, Alberta, 10 June 1992

The structure and functions of the traditional lodge provides a model for the exercise of self-government. We call upon the chiefs and councils and their representative organizations...to take immediate action to institute structures and processes that will provide opportunity for full and equal participation for First Nation elders, youth, women...in the development of self-government...[and] that the development of self-government structures, institutions, processes and policies be guided by traditional Aboriginal values, customs and practices.

Marilyn Fontaine
Aboriginal Women's Unity Coalition
Winnipeg, Manitoba, 23 April 1992

I don't believe that Indian self-government, or Indian self-determination should be merely a transferring of what is there. We need to create something. We need to look back to see where we've been and to put in place once again a mechanism that will perpetuate a good, healthy life for our future generations.

Alma Brooks
Wabanoag Medicine Lodge
Kingsclear, New Brunswick, 19 May 1992

Unfortunately, the imposition of southern values, laws and institutions on Inuit society has resulted in social, political and economic chaos in our communities. Women have suffered doubly for we lost status in our own society and were subjected to the patriarchal institutions born in the south. Until a proper balance is achieved among

Inuit men and women, mechanisms must be put into place to ensure that women are equally represented in all decision-making processes and on all decision-making bodies.

Martha Flaherty
President, Pauktuutit
Ottawa, Ontario, 1 November 1993

We also need a system of responsible government...a system of government that is a more accountable, representative method of conducting government, which has recognizable and respected rules of conduct.

Bernice Hammersmith
Provincial Secretary, Metis Society of Saskatchewan
La Ronge, Saskatchewan, 28 May 1992

A number of Aboriginal women identified themselves as members of nations rather than bands:

The Native Women's Association of Canada has stated previously and maintains that self-government should be granted...to nations, not to band councils....Each band council does not represent a nation....Any self-government agreement must be negotiated on a nation-to-nation basis.

Sharon McIvor
Native Women's Association of Canada
Toronto, Ontario, 26 June 1992

Quite often, our association is regarded as a special interest group. That bothers me because we are not a special interest group. We are members of a nation, and our organization represents many nations.

Marlene Pierre
Ontario Native Women's Association
Thunder Bay, Ontario, 27 October 1992

I think probably if the leaders had taken time to reflect and meditate on what those traditional values are that we would have the development of Aboriginal governments based on the principles of nationhood and not on the corporations acts of the provinces...[and that would accept] and welcome women's views as not just a particular lobby group's views but as a view of part of the nation, as part of the people, that women have real needs and have real answers to problems.

Sandra DeLaronde
President, Metis Women of Manitoba
The Pas, Manitoba, 19 May 1992

Even now as they talk self-government, they talk about imposed systems. That's for us to decide as nations, but we must organize into nations again, not as band councils.

Livina Lightbown
Vancouver, British Columbia
3 June 1993

In discussing self-government institutions and processes, Aboriginal women expressed views that focused on ensuring inclusiveness of all citizens of a nation:

In terms of what self-government might look like...first of all, we have to look at really developing a very basic philosophy of how people should be treated...that government has to be very sensitive to the needs of all its citizens.

Kathy Mallet
Co-ordinator, Original Women's Network
Winnipeg, Manitoba, 23 April 1992

The incorporation of the whole circle must be viewed as the point of reference to guarantee the survival of our peoples as nations. The extended family concept must be inclusive and applied not only to the citizens on the traditional homelands, but also to our people in the inner cities, prisons and smaller communities. Shared leadership responsibilities must become more fluid, which will allow a more positive approach to begin addressing many of the social problems that impact on our people daily. We have to begin to take a more holistic approach to these social issues.

Carol Gauthier
Shingwauk Anishnabek Student Society
Sault Ste. Marie, Ontario, 11 June 1992

They also spoke about the need to ensure that self-government models incorporate traditional principles and values:

The Aboriginal community needs to have the opportunity to come together in all its diversity, to undergo a values clarification process within the context of reviving traditional values. After all, violence is not a traditional value.

Marilyn Fontaine
Aboriginal Women's Unity Coalition
Winnipeg, Manitoba, 23 April 1992

Above all, First Nations, Inuit and Métis women expressed the need to ensure that Aboriginal governments are accountable to their citizens through mechanisms designed to ensure fairness, trust, equality and justice:

I firmly believe that self-government based upon the inherent right to be self-determining must hear the weaker voices as well as the stronger voices. Self-government must be built upon the foundation of all Aboriginal people...[and] must provide for those people in need. Self-government must be built upon fairness and equality.

Dorothy McKay
Big Trout Lake, Ontario
3 December 1992

If we are to put...self-government and our own policing and administration...in place, we must ensure that all our people will have a means to take their complaints forward. We must ensure that all our administration and self-governing is accountable to ensure that the basic rights and freedoms our grandfathers and our mothers suffered starvation for will be assured....We must protect all of our people's rights. We are being blinded by the terminology being used today that helps to divide us, such as status and non-status, on-reserve, off-reserve. What is particularly irksome for me is the irrationality behind defining the level of status a person has by your gender or where you sleep or hang your hat and by your proximity to band politics.

Linda Ross
Kingsclear Indian Band
Kingsclear, New Brunswick
19 May 1992

We have to be on guard against the danger of reproducing the same paternalistic system that has been so often criticized. Moreover, if we create agencies or councils without really developing them and defining their powers, we will make the mistake of delegating responsibilities without conferring on these bodies the authority required to fulfil their mandate. What seems of utmost importance, however, is to establish an appeal system for cases where individuals feel that their rights have been infringed. [translation]

Jeannette Boivin
Director, General Council of Atikamekw Women
Manouane, Quebec, 3 December 1992

Many Aboriginal women spoke critically about the development of self-government. Although they support self-government, Aboriginal women emphasized the need for healing in their communities:

Most women supported fully the move toward self-government and yet had many concerns and fears about the fulfilment of that right for Aboriginal peoples. Why? Why do women feel such ambivalence towards the idea of self-government? The answer is clear to women....We have to change our priorities. We must have personal and community healing.

Lynn Brooks
Executive Director, Status of Women Council of the N.W.T.
Yellowknife, Northwest Territories, 7 December 1992

Some Aboriginal women felt they were full and equal partners in self-government discussions, but many women expressed fears that new regimes or systems could develop that would perpetuate patterns of exclusion. Aboriginal women and others spoke about situations in which they have been ignored, intimidated, mistreated and excluded:

If the question of Aboriginal self-government was raised at this assembly today, the results would be the majority lacking enough topical information to render an informed opinion on the subject. We view this communication gap between the Aboriginal elites and the grassroots people as a major flaw in the whole negotiating process on Aboriginal self-government.

Carol Gauthier
Shingwauk Anishnabek Student Society
Sault Ste. Marie, Ontario, 11 June 1992

The response of the Assembly of Manitoba Chiefs to some of the issues that we have raised has also raised a number of serious considerations to us. It has brought to the foreground the potential for the abuse of human rights in the existing political and service delivery structures of Aboriginal government. It highlighted the lack of democratic mechanisms that would allow for the full and equal participation of women and off-reserve people in decisions that concern and affect them. It has also served to demonstrate that a dangerous capacity for the abuse of power and the exercise of undue influence is greatly enhanced and facilitated within a political structure that has no mechanism for the democratic process of appeal and no meaningful facility for accountability to its constituents.

Marilyn Fontaine
Aboriginal Women's Unity Coalition
Winnipeg, Manitoba, 23 April 1992

I would say that there is a real need for the entrenchment of women's rights within self-government. The one thing I hear from women in the communities as well is that there is a real lack of enough advocates. There are advocates, but a lack of enough advocates for their concerns. Often times, things are brought forward to band councils at the community band or regional level and their concerns don't go any farther than that.

> Sarah Kelleher
> N.W.T. Family Services
> Yellowknife, Northwest Territories, 7 December 1992

In some cases, projects initiated by Aboriginal women faced opposition in their communities:

> We ran across many barriers to healing. We found we had to overcome mistrust by families, by friends, community members and service providers. We were perceived as a threat to existing relationships, friendships, jobs and authority....In the circle, we began to learn how to communicate with each other. Trust was built, and we started to support one another....We have many strengths as Aboriginal people, especially the women who have helped us to survive as Anishnabek....Our solutions are: Remove the barriers that prevent personal, collective or community healing. The healing has to be put into the hands of the women first.

> Deborah Herrmann
> Co-ordinator, Kettle Point Caregivers
> London, Ontario, 12 May 1993

Some Aboriginal women pointed to barriers raised by community leadership, which is often male-dominated. Other Aboriginal women see themselves as being excluded from decision-making processes:

> These initiatives, for whatever reasons, are found to be intimidating and threatening to the male-dominated organizations that claim to represent us. In many situations, these organizations have come to oppose the initiatives of the community-based Métis women. They are in the process of negotiating self-governance while they actively try to exclude their female counterparts.

> Melanie Omeniho
> Women of the Metis Nation
> Edmonton, Alberta, 15 June 1993

During our hearings, the Aboriginal Women's Council of Saskatchewan spoke about the results of their research project, which involved interviews with 74 Métis and First Nations women ranging in age from 17 to 58.[98] They found that many women know little about self-government and feel powerless because decisions are made without them. Programs or services are introduced without their involvement being requested or encouraged.

Furthermore, the interviews revealed that some women had been thrown out of meetings or shunned for attempting to join in. Many women feared repercussions for expressing their views and did not want to be identified by name in the study. Some women reported being fired from their jobs as punishment for speaking out. Because the women knew little about self-government, they based their judgement on past negative experiences, such as the implementation of Bill C-31, and feared a similar trampling of rights under future self-government arrangements. Still, some hoped that change would bring about a better life that would empower their people and strengthen the cohesiveness of their nations.

Some Aboriginal women focused their concerns on the existing leadership, indicating that shifts in attitude and behaviour among some male leaders are required:

> Native women have been bearing tremendous burdens in their family, in the home, as well as outside the home, in the workplace and in the political arenas of this country. In order to eliminate the sexism and the racism that is directed at Aboriginal women, we have to see a concerted effort on the part of Native male leadership in this country.
>
> Brenda Small
> Moose Factory, Ontario
> 9 June 1992

> I would like to point out, to have somebody at least acknowledge the fact that these people have been elected or appointed to those positions of authority or power and that they need to remember who put them there and what they're there for. They need...to listen to those voices because sometimes our leaders get too high or too distant from our communities and they no longer hear what is important at the community level....I know there are not very many chiefs and councillors here from our communities and that concerns me somewhat because it is important that they hear it. But what we want to do at the United Indian Councils communities is turn that circle around so that our leaders are not at the top and we're not looking up at them, but that they remember that they are servants of the people and they are there to espouse our viewpoints and to support and represent us.
>
> Cynthia C. Wesley-Esquimaux
> Vice-Chief, United Indian Councils
> Orillia, Ontario, 13 May 1993

It was apparent in what we heard from Aboriginal women that fairness, inclusiveness, and accountability in Aboriginal governments are of paramount importance. In Volume 1, Chapter 16, we set out the basic principles necessary to achieve a renewed relationship – recognition, respect, sharing and responsibility. These principles are also key to the relationship between Aboriginal men and women.

Testimony has revealed the strong determination of Aboriginal women to be fully involved in the negotiation and development of self-government in their communities and nations. Only if this happens can they ensure that their families are healthy and secure, living in an environment where the primary values are inclusiveness, fairness and respect:

> We believe that, because it has to be a community-upward process to develop self-government, we have to make sure that the elders, our grandmothers and our grandfathers, the women, the young people in the community, are brought in to talk....They have to come and talk about what they feel their future is in the framework of self-government....I want to get rid of the division and the derision in the communities and start opening up those lines of communication right at the community level.
>
> Marlene Pierre
> Ontario Native Women's Association
> Thunder Bay, Ontario, 27 October 1992

> We must have faith in the ability of our nations to control our destiny. An Aboriginal government must be responsible. Every form of government is judged on how its people are treated. Assuming control of a band's membership is the first step toward political autonomy. To become a people who govern themselves, we must co-operate in developing institutions in our communities, with the participation of all our members. We must not repeat the injustices suffered by many of our members under the *Indian Act*. We must be a model of a more equitable system. [translation]
>
> Mèrilda St. Onge
> Women of the Montagnais Nation
> Sept-Îles, Quebec, 19 November 1992

Many Aboriginal societies were more egalitarian before contact than they are today. Women had important roles in the social, economic and political life of their community. They were the wisdom-keepers. They selected chiefs. They taught their children about the nature and qualities of a leader. They were responsible for resolving internal disputes and healing their communities. Aboriginal women continue to feel strongly about their place in Aboriginal society in the future.

> Their responsibilities stretch all the way from cradle to grave. Our women are the mothers, the providers, the wife, the decision maker, community leader; and these many roles require them to keep a careful balance.
>
> Rita Arey
> President, N.W.T. Status of Women
> Inuvik, Northwest Territories, 6 May 1992

In assuming these responsibilities as well as meeting the challenges of implementing self-government, contemporary Aboriginal women continue to struggle to establish a role for themselves. The family-based consensus process once used in many First Nations communities has been displaced by majority-based electoral systems that have altered the roles of women, elders and other members of the community. These electoral systems have shattered consensus, alienated the community from decision making, and bred distrust of leaders and officials. Decision-making processes must be accessible and responsive to the views of the people as a whole, to communities, families and individuals.

We have seen that more and more Aboriginal women are taking on positions of leadership in social, economic, cultural and political institutions. We expect this trend to continue.

> The increased political participation of Aboriginal women testifies to the increased willingness of Aboriginal women to participate in decisions aimed at improving the living conditions of not only their families but their communities and their nation. [translation]
>
> Michèle Rouleau
> Quebec Native Women's Association
> Montreal, Quebec, 27 May 1993

> I think women now have to start working...on changing those very ideals that our politicians hold. They have to hold their politicians accountable and a little more responsible to the social needs. How can we advance as a people and as a society if we can't even look in our own backyard....We have to start taking that responsibility.
>
> Margaret M. Eagle
> Yellowknife, Northwest Territories
> 7 December 1992

Aboriginal women are also ready to define codes of conduct they see as crucial to responsible leadership.

> In 1992, Pauktuutit's annual general assembly passed a resolution calling on all Inuit organizations to develop and implement codes of conduct for their leadership. These codes are to be developed with the active participation of Inuit women....Inuit women have been very clear about what they expect from their leadership. Good leaders have...the following qualities: fairness, high moral standards, commitment, honesty, the respect of their communities, kindness, understanding and the willingness to listen. Characteristics and behaviours which are unacceptable in leaders include dishonesty, insensitivity, unfairness, abuse of alcohol or drugs, wife battering, child abuse, racism, prejudice.
>
> Martha Flaherty
> President, Pauktuutit
> Ottawa, Ontario, 1 November 1993

In Volume 2, Chapter 3, we noted that a government must have three basic attributes: legitimacy, power and resources. Legitimacy refers to public confidence in and support for government. It depends on such factors as the way the structure of government was created, the manner in which leaders are chosen, and the extent to which the government advances public welfare and honours basic human rights. To put in place fully legitimate governments, Aboriginal peoples must enjoy the freedom, time and resources to design their own political institutions, through a genuinely inclusive process that involves consensus building at the grassroots level.

The capacity to exercise self-determination is vested in Aboriginal nations that share a collective sense of identity. There is a pressing need for nations to reconstitute themselves as modern political units. We agree with the views of many Aboriginal women who spoke about the need to rebuild nations.

In our discussion of governance, we noted that there are many ways for Aboriginal nations to conduct their internal affairs to ensure fairness and accountability. Aboriginal governments could establish charters or other instruments to protect individual rights and curb abusive uses of power by government. Whatever measures are adopted, Aboriginal women must be actively involved in their development and implementation.

As Aboriginal women continue to voice their concerns and take action at the community and regional level, other developments are occurring. The involvement of women in the design and development of a new government for Nunavut is a good example. The Nunavut Implementation Committee (NIC) responded to concerns expressed by Inuit women by considering ways to ensure balanced representation of men and women in elected positions. In a December 1994 discussion paper, NIC commissioners committed themselves to the principle of sexual equality.[99] The discussion paper notes that women make up just over half the population but are systematically under-represented in politics. The paper acknowledges that women have always played a prominent role in Inuit society. Communities in the eastern Arctic could not function without the contributions made by women – in the home, in the workplace, and in a wide range of organizations. But women remain significantly under-represented in electoral politics; only one of the 10 MLAs for the Northwest Territories from the eastern Arctic (the area that will become Nunavut in 1999) is a woman.

The NIC proposed that the future Nunavut legislative assembly guarantee balanced participation of men and women by having two-member constituencies. The familiar 'first past the post' system would continue to be used, but voters would choose two members in each riding, one woman and one man. The model could work whether consensus government or a party politics system was used.

The Nunavut Implementation Committee acknowledged the work of Pauktuutit and an informal network of prominent Inuit women leaders as well as the support of many Inuit men who believe in equal participation of women in politics. The committee noted that these people have helped create a social and political climate amenable to the discussion of sexual equality in electoral politics.

More generally, Aboriginal women are actively pursuing discussions on self-government and other major issues on their own, at conferences, meetings and workshops:

> We are looking for solutions to improve the situation in terms of the relationship between the men and the women....There has to be a process in place whereby the women are recognized equally and where they will be invited and respected to participate and to have input on matters that affect them.
>
> Marguerite Saunderson
> Northern Women's Resource Services
> Thompson, Manitoba, 1 June 1993

And it is apparent that they are determined to accomplish their goals:

> We also have to recognize that within our own nations, there has to be a healing and building and bonding of women and men for the betterment of the nations...that we will not allow ourselves to be put into the back rooms anymore by ourselves...that we need and want to be at the table for the future of the Métis Nation and Aboriginal nations; that within our nations as well, our current leadership has to take note of that fact and that they include women in all aspects of negotiation.
>
> Sandra DeLaronde
> President, Metis Women of Manitoba
> Winnipeg, Manitoba, 3 June 1993

Aboriginal women's participation in developing self-government is absolutely crucial. The model developed by the Nunavut Implementation Committee is an example of how one group is pursuing a style of governing that attempts to ensure a balance between male and female participation.

Aboriginal women seek to maintain or regain their position of respect, and some Aboriginal men have acknowledged this emerging phenomenon:

> It means we will elevate the women. They will be given the right to elevate chiefs as well as also to depose their chiefs. That's the kind of power. They will be the backbone of the Great Law. That's the way it's going to be. [translation]
>
> Chief Jacob (Jake) Thomas
> Cayuga Nation
> Akwesasne, Ontario, 3 May 1993

> [T]he spiritual law, the law of reality...is outside here. If nations don't make their law accordingly, they will fail eventually because no human

being is capable of changing that particular law. Our people understood that. That is why we are having a planting dance now. That is why we will have a dance for the strawberries, the beans, the green corn, the harvest. Why? Because we understand thanksgiving, where it comes from – the earth, the mother. That is why women are fundamentally important in government – their perspective, their compassion, their choice, their attitudes toward family. The leaders that they choose are like them; otherwise, they wouldn't choose them.

Oren Lyons
Iroquois Confederacy
Akwesasne, Ontario, 3 May 1993

8. THE FAMILY

The living conditions of many Aboriginal women are marked by continuing discrimination, exclusion and powerlessness. In Volume 3, Chapter 2, we recommended that governments responsible for the application of laws, regulations and practices affecting Aboriginal people on-reserve, on Aboriginal territories and in emerging structures of self-government ensure that the rights of women to protection from discrimination on the basis of sex are observed through

- the review and, where necessary, revision of current laws, regulations and practices to ensure sexual equality; and
- the application of standards of sexual equality in drafting procedures for nation building, enacting laws, and applying regulations under Aboriginal government jurisdiction.

In maintaining their responsibilities to their families, however, Aboriginal women continue to face other difficulties. The testimony of Aboriginal women reveals that they are often both the mainstay of the family unit and the catalyst for change:

It is true that Inuit women are working outside of the home in increasing numbers, and they are also actively involved in the myriad of committees and boards which have sprung up in most communities. But women have maintained their responsibilities in the home and for child rearing. Furthermore, women are unofficially filling the gaps in social services in the north. More and more women are taking on a caregiving role at the community level, counselling and supporting friends and family members in crisis.

Martha Flaherty
President, Pauktuutit
Ottawa, Ontario, 1 November 1993

Some Métis women face problems of isolation in rural and remote communities. They are often the primary caregivers if there are children involved, and too often they must leave their home community to access education and training institutions.

Pat Harper
Metis Women of Manitoba
Winnipeg, Manitoba, 22 April 1992

A primary concern for Aboriginal women is the well-being of their children. As we pointed out in our chapter on the family, this was a prominent theme in presentations made to the Commission. A second theme revolves around the perception that healthy families are at the core of the renewal process:

> During the inquiry, we have tried to listen to our children. All children need to be healthy, they need to be loved and cared for. In many ways, this inquiry and our desire to change expresses the hope that we will find the strength to help our children.

Chief Katie Rich
Sheshatshiu, Newfoundland and Labrador
17 June 1992[100]

In sharing their views about care of the family, Aboriginal women spoke about midwifery, child care and concerns about youth, the elderly and ways of making a living.

8.1 Birth and Midwifery

Inuit women described the importance of midwifery and the problems they face in having this long-practised tradition recognized. (The issues surrounding midwifery are also covered in Volume 3, Chapter 3.) A research report prepared for us demonstrated that the traditional practice of midwifery was

> integral to a way of life in which birth was experienced close to the land...and was not only essential to the physical survival of successive generations, but also served to foster significant social relationships among those who participated in the life cycle event of birth. The legacy of traditional midwifery knowledge, passed from one generation to another, continues to be regarded as an important conveyor of cultural knowledge and identity, and as a source of esteem among Aboriginal women.[101]

Martha Greig of Pauktuutit pointed out in her presentation that, until recently, Inuit women gave birth on the land. This practice began to change during the 1950s and 1960s when families moved from their traditional camps into permanent settlements. In the settlements, births took place at the nursing station, often with a nurse-midwife and Inuit midwives in attendance. By the 1970s the federal government had decided that all births should take place in hospitals. Inuit women living in communities without hospital services were evacuated by air to a regional centre like Iqaluit or to southern Canada. Today, almost all Inuit children are born in a regional hospital far from home and family.

The research study points out that the current debate about the future of midwifery in the north raises questions about appropriate legislation, mechanisms of registration and licensing, educational requirements and models of training, as well as questions about safety, acceptable levels of risk, and financial costs. It goes on to note that many of these questions remain unanswered, while little effort is being put into the development of concrete midwifery options. Aboriginal women have been absent or under-represented in the power structures that retain control over maternity health services, but they are playing a lead role in efforts to change the situation:

> Unfortunately, the debate we often find ourselves engaged in is premised on a disrespect for our history and for the knowledge and skills which many of our elders still posses. We often find ourselves on the defensive, endlessly declaring that we, too, are concerned about maternal and infant mortality rates. We have not been allowed to engage in this debate as equals....Changes [need to be] made to the health care system to allow women to regain control of pregnancy and childbirth. In many areas, this may mean the development of regional birthing centres; in others, it might mean providing nursing stations, with the necessary staff and equipment to safely accommodate childbirth. In all cases, it means utilizing the skills of Inuit elders as teachers and midwives and setting up training or apprenticeship programs.

> Martha Greig
> Vice-President, Pauktuutit
> Ottawa, Ontario, 1 November 1993

The maternity project of the Inuulitsivik Health Centre (IHC) in Povungnituk, northern Quebec, has been cited as an excellent example of a program designed to restore legitimacy to the role of elders. During the Commission's round table on health and social issues, Aani Tuluguk presented information about how the IHC maternity project came into being.[102] Created in 1986 in response to a proposal from the local Aboriginal women's association and with the help of a supportive physician, the project involves Aboriginal and non-Aboriginal midwives working in collaboration with other health professionals. They provide a full range of health services to pregnant women in the region. Program results to date indicate that midwifery practice in the north can be effective and beneficial to the health of mothers and babies and to the family unit as a whole.

Aboriginal women's organizations in the north have been leading the call for a return to midwifery. As pointed out in the research study prepared for the

Commission, "the issue of midwifery in the North will not be adequately addressed until Aboriginal women are themselves full participants in the discussions".[103]

In Volume 3, Chapter 3, we recommended that the federal government and provincial governments collaborate to develop community birthing centres in First Nations and Inuit communities. We also recommended that traditional and bio-medical practitioners continue to engage in dialogue, with two objectives: enhancing mutual respect and discussing areas of possible collaboration. (For a more thorough discussion of issues around traditional healing, see Volume 3, Chapter 3, Appendix 3B.)

8.2 Child Support and Child Care

Among all the issues addressed in our discussion of the family (Volume 3, Chapter 2), two were seen as requiring immediate attention. The first one concerned difficulties in enforcing child support orders:

> The single mothers are very frustrated because the fathers are not being supportive for the children....Maybe the community can garnishee their wages.
>
> Margaret A. Jackson
> Sudbury, Ontario
> 31 May 1993

The difficulty relates in part to jurisdiction. Where the support recipient, or the child for whom support is payable, is an Indian within the meaning of the *Indian Act*, enforcement action can be taken against another Indian person's property or wages earned on a reserve. If neither the support recipient nor the child is an Indian within the meaning of the act, however, the income earned by an Indian person on a reserve cannot be garnisheed or subject to a support deduction order, nor can the individual's property on a reserve be seized.

A further difficulty is a reluctance on the part of some chiefs and band councils to comply with enforcement actions, particularly notices of garnishment. The experience in Ontario, for example, is that some bands refuse even to provide information that may assist in the enforcement of a support order or notice of garnishment.[104]

Consistent with our recommendations in Volume 2, we proposed in Volume 3 that jurisdiction over child welfare and family matters (among others) be affirmed as matters falling within the core jurisdiction of self-governing Aboriginal nations. We also recommended that Aboriginal nations or communities establish family law committees, with Aboriginal women as full participants. These committees would study issues such as

- the interests of family members in family assets;
- the division of family assets on marriage breakdown;

- factors to be considered in relation to the best interests of the child, as the principle is applicable to Aboriginal adoption;
- rights of inheritance pertaining to wills, estates and intestacy; and
- obligations regarding spousal and child support.

The second issue requiring immediate attention is the difficulty of obtaining child care. The lack of accessible and affordable child care is particularly problematic in urban areas. Since urban Aboriginal women usually do not have the extended family and community networks available to women in rural communities, they need access to child care if they wish to seek employment or further education. In urban areas, a significant proportion of Aboriginal families are headed by sole-support mothers. Lack of child care can thus become a barrier to employment:

> Often poor, without work, with little education and with dependent children, they [Aboriginal women] are isolated and particularly ill-equipped to confront a life setting that is very remote from their first culture. The young women think that in the city everything will be easier, that they will be able to find work, a boyfriend and offer a better life to their children....But the reality that awaits them is quite different. [translation]
>
> Éléonor Hoff
> Quebec Native Women's Association
> Montreal, Quebec, 27 May 1993

Aboriginal women in all parts of the country spoke about the need for culturally appropriate child care facilities and the resources to maintain them.

> A lot of women...are going through hardships and a lot of times we have tried to keep the daycare centre open but, according to the law, it is impossible...because it has to look nice and it has to meet government standards....We feel we can maintain a daycare centre on our own....We started one and the women's group ended up losing money, and that money we have raised, which never came from the government, we spent on a daycare centre.
>
> Anna Samisack
> President, Atiraq Women's Group
> Inukjuak, Quebec, 8 June 1992

Child care is as much an economic development issue as a social issue. Child care is an integral factor in an individual's road to self-reliance and in community economic development and health. Although the impact of inadequate or unavailable child care is felt mainly by women, it affects the whole family and the community. At the centre of it all are the children – the men and women of the future.

In Volume 2, Chapter 5, which deals with economic development, we made several recommendations concerning child care. We recommended that Aboriginal, federal, provincial and territorial governments enter into agreements to establish roles, policies and funding mechanisms to ensure that the child care needs of Aboriginal parents are met in all Aboriginal communities. We also recommended that the federal government continue funding research and pilot projects under the Child Care Initiatives Fund until alternative, stable funding arrangements for child care services can be arranged. Third, we recommended that Aboriginal organizations and governments assign a high priority to the provision of child care services in conjunction with major employment and business development initiatives and the restructuring of social assistance programs. Finally, we recommended that provincial and territorial governments amend their legislation respecting the licensing and monitoring of child care services to make the standards for certification and facilities more flexible.

We also recommended that in developing and implementing child care strategies, governments pay particular heed to the child-rearing philosophies and practices of Aboriginal peoples.

8.3 Concern about Youth

First Nations, Métis and Inuit women are concerned about their young people and note that there seems to be a lack of involvement of youth in community life and decision making. (See Chapter 4 in this volume for our analysis and recommendations concerning Aboriginal youth.)

> In 1986, 44 per cent of the Inuit were under 15 years of age. This large group of people, future talent, is neither recognized nor fully utilized in today's society. Many of the youth are in conflict with their parents, since they are caught in the transitional stage. They are pulled in two different directions – trying to follow their parents' traditional lifestyle, and trying to prepare themselves for today's modern technological society.
>
> Ineaq Korgak
> Executive Director, Baffin Regional Health Board
> Iqaluit, Northwest Territories, 26 May 1992[105]

The concerns of Inuit women about their young people were also expressed in a study undertaken for Pauktuutit.[106] The most serious problem is a lack of identity and a sense of confusion rooted in the conflict between Inuit and non-Aboriginal cultures. The study noted that the problems of a society in transition seem to be more visible among youth. However, in spite of problems facing Inuit youth, there is confidence in their ability to overcome obstacles:

> While our communities are going through difficult times, our culture remains vibrant and capable of adapting. Our 'cultural glue' is

strong, and a future which combines the best of the old with the best of the new is not just a cliché – it is achievable.

Rosemarie Kuptana
President, Inuit Tapirisat of Canada
Toronto, Ontario, 26 June 1992

Concern was expressed about racism in urban settings and its effects:

We face racism in the schools. Our children don't feel good about themselves when they come home and that is all held in here. By the time they are teenagers, they are lashing out at their own people.

Vicki Wilson
Aboriginal Women's Council of Saskatchewan
Saskatoon, Saskatchewan, 28 October 1992

In Chapter 7 of this volume, where we examine urban perspectives, we recognize that one of the most difficult aspects of urban life for Aboriginal people is dealing with the personal impact of racism. In testimony before the Commission, it became apparent that Aboriginal women often play a lead role in combatting racism and facilitating change:

As women, we need to promote a sense of personal and group identity. A positive self-concept is developed by how we see ourselves and how we think others see us. By promoting recognition of our cultural heritage, we will increase our pride and self-acceptance. As women, we have the power to end racism by redefining and implementing appropriate ways of honouring cultural diversity in our daily interactions with our children. Our own Métis children will be stronger and richer people for our efforts.

Betty Ann Barnes
Director of Social Services
Nechako Fraser Junction Metis Association
Prince George, British Columbia, 31 May 1993

Motivating Native children on their future goals is something I practise with the students I work with at the elementary level. The momentum of their dreams and ambitions has to be cultivated at the elementary level and maintained and nurtured through the secondary level.

Colleen Wassegijig
Toronto, Ontario
3 November 1992

Aboriginal women reminded us that the youth of today will assume much of the responsibility for implementing a renewed relationship between Aboriginal and non-Aboriginal people in Canada. The views and aspirations of Aboriginal youth are therefore vitally important and are addressed in Chapter 4 of this volume.

8.4 Concern about the Elderly

Concern about youth was paralleled by a concern about the elders and senior citizens of Aboriginal communities. As one speaker noted, the living conditions of seniors require immediate attention:

> There are too many of our elderly that are being neglected in hospitals, in homes, or not even homes, in rooming houses. We have rooming houses with some of our elderly who need personal care, who live in one room with a little hotplate, and just one single bed and a wooden chair.
>
> Dorothy Betz
> President, KeKiNan Centre
> Winnipeg, Manitoba, 22 April 1992

In our discussion of the family (Volume 3, Chapter 2), we pointed out that Aboriginal seniors are particularly vulnerable to economic abuse. Elderly persons derive their income mainly from pensions or social assistance, supplemented by food from the bush or gardens. Some children and grandchildren include pensioners in the sharing network, helping out with daily tasks in exchange for financial and other assistance. But in some cases, people exploit and even terrorize the elderly.

The KeKiNan Centre is an example of leadership by Aboriginal women in developing holistic approaches to improving the quality of life for Aboriginal people. Started by the Manitoba Indian Nurses Association and the Indian and Metis Senior Citizens Group of Winnipeg, it is the first senior citizens home for Aboriginal people in urban Canada. The original goal was to develop a geriatric care centre for Aboriginal elders in Winnipeg. However, the proposal was adapted to include enriched (or supportive) housing (30 units) in addition to the personal care (geriatric) units. The first tenants of KeKiNan moved in on 1 December 1991.

The philosophy of KeKiNan is to ensure that the elderly

- are part of the decision-making process;
- live in conditions of safety, security, dignity and comfort;
- have opportunities to fulfil their interests and to be productive within the community; and
- have access to health, social and all other services equivalent to those available to others, provided within and by persons representing an atmosphere of cultural understanding and respect.

The approach adopted by KeKiNan was echoed in other parts of the country:

> Our elders need to become more active in healing, being a positive role model, teaching the younger generations about our culture and traditions. Give the healthy elders a chance to be counsellors in the community. It is our belief that we learn from the stories told by our grandmothers and grandfathers. This has been lost and must be

brought back. A retirement centre for elders that have no family to provide a safe, secure and healthy environment: such a centre would provide shelter, medication, traditional foods and entertainment and be Aboriginally staffed.

Lillian George
Program Director
Sexual Abuse Treatment Services Program
Prince George, British Columbia, 31 May 1993

8.5 Making a Living

The Aboriginal population has increased sharply in recent years, in part because of high birth rates and decreasing rates of mortality. As a result, the working-age population is growing rapidly and is projected to continue to do so in the coming years.

As of 1991, the labour force participation rate for Aboriginal women was higher than that of Aboriginal men. Many more Aboriginal women are entering the work force. Some hold leadership positions in emerging or established Aboriginal training and economic development institutions and are thus very conscious of the problems facing Aboriginal women. For example, Isabelle Impey, president of the Metis Women of Saskatchewan, is executive director of the Gabriel Dumont Institute of Native Studies and Applied Research, which promotes the renewal and development of Métis culture and the design and delivery of education and cultural programs and services. She spoke about some of the frustrations Métis women encounter:

> We have found that many students who enrol in our courses are single parents with one or more dependants. If such a student graduates from Teachers Training Program, for example, we have found that it takes 14 years to pay off the student loan from the year they started. That means she is living under the poverty level when she gets her first job....She cannot provide for her family's needs and the cycle of poverty is maintained....Sometimes it is more beneficial...to go to Social Assistance and get the benefits of subsidies and child care rather than go in a classroom and teach; and it is unacceptable that they are in that position today.

Isabelle Impey
Executive Director
Gabriel Dumont Institute of Native Studies and Applied Research
Saskatoon, Saskatchewan, 12 May 1993

Many Aboriginal women see their economic endeavours as contributing to community development:

> We do not see the point of a few individuals or families becoming rich if the rest of the community is experiencing unemployment and poverty. Most government economic development programs and

strategies are designed to assist those few individuals who can manoeuvre the system; they are not designed with community development in mind....Moreover, they are not designed with women in mind.

Simona Arnatsiaq-Barnes
Economic Development Officer, Pauktuutit
Ottawa, Ontario, 2 November 1993

Two projects described by Arnatsiaq-Barnes illustrate the holistic way Inuit women approach economic development. In Arctic Bay, the women's group established a facility that includes a sewing centre and a child care centre. The second project, started by the women's group in Igloolik, is a plan to develop a facility that will make and sell traditional clothing and offer peer counselling services for victims of family violence. In pursuing their goals, the women in Igloolik stated that they were not prepared to separate their needs artificially in order to fit into existing programs and funding guidelines.

Economic Development for Canadian Aboriginal Women (EDCAW) is a non-profit organization representing the interests of Aboriginal women in economic development. Its mission is "to restore the quality of life of Aboriginal people through the increased participation of Aboriginal women in the Canadian and world economies". Having consulted extensively with Aboriginal women, EDCAW identified a number of business development barriers: access to conventional lending institutions; raising seed financing; gaining soft asset financing; and access to financial training and business skills.

Socio-economic indicators strongly suggest that Aboriginal women are less likely to pass the standard loan criteria used by financial institutes. Also, the majority of Aboriginal women-owned businesses are in the micro and small business sector....[M]any financial institutions are inaccessible to northern and rural Aboriginal communities. Aboriginal women have little or no comfort level or experience in establishing a relationship with their financial institution....Further, without the savings component of a financial service, equity for a business idea can never be saved....

These gaps can be bridged if we keep one important principle in mind, and that is...that Aboriginal women who want to be in business must not continue to be kept outside of the economic mainstream. Aboriginal communities and Aboriginal economies will not develop without the full participation of Aboriginal businesswomen and their businesses.

Pat Baxter
National Co-ordinator
Economic Development for Canadian Aboriginal Women
Ottawa, Ontario, 1 November 1993

Aboriginal women involved at the community or nation level stated that their vision of economic development includes ensuring that their people are healthy, educated and full participants:

> [We] would like to share with you the vision on economic development as established by the Gitksan-Wet'suwet'en people. This came about from a number of community consultation meetings which started in September of 1990. The Gitksan-Wet'suwet'en people were concerned about economic development. People will be healing or healed of social and spiritual disease. An inventory of people's skills will be taken. Education and training...will continue to take place....Management will be based on the Gitksan and Wet'suwet'en systems, our system of Aboriginal self-government. The Gitksan and Wet'suwet'en house groups will be healthy....Our mandate is to act as a catalyst for encouraging increased participation by the Hereditary House Groups, by the communities and by individuals in the development of a sustainable economy.
>
> Violet Gellenbeck
> Executive Chairperson
> Gitksan and Wet'suwet'en Economic Development Corporation
> Kispiox, British Columbia, 16 June 1992

Aboriginal governments need to regain effective control of their economies if they are to pursue forms of development appropriate to their culture and needs. To do so, they need powers in the economic realm as governments. They also need to be able to shape their economies through their own economic development institutions. We therefore recommended in Volume 2, Chapter 5 that federal, provincial and territorial governments enter into long-term economic development agreements with Aboriginal nations (or institutions representing several nations) to provide multi-year funding to support agreed economic development goals and principles. Women must have an active role in shaping these institutions and processes, so that their perspectives are incorporated in economic development and they have equal opportunities to benefit from it.

In addition, because women are particularly active in the small and micro-business sector, the business development activities of Aboriginal nations must pay special attention to their needs. In our discussion of economic development, we therefore highlighted the importance of lending and support programs for micro-businesses and noted the contributions that very small businesses can make to the economic development of a community – and to providing business-related income for women in particular. We also called for the further development of micro-lending programs as an important tool for the development of very small businesses.

On the issue of access to equity capital, Economic Development for Canadian Aboriginal Women recommended that the mandates of Aboriginal capital corporations (ACCs) be expanded so that all Aboriginal women have access, that more

Aboriginal women be included in the decision-making process of ACCs, and that ACCs design specific programs and services for Aboriginal women.[107] In Volume 2, Chapter 5, we recommended that ACCs take appropriate steps, with the assistance of the federal government, to improve their administrative efficiency, their degree of collaboration with other ACCs, and their responsiveness to Aboriginal clients.

Our analysis of employment development in Volume 2, Chapter 5 emphasized the need for an integrated effort to get Aboriginal people into real, sustainable jobs. We recommended a special employment and training initiative, using existing levers where they work and improving on them where they have not worked (especially employment equity, a program with the potential to help Aboriginal women gain a foothold in the employment market).

We examined education and training in Volume 3, Chapter 5. Key recommendations of interest to Aboriginal women include recognizing the right of Aboriginal peoples to establish their own education systems at all stages of life. Self-government in education includes the capacity to make laws, set standards, establish policies and introduce regulations in all areas related to the education of Aboriginal citizens. We also recommended that Aboriginal governments assume responsibility for all aspects of adult education and job-related training, including program design and criteria, language of instruction, and internal allocations of funds. It is expected that Aboriginal women will be fully involved in the implementation of these recommendations.

Our public consultations and research revealed the wide and diverse range of organizations, groups and networks of Aboriginal women. Some of the organizations have existed for many years, while others are quite new. The knowledge and skills base accumulated among these groups could be used to greater effect – to identify gaps and to encourage further development of ideas, strategies and processes important to Aboriginal women. A data base or inventory of existing Aboriginal women's groups and the work they are doing would be invaluable in ensuring that experiences and skills are shared as widely as possible.

RECOMMENDATION

The Commission recommends that

Inventory of Aboriginal Women's Groups

4.2.3

Aboriginal governments and planning bodies with a mandate to develop new structures for human services undertake, in collaboration with women's organizations, an inventory of existing services, organizations and networks with a view to building on existing strengths and ensuring continuity of effort.

9. CONCLUSION

At our public hearings in Calgary, Gerri Many Fingers echoed the feelings of many Aboriginal women about the future they envision for their children and their role in making that vision a reality:

> We are seeking a life of hope for our children, a life of freedom from mental abuse, physical abuse, drugs, racism, sexism....We are aware of the political, social, mental and spiritual issues which our people are facing and confronting each day, whether we live on the reserve or off the reserve....We are the very soil, the fertile soil, which makes, creates and nurtures our future. We are the ones who can give our people a sense of security through our homes and environment....We are the ones who can and must integrate ourselves, our families and our communities. We are all part of each other and cannot be separated, as has happened to a very large degree in the past. Our very existence, our very role, dictates to us to change to a life of brightness, hope, security and love.
>
> Gerri Many Fingers
> Executive Director
> Calgary Native Women's Shelter Society
> Calgary, Alberta, 26 May 1993

In this chapter, we have examined the position and role of Aboriginal women under existing social conditions and legal arrangements and in the future. Although today they sometimes have to struggle to be heard, women once enjoyed a prominent and respected place in many Aboriginal communities. Testimony at our hearings and in the research studies prepared for us provides insight into the life stories of Aboriginal women and the events that changed their situation.[108]

The women's voices heard in this chapter have many commonalities, despite diverse cultural backgrounds and geographic locations. They share an overriding concern for the well-being of their children, families, communities and nations, a concern that encompasses all the issues in our mandate, from education to justice, lands and resources to governance, health to the environment. As their testimony reveals, Aboriginal women have often been excluded – from their home communities, from decision making, and from having a say in their future and their children's future. Their determination to change this situation – to be included in these areas and more – is the powerful message we received.

Whether their concerns related to the *Indian Act*, health and social services, family violence, fairness and accountability in governance, or the well-being of the family, Aboriginal women are demonstrating courage and resilience in acting to secure the kind of future they want to see for the generations yet unborn. We heard them speak of the need for governments and other Aboriginal people to acknowledge, recognize and respect their contributions and to find meaningful ways to include all citizens in the task of rebuilding Aboriginal nations.

As the givers of life, custodians of culture and language, and caretakers of children, Aboriginal women want to work co-operatively with others, despite the obstacles that often stand in the way. They want to repair relationships among Aboriginal people in their communities so as to rebuild strong nations.

Aboriginal women have a particular genius for survival. They have endured many changes. They have made and continue to make significant contributions to improving the quality of life for Aboriginal people. They are speaking out on a range of issues and demonstrating leadership by pursuing community-based initiatives to empower themselves and, in turn, their families and communities. Their approaches to problem solving and decision making are holistic. Their vision of the future is one of inclusion, based on values of kindness, honesty, sharing and strength through mutual support.

As Aboriginal peoples develop and implement self-government, the perspectives of Aboriginal women must guide them. We offer encouragement to the Aboriginal women who came forward to speak to us, and particularly to those who could not. We acknowledge the contributions of Aboriginal women across the country; they have a critical role in providing leadership at the community and nation level. Aboriginal women are the guardians of the values, cultures and traditions of their peoples. They have a vital role in facilitating healing in families and communities. They are anxious to share their wisdom, kindness, honesty and strength with Aboriginal men so that together they can regain the self-confidence and self-esteem needed to rebuild nations governed by wise leaders dedicated to the welfare of their people and the cultural, spiritual and economic viability of their communities.

NOTES

1. Nongom Ikkwe of the South East Region, Manitoba, "Aboriginal Women's Perspective on Self-Government", brief submitted to the Royal Commission on Aboriginal Peoples [RCAP] (1993), p. 2. For information on briefs to RCAP, see *A Note About Sources* at the beginning of this volume.

2. Rowena General (Katsitsakwas), "A Case Study of the Traditional Roles of Women in Collective Decision Making in the Mohawk Community of Ahkwesa'hsne", research study prepared for RCAP (1993) [note omitted]. For information on research studies prepared for RCAP, see *A Note About Sources* at the beginning of this volume.

3. K. Knight, "Roles of Women in Decision Making (Kuujjuaq)", research study prepared for RCAP (1994).

4. This projection for 1996 is based on the extension of recent trends in birth, death and migration rates among Aboriginal groups before 1991. A full description can be found in Mary Jane Norris, Don Kerr and François Nault, "Projections of the

Population with Aboriginal Identity in Canada, 1991-2016", research study prepared by Statistics Canada for RCAP (1995).

5. K. Williams, "An Assessment of Historiographical Writings on First Nations Women in Canada", University of Ottawa, 16 December 1992, p. 1. This paper provides historical information on the position and role from a number of nations, including the Huron, Montagnais-Naskapi, Iroquois, Tlingit, Tsimshian, Nootka, Chipewyan, Mi'kmaq and Carrier.

6. Alison Prentice et al., eds., "The First Women", in *Canadian Women: A History* (Toronto: Harcourt Brace Jovanovich, 1988), p. 32.

7. Osennontion and Skonaganleh:rá, "Our World", *Canadian Woman Studies*, 10/2 and 3 (Summer/Fall 1989), pp. 12-14.

8. Winona Stevenson, "Aboriginal Women's Studies: The State of the Field and a Call for Research", research study prepared for RCAP (1992).

9. The exception here is the Labrador Inuit who were converted to Christianity by the Moravian missionaries beginning in 1771. As early as 1791, converted Inuit had to promise to send their children to school. Inuit were educated in Inuktitut under the direction of the Moravian missionaries until the province of Newfoundland took over the education system in 1949. See Tim Borlase, *Labrador Studies: The Labrador Inuit* (Happy Valley-Goose Bay, Newfoundland and Labrador: Labrador East Integrated School Board, 1993), p. 203.

10. Pauktuutit, *Arnait: The Views of Inuit Women on Contemporary Issues* (Ottawa: Pauktuutit, 1991), p. 6.

11. Nancy Wachowich et al., "Unikaavut: Our Lives, Stories from the Lives of Three Generations of North Baffin Inuit Women", research study prepared for RCAP (1994).

12. Janet Mancini Billson, "Violence Toward Women and Children", in *Gossip: A Spoken History of Women in the North*, ed. Mary Crnkovich (Ottawa: Canadian Arctic Resources Committee, 1990), p. 152.

13. Russel Lawrence Barsh and James Youngblood Henderson, *The Road: Indian Tribes and Political Liberty* (Berkley: University of California Press, 1980), p. vii.

14. Ovide Mercredi and Mary Ellen Turpel, *In The Rapids: Navigating the Future of First Nations* (Toronto: Viking, 1993), pp. 88-89.

15. S. Prov. C. 1850, c. 42., s. 5:

> And for the purpose of determining any right of property, possession or occupation in or to any lands...the following classes of persons are and shall be considered as Indians....
>
> *First* – All persons of Indian blood reputed to belong to the particular Body or Tribe of Indians interested in such lands, and their descendants:
>
> *Secondly* – All persons intermarried with such Indians and residing amongst them, and the descendants of all such persons:

Thirdly – All persons residing among such Indians, whose parents on either side were or are Indians of such Body or Tribe, or entitled to be considered as such: And

Fourthly – All persons adopted in infancy by such Indians, and residing in the village or upon the lands of such Tribe or Body of Indians, and their descendants:

Parallel legislation in Upper Canada, *An Act for the protection of the Indians in Upper Canada from imposition, and the property occupied or enjoyed by them from trespass and injury*, S. Prov. C. 1850, c. 74, s.10 simply noted that the act applied to "Indians and those who may be intermarried with Indians...."

16. *An Act to repeal in part and to amend an Act, intituled, An Act for the better protection of the Lands and property of the Indians of Lower Canada*, S. Prov. C. 1851, c. 59, s. 2 stated that

the following persons and classes of persons, and none other, shall be considered as Indians....

Firstly. All persons of Indian blood, reputed to belong to the particular Tribe or Body of Indians interested in such lands or immoveable property, and their descendants:

Secondly. All persons residing among such Indians, whose parents were or are, or either of them was or is, descended on either side from Indians or an Indian reputed to belong to the particular Tribe or Body of Indians interested in such lands or immoveable property, and the descendants of all such persons: And

Thirdly. All women, now or hereafter to be lawfully married to any of the persons included in the several classes hereinbefore designated; the children issue of such marriages, and their descendants.

17. S. Prov. C. 1857, c. 26.

18. Department of Indian Affairs and Northern Development [hereafter DIAND], *Identification and Registration of Indian and Inuit People* (Ottawa: 1993).

19. Sally Weaver, "First Nations Women and Government Policy 1970-92: Discrimination and Conflict", in *Changing Patterns: Women in Canada*, 2nd edition, ed. Sandra Burt, Lorraine Code and Lindsay Dorney (Toronto: McClelland and Stewart, 1993), p. 98. Weaver notes in this regard:

Traditionally, the predominant principle of descent among the tribes was bilateral – meaning that descent was traced equally through both the mother's and the father's relatives. Next most common was matrilineal descent, the tracing of descent through the female line. Patrilineal descent was much less common.

20. *An Act providing for the organisation of the Department of the Secretary of State of Canada, and for the management of Indian and Ordinance Lands*, S.C. 1868, c. 42, s.15. The definition was virtually identical to that in the 1850 Lower Canada legislation (see note 15).

21. *An Act for the gradual enfranchisement of Indians, the better management of Indian affairs, and to extend the provisions of the Act 31st Victoria, Chapter 42,* S.C. 1869, c. 6.

22. Some of these measures were as follows: instituting a system of individual property holding on reserves; permitting the imposition of the three-year elective system for chiefs and councillors on chosen bands; limiting the powers of elected councils to a list of relatively minor matters, all subject to official confirmation; providing that an enfranchised Indian man could draw up a will regarding his land in favour of his children, but not his wife, in accordance with provincial law. Originally designed for the more 'advanced' Indians of Ontario and Quebec, this legislation was later extended to Manitoba and British Columbia and eventually to all of Canada.

23. Letter from Hector Langevin to Sawatis Anionkiu Peter Karencho and other Iroquois Indians, Caughnawaga, Quebec (20 August 1869), National Archives of Canada [NAC], Record Group [RG] 10, Vol. 528. See also D.E. Sanders, "The Bill of Rights and Indian Status" (1972) 7 U.B.C. L. Rev. 81 at 98.

24. In the modern version of the *Indian Act,* location tickets have been replaced by certificates of possession and occupation. The concept in the modern act is similar to that in the 1869 legislation, however.

25. Objections were raised early on by Aboriginal groups. In 1872, the Grand Council of Ontario and Quebec Indians (founded in 1870) sent the minister in Ottawa a strong letter that contained the following passage:

    They [the members of the Grand Council] also desire amendments to Sec. 6 of the Act of [18]69 so that Indian women may have the privilege of marrying when and whom they please, without subjecting themselves to exclusion or expulsion from their tribes and the consequent loss of property and rights they may have by virtue of their being members of any particular tribe. (NAC RG10, Red Series, Vol. 1934, file 3541)

    These requests, of course, went unheeded. See also John Leslie and Ron Maguire, eds., *The Historical Development of the Indian Act* (Ottawa: Department of Indian Affairs and Northern Development, Treaties and Historical Research Centre, 1978), p. 55.

26. J.R. Miller, *Skyscrapers Hide the Heavens: A History of Indian-White Relations in Canada* (Toronto: University of Toronto Press, 1989), pp. 194-195.

27. *An Act to further amend "The Indian Act, 1880",* S.C. 1884, c. 27, s. 5.

28. *An Act to amend the Indian Act,* S.C. 1920, c. 50, s. 2.

29. Letter from Deputy Superintendent General Scott to Arthur Meighen, Superintendent General of Indian Affairs (12 January 1920), reprinted in NAC RG10, Vol. 6810, file 470-2-3, vol. 7. See also Leslie and Maguire, *The Historical Development of the Indian Act* (cited in note 25).

30. *An Act to amend the Indian Act,* S.C. 1920, c. 50, s. 3. The provision was repealed in 1922 but reinstated in 1933 and retained in modified form until 1961, when

it was finally removed permanently in *An Act to amend the Indian Act*, S.C. 1961, c. 9, s. 1.

31. *The Indian Act*, S.C. 1951, c. 29, ss. 11(c)-(e) of the amended act all refer to the male line of descent as criteria for registration as an Indian.

32. DIAND, Memorandum of 2 July 1968, as described in Kathleen Jamieson, *Indian Women and the Law in Canada: Citizens Minus* (Ottawa: Supply and Services, 1978). The red ticket system is also referred to and described in the recent decision of the Federal Court of Canada in *Sawridge Band* v. *Canada*, [1995] 4 Canadian Native Law Reporter 121.

33. *An Act to amend the Indian Act*, S.C. 1956, c. 40, s. 6(2).

34. *An Act to amend the Indian Act*, S.C. 1956, c. 40, s. 26.

35. Jamieson, *Indian Women* (cited in note 32).

36. *Report of the Royal Commission on the Status of Women in Canada* (Ottawa: Information Canada, 1970), pp. 237-238. For a discussion of the background to the issue see Douglas Sanders, "The Renewal of Indian Special Status", in Anne F. Bayefsky and Mary Eberts, eds., *Equality Rights and the Canadian Charter of Rights and Freedoms* (Toronto: Carswell, 1986), p. 529.

37. *Re Lavell and Canada (A.G.)* (1971), 22 D.L.R. (3d) 182 (Ont. Co. Ct.). See also Weaver, "First Nations Women" (cited in note 19).

38. *Lavell* v. *Canada (A.G.)* [1971] F.C. 347.

39. *Bedard* v. *Isaac* [1972] 2 O.R. 391 (Ont. H.C.).

40. *Lavell* v. *Canada (A.G.)*; *Isaac* v. *Bedard* [1974] S.C.R. 1349. For the majority (5-4), Justice Ritchie held that there was no impermissible discrimination. He distinguished (at p. 1372) between this case and that of *R.* v. *Drybones*, [1970] S.C.R. 282, on the basis that, as criminal law, the alcohol provisions in the *Indian Act*

> could not be enforced without denying equality of treatment in the administration and enforcement of the law before the ordinary courts of the land to a *racial group*, whereas no such inequality of treatment between Indian men and women flows as a *necessary result* of the application of section 12(1)(b) of the *Indian Act*. [emphasis added]

No one quite knows what this passage means, but it may refer to the fact that Indian women have a choice regarding whom they marry, so that subsection 12(1)(b) does not become a factor for Indian women as a *necessary result* of being an Indian woman. This dubious rationale has convinced few legal scholars. The case is usually cited for the proposition that Parliament can discriminate against certain classes of people, in the context of the *Canadian Bill of Rights* at least, in the pursuit of otherwise valid federal objectives. See Jack Woodward, *Native Law* (Toronto: Carswell, 1989), p. 146.

41. See Weaver, "First Nations Women" (cited in note 19).

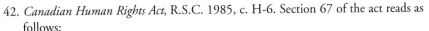

42. *Canadian Human Rights Act*, R.S.C. 1985, c. H-6. Section 67 of the act reads as follows:

> Nothing in this Act affects any provision of the *Indian Act* or any provision made under or pursuant to that *Act*.

43. [1981] 2 Human Rights Law Journal 158; 68 I.L.R. 17. Canada was criticized by the Human Rights Committee established pursuant to the *International Covenant on Civil and Political Rights* to which Canada is a signatory. The Covenant is one of the documents that influenced the development of the Charter and it contains many human rights provisions similar to Charter protections. The Human Rights Committee took aim at section 12(1)(b) and found that it unjustifiably denied Sandra Lovelace, who had lost Indian status and band membership upon marrying out, her rights under section 27 of the Covenant as a member of an ethnic minority to enjoy her culture and language in community with other members of her band. The Committee did not find the loss of status attendant upon her marrying out to be reasonable or necessary to preserve the identity of the Tobique Band of which she had been a member. The case is discussed in Anne F. Bayefsky, "The Human Rights Committee and the Case of Sandra Lovelace" (1982) 20 Can. Y.B. Int'l L. 244.

44. This is subject to the minor exception that in cases where bands admit persons without Indian status to band membership, such persons are deemed to be status Indians for certain purposes under the *Indian Act* pursuant to section 4.1. Thus, the *Indian Act* will apply to such persons as if they were 'Indians'. It is important to note in this regard that the provision is only for purposes of sections associated with reserve residency and does not include deemed Indians for other purposes, such as funding from the federal government or post-secondary education benefits. For these and related purposes, only status Indians are counted.

45. In 1994, the requirement in section 77(1) that the elector must be "ordinarily resident on reserve" was struck down at trial in an action brought by off-reserve band members in *Corbiere* v. *Canada* [1994] 1 C.N.L.R. 71. (The trial decision was under appeal at the time of writing.)

46. DIAND, *Impacts of the 1985 Amendments to the Indian Act (Bill C-31): Summary Report* (Ottawa: Supply and Services, 1990) (hereafter, *Bill C-31 Summary Report*).

47. *Bill C-31 Summary Report*, p. ii.

48. *Bill C-31 Summary Report*, p. 5.

49. *Bill C-31 Summary Report*, p. 6.

50. *Bill C-31 Summary Report*, pp. 9 and 12.

51. Figures supplied by DIAND liaison office, 5 July 1995.

52. According to *Bill C-31 Summary Report*, p. iii, 90 per cent of Bill C-31 registrants still live off-reserve.

53. *Bill C-31 Summary Report*, p. 17.

54. *Bill C-31 Summary Report*, p. iii.

55. *Bill C-31 Summary Report*, p. ii. The precise figure is 77 per cent.

56. *Bill C-31 Summary Report*, p. iv.

57. *McIvor* v. *Registrar DIAND*, BCSC no. CC5/89. According to information received from the federal department of justice as of October 1995, this case is continuing.

58. Bands created since 1985 have not been declared bands in the sense in which the term is used in the *Indian Act.* Rather, they are said to result from the minister's power under section 17 to "amalgamate" or to "constitute" new bands from existing bands. According to information received from the DIAND registrar, the last band created by declaration of the governor in council was the Conne River band of Newfoundland in 1984.

59. *Privacy Act*, R.S.C. 1985, c. P-21; *Bill C-31 Summary Report* (cited in note 46), p. 6.

60. Manitoba, Public Inquiry into the Administration of Justice and Aboriginal People. *Report of the Aboriginal Justice Inquiry of Manitoba*, Volume 1: *The Justice System and Aboriginal People* (Winnipeg: Queen's Printer, 1991), p. 204.

61. Assembly of First Nations/Native Women's Association, "Joint Statement on Bill C-47", 22 June 1984. Bill C-47 was the precursor to Bill C-31. The joint statement lists eight specific points relating to the right of First Nations to define their own citizenship.

62. Minutes of Proceedings and Evidence of the Standing Committee on Indian Affairs and Northern Development Respecting: Bill C-31, An Act to amend the *Indian Act* (Ottawa, 14 March 1985), Issue No. 16, pp. 7-8.

63. Stewart Clatworthy and Anthony H. Smith, "Population Implications of the 1985 Amendments to the Indian Act", research study prepared for the Assembly of First Nations (Ottawa: 1992), pp. vii-viii [emphasis in original].

64. *Indian Act*, R.S.C. 1985, c. I-5, s. 10.

65. *Indian Act*, s. 2(1). This definition may be affected by the outcome of the appeal in the case *Corbiere* v. *Canada* (cited in note 45).

66. This may also be affected by the outcome of the appeal in *Corbiere* v. *Canada.*

67. Clatworthy and Smith, "Population Implications" (cited in note 63), p. 20. The authors note in this context that "one motivation for passing a code was to exclude from membership a portion of the C-31 registrant population".

68. In the *Indian Act* of 1985, section 77(1) contains the band council election requirement that electors be "ordinarily resident on the reserve".

69. *Bill C-31 Summary Report* (cited in note 46), p. iv.

70. *Bill C-31 Summary Report*, pp. 24-25, 43.

71. The Congress of Aboriginal Peoples drew attention to this problem in early 1985. They proposed that the codes be published in the *Canada Gazette* or in a special

Aboriginal Gazette, and had their views tabled at an intergovernmental meeting in Quebec City. See Congress of Aboriginal Peoples, "A National Aboriginal Registry", Document: 830-507/009 tabled at the Federal-Provincial-Territorial Meeting of Ministers Responsible for Native Affairs and Leaders of National Aboriginal Organizations (Quebec City, 17-18 May 1994).

72. According to information received from the federal justice department, about a dozen cases concerning Bill C-31 and its impact are under litigation.

73. *Sawridge Band* (cited in note 32), p. 127. At time of writing, an appeal had been filed.

74. Clatworthy and Smith, "Population Implications" (cited in note 63), pp. 18-19.

75. According to Clatworthy and Smith, "Population Implications", p. vii, restrictive membership codes will have the following impact:

> While the registered Indian population is likely to increase for perhaps two generations, it will eventually begin to decrease. In our view the issue is not whether this will occur, but when and how quickly. Estimates of the rate of future out-marriage (or Indian to non-Indian parenting) are the critical factor. If we assume that the current rate (34 per cent) will increase by 10 percentage points over the next 40 years, then the beginning of Indian population decline is 50 years, or two generations, into the future. Membership declines under two-parent [membership] codes begin within a generation.

76. Subsection 10(2) of Bill C-31 states that a band "may...provide for a mechanism for reviewing decisions on membership". It is generally accepted that the word "may" is permissive and not mandatory in the context in which it is used.

77. The examples presented are drawn from Clatworthy and Smith, "Population Implications" (cited in note 63), pp. 54-72.

78. *Bill C-31 Summary Report* (cited in note 46), pp. 15-16.

> Respondents were asked to think back to when they first applied for registration/restoration and to state why it was important for them to apply. All comments were recorded. The reasons most often cited related to personal identity (41 per cent); 21 per cent referred to culture or a sense of belonging. A total of 17 per cent of registrants gave the correction of injustice as a reason, while 7 per cent referred to aboriginal rights....
>
> Respondents over 25 years of age were more likely than younger registrants to refer to cultural and personal identity and the need to correct injustice as reasons for applying for status. Younger registrants expressed more interest in educational benefits and were more apt to report that their families applied for status or asked them to do so.

79. *Bill C-31 Summary Report*, pp. 27-28.

80. B.C. Native Women's Society, "Aboriginal Women and Divorce", brief submitted to RCAP (1993), p. 11.

81. *Derrickson* v. *Derrickson*, [1986] 1 S.C.R. 285.

82. B.C. Native Women's Society, "Aboriginal Women and Divorce", p. 12.

83. Clatworthy and Smith (cited in note 63).

84. Anduhyaun, "Our Role in Creating the Future Aboriginal Women Want", brief submitted to RCAP (1992), pp. 2-3.

85. Anduhyaun, "Our Role", p. 11.

86. Indigenous Women's Collective of Manitoba, "Report on the Indigenous Women's Perspective in Manitoba", brief submitted to RCAP (1993), p. 3.

87. Ontario Native Women's Association, "Breaking Free: A Proposal for Change to Aboriginal Family Violence" (Thunder Bay, Ontario, 1989). The study reported that eight out of 10 Aboriginal women had personally experienced violence. Of these women, 87 per cent had been injured physically and 57 per cent had been sexually abused.

88. RCAP, *Choosing Life: A Special Report on Suicide Among Aboriginal People* (Ottawa: Supply and Services, 1995), p. 16 and following.

89. See RCAP, *Bridging the Cultural Divide: Aboriginal People and Criminal Justice in Canada* (Ottawa: Supply and Services, 1996), Chapter 4, "Ensuring the Safety of Women and Children in Aboriginal Justice Systems", p. 269.

90. Jean Goodwill, "Historical Overview of Social, Political, Cultural and Economic Aboriginal Women's Organizations in Canada", research study prepared for RCAP (1993).

91. First Nations Eagle Women's Circle, newsletter of the Indian Homemakers' Association of B.C. (May 1993), p. 12. Information on this association was also tabled at the Commission's public hearings in Vancouver on 3 June 1993.

92. Provincial-territorial associations continued to develop and, with the exception of the Métis National Council of Women, the following groups applied for and received funding from the Commission's Intervener Participation Program (the Métis National Council of Women provided a presentation under the auspices of the Métis National Council):
    B.C. Native Women's Society, incorporated in 1969
    Aboriginal Women's Council of Saskatchewan, 1971
    Ontario Native Women's Association, January 1972
    Nova Scotia Native Women's Association, early 1970s
    New Brunswick Native Indian Women's Council, formed in early 1970s, incorporated in July 1983
    Native Women's Association of Canada, 1974
    Aboriginal Nurses Association of Canada, 1976
    Femmes autochtones du Québec/Quebec Native Women's Association, May 1978
    Native Women's Association of the Northwest Territories, 1978
    Aboriginal Women's Council (B.C.), formed in March 1984

Pauktuutit (Inuit Women's Association of Canada), March 1984
Indigenous Women's Collective of Manitoba, 1986
Nongom Ikkwe, 1987
Women of the Metis Nation (Alliance), Alberta, March 1988
Economic Development for Canadian Aboriginal Women, July 1991
Metis Women of Manitoba, December 1991
Métis National Council of Women, 1992
For more information, see *Intervener Participation Program: Final Report* (RCAP: 1994).

93. Pauktuutit, *Arnait* (cited in note 10).

94. The national Métis organization, the Métis National Council, was not formed until 1983.

95. *Native Women's Association of Canada* [hereafter NWAC] v. *Canada* (1992), 2 F.C. 462.

96. *NWAC* v. *Canada* (1992) 3 F.C. 192 at 212.

97. *NWAC* v. *Canada*, [1994] 3 S.C.R. 627 at 664-665.

98. Aboriginal Women's Council of Saskatchewan, brief submitted to RCAP (1993).

99. Nunavut Implementation Commission, "Two-Member Constituencies and Gender Equality: A 'Made in Nunavut' Solution for an Effective and Representative Legislature", discussion paper released by the NIC, 6 December 1994.

100. See also The Innu Nation and Mushuau Innu Band Council, *The People's Inquiry Report Gathering Voices: Finding Strength to Help Our Children* (Utshimasits, Ntesinan, June 1992).

101. Lesley Paulette, "Midwifery in the North", research study prepared for RCAP (1995).

102. See Aani Tuluguk, "The Inuulitsivik Health Centre and its Maternity Project", in *The Path to Healing: Report of the National Round Table on Aboriginal Health and Social Issues* (Ottawa: RCAP, 1993), pp. 239-240.

103. Paulette, "Midwifery in the North" (cited in note 101).

104. Ontario Ministry of the Attorney General, correspondence with RCAP, 9 September 1993.

105. As of 1991, 42.1 per cent of Inuit were under the age of 15; see Norris, Kerr and Nault, "Projections of the Population" (cited in note 4).

106. Pauktuutit, *Arnait* (cited in note 10).

107. Economic Development for Canadian Aboriginal Women, "The Access to Financial Institutions by Aboriginal Business Women", brief submitted to RCAP (1993).

108. A number of research studies were prepared for the Commission on the lives of Aboriginal women, including Cynthia Dunnigan, "Three Generation Life History Study of Metis Women in Alberta" (1993); Camil Girard, "Culture and Intercultural Dynamics: The Life Stories of Three Women from Saguenay-Lac-Saint-Jean", (1994); Vicki English-Currie, "Three-Generational Study: Grandmother, Mother, Daughter – Indian Residential Schools: Grandmother, Mother, Daughter Speak" (1994); Tammy Anderson Blumhagen and Margaret Seguin Anderson, "Memories and Moments: Conversations and Re-Collections, Life History Project" (1994); Giselle Marcotte, "Métis, C'est Ma Nation. 'Your Own People,' Comme on dit: Life Histories from Eva, Evelyn, Priscilla and Jennifer Richard" (1995); Emily Masty, "Women's Three Generations: Life History Project in Whapmagoostui, Quebec" (1995); and Nancy Wachowich et al., "Unikaavut: Our Lives, Stories from the Lives of Three Generations of North Baffin Inuit Women" (1995).

3

ELDERS' PERSPECTIVES

One of the things that we found out...as we talked with many different groups, is the common motif that occurs all over the place which makes reference to Turtle Island. Turtle Island encompasses the whole North American continent, Ellesmere Island in the north representing the head, Labrador representing one of the flippers, Florida another flipper, Mexico the tail, California another flipper, Alaska another flipper, and then the shell is divided into 13 areas. There is a custodian in each area – and we belong to one of them. In our language we use the word *Spoo-pii* to describe the Turtle, which means an area which is high.

This area that you are in right now, what we have here is that the water flows off in all directions from this area, which represents the high spot. All these areas, as in the live turtle, are what represents our sacred constitution, the Constitution of Turtle Island....

This Constitution has been there for a long time. It still exists. We can still utilize it, which we do. It has its own legal system; it has its own economic system; it has its own education; it has its own philosophy; it has its own language; it has its own logic. We can utilize those things. We have been doing it for the last 500 years. It's nothing new. It is something that, if more people realized what it was and realized it's not a threat, it's who we are, it's what we are, it is something that is very real and we can use it. I use it every day.

Stan Knowlton, Sik-ooh-Kotoki Friendship Society
Lethbridge, Alberta, 25 May 1993[*]

---

[*] Transcripts of the Commission's hearings are cited with the speaker's name and affiliation, if any, and the location and date of the hearings. See A Note About Sources at the beginning of this volume for information about transcripts and other Commission publications.

THE LAND WE OCCUPY is known to First Nations people as Turtle Island. The relationship of Aboriginal people to Turtle Island is governed by rules and principles formed in the distant past. Aboriginal people believe the Creator preordained how that relationship should be and provided the tools and the means to live a life that expresses that relationship. The nature of that relationship with the Creator, the natural world, the animal world and other human beings is described in Aboriginal languages, which are seen as gifts from the Creator. For thousands of years, each generation learned the lessons of Turtle Island from preceding generations. The ancient wisdom, the traditions, rituals, languages and cultural values were passed on and carried forward. In this process, a primary role was played by the Elders, the Old Ones, the Grandmothers and Grandfathers. As individuals especially knowledgeable and experienced in the culture, they were seen as those most closely in touch with the philosophical teachings of life lived in harmony with the Creator and creation.

Guided by the teachings of the Old Ones, the people survived and flourished. Great nations coexisted. Extensive trade networks thrived. Alliances and confederacies formed for mutual interest, and complex international relationships emerged. Compatible attitudes toward the Creator and Mother Earth formed the basis of agreements among nations. Rules of conduct, whether in peace or in war, governed behaviour.

Then there came a great change. About 500 years ago, strangers from across the ocean sailed to this ancient land – Turtle Island – and called it 'the New World'. To the newcomers, this was unexplored country. They knew little about the original inhabitants, whose footsteps had worn a patchwork of paths and trails across the continent. When eventually they did come to know the First Peoples, the newcomers understood little of their laws and customs and the values that underlay their relationship to Turtle Island:

> The Great Land of the Inuit is the sea, the earth, the moon, the sun, the sky and stars. The land and the sea have no boundaries. It is not mine and it is not yours. The Supreme Being put it there and did not give it to us. We were put there to be part of it and share it with other beings, the birds, fish, animals and plants.[1]

The new arrivals had quite different beliefs and sought to promote their beliefs in the hope that the original inhabitants would come to see things their way. It did not happen. The Old Ones continued to teach the ancient wisdom about the way to live, how to relate to the Creator, and how to coexist with their brothers and sisters of the plant and animal world. The lessons of how the Creator intended people to live with one another persisted.

These teachings form part of the intellectual tradition of the Aboriginal nations of Canada. They are the foundation upon which an Aboriginal com-

munity is built. Aboriginal peoples' understanding of their relationship to
Canada and Canadian society is shaped by these teachings. To appreciate fully
Aboriginal peoples' view of this relationship, we must look at the philosophy that
informs it.

In this chapter, we hope to shed some light on this North American intellectual tradition. The Commission was instructed to investigate and make recommendations regarding the position and role of Aboriginal Elders. We gave
close and careful attention to the Elders who spoke to the Commission, both at
our public hearings and through written submissions. We also devoted a portion of our research to investigating issues raised by the Elders and exploring their
perspectives on these issues.

This chapter is an attempt to convey their perspectives. We do not intend
to homogenize the many world views embraced by Aboriginal peoples. We recognize, however, that there are common human problems for which all societies
– if they are to survive – must find solutions, and that there are a limited
number of solutions to them. Aboriginal peoples share some common values
because of their experience of life as peoples rooted in the land.

The Elders spoke to us of their deep concern about the lack of knowledge
of non-Aboriginal Canadians about Aboriginal peoples, their culture and history.
They believe this is directly responsible for the current misunderstandings between
First Peoples and other Canadians. We hope to convey in this chapter the message of the Elders. It is a message rooted in the past but speaking to the future.

1. Who are the Elders?

> Elders are respected and cherished individuals who have amassed a
> great deal of knowledge, wisdom and experience over the period of
> many, many years. They are individuals who have also set examples,
> and have contributed something to the good of others. In the process,
> they usually sacrifice something of themselves, be it time, money or
> effort.[2]

> Elders, Old Ones, Grandfathers and Grandmothers don't preserve the
> ancestral knowledge. They live it.[3]

Elders are generally, although not exclusively, older members of the community.
They have lived long and seen the seasons change many times. In many
Aboriginal cultures, old age is seen as conferring characteristics not present in
earlier years, including insight, wisdom and authority. Traditionally, those who
reached old age were the counsellors, guides and resources for the ones still finding their way along life's path. Elders were the ones who had already walked a
great distance on this path and were qualified to advise based on their knowledge of life, tradition and experience.

In the Ojibwa world view, there are Four Hills of Life: infancy, youth, adulthood and old age. For an individual to live a full life, he or she must pass through experiences unique to each stage of life. This personal and spiritual evolution culminates in old age, generally a time of wisdom and reflection. Among the Gwich'in, people are considered old only when they have seen five generations. It is then that an individual can be considered an Elder. The Old Ones have received gifts they can return to the community: the gifts of experience and knowledge.

Age itself does not make one an Elder, however. Most Aboriginal peoples have a special word or name for Elders that distinguishes them from what we would call senior citizens. In Inuit communities, for example, elderly people are called *inutuqak*, but those considered Elders are referred to as *angijukqauqatigiit*, a 'union of leaders'.

Elders have special gifts. They are considered exceptionally wise in the ways of their culture and the teachings of the Great Spirit. They are recognized for their wisdom, their stability, and their ability to know what is appropriate in a particular situation. The community looks to them for guidance and sound judgement. They are caring and are known to share the fruits of their labours and experience with others in the community.

> The communities will define who they have as...community Elders. But in the true sense of Elders, they are people who are spiritual leaders, who have dedicated their lives and continue until they go to the Spirit World....They live the culture, they know the culture, and they have been trained in it. These are the true Elders. We have some Elders you might never, ever hear of. They stay in the bush, they stay in their communities, but they are Elders. They are spiritual Elders, and they live that way of life.
>
> Elder Vern Harper
> Toronto, Ontario
> 25 June 1992

For the Mohawk Nation, Elder is a sacred title. The Ojibwa word for Elder, *Kichenishnabe*, means 'Great People'. To Inuit communities in the Keewatin region of the Northwest Territories, Elders are "those who are able to see what they used to do and what they remember from what they learned from their parents and grandparents".[4]

While Elder is a distinguished title, traditional Elders do not seek status; it flows from the people. Communities elevate their Elders, but the Elders keep their feet planted firmly and humbly on the ground. Even though they have walked far down life's path, they feel young in relation to their culture's ancient knowledge. "Even me, I am an Elder now, but I am still learning yet," said Virginia Alexander of the Nak'azdli Elders' Society at our hearings in Stoney Creek, British Columbia.

The teachings they have learned began with the Creator and have been passed on from generation to generation. Said Ojibwa Elder Alex Skead at our hearings in Kenora, Ontario, "As an Elder, I am grandfather of all you people here. I am seventy years of age and I still feel very small. So much things to learn in life".

Elders will step to the fore, but often only when asked. It is the community's responsibility to seek out the Elders' gifts of knowledge and insight. Elders are rooted in the morals of the Creator. They are the conscience of the community:

> When we talk about economics and we talk about development and we talk about money, we have to balance that with reality. We have to balance that with quality of life, with peace, with community. I think if there is anything that Indigenous people have to offer this Commission, it is that perspective. And it is fundamentally important for survival. Every question that is political is also moral. Every question. And you have to answer it morally. That brings responsibility to governance and governors and people.
>
> Elder Oren Lyons
> Onondaga Chief and Faithkeeper
> Iroquois Confederacy
> Akwesasne, Ontario, 3 May 1993

Elders are neither prescriptive nor intrusive in their teachings. They live their lives by example, according to the laws of the Creator. When asked in an appropriate manner, they offer their teachings. They will recount the stories and legends that flow through their culture but will not impose their personal interpretations of the lessons to be drawn from them.

They are good listeners, a quality born of humility and patience. For people with an oral tradition, listening is an important and essential skill. One does not presume to know; one listens and learns. As the Elders say, the Creator gave us two ears but only one mouth. An Ojibwa Elder told us:

> You can be very, very knowledgeable about book learning and everything, but that does not mean you have wisdom. You have to listen to what the people talk, how they talk, and what they say.
>
> Elder Dominic J. Eshkawkogan
> Ojibway Cultural Foundation
> Sudbury, Ontario, 31 May 1993

Elders can be men or women. Both have many common responsibilities as the keepers of wisdom, but it is acknowledged that men and women have different and distinctive life experiences. In some situations, their roles and responsibilities are different:

> We also like to involve, as much as possible, our Elder traditional midwives. The Elder woman is a traditional midwife, and the training of the community midwife is done both in the modern hospital

way and the traditional way. There is a balance as much as possible between the two, so that the community midwife retains the traditional values.

Aani Tuluguk
National Round Table on Aboriginal Health and Social Issues
Vancouver, British Columbia
11 March 1993

The women's role within the Elders, my grandmother's role and my aunts' roles, we were almost like hidden leaders, as we used to learn in community development days.

Everybody that needed advice went to my mother, went to my aunts, went to my grandmother. Even the men, when they went to the meetings and organizing, they never went before we had a meeting and a gathering of the total family unit, the total community unit, and the women told the men what to say. It was a consensus of the total family unit.

Senator Thelma Chalifoux
Metis Nation of Alberta
Winnipeg, Manitoba, 22 April 1992

In the Métis Nation, the title 'Senator' is bestowed on individuals in recognition of their knowledge and insight. It carries many of the same connotations as the term Elder in First Nations cultures. In some Aboriginal societies Elders are called Grandmother and Grandfather, titles that acknowledge their role as teachers and wise ones. These familial designations also allude to the important role of Elders in raising children. Elders apply their spiritual understanding of relationships among the elements of creation to relationships within the family and the community. The Commission heard about how this happens in some Inuit communities:

Children learned respect from Elders....From ten years on, more responsibility was placed on the child. Boys and girls had different chores to do. They were encouraged to help Elders with their tasks. They began to learn the importance of co-operation and social aspects of traditional Inuit lifestyles.

Elder James Panioyak
Cambridge Bay, Northwest Territories,
17 November 1992

Both Elders and parents had a role in rearing and teaching the children. We were taught to respect all our peers; respect and obey the rules; respect and knowledge for the life and ways of all of the animals, killing only the mature and/or only what was required; respect and knowledge of weather-related elements and the lay of the land. We learned the language, life, survival and hunting skills. We learned to respect others, share with each other and care for one another.[5]

Presenters of all ages spoke passionately about the importance of Elders in contemporary society. As many Aboriginal people rediscover themselves in their culture, Elders are seen as living connections to the original teachings of the Creator. Some presenters commented on the seemingly diminished role Elders have in modern Aboriginal society, viewing this as a reflection of the breakdown of traditional Aboriginal culture:

> It seems that time has taken its toll with the new ways. Our Elders' ways and teachings have now become unheard by young generations. Their once powerful guidance and sense of direction were completely ignored. 'We are now lost'. There was, it seemed, no hope. We cannot go back into the past.
>
> We don't know where this fast stream of life is taking us. Even our spiritual medicine, our guidance of the Dene ways have left us. We are now in limbo.
>
> Robert Norwegian
> Foothills Pipe Lines
> Calgary, Alberta, 27 May 1993

It is precisely because of this loss of direction that many Aboriginal people are looking to Elders for guidance. It is said that Elders remind us of our responsibility to the future. Looking to the future and not the past, their teachings become the foundation on which to build healthy, self-determining communities.

2. The North American Intellectual Tradition

> The knowledge, this thing called knowledge – I know we can learn some things in school, but the real knowledge comes from the Creator. The knowledge that grows in the mind comes from the Creator. The one who created all the people....The things that we know now in our lives, in our mind, it comes from the Creator, not from our fellow human beings. [translation]
>
> Steven Chapman
> Big Trout Lake First Nation
> Big Trout Lake, Ontario, 3 December 1992

Elders approach all issues through the traditional teachings of their culture, teachings seen to emanate from the Creator. Because the knowledge a person receives

is given by the Creator, it is considered sacred. As learning continues throughout one's life, so life itself is a sacred ceremony.

> In our teachings, your spirit lives forever. It is only using this vessel
> for the period of time it is in this realm on Mother Earth. And
> when we were placed here on Turtle Island, the Creator promised us
> forever that life and that love.
>
> He promised us all of those things that we would ever need to
> go to that beautiful place. Everything you will ever need is there for
> you. If you get sick, your medicines are there. Your food is there with
> those animals, with the fish, with the bird life. Those trees, those
> rocks, that water that gives all life, the life blood of our Mother, the
> Earth, flows in the rivers, lakes and streams and brooks and creeks.
> That is our lifeblood. You will nourish from that. All life nourishes
> from that.

Elder Roger A. Jones
Shawanaga First Nation
Sudbury, Ontario, 1 June 1993

The North American intellectual tradition is an ancient system of knowledge that takes its meaning from a set of assumptions about the world and how
it operates. These assumptions have governed Aboriginal nations for thousands
of years. They address the basic philosophical questions posed in other intellectual
traditions. Who is God, the Creator? How was the world formed? What are the
rules of appropriate behaviour? The answers, sometimes different from those
arrived at in other intellectual traditions, are no less profound.

The thinker in the North American intellectual tradition has, in the words
of James Dumont, "an all-around vision" in contrast to the "straight-ahead
vision" of modern thought.[6] Areas such as the study of dreams and the knowledge of spiritual planes do not form part of the western intellectual tradition but
are integral to the all-around vision. Because of differences such as these, it can
prove difficult to discuss the Elders' holistic way of explaining phenomena with
those trained in a linear way of thinking. For the 'all-around' thinker, the natural and supernatural intertwine. Past, present and future mesh in the life of an
individual. The realm of the sacred becomes part of everyday experience.

This spiritual aspect of knowledge is central to the North American intellectual tradition. Knowledge is sacred, a gift from the Creator. This affects how
knowledge is protected and used, as well as how it is acquired and validated.

In Aboriginal societies, those who have this knowledge can 'see' in ways
generally not possible in western societies, grounded as they are in a linear view
that seeks understanding in terms of continuums, opposites and specific categories. The linear approach to knowledge leads one to think of isolated causes

and effects, of what happened and in what order. The relational approach to knowledge sees the relationship among things as well as the unity and integrity of things. Such a way of seeing is called holistic. A non-Aboriginal academic compares the two approaches:

> [T]he methods of [western] science are essentially reductionist, that is to say, they seek to understand organisms or nature by studying the smallest or simplest manageable part or sub-system in essential isolation....Traditional knowledge seeks to comprehend such complexity by operating from a different epistemological basis. It eschews reductionism, placing little emphasis on studying small parts of the ecological system in isolation....
>
> [T]he non-western forager lives in a world not of linear causal events but of constantly reforming, multi-dimensional, interacting cycles, where nothing is simply a cause or an effect, but all factors are influences impacting other elements of the system-as-a-whole.
>
> Linear approaches to analysis cannot be applied to cyclical systems and, as everyone now realizes, ecosystems are in fact complex cycles of re-circulating energy, matter and relationships.[7]

For many Aboriginal people, knowledge – like all things – emanates ultimately from the Creator. But usually a distinction is made between two kinds of teachings. *Objective knowledge* comes directly from the Creator. It is the source of the sacred laws that govern relationships within the community and the world at large. It is the source of the traditions and sacred ceremonies. It tells one how to lead a good life.

Equally valid is knowledge that comes through experience gained in the physical world. This is *subjective knowledge*, the knowledge acquired by doing. It is how children learn to hunt, make tools or gather medicines. They watch and, at some point, make their own attempt (often under the watchful eye of a parent or Elder). As they gain experience, their skills are refined. This kind of knowledge is subjective because it can change: an individual may find a better way of doing things. This learning and refining can continue throughout a lifetime. In many Aboriginal cultures, knowledge is often suspect if it is founded on events outside one's personal experience.

For Aboriginal peoples, both types of knowledge inform everyday life. To illustrate the point, imagine a hunting party. The skills used to track and bring down the animal are rooted in experience, learned in the subjective realm. Objective knowledge, directly traced back to the Creator, teaches that the spirit of the slain animal must be honoured and thanked. The ceremony itself is a teaching from the Creator. Objectivity and subjectivity intertwine like a braid in the daily act of living.

3. Cultural Wisdom and the Oral Tradition

Traditional wisdom is both content and process. It speaks of how things should be done as well as what should be done. It is normative. It embodies the values of the people in the lessons that are taught. What is right and appropriate can be found in the teachings.

The North American intellectual tradition is, for the most part, an oral one. This means that the transmission of knowledge is an interpersonal and, often, intergenerational process. All that must be remembered must be spoken aloud. The relationship between the speaker and the listener is a personal one. They share an experience. Each person hearing the stories of the past feels the pain, joins in the laughter, and relives the victories as a part of his or her own experience. The past, present and future become one:

> The human voice leaves a lasting imprint on human memory and feelings, because so much heart and spirit can be communicated through the voice, like no other medium.
>
> I resist writing down the stories and legends of our past because I have experienced the value of sharing them through close human contact. I also respect that the spoken word is sacred and powerful because I have seen instances where hearts were moved into action simply through listening to the voice of a storyteller. I have witnessed people change after listening to their past speaking to them through storytelling.
>
> There is a particular kind of magic or force that reaches out from a storyteller and touches something deep inside a listener, to respond. I have been led to believe that we carry some ancient memory inside ourselves that only the human voice can unlock and awaken, but how this happens I cannot explain.[8]

In the western intellectual tradition, the emphasis is on the written word. Reality is objectified on the pages of a book. Marshall McLuhan, who could be called an Elder of the western tradition, noted the subtle yet profound effect the shift to the written word had on western consciousness:

> Western history was shaped for some three thousand years by the introduction of the phonetic alphabet, a medium that depends solely on the eye for comprehension. The alphabet is a construct of fragmented bits and parts which have no semantic meaning in themselves, and which must be strung together in a line, bead-like, and in a prescribed order. Its use fostered and encouraged the habit of perceiving all environment in visual and spatial terms – particularly in terms of a space and of a time that are uniform,

c,o,n,t,i,n,u,o,u,s

and

c-o-n-n-e-c-t-e-d.

The line, the continuum – this sentence is a prime example – became the organizing principle of life....'As we begin, so shall we go'. 'Rationality' and logic came to depend on the presentation of connected and sequential facts or concepts.

For many people rationality has the connotation of uniformity and connectiveness. 'I don't follow you' means 'I don't think what you're saying is rational'.

Visual space is uniform, continuous, and connected. The rational man in our Western culture is a visual man. The fact that most conscious experience has little 'visuality' in it is lost on him.[9]

The mind-set described here is wrapped around empirical evidence and the 'burden of proof'. There is little room for reconciliation between this view and the Aboriginal world view, which accommodates the physical and the metaphysical.

Oral societies depend on cultural memory. Each person carries his or her personal story but also those of parents and grandparents. Elders link the coming generations with the teachings of past generations. The cultural teachings are the foundation of Aboriginal peoples' identity. If the culture is allowed to die, the identity of the people is buried with it.

4. WHEN CULTURES COLLIDE

Our languages, our spirituality and everything that we are – that was given to us and that was carried before by our ancestors, our grandparents who have passed on. When they couldn't carry it any longer and they went to join that spirit world, they handed it to us and they said, 'Now you are the real ones. You have to carry it.' Now they are in the spirit world. They are our past.

Charlie Patton
Mohawk Trail Longhouse
Kahnawake, Quebec, 6 May 1993

Traditional knowledge consists of a world view, organizing principles of life, laws of behaviour, and a knowledge of the sciences, from archaeology to zoology, framed and presented in a unique way through the power of the spoken word. The spoken word, itself a gift of the Creator preserved by the Elders, is the fabric out of which the pattern of the culture is fashioned. This is the content of Aboriginal cultures. Here we will touch on some aspects of culture, but for further exploration, see Volume 1, Chapter 15.

Cultures are dynamic, not static – they evolve, adapting to new conditions. But if their essence is not interfered with, they change in ways that leave the core values intact. They build on new knowledge and past achievements, but their foundation remains fundamentally sound. Aboriginal cultures have struggled to maintain their traditional values and knowledge despite aggressive external attempts to destroy cultural integrity.

The western intellectual tradition is perceived to be the standard by which knowledge is measured, the superior tradition. Western cultures have considered themselves more advanced (their societies being 'nations', for example, and Aboriginal societies, 'tribes'). Simply stated, the western way is seen as the right way and if Aboriginal peoples are to advance and enter the modern world, they must abandon the North American intellectual tradition (categorized not as an intellectual tradition but as 'ritual', 'magic', 'folkways').

For most Aboriginal people, this deculturalization has been too great a price to pay for modernization. Moreover, it is an unnecessary sacrifice. A return to traditional values does not mean turning back the clock. Many people live their lives according to other great teachings and philosophies, some of which are thousands of years old. Elders are crucial if traditional knowledge and values are to become a source of strength and direction in the modern world:

> Elders are the carriers of knowledge of our culture and our Nations. They should be listened to because the teachings are from their ancestors and are the 'way of life'.[10]

The most powerful message heard by the Commission about Elders was that Aboriginal people see their Elders as a contemporary link to traditional knowledge. Elders are the keepers of the traditional culture. They know the teachings of the ancestors – the ceremonies, rituals and prophesies, the proper way to behave, the right time for things to happen, and the values that underlie all things. Elders are essential to the perpetuation and renewal of the traditional way of life.

Many presenters told us that any new institutions – if they are to be genuinely Aboriginal institutions – must have at their core the teachings of traditional knowledge. Aboriginal Elders can make important contributions in this area. They hold the knowledge that is essential to design and sustain new institutions and practices. Elders must be included in the construction of new institutions.

RECOMMENDATION

The Commission recommends that

Participation in
Nation Building

4.3.1

Aboriginal, federal, provincial and territorial governments acknowledge the essential role of Elders and the traditional knowledge that they have to contribute in rebuilding Aboriginal nations and reconstructing institutions to support Aboriginal self-determination and well-being. This acknowledgement should be expressed in practice by

    (a) involving Elders in conceptualizing, planning and monitoring nation-building activities and institutional development;

    (b) ensuring that the knowledge of both male and female Elders, as appropriate, is engaged in such activities;

    (c) compensating Elders in a manner that conforms to cultural practices and recognizes their expertise and contribution;

    (d) supporting gatherings and networks of Elders to share knowledge and experience with each other and to explore applications of traditional knowledge to contemporary issues; and

    (e) modifying regulations in non-Aboriginal institutions that have the effect of excluding the participation of Elders on the basis of age.

Throughout this chapter, we consider how traditional knowledge and culture – and the repositories of that knowledge and culture, the Elders – can be reintegrated into Aboriginal institutions.

5. Traditional Culture in the Modern World: The Elders' Role

5.1 The Context

> Our way of life is so different. The two lives – the Native life and the white life – are different.
>
> Tonena McKay
> Big Trout Lake First Nation
> Big Trout Lake, Ontario, 3 December 1992

Aboriginal knowledge – the North American intellectual tradition – is indigenous to this land. It sustained Aboriginal cultures for thousands of years, enabling them to thrive and grow strong. Strangely, this fundamental truth eludes most Canadians, who seem to believe that knowledge arrived with the Europeans. Government, laws, education, religion and history itself are thought to have been transplanted to the continent with the first settlers. History books, written from the perspective of the newcomers, do nothing to counteract this misguided impression.

Elders deplore the fact that most Canadians do not learn about Aboriginal peoples and their ways of life, information that would help them understand issues from the Aboriginal perspective. Many Elders say this knowledge is vital to bridging the gap of understanding between Aboriginal and non-Aboriginal Canadians. The Elders who spoke to us often provided teachings they considered a starting point for mutual understanding.

Experts on relationships, Elders understand better than most people the original relationship that existed between Aboriginal peoples and other Canadians. For the Mohawk Nation, the nature of this relationship is symbolized by the Two Row Wampum:

> From the beginning we realized that the newcomers were very different from any other people who lived on Turtle Island. Consequently, our people proposed a special agreement to be made between the two parties. It is an initial guide for developing relations between ourselves and any other nations. It is the timeless mechanism. Each succeeding generation is taught the importance of the *Kaswentha,* or Two Row Wampum, for generations to follow.
>
> As you can see, the background of white wampum represents a river. The two parallel rows of purple wampum represent two vessels travelling upon the river. The river is large enough for the two vessels to travel together. In one vessel can be found the Kanien'kehaka, and in the other vessel the European nations. Each vessel carries the laws, traditions, customs, language and spiritual beliefs of the respective nation.
>
> It shall be the responsibility of the people in each vessel to steer a straight course. Neither the Europeans nor the Kanien'kehaka shall intersect or interfere with the lives of the other. Neither side shall attempt to impose their laws, traditions, customs, language or spirituality on the people in the other vessel. Such shall be the agreement of mutual respect accorded in the Two Row Wampum.
>
> Edward J. Cross
> Chairman, Kanien'kehaka Raotitiohkwa Cultural Centre
> Kahnawake, Quebec, 5 May 1993

Elders see the differences in perceptions and the resulting issues of contention. Testifying at our hearings in Port Alberni, British Columbia, Moses Smith, an Elder of the Ehattesaht community, spoke of the "audacity of the whiteman" to say that he was giving land to the Indians when the land was not his to give. The land was put there by the Creator to be used with respect by the original peoples; the concept of ownership of the land, as understood in western law, is not part of the traditional world view. At our hearings in Maniwaki, Quebec, Elder Mike Chabot explained that the *Indian Act* undermined the moral authority of some traditional chiefs because they were no longer recognized as community leaders by the government. The act also prescribed and limited the powers of the elected chief and council.

Understanding the world holistically, Elders know that relationships must be in balance and harmony. They see that the relationship between Aboriginal and non-Aboriginal peoples in Canada is out of balance. Harmony must be restored.

5.2 Freedom to Live a Traditional Spiritual Life

> Our traditional spiritual beliefs are not a religion. Ours is a holistic spiritual way of life. This spiritual way of life is our traditions, beliefs and government.
>
> Dennis Thorne (Tungán Cikala)
> Edmonton, Alberta, 11 June 1992

Elders told the Commission of the hardships they face in trying to live the way of life they inherited from their ancestors. For Aboriginal peoples, spirituality permeates all aspects of life. Life itself is a sacred ceremony, each moment alive with awareness of the presence of the Creator in the gifts of Mother Earth.

In the modern era, however, the sacred laws of Manitou, the Creator, have been impinged upon by the legal constructs of the new arrivals. Dennis Thorne, an Oglalah Sioux, described the problems confronting those trying to live a traditional life under these foreign precepts.

> When traditional spiritual people cross the border to come to Canada or go to the U.S., we are molested and harassed by border customs....Another question asked [us] is: do we have any animal parts? When I cross the border I may have eagle feathers, eagle wings, eagle bone whistle, eagle claws, bear grease, buffalo fat, animal skins – these are used for ceremonial purposes – as well as many medicinal plants and herbs. Again, I have no recourse or protection....
>
> Our sacred sites, such as medicine wheels, petroglyphs, rock paintings, fasting places, pipestone quarries, mounds and other ceremonial places are all controlled by man-made and non-Native institutions. Traditional people do not want to be tourists to their culture but have access for spiritual practice and beliefs. Many traditional people do not have their own land today. We are charged by different agencies if we pick medicines or cut willows for ceremonial purposes in national or provincial parks. They are often the only clean places left to pick medicines.
>
> Dennis Thorne (Tungán Cikala)
> Edmonton, Alberta, 11 June 1992

Others reiterated concerns that access to the trees, animals and natural resources necessary to conduct ceremonies be available to traditional people without the need to obtain licences or the threat of being arrested. Commissioners were asked for assurances that sacred sites would be protected and access to them guaranteed. People from Treaty 4 and Treaty 8 communities also explained that the mountains – sites where sacred ceremonies are performed – were never a part of the treaty negotiations. These sites are not part of reserves but are on what are now deemed provincial and federal Crown lands.

For these compelling reasons, the Commission urges reconciliation to ensure that Aboriginal people have the freedom to practise their traditional spirituality. In Volume 2, Chapter 4 we set forth recommendations aimed at achieving this goal through the reallocation of lands and resources and the re-establishment of Aboriginal authority over traditional lands.

One mechanism we recommend is the use of co-management boards to ensure Aboriginal involvement and consultation regarding traditional lands. Sometimes referred to as joint stewardship, joint management, or partnership, co-management has come to refer to institutional arrangements where governments and Aboriginal groups (and sometimes other parties) enter into formal agreements specifying their respective rights, powers and obligations with respect to the management and allocation of resources in a given area of Crown lands.

The term co-management has been used loosely to cover a variety of institutional arrangements, ranging from consultation to the devolution of administrative if not legislative authority to multi-party decision-making bodies. It is essentially a form of power sharing, although the relative balance among parties and the specifics of the implementing structures can vary a great deal. Most (but not all) examples of co-management to date involve Aboriginal parties in a central role, either sharing power with governments exclusively or in conjunction with interested parties.

What exists today is a compromise between the Aboriginal objective of self-determination or self-management and government's objective of retaining its management authority. This compromise is not one between parties of equal power, however, and Aboriginal peoples regard co-management as an evolving institution.

Whatever mechanisms or institutions are in place to govern land use, Elders must have a say in designing policies and procedures aimed at preserving and protecting sacred sites and traditional lands.

RECOMMENDATION

The Commission recommends that

Protection of
Sacred Sites

4.3.2

Aboriginal Elders be involved in the formulation and implementation of policies for the preservation and protection of sacred sites. In co-management situations, Elders should be board members.

5.3 Elders in Culture, Language and Values

> Does it confuse you when I refer to animals as people? In my language, this is not confusing. You see, we consider both animals and people to be living beings. In fact, when my people see a creature in the distance, the thing they say is: *Awiiyak* (Someone is there). It is not that my people fail to distinguish animals from people. Rather, they address them with equal respect. Once they are near and identify the creatures' shadows, then they use their particular name.
>
> Alex McKay
> McMaster University
> Toronto, Ontario, 25 June 1992

Aboriginal people know the power of the spoken word. This is the essential component of the teachings in the oral tradition. Language captures our perception of the world around us and how we relate to this world. Aboriginal languages pass on what it means to be Odawa, Métis or Innu by embracing the knowledge and developing the systems of interpretation transmitted therein. Language provides meaning. But meaning is derived not simply from words; it also comes from the structure of the language, the way words are put together. (A more comprehensive discussion about Aboriginal languages is found in Volume 3, Chapters 5 and 6. Here we touch on the importance of language specifically from the Elders' perspective.)

Michif, the language of the historical Métis Nation, reflects the Métis culture, embodying aspects of both European and Aboriginal cultures. In Michif, nouns are drawn from the French language while verbs are from the Cree. This makes for a language consisting of two completely different components with separate sound systems and rules governing syntax. The blending of the cultures has created a language unique in the world.[11]

Aboriginal languages also embody cultural understandings of the relationship between things and of life as dynamic, in a state of flux, with cycles of birth, growth, death and renewal. Cycles recur but are never completely predictable. As Blackfoot scholar Leroy Little Bear notes:

> Constant motion is inherent in the Native thought process, and consequently many Native languages, such as Blackfoot, are very action- or verb-oriented. We've always thought in terms of energy, energy fields and constant motion.[12]

Marie Battiste describes how her language, Mi'kmaq (which is also verb-based), embraces the Mi'kmaq way of seeing the world:

> [Mi'kmaq] is built around relationships, and the relationships of people to each other are more important than anything else....

In Mi'kmaq, everything operates from the basis of verbs, and verbs are complicated by all of the other elements around them which show relationships. So the most important element of the language is the verb because everything is connected to it and all the other words can be shifted around because of that.

There is an animate and an inanimate relationship and this inanimate relationship relates to how close we have [felt] to some things. The relationship of objects around us, those that have had an intimate relationship have an animate relationship, and those things that haven't have an inanimate relationship. But they have nothing to do with 'living' and 'dead'.

Marie Battiste
Mi'kmaq Cultural Curriculum Co-ordinator,
Eskasoni School Board
Eskasoni, Nova Scotia, 7 May 1992

Conversely, the dominant non-Aboriginal languages in Canada – French and English – are noun-based. The emphasis is on things. While appropriate for communicating the western perspective, these languages, in the eyes of Aboriginal people, fail to capture the essence of the Aboriginal way of seeing the world:

> To call something a tree is, as I perceive what has been shared with me, to impose a man-invented label on a man-invented stage in the transformation process from seed, to shoot, to sapling and then on to the bark-losing, root-withering, core-rotting and falling-to-earth-to-become-part-of-the-soil stages that follow. In fact, words like "seed", "shoot" and "sapling" are the same, just words, arbitrarily fastened by English-speakers onto artificially "frozen" moments of continuous change. In reality, according to the Algonkin speaker, the only thing that has "died" is what we created in the first place: the tree-concept which we imposed upon that one 'segment' of the spiritual continuum. Put another way, we *disconnected* a segment of the transformation process, froze it with the label "tree", then lamented its passing.[13]

In Inuktitut, the language spoken by Inuit, there are no separate terms to denote the sex of a person or animal. In addition, the language embraces a way of seeing the world in which each thing, animal and human being is accorded an equal status.

These subtle distinctions are often lost when Aboriginal languages are translated into English or French. Aboriginal languages are essential tools for describing, teaching and passing on traditional wisdom:

> We cannot protect our culture and our ceremonies unless we have our language....There are many things that I cannot find the words for

in English. In the language, it has a real essence that can't be expressed in English.[14]

The difficulty of translating Aboriginal languages is not limited to specific words. It extends to the concepts embedded in the words, concepts that may not be consistent between Aboriginal and non-Aboriginal speakers. Words like 'justice' carry with them a great deal of conceptual, moral and philosophical weight. The concept of justice varies with a society's ideas of what is just and fair. We may be able to find an Aboriginal equivalent for the word justice, but the underlying meaning may be quite different.

Elders play a critical role in the retention, renewal and celebration of Aboriginal languages. They know the precision of usage. They are, in western terms, the linguistic professors of their culture. The Elders addressing the Commission were passionate about their language. They stressed the use of Aboriginal languages as the only way to ensure accuracy in transmitting the North American intellectual tradition. They spoke of the failure of the schools to teach Aboriginal languages. They decried the loss of language as a threat to Aboriginal culture:

Right now, we are beginning to face a problem within our culture. Our language gradually is being pushed back to the point where our children regard the English language as their first language. Years ago, our Elders had one language which is the Inuit Inuktitut language.

Then my generation was sent to school and we were taught to speak English to the point where we weren't allowed to speak our mother tongue. If we did, a punishment was in order. Some of us were fortunate to keep our language and adapt to the English language as well.

Today, our children have one language just as our Elders have one language. But our children's language is the English language. I think that is the most significant problem we are facing today. It is the lack of communication between our Elders and children.

Presently, we don't have a written form of literature in our Inuit Inuktitut dialect to maintain our language. The present school system does not have the proper criteria to develop and maintain our language. The school system provides language, but the language that is being taught is in the eastern dialect. Parents are not maintaining the language at home as much as they used to.

Elder James Panioyak
Cambridge Bay, Northwest Territories
17 November 1992

Elders entreated young people to learn the languages, not simply to preserve them but to learn as well the social and psychological aspects of the culture that speaks the language. One learns when, to whom and about what it is appropriate to talk. These patterns of discourse become so natural that it is easy to forget they are culturally specific. Thinking in the language is the sign of a mature language speaker. Dreaming in the language is another sign of a fluent speaker. Thinking and dreaming in a language mean that the speaker has internalized the principles for organizing the world that underpin that language.

Many Aboriginal languages are in danger of being lost forever. (In Volume 3, Chapter 6 we provide more detail on the current state of Aboriginal languages and recommendations for retaining and increasing Aboriginal language use.) Ways must be found to ensure that the Elders' words are heard by the coming generations. Otherwise, the words – and everything that the words convey – will be lost. This recognition of the interrelatedness of culture, language and values speaks loudly for the inclusion of Elders in the consideration of these matters. More and more Aboriginal people are expressing a desire to learn about their culture and history. Traditions can be learned without knowing an Aboriginal language. But it is the Elders' dream that those who wish to understand the Aboriginal world view will not only learn the traditions and teachings but also learn to speak, think and dream as Aboriginal people.

5.4 Elders in Education

> Traditionally, education was not schooling. Learning for survival happened during all the waking hours, each and every day, and all life long. Learning occurred through life experience – not in abstraction or set apart from on-going activities.[15]

Education was the topic most talked about by the Elders appearing before the Commission. Education is what shapes young minds, and Elders have a passionate concern for the future of Aboriginal children and the Aboriginal way of life. Many spoke of the traditional education they had experienced and of their vision for the future. They want education to respect their skills, knowledge and traditions. They want the children of tomorrow to know themselves as Aboriginal people.

Unfortunately, this view often collides with the western approach to education and its assumptions about what skills, knowledge and values constitute a good education. In the western tradition, Aboriginal knowledge is often slighted as inferior or irrelevant.

Slowly, some are beginning to recognize the important contributions Elders can make in the school system. Lakota scholar Beatrice Medicine notes: "All individuals involved with Native education will benefit effectively using Elders metaphorically as bridges between two cultural domains."[16] Winnipeg's community and race relations co-ordinator offered this idea:

> Elders are considered guardians of Aboriginal cultures, and their role in cultural and language development in all school systems, at

all academic levels, must be acknowledged. They must be accorded the professional status and appropriate compensation.

Elders, by their wisdom and experience, can teach about tradition, history, culture, values, customs, role models and symbols of respect. They can fill the need for closer interaction between youth and Elders and act as resource persons in the areas of language and cultural programs. They could give support, advice and guidance to education staff and students by sharing their wisdom, philosophy, knowledge and experience. They could provide tutoring, story telling and language instruction. They can provide teachings about positive contributions made by Aboriginal people in history.

> Harold Rampersad
> Co-ordinator, Community and Race Relations Committee
> City of Winnipeg
> Winnipeg, Manitoba, 3 June 1993

In Volume 3, Chapter 5 we recommended that Elders be reinstated to an active role in educating Aboriginal children and youth and that they be compensated in a manner that shows respect for their unique knowledge and skills. But we acknowledge that tensions remain between what people want Elders to do, what Elders want to do, and what existing school structures will allow. Some Elders spoke of being angry and frustrated in their attempts to teach their knowledge in a school setting. Traditionally, Elders taught by doing, and young people learned from them by doing. The world around them was the classroom. Elders would rather offer their teachings in culture camps, on the trapline, or in their own facilities.

> More than once I have approached younger people and I have gone out hunting with younger people by teaching them – sometimes they really don't know how to go out hunting. But I've gone out hunting with them. That way they learn the language and the culture more, by going out hunting with them. I feel that they should go out in the land in order to teach them both worlds. [translation]

> Elder Lucassie Nutaraluk
> Chairman, Kalugiak Elders Group
> Iqaluit, Northwest Territories, 25 May 1992

Many Elders are ready and willing to teach the traditional skills of living on the land. These skills – hunting, trapping, fishing, harvesting and gathering food, herbs and medicines, shelter and fire building – need not be learned in the classroom and, in fact, are best learned out on the land. This is practical knowledge that not only promotes understanding of the land but also helps to ensure survival.

Elders' roles in education are not limited to teaching language and traditional skills. Modern science is beginning to recognize and validate the Aboriginal conception of the universe. This ancient philosophy of the nature of the cosmos is consistent with many of the fundamental principles set forth in modern science, particularly quantum physics and its offshoot, chaos theory:

> It turns out that those concepts in quantum physics are very similar to concepts that North American Indians have always had – Native Science, for lack of a better name....
>
> [The] notion of constant motion, which the quantum physicists sometimes talk about in terms of chaos theory, we've always talked about in terms of the trickster. In other words, the whole notion of chaos is not new to us at all. We've always known the trickster....
>
> The notion of observer-created reality is also incorporated into Native thinking. The notion of relationships, relational networks, is very important, too. This discovery of time and space being the same is old hat in Blackfoot. We've always thought about it that way. If I were talking about somebody I see in the distance over there or somebody I saw several days ago, I'd talk about them in the same way. Time and space have always been the same thing in Blackfoot, in Cree and in many other Native languages.[17]

"Native science" can offer valuable insights and teachings in areas such as astronomy, medicine, pharmacology, biology, mathematics, and environmental studies, to name but a few.

Disagreements remain between Aboriginal and non-Aboriginal people about what needs to be taught and how best to teach it. In the short term, deliberate efforts will have to be made to help Elders and school personnel bridge this cultural gap. An example can be found in the work of the Saskatchewan Indian Federated College:

> Over the years, we have had the Elders of the Indian communities play a very important role in terms of advising us about the way in which we should lay the foundation of our programs. They pointed out to us very strongly the importance of our values and the importance of our keeping our values and incorporating our values in the curriculum. We've had a lot of opportunity to discuss our curriculum developments with the Indian communities and so we are very convinced that the curriculum is very responsive to the communities.
>
> Blair Stonechild
> Dean, Saskatchewan Indian Federated College
> Regina, Saskatchewan, 10 May 1993

The role of Elders in education is not limited to direct instruction and curriculum development. Elders in the modern context are happy to be involved even peripherally in the education of young people in their community. They see education as important and necessary. In some northern and remote communities, Elders are known to walk through the streets in the early hours of the morning, watching for bear or wolf tracks, ensuring the roads and paths are safe for school children. Elders are not asked to take on this responsibility. They simply do it.

New models of education are necessary for Aboriginal students if they are to learn about their culture and to take their place as Aboriginal people in contemporary Canada. Elders have a role in developing these new models and in implementing the teaching of the subject matter. The nature of the North American intellectual tradition, the way traditional knowledge is taught and learned, and the complexities of Aboriginal languages are all pertinent to the development of new models. Elders can make important contributions in all these areas.

5.5 Elders in Justice

Traditional knowledge, with its holistic view of the individual, the world and the individual's place in the world, contains precepts of order, of what is right and appropriate behaviour. The world view of a given Aboriginal people sets limits on what is allowed and not allowed. The world view frames the relationship between human beings and the Creator, between human beings and the physical world, the plant world and the animal world. Some nations codify the rules of conduct, as in the Iroquois Great Law of Peace. Others imbue children with the moral code through legends, stories and examples. Language further describes the values and ethical positions expected. In this way, Elders are teachers of ethics. These ethics were the foundation of traditional justice.

Justice in traditional societies focused not on punishment but on restoring harmony to the community. Rules and well-established social mores were in place to keep conflict to a minimum. An Elder provides an example common to Inuit societies in Labrador:

> The Elders had rules related to hunting parties; for instance, if there was only one animal killed, they had clear-cut guidelines indicating who owned the kill. The hunter who killed the seal did not necessarily own it; another may have first harpooned it without killing [it], or it may have been killed at [another hunter's] seal breathing hole, in which case the kill belonged to the former. The animal was cut and divided among the hunting party with precise rules/knowledge as to who got how much and exactly what part of the animal in accordance to what role each hunter had partaken in the kill.[18]

When conflict arose, Elders often acted as mediators. They would listen to all who wanted to speak on the matter at hand before determining what must be done. The prescribed action was always aimed at restoring balance and harmony to relationships within the community. The first priority was to keep the circle – the community – strong. This is why in many Aboriginal societies, the worst form of punishment was banishment, used only as a last resort:

Every one might act different from what was considered right [if they chose] to do so, but such acts would bring...the censure of the nation, which [was] dreaded more than any corporal punishment that could be inflicted....

This fear of the nation's censure acted as a mighty band, binding all in one social, honourable compact. They would not as brutes be whipped into duty. They would as men be persuaded to the right.[19]

Recent studies show that traditional Aboriginal concepts about justice and truth collide and conflict with those underpinning the non-Aboriginal justice system.[20] In many Aboriginal languages, there is no word for or concept of guilt as understood in European law. In Inuktitut, for example, the word 'guilt' connotes 'blame'.[21] Even when Aboriginal people use the English or French words, the meaning is not consistent.

Two approaches have emerged in efforts to adapt the justice system to the needs of Aboriginal people: modifying the existing system to make it culturally more appropriate for Aboriginal people, and instituting distinct Aboriginal systems. The role of Elders is critical to both approaches. The justice system is an area where Elders have found the most opportunity in recent years to effect change – they work in prisons and with a broad range of community programs, participate in community sentencing and act as justices of the peace. Successes and lessons learned in these areas can direct policy makers to other suitable avenues for Elders' participation and collaboration.[22]

5.6 Elders in Governance

What is sovereignty? Sovereignty is difficult to define because it is intangible, it cannot be seen or touched. It is very much inherent, an awesome power, a strong feeling or the belief of a people. What can be seen, however, is the exercise of Aboriginal powers. For our purposes, a working definition of sovereignty is the ultimate power from which all specific political powers are derived. Sovereignty is inherent. It comes from within a people or nation. It cannot be given to one group from another. Ideally, sovereignty is the unrestricted right of a people to organize themselves in social, cultural, economic and political patterns that meet our needs. It is the inherent right of our people to define ways and means in which to utilize our lands, sovereign and traditional territories, held and set aside for our own use and benefit.

Elder Roger Jones
Councillor, Shawanaga First Nation
Sudbury, Ontario, 1 June 1993

No matter what is said about the issue of self-government, when we marry our own children and we bury our own dead, then we are self-governing. Until then, we are not.

> Elder Michael Thrasher
> Winnipeg, Manitoba
> 21 April 1992

Elders look at their people as self-governing from time immemorial, as people who never surrendered their autonomy. Elders believe that

> Sovereignty comes from the Creator. The Creator placed us on this land and gave us laws to live a good life and to live in peace and harmony with one another and with all creation.

> Elder Vernon Roote
> Deputy Grand Chief, Union of Ontario Indians
> North Bay, Ontario, 10 May 1993

In the past, as we have seen, Aboriginal societies were self-governing nations and conducted themselves as such. Confederacies, leagues and alliances were formed, trading networks were developed and maintained, and rules of law governed within the nations. For Elders, sovereignty in the modern context means exercising self-government. This means returning to the laws of Creation and exercising Aboriginal law:

> But we must recognize that and respect it. And we must bring back these tools that we were given by the Creator. That is our strength. This is inherent. This is our inherent right. Those drums that are in your community are the heartbeat of the people. Those pipes, those sweat lodges, those teaching lodges.

> Elder Roger Jones
> Councillor, Shawanaga First Nation
> Sudbury, Ontario, 1 June 1993

Let us develop self-government along traditional lines with a place for the hereditary Chiefs and Councils. Let us provide our Elders with the respect they deserve. Let us listen to the wisdom of their voices and share in respect for our territories. Let us govern ourselves along the holistic principles that have traditionally provided balance in our lives and spirits. Let us be guided by the words healing, trust and protection.

> Ray Prince
> General Director, Northern Region
> National Aboriginal Veterans Association, B.C. Chapter
> Prince George, British Columbia, 31 May 1993

Elders, grounded in traditional knowledge, can lead the struggle to re-establish culturally appropriate models of governance. They are explicit about their desire to play a role, as stated by an Innu Elder:

> We would like to be given a chance to control our own lives, to do things that are necessary to our way of life. [translation]
>
> Elder Simeo Rich
> Sheshatshiu, Newfoundland and Labrador
> 17 June 1992

5.7 Elders in Traditional Health and Healing

Elders tell us that healing is a spiritual process not confined solely to medicine and biology. The view is holistic. Like the three strands that form a braid of sweetgrass, the mind, body and spirit are intertwined, and each must be healthy and in balance. If one strand is weak, the braid is undone. As one Elder told us:

> Healing means mending bodies and souls. It also means rekindling the flames that strengthen our Native spirituality. It means physical, mental, psychological and emotional well-being. This is known in Native healing circles as the holistic approach to healing.
>
> Elder Byron Stiles
> Orillia, Ontario
> 13 May 1993

Elders are sought-after to treat unhealthy individuals, those whose spirits seem to be out of balance. They listen to the individual and consult with those close to him or her. They consider the mind, the body, and the spirit. Sometimes an Elder will conduct an appropriate ceremony before prescribing treatment. Treatment itself might consist of administering traditional medicine, conducting a ceremony for the individual and some or all members of the community, or both.

The underlying philosophy is that health is maintained by following the Creator's instructions for living a good life. Ceremonies – the sweat lodge, fasting – are ways of maintaining a connection with the Creator. Traditional medicines are used when necessary and are seen as gifts from the Creator:

> There is not a flower that buds, however small, that is not for some wise purpose.
>
> There is not a blade of grass, however insignificant, that the Indian does not require.
>
> Learning this, and acting in accordance with these truths, will work out your own good, and will please the Great Spirit.[23]

Examples abound of the success of traditional healers providing treatment through all stages of life:

I never saw a doctor while I was delivering all these children. I had to use a midwife while I was delivering these children....We had our own traditional doctors. I guess they were termed medicine men back then, but they assisted, they helped us, they healed us using traditional herbs and medicines. We never encountered any problems when we, as women, were delivering our own children because we had experienced people who deliver children who had a lot of experience being midwives. [translation]

Elder Juliette Duncan
Muskrat Dam First Nation
Big Trout Lake, Ontario, 3 December 1992

My First Nations believe in our medicine. I take this birch sap for arthritis and I don't have it. I brought this birch sap three years ago and I drank it. I have got to be away, so I am teaching my son to get it, because it is just a few days that it is in, and then there will be no more sap.

Elder Pearl Keenan
Commissioner for the Day
Teslin, Yukon, 27 May 1992

Traditional healers have always been trusted in Aboriginal communities. For some Elders, it is western medicine that is suspect. They have seen people become addicted to western medicines or be subjected to uncomfortable or painful treatments with little or no positive result. Carl Hammerschlag, a physician who has worked with the Hopi people in Arizona, explains the difference between western-trained medical doctors and traditional healers in the following way:

Contemporary medical training arms us factually but numbs us emotionally. This leads to people's distrust of doctors, which is reflected in the rise of malpractice suits. People are angry at the sad truth that you can be a doctor and not a healer. A good doctor can make the right diagnosis and treat the patient and if she's a great doctor, then she will also add a preventive component so the patient learns to minimize future exposure. But a healer can do all that and, in addition, help patients understand something about why they get sick, about their place in the world, and about their relationships with others, even the universe.[24]

Elders feel their traditional healing practices are being threatened on a number of fronts. The greatest concern for Elders is the encroachment of governments upon this sacred domain. An Ojibwa Elder stated:

On 19 December 1992, there was an introduction of a paper at the federal level to ban 64 therapeutic herbs from stores. When I read that I said, 'Well, they are going to have to have one police on me all the time because whenever I leave the house to go and pick medicines they are going to have to watch what I pick and they are going to have to teach that cop or person how to identify those medicines I am going to pick, because I am going to continue to use those medicines, regardless of what the government does....[H]ow do they know it is harmful? We, as Native people, have been using these remedies for thousands of years and some of us extend our life with that. It does not harm us.

Elder Dominic Eshkawkogan
Sudbury, Ontario
31 May 1993

Elders told us that these regulations, coupled with regulations that restrict their access to parks and sacred places where healing ceremonies are performed and medicines gathered, strike at the core of their beliefs and violate their spiritual essence. Policies must be developed through close consultation with representative Elders and Elders' organizations.

RECOMMENDATION

The Commission recommends that

Access to Public Lands for Traditional Purposes

4.3.3

Federal, provincial and territorial governments

(a) recognize Aboriginal people's right of access to public lands for the purpose of gathering traditional herbs, plants and other traditional medicines where the exercise of the right is not incompatible with existing use; and

(b) consult with Aboriginal governments on guidelines to govern the implementation of this right.

Elders have expressed concern about the current interest in Aboriginal spirituality, sparked to some degree by advocates of new age spirituality. Elders believe that traditional healing practices are being eroded by self-proclaimed 'Elders' who are not grounded in the traditions. Some Elders expressed alarm at the careless use of healing circles.

The problem with the healing circles, as the Elders perceive it, is that you have people who give a smidgen of tradition, of teaching, under the guise of traditional healing.

Elder Hugh Dicky
London, Ontario
12 May 1993

This raises questions. How is it decided who can perform certain ceremonies, practise certain rituals, sing certain songs, or organize and conduct healing circles? Who determines the qualifications of those calling themselves medicine people, traditional healers or Elders? The issue of self-regulation among traditional healers is something Elders themselves should address within the larger Aboriginal community. There are Elders' societies and organizations, both formal and informal, at the local, regional and national levels. For example, the Nak'azdli Elders' Society is active in British Columbia; internationally, the Three Fires Society is a large North American spiritual organization based on the teachings of the Midewewin Grand Medicine Society. These and other groups might wish to discuss criteria or procedures for recognition of traditional Elders. Ultimately, it is Aboriginal people who will determine who their Elders are. For Aboriginal people and their Elders, community recognition is the most reliable determining factor. Aboriginal health and healing issues, including ways to strengthen and enhance traditional approaches to healing and incorporate traditional healing into the mainstream health care system, as well as the Commission's recommendations in this area, are examined in detail in Volume 3, Chapter 3.

5.8 Elders in Social Issues

Traditional societies were founded on reciprocal relationships. Respect and responsibility – to one's self, the community and the Creator – were fundamental values that held society together. They were the bond that transformed a collection of people into a community. People cared for each other. Everyone had a role:

> The Elders were there as a man or woman to guide the society using the accumulated wisdom from a long life. The youth presented the hope and aspirations of a culture who learned by sense and imitation. The woman held the central and most honoured role as the bearer of life and man held the envious role of the protector, to preserve and maintain the continuity of the family unit.
>
> Chief Edmund Metatawabin
> Fort Albany First Nation
> Timmins, Ontario, 5 November 1992

Daily activities, ceremonies and rituals helped strengthen these roles and foster a sense of community. There were formal and informal rules guiding community life that worked to prevent disputes while strengthening the social bond among community members. Each Inuit community had its chief Elder:

> There were established trapping and fishing camps outside of the community with each camp having its own leader, sub-leaders and

territory. People using nets or traps for cod, salmon, or seals had rights to certain berths....[O]ther fur trappers had rights to certain areas. All other areas, excluding established camps, were used as general hunting grounds for seal, fish, caribou, fox, etc.[25]

Métis communities were organized with equally specific roles and responsibilities:

Métis social organization was communal and democratic. During the buffalo hunt, for example, they would get together and, for that specific purpose, would organize a provisional government with a president, captains and soldiers. In 1840 a massive hunt was recorded where there were 1,630 people using 1,210 Red River carts. A hunt of that size had to be highly organized and very disciplined. Everything had to be very precise.[26]

When Elders look at their communities today, they no longer see a place where everyone has a role. Traditions have been eroded, and the values that once bound society together have been lost or abandoned. There is no harmony; the circle has been broken. Instead, they see alcoholism, substance abuse, violence within families, unemployment, welfare, economic instability, and suicide. They also see the causes of these ills:

There is no mystery on the phenomenon of high suicide rates among our youth. Despair and hopelessness are intolerable in the lives of any human being. This situation is especially critical when the loss of individual self-worth occurs simultaneously with the rapid disintegration of our supporting culture.

Elder Jack Brightnose
Lac Seul First Nation
Big Trout Lake, Ontario, 3 December 1992

Elders believe firmly that the solution is a return to cultural teachings. Instead of feeling shame as Aboriginal people, youth and others would find in their Aboriginal identity a source of pride and strength.[27]

Elders act when they can to address pressing social needs at the community level. They are limited by inadequate facilities and resources, but they do what they can. An Ojibwa Elder told the Commission of his own efforts:

We should work together and get along with one another. Help each other. When somebody's down, pull him up. That's what happened when I was working the street patrol. I found a lot of my brothers lying in the gutter. I pull them up, stand him up, take him to detox. Maybe he'll fall again. Get him up again. That's the way we do it and then that's the way they should live. Help one another, work together, so we have a good country.

Elder Alex Skead
Winnipeg, Manitoba
22 April 1992

Respect, responsibility, caring and sharing are the solutions Elders bring to the social problems of Aboriginal people. They believe that the breakdown of Aboriginal societies and the consequent loss of cultural values are at the root of these problems. Restoring, renewing and strengthening cultural values is the solution they put forward. It is one in which they will have an active role as the carriers and teachers of those values.

5.9 Elders, Lands and Resources

My grandfather tried hard to keep his visions and dreams going in the family. When he was seven, the family left him at the summer camp to explore and know the ways of nature. All his peers were doing the same. He told me during this time he ate berries and squirrels. His communion with the trees started. The spruce provided him with comfort and warmth.

The rocks spoke to him of their resilience and power. The water spoke to him of its reflectivity, purity and power. This was my grandfather's vision. During the summer my grandfather met a bear cub without its mother and they became friends.

For 16 years, my grandfather's brother the bear came to live and play with him. My grandfather's hand was paralyzed because the bear bit him when they were wrestling. Pete, my grandfather, never hurt this bear till then. Grandfather gave the bear a bleeding nose. They never hurt each other till the bear died. My grandfather was sad.

Ron Momogeeshick Peters
Toronto, Ontario
2 November 1992

Elders tell us that Aboriginal people have a special relationship to the land, that they belong to the land, which the Creator provided for them and their children. The Creator placed on the land all that Aboriginal people would need to survive in harmony and balance with nature. For Aboriginal people, land is deeply intertwined with identity:

The concepts of territory, traditions and customs are not divisible in our minds. In our language we say: *THO ION nDEH SHU! TEN!*....That is, 'Our territory, our customs, and our traditions'....The question of the fundamental principles of the Long House is that, when we talk about the land, we say: *ONGWAnDUWEN ONWENTSA*. That is, 'Our Mother Earth'. It cannot be bought, it cannot be sold, it cannot be cashed in, because it is our mother – and you don't sell your mother. [translation]

Michel Gros-Louis (Taré Dan Dèh)
Akiawenrak Long House
Wendake, Quebec, 17 November 1992

There is not a lake or mountain that [does not have] connected with it some story of delight or wonder, and nearly every beast and bird is the subject of the story-teller, being said to have transformed itself at some prior time into some mysterious formation – of men going to live in the stars, and of imaginary beings in the air, whose rushing passage roars in the distant whirlwinds.[28]

The concept of territory has a special meaning to the Algonquin people:

It is the foundation of everything. Without territory, there is no autonomy. Without territory, there is no home. The reserve is not our home. I am territory. Language is territory. Belief is territory. It is where I come from. Territory can also vanish in an instant. Before the colonization of the Abitibi our ancestors always lived on the territory. My grandfather, my grandparents and my father lived there. This is the territory that I am talking about....

I live on the territory there, but it is not a reserve. I stay on the reserve from time to time, but I live on the ancestral hunting and fishing grounds where my father lived and died. [translation]

Oscar Kistabish
Val d'Or, Quebec
30 November 1992

The Elders tell us that the Creator made Aboriginal people the caretakers and stewards of the land. The people were told by the Creator to respect the gifts of the world around them.

I have the responsibility to use the Creator's gifts in a respectful way. That is why I will take only what I truly need and I will use all of what I take. I will not waste. When I pick medicine plants, I leave two for every one I pick. This way, I make sure the next person has medicine to pick, and I also ensure the sacred medicines will not disappear.

When I pick medicine, cut wood or take an animal or fish – indeed, whenever I take from Creation – I give thanks. I'm not sure if what I take has feelings as I do, or if it has the capacity to understand or communicate as I can. But, it is certainly alive. It grows and perpetuates itself. It plays a vital role in the Circle of Life and, eventually, it dies. When it gives of itself, I perform a ceremony to honour the gift of its power. In order to properly honour this relationship, I kindle a fire and offer *Oienkwenonwe* (Sacred Tobacco) so that the spirit of that which I have taken may hear my words and thoughts. The relationship between us is an intimate and personal one.[29]

Traditional knowledge of the ways of the land was rooted in an understanding of the holistic, interrelated nature of the earth's ecosystems, of the Circle of Life.

> Their philosophy is that all things are connected, that you cannot isolate one part of water, for instance, sport fishing. They don't see it that way. When they talk about water, they talk about everything that is connected to water. It starts with the smallest living thing right on up to the largest.
>
> They talk about water as being a big chain in a big circle, and we are part of that circle. We have to look after everything that is within that circle. If we destroy anything within that circle, we destroy ourselves.
>
> Albert Saddleman
> Kelowna, British Columbia
> 16 June 1993

Some Elders say that the only people who truly own the land are the generations yet unborn. Once born, you no longer own the land. Instead, it becomes your responsibility to take care of the land for its rightful owners: the coming generations.

Elders tell us that currently fashionable terms such as 'environmentally friendly' and 'sustainable development' are ancient concepts inherent in Aboriginal societies. The Iroquois people, for example, used to plant corn, beans and squash together. In this way, the 'Three Sisters', as they were known, were much less susceptible to the ravages of disease and insects.

The special relationship between Aboriginal peoples and land has been written about in considerable detail in recent years. Traditional ecological knowledge is being acknowledged and given recognition by scientists worldwide. Yet collaboration with people who have this traditional knowledge is only starting to happen now. A 1990 environmental impact study prepared for the Canadian Environmental Assessment Research Council noted the relevance of the Inuit system of classifying animals according to their relationships within the ecosystem as a whole:

> Although ecological classification is a relatively recent development in the Western scientific tradition, it has long been a fundamental organizing principle for the traditional Inuit taxonomy....The Inuit system of classification reveals a strong ecological logic and reflects

a dichotomy of land and sea which is a central theme in traditional Inuit mythology and world-view.[30]

Inuit in the southeastern Hudson Bay region divide animals – *umajuit* – into six main subdivisions. *Puijiit* are 'those that rise to the surface' (such as seals, whales and walrus); *pisutiit*, or 'those that walk', include polar bear, caribou and foxes; *timmiaq* are the large birds, including loons, swans, hawks and ptarmigans; *qupauak* are the songbirds, shorebirds and other small birds; *iqaluit* includes large motile fish such as Arctic char, brook char, lake char and whitefish; and *irqami-utait*, a diverse group of bottom-dwelling marine organisms, that includes fish, clams, sea urchins and seaweeds.

The report notes the 'ecological logic' of this system, a system that directly reflects the Inuit world view. Mammals are grouped into those of the sea and those of the land. Large birds are distinguished as water-seekers or land-seekers, and free-swimming fish are separated from bottom dwellers. The author states:

> The development of a classification system based upon ecological principles is a product of viewing the natural world from an ecological perspective. Recognition of traditional knowledge on the basis of scientific value rather than expediency will advance our understanding of arctic ecosystems and improve our ability to protect them, as well as helping sustain a culture with deep roots in the northern ecosystem.[31]

Elders are alarmed by the short-sighted approach to development now so prevalent. They foresee dire consequences if the approach does not change dramatically. Simply put, Elders believe we are destroying ourselves:

> As we see things now, our earth is dying. It is gradually being destroyed. Every second the human race is producing poisons, with many of the emissions destroying the vegetation which directly affects the wildlife that our people rely on for survival.
>
> Much of the development that is going on is considered by modern economists and politicians to be economic growth. The way our Elders see it, it is the destruction of our Mother Earth. And without Mother Earth we have nothing. We must consider the environment over economy, and at the same time realizing that there must be a balance.
>
> Elder Clarence Apsassin
> Elders' Program Co-ordinator, Treaty 8 Tribal Association
> Blueberry River Reserve
> Fort St. John, British Columbia, 20 November 1992

Elders believe there is only one solution: living life according to the Creator's instructions. The Creator's guidance ensured that the land, sea and sky, and all creatures dwelling there, would remain for future generations. The Creator's instructions provided for maintenance and care of the earth. Long before government imposed its rules and regulations, Aboriginal peoples had their own systems of territorial use and maintenance:

> Each family had its own district where they belonged and owned the game. That was each one's stock, for food and clothes.
>
> If another Indian hunted on our territory we, the owners, could shoot him. This division of the land started in the beginning of time, and always remained unchanged. I remember about twenty years ago some Nipissing Indians came north to hunt on my father's land. He told them not to hunt beaver. 'This is our land,' he told them; 'you can fish but must not touch the fur, as that is all we have to live on.' Sometimes an owner would give permission for strangers to hunt for a certain time or on a certain tract. This was often done for friends or when neighbours had a poor season. Later the favour might be returned.[32]

Systems for managing lands and resources were based on spiritual as well as ecological principles:

> Included in the spiritual laws were the laws of the land. These were developed through the sacred traditions of each tribe of red nations by the guidance of the spirit world. We each had our sacred traditions of how to look after and use medicines from the plant, winged and animal kingdoms. The law of use is sacred to traditional people today.
>
> Dennis Thorne (Tungán Cikala)
> Edmonton, Alberta
> 11 June 1992

Most Elders want to see co-management of natural resources such as wildlife, oil and gas, forests, water and minerals. Aboriginal people with traditional knowledge must also have more control over laws regarding jurisdiction of their traditional territories. An Innu Elder told us:

> [W]e're saddened by the government regulations, what we have to put up with. In the early days we didn't have to put up with any of this. There was no such thing as rules and regulations, government regulations, in the bush because of hunting and living the way we used to live.
>
> The Innu didn't change the way they live, or haven't changed. It is the government that is changing us, that wants us to live the way they live. But we can't do that. We have to maintain our way of living as well. If they hadn't bothered with the people in our communities in the early days, we would still have what we had in the past.
>
> Elder Elizabeth Penashue
> Sheshatshiu, Newfoundland and Labrador
> 17 June 1992

6. A Call to Action

We can never lose our way of life. We cannot let it go. We have to stand up for our way of life. All of us.

Elder Madeline Davis
Fort St. John, British Columbia
19 November 1992

The voices of the Elders who appeared before the Commission amounted to a collective call to action. They are calling for a revolution in the thinking of non-Aboriginal people. Elders, as the visionaries of Aboriginal society, bring a compassionate approach to the future. The future is tied to the past and present. The future is now. An Ojibwa Elder explains:

The Grandfathers and the Grandmothers are in the children – whose faces are coming from beneath the ground.[33]

Although the Elders who spoke to us were from many different traditions, nations and peoples, they had amazingly similar things to say. The intellectual traditions reinforced each other. First Nations, Métis and Inuit Elders spoke as one, looking to the future through the prism of traditional knowledge. They have much to teach us:

Each time one of these people passes on, a book closes. We don't have a record of it any more.

Elder Michael Thrasher
Winnipeg, Manitoba
21 April 1992

While most Elders were hopeful for the future, there was urgency in their message. The time has come to think about the future we are making for ourselves and our children. Will this be the last generation to live off the land, to speak the ancestral languages? Or will we see cultural rebirth in Aboriginal nations? What is to become of the North American intellectual tradition? If present trends continue, the situation looks bleak. Elders fear there will be no Aboriginal languages written or read, or even spoken, within the next quarter-century. A majority of Aboriginal people will be living in urban centres, away from their traditional homelands. In the name of resource development, bulldozers will continue to encroach on traditional territory, rending the land, leaving special cultural places unrecognizable.

Canadians must acknowledge the urgency of the situation and begin to act now. In some communities, it is already starting:

There was a time in the history of the Anishnabe people we nearly lost all of these things that we once had as a people, and that road narrowed. We could cite many reasons why that road narrowed, and we almost lost all of our culture. But today we strive to remind our people of those stories once again, to pick up that work that we as Anishnabe people know. It is our work and we ask no one to do that work, for it is our responsibility to maintain those teachings for our people.

Charlie Nelson
Mejakunigijique Aneebedaygunib [phonetic]
Roseau River, Manitoba, 8 December 1992

It is a time for Aboriginal people to make decisions. If the language is important, it must be spoken. If the ceremonies are important, they must be practised. If the knowledge is important, it must be retrieved, passed on and applied. If the sacred places are important, they must be saved. If Elders are important, they must be involved fully and centrally in matters of education, health, justice, self-government – in all institutions and decisions affecting the present and the future of Aboriginal peoples.

The Commission concludes that traditional culture is an important and defining characteristic of Canadian society and that Canadians must support Aboriginal peoples in their efforts to maintain their culture. Elders are the source and the teachers of the North American intellectual tradition. If they are lost or ignored, it is lost:

> We are grateful to our Elders, our grandmothers and grandfathers for their generosity and kindliness in sharing with us their wisdom and knowledge. We are grateful for the example they set for us as keepers of the culture and traditions and values of our people. The strength, courage and dignity that they exemplify are a constant source of inspiration. Their continued commitment to the survival of our languages, their concerns about the environment and the healing of our people is important to the future of our people. Our leaders, our young people and those yet unborn must have access to this knowledge and wisdom if we are to survive as strong and healthy communities.
>
> Their accumulated reservoir of knowledge and wisdom is freely offered to the living generations of the people in an effort to help us communicate harmoniously with our past, present and future. Besides the accumulated reservoir of knowledge that the Elders share with us, we too have a responsibility to assure the Elders of our support and to provide a process of binding with us and with the youth. We need to be connected. We need to assist them in their journey as they get older. Our Elders need to be and want to be in touch with what is happening.[34]

Notes

1. Sam Metcalfe, personal communication with staff of the Royal Commission on Aboriginal Peoples [RCAP], 2 February 1995.

2. Terry Lusty, "Defining a 'True' Native Elder", *Native Journal* 2/4 (May/June 1993), pp. 1 and 3.

3. Harvey Arden and Steve Wall, *Wisdom Keepers: Meetings with Native American Spiritual Elders*, ed. White Deer of Autumn (Hillsboro, Oregon: Beyond Words, 1990).

4. Ollie Ittinuar, Chairman, Inuit Cultural Institute, RCAP transcripts, Rankin Inlet, Northwest Territories, 19 November 1992.

5. Metcalfe (cited in note 1).

6. James Dumont, "Journey to Daylight-Land: Through Ojibwa Eyes", *Laurentian University Review* 8/2 (February 1976), pp. 31-32.

7. Milton M.R. Freeman, "The Nature and Utility of Traditional Ecological Knowledge", *Northern Perspectives* 20/1 (Summer 1992), pp. 9-10.

8. Esther Jacko, "Traditional Ojibwa Storytelling", in *Voices: Being Native in Canada*, ed. Linda Jaine and Drew Hayden Taylor (Saskatoon: University of Saskatchewan, Extension Division, 1992), p. 66.

9. Marshall McLuhan and Quentin Fiore, *The Medium is the Massage* (Toronto: Random House, 1967), pp. 44-45. Lest some readers think this citation contains a typographical error (and a humorous one at that), note that McLuhan coined the phrase "The medium is the message" in his 1964 book, *Understanding Media*. Never one to overlook a good pun, McLuhan titled a 1967 recording *The Medium is the Massage* and used this title again for the work cited here.

10. Elder Peter O'Chiese, speaking at the Eleventh Annual Traditional Peoples' Gathering, Trent University, Peterborough, Ontario, 18-20 February 1994.

11. Pieter Jan Bakker, "'A Language of Our Own': The Genesis of Michif, the Mixed Cree-French Language of the Canadian Métis", PH.D. dissertation, Drukkerij Universiteit van Amsterdam, 1992, pp. 1-2.

12. Leroy Little Bear, "What's Einstein Got to Do with It?", in *Continuing Poundmaker and Riel's Quest: Presentations Made at a Conference on Aboriginal Peoples and Justice*, comp. Richard Gosse, James Youngblood Henderson and Roger Carter (Saskatoon: Purich Publishing, 1994), p. 70.

13. Rupert Ross, "Surfing the Flux: Exploring the Roots of the Aboriginal Healing Process" (unpublished draft, September 1994), p. 21.

14. Rose Auger, "Native Spirituality, Healing and Languages", in *Wisdom and Vision: The Teaching of Our Elders*, Report of the National First Nations Elders Language Gathering, Manitoulin Island, Ontario, 21-25 June 1993, p. 43.

15. *Dene Kede – Education: A Dene Perspective*, Dene Kede Curriculum Guide (Yellowknife: Northwest Territories Education Development Branch, 1993), p. xxvi.

16. Beatrice Medicine, "My Elders Tell Me", in *Indian Education in Canada*, Volume 2: *The Challenge*, ed. Jean Barman, Yvonne Hébert and Don McCaskill (Vancouver: University of British Columbia Press, 1987), p. 151.

17. Little Bear, "What's Einstein Got to Do With It?" (cited in note 12), p. 70.

18. Metcalfe (cited in note 1).

19. G. Copway (Kah-Ge-Ga-Gah-Bowh, Chief of the Ojibwa Nation), *The Traditional History and Characteristic Sketches of the Ojibway Nation*, facsimile edition (Toronto: Coles, 1972), p. 144. Originally published London, England: Charles Gilpin, 5 Bishopsgate Without, 1850.

20. Fred Ahenakew, Cecil King and Catherine Littlejohn, "Indigenous Languages in the Delivery of Justice in Manitoba", a paper prepared for the Aboriginal Justice Inquiry of Manitoba, 9 March 1990, p. 25.

21. Metcalfe (cited in note 1).

22. For a more detailed discussion of existing initiatives and programs designed to make the justice system culturally more appropriate for Aboriginal people – including the role of Elders in the justice system – see the Commission's report *Bridging the Cultural Divide: A Report on Aboriginal People and Criminal Justice in Canada* (Ottawa: Supply and Services, 1996). The report also includes the Commission's recommendations regarding Canada's criminal justice system and Aboriginal people.

23. Copway, *The Traditional History* (cited in note 19), p. 175. Here, Copway is relating oral history on the origins of traditional medicine and healing in Ojibwa society.

24. Carl A. Hammerschlag, *The Theft of the Spirit: A Journey to Spiritual Healing with Native Americans* (New York: Simon and Schuster, 1993).

25. Metcalfe (cited in note 1).

26. Clem Chartier, "Métis Perspective on Self-Government", in *Continuing Poundmaker and Riel's Quest* (cited in note 12), p. 84.

27. The Commission examined the issue of suicide among Aboriginal people in a special report, *Choosing Life: Special Report on Suicide Among Aboriginal People* (Ottawa: Supply and Services, 1995).

28. Copway, *The Traditional History* (cited in note 19), p. 95.

29. Kanatiio (Allen Gabriel), brief submitted to RCAP (1995), p. 8.

30. Douglas J. Nakashima, *Application of Native Knowledge in EIA: Inuit, Eiders and Hudson Bay Oil* (Montreal: Canadian Environmental Assessment Research Council, 1990), p. 5.

31. Nakashima, *Application of Native Knowledge*, p. 5.

32. Aleck Paul, quoted in Peter Nabakov, ed., *Native American Testimony: A Chronicle of Indian-White Relations from Prophecy to the Present, 1492-1992* (New York: Viking, 1991), p. 87.

33. Ojibwa Elder Eddie Benton-Banai, quoted in Arden and Wall, *Wisdom Keepers* (cited in note 3), p. 10.

34. Mary Lou Fox, Director, Ojibwa Cultural Foundation, West Bay First Nation, "Proposed Programs/Activities", April 1994-March 1995, pp. 2-3; see also RCAP transcripts, Sudbury, Ontario, 31 May 1993.

4

THE SEARCH FOR BELONGING: PERSPECTIVES OF YOUTH

Our vision is to be happy. We want to relax and have dreams and laugh. We want to love and talk. We want more Indian counsellors. We want nobody to hurt us and make fun of us. We want to feel safe. We want our own police. We want a justice system that works. We want to know our Native culture. We want to respect each other. We have to have a better future.

Robert Quill
Coldwater Band School
Merritt, British Columbia, 5 November 1992*

1. THE VISION OF ABORIGINAL YOUTH

YOUNG ABORIGINAL PEOPLE are deeply concerned about the future because it is their future. They speak of concerns rooted in the here and now, with an eye to what can be done today to build a better tomorrow.

The Commission's terms of reference instructed us to investigate and make concrete recommendations concerning the situation of Aboriginal youth. We heard from hundreds of young people – at our public hearings, through written submissions, through specially convened youth circles, and during visits to schools, child care centres and many other facilities. In addition, the Commission's research division included a youth team to focus on the issues and concerns of young Aboriginal people. Through these many channels, the Commission attempted to come to grips with the hopes, dreams and fears of Inuit, First Nations and Métis youth.

---

* Transcripts of the Commission's hearings are cited with the speaker's name and affiliation, if any, and the location and date of the hearing. See A Note About Sources at the beginning of this volume for information about transcripts and other Commission publications.

We were encouraged to see that Aboriginal youth, when presented with a problem, immediately tend to look for solutions that are practical and feasible, and that will work at the community level. It became clear that for young Aboriginal men and women, community development is not about infrastructure, but about people, and about building a stronger community. By and large, they are not concerned with perceived political or administrative impediments; they do not worry about overlapping jurisdictions, competing programs or other bureaucratic hurdles. They feel these political obstacles are immaterial, creations of a system that has largely failed Aboriginal people.

Politically and culturally, many Aboriginal youth identify with an Aboriginal nation. When they gather, they are not concerned about who has 'Indian' status – or how they acquired it – and who does not, about who lives on-reserve and who does not. They do not identify with labels fabricated for administrative purposes by governments. They are first and foremost Mi'kmaq, or Inuit, or Métis or Saulteaux – they are members of an Aboriginal nation. They want organizations that represent their true nationhood.

Yet they recognize that, as Aboriginal people, they have common bonds. They share the legacy of a colonial past. Their peers and their communities face many of the same challenges. They are willing to work together to address the common concerns of Aboriginal peoples everywhere. They would like their organizations to share in this co-operative effort:

> You know, we don't need money all the time. What we need is our nation, our people, our communities to come together as one and to work together as one, to sit down and say, "Okay, this is what we've got to do". The government is obviously not doing anything, so we'll just never mind the government for now. We'll shift that off to the side....It's our people who are in trouble. We have to work as one people, one nation. We must do that. It's extremely important.
>
> Stan Wesley
> Moose Factory Youth Group
> Moose Factory, Ontario, 9 June 1992

Youth believe in themselves as Aboriginal people, and believe that this identity is within them wherever they go. They assert that their rights are not restricted to a reserve or traditional homeland, but remain with them no matter where they choose to live. The term 'community' appears often in this chapter. It is used in the broadest sense. It is not simply a physical space; it refers to any group of people who share ways of being together. Hundreds of distinct Aboriginal communities are identified on the map, yet there are many hundreds of equally distinct communities that are not identified by borders. There are communities of students, of co-workers, in prisons, and on the streets of urban Canada.

Aboriginal youth spoke to the Commission about many issues from fresh and unique perspectives. It would be a mistake to try to compress these voices into a single note or tone. But all Aboriginal young people have at least some common concerns. They are the current generation paying the price of cultural genocide, racism and poverty, suffering the effects of hundreds of years of colonialist public policies. The problems that most Aboriginal communities endure are of such depth and scope that they have created remarkably similar situations and responses among Aboriginal youth everywhere. It is as though an earthquake has ruptured their world from one end to another, opening a deep rift that separates them from their past, their history and their culture. They have seen parents and peers fall into this chasm, into patterns of despair, listlessness and self-destruction. They fear for themselves and their future as they stand at the edge.

Yet Aboriginal youth can see across this great divide. Their concern about the current crisis is leavened with a vision of a better tomorrow. They spoke often of empowerment, a process brought on by healing and community development:

> In our society the practice of self-cleansing was deemed an honourable ritual which was not confined only to the individual, but also practised at the clan and community level. To begin our healing process as Aboriginal people we must first undergo a cleansing process. We must begin prioritizing the issues that will require our utmost efforts and resources. We feel the most important resource base we have as Aboriginal people is our people.
>
> Carol Gauthier
> Shingwauk Anishinabek Student Society
> Algoma University
> Sault Ste. Marie, Ontario, 11 June 1992

Through empowerment, individuals become mentally, physically, emotionally and spiritually healthy. They come to recognize themselves as valuable members of the community. They work to make their community stronger, and in doing so they help other members of the community empower themselves. The process is a continuum or circle – the symbol common to many Aboriginal cultures. How to achieve the empowerment of Aboriginal youth and communities was a central preoccupation for the young people who spoke to the Commission. It is the primary focus of this chapter, which is based largely on the words of Aboriginal youth. But because of its implications for future generations, the chapter speaks to the concerns of all Aboriginal people, regardless of age.

2. THE REALITY FOR ABORIGINAL YOUTH: AN OVERVIEW OF CURRENT CONDITIONS

2.1 An Aboriginal Youth Profile

The majority of Aboriginal people in Canada – 56.2 per cent, or some 405,200 people – are under the age of 25.[1] By contrast, only 7.3 per cent are 55 years of age or older. For societies struggling to reclaim their traditional languages and ways of life, this puts tremendous pressure on the older generations.

The Aboriginal population in Canada is much younger than the non-Aboriginal population. Children – from newborns to age 14 – make up 36.5 per cent of the Aboriginal population but only 21.1 per cent of the Canadian population. Youth – those 15 to 24 years of age – account for 14.2 per cent of the Canadian population but 19.8 per cent of the Aboriginal population (see Table 4.1). This definition of youth is consistent with that used by Statistics Canada, the Organisation for Economic Co-operation and Development and the United Nations Educational, Scientific, and Cultural Organization. When citing statistics in this chapter, we adhere to a strict definition of children, that is, people up to the age of 14. When not citing statistics, we use such terms as 'young Aboriginal people' and 'Aboriginal youth' to apply to all Aboriginal people under the age of 25.

The urban context is crucial to understanding the present situation of Aboriginal youth. Almost half (45 per cent) of all Aboriginal people under age 25 live in non-reserve urban centres (defined as a population of at least 1,000 and a density of 400 people per square kilometre; for purposes of the Commission's work, urban areas exclude reserves that may be within the geopolitical boundaries of urban areas). Of these, the majority (40.4 per cent) live in urban areas with populations of more than 100,000 – cities such as Montreal, Toronto, Winnipeg, Saskatoon, Edmonton and Vancouver.[2] Well over half the status and non-status Indian and Métis youth in urban areas live in large cities.[3] The exception is Inuit youth, almost 80 per cent of whom live in northern communities; of Inuit youth in urban areas, 21.2 per cent live in large cities.

The number of young Aboriginal people in urban areas varies from city to city. The 1991 Aboriginal peoples survey indicated that there were 3,260 Aboriginal people under the age of 25 in the Ottawa-Hull area. Winnipeg, a city known for its large Aboriginal population, had more than 20,000 young Aboriginal people. The Aboriginal youth population of Edmonton was reported as about 17,000, while in other large cities the numbers ranged from 5,000 to 10,000.[4]

A gradual greying of the Aboriginal population will occur over the long term. The current birth rate is much lower than it was in the 1960s. The proportion of the Aboriginal population 14 years of age and under is expected to decline from 36.5 per cent in 1991 to 24.4 per cent in 2016. The age group from 15 to 24 will stay at 20 per cent until the turn of the century, but will gradually drop to 16 per cent by 2016. In terms of numbers, this population will rise from an estimated 142,400 in 1991 to a projected high of 189,100 by the year 2011, and will then fall to 175,500 by 2016. Demographically, Aboriginal youth will remain a significant force. In 2011, those aged 20 to 24 will represent the largest five-year age group in the Aboriginal population (98,900), and those aged 15 to 19 the second-largest (90,200).

TABLE 4.1
Age Distribution of the Aboriginal Identity and Canadian Populations, 1991

Age Group	Aboriginal[1]	Canadian[2]
	%	%
0-14 years	36.5	21.1
15-24 years	19.8	14.2
25-34 years	18.5	17.9
35-54 years	17.9	27.1
55+ years	7.3	19.7

Notes:
1. Figures have been adjusted to account for undercoverage of the population. For a more complete discussion see Volume 1, Chapter 2, and M.J. Norris et al., "Projections of the Population With Aboriginal Identity in Canada, 1991-2016", research study prepared by Statistics Canada for the Royal Commission on Aboriginal Peoples (February 1995).
2. Includes Aboriginal and non-Aboriginal persons.

Source: Statistics Canada, "Mother Tongue: 20% Sample Data", Catalogue no. 93-333, 1992.

2.2 The Importance of Listening to Aboriginal Youth

A lot of things that have been put in place for youth don't work because they haven't consulted youth themselves. It is time for us to start doing things as young people because no one is going to do it for us. We can't wait for the government or the community to do things. We have to work with them.

Tonya Makletzoff
Yellowknife, Northwest Territories
10 December 1992

Youth, it seems, are somewhat wary of government-designed solutions, even those of Aboriginal governments. In the past, programs designed to assist them have been scattered and often misdirected. They feel their concerns are not taken seriously by their leaders and their communities. When they speak out, their voices go unheard. Feeling marginalized, excluded or devalued, some have lost faith in their communities. Aboriginal governments have to become more accountable to their communities and to youth. Through hundreds of hours of testimony and thousands of pages of presentations to the Commission, it became clear that the priorities of youth are healing, education, employment, culture and identity, and recognition of and involvement in the institutions that affect their lives. Their numbers in the population of today and their role in shaping and leading their communities and nations tomorrow make it essential for governments – Aboriginal and non-Aboriginal alike – to listen to their concerns and act on their priorities.

3. TOWARD WHOLE HEALTH

We know, Grandfather, that you gave us a sacred power,
But it seems like we didn't know its purpose.
So now we've learned as we sat together:
The name of the power is Love –
Invincible, irresistible, overwhelming power.
The power you gave us we are going to use.
We'll dry the tears of those who cry
And heal the hurts of them that are hurting.
Yes, Grandmother,

We'll give you our hands,
And our hearts and our minds and our bodies.
We dedicate our lives to affirmation.
We will not wait nor hesitate.
And as we walk on this sacred earth,
We will learn together to celebrate
The ways of peace, and harmony, and tranquillity
That come
From diminishing that negative, evil power within us
And in the world around us.
Thank you, Grandfather, for this prayer.

3.1. The Need for Whole Health

This prayer opened Youth Forum – A Voice for the Future, held in the Inuit community of Hopedale, Labrador, in February 1993.[5] Hopedale and its neighbour to the north, the Innu community of Davis Inlet, are among the many Aboriginal communities still struggling to wrest from the government of Canada basic services that were promised decades ago. Years of neglect have left today's youth in need of not just physical amenities but also holistic healing that focuses on the four pillars of the individual's being: spirit, mind, body and emotions. Unless a holistic approach is taken, the despair that has gripped Aboriginal communities will not let go.

A recent example is illustrative. Davis Inlet gained national prominence in January 1993 when television stations across the country broadcast videotape images of six youths attempting suicide. Canadians were shocked, and rightly so. In all, 17 youths – including the six who had attempted suicide – needed urgent treatment for the substance abuse that was destroying them, and they were eventually taken to the Poundmaker Lodge in Alberta. Yet when the youth returned to the community, many resumed substance abuse. Their bodies had been healed, but there was nothing to nourish their minds, emotions or spirits. To have a lasting effect, healing must address not only individuals but also the community. The initiative to heal must come from and be rooted in the community. These are perhaps the most important lessons of the Davis Inlet experience.

Healing is the first step on the road to empowerment. Youth believe that this healing process builds the strength they need to face all other challenges:

> We feel that the healing will come from within the community. Along with a realistic resource base, we have the tools to heal our people.
>
> Desmond Peters Jr.
> Student, Aboriginal Governments Program, University of Victoria
> Victoria, British Columbia, 22 May 1992

In many Aboriginal societies, the Medicine Wheel is the symbol of holistic healing, embodying the four elements of whole health:

- spiritual health, which can mean many things, depending on the individual's approach to spirituality, and may include participating in ceremonies, gaining traditional knowledge, and exploring spiritual heritage;
- mental health, which includes education, knowledge of Aboriginal history and cultural contributions, and activities that promote self-confidence;
- physical health, including nutrition, sports and recreation, and cultural activities; and
- emotional health, gained through access to sharing circles, counsellors and elders.

A return to traditional forms of healing is not regression but a resumption of the path that sustained Aboriginal people and nations for generations. The Commission recognizes, however, that reintroducing traditional healing methods can cause tension in communities and must therefore be done with community support and with great sensitivity.

Youth have begun to benefit already from a holistic approach to healing at several locations. Young women's teachings are offered at Matootoo Lake, a site for traditional healing near the Peguis First Nation in Manitoba. Matootoo Lake was chosen because traditional teachers and elders say that healers used to come to the area to pick medicinal plants and build sweat lodges. (*Matootoo* is the Ojibwa word for sweat lodge.) The teachings offered at Matootoo Lake prepare young women for the emotional, physical and spiritual transition to womanhood. A major goal of the program is to reduce unplanned pregnancies by helping young women acquire confidence in their ability to deal with sexuality. A parallel program for boys is designed to enhance their self-esteem, develop respect for girls and women and raise awareness of issues such as violence against women. The program has a great deal of local credibility, and the demand for services outstrips availability.[6]

Culture, sports and recreation, counsellors, peers, elders, parents, family and governments all play a role in healing Aboriginal communities. When approaches to healing address the individual and the community holistically, whole healing can take place. We discuss the holistic approach to healing at greater length in Volume 3, Chapter 3.

We turn now to approaches that will enable youth to heal themselves and find the spiritual, mental, physical and emotional health they seek.

3.2. Spiritual Health

> The first time I heard the drum it was like a magnet pulling me to it. When I hear the drum and the songs it makes me want to get up and dance. When you're near the drum you can feel it in your heart because it's your heartbeat. It's only natural for a person to want to dance because it is the first sound you hear – your mother's heartbeat.
>
> Vera Wabegijic
> National Youth Representative
> National Association of Friendship Centres
> Ottawa, Ontario, 5 November 1993

For many Aboriginal people, spiritual health is directly related to reclaiming their traditions, culture and language. During the Commission's hearings, Aboriginal youth spoke more often about culture and identity than about anything else in the Commission's mandate. The research studies and youth circles sponsored by the Commission revealed these themes as well. No matter where the community, no matter who the speaker, Aboriginal youth spoke with a single voice about what culture means to them and about its place in the healing process. Cultural identity imbues all four areas of healing.

Understanding themselves as Aboriginal people is important to youth because it directly affects their self-esteem, which in turn affects their motivation to strive for a better tomorrow. Aboriginal youth have been bombarded by negative images of their people: inaccurate portrayals in the media, in old (and not so old) movies and television shows, and in school curricula that distort or ignore the contributions of Aboriginal cultures. They also face day-to-day, street-level racism and government and public policies that continue to devalue Aboriginal people and culture. They see members of their communities ravaged by substance abuse and physical abuse and they wonder, is that what it means to be an Aboriginal person?

The importance of a secure sense of identity cannot and should not be downplayed or dismissed. Identity confusion or lack of identity is a major risk factor for suicidal behaviour among young Aboriginal people, as we pointed out in *Choosing Life: Special report on suicide among Aboriginal people:*

> In speaking to Commissioners, Aboriginal youth described both exclusion from the dominant society and alienation from the now

idealized but once-real 'life on the land' that is stereotypically associated with aboriginality. The terrible emptiness of feeling strung between two cultures and psychologically at home in neither has been described in fiction and in art, as well as in testimony given before the Commission. If they have few positive role models or clear paths to follow, Aboriginal youth may be forced to turn to one another, building tight bonds against a hostile world. Their inward-looking subculture may reinforce hopelessness and self-hate, and their only exits may appear to be the oblivion of drugs and alcohol – or death.[7]

Giving Aboriginal youth the opportunity to learn about their language, culture and traditional values teaches them that they are valid and valued individuals and that they can be proud – not ashamed – of their culture and the contributions Aboriginal people have made. Youth who gain a positive sense of self come to see their future as worth fighting for. Grounded in their culture, they can work as Aboriginal people to make a better tomorrow:

> When I hear elders talking about our culture and traditions, it moves me. Their words strengthen me and inspire me. The teachings that have been passed on to me help me along the path I have chosen. It helps focus my mind and encourages me to do my best every day.
>
> Vera Wabegijic
> National Youth Representative
> National Association of Friendship Centres
> Ottawa, Ontario, 5 November 1993

Four key themes emerged from what youth told the Commission regarding culture:

- the loss of culture and identity through denial and suppression;
- the importance of language;
- the role of parents and elders; and
- the challenge of moulding non-Aboriginal institutions to reflect Aboriginal values.

Aboriginal youth know their culture is more profound than a lifestyle, that it taps into the very heart of their people and their spirituality. Yet they feel their cultures are threatened, and they cling to them as the key to survival. Many feel that the traditions defining their identity are being forgotten by all but a few elders:

> Many of our parents think they are worthless. Many of them do not have the heart to serve as a stable source of love and discipline. We are experiencing a breakdown in traditional family values. We are not making human beings human. Educate us to be a guide, a friend, a

companion to our parents, our people and to all Canadians. Children have dreams. Children trust grown-ups. Please don't let us down.

Tara Lindsay
Iqaluit, Northwest Territories
25 May 1992

I have a grandfather who is 80 years old and I have been growing up with him for my 18 years. I cannot speak my language. I try. But I love him more than anything, and there's communication there....you can feel the love between us and I can rub his hand and we know we understand each other. But there is something missing when we cannot listen to the stories they have to tell, or explain how you are feeling about something. And it's very frustrating for me, knowing that this very important part of my culture is being lost.

Christina Delaney
Moosonee, Ontario
10 June 1992

This sense of loss coloured virtually every statement that youth made to the Commission. For some it was the focus of their message. For others, the sense of loss was muted or overwhelmed by strong cultural pride. Our hearings often revealed these two poles: the devastation felt among youth in Aboriginal communities, and the yearning for identity through a revived and invigorated culture. This duality is played out in the lives of many young Aboriginal people.

One of the Commission's research projects revealed this yearning for identity through 'Sonny', a young Aboriginal man who abused alcohol and drugs.[8] Sonny eventually rediscovered his sense of self through identification with his culture. At a Native Friendship Centre he was introduced to songs, dances, ceremonies and other cultural practices. Eventually Sonny was able to turn his life around, through renewed pride and self-esteem. His culture was like a key, unlocking his capacity to heal himself.

Like Sonny, many Aboriginal youth who come into conflict with the law are either unaware of their cultural roots or seeking to find them. The over-representation of Aboriginal youth in the justice system suggests other problems, including high unemployment and a perceived lack of opportunity, the absence of positive role models, low self-esteem, and the effects of racism and cultural devaluation.

Youth interviewed as part of a Commission research project said they were proud of their culture, but most of them did not even know their culture until they were exposed to it at the Edmonton Young Offenders Centre.[9] It is both sad and ironic that some youth discover their culture only behind the walls of a prison. 'Missy', a former street youth in Vancouver, asked: "Why are counselling and Aboriginal culture suddenly provided *after* youth have landed on the street? It gives kids the wrong message – if you're behaving yourself, you're doing okay in school, you're at home and you don't run away...you don't deserve these things".[10]

The urban context

> We believe our heritage, culture and religion are what make us human beings. It is very difficult in the city to learn these things because many of the knowledgeable people who know about it and can help us with it don't live here. We must have help and resources so that we can reach out to these people and build connections between us and them.
>
> Jolene Wasteste
> Regina, Saskatchewan
> 10 May 1993

The search for culture and identity can be especially difficult in urban areas. Aboriginal youth living in cities face different challenges in trying to heal themselves. They are a minority in a sea of cultures. They must seek out or create their own communities to develop a sense of who they are as Aboriginal people:

> You are living two lifestyles when you live off-reserve....I was brought up to know two cultures, but I am one or the other. I am always thought of as one or the other.
>
> Judie Acquin
> Fredericton, New Brunswick
> 16 June 1993

Some Aboriginal youth were born in the city, but over the years there has also been substantial migration of Aboriginal people from rural or reserve communities to urban areas. Young people leave their communities for many reasons: their parents move, they decide to flee abusive situations, they want a higher quality of secondary education than is available closer to home, or they enter post-secondary institutions.

Urban youth do not want to be seen as traitors to their home communities. Many have a deep commitment to helping strengthen and enrich their communities. In some cases, they would stay if the community offered them the opportunities they seek. But to gain the necessary skills and resources – through education, work, and health care – they sometimes have to move to an urban environment for at least a few years. For some, the city becomes their community.

Once in the city, they find new pressures and challenges. Substance abuse is one of the most pervasive problems facing Aboriginal youth. Like the high rates of incarceration, however, substance abuse is symptomatic of a deeper malaise: loss of identity and low self-esteem. In urban centres these feelings can be amplified if there is no readily apparent Aboriginal community to turn to for support.

While trying to come to grips with their Aboriginal identity, Aboriginal youth are bombarded with the images and sounds of the dominant society. Television and advertising seldom include Aboriginal content, while satellites beam images of non-Aboriginal culture into homes in remote areas across the country. Non-Aboriginal culture pervades the life of Aboriginal youth.

Youth in smaller communities are exposed to non-Aboriginal culture through television, educational curricula and teachers. But youth in urban centres are surrounded by it. They live and experience it directly. While some can balance an urban lifestyle with their traditions and culture, others feel they are drowning in the mainstream.

Culture and identity

Youth told the Commission that they must have opportunities to explore and live their culture. Not all want to return to a traditional lifestyle; for many, especially those living in cities, this is highly unlikely. Yet they want to learn about the values and beliefs of their people and what it means to be an Aboriginal person in the modern world. They want to learn Aboriginal languages and celebrate their cultures through traditional practices and ceremonies. This need not be done to the exclusion of non-Aboriginal culture. Cultures are not static; they evolve over time. Young people want to learn the values and wisdom that sustained their ancestors long ago – values and wisdom they can use to guide their behaviour in today's world. They want to face the future as Aboriginal people.

The home is where such practices and values are traditionally transmitted. But some youth told the Commission that their parents no longer have the necessary knowledge. Elders and support networks, where they exist and when they can be located, can help. There is a need for facilities and programs where youth can gather and learn. This is particularly important for those who are making the transition from reserves or remote communities to the city. Youth recommended to the Commission that a variety of facilities to meet their cultural needs be established.

Among their suggestions was to set up Aboriginal youth centres. These centres would be a co-operative effort among community leaders, educators and government officials to give young people the qualities and skills needed to be leaders in the community. Aboriginal elders and others recognized as knowledgeable in the culture should have a role in planning and implementing programs. The centres would combine voluntarism and government-funded programs to enhance traditional knowledge and skills, offer enhanced academic and technical training, expose youth to professional and government environments, and foster a spirit of service. In cities, the centres should also provide counselling and support for youth moving from home communities to the urban environment.

The centres should, as much as possible, use existing resources in order to limit financial dependence. They could be established in existing facilities such as friendship centres, community centres, cultural centres and schools.

RECOMMENDATION

The Commission recommends that

Cultural Centres   **4.4.1**
for Youth   Youth centres be established on reserves and in communities, including urban communities, where there is a significant Aboriginal population. Where cultural centres exist they should develop a specific youth component, including cultural and recreational programs.

In Chapter 7 of this volume, we recommend a number of ways to support and enhance Aboriginal cultural identity in urban areas. One recommendation is that land dedicated to Aboriginal cultural and spiritual needs be set aside in urban areas. Where feasible, youth centres could be established on or near this land.

Young Aboriginal people also spoke of the need for youth shelters or facilities to provide a safe place for youth suffering from mental, emotional and physical abuse – with counsellors to help them deal with the difficult years of adolescence and young adulthood:

> I believe right now in my community there is too much violence, there is too much death, suicide. With these kinds of things, I don't see why the federal government or the provincial government can't come up with a crisis centre for this kind of problem.
>
> Randy Nepoose
> Hobbema, Alberta, 10 June 1992

They want shelters that offer cultural activities and programs that build self-esteem and provide a sense of belonging. Youth centres can meet some of these needs, as can the Aboriginal healing lodges and healing centres we recommended in Volume 3, Chapter 3.

Aboriginal youth also recommended youth camps – places where they can get back to the land and learn about themselves and their culture. Rediscovery Camps provide one model. The first, on Haida Gwaii (Queen Charlotte Islands), in British Columbia, was launched in 1978. It was established under the guidance of local elders as a way to combat growing problems of substance abuse, juvenile delinquency and family disruption.

Rediscovery Camps now constitute a broad network of affiliated programs spanning several countries, including Canada, the United States and New Zealand. They are generally for youth between eight and 17 years of age and have a mix of Aboriginal and non-Aboriginal participants. They take place in wilderness areas near participants' home communities. The youth are taken out on the land for a week or more to learn survival and wilderness skills and traditional ways. The skills are relevant to the local environment; if the camp is near water, for instance, fishing and canoeing may be emphasized.

A unique feature of the camps is the emphasis on traditional knowledge. Members of the local community participate as guides, cooks or group leaders, and elders play an integral role as well:

> Native elders naturally assume the respected head position of a Rediscovery extended family. The original organizers felt that the elders would benefit the program most through their songs, stories, crafts, and skills. In addition to this, the elders have proven to be the program's most effective counsellors, transcending any generation gap between themselves and the coolest of teenagers....[Elders] appear as loving and caring grandparents – which is exactly what they are.[11]

The elders ensure the traditional knowledge and skills imparted are authentic – another key feature of the Rediscovery model.

> The camp has taught me so much for being grateful for the beauty of this earth, respect for mother nature, and respect for my elders.[12]

Rediscovery Camps bring together Aboriginal and non-Aboriginal youth to increase understanding and awareness and to build bridges between cultures. Of course, some Aboriginal youth know as little about Aboriginal cultures as non-Aboriginal youth do. For those looking to learn about themselves, Rediscovery provides an opportunity to learn about their culture in a traditional environment. Any Aboriginal community could adapt the Rediscovery model for its own youth, incorporating a strong focus on its own culture and traditional practices.

This is already happening in some communities. The Avataq Cultural Institute in Nunavik, the Inuit territory in northern Quebec, runs a traditional Inuit summer camp in Inukjuak. In New Brunswick there is a summer camp that provides cultural enrichment for Maliseet and Mi'kmaq students. These initiatives and the Rediscovery Camps provide models for communities wishing to pass on traditional knowledge in a traditional way.

RECOMMENDATION

The Commission recommends that

Cultural Camps for Youth **4.4.2**

Federal, provincial and territorial governments provide funding for community initiatives to establish Aboriginal youth camps that would

(a) pursue cultural activities linking youth with elders through the development of traditional skills and knowledge;

(b) promote a healthy lifestyle (counselling, fitness and nutrition); and

(c) encourage positive social interaction between Aboriginal youth of different nations and between Aboriginal and non-Aboriginal youth.

These camps would provide an excellent way to begin to establish cultural identity and to instil the confidence Aboriginal youth will need to confront the challenge of rebuilding their communities. Each young person will have to choose his or her own path to healing. But establishing cultural identity should be considered a priority and a major step in the healing process.

Communities, too, must direct their own healing, but they often need support. No one magic recipe will work in all communities; each must establish its own needs and find the methods and type of support to address those needs. Activities such as drumming and dance groups, pow-wows, language classes, and youth and elder gatherings have all been helpful in spiritual healing by various communities. Yet, the "unfortunate reality is that these vital activities are the types of initiatives that governments seldom fund. These are the soft areas, the intangible areas, at least as considered by government officials, because their results appear hard to measure".[13] What is not difficult to measure, though, is the devastation that results when youth do not have access to such activities.

3.3 A Healthy Mind

Aboriginal youth who spoke to the Commission told us that education is the key that unlocks the door to the future – a future where Aboriginal nations will be prosperous, self-determining entities. Youth feel that education has two purposes: to build and enhance their understanding of themselves as Aboriginal people; and to prepare them for life in the modern world. They want to acquire traditional knowledge and skills, but they also want to be educated in accounting, engineering, physiology, business administration and many other fields. The two kinds of knowledge are complementary; youth armed with a quality education can take their place as Aboriginal people in the modern world.

Language and education

I believe that all Aboriginal people should be able to speak their own language because it gives them a sense of pride of who we are as Aboriginal people. I also feel that the younger generation should learn how to speak the language because it is part of our identity and culture. Our language is our last means as to who we are as Native people. As an individual, I truly wish I could speak Ojibwa. Not knowing my language makes me feel sad because I am not able to communicate with people who speak the language. However, I am working on it. Whenever I go to my grandparents' home, they usually speak to me in our language. My mother is also teaching us what she knows. I am paying more attention in our Ojibwa classes taught to us in school.

Jill Henderson
Fort Alexander, Manitoba
30 October 1992

Aboriginal youth who want to reclaim their culture recognize that culture begins with language. Many Aboriginal people told the Commission that without the language, the culture will be lost:

Language is the essence of a culture. Languages are vehicles for the transmission of values, culture and literature. They shape perceptions, an understanding of self, culture, heritage and world view.

Mary Noey
La Ronge, Saskatchewan
28 May 1992

Maintaining Aboriginal language is easier in northern communities than it is in other parts of the country. Only 8.6 per cent of Aboriginal children in southern Canada can speak an Aboriginal language (see Volume 3, Chapter 5).

Preserving and reviving Aboriginal languages will take the combined efforts of individuals, families and community institutions. Youth recognize that some parents did not pass on an Aboriginal language because they thought English or French was the language of the future. Many of these parents were raised in an environment where Aboriginal languages were not valued by the dominant culture – indeed, were actively suppressed in some cases. Youth today realize that language is the glue that holds cultures together; languages must not only be preserved, they must be kept alive.

Aboriginal youth want their languages respected in the educational system and in the community at large. Nunavik is a good model. There, under the Kativik School Board, Inuktitut is the first language of instruction in the early grades and is taught as a subject in the upper grades. Inuktitut is heard up to six or seven hours a day on radio, and the Inuit Broadcasting Corporation works with regional bodies to produce five and a half hours of Inuktitut programming each week. Regional magazines, newsletters and official reports are printed in Inuktitut. The Kativik School Board has developed curriculum material to support oral and written language instruction.

This approach to language and language education is no doubt easier to implement in an Aboriginal people's home territory where there is a single linguistic tradition. In centres where more than one language is used – particularly in urban areas – it is more of a challenge to provide language support for everyone. In Vancouver, parents who want their children to learn an Aboriginal language through the school system can approach the school board with an application for a locally developed course. They can also suggest the name of a member of the linguistic community who is recognized as an Aboriginal language teacher by the B.C. College of Teachers. The course need not be taught in the classroom; it can be home-based or in a community setting.

Aboriginal students want their languages given the same status as English and French in the educational system. They want to be able to learn their languages in schools and to receive recognition and credit for their efforts. Some said that Aboriginal students should be given the option of studying their own language in lieu of French or English – in school, at home or in the community (as in the Vancouver model). This could be done in co-operation with local friendship centres, community centres or, where they exist, Aboriginal language associations.

The revival of Aboriginal languages should be recognized as an integral component of healthy communities. The revitalization of the indigenous languages of North America should be supported by efforts such as those we recommend in Volume 3, Chapters 5 and 6. Wherever possible, institutions serving Aboriginal people should use the relevant language or languages.

Culturally appropriate education

Education can be an agent of cultural survival or cultural disintegration. Recognizing the significant role of educational institutions, Aboriginal youth feel the time has come for Aboriginal communities to control these institutions. In fact, Aboriginal peoples have been calling for Aboriginal control of education – and community involvement in the education of their youth – since at least 1972, when the National Indian Brotherhood presented its landmark policy paper, *Indian Control of Indian Education* to the minister of Indian affairs.

Education can be used to pass on the values and customs of the community. Children can be infused with their culture and grow to become healthy, valuable, contributing members of society. The word education derives from the Latin, *educere*, which means to draw out; education should draw out what exists in the child. Yet in the past, education was used to crush what exists in the Aboriginal child:

> Unfortunately, the system of education that the Innu received from the non-Innu society has contributed very much to the disintegration of the Innu society.[14]

> I remember my first day of school when the bus was coming....My mother had me all ready. My hair was braided. I had red ribbons....I

stood at the road and it was a big day and I was afraid. My mother said, "Here comes the bus. You will be all right, Sherry Lynn. And remember – try to act like them." That's what she told me.

Sherry Lawson
Orillia, Ontario
13 May 1993

I see this as genocide. What better way to kill a people than to rob them of their chance for a good education, taking away the opportunity for us to make something of ourselves.

Lisa Raven
Hollow Water Band, Wanipigow School
Winnipeg, Manitoba, 23 April 1992

Some youth would prefer schools set up by and for Aboriginal people. They see such schools as refuges from racism and from mainstream educators, some of whom are ignorant of Aboriginal culture and its importance to youth. When asked why Aboriginal students were failing in the Vancouver school district, one teacher replied, "When are natives going to realize that they need to give up their culture and join the rest of society?"[15]

Learning about and reviving traditions does not mean turning back the clock. Students, and youth in general, simply want to know themselves as Aboriginal people and to use cultural values to guide them in today's world. It is no surprise that Aboriginal students in that same Vancouver school district, when asked what keeps them from completing secondary studies, responded with remarks such as "ashamed and embarrassed to be Indian", "racism", "alcohol and drug abuse", and "no support from home". Parents responded, "Schools do not prepare our children for life in our culture or life in today's society".[16]

Parents and grandparents certainly have a role in transmitting culture; in some cases, however, they may not have the knowledge necessary to do so. The reality is that, for many, both the problem and the solution are in the classroom.

Unfortunately, Aboriginal children are not staying in school, and their level of formal education lags behind that of the general population. As shown in Table 4.2, compared to the general Canadian population, fewer Aboriginal youth complete their studies at any level of the education system. Among Aboriginal youth aged 15 to 24 not attending school, 68.5 per cent did not complete high school, and once Aboriginal youth drop out of school they are less likely to return; two-thirds of Aboriginal men and 60 per cent of Aboriginal women aged 15 to 24 do not complete high school or take adult upgrading after dropping out.

For Aboriginal youth, remaining in school can be a lonely, isolating and degrading experience. Those attending Canadian universities often find them unresponsive to their needs. Students spoke of the low expectations of them on

TABLE 4.2
Aboriginal Identity and Canadian Populations Aged 15-24
No Longer Attending School, by Highest Level of Education, 1991

Level of Education	Aboriginal	Canadian[1]
	%	%
Grade 8 or Less	15.8	5.4
High school (no certificate)	42.7	31.5
High school certificate	15.5	26.3
Non-university (no certificate)[2]	11.3	9.6
Non-university certificate	7.4	15.0
University (no degree)	5.9	7.9
University degree	0.6	4.4

Notes:
1. Includes Aboriginal and non-Aboriginal persons not attending school full-time.
2. Such as a trade school offering plumbing, carpentry certification, etc.

Source: For Aboriginal identity population, Statistics Canada, 1991 Aboriginal Peoples Survey, custom tabulations, 1994; for Canadian population, Statistics Canada, 1991 Census, "Educational Attainment and School Attendance", Catalogue no. 93-328, 1991.

the part of professors, university personnel and community members.[17] Students at the University of Alberta called for the formation of a World Indigenous University as a vehicle for healing. Their vision is of "a place of healing, one where people could touch each other emotionally, physically, spiritually and mentally, a place where critical thinking was the norm and sensitivity was expected".[18]

We agree that forming such an institution is a worthwhile goal. In Volume 3, Chapter 5, we recommend establishing an Aboriginal Peoples' International University (APIU). It would promote traditional knowledge and scholarship, undertake applied research related to Aboriginal self-government, and offer information dissemination services. We see it as an Aboriginal-controlled network of co-ordinated regional institutions and programs representing the diverse cultural and linguistic traditions of First Nations, Inuit and Métis people.

APIU would articulate a unifying vision within which people of diverse traditions could pursue the study of traditional knowledge at its most complex. It would contribute to the efforts of many communities and leaders to restore elders to a place of honour as the first teachers and scholars of Aboriginal peoples. It would give Aboriginal and non-Aboriginal researchers, professionals and scholars opportunities to meet elders and study with them. It would expand the boundaries of knowledge by developing frameworks of analysis and interpretation defined by Aboriginal values and perspectives. Aboriginal graduate students would be able to pursue options rooted in Aboriginal intellectual and spiritual traditions instead of in western traditions only. Such an institution would benefit not only Aboriginal people, but people from all over the world.

Post-secondary education is just one area of concern. Educational institutions must become more receptive to what Aboriginal students say they want from the education system: schools that recognize and acknowledge Aboriginal culture and curricula that validate the contributions of Aboriginal people. Modest curriculum improvements have been made over the past 15 years, but they have been far too slow in coming and have not been introduced systematically in all parts of the country. Changes often gloss over or avoid the fundamental changes needed to create curricula rooted in Aboriginal understandings of the world in subjects such as history, art, health, mathematics and the sciences. Aboriginal content is usually in the form of add-on units to 'enrich' existing content; it does not tackle the core assumptions, values and logic of existing curricula. Language and culture classes can be added to a school's program without altering the basic content of classes in English, French, science, math or social studies.

The Akwesasne science and mathematics program is a good example of reshaping curriculum to reflect Aboriginal values. It began as a pilot project in 1988 in the Mohawk community of Akwesasne, which straddles the borders of Ontario, Quebec and New York state. Joining together to carry out the project, which they call the Mohawk Way to Go to School, were the Aboriginal Health Professions Program of the University of Toronto, the board of education of the Mohawk Council of Akwesasne, and the General Vanier Secondary School of the Stormont, Dundas and Glengarry public school board (Ontario). The goal was to find an approach that would give students a solid base in science and mathematics without supplanting traditional Aboriginal values and knowledge.

A curriculum for grades seven to nine has been developed through the efforts of Mohawk health and science professionals, elders, spiritual leaders, parents and community members. The content reflects Mohawk contributions to science and math, both historically and in the present. Science themes integrate the earth, trees, animals, birds, agriculture, food, water, cosmology, and Mohawk ways of knowing. Math themes include cultural values, sacred circles, ceremonial significance, space, time, measurement and distance concepts, puzzles, games, and environmental applications for math. One striking aspect of the program is that teaching and learning methods are being analyzed to determine what works best for Mohawk children. Traditional Mohawk teachers have their own approach to instruction, which is being studied in an effort to understand why it is so effective.

The Akwesasne science and mathematics program has several features worth noting. The curriculum has Aboriginal knowledge and beliefs at its core. These are central to the curriculum – they are not add-ons. The curriculum is holistic; rather than separating aspects of the environment into smaller component parts, the interrelatedness of entire ecosystems is examined. The curriculum includes experiential components that tie theory learned in the classroom to the real world outside the school doors. For example, students monitor environmental problems in the community. In this way, the relevance of the knowledge being acquired is explicit.

The experiential aspect of learning and the holistic approach to teaching both reflect an Aboriginal world view. The curriculum does not reject western science and mathematical concepts, but it does not hold them up as the only truth. Instead, they are seen as another way of looking at the world. In certain respects, the two approaches have complementary strengths; the underlying values and assumptions of both Mohawk and western world views are made visible.

A final aspect of this program is community involvement, which was present when the program was being developed and continues as it evolves. The community can be a resource in initiating change in the educational system, especially in the face of weak government support.

Other examples of culturally relevant approaches to education are detailed in Volume 3, Chapter 5. They include the Dene Kede curriculum and the Inuuqatigitt curriculum in the Northwest Territories, and the SIMA7, Come Join Me camp program. Cultural programs can be added to the curriculum or, in some cases, the whole curriculum can be developed around a cultural core. The most established cultural programming is happening in schools governed by Aboriginal-controlled boards, such as the Kativik School Board in Nunavik and the divisional boards in the Northwest Territories.

The Children of the Earth High School in Winnipeg, Manitoba, offers a strong cultural core as well as specific support programs that are provincially funded. The Ile-a-la-Crosse School Board in northern Saskatchewan operates a school with classes from junior kindergarten to grade 12. Métis values, history and culture are an integral part of the curriculum, and the Michif language is taught as a credit course. The school also offers support services such as a daycare facility, a dental clinic and a public library.

At the post-secondary level, the Saskatchewan Indian Federated College (SIFC) has provided excellent programs for Aboriginal youth for many years. It has succeeded where millions of dollars in mainstream education have failed. Established in 1976, SIFC is the only Aboriginally controlled university college in Canada federated with an accredited degree-granting university. The college is academically federated with the University of Regina, ensuring that all regulations respecting admissions, hiring of faculty and academic programs meet University of Regina degree standards. Its board of governors includes representatives from each tribal council in Saskatchewan, as well as representatives from the University of Saskatchewan, the University of Regina, the Department of Indian Affairs and Northern Development, the Saskatchewan education department, and SIFC faculty and students.

The faculty is led by Aboriginal professors who have doctorates and master's degrees. Initially, the college focused on developing programs in

Aboriginal studies, including Aboriginal art, languages, teacher education and social work. Programs for Aboriginal people in management and administration, communications, arts and health care followed in the early 1980s. More recently, in response to the needs of Aboriginal communities, SIFC has established a school of business and public administration and a department of science to encourage more students to enter science-based professions in the areas of health, engineering and agriculture. Aboriginal culture is also promoted outside the classroom. Elders conduct pipe ceremonies every morning and meet the students individually to help them learn about their heritage.

The Gabriel Dumont Institute, also in Saskatchewan, was held up as a model of a community-based institution incorporating Aboriginal values and language:

> The [Gabriel Dumont Institute's] delivery model of post-secondary education to Métis people is highly regarded by the participants as an effective model for the development of Métis post-secondary education. Of essential importance to the delivery of Métis post-secondary education, as pointed out repeatedly by many participants, are three elements: community-based programming, retention of Métis languages and culture, and vocational orientation of education.[19]

Aboriginal youth told the Commission that these are the kinds of institutions that can meet their needs. They want more of these facilities and want them supported at a level that enables them to meet the demand for services.

Such sweeping changes may not be possible in schools that serve students from many different cultures. Nevertheless, Aboriginal youth believe every Canadian school should have a curriculum that incorporates the history and contributions of the original inhabitants of this land. Too often, the contributions of Aboriginal people are left out of the history books or treated in a cursory or dismissive way; their science and intellectual traditions are missing completely.

Aboriginal youth want to attend schools that teach Aboriginal perspectives as part of Canadian history. They want to learn in an environment where the contributions of Aboriginal peoples are recognized and respected and where teachers recognize and respect the culture and aspirations of Aboriginal students:

> The students of the Mushkegowuk Student Services think to make a better Canada that all Canadians should be educated on Native culture and history, so they'll know how we lived before the Europeans arrived and how we live today. And they would notice how quickly we changed from the time when the Europeans came....Start at an early age teaching the non-Natives about the Natives.

> Gaby Bird
> Moose Factory, Ontario
> 9 June 1992

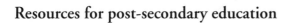

Resources for post-secondary education

Education being a right for Aboriginal people has to be constitutionally protected – protected for all Aboriginal people. Through education
the visions of those from the past will be unfolded. But also the visions
Aboriginal leaders have today will be realized by future generations.

> Walter Madonick
> Canadian Federation of Students
> The Pas, Manitoba, 20 May 1992

The curriculum and program changes described in the preceding sections are
designed to keep students in the classroom. But for Aboriginal youth seeking post-
secondary education, simply getting into the classroom can be a problem. This situation could escalate as more and more youth (and adults) look to post-secondary
education to improve their career options and job opportunities. The next generation might be able to break through the cycles of poverty and dependency that have
consigned Aboriginal peoples to the margins of society. Aboriginal youth see post-
secondary education as a critical link in this chain of transformation. The lack of
financial means to acquire this education is often a barrier, however.

For First Nations students, the federal government has been the most
important source of financial assistance. The Northwest Territories has funded
university education for all residents, including First Nations, Inuit and Métis
people. The Yukon also provides education subsidies, but at a lower rate than
the Northwest Territories.

Aboriginal youth generally decried the lack of funding available for students
to attend post-secondary institutions:

> The cutbacks and capping of post-secondary funding have caused prob-
> lems for many students. The funding criteria restrict many students to
> eight-month funding support. The result of this is students have to take
> a heavier course load, forgoing the option to achieve a higher grade point
> average which is necessary in order for the students to enter into a spe-
> cialized program such as medical school, law school, et cetera....

> Margaret King
> President, Native Student Union, University of Manitoba
> Winnipeg, Manitoba, 22 April 1992

> [The Indian affairs department] will only fund a student once in each
> level, therefore limiting a student's access to another degree at the same
> level....I would have to find alternate sources to finance my studies.
> But, in fact, the government is responsible for all my education.

> Claudine Louis
> Hobbema, Alberta
> 10 June 1992

For Métis youth and some First Nations youth without strong ties to home communities, funding for post-secondary education is extremely limited.

There was also concern about the limits on the types of programs funded. One student noted that under the current guidelines he could not get funding for training to be a pilot:

> I feel that all Aboriginal people should be given the same opportunity to choose their own careers....[I] have found it cost around $50,000 for five years of university. It cost $53,000 for a two-year flying program, plus you come out with 16 transferrable university credits. Over the short term, yes, flying is more expensive, but over the long term it costs about the same amount of money.
>
> Arthur Williams
> Happy Valley-Goose Bay, Newfoundland and Labrador
> 16 June 1992

Beyond funding, Aboriginal students say they need more support and resources to continue their education. Single mothers, in particular, would like to have low-cost or subsidized daycare.

We examined the issues surrounding funding for post-secondary education and the different situations of First Nations, Métis and Inuit youth in Volume 3, Chapter 5, and recommended that

- the government of Canada affirm its obligation to provide a full range of education services to treaty nations where such a right appears in treaty texts, related documents or oral accounts of treaty agreements;
- existing student benefits continue for First Nations and Inuit post-secondary education, along with additional resources to address increased costs and to meet the higher level of demand for post-secondary education; and
- that a scholarship fund be established for Métis and other Aboriginal students who do not have access to post-secondary education financial support.

For a more detailed analysis of these and other issues in education and the Commission's recommendations, see Volume 3, Chapter 5.

3.4 A Healthy Body

Physical fitness, sport and recreation

Many of today's Aboriginal leaders were heavily involved in sports and recreation as youngsters. Associate Chief Judge Murray Sinclair of the Manitoba provincial court and a former member of Parliament from Alberta, Willie Littlechild, both studied physical education before becoming lawyers. Littlechild states that sports and recreation are crucial for Aboriginal youth:

The most critical area of sports for Native peoples is still the development of leadership....There is still a great need to develop sports administrators, coaches, officials and recreation directors that would serve the unique concerns of Native communities.[20]

Promoting Aboriginal athletes as role models can inspire young people to participate in sports and recreation programs. Mohawk athlete Alwyn Morris, gold and bronze medal winner in kayaking at the 1984 Olympics, and former Pittsburgh Penguin left-wing Ted Nolan, an Ojibwa from the Garden River Reserve in Ontario, have both taken part in the National Native Role Model Program. The program involves promotional events and speaking tours dealing with issues such as education and drug and alcohol awareness.

Aboriginal athletes build bridges to the broader Canadian community. When they compete, they join the multicultural community of sports and sports enthusiasts. Their involvement can instil pride in Aboriginal people of all nations and give Aboriginal people a national and international presence. In 1990, track-and-field fans around the world cheered as Angela Chalmers, a member of the Birdtail Sioux First Nation community in Manitoba, became the first woman in the history of the Commonwealth games to win both the 1,500- and 3,000-metre races. She went on to win a bronze medal at the 1992 summer Olympics in Barcelona, Spain. Other examples abound. Indeed, the history of sports is studded with the names of Aboriginal athletes: Tom Longboat (marathon), George Armstrong and Jim Neilsen (NHL hockey), Sharon and Shirley Firth (Olympic cross-country skiers), and Jack Jacobs (NFL and CFL football), to name only a few. When Aboriginal athletes compete, they send a strong message that their people are part of the fabric of the Canadian and international communities. They are role models for youth of all nations.

Young people appearing before the Commission emphasized the need for sports and recreation opportunities. We refer to sports and recreation in the broadest sense, including physical activity, leadership training, coaching, recreation program training, participation in cultural activities, and dramatic and musical pursuits. Sports and physical pursuits are important to many Aboriginal youth because they have high energy levels and, in some circumstances, too much time on their hands. Boredom can be a major problem in communities with few resources. The Metis Nation of Alberta noted that most "Métis youth do not have access to even the most modest recreational facilities to relieve their boredom and frustration often associated with a lifestyle plagued by poverty".[21] Many youth spoke about this concern:

There are many problems surrounding us, one of which is that there seems to be nowhere to go or nothing to do. Inuvik's youth have talked about a facility for us to go to, one with counsellors and a program co-ordinator. In this centre we would like to see a leisure and sports complex as a joint facility – some place where we can sit and enjoy each other's company or get involved in activities.

Cheryl Greenland
Gwich'in Youth
Inuvik, Northwest Territories, 5 May 1992

The absence of adequate recreation facilities and leisure activities is creating a pressing situation in many Aboriginal communities, where the large number of youth, their high and early school drop-out rates and the lack of jobs are a potentially explosive combination. In the absence of leisure opportunities, substance abuse may be their only escape from crushing boredom and dreary surroundings.

As discussed earlier, substance abuse is a pervasive problem among Aboriginal youth.A study of Haida youth by the community of Old Massett, British Columbia, for example, found that substance abuse was their greatest problem. "The most common health recommendation was to have a recreation facility created especially for youth to give them an alternative to drinking and drug use."[22] This sentiment was echoed by youth from other communities as they spoke at our hearings:

The youth today need productive activities, a place to stay where they can work together and spend time....If they have a place to go and things to do it will be less likely for them to be involved in drug and alcohol abuse. As soon as they do something worthwhile, their self-confidence will build and they will feel better about themselves.

Kathy Nelson
Roseau River, Manitoba
8 December 1992

Sports and recreation can be effective instruments for youth to use in building their communities. Sport, like other activities involving goal-setting and discipline, can spill over into other aspects of a person's life. The Aboriginal view of games is a holistic one, involving culture, education, health and spiritual significance.[23]

Some youth "want and need to learn and incorporate a more traditional way...[and] sports are a recreation activity as well as a method of enhancing cultural retention".[24] These activities promote leadership development, along with cultural awareness and traditional values. Lacrosse, Inuit high-kicking and water sports such as kayaking and canoeing are all examples of sports and recreation activities rooted in traditional culture.

The Arctic Games bring athletes together to compete in mainstream and traditional sports and games. The traditional events include seal skinning, tea boiling, fish cutting, one-footed and two-footed high kicks, and head pulls. Here the emphasis is not on the elite athlete or a 'winner take all' mentality; often, competitors actually teach each other during the competition.

The First Nations Running Club is a good example of youth attempting to build a community across Canada and, at the same time, learn about their traditional culture through sport:

> To the Indians, running was a way to communicate over long distances and an essential part of fighting and hunting. However, it was also a game and a way of instilling values, developing strong wills and of connecting with the forces of the universe....
>
> Running without rest [was] a means of purification....running was far more than sport and entertainment for the Indians, it was a search for the meaning and essence of life itself.
>
> It is the race of the individual against the limits of his own flesh and it is the unending race of all humanity with the wonder of creation. No man shall win, no man shall lose; but as each walks away, his broad chest heaving, his knees trembling, it is with the ecstatic look in his eyes of one who has spent himself to the full and before he faltered, seen over the horizon is the mystic glow of his final victory.[25]

Many youth are unaware of the traditional significance of running in some Aboriginal nations. One of the goals of the First Nations Running Club is to "empower native youth to lead successful lives in [a non-Aboriginal] society by developing a clear cultural foundation of values and identity". The club began in Red Lake, Ontario, in 1988. Runners have participated in a number of events, including the 1991 Sacred Run, part of the Manitoba Marathon. It was here that club members met youth from the Salish Nation, the Anishnabe and the Iroquois Confederacy. The club now has chapters in British Columbia, Alberta, Saskatchewan, Manitoba, Quebec and Ontario and is seeking to establish chapters across the country. At the national office in the community of the Cape Croker-Chippewas of Nawash, a running camp offers youth and elders a place to come and share traditional teachings.

Northern Fly-In Sports Camps (NFISC) provide summer recreation programs for children and youth, with the goal of developing social and leadership skills.[26] In operation since 1986, the program was originally funded through a one-time University of Manitoba Outreach grant and various donations. The key to NFISC's success is inter-agency co-operation, with members of the wider community participating in designing and implementing the program. The RCMP, for example, is involved with NFISC and has noted a significant drop in crime rates in communities where the program is in operation.[27]

However, over the long term such programs can be successful only when they are grounded in and sustained by the community. Even with ample facilities and supplies, recreation programs cannot simply be willed to work. Within the community there must be motivated and qualified leadership among youth who can organize and inspire their peers.

At the Selkirk Friendship Centre Youth Club in Manitoba, a full-time co-ordinator plans social, recreational, educational and cultural activities. The program is funded through the Community Action Program of the National Drug Strategy. Activities focus on drug abuse prevention and, notably, the program accepts not only abstainers but strivers as well (individuals who use drugs occasionally but are trying to break free).

The Rediscovery Camp model (mentioned earlier in relation to spiritual health) can also be used to foster self-esteem and cultural identity while contributing to physical development. The camps enhance outdoor skills, traditional land-based skills, and cultural and environmental awareness, and the daily regimen contributes to physical fitness and well-being. The activities vary depending on the surrounding environment. In Fort McMurray in northern Alberta, students canoe, hunt small game, fish, hike and learn to set up camp. In coastal British Columbia, young people can develop backpacking skills and ocean-related skills such as fishing and swimming. A spin-off benefit is the employment Rediscovery Camps have created in Aboriginal communities, as participants go on to become guides, leaders and trainers.

The Canadian Outward Bound School has worked with Aboriginal schools in running youth programs. Community members in Big Trout Lake, Ontario, have created their own land-based program. Elders there take out on their traditional land about 40 young people for several weeks at a time during each of the four seasons. The Avataq Cultural Institute in Nunavik operates a traditional Inuit summer camp in Inukjuak each year, and a similar camp is operated by the community of Kuujjuak. On the northern coast of Labrador, high school athletes gather twice each year (in fall and winter) for a week of sports competition. The events include traditional Inuit games. The games are rotated among participating communities, giving students an opportunity to travel and meet their peers in other areas. Similarly, Aboriginal games have been held in Quebec each year since 1991. Many youth enjoy the healthy competition and see these events as something to look forward to in the school year.

Sports and recreation contribute to healing in a holistic way. Participation enhances physical development and increases awareness of fitness and nutrition. But when youth also operate the programs, a momentum seems to build, tapping into their energy and creativity. They develop leadership skills, as well as communication, fund-raising and organizing skills they can apply to their personal and community endeavours in other areas besides recreation.

In Old Massett Village, Haida youth practise traditional dancing at the Davidson Longhouse several times a week. In addition, 40 youth paddled in ocean-going canoes to Bella Bella, a Heiltsuk community on British Columbia's central coast, for the revival of the great west coast tradition of inter-nation canoe gatherings. From start to finish, youth carried the day. They were responsible for making and painting their own paddles and learning songs and dances to perform for the host village.

Youth also participate in the All Native Basketball Tournament in Prince Rupert and the Christmas Classics Tournament, hosted by Old Massett. Students there are asking for more organized sporting events for men and women and cultural classes to teach traditional skills such as carving, weaving, Haida dancing and food preparation. They also want "workshops for the youth regarding issues such as self-esteem, drug and alcohol abuse, family violence, peer pressure, career and education, and communication skills".[28]

The Old Massett programs succeeded because basic facilities were available to house the programs; the holistic approach guided program development and allowed people with different skills and abilities to participate; and youth were able to exercise leadership and initiative.

A similar example is the Chevak Village Youth Association in Alaska, where "the local community has taken over the organization and adapted its goals and activities to the local norms". Like the best of holistic programs, it serves a number of educational, social and economic functions for youth. It was created and run entirely by Aboriginal youth to address a situation where "hanging out, visiting, playing basketball and snow machining pretty well exhausted the leisure activities available to the youth of Chevak".[29]

All these activities and organizations are proof that youth can be the solution, if they are not simply regarded as 'the problem'. When governments and communities make the leap of faith to assist youth, youth respond. Solutions do exist, and communities can implement them – sometimes despite government inaction. Yet attempts to take action often meet a host of obstacles. Some initiatives that have shown real results have been dismantled because of shifting government priorities, or programs have broken down because of inadequate financial resources.

In communities where there are recreational facilities, the need for leadership is acute. The Arctic College offers a two-year program to train recreation leaders, with a curriculum that includes communications, management, programming, leadership, facilities management, marketing, anatomy, physiology and social psychology. The Northern Recreation Director Training Program (NRDTP) is a combined program of the Manitoba departments of education and training (New Careers North), culture, heritage and citizenship, and northern affairs. It provides training for adults who may have had difficulties with the educational system in the past.[30] Young Aboriginal people want to see programs such as NRDTP and the Arctic College Recreation Leaders Program supported and expanded so they are accessible to everyone interested in this field.

Given the success of these initiatives, it is regrettable that similar efforts are not being made across Canada. Neil Winther, who was among the founders of Northern Fly-In Sports Camps, states, "The farther one moves up the bureaucratic ladder (provincial or federal) the less evidence one finds for support". Attempts to develop a Manitoba Aboriginal sports and recreation association have been slowed because "this organization could be seen as a threat to the existing provincial sport organizations, which have done little to target Aboriginal people, even though it is obvious that Aboriginal people have the greatest need for sport".[31] Given the number of Aboriginal youth and the factors that make them vulnerable to physical and social dysfunction, sustained efforts are needed to make sports and recreational facilities and leadership programs widely accessible. The first step would be to establish a body to advise federal, provincial, territorial and Aboriginal governments on how best to meet sports and recreation needs in Aboriginal communities. This advisory council should have a membership drawn from among Aboriginal sports and recreation professionals, administrators, and co-ordinators across the country. Non-Aboriginal professionals with expertise in this area could also participate. Each province and territory must be represented. With the help of provincial, territorial and federal funding, council members could co-ordinate needs assessments and consult Aboriginal communities to determine their sports and recreation priorities.

The advisory council would then direct resources so that communities can develop, implement and sustain their own programs. This would include acquiring equipment and facilities and building capacity within the community – in particular, leadership and recreation training. The council should not dictate or impose programs developed centrally. The record shows that most successful initiatives are community-driven.

For example, the advisory council could develop a program to provide the expertise of trained recreation programmers to travel to communities and give presentations or workshops on subjects such as how to set up and run a recreation sports league. This way, skills and knowledge would stay with the community after the experts had left. Aboriginal athletes – many of whom are role models for Aboriginal youth – could be recruited for this purpose. Programming must be implemented and sustained by the community, however.

A floor hockey league is a good example of a program that can be set up, even in a community with limited resources; equipment needs are minimal, many youth are familiar with the general rules of the game, and if there is no recreation facility, any building with an open floor can be used. Many other sports can be adapted to suit the resources the community has available.

Such programs can begin now to meet the sports and recreation needs of Aboriginal youth; there need not be a long wait while funding is secured or recreation complexes are built. Meanwhile, planning should be under way to develop resources and expertise for the long term.

RECOMMENDATIONS

The Commission recommends that

Aboriginal Sports and Recreation Advisory Council

4.4.3

The federal government, through the Minister of State for Fitness and Amateur Sport, establish and fund an Aboriginal sports and recreation advisory council to advise – in consultation with regional, provincial and territorial sports and recreation organizations – federal, provincial, territorial and Aboriginal governments on how best to meet the sports and recreation needs of Aboriginal people (including those living in urban areas).

Sports and Recreation Initiatives

4.4.4

The proposed Aboriginal sports and recreation advisory council promote programs and initiatives that are

(a) community-driven, based on needs identified by the community, with programming developed or modified by the community to meet the community's needs;

(b) sustainable, as opposed to one-time tournaments or events; and

(c) capacity builders aimed at providing instruction in recreation programming, leadership development and coaching skills.

The federal government would fund the council. Provinces now provide the bulk of funding for sports and recreation initiatives in their areas, so they would be expected to help cover the cost of initiatives taking place within their boundaries.

Aboriginal people will have to work with the federal, provincial and territorial governments to decide the form, structure and membership of the advisory council. Aboriginal experts in the field – sports and recreation programmers, co-ordinators, administrators, researchers, and Aboriginal youth representatives – at the community, provincial and national levels should meet with ministers of sports and recreation to address organizational concerns. An intergovernmental meeting of these ministers would provide a forum for discussion among all the parties involved.

RECOMMENDATION

The Commission recommends that

Intergovernmental
Forum within 1
Year of Report
4.4.5

A meeting of ministers responsible for sports and recreation be convened within one year of the publication of this report to discuss the form and structure of the proposed Aboriginal sports and recreation advisory council, and that Aboriginal youth and Aboriginal experts in the field – recreation and sports programmers, co-ordinators, administrators and researchers – be invited to take part in this discussion.

A co-ordinated and concerted effort to provide constructive outlets for the energy and enthusiasm of Aboriginal youth, and at the same time develop their leadership skills and self-esteem, can go a long way toward improving the health of Aboriginal communities.

Aboriginal youth and HIV/AIDS awareness

Another serious health concern of Aboriginal youth is Acquired Immune Deficiency Syndrome (AIDS). Research conducted for the Commission suggests that "Aboriginal youth are at a high risk of acquiring HIV infection because they are sexually active and often engage in unprotected sex, as evidenced by the high number of teenage pregnancies; they are under strain of peer pressure to use and abuse alcohol and a variety of substances; some have been sexually abused; some are homeless, transient and street dwellers".[32] This statement is supported by the 1990 study on AIDS and the Aboriginal population. Researchers found that Aboriginal communities are particularly susceptible to transmission through heterosexual contact and that the youth population is highly vulnerable.

Recent data indicate that in terms of confirmed (and surviving) cases of HIV infection, 69 of the 2,597 Canadians diagnosed as of January 1993 were Aboriginal, based on self-definition and physicians' records.[33] While this number is relatively small, it represents three times the number of diagnosed cases since the first report of the Joint National Committee on Aboriginal AIDS Education and Prevention in 1990.

Despite this, little has been done to date to address the issue. The root problems – abuse, homelessness and drug use – and possible solutions are discussed elsewhere in this report. We focus here on the need for educating Aboriginal youth about AIDS and all sexually transmitted diseases.

Aboriginal youth want to see more AIDS awareness strategies and programs designed specifically for them. These strategies must include education on reducing the risk of contracting HIV. Similar initiatives should be launched for awareness and prevention of sexually transmitted diseases. Youth themselves can be tapped as a resource in developing and implementing programs. A discussion of HIV/AIDS and the Aboriginal population in general can be found in Volume 3, Chapter 3.

3.5 Emotional Health

In a healthy community environment, youth in distress would be able to turn to an accessible and co-ordinated support network. They would be able to talk with parents, elders and peers about their concerns and problems. They would be able to contribute to sharing circles and take part in traditional ceremonies. But for many Aboriginal youth, elders are difficult to reach because they are so few, language is often a barrier to communication, parents are still weighed down with their own burdens, and the friends a young person needs are wrestling with their own problems.

The most urgent need for youth in distress is to speak with someone they can trust, someone who can readily understand and empathize with them. Youth crisis centres, friendship centres – indeed, any facility used by Aboriginal youth – should have a 'youthful face'. Wherever possible, young Aboriginal people should be recruited to work as counsellors in these facilities and to staff information and crisis lines.

Youth recognize, too, that elders have much to offer, and they want them to be an integral part of their lives. Yet there are few ways to involve elders in the lives of urban Aboriginal youth. This is an immediate concern because the number of elders with comprehensive knowledge of the language and traditions is declining quickly. They are a small proportion of the Aboriginal population; if their knowledge is not passed on, it will disappear with them:

> There should be a sense of – not independence or dependence – but interdependency, because traditionally elders provided a lot of the basic necessities so that young people can have their needs met. And that has to continue, but sometimes that is lost in some families....There should be contributions from elders and parents...but not controlled by those people.

Delbert Majer
Saskatchewan Metis Addictions Council
Regina, Saskatchewan
10 May 1993

Elders must be involved in the holistic healing of youth. They have much to offer the spirit, the mind, the body and the emotions. They have an important role in teaching traditional culture and values. Aboriginal youth want to see the elders and their knowledge integrated into all aspects of community life, including education, health, justice and governance. They feel the elders' teachings should help inform the guiding principles of community life. In Chapter 3 of this volume we discuss a number of ways to bring elders and youth together.

4. MAKING A DIFFERENCE: EMPOWERING ABORIGINAL YOUTH

4.1 Empowerment

> We could go on forever talking about solutions, but if we are just going to talk and we are not going to do anything, then these solutions mean nothing.

> Tonya Makletzoff
> Yellowknife, Northwest Territories
> 10 December 1992

Healthy Aboriginal youth are ready to face the challenges that confront their communities and to find the solutions that will make their nations strong. Youth told the Commission emphatically that they need to be recognized by and involved in the institutions that affect their lives. They want to empower themselves by acquiring the skills and capacities that will enable them to solve their own problems. Many of the healing initiatives described in this report will help them gain the necessary spiritual, mental, physical and emotional qualities. Having discovered their inner resources, they will develop the lasting solutions needed by their communities. This is why Aboriginal youth are demanding that their voices be heard.

Aboriginal youth say they need to be empowered individually, politically and economically. Individual empowerment means that young people must be healthy as individuals, able to help themselves and others. Political empowerment would enable them to speak out, take a stand on the issues that they care about, and work together at the local, national and international levels. Economic empowerment would ensure that they acquire the skills needed to contribute as valuable members of their communities and nations.

Youth are willing to roll up their sleeves and work hard to rebuild. But they want to do more than that. They want to help develop the initiatives, the ideas, and the organizations necessary to sustain successful programs. They want a say in planning and implementing community development, in laying the groundwork for the future.

4.2 Recognition and Involvement

If each young person is seen as a star in the cosmos, then empowerment is the process through which those stars become a constellation. Many connections must be made to restore Aboriginal communities. Youth need to be involved in governance and local administration of communities, and they need ways to express themselves collectively, to communicate with each other across vast distances, to talk to their peers in communities accessible only by air or winter road. They look beyond borders and realize that some of the problems plaguing their communities are not unique to Canada – they are present wherever Indigenous peoples have been colonized.

Young Aboriginal people must have the means to develop deep roots in their communities. Concurrently, they must be allowed to branch out and assume a place in society at large. Some will find a role in home communities; others will leave but still retain roots at home. Nearly 45 per cent of Aboriginal youth live in cities, but a significant proportion have spent at least some of their growing years in small communities. Many have a personal commitment to making their communities of origin better places in which to grow up and live.

Various organizations have worked with Aboriginal youth in co-operative efforts aimed at empowerment. The National Association of Friendship Centres (NAFC) is an example. Youth have participated in its annual general meetings since 1984 and have representatives on national and provincial boards of directors.[34] Youth forums have been held at all NAFC annual meetings since 1989. NAFC has planned, organized and hosted numerous activities designed to benefit youth and children – culturally based programs such as drumming and dance groups, pow-wows, the Little Beavers program, language classes, and gatherings for youth and elders.

At the behest of young people, NAFC established the Aboriginal Youth Council in September 1994. It is composed of an executive council and four representatives from the northern, western, central and eastern regions of Canada (with plans to expand the council to include representation from each province and territory). All the executive and regional representatives are Aboriginal youth. The purpose of the council is to strengthen the voice of Aboriginal youth within NAFC and in the country at large and to direct NAFC initiatives geared to Aboriginal youth.

The main goals of the Aboriginal Youth Council are

- communication among Aboriginal youth of all nations;
- training and development for Aboriginal youth;
- involvement of Aboriginal youth at all levels of the friendship centre movement; and
- preservation, promotion and protection of Aboriginal cultures and heritage.

Of particular importance to the council is establishing a national database of individuals, groups and government bodies dealing with Aboriginal youth and youth issues. Sharon Visitor, NAFC's youth intervener co-ordinator, says the database is a necessary first step to mobilizing Aboriginal youth. She notes that because of government funding cuts, some centres cannot afford to send youth to the annual general meetings. "We want to motivate the youth to get them out and find their own resources, and to organize their own events", such as youth forums and workshops.[35] The database will help to put youth in contact with others who have those resources and skills. As well, it will be a national networking resource.

Inuit Tapirisat of Canada (ITC) has worked with its young constituents. A national Inuit youth conference in northern Quebec in November 1994 drew 80 delegates from across the north. The delegates formed the National Inuit Youth Council, and its president now has a seat on the national board of Inuit Tapirisat. ITC was quick to accept a youth representative on its board and favours more youth involvement in the organization.[36]

The drive among youth to share and communicate with one another is a motivating factor behind a relatively new international youth organization, the Inuit Circumpolar Youth Council. The council has its origins in a resolution brought forward at the 1992 general assembly of the Inuit Circumpolar Conference (ICC) calling for greater youth involvement. The executive council felt that if ICC was to follow through on this resolution in the spirit in which it was brought forth, then it must let youth take the initiative.

The Inuit Circumpolar Youth Council was officially formed in the fall of 1994. It includes representatives from Canada, Greenland, Alaska and Russia. Its focus is to consider issues before ICC from the perspective of youth. Generally, the council is pushing for greater youth involvement in ICC and wants to direct attention to the special concerns of Aboriginal youth. Because of its international nature, it is particularly interested in enhancing communication among Aboriginal youth in different countries.[37]

For many Aboriginal youth, the key to a better future is communication and networking. By sharing their concerns, youth can compare notes and arrive at possible solutions to problems. In some cases, the solutions are already out there; it is simply a matter of getting the information. Communication also fosters a sense of solidarity, of a shared mission and commitment among Aboriginal youth:

> At this present time, myself and many other Aboriginal youth feel that we can unite all Aboriginal youth from across the island and Labrador to form one unique group with different backgrounds, cultures, customs....The Aboriginal people have to work together....
>
> Yance Sheehan
> St. John's, Newfoundland
> 22 May 1992

The Internet is one way for Aboriginal youth in Canada and around the globe to communicate with each other. As more schools, libraries and other institutions acquire this resource, Aboriginal youth must be trained and encouraged to use it. Youth in remote and rural areas in particular will benefit from the information superhighway, but it will enable all youth to share their concerns and aspirations and to learn more quickly about how others have achieved success in building their communities.

Access to national and international databases could provide youth with information that will help them take charge of their own problems and develop solutions for their own communities. Such databases contain demographic and other statistical information, contacts for funding and service agencies, and information about employment opportunities, technical and human resources, educational opportunities, and cultural and recreational activities. As more government departments, individuals, and private and public organizations go online, these databases will expand to make more and more information available to Aboriginal youth.

In Volume 3, Chapter 5 of this report, we recommend establishing an electronic clearinghouse for information exchange between Aboriginal people worldwide. This network would link rural and urban communities around the world. Information could be made available from electronic archives, Aboriginal resource centres, libraries, and government and non-government organizations. Users would be able to locate relevant resources and contact communities or individuals directly. Aboriginal communities could ensure access by installing public computer terminals in a school, adult education building, library or other public facility.

Aboriginal youth and their concerns should also be represented more often in the mass media. CBC radio in particular offers a network that is widely accessible to Aboriginal communities in all parts of the country. Private broadcasters should also be encouraged to increase their commitment to programming for Aboriginal youth. In both cases, commitments to Aboriginal programming should not be met by burying these programs in late-night or early-morning spots.

We examine this situation in some detail in Volume 3, Chapter 6, where we recommend that public and private media give greater access to Aboriginal media products. The CBC in particular should have a mandate to purchase and broadcast Aboriginal programming from independent Aboriginal producers and to create English- and French-language versions of Aboriginal programs for regional and national distribution. The Canadian Radio-television and Telecommunications Commission (CRTC) also has a role to play. Licences issued by the CRTC to public and commercial broadcasters for regions with significant Aboriginal populations should include conditions guaranteeing fair access to and distribution of Aboriginal and Aboriginal-language programs.

Finally, getting more Aboriginal people involved in the media will help increase and improve programming about them and their concerns. We recommend that public communications and cultural agency policies, as well as employment equity plans in both private and public media, address the need for training and better representation of Aboriginal people. (Specific recommendations and supporting details are in Volume 3, Chapter 6 of this report.)

Canada has been active internationally in human rights development and Aboriginal issues. In 1985 it sponsored a series of activities for International Youth Year to help young people across Canada know themselves better and become aware of their potential contributions to society. Aboriginal youth participated in these events, and their organizations continue to play a key role in the international Aboriginal youth movement.

Healing Our Spirit Worldwide was a conference held in Edmonton in 1992. The Saskatoon Youth Advisory Council played an important role in developing and organizing the event. The Cree Nation Youth Council of Quebec helped organize the 1992-1993 World Indigenous Youth Conference, held in Quebec City. The goal was to bring together more than 2,000 Indigenous youth, along with their elders, to examine social and economic problems and to discuss solutions. Other goals included establishing permanent networks, developing more peaceful relationships with non-Indigenous people, increasing youth involvement, and drafting a universal declaration of Indigenous rights. In June 1993 the International Youth Assembly was held in the Little Black River First Nation community and in Winnipeg, Manitoba. More than 150 youth from five countries attended the assembly. The three main topics of discussion were healing, education and empowerment. These activities demonstrate the ability of youth to organize themselves nationally and internationally, to address areas of concern, and to take responsibility for their own healing.

4.3 Economic Empowerment

Many Aboriginal youth see themselves facing an economic wasteland. They see high unemployment rates, inadequate training and a lack of meaningful jobs. Their unemployment rate is 31.8 per cent, more than double that of non-Aboriginal youth (15.1 per cent).[38] Added to this is pressure to choose between the traditional way of life and the modern world, the implication being that there is no way to accommodate the two worlds. Many youth are beginning to reject this argument. They want employment, but they seek employment that contributes to the community, not just to the gross national product. The economic empowerment of Aboriginal youth involves building a bridge between the wage and non-wage economies.

An example of this type of bridging is where young people earn sweat equity by volunteering in the construction of houses for the community. Federal programs with a sweat equity component do exist; there should be more of them in Aboriginal communities. Programs should be flexible to accommodate the needs of various communities. Sweat equity programs would achieve much-needed improvements in community infrastructure and could also have the added benefit of facilitating healing for individuals and the community at large. Many Aboriginal communities face severe housing shortages. Aboriginal youth are often looking for meaningful work, but the community offers little opportunity for employment. Sweat equity housing programs could thus meet the needs of youth and of communities.

Under these programs, people 'invest' by contributing their labour to the construction of other community members' houses. The sweat equity they build can later be exchanged for help in building their own houses. A model for such programs is Habitat for Humanity, a non-profit non-governmental organization founded in 1976. Habitat for Humanity Canada, established in 1985, describes its activities as follows:

> Through volunteer labor, efficient management and tax-deductible donations of money and materials, Habitat builds and rehabilitates homes with the help of the home-owner (partner) families. Costs differ relative to location, labor and materials. Currently, a three-bedroom Habitat house in Canada costs between $50,000 and $80,000. Habitat is a joint venture in which those benefitting from it participate directly in the work. Each homeowner family must invest 500 hours of unpaid labor or "sweat equity" in the construction of their and others' homes. This reduces cost, increases pride and fosters positive relationships.[39]

This approach could be adapted and modified specifically for Aboriginal people and communities. In addition to earning sweat equity toward a house, youth would learn and refine marketable skills. The community's housing needs would be met, more and better houses could be built for the same amount of money, and employment opportunities would be created in the community. Finally, and perhaps most important, community bonds are strengthened through such co-operative efforts; as people build homes, they are building a community.

This type of program could be accommodated by modifying current funding programs for housing construction in Aboriginal communities. A more detailed discussion of housing issues is presented in Volume 3, Chapter 4. In the same volume, Chapter 3, we discuss other initiatives that help build and strengthen bonds within the community.

RECOMMENDATION

The Commission recommends that

Co-operative Home Construction

4.4.6

Co-operative home construction, based on the Habitat for Humanity model, be initiated in Aboriginal communities to provide housing, employment and construction skills for Aboriginal youth.

A trained and qualified Aboriginal work force benefits not only the Aboriginal community but also the wider economic community. Aboriginal youth are the fastest growing population segment in Canada. Increasing numbers are reaching work force age, yet they are not being equipped with the skills needed to participate in the labour market.

The Aboriginal population is an important source of new employees. In Manitoba, for example, it is projected that Aboriginal youth will account for about 16 per cent of all young people reaching work force age (15 to 19) between 2001 and 2016. In Saskatchewan, their proportion will grow from 15.3 per cent in 2001 to 19.3 per cent in 2016.[40] An investment in training for Aboriginal youth will benefit individuals but will also be essential to achieve the necessary level of competence in the work force as a whole.

For Aboriginal nations, education and training are especially important in implementing self-government. A trained work force will be needed to plan and deliver services previously provided by governments. Education and training to develop management and administrative skills will be crucial to a smooth transition. These skills will be necessary to organize and manage local government services and to facilitate the building of infrastructure to support community development.

Equipped with these skills, Aboriginal youth will be able to participate in the labour force anywhere, whether they choose to use their skills in their communities of origin or to travel to other areas of the country. To ensure adaptability in the labour market, they must be equipped with certifiable skills that are broadly based and portable.

The Commission examined these issues and set out a plan for Aboriginal employment development in Volume 2, Chapter 5. Topics discussed there include a special employment and training initiative aimed at major employers who can provide the kinds of jobs and work experience critical to developing the self-governing capacity of Aboriginal nations; employment equity initiatives for a much broader range of employers; employment services; employment opportunities in Aboriginal communities; the reduction of obstacles to employment, such as lack of child care; and job creation in Aboriginal communities.

Economic empowerment means Aboriginal youth will have a say in developing and running employment and other economic programs targeted to them. In some areas, youth can be directly involved: youth counsellors, recreational leaders, teaching assistants and health providers should all be recruited from the ranks of youth. In urban centres, youth should be sought out for employment as street workers and to staff friendship centres. They should also work in transition houses that help youth from small or isolated communities adjust to life in the city. All these initiatives require qualified and experienced leadership. But they also require the enthusiasm, energy and empathy that youth demonstrate in abundance.

5. Consolidation:
A Framework for a Canada-Wide
Aboriginal Youth Policy

5.1 The Need for a Canada-Wide Policy

The lack of a coherent policy on Aboriginal youth, as well as the absence of clear goals and priorities, has left some youth frustrated and disillusioned in their dealings with government. Money and resources have been devoted to a variety of programs over the past quarter-century without any clear policy direction. Programming is fragmented, scattered and reactive. There is no framework and few clear driving principles. Generally, Aboriginal youth programs have been driven by other initiatives (such as those developed under the *Young Offenders Act* or job-creation programs) or occur in response to very specific situations (such as training Aboriginal health care workers to deal with AIDS or family violence). There is no encompassing framework to guide programming specifically for youth. Youth do not expect special treatment, but their pivotal role in their communities suggests a need for programs that recognize their specific needs, aspirations and concerns.

In addition, Aboriginal youth face crisis situations that must be addressed immediately. Federal programs have tended to focus on employment, training and education. While these are important, usually initiatives concerning them have been developed in the context of wider programs aimed at all youth. Unless the special needs of young Aboriginal people are considered, programs that are inappropriate for their specific circumstances or culture may be initiated, resulting in money being spent but problems remaining unsolved.

The provinces have been dealing with the issues confronting Aboriginal youth for years now through corrections, social services and education systems. Provincial Aboriginal programming appears somewhat more focused than federal programming. In particular, some of the western provinces have made efforts to complement programs in the correctional field with social programming for families and youth. Saskatchewan and the Northwest Territories appear to have had the greatest success to date in placing youth programs in a larger policy context.

For their part, Aboriginal organizations have been working to integrate youth in their decision making and to reaffirm their commitment to youth.

At its 1989 and 1992 general assemblies, the Inuit Circumpolar Conference passed a number of resolutions concerning Inuit youth, calling for their recognition within the organization. The conference has a section on Inuit youth in its *Principles and Elements for a Comprehensive Arctic Policy.* It contains 20 clauses that could guide government efforts to develop a similarly comprehensive approach. The following selection of principles shows the potential scope of such a document:

> The strategy should encompass direct youth participation and action at regional, national and international levels, as appropriate. In addition, youth programs should be designed so that a significant portion of the responsibility is placed on Inuit youth.
>
> Considering that youth (24 years or less) make up over 50 percent of the population in circumpolar regions, it is necessary that they actively participate in political and other decision-making processes....
>
> Moreover, contributions of young people to society should be recognized and highlighted. Through collective efforts and improved communication, both among youth, and between youth and other members of the Inuit community, major steps must be taken to overcome the barriers to youth participation. The Arctic policy must consider ways for new and existing northern institutions to better respond to the needs and aspirations of young people and provide for their involvement. Mechanisms must also be established to monitor and assess government policies and programs in terms of their impact on younger generations. Where necessary, new initiatives and opportunities to enhance youth development and address youth priorities must be introduced.[41]

The Cree Nation Youth Council of Quebec was established in 1990 as a consultative organization to the Cree Regional Authority/Grand Council of the Crees (Quebec). Its mandate comes from an assembly of Cree youth, a regional body composed of representatives from nine Cree communities.[42] Aboriginal communities are starting to focus their energies on youth; Canadian governments can join them as partners.

If Aboriginal youth are to become leaders in their communities, they have to learn about leadership, about themselves and about each other. Meetings, exchanges and leadership development are vitally important to this generation. Yet these kinds of initiatives have been virtually absent from federal programs. A model for such programs is a youth service project launched under the U.S. *National Community Service Act.* It is called Gadugi (a Cherokee concept embracing service within a family, clan or community based on a common bond of tribal identity). Gadugi was developed as a national Indian youth leadership project. Particularly instructive are the principles that guide the program; they are derived from key values common to Aboriginal peoples in North America:

• Family: Special attention and concerted effort are needed to restore the strength of the family within Native American culture.

- Service to Others: Cultivating the spirit of service provides young people with an opportunity to transcend self-centredness, to develop genuine concern for others, and to put into action positive attitudes and skills.
- Spiritual Awareness: A return to spiritual values, be they Christian or traditional, will provide young people with a constant source of inner strength, self-knowledge, perspective and love for others.
- Challenge: There is value in involving youth in risk-taking activities, where they are called upon to tap into and stretch their own capabilities.
- Meaningful Roles: These are essential in order to develop positive social skills and a sense of self-worth.
- Recognition: The turning points of youth are often referred to as "rites of passage" and need to be acknowledged and celebrated.
- Responsibility: A strong sense of personal responsibility is a vital element in the development of capable young people.
- Natural and Logical Consequences: Nature is often the best teacher, and young people must not be over-protected from reality.
- Respect: Respect fosters a sense of relationship and unity with the universe.
- Dialogue: Talking about what happened, analyzing why it is important, and determining how we can learn from the experience helps young people internalize their experience and use what they learn in other situations.[43]

Aboriginal youth programs should be aimed at all Aboriginal youth, no matter where they live or to which nation they belong. In the past, distinctions have denied groups such as Métis youth access to services and support. Equally important, distinctions based on artificial categories such as 'Indian' status obscure more important differences that exist at the community level. Not all status Indian communities face the same problems, and the circumstances of Inuit youth can in some cases be quite similar to those facing Métis youth. The important differences are local, and programs should be developed that are flexible enough to respond to local conditions.

Young Aboriginal people want to strengthen communities by empowering themselves and others. It is they who will start the journey toward self-determination and community development. Healthy local communities are better able to reach out to the larger community around them. Building a new relationship between Aboriginal and non-Aboriginal people in Canada depends on young people and on their vision and commitment to a new path, to a wider, more inclusive circle.

5.2 The Policy Framework

Aboriginal youth have tremendous energy and potential. The role of public policy should be to help build spirit and leadership so that they can confidently assume their place as the living future of Aboriginal societies. There is an urgent need for a co-ordinated, comprehensive policy framework to guide existing programs in a concentrated effort to deal with problems and develop opportunities.

RECOMMENDATION

The Commission recommends that

Canada-Wide 4.4.7
Policy Framework Federal, provincial and territorial governments develop and adopt, through the leadership of the Ministry of State for Youth, and in close consultation with Aboriginal youth and their representative organizations, a comprehensive Canada-wide policy framework to guide initiatives and programs directed to Aboriginal youth.

Based on careful consideration of what Aboriginal youth told the Commission, we propose the following guide to establishing the framework for a Canada-wide Aboriginal youth policy, in the form of key program areas, goals, and a process for developing and implementing a holistic policy.

Key program areas

To focus the policy, we identified key program areas based on what we heard from Aboriginal youth and on our own examination of the issues.

RECOMMENDATION

The Commission recommends that

Key Program Areas 4.4.8
Key program areas for a Canada-wide Aboriginal youth policy be education, justice, health and healing, sports and recreation, and support programs for urban Aboriginal youth:
(a) Education in the broadest sense must be a priority, with greater efforts to develop a culturally appropriate curriculum that reinforces the value of Aboriginal culture. Transformative education – which uses students' personal experiences as a springboard for deeper analysis and under-

standing of the world around them – should be considered in developing initiatives in education.

(b) The justice and corrections system has a substantial impact on youth. New programs should be developed and existing programs modified to focus on reintegrating youth into the community through approaches that reflect Aboriginal culture.

(c) Health and healing must reflect the needs of Aboriginal youth, particularly in the areas of counselling and support.

(d) Sports and recreation must be treated as an integral part of Aboriginal youth policy. Increased resources for facilities and programming are needed, as are trained people to coordinate sports and recreation programs for Aboriginal youth. Also, the sports community – athletes and fans – must be seen as a way to build and strengthen relationships among Aboriginal and non-Aboriginal people.

(e) Aboriginal youth in urban areas need innovative programs to help them bridge the traditional and urban worlds and support their choices about where and how to live.

Canadian governments should consult and collaborate with Aboriginal governments and organizations and Aboriginal youth and their organizations, in designing and delivering programs.

Goals

Overarching goals are needed to guide development of the policy. Aboriginal youth, working with the other parties involved, will have to set specific goals for what they hope to achieve through the policy. The following should be used to guide and develop initiatives in all program areas:

- Youth must participate actively in political and decision-making processes at all levels. They must be seen as, and be encouraged to be, valuable members of society, not simply a group requiring attention and assistance. Moreover, young people's contributions to society must be recognized and highlighted.

- A key goal of all Aboriginal youth programs should be to provide the tools and resources youth need to develop their leadership potential, enhance their awareness of culture and traditions, gain self-esteem and confidence, and learn the value of working together.

- A central concern of Aboriginal peoples is that cultural and spiritual rebirth proceed alongside economic development. Aboriginal youth do not see economic development as an end in itself. They see it as a means for Aboriginal people to support their communities and express daily in a thousand small acts who they are and what they aspire to be.
- Youth must be trained for involvement in nation building. The relationship between economic development and cultural rebirth is seen most clearly in the move to self-government and building the institutions of self-government. Such institutions will be self-sustaining and will be rooted in the values of traditional culture. Training and employment needs must include skills and abilities that will help Aboriginal people become self-governing.
- While employment and training programs are important, governments should pay equal attention to the cultural and spiritual development of youth by supporting initiatives in those areas. To facilitate cross-cultural dialogue among youth across regional, national and international lines, youth exchange programs, conferences, seminars and workshops should receive sponsorship.

RECOMMENDATION

The Commission recommends that

Developing and
Implementing
Youth Policy

4.4.9

All governments pursue the following goals in developing and implementing a Canada-wide Aboriginal youth policy: youth participation at all levels, leadership development, economic development and cultural rebirth, youth involvement in nation building, and cultural and spiritual development.

Process

To monitor progress toward these goals and to set new goals where warranted, there should be a regular assembly where participants can assess progress to date. In some cases, new approaches or strategies for meeting goals may be developed if participants feel there is a need. Also, as programs and initiatives evolve, and as new priorities arise, new policies and programs can be put forward.

Youth delegates would be selected from various regional, provincial, territorial and national organizations; representatives from federal, provincial and territorial departments dealing with concerns of Aboriginal youth, and selected representatives from the public and private spheres should also be invited to attend. An Aboriginal youth conference organizing committee, in consultation with its constituents, would chose these representatives.

RECOMMENDATION

The Commission recommends that

Monitoring **4.4.10**
Progress and
Setting Priorities The federal government provide funding for a biennial conference of Aboriginal youth delegates and invited representatives
from government and non-government organizations, the purpose of which would be to

(a) review progress over the preceding 24 months on goals
established under the Canada-wide Aboriginal youth
policy; and

(b) set priorities for new policies and programs where a need
is identified by delegates.

The first such conference should be held within two years of the release of
this report and would be the organizing conference at which Aboriginal youth
delegates can develop this initiative. Issues of importance and urgency will be
identified, and organizational issues and activities can be planned in preparation
for the first biennial Aboriginal youth conference. The initial co-ordination
among representative organizations can be handled by an appropriate branch of
the federal government, such as Youth Services Canada (Human Resources). The
organization and structure of the conference should be established by a representative Aboriginal youth organization chosen by the parties involved. We
suggest that the organization of subsequent biennial conferences be rotated
among Aboriginal youth organizations.

6. CONCLUSION

> I believe now is our time. Now is our time. We are starting to be
> looked at now and I believe we can really make a difference now
> because we are finally standing up.
>
> Randy Nepoose
> Hobbema, Alberta
> 10 June 1992

If the quest of Aboriginal youth could be summed up in one word, that word
would be 'empowerment'. In this chapter we have documented some of the serious obstacles to empowerment, but also the many efforts of Aboriginal youth
and institutions to take charge of their future. Youth want to take hold of their

future, not be dragged unwillingly to an unknown destination. They want to be able to shape the world they will inherit; they want a say in what kind of world that will be.

In the words of the National Aboriginal Youth Career and Awareness Committee, as steps are taken to heal communities, "self-government and self-determination will fall naturally into place. Each issue has a time and place that will allow it to nurture and flourish".[44]

The development of healthy, vibrant Aboriginal communities in Canada can serve as a model to the world. Aboriginal youth look at the problems and ask, why? Then they take the next important step, which is to articulate solutions grounded in their cultures and traditions, solutions that reflect who they are and what they have to contribute to Canada and the world. Looking at those solutions, the question then becomes, why not?

Aboriginal youth want to be the solution, not the problem. Healing youth today will lead to their empowerment tomorrow. With empowerment, they will have the mental, physical, emotional, and spiritual energy to help those around them: their peers, their parents, and their communities. The circle of wellness will grow.

Notes

1. Mary Jane Norris, Don Kerr and François Nault, "Projections of the Population with Aboriginal Identity in Canada, 1991-2016", research study prepared for the Royal Commission on Aboriginal Peoples [RCAP] by Statistics Canada (1995). For information about research studies prepared for RCAP, see *A Note About Sources* at the beginning of this volume. Unless otherwise indicated, statistics cited in this chapter are taken from this source.

2. Statistics Canada, 1991 Aboriginal peoples survey (APS), custom tabulations, 1994.

3. Statistics Canada, 1991 APS, custom tabulations. The data are not adjusted for undercoverage in the survey.

4. Statistics Canada, "Age and Sex: Aboriginal Data, 1991", Catalogue No. 93-327, 1993, Table 2.

5. RCAP organized its own series of youth forums and youth circles in cities across the country, including Vancouver, Lethbridge, Regina, Ottawa, Montreal, Fredericton and Halifax.

6. Benita Cohen, "Health Services Development in an Aboriginal Community: The Case of Peguis First Nation", research study prepared for RCAP (1994).

7. RCAP, *Choosing Life: Special Report on Suicide Among Aboriginal People* (Ottawa: Supply and Services, 1995), p. 30.

8. Kathleen E. Absolon and R. Anthony Winchester, "Urban Perspectives, Cultural Identity Project, Victoria Report: Case Studies of 'Sonny' and 'Emma'", research study prepared for RCAP (1994).

9. Chris Lafleur, "Edmonton Youth Perspectives Project", research study prepared for RCAP (1993).

10. Lauri Gilchrist and R. Anthony Winchester, "Urban Perspectives: Aboriginal Street Youth Study, Vancouver, Winnipeg and Montreal", research study prepared for RCAP (1995). The story of 'Missy' is recounted in *Choosing Life* (cited in note 7), pp. 31-36.

11. Thom Henley, *Rediscovery, Ancient Pathways – New Directions: A Guidebook to Outdoor Education* (Vancouver: Western Canada Wilderness Committee, 1989), p. 34.

12. Chippewa girl, age 15, quoted in Henley, *Rediscovery*, back flap.

13. National Association of Friendship Centres, "Intervener Participation Project: Final Report to the Royal Commission on Aboriginal Peoples" (1993). (The NAFC appeared at RCAP public hearings in Ottawa on 5 November 1993.) For information about briefs submitted to RCAP, see *A Note About Sources* at the beginning of this volume.

14. Armand McKenzie, "Everything has been said, we all know the solutions...a time to change and a time to act: Foundation Analysis of the Political Development of the Innu of Ntesinan", research study prepared for RCAP (1993).

15. Lorna Williams, Sharon Wilson, Adeline Saunders and Patrick Maxcy, "Elementary Education Study: Vancouver Inner City Project, Feuerstein's Instrumental Enrichment and Related Applied Systems", research study prepared for RCAP (1993).

16. Williams et al., "Elementary Education Study".

17. Saskatchewan Indian Federated College [SIFC], "Aboriginal Post-Secondary Education: Indigenous Student Perceptions", research study prepared for RCAP (1994).

18. SIFC, "Aboriginal Post-Secondary Education".

19. John Dorion and K.R. Yang, "Métis Post-Secondary Education", research study prepared for RCAP (1993).

20. W. Littlechild, *Sport and the Native Population, A Proposed Sport Development Policy*, Sport Issue Papers Volume 2 (Edmonton: Alberta Recreation and Parks, 1981), p. 590.

21. Metis Nation of Alberta Association, brief submitted to RCAP (1993), p. 21.

22. Lucille Bell, "1993 Youth Perspectives Report of Old Massett", research study prepared for RCAP (1993).

23. Donald J. Mrozek, "Games and Sport in the Arctic", *Journal of the West* 26/1 (January 1987).

24. Neil Winther, "A Comprehensive Overview of Sport and Recreation Issues Relevant to Aboriginal Peoples in Canada", research study prepared for RCAP (1994).

25. "First Nations Running Club", brief submitted to RCAP (1992), p. 1.

26. Winther, "A Comprehensive Overview of Sport and Recreation Issues" (cited in note 24).

27. Initiatives such as these are explored in the Commission's special report, *Bridging the Cultural Divide: A Report on Aboriginal People and Criminal Justice in Canada* (Ottawa: Supply and Services, 1996) and in our discussion on education in Volume 3, Chapter 5.

28. Bell, "1993 Youth Perspectives Report of Old Massett" (cited in note 22).

29. McDiarmid, quoted in Winther, "A Comprehensive Overview of Sport and Recreation Issues" (cited in note 24).

30. Winther, "A Comprehensive Overview of Sport and Recreation Issues".

31. Winther, "A Comprehensive Overview of Sport and Recreation Issues".

32. Robert Imrie and David Newhouse, "Aboriginal People and HIV/AIDS in Canada", research study prepared for RCAP (1994).

33. Imrie and Newhouse, "Aboriginal People and HIV/AIDS". More recent figures indicate that Health Canada was aware of 176 cases of AIDS among Aboriginal people in January 1996. See Warren Goulding, "Behind the Statistics", *Maclean's,* 15 July 1996.

34. NAFC, "Final Report" (cited in note 13).

35. Sharon Visitor, NAFC Youth Intervener Co-ordinator, interview with RCAP, Ottawa, Ontario, 7 June 1995.

36. Jimmy Onalik, Youth Co-ordinator, Inuit Tapirisat of Canada, interview with RCAP, Ottawa, Ontario, 5 June 1995.

37. Frank Anderson, Inuit Circumpolar Conference Youth Liaison Worker, interview with RCAP, Ottawa, Ontario, 7 June 1995.

38. Don Kerr and Andy Siggner, "Canada's Aboriginal Population, 1981-1991", research study prepared for RCAP (1995). The unemployment rate was 32.1 per cent for Inuit youth, 28.2 per cent for Métis youth, 25.7 per cent for the non-status Indian population, and 40.4 per cent among status Indians.

39. Habitat for Humanity Canada, "Quick Facts" and "General Information", brochures (November 1995).

40. Norris et al., "Projections of the Population" (cited in note 1); Statistics Canada, "Projections of the Canadian Population", unpublished, 1995; and Statistics Canada, 1991 Census, Catalogue No. 93-33, 1992.

41. Inuit Circumpolar Conference, *Principles and Elements for a Comprehensive Arctic Policy* (Montreal: Centre for Northern Studies and Research, 1992), p. 87.

42. Kenny Loon, "Foundation Analysis of the Political Development of the Crees of Quebec", research study prepared for RCAP (1993).

43. Rich Willits-Cairn and James C. Kielsmeier, eds., *Growing Hope: A Sourcebook on Integrating Youth Service into the School Curriculum* (Roseville, Minn.: National Youth Leadership Council, 1991), p. 8. NIYLP projects included helping the Pueblo of Picuris rebuild a 250-year-old adobe church by contributing 300 hand-made bricks, repairing and constructing trails and tending to Anasazi ruins at the El Morro National Monument, visiting scenic Navajo sites in Canyon de Chelly to learn about the destruction wrought by Kit Carson and the U.S. army in the 1860s, and starting a tradition of replanting peach trees in the area.

44. National Aboriginal Youth Career and Awareness Committee, brief submitted to RCAP (1993), p. 14.

5

MÉTIS
PERSPECTIVES

ABORIGINAL POLICIES OF THE GOVERNMENT of Canada reflect the mistaken view that there are only two major groups of Aboriginal peoples in Canada, First Nations and Inuit.[1] The Métis are distinct Aboriginal peoples, neither First Nations nor Inuit. Although their early ancestors included First Nations people and (in the case of the Labrador Métis) Inuit, they have been independent peoples for generations. (See Volume 1, Chapter 6 for a brief introduction to Métis history.)

1. THE OTHER ABORIGINAL PEOPLES

In 1982, the constitution of Canada was amended to state that Canada's Aboriginal peoples include the Métis. Métis people did not need to be told that: they have always known who they are. They have always known, too, that Canada would be a different place today if they had not played a major role in its development. Modern Canada is the product of a historical partnership between Aboriginal and non-Aboriginal people, and Métis people were integral to that partnership.

Intermarriage between First Nations and Inuit women and European fur traders and fishermen produced children, but the birth of new Aboriginal cultures took longer. At first, the children of mixed unions were brought up in the traditions of their mothers or (less often) their fathers. Gradually, however, distinct Métis cultures emerged, combining European and First Nations or Inuit heritages in unique ways. Economics played a major role in this process. The special qualities and skills of the Métis population made them indispensable members of Aboriginal/non-Aboriginal economic partnerships, and that association contributed to the shaping of their cultures. Using their knowledge of European and Aboriginal languages, their family connections and their wilderness skills, they helped to extend non-Aboriginal contacts deep into the North American interior. As interpreters, diplomats, guides, couriers, freighters, traders and suppliers, the early Métis people contributed massively to European penetration of North America.

The French referred to the fur trade Métis as *coureurs de bois* (forest runners) and *bois brulés* (burnt-wood people) in recognition of their wilderness occupations and their dark complexions. The Labrador Métis (whose culture had early roots) were originally called 'livyers' or 'settlers', those who remained in the fishing settlements year-round rather than returning periodically to Europe or Newfoundland. The Cree people expressed the Métis character in the term *Otepayemsuak*, meaning the 'independent ones'.

1.1 Nation-to-Nation Relations

As we have stated throughout this report, the only satisfactory resolution of contentious Aboriginal issues can be one that is negotiated between the representatives of appropriate Aboriginal and non-Aboriginal governments. No remedial steps, however benevolently intended, should be taken without prior approval of Aboriginal people. The independence of Métis peoples dictates that the nation-to-nation approach is as appropriate in dealing with them as it is for First Nations and Inuit.

RECOMMENDATION

The Commission recommends that

Nation-to-Nation 4.5.1
Approach   Political negotiation on a nation-to-nation or analogous basis be the primary method of resolving Métis issues.

Aboriginal collectivities claiming to be nations of Métis people should be recognized under the same recognition policy and using the same criteria as applied to all Aboriginal peoples (see Volume 2, Chapter 3). To justify this conclusion it is necessary to demonstrate that Métis nations are distinct from First Nations and Inuit. Applying the policy will require the identification of mature Métis nations and a procedure for dealing with Métis communities that have not yet attained the status of nation. An understanding of the nature of Métis identity is essential to these determinations. We address each of these matters in succeeding sections.

1.2 Métis Identity

Identity, whether of an individual or a people, is always a sensitive and complex matter. A person can be identified simultaneously as Métis, Aboriginal, Albertan,

Canadian and female, among other identities. For some, being Métis is a vital part of who they are; for others, it is less significant. Being Métis, moreover, can mean different things in different contexts: one context may speak to an individual's inner sense of personal identity; another may refer to membership in a particular Métis community; a third may signal entitlement to Métis rights as recognized by section 35 of the *Constitution Act, 1982*. Throughout the following discussion of Métis identity, the meaning of the term is governed largely by the context in which it is used.

The determination of Métis identity (and indeed Aboriginal identity) is not merely a question of genetics. A Métis person certainly has both Aboriginal and non-Aboriginal ancestry, but ancestral links may also be non-genetic. They sometimes involve marriages or adoptions, family links that are as deeply cherished as blood connections.

Ancestry is only one component of Métis identity. Cultural factors are significant; a people exists because of a common culture. When someone thinks of themselves as Métis, it is because they identify with the culture of a Métis people; and when a Métis people accepts someone as a member, it is because that person is considered to share in its culture. A comment to the Commission from Delbert Majer makes the point:

> I'll say I'm Métis or other young people that I know that are Métis have been confronted with the same question: 'Oh, I didn't think you were Métis. You don't look it.' You know, it's not a biological issue. It's a cultural, historical issue and it's a way of life issue; and it's not what you look like on the outside, it's how you carry yourself around on the inside that is important, both in your mind and your soul and your heart.
>
> Delbert Majer
> Saskatchewan Metis Addictions Council
> Regina, Saskatchewan, 10 May 1993*

When the subject of Aboriginal identity is discussed, reference is sometimes made to rational connections and objective criteria, such as place of residence, languages spoken, family links and community involvement. These are matters of evidence. They are guides to helping people decide whether someone who claims association has a genuine connection with the people. No one objective factor can ever be conclusive by itself; even when weighted for value, objective measures cannot be applied mechanically. In the end it comes down to two key elements – ancestry and culture – and their acceptance by both the individual and the people.

---

* Transcripts of the Commission's hearings are cited with the speaker's name and affiliation, if any, and the location and date of the hearings. See A Note About Sources at the beginning of this volume for information about transcripts and other Commission publications.

It is primarily culture that sets the Métis apart from other Aboriginal peoples. Many Canadians have mixed Aboriginal/non-Aboriginal ancestry, but that does not make them Métis or even Aboriginal. Some of them identify themselves as First Nations persons or Inuit, some as Métis and some as non-Aboriginal. What distinguishes Métis people from everyone else is that they associate themselves with a culture that is distinctly Métis.

Historically, Métis cultures grew out of ways of life dictated by the resource industry roles of the early Métis. For those who served the fur trade, the birth of the unique Métis language, Michif, was a consequence of using both French and Indian languages. The need to travel inspired mobile art forms: song, dance, fiddle music, decorative clothing. The periodic return to fixed trading bases, the seasonal nature of the buffalo hunt and discriminatory attitudes all shaped settlement patterns. For Métis people of the east, seasonal hunting and gathering expeditions combined with influences that stemmed from a fishing economy. In all cases, the cultures developed organically, their characteristics determined by the social and economic circumstances that germinated and nourished them.

Those shaping circumstances have changed over time, as have aspects of collective Métis cultures and individual lifestyles. The changes have been minimal for some and dramatic for others. A few have experienced a complete loss of Métis identity; others have rediscovered ancestral Métis connections. Some maintain their forebears' day-to-day participation in hunting, fishing, trapping and gathering while others engage in these traditional pursuits only on a recreational basis. Métis cultures themselves have changed: barbecues are often used instead of campfires, and jigs are sometimes played on electric keyboards. Despite the evolving nature of resource use and the diversity of modern Métis lifestyles, the celebration of original Métis cultures remain central to all who retain their Métis identity.

Individual identity is a matter of personal choice. One can identify with any people or nation, whether or not there is an objective reason for doing so and whether or not that people or nation agrees. For acceptance of that identification, however, it is necessary to win the approval of the people or nation with which one identifies. It would be inappropriate for anyone outside that nation to intervene. Therefore, when a government wishes to know a nation's membership for the purpose of engaging in nation-to-nation negotiations, it can legitimately consider only two criteria: self-identification and acceptance by the nation.

This does not mean that other governments can never legitimately concern themselves with who is or is not Métis. Suppose that the government of Canada agreed through negotiation to provide a benefit to Métis residents of a particular area. In the absence of an agreed definition of Métis, it would be necessary for the government to decide who did and did not qualify for the benefit. Or if, pending the negotiated settlement of a Métis issue, it were agreed that a government should administer a program related to the issue, the program's beneficiaries would necessarily have to be identified. It might also be appropriate for a government to identify the membership of an Aboriginal nation in order to assess the ramifications of a decision recognizing its status as a nation. Beyond such purposes, the composition of an Aboriginal nation should be the business of no one other than that nation and its members.

RECOMMENDATION

The Commission recommends that

Métis Identity **4.5.2**
Every person who
(a) identifies himself or herself as Métis and
(b) is accepted as such by the nation of Métis people with which that person wishes to be associated, on the basis of criteria and procedures determined by that nation
be recognized as a member of that nation for purposes of nation-to-nation negotiations and as Métis for that purpose.

1.3 Métis Cultures and Communities

The mandate of the Commission extends to all Aboriginal peoples, however they may be designated by themselves or by others. Where a particular group of Aboriginal persons has chosen a name for itself, we feel obliged to respect that choice; any other response on our part would be unacceptably intrusive. For that reason, we use the term Métis in reference to the Labradorians and others beyond the Métis Nation homeland who so describe themselves. On the other hand, in deference to the legitimate concerns of Métis Nation members who trace their roots to the western fur trade, we have tried to differentiate these two Métis worlds as much as possible by referring to one as the Métis Nation and to the other by terms such as other Métis, eastern Métis, Labrador Métis and so on. This chapter is organized along those lines, with the introductory material followed by discussions of the Métis Nation and other Métis.

There are many distinctive Métis communities across Canada, and more than one Métis culture as well. Geographically, the homeland of the Métis Nation embraces the three prairie provinces as well as parts of Ontario, the Northwest Territories, British Columbia, and the north central United States. Another Métis people, at least as old as the Métis Nation, is located in Labrador and has maritime traditions. Although the origins of that population are venerable, the application of the term Métis to it is relatively recent. Other Métis

TABLE 5.1
Métis Origin and Aboriginal Identity Populations, 1991

	Origin	Identity
Newfoundland and Labrador	1,605	2,075
Prince Edward Island	185	—
Nova Scotia	1,590	225
New Brunswick	975	100*
Quebec	19,480	8,690
Ontario	26,905	12,055
Manitoba	45,575	33,230
Saskatchewan	32,840	26,995
Alberta	56,310	38,755
British Columbia	22,295	9,030
Yukon	565	190*
Northwest Territories	4,310	3,895
Canada	212,650	135,265

Notes:
These figures are unadjusted for undercoverage in the census. Because the Commission has not made any adjustment to the Métis population count in the 1991 census to take account of undercoverage, the unadjusted population counts of Métis in the Aboriginal Peoples Survey are used to facilitate the comparisons made in this table. The adjusted Métis count, used elsewhere in this chapter, is 139,400.
— Figures suppressed because of small size; their coefficient of variation is higher than 33.3%.
* Figures to be used with caution; their coefficient of variation is between 16.7% and 33.3%.

Source: Statistics Canada, *Age and Sex: Aboriginal Data*, catalogue no. 94-327 (March 1993); Census Table 1, Aboriginal Peoples Survey, Table 1.

communities are found in Quebec, Ontario, Nova Scotia, New Brunswick, British Columbia and the North. Some have significant links to the western Métis Nation while others do not. A comparison of the size and distribution of these other Métis populations with those of the Métis Nation and the Métis of Labrador is shown in Table 5.1.

The Métis population of Newfoundland is located mostly in Labrador. Identifying the Métis Nation population is more difficult. Some think that only the figures for the prairie provinces should be included, while others would include some or all of the figures for Ontario, British Columbia and the northern territories. This variation in approach stems from fundamental differences in interpretation of the term Métis and the make-up of the Métis Nation. Unadjusted 1991 Aboriginal peoples survey (APS) data show that the Métis Nation is without doubt larger than the Labrador group, no matter how one counts them: 98,980 if only prairie residents are counted; 111,565 if half the

Ontario, British Columbia and territorial figures are added; 124,150 if all Ontario, British Columbia and territorial Métis are included.[2] While the figures represent the number of persons who identified themselves as Métis in the APS, the number reporting Métis ancestry in the 1991 census was considerably higher.

These statistics can be strongly influenced by circumstances, as shown dramatically in the Newfoundland figures, which seem at first glance to show an impossible situation: more persons reported Métis identity than have Métis ancestral origins. The explanation for the discrepancy appears to be that, when asked to specify their origins, some Labrador Métis chose to answer the origin question on the census form in terms of their early Inuit or Innu ancestry, while they identified themselves as Métis in the APS. Many Labradorians probably reported Métis identity in the APS because of the high-profile organizational and advocacy activities of the Labrador Métis leadership at the time the survey was being conducted. Advocacy activities in other provinces and territories could have a similar impact on future statistics for those areas.

Identifying Métis persons

The appropriateness of applying the term Métis to everyone covered by Table 5.1 is the subject of much dispute. Many members of the Métis Nation believe that, because the term has been associated most often with them and their ancestors, they have a right to its exclusive use. They believe other Canadians of mixed Aboriginal/non-Aboriginal ancestry and culture should be described in some other way. Persons in the latter category point out that in terms of dictionary definitions, 'métis' simply means 'mixed'. They point to early historical references to the term on maps of areas outside Métis Nation territory and contend there is evidence that when the term was inserted in the constitution in 1982, it was intended to apply to all Métis people. The controversy has legal, social, cultural and political dimensions. The legal aspects are discussed later in the chapter.[3]

Socially and culturally speaking, if people consider themselves Métis and those with whom they associate agree, it does not really matter what others think. Politically speaking, if those in the disputed categories can obtain places at the relevant bargaining tables or participate in political processes, the validity of their legal claim as distinct Métis peoples will be beside the point. If, for example, the Métis National Council and the Metis Nation of Ontario agree that all Ontario Métis constitute part of the Métis Nation, the governments of Canada and Ontario do not have to agree. Similarly, if the federal government chooses to offer its Métis-specific programs to the Labrador Métis, it does not matter if the political leaders of the Métis Nation concur in the decision. Assuming that fair and justiciable qualifying criteria exist, if one order of government makes a decision that could have significant impact on the other (for example, by expanding the number of beneficiaries under a program), the other order is free to accept or reject the decision for its own reasons.

Apart from the laws relating to trade names, corporate names and fraud, there is nothing to prevent any group of people from calling themselves whatever they wish. While it is true that the term Métis has been associated with the Métis Nation of the west much more commonly than with any other group, the Labrador Métis and others who now consider themselves Métis within the meaning of section 35 of the *Constitution Act, 1982* are entitled to refer to themselves as Métis (although not as members of the Métis Nation) if they choose.

Recognition of nationhood

There are sharp differences of opinion about the nation status of communities other than the Métis Nation. Although it is not easy to list definitively all the essential attributes of peoplehood or nationhood, they certainly include social cohesiveness, collective self-consciousness, cultural distinctiveness and effective political organization. While many are convinced that some of the other Métis collectivities already possess these essential attributes of nationhood, others doubt that stage has been reached by any community outside the Métis Nation. The Commission is not in a position to resolve that controversy.

Recognition of nationhood is an essentially political function about which we commented at length in Volume 2, Chapter 3. Having recommended a general recognition policy for application to all Aboriginal nations, it would be inappropriate for us to attempt here to settle controversial questions relating to the status of particular groups within the Métis population of Canada. That said, we do intend to offer a few observations on the subject of Métis nationhood for those whose task it will be to implement the recognition policy.

The Métis Nation and the Labrador Métis

Application of the recognition policy is not likely to cause any problems for the Métis Nation. Its long-standing existence as a people and as a nation seems to us indisputable. It is widely acknowledged that the Métis Nation is culturally distinct and that it has demonstrated social cohesiveness as well as political determination and effectiveness throughout its eventful history. The Métis Nation's political representatives are completely appropriate participants in intergovernmental negotiations concerning Métis issues. The Métis National Council, representing a large sector of the Métis Nation, proved its competence in that role during the deliberations that produced the draft Métis Nation Accord as part of the Charlottetown Accord deliberations. The Native Council of Canada (NCC) had previously negotiated the inclusion of Métis in section 35 of the *Constitution Act, 1982*. We believe that the Métis Nation is a suitable unit for the exercise of Aboriginal self-government. We say nothing about the question concerning which communities constitute the Métis Nation, of course; that is to be determined by the nation and each community.

Although we have less information about the Métis people of Labrador, we believe that they are probably also in a position to exercise the rights and powers of nationhood. Certainly, the Labrador Métis community exhibits the historical rootedness, social cohesiveness and cultural self-consciousness that are essential to nationhood, and they are developing a political organization that will allow them to engage in effective nation-to-nation negotiation and to exercise self-government. While the way of life of the Labrador Métis is very similar to that of Labrador Inuit and Innu, the Métis culture is sufficiently distinct to mark them as a unique people, and in our view they are likely to be accorded nation status under the recognition policy we propose.

Other Métis communities

The Commission has not formed an opinion about the nationhood of other Métis communities. It is possible that some communities could qualify under the recognition policy and that those that cannot do so now will be able to do so at a later time as their cultural and political situations evolve.

The issue of nationhood must be approached with caution. We know much more about the Métis Nation and the Labrador Métis than we do about the other Métis groups. That is why we have recommended the application of a general recognition policy when the validity of any Aboriginal nation is called into question.

In the meantime, it may be possible for effective negotiations on some Aboriginal matters to be conducted by or on behalf of Métis communities that are in the process of emerging as nations. Few would doubt the legitimacy of NCC's efforts to have Métis people included in the *Constitution Act, 1982;* yet few would contend that those affected by the provision, apart from the Métis Nation and the Labrador Métis, possessed full nationhood at the time. That was a matter about which Métis opinion across Canada was all but unanimous, so NCC's representativeness on the question was indisputable. The legitimacy of NCC's role in the negotiations would have been very different if the subjects negotiated had been more controversial. For example, if NCC had attempted to relinquish Aboriginal rights on behalf of other Métis, or to create governing bodies for them, its attempts would surely not have been valid.

It may be that, for the purpose of negotiations concerning Métis collectivities that are emerging as nations, the only relevant question is whether the negotiating organization has a mandate to negotiate on behalf of those it purports to represent. In other words, rather than asking whether the organization in question can properly act in a governmental capacity, one would ask only whether it has a political mandate to negotiate on a particular question. In our view, satisfactory progress in the negotiation of some Métis issues may require this pragmatic approach rather than an all-or-nothing focus on nationhood.

Admittedly, in the absence of full nationhood, it would be difficult to determine which organizations governments should recognize for purposes of particular negotiations. The guidelines for such decisions would likely be the nature of the issue to be negotiated, the size, stability and significance of the organization's constituency, the group's access to satisfactory representation by an existing Aboriginal nation, the attitudes of other Aboriginal participants in the negotiations, and common sense.

In some cases, the decision would be obvious. Suppose that federal and provincial governments proposed to discuss a constitutional amendment or changes in legislation or policy that could affect the rights of all Canadian Métis but that the representatives of the Métis Nation and the Labrador Métis had no mandate to speak for anyone beyond the geographic boundaries of their respective homelands. It would then be imperative to invite to the bargaining table representatives of other Métis communities.

A more problematic situation would arise where a large group of self-identified Métis people disputed its exclusion from membership in a nation or demanded separate participation in negotiations. Generally speaking, such demands should be ignored by external governments if the citizenship process of the nation includes fair criteria and an effective appeal procedure, because matters of membership and representation within a nation should be resolved by the nation itself. If, however, a major component of the Métis population (for example, most of the Métis people of one province or a majority of the female population) renounced or was denied association with a nation or its political structures, or sought separate participation in negotiations, a more challenging situation would present itself, calling for sensitivity to both the position of the excluded minority and the autonomy of the nation.

1.4 Protection under Section 35

Another identity issue that divides Métis people to some extent relates to their legal status under section 35 of the *Constitution Act, 1982.* That historic amendment to the constitution of Canada recognized and affirmed existing rights of the "Aboriginal peoples of Canada" and certified that the Métis are among those peoples. What it did not make clear was who Métis people are for purposes of section 35. Some believe that the term Métis in section 35 was intended to cover only the Métis Nation. Others interpret it to mean that it applies to all who consider themselves Métis.[4]

The legal definition of Métis cannot be resolved without a Supreme Court of Canada ruling. Whatever the Supreme Court eventually decides, though, the practical legal consequences are likely to be the same, because section 35 unquestionable covers *all* "Aboriginal" peoples. That "Aboriginal" is not exhausted by the phrase "Indian, Inuit and Métis" is made clear by the word "includes" in section 35(2). Therefore, even if Aboriginal peoples outside the Indian, Inuit and

Métis Nation categories are not "Métis" for purposes of section 35, they nevertheless have the full protection of that section since they are indisputably "Aboriginal". That logic has not been disputed by the government of Canada or of a province, and unless it was, we would see no need for further amendment to section 35, as some eastern Métis have proposed.

1.5 Coverage under Section 91(24)

A significant identity dispute between Métis people and the federal government centres on the meaning of section 91(24) of the *Constitution Act, 1867*, which gives Parliament exclusive jurisdiction with respect to "Indians, and Lands reserved for the Indians". Does the word 'Indians' embrace Métis people? The government of Canada has consistently said it does not and has refused to acknowledge its jurisdiction over Métis matters (although it has initiated certain programs for the benefit of Métis in recent years). Métis people have said that section 91(24) applies to them and have accused the federal government of discrimination in excluding them from social benefit programs available to other Aboriginal peoples. This question also has not been decided by the courts.

We are convinced that all Métis people, whether or not they are members of full-fledged Aboriginal nations, are covered by section 91(24). There are several reasons for that conclusion. The first is that at the time of Confederation, use of the term 'Indian' extended to the Métis (or 'halfbreeds' as they were called then). This can be seen, for example, in section 31 of the *Manitoba Act, 1870* and in section 125(e) of the *Dominion Lands Act 1879*, both of which made provision for land grants to "halfbreed" persons ("Métis" in the French versions) or in connection with the "extinguishment of *Indian* title" [emphasis added]. The Supreme Court of Canada held as early as 1939 that Inuit ("Eskimos") are included within the scope of section 91(24) because the section was intended to refer to "all the aborigines of the territory subsequently included in the Dominion",[5] and there is every reason to apply the same reasoning to Métis people. Most academic opinion supports the view that Métis are Indians under section 91(24),[6] and a recent commission of inquiry in Manitoba reached the same conclusion.[7] We support this view.

In light of the consistent refusal of the government of Canada to concur with that conclusion, however, it might be advisable to remove all possible doubt by an amendment to section 91(24), as the government of Canada agreed to do in the Charlottetown Accord. Sections 54 and 55 of the accord contained proposals for such an amendment:

> 54. Section 91(24).
> For greater certainty, a new provision should be added to the Constitution Act, 1867, to ensure that Section 91(24) applies to all Aboriginal peoples. The new provision would not result in a reduc-

tion of existing expenditures on Indians and Inuit or alter the fiduciary and treaty obligations of the federal government for Aboriginal peoples. This would be reflected in a political accord...

55. Métis in Alberta/Section 91(24).
The Constitution should be amended to safeguard the legislative authority of the Government of Alberta for Métis and Métis Settlements lands.

To eliminate doubt about the inclusion of Métis people in section 91(24) as it is now worded, the governments of Canada and the provinces should, after consulting with appropriate representatives of Métis and other affected Aboriginal peoples, formulate an amendment to section 91(24) that will ensure their inclusion. Failing that, the government of Canada should refer the meaning of the present section to the Supreme Court of Canada in a constitutional reference.

RECOMMENDATION

The Commission recommends that

Section 91(24) **4.5.3**
Coverage The government of Canada either
   (a) acknowledge that section 91(24) of the *Constitution Act, 1867* applies to Métis people and base its legislation, policies and programs on that recognition; or
   (b) collaborate with appropriate provincial governments and with Métis representatives in the formulation and enactment of a constitutional amendment specifying that section 91(24) applies to Métis people.
If it is unwilling to take either of these steps, the government of Canada make a constitutional reference to the Supreme Court of Canada, asking that court to decide whether section 91(24) of the *Constitution Act, 1867* applies to Métis people.

1.6 Economic and Social Profile

The 1991 census and the Aboriginal peoples survey (APS) that followed it painted a gloomy picture of Métis economic circumstances. Overall, Métis are a little better off than Aboriginal people generally but much worse off than most non-Aboriginal Canadians. Their health, safety, longevity and cultural stability are all threatened by their economic situation.

TABLE 5.2
Selected Labour Force Activity Indicators, Population Age 15+, 1991

| | North American Indian | | Métis | Inuit | Total Aboriginal | Total Population |
	On-reserve	Non-reserve				
	%	%	%	%	%	%
Employed	31.4	46.5	49.4	42.9	43.0	61.1
Unemployed	14.0	14.2	13.7	14.3	14.0	6.9
Not in labour force	54.0	39.0	36.6	42.4	42.6	32.1
Participation rate	45.3	60.7	63.1	57.2	57.0	67.9
Unemployment rate	30.8	23.4	21.7	25.0	24.6	10.2

Source: Statistics Canada, 1991 Aboriginal Peoples Survey, catalogue no. 89-534; 1991 Census, catalogue no. 93-324.

TABLE 5.3
Income Distribution, Population Age 15+, 1991

| Total Income | North American Indian | | Métis | Inuit | Total Aboriginal | Total Population |
	On-reserve	Non-reserve				
	%	%	%	%	%	%
Under $2000	28.7	24.0	22.9	27.7	25.2	14.4
$2,000 to $9,999	35.5	26.4	26.4	29.7	30.0	19.6
$10,000 to $19,999	22.2	22.7	24.1	19.8	22.8	22.3
$20,000 to $39,999	11.9	20.3	20.1	16.0	17.8	28.2
$40,000 and over	1.7	6.6	6.5	6.8	5.3	15.4

Source: Statistics Canada, 1991 Aboriginal Peoples Survey, catalogue no. 89-534; 1991 Census, catalogue no. 93-331.

It will not come as a surprise that unemployment leads the economic difficulties of Métis people. Although the unemployment rate for Métis individuals (21.8 per cent) is lower than for Aboriginal persons (30.8 per cent), it is more than double the Canadian average (10.2 per cent) (see Table 5.2).

When annual income levels are examined (see Table 5.3) an equally dismal picture emerges: Métis people are represented more heavily than other Canadians

TABLE 5.4
Selected Social Problems Reported by Aboriginal Identity Population, 1991

	Total Aboriginal	North American Indian		Métis	Inuit
		On-reserve	Non-reserve		
	%	%	%	%	%
Unemployment	67.1	78.3	60.2	66.9	74.5
Family violence	39.2	44.1	36.4	39.0	43.5
Suicide	25.4	34.4	20.4	21.6	41.2
Sexual abuse	24.5	29.0	21.8	23.0	35.1
Rape	15.0	16.4	13.3	14.6	25.0
Alcohol abuse	61.1	73.2	56.0	58.8	57.6
Drug abuse	47.9	58.8	43.2	45.2	49.0

Note: Percentage of respondents reporting each phenomenon as a problem in their community.
Source: Statistics Canada, 1991 Aboriginal Peoples Survey, catalogue no. 89-533.

TABLE 5.5
Percentage of Aboriginal Identity Population Age 15+ that Reported Receiving Social Assistance, 1991

Duration	North American Indian		Métis	Inuit	Total Aboriginal
	On-reserve	Non-reserve			
	%	%	%	%	%
1 to 6 months	10.6	7.8	7.5	8.2	8.5
7 to 12 months	28.1	15.8	13.6	14.1	18.4
Total	41.5	24.8	22.1	23.5	28.6

Source: Statistics Canada, 1991 Aboriginal Peoples Survey, catalogue no. 89-534.

in the income categories below $20,000 per annum; in higher income categories, they fall sharply behind other Canadians. In annual incomes of $40,000 and over, for example, we find 15.4 per cent of Canadians but only 6.5 per cent of Métis people. Off-reserve Indians are represented in almost the same relationship as Métis people in the categories above $20,000.

Economic stress breeds social stress, and the economic hardship of Métis people relative to other Canadians is reflected in a correspondingly higher inci-

TABLE 5.6
Business Ownership, Aboriginal Identity and Canadian Populations Age 15+, 1991

	North American Indian		Métis	Inuit	Total Aboriginal	Total Population
	On-reserve	Non-reserve				
	%	%	%	%	%	%
Have previously owned	5.3	9.2	12.1	4.3	8.4	
Currently own	3.3	5.2	6.4	2.6	4.8	9.9
Are considering owning	7.3	9.6	8.9	10.1	8.8	

Source: Statistics Canada, 1991 Aboriginal Peoples Survey, catalogue no. 89-534; 1991 Census, catalogue no. 93-326.

dence of social problems. When the APS asked Métis respondents in 1991 to indicate which of several social issues were problems in their communities (see Table 5.4), the problems they cited most frequently were unemployment (66.9 per cent), alcohol abuse (58.8 per cent), drug abuse (45.2 per cent) and family violence (39 per cent). While Métis statistics for these perceived problems are marginally lower than for the general Aboriginal population, they are consistently higher by a greater margin than those reported by Indian people living off-reserve.

Among the few bright notes in Métis economic statistics are two indicators of the entrepreneurial spirit noted by the Cree when they called Métis people 'the independent ones'. The proportion of Métis people reporting receipt of social assistance in 1991 (22.1 per cent), although unacceptably high, was lower than for all Aboriginal persons (28.6 per cent) (see Table 5.5). In statistics for business ownership, the rate of Métis ownership (6.4 per cent) is well ahead of that for all Aboriginal groups (4.8 per cent) (see Table 5.6).

Education holds the key to harnessing the independent Métis spirit to improve their future social and economic circumstances. Although Métis people have slightly more formal education on average than either Inuit or Indian people living on-reserve, their educational attainment is lower than that of Indian people living off-reserve and markedly below that of Canadians generally (see Table 5.7). Of the Métis population, 19.1 per cent have fewer than eight years of schooling, compared to only 11.8 per cent of Canadians generally. While 12.2 per cent of Canadians hold university degrees, only 3.3 per cent of Métis persons do. In all certificate or degree categories, from high school to university, as well as in university attendance, Métis people are significantly less well represented than Indian people living off-reserve.

TABLE 5.7

Highest Level of Education, Aboriginal Identity and Canadian Populations Age 15-64 No Longer Attending School, 1991

Highest Level of Education	North American Indian		Métis	Inuit	Total Aboriginal	Total Population
	On-reserve	Non-reserve				
	%	%	%	%	%	%
Less than grade 9	39.6	16.0	19.1	46.6	25.4	11.8
Secondary, no certificate	29.9	33.9	34.2	20.1	32.1	22.8
Secondary certificate	8.3	15.5	14.8	8.7	12.8	21.2
Non-university, no certificate	6.9	8.3	8.5	8.6	8.0	6.2
Non-university certificate	10.6	16.2	15.3	13.2	14.1	17.9
University, no degree	3.4	6.1	4.4	1.8	4.7	7.9
University degree	0.9	3.6	3.3	—	2.6	12.2

Note:
— Figures suppressed because of small size; their coefficient of variation is higher than 33.3%.
Source: Statistics Canada, 1991 Aboriginal Peoples Survey and 1991 Census, custom tabulations.

TABLE 5.8

Aboriginal Language Use, Aboriginal Identity Population Age 15+ 1991

	Total Aboriginal	North American Indian		Métis	Inuit
		On-reserve	Non-reserve		
	%	%	%	%	%
No longer speak	6.1	5.3	7.1	5.8	2.9
Would like to learn	88.2	88.4	92.5	83.0	88.0
Never spoke	54.9	28.0	65.3	73.7	21.9
Would like to learn	74.9	73.6	86.8	72.5	73.6

Source: Statistics Canada, 1991 Aboriginal Peoples Survey, catalogue no. 89-533.

A distressing pattern of cultural loss also emerges from the statistics on Métis use of Aboriginal languages and Métis participation in traditional

TABLE 5.9
Aboriginal Identity Population Age 15+ Who Listen to or Watch Selected Media in an Aboriginal Language, 1991

	Radio	Recordings	Television	Videos
	%	%	%	%
Total Aboriginal	25.3	19.1	33.9	15.1
North American Indian				
On-reserve	40.0	28.9	37.9	22.1
Non-reserve	14.0	13.9	27.4	11.3
Métis	16.6	9.8	31.2	9.4
Inuit	78.0	49.3	81.0	34.1

Source: Statistics Canada, 1991 Aboriginal Peoples Survey, custom tabulations.

Aboriginal activities. A much higher percentage of Métis adults than those of other Aboriginal groups reported having ceased to speak (5.8 per cent) or never having spoken (73.7 per cent) an Aboriginal language (see Table 5.8). However, 72.5 per cent of those people expressed a desire to learn an Aboriginal language (this contrasts with nearly 87 per cent of non-reserve North American Indians). The percentage of Métis adults who reported listening to or watching selected media such as radio, television, recordings or video tapes in an Aboriginal language was lower than in every other Aboriginal group (except for North American Indians residing off-reserve; see Table 5.9).

Other aspects of Métis culture are also seriously at risk. Métis participation in traditional Aboriginal activities, especially in the areas of the Métis Nation, is dramatically lower than for other Aboriginal groups (see Table 5.10). The Métis participation rate overall is 39.8 per cent for those 15 and over. While significant numbers of Métis continue to follow traditional lifestyles, those numbers will probably diminish over time. For most people, their Métis heritage is a source of enrichment that does not demand that they pattern their thoroughly modern lives on the past. When we speak of participation in traditional Aboriginal activities, we refer, for the most part, to activities that are cultural, spiritual, ceremonial or recreational in nature. While they may not affect the bread-winning capabilities of most, their contribution to the quality of modern Métis life is of cardinal importance. (See the discussion of education, culture and language later in the chapter.)

Ways to improve the situation of Métis cultural loss are suggested by the reasons respondents gave for not taking part in traditional Aboriginal activities (see Table 5.11). The two most frequently cited reasons are a lack of opportunity to participate (availability) and a lack of traditional knowledge. If Métis

TABLE 5.10
Participation in Traditional Activities, Aboriginal Population Age 15+, 1991

	North American Indian				Métis		Inuit		Total	
	On-Reserve		Non-Reserve							
	#	%	#	%	#	%	#	%	#	%
Newfoundland and Labrador	170	49.3	750	41.8	985	71.9	1,790	62.5	3,570	57.4
Prince Edward Island	90	66.7	—	—	—	—	—	—	145	40.3
Nova Scotia	1,970	56.1	820	41.4	—	—	—	—	2,825	50.0
New Brunswick	805	45.4	515	38.0	—	—	—	—	1,350	41.9
Quebec	10,120	75.2	5,750	38.7	2,140	34.4	3,310	81.6	21,030	55.4
Ontario	8,910	64.9	20,130	37.8	2,530	33.2	265	64.6	31,660	42.6
Manitoba	11,280	55.9	8,415	42.5	7,660	35.7	—	—	27,220	44.3
Saskatchewan	10,470	64.1	9,590	54.9	6,765	43.1	—	—	26,705	54.2
Alberta	8,110	67.0	11,625	44.3	9,770	42.4	260	66.7	29,365	48.0
British Columbia	14,285	71.0	18,995	46.8	1,850	31.2	—	—	34,560	52.6
Yukon	195	90.7	1,890	70.5	75	—	—	—	2,175	71.4
Northwest Territories	115	88.5	4,845	79.6	1,635	65.3	9,680	80.0	16,215	78.2
Canada	66,510	65.2	83,390	44.8	33,460	39.8	15,410	74.1	196,830	50.6

Note:
— Figures suppressed because of small size.
Source: Statistics Canada: 1991 Aboriginal Peoples Survey, catalogue no. 89-533.

TABLE 5.11

Reasons for Not Participating in Traditional Activities, Aboriginal Identity Population 15+, 1991

	North American Indian	Métis	Inuit
	%	%	%
Availability	35.9	32.6	33.8
No time	15.9	16.8	18.3
Lack of traditional knowledge	15.3	19.7	9.2*
Legal problems	0.9	1.0*	—
Cost	1.5	1.1*	—
Health	3.8	4.2	8.9*
Personal reasons	7.1	7.1	9.6*
No desire	4.2	5.1	4.0*
Lack of information	9.4	11.1	—
Don't know/refused	12.4	7.9	16.1
Other	2.5	1.8	—

Note:

* Figures to be used with caution; coefficient of variation is between 16.7% and 33.3%.

— Figures suppressed because of small size; coefficient of variation is higher than 33.3%.

Source: Statistics Canada, 1991 Aboriginal Peoples Survey, custom tabulations.

people are to participate more fully in Aboriginal culture, the assistance they need includes greater opportunities to participate and the provision of better information about what is available.

A final demographic fact is that fully 65 per cent of Métis people live in urban areas, compared to 34 per cent of the registered North American Indian population. Only non-registered Indians (69 per cent) are more heavily represented in cities. Table 5.12 indicates that Winnipeg and Edmonton are home to much larger Métis populations than other cities in Canada.

1.7 Métis Rights

The often inadequate consideration of Métis rights and the present status of these rights are addressed at length in Appendices 5A, 5B and 5C to this chapter and briefly later in the chapter. However, there are two issues we wish to highlight now.

We believe that Métis, as Aboriginal people, are entitled to exercise Aboriginal rights. Section 35(2) of the *Constitution Act, 1982* lists Métis among

TABLE 5.12
Métis Identity Population by Age, Selected Metropolitan Areas, 1991

	0-14 years		15-24 years		25-54 years		55+ years		Total
	#	%	#	%	#	%	#	%	#
Montreal	—	—	—	—	785*	47	—	—	1,675
Ottawa-Hull	395*	28	295*	21	650	46	—	—	1,425
Toronto	—	—	—	—	—	—	—	—	1,430*
Winnipeg	5,315	36	3,330	22	5,475	37	870*	6	14,990
Regina	1,490	40	695*	19	1,295	35	235*	6	3,720
Saskatoon	2,500	45	1,025	18	1,865	33	—	—	5,585
Calgary	1,435	34	880*	21	1,755	41	—	—	4,285
Edmonton	5,250	39	2,545	19	5,045	37	675*	5	13,515
Vancouver	1,180	29	810*	20	1,765	43	315*	8	4,070

Notes: Métis population is not adjusted for undercoverage in the 1991 Aboriginal Peoples Survey.
— Figures suppressed because of small size; their coefficient of variation is higher than 33.3%.
* Figures to be used with caution; their coefficient of variation is between 16.7% and 33.3%.

Source: Statistics Canada, Aboriginal Data: Age and Sex, catalogue no. 94-327 (1993).

Canada's Aboriginal peoples, making it clear that they have the same autonomous entitlement to exercise Aboriginal and treaty rights as other Aboriginal peoples.

Our other preliminary observation about Métis rights is that they are both legal and moral/political in nature. In our later discussion of Métis rights, it will be seen that for historical reasons, *legal* entitlements vary from one Métis group to another. It will also be seen that most if not all Métis legal claims are open to debate, although the grounds for disputing them differ with the situation. Common to most situations, however, is an indisputable *moral* claim to restitution. That moral claim is based on inexcusable governmental handling of Métis land rights over the years, as well as continuing discrimination and neglect experienced at the hands of the government of Canada by Métis people.

The experience of discrimination is common to all Métis people. It has contributed largely to their present problem, and it strengthens both their legal and their moral claims to entitlements. This problem is not unique to Métis, of course; every Aboriginal person is familiar with discrimination. Their situation does, however, have some unique characteristics.[8] Although most Métis people are or have been involved in both the Aboriginal and non-Aboriginal worlds, many have never felt fully accepted by either world. That is one reason why their forebears established separate Métis settlements. While prejudice has affected many aspects of their lives, the worst and least excusable form it has taken has been discriminatory governmental policies, especially on the part of the government of Canada.

At the core of official federal government discrimination has been the government's consistent refusal to acknowledge that Métis matters fall within its jurisdiction under section 91(24) of the constitution. While that section does not refer explicitly to Métis people, there is strong legal reason to believe that section 91(24) applies to *all* Aboriginal persons. The government of Canada's refusal to accept that argument has had serious discriminatory consequences, both personal and collective, for Canadian Métis.

Except in the northern territories, Métis people often have been deprived of post-secondary educational assistance and benefits ranging from health care to economic development and cultural support programs available to other Aboriginal peoples. On one occasion, the federal government's refusal to deal with Métis concerns tied the hands of a provincial government trying to help: as discussed later in this chapter, when the Alberta government requested federal co-operation to enact a constitutional amendment to entrench the Alberta Metis Settlements, the government of Canada refused to help.

Of the many measures needed to ensure that Métis people receive fair treatment in the future, one of the most fundamental is the elimination of discrimination in all forms. The refusal by the government of Canada to treat Métis as full-fledged Aboriginal people covered by section 91(24) of the constitution is the most basic current form of governmental discrimination. Until that discriminatory practice has been changed, no other remedial measures can be as effective as they should be.

2. THE MÉTIS NATION

2.1 The History

Ancestors of today's Métis Nation people established communities in parts of what is called the Métis Nation homeland in north central North America. The better-known settlements were at Sault Ste. Marie in present-day Ontario, at Red River and White Horse Plains in present-day Manitoba, at Pembina in present-day North Dakota, at Batoche in present-day Saskatchewan, and at St. Albert in present-day Alberta.[9]

The culture of those early forebears derived from the lifestyles of the Aboriginal and non-Aboriginal peoples from whom the modern Métis trace their beginnings, yet the culture they created was no cut-and-paste affair. The product of the Aboriginal-European synthesis was more than the sum of its elements; it was an entirely distinct culture.

A fine example of that cultural distinctiveness is Michif, a unique language that blends components of French and Aboriginal languages in a novel way. A recent study of the language by a Dutch linguist says this about Cree-French Michif:

> It is a mixed language drawing its nouns from a European language and its verbs from an Amerindian language...No such mixture of two languages has been reported from any [other] part of the world....Michif is unusual if not unique in several respects among the languages of the world. It poses challenges for all theories of language and language contact....Michif challenges all theoretical models of language. It is a language with two completely different components with separate sound systems, morphological endings and syntactic rules....The impetus for its emergence was the fact that the bilingual Métis were no longer accepted as Indians or French and they formulated their own ethnic identity, which was mixed and where a mixed 'language of our own' was considered part of their ethnicity.[10]

The right to pursue a distinct Métis way of life was not won easily. When the Hudson's Bay Company sponsored agricultural settlement at Red River, the intrusive policies of the company's governor of Assiniboia in 1815 and 1816 threatened the fur trade activities of the rival Northwest Company and its Métis employees and associates. The violent confrontations that resulted culminated in the bloody Battle of Seven Oaks, in which a party of Métis and First Nations warriors headed by Métis leader Cuthbert Grant defeated an armed force led by Governor Semple. Twenty-one members of the company's force, including the

The Battle of Seven Oaks

Would you like to hear me sing
Of a true and recent thing?
It was June nineteen, the band of Bois-Brulés
Arrived that day,
Oh the brave warriors they!

We took three foreigners prisoners when
We came to the place called Frog, Frog Plain.
They were men who'd come from Orkney,
Who'd come, you see,
To rob our country.

Well, we were just about to unhorse
When we heard two of us give, give voice.
Two of our men cried, "Hey! Look back,
look back
The Anglo-Sack
Coming for to attack"....

Now we like honourable men did act,
Sent an ambassador – yes, in fact!
"Monsieur Governor! Would you
like to stay?
A moment spare –
There's something we'd like to say."

Governor, Governor, full of ire.
"Soldiers!" he cries, "Fire! Fire."
So they fire the first and their muskets roar!
They almost kill
Our ambassador!

When we went galloping, galloping by
Governor thought that he would try
For to chase and frighten us Bois-Brûlés.
Catastrophe!
Dead on the ground he lay.

You should have seen those Englishmen—
Bois-Brûlés chasing them, chasing them.
From bluff to bluff they stumbled that day
While the Bois-Brûlés
Shouted "Hurray!"

Tell, oh tell me who made up this song?
Why it's our own poet, Pierre Falcon.
Yes, she was written, this song of praise,
For the victory
We won this day.
Yes, she was written, this song of praise—
Come sing the glory
Of the Bois-Brûlés.

Source: Margaret Arnett MacLeod, comp. and ed., *Songs of Old Manitoba* (Toronto: Ryerson Press, 1959), pp. 5-9, translated by James Reaney.

governor, were killed in that clash. One Métis person died. The victory was celebrated in song by Pierre Falcon, the irreverent nineteenth century Métis bard (see box).

In 1849, the Hudson's Bay Company again tried to restrict Métis fur trading, this time by prosecuting Métis trader Guillaume Sayer in its own court for allegedly violating its trade monopoly. A massive demonstration of Métis people in and around the Red River courthouse resulted in a decision that did not impose any penalty on Sayer. It thus conveyed a clear message that the company's trading monopoly was no longer enforceable. A Métis observer in the courthouse shouted to his confrères outside the building, "Le commerce est libre!", and history concurred.[11]

One of the principal organizers of the Métis demonstration at the Sayer trial was Louis Riel, Sr., born at Ile-a-la-Crosse and prominent at Red River. His son, Louis David Riel, would later come to national and international attention as the leader of Métis resistance that would affect Canadian history in funda-mental ways.

The first Riel Resistance began in 1869 with an ill-advised attempt by the government of Canada to open for Canadian and European immigration parts of the prairies it had purchased from the Hudson's Bay Company.[12] The gov-ernment had not consulted those who already lived in the area, most of whom were First Nations and Métis people, but sent surveyors to Red River to prepare for a new system of land distribution, even before the transfer to Canada was com-plete. Métis people, who felt their land holdings threatened, ordered the survey-ors to cease their activities and organized a common response with other residents to the incursions of the government of Canada. The newly formed provisional government, headed by Louis Riel, Jr., dispatched a delegation of Red River rep-resentatives to Ottawa to negotiate the terms of the area's entry into Canada. John

Misfortunes of an Unlucky 'King'

Now where in all the country
Could e'er be found again,
A tale as sad as this one
Of McDougall and his men?
Now as I sing, draw near,
If this, my song, you'd hear.

He journeyed to our region—
He thought it his estate;
The good man there would govern
Like an Eastern potentate;
This land for him was free,
By Cartier's decree.

From Canada he started;
His heart with hope did swell;
With confidence he stated,
"Out there we'll all live well,
With joy and rapture sing,
At last I am a king".

This minister so faithful
Was far from finding out,
That facts as he foretold them
Would never come about;
Delusions he would know—
Illusions turned to woe!

His kingdom lies before him,
He starts to enter it;
A man cries out to stop there—
"This thing we'll not permit;
My friend, you need not fear
Provided you stop here."

Astonished by the firmness
Of rebels brave and bold,
With threats he tries to conquer,
"You'll do as you are told."
His actions are in vain—
He won't have his domain....

In dreams he wears a crown still
And never knows defeat;
The only throne he has now
Has a hole cut in the seat:
And this today he owns;
He needs no other thrones.

As soon as the officials
Find out their plan fell through,
Will they turn black with laughter?
Will they know what to do?
They did not have their way,
Thanks to the Bois-Brûlés!

Source: Margaret Arnett MacLeod, comp. and ed., *Songs of Old Manitoba* (Toronto: Ryerson Press, 1959), translated by Robert L. Walters.

Bruce was the designated president at first, with Riel as secretary, but Riel played a central role from the start and eventually was made president in name as well as fact. Local demands were embodied in a 'Bill of Rights' that the delegates carried with them. In the meantime, a party of Canadian officials, including the new governor-designate, was intercepted by an armed Métis force and ordered to stay out of the territory.

Again, the minstrel Pierre Falcon chronicled the events (now remembered by the place name La Barrière, just south of Winnipeg). He took particular delight in the turning back of governor William McDougall and his entourage. McDougall was a rather pompous fellow, and Falcon made the most of his predicament.

The negotiations in Ottawa were tough, but persistence on the part of the Red River representatives, especially Abbé Ritchot, resulted in a deal. A statute of the Parliament of Canada (the *Manitoba Act*) and written and verbal promises to Ritchot from the prime minister's right-hand minister, Sir George-Étienne Cartier, met most of the demands of the Red River community:

- full provincehood rather than mere territorial status for Manitoba;
- guarantees for the French language and for Roman Catholic schools;
- protection for settled and related common lands;
- distribution of 1.4 million acres of land to Métis children "towards the extinguishment of the Indian title to the lands in the province" and (so Ritchot understood) to ensure the perpetuation of Métis communities in Manitoba; and
- amnesty for those who had participated in the resistance and formed the provisional government.

When Ritchot reported on the promises made to him at Red River, the provisional government's legislative assembly wholeheartedly endorsed the agreement.

The *Manitoba Act, 1870* was enacted by the Parliament of Canada (and the next year given constitutional status by the British Parliament in the *Constitution Act, 1871*). Louis Riel and many Métis believed the Métis-related provisions of the *Manitoba Act,* supplemented by the other promises, to be the equivalent of a treaty.[13] However, the Red River Métis were soon given indications that their 'treaty' with Canada would not be fully honoured.

The death of Thomas Scott at the hands of the provisional government resulted in Canadian troops being dispatched to Red River. The soldiers terrorized Métis residents of Red River and killed at least one, Elizéar Goulet. Louis Riel, far from being celebrated as the father of the new province, was forced to flee to exile in the United States. Riel was subsequently elected three times in succession to the Parliament of Canada, but he was not permitted to take his seat.[14]

Implementation of the promises made to Métis people in the *Manitoba Act* and accompanying agreements was grossly inadequate (see Appendix 5C). Decades-long delays were common in the distribution of land and the confirmation of existing holdings, and in the meantime much choice land was allocated to newcomers. Standards set for the confirmation of land holdings were inconsistent with the seasonal and non-agrarian occupancy patterns of many Métis. 'Title extinguishment' land grants were widely dispersed rather than being concentrated in areas contiguous to existing Métis settlements, thus frustrating Métis dreams of a cohesive homeland. Distributing Métis land entitlements as scrip created opportunities for unscrupulous land agents and even government officials to defraud Métis landholders. The activities of Robert Lang, a federal official who extorted bribes for prompt settlement of Métis claims, were known to Prime Minister Macdonald by April 1883, but Lang remained on the government payroll for a further two years and was never prosecuted.[15]

Although such cases of fraud and extortion by government authorities were relatively rare, it was common for officials to turn a blind eye to unfair dealings in which private operators were involved. Gilbert McMicken, the first dominion lands agent appointed by the federal government to supervise the distribution of western lands, invited his son to set up a real estate office in the same building and later traded in Métis scrip himself shortly after resigning from his post. His partner in some of those transactions was former Manitoba lieutenant-governor, Alexander Morris.[16] Even the chief justice of the province, E.B. Wood, who once described the "half breed reserves" as "a curse to the country", profited personally from them.[17]

The government of Canada owed a fiduciary duty to the members of the Métis Nation, as to all Aboriginal people. The government was legally responsible to act in the best interests of Métis people and not to place its own interests, or those of non-Aboriginal persons, ahead of Métis interests. Its tolerance or reckless ignorance of, and occasional complicity in, the schemes by which many Métis people were effectively stripped of their *Manitoba Act* benefits is difficult to reconcile with that fiduciary responsibility.

Error and confusion were so widespread that both Parliament and the legislature of Manitoba enacted remedial legislation. Much of it was designed to relieve officials and others from liability for irregularities or illegal acts. More often than not, this legislation made things worse for the Métis population. One scholar has expressed the view that many of the statutes were unconstitutional.[18]

Even legislation that purported to be for the benefit of Métis people sometimes introduced problems. Section 31 of the *Manitoba Act* called for 1.4 million acres to be divided "among the *children* of the half-breed heads of families" [emphasis added]. The purpose of this distribution was stated to be "towards the extinguishment of the Indian Title to the lands in the Province" and "for the benefit of the families of the half-breed residents" (see Appendix 5C). The ambiguity of the wording made it unclear whether the distribution of land should be restricted to children (those who in 1870 were not yet heads of families) or should include heads of families as well. The reference "for the benefit of the families" as well as the history of the negotiations supported the broader application,[19] but the government of Canada chose to exclude heads of families. Subsequently, in the face of Métis protests, Parliament enacted a statute giving Métis heads of families a right to scrip toward the extinguishment of Indian title.[20] However, that statute also gave equivalent benefits to long-time non-Aboriginal settlers, on the grounds that they had contributed as much to the development of the area as Métis old-timers. That Métis people and non-Aboriginal settlers were treated alike meant that the scrip given to Métis heads of families could not be construed to be for the purpose of extinguishing Indian title; it was no more than a grant in recognition of the contributions made by *all* old settlers. A strong legal argument can therefore be made that the Aboriginal title of Métis heads of families was never extinguished.

In fact, the Métis Nation disputes that the Aboriginal title of *any* Manitoba Métis person can be considered extinguished (see Appendix 5C). Of the more than 1.4 million acres of vacant Crown land distributed in compliance with the *Manitoba Act* and related legislation, only a small percentage ended up in Métis hands. According to Sir John A. Macdonald, "apparently despairing of ever receiving patents for their lands, the majority of the claimants had disposed of their rights for a mere song to speculative friends of the Government...."[21]

The Métis believe, and historical events corroborate, that the bargain struck in 1870 between representatives of the government of Canada and the Red River delegation intended that the Aboriginal title to the land occupied by Manitoba Métis would be surrendered in return for land grants and other measures to preserve a Métis nation with a cohesive land base. It is clear that this did not happen. Since the government failed to live up to its part of the bargain, it is not surprising that the Manitoba Métis deny their forebears ever surrendered their Aboriginal title to land.

The despair that Macdonald recognized led to more than just selling what seemed like useless scrip for "a mere song". It led many Métis to abandon Manitoba altogether, to move westward and northward, where several Métis communities already existed, suggesting that it might still be possible to establish an autonomous Métis homeland. The flood of immigration and an epidemic of chicanery had ruled out the dream in Manitoba, but it would not be long before this dream too would be shattered.

The *Manitoba Act* applied only to the land in the original province of Manitoba, an area so small at the time that it was dubbed the 'postage stamp province'. It was necessary for Parliament to pass a further statute – the *Dominion Lands Act* – to deal with lands in the vast Northwest Territories that Canada acquired from the Hudson's Bay Company (see Appendix 5C). The first version of that act, passed in 1872, made no reference to Métis rights, although it did stipulate that land should not be disposed of for agricultural, lumbering or mining purposes until Indian title had been extinguished,[22] a requirement that would be violated often in the years to come. It was not until 1879 that the act was amended to permit land grants to be made to Métis persons living in the Northwest Territories outside Manitoba in July 1870, in connection with the extinguishment of the Indian title. A further six years passed before any steps were taken to implement that provision.

The *Dominion Lands Act* was very different from the agreement made with the Manitoba Métis people. In the first place, it was not an agreement at all, since the Métis were never consulted about it. Nor did it have the constitutional authority given to the *Manitoba Act* by the *Constitution Act, 1871*. In any case, although it recognized the existence of Indian title, it granted no direct rights but rather empowered the government of Canada, in its absolute discretion, to make extinguishment land grants, unspecified as to size, "to such persons, to such extent and on such terms and conditions, as may be deemed expedient".[23]

The order in council necessary to implement that provision was not passed until March 1885. By then it was too late to prevent impending tragedy. Métis concern for the protection of their lands had intensified by the month as land-hungry newcomers flooded into the prairies. The situation was made worse by the sudden disappearance of the buffalo in the early 1880s. In 1884 the Saskatchewan Métis persuaded Louis Riel to leave his exile in Montana and move with his family to Batoche, in the heart of Saskatchewan Métis country, to organize negotiations with the government of Canada. The negotiations proved fruitless, and Riel persuaded his people once more to form a provisional government with himself at the helm and to establish a military force of plainsmen skilled in the arts of the buffalo hunt, with the legendary Gabriel Dumont as adjutant. The plains peoples, who had been placed in similarly desperate straits by the buffalo famine, were also preparing for violent confrontation, if necessary, under the strong leadership of Big Bear and Poundmaker.

The federal government reacted by sending a powerful military expedition to the Northwest in the spring of 1885, and the stage was set for disaster.[24] Although Métis and Indian forces met with some success in early skirmishes, government troops scored a decisive victory at Batoche. After Riel's surrender, they went on to crush the Indian resistance. Big Bear and Poundmaker were both sentenced to three years' imprisonment. Louis Riel, after a dramatic and controversial trial and an unsuccessful appeal, was hanged for treason at Regina on 16 November 1885. Dreams of an autonomous western Métis homeland did not die with Riel, however; his martyrdom continues to inspire progress toward that goal.

A large quantity of prairie land (160 acres for Métis heads of families and 240 acres for each of their children, including land they already possessed) was distributed by means of a scrip system in later years under the authority of the Métis land provision of the *Dominion Lands Act 1879* (see Appendix 5C). As in Manitoba, however, very little of the land ended up being owned by Métis people. Delays, inefficiencies, inequities and outright scams were almost as common in the administration of the *Dominion Lands Act* as in that of the *Manitoba Act*. The land to which the scrip entitled them and the land registry offices where allocations had to be processed were so far from the Métis claimants' homes that they felt the only value they could get from the scrip was whatever price a land agent was willing to offer them.

Complaints about maladministration of *Dominion Lands Act* benefits have fallen mostly on deaf ears. Government commissions appointed to investigate Métis complaints resulted in little redress. Although it has been over a century since Louis Riel was hanged for seeking a just resolution of Métis claims, those claims remain largely unresolved. Métis people whose ancestors resided in the 1880s in areas of the old Northwest Territories outside the original postage stamp province of Manitoba believe that they are in a strong legal position. Since their Aboriginal title has never effectively been extinguished, they say they continue to hold it. If there is any difference between them and the *Manitoba Act* Métis, it is that their legal position seems stronger, since there was not even a pretence of obtaining their consent to the enactment of the *Dominion Lands Act*.

Litigation is currently under way on behalf of the Métis populations of Manitoba and Saskatchewan for vindication of what they believe to have been the suppression of their constitutional rights. We are advised that similar litigation is also being considered in Alberta.

Some Canadians think that Métis Nation history ended on the Batoche battlefield or the Regina gallows. The bitterness of those experiences did cause the Métis to avoid the spotlight for many years, but they continued to practise and preserve Métis culture and to do everything possible to pass it on to future generations.

It has not been easy. Increasing immigration and development consumed their historical lands at a distressing rate. Increasingly restrictive hunting laws, with which they were required to comply despite their Aboriginal heritage, made it more and more difficult to follow traditional pursuits. While they were never well off, Indian people at least had their reserves and benefited from various social services provided by the government of Canada. Not so the Métis. In the early twentieth century, the circumstances of the Alberta Métis were "especially grim in the central and north-central regions....Game was scarce, prohibitively expensive fishing licences were required, and white settlement was spreading remorselessly. The majority of the Metis were reduced to squatting on the fringes of Indian reserves and white settlements and on road allowances".[25] The 'independent ones,' who had been the diplomats and brokers of the entire northwest were now being referred to as the 'road allowance people'.

In 1930 the government of Canada agreed to transfer to the prairie provinces ownership of public lands in those provinces. All other provinces had owned their public lands from the moment they entered Confederation, but this had been denied to Manitoba, Saskatchewan and Alberta to facilitate the federal government's prairie settlement policies.

When the undistributed residue of prairie public lands was finally conveyed to the provinces by the *Natural Resource Transfer Agreements* (given constitutional authority by the *Constitution Act, 1930*), the arrangement included promises concerning Aboriginal use of land. One of those promises obligated the provincial governments to respect the rights of "Indians" to hunt, trap and fish "for food at all seasons of the year on all unoccupied Crown land and other land to which they have a right of access".[26] Although a strong legal, moral and political case can be made in support of treating Métis as Indians for the purpose of exercising this essential right, the provinces have never been willing to acknowledge that Métis people have that right. (For more on this subject, see Appendices 5B and 5C, especially the section on the *Ferguson* case in Appendix 5C.)

Some Métis settlements survived in the prairies, and in time more would be established. Developments in Alberta were particularly noteworthy.[27] There the provincial government showed itself willing, unlike the governments of Canada and other provinces, to help Métis people improve their lot. Taking lessons from an unsuccessful turn-of-the-century attempt by the Catholic church and the federal government to establish a Métis colony at St. Paul des Métis, and belatedly accepting the recommendations of a subsequent provincial royal commission concerning the 'Métis problem', the Alberta legislature in 1938 provided for the establishment of a number of Métis settlements on public land provided by the provincial Crown.[28]

Eight of the original 12 settlements still exist. Although some of the assumptions underlying their creation were condescending and racist, and although the initial arrangements were undemocratic, the Alberta Metis Settlements constituted the first (and still the only) assured collective Métis land base in Canada. After years of evolution toward greater autonomy, the settlements were substantially reorganized and entrenched in the Alberta constitution in 1990.[29]

Unfortunately, the constitutional validity of some of Alberta's efforts is being disputed, and the province has been unsuccessful in obtaining federal government assistance to resolve the problem. The uncertainty springs from two controversial constitutional questions:

- Does a provincial legislature have jurisdiction to enact laws relating to Métis matters in light of federal jurisdiction over "Indians, and Lands reserved for the Indians" under section 91(24)?
- Can a provincial legislature bestow group land rights in a manner that will ensure that they are constitutionally protected from abolition or abridgment by subsequent legislation?

Both difficulties could be avoided by co-operation between the legislature of Alberta and the Parliament of Canada, but such co-operation has not been forthcoming. We return to this question later in the chapter.

Although Riel's provisional government was smashed at Batoche in 1885, other Métis organizations have developed over time, for limited purposes at first, but with gradually expanding mandates. A group called the Union nationale métisse de Saint-Joseph du Manitoba was formed in St. Vital (the Manitoba community where the Riel family lived) in 1887, for the purpose of correcting the public record about Métis history. After many years of research, that organization published *L'Histoire de la Nation Métisse dans l'Ouest Canadien*, by A.-H. de Tremaudan, in 1935.[30]

The first important post-Batoche Métis political organization had its origins in the concerns of Métis residents of Fishing Lake, Alberta, in 1929. Plans to open the area for settlement and to transfer control of prairie natural resources from the federal government to the provincial governments attracted the attention of many Métis throughout the province of Alberta. In December 1932, a founding convention held in St. Albert established the Métis Association of Alberta. The association was instrumental in persuading the Alberta government to establish the Metis Settlements, and it has since worked tirelessly to improve the situation of Alberta's Métis population.

The Saskatchewan Metis Society was formed in 1938. It lobbied the government of Canada for a just resolution of Métis land claims and for federal support for Métis agricultural and industrial enterprises. Those efforts were unsuccessful, but the society's activities resulted in greater receptivity to Métis concerns by the Saskatchewan government. In 1944 the province made available eight townships at Green Lake for Métis settlement, supplementing a number of Métis farms it had established previously.

In 1965 the Lake Nipigon Metis Association was formed by Métis from northwest Ontario, primarily to do something about the plight of area Métis fishermen. That led to the creation of successive organizations, including the Ontario Metis and Non-Status Indian Association (now the Ontario Metis Aboriginal Association) and, most recently, the Congress of Aboriginal Peoples and the Metis Nation of Ontario.

Although the original Saskatchewan Metis Society had been based in the southern part of the province, it was subsequently matched by a northern organization, the Metis Association of Saskatchewan. In 1967, these two organizations amalgamated as the Metis Society of Saskatchewan (now the Metis Nation of Saskatchewan), which has become one of the most effective Métis political groups in Canada. Also in 1967, the Métis of Manitoba formed the Manitoba Metis Federation, uniting various existing groups and providing a strong Métis voice.

In British Columbia, the first organization representing Métis people (also non-status Indians) was formed in 1970. Today, British Columbia Métis are represented by several organizations, including the Metis Nation in British Columbia, a broadly based coalition of Métis associations. In 1972 the descendants of Métis people from trading posts along the Mackenzie River established what is now known as the Metis Nation of the Northwest Territories.

In 1970 an important national amalgamation of forces took place with the creation of the Native Council of Canada (NCC, now the Congress of Aboriginal Peoples). Métis organizations of Alberta, Saskatchewan and Manitoba came together in the NCC to give them and non-status Indians a single national voice for the first time. That national voice was effective in many ways. For example, it increased the pressure on the government of Canada to include Métis in benefit programs available to other Aboriginal persons. By that time, the government had begun to make certain programs accessible to Métis everywhere in Canada (usually in common with non-status Indians). The NCC also pressed the land claims and other constitutional concerns of the Métis, and although the federal government continued to assert that Métis rights had been extinguished by the *Manitoba Act* and the *Dominion Lands Act*, it did agree to fund land claims research.

The NCC's greatest achievement, in collaboration with other Aboriginal organizations, was to persuade federal and provincial politicians to agree to the entrenchment of "the existing Aboriginal and treaty rights of the Aboriginal peoples of Canada" in section 35 of the *Constitution Act, 1982*, and to insist that Aboriginal peoples be defined in section 35(2) to include Métis people.

NCC representation of both Métis and non-status and off-reserve Indians (paralleling federal government policies at the time) created internal stresses. Those stresses resulted in 1983 in the withdrawal from NCC of most of the major Métis organizations of the west, who immediately formed a new national organization, the Métis National Council (MNC).

The MNC pressed for full participation of the western Métis (whom they consider the only people entitled to be called Métis) at the constitutional bargaining table of first ministers, who were engaged at the time in discussions concerning future constitutional changes that would affect the Aboriginal peoples of Canada. When federal authorities resisted inviting the MNC to the constitutional table, the MNC sued in the courts. It eventually won its place at the table in an out-of-court settlement.[31]

The MNC's participation in the constitutional negotiations resulted in agreement being reached in May 1992 on the outline of a pact known as the Métis Nation Accord.[32] It was part of a larger agreement, the Charlottetown Accord; like the larger accord, it was subject to ratification by the Canadian electorate in a referendum.

The Métis Nation Accord was described as follows in the Charlottetown Accord:

56. Métis Nation Accord(*)
The federal government, the provinces of Ontario, Manitoba, Saskatchewan, Alberta, British Columbia and the Métis National

Council have agreed to enter into a legally binding, justiciable and enforceable accord on Métis Nation issues. Technical drafting of the Accord is being completed. The Accord sets out the obligations of the federal and provincial governments and the Métis Nation.

The Accord commits governments to negotiate: self-government agreements; lands and resources; the transfer of the portion of Aboriginal programs and services available to Métis; and cost sharing agreements relating to Métis institutions, programs and services.

The asterisk indicated that the consensus was "to proceed with a political accord", although the final product was to be "legally binding, justiciable, and enforceable". A best-efforts draft legal text for such an accord was concluded by representatives of the Métis and of federal, provincial and territorial governments on 7 October 1992. The complete text of that draft appears in Appendix 5D. The Métis Nation Accord died in the fall of 1992 when the Charlottetown Accord was rejected by voters. However, the attainment of a similar working agreement for Métis issues has not died as a goal of Métis people.

Also lost when the Charlottetown Accord foundered were the proposed texts of constitutional amendments that would have confirmed that Métis people are covered by section 91(24) and would have protected the position of Alberta's Metis Settlements:

54. Section 91(24)
For greater certainty, a new provision should be added to the *Constitution Act, 1867* to ensure that Section 91(24) applies to all Aboriginal peoples. The new provision would not result in a reduction of existing expenditures by governments on Indians and Inuit or alter the fiduciary and treaty obligations of the federal government for Aboriginal peoples. This would be reflected in a political accord(*).[33]

55. Métis in Alberta/Section 91(24)
The Constitution should be amended to safeguard the legislative authority of the Government of Alberta for Métis and Métis Settlement lands. There was agreement to a proposed amendment to the *Alberta Act* that would constitutionally protect the status of the land held in fee simple by the Métis Settlements General Council under letters patent from Alberta.

While the text of the first of these proposed constitutional amendments would be subject to further political negotiation, the second was fleshed out in detailed legal language in sections 12 and 23 of another draft prepared by officials of governments and Aboriginal organizations and made public 9 October 1992. The draft texts are contained in Appendix 5E. The issues involved in the Charlottetown Accord controversy were certainly very complex, but there can be no doubt that the failure of the accord was a major setback for the Métis Nation.

We have already proposed action to deal with the federal government's past reluctance to accept the application of section 91(24) to Métis people (Recommendation 4.5.3), and we also make a recommendation concerning the Alberta Metis Settlements (Recommendation 4.5.4). It will also be important for the federal government and the governments of those provinces and territories within which parts of the Métis Nation homeland lie to demonstrate their good faith by entering negotiations as soon as possible with representatives of the Métis Nation to conclude a Métis Nation Accord as a foundation for future nation-to-nation relations.

2.2 Looking at the Present, Looking Toward the Future

The Métis Nation includes by far the largest proportion of Canada's Métis population. Even if it embraces only the prairie provinces, the Métis Nation includes 98,980 persons who claim Métis identity, which is 73 per cent of the Métis in Canada (see Table 5.1). Although there are differences of opinion about precisely how far the Métis Nation extends beyond its prairie core, there is wide agreement that it includes some portions of Ontario, the Northwest Territories and British Columbia. If only half of the disputed areas were considered to be part of the Métis Nation, its population would be 111,575 or 82 per cent of the Canadian total. If all disputed lands were included, the numbers would rise to 124,150 and 92 per cent respectively. These figures take no account, of course, of Métis people living in parts of the United States that once were part of the historical Métis homeland.

It is not for the Commission to say which Métis communities in the disputed areas form part of the Métis Nation and which do not. These are matters to be determined by the Métis Nation and the communities themselves. What we can say is that the Métis Nation is the most significant Métis collectivity in Canada. It unquestionably constitutes an Aboriginal people within the meaning of section 35 of the *Constitution Act, 1982* and an Aboriginal nation for purposes of negotiations with other governments.

We noted earlier that 64.6 per cent of Canada's Métis population lives in cities; the western cities of Winnipeg and Edmonton include an especially high proportion of Canadian Métis (29 per cent of the entire prairie Métis population, Table 5.12). Accordingly, urban land areas are potentially part of Métis land bases. (More information and recommendations regarding the Métis and an urban land base can be found in Volume 2, Chapter 4 and Volume 4, Chapter 7.) These facts, however, should not cause us to lose sight of the importance to all Métis, particularly members of the Métis Nation, of a rural land base. The Métis Nation culture is an Aboriginal culture, rooted in the land, and almost all who self-identify as Métis attach great value to the practice and preservation of traditional land-based activities, regardless of where they live.

The 35.4 per cent of Métis persons who live in rural areas represent many individuals and a number of distinct communities. While some of the rural population is scattered, high concentrations exist in a few locations, notably the Metis Settlements of Alberta and several predominantly Métis communities in other parts of the Métis Nation homeland. Those communities may well hold the key to preserving and perpetuating Métis culture for the future.

There is reason to be optimistic about the success of Alberta's Metis Settlements and their value as models for Métis communities on other land bases in the years to come.[34] When Commissioners visited the Elizabeth Settlement, we were given a detailed description of the history and contemporary operation of Metis Settlements by Ken Noskey:

> I believe that the experience which we have had with the Metis Settlements legislation points to some wider lessons which might be of assistance to all Aboriginal peoples in Canada as they move towards greater political control of their own communities....
>
> I would not want to leave the impression that the Metis Settlements legislation has ushered in a perfect world; not surprisingly, that is far from the truth or the case. As I have mentioned, the Metis Settlements General Council has recently established with the government of Alberta a joint review process to examine how effectively the legislation is meeting the goals established for it and what provisions should be changed.
>
> I do believe, however, the settlements have achieved significant things with this legislation and that it provides a stepping stone to greater autonomy and higher levels of economic and social development in our communities. With regard to lessons which other jurisdictions might learn from our experience my short answer would be this: The transition to self-government on the part of Aboriginal communities can be most effectively addressed if it is done in co-operation with all levels of government: Aboriginal, provincial and federal. Only in such situations can resources be used with maximum efficiency in what is bound to be a difficult, demanding and expensive process.
>
> Ken Noskey
> Metis Settlements General Council
> Elizabeth Metis Settlement, Alberta, 16 June 1993

The experience of the Alberta Metis Settlements is instructive. It is not conclusive, of course, since although the settlements are undoubtedly showing the way in some areas of Métis self-government, their institutions and processes are still evolving, and other Métis communities may prefer to develop along different lines. There is nevertheless much to learn from the pioneering attempts, both successful and unsuccessful, of the Alberta settlements.

It is unfortunate that the failure of the Charlottetown Accord prevented implementation of constitutional amendments to remove doubt about the constitutional status of Alberta's Metis Settlements and their lands. The best-efforts draft of October 1992 suggested wording for amendments to the *Constitution Act, 1867*, and the *Alberta Act, 1905*, which, if enacted, would have empowered Parliament and the Alberta legislature to make laws concerning Métis people and settlements in the province. They would also have provided constitutionally entrenched protection for settlement lands (see Appendix 5E). In our view, there is no reason to delay the enactment of these important amendments any longer. They could be brought into being by collaborative efforts of federal and Alberta authorities. No further time should be lost in doing so.

RECOMMENDATION

The Commission recommends that

Constitutional
Confirmation of
Alberta Metis
Settlements

4.5.4

The substance of the constitutional amendments relating to the Metis Settlements of Alberta, referred to in section 55 of the Charlottetown Accord and contained in sections 12 and 23 of the Draft Legal Text of 9 October 1992, be enacted as soon as possible by joint action of the Parliament and government of Canada and the legislature and government of Alberta.

Women

Women have special concerns in rural and urban communities of the Métis Nation as well as in its political organizations. Those concerns often find effective expression, because women are active in Métis Nation communities and organizations. Sometimes, however, Métis women share the sense of exclusion that is still too familiar among women in many sectors of Canadian society.

Views are sharply divided on this issue. Sheila Genaille, then president of the Metis National Council of Women, told the Commission that

> Métis women had and continue to have a prominent role in the ongoing development of the Métis Nation. Our contemporary organizations have a strong participatory Métis women's component....Our perceptions of the roles of the Métis women's provincial and national organizations differ from some of the roles that other

Aboriginal women's groups have taken. Today, Métis women continue to be full partners and are an integral component to the continued success of the Métis Nation.

Sheila Genaille
Metis National Council of Women
Slave Lake, Alberta, 27 October 1993

On the other hand, according to Betty Ann Barnes,

Métis women have not been included as representatives of Aboriginal people. Governments must realize that male-dominated Aboriginal organizations do not represent the interests of most Aboriginal women and should not be seen as acting on women's behalf. Aboriginal rights of women are already being violated in their communities today, and without the involvement of women at a political level, we Aboriginal women will continue to live in oppressive conditions.

Betty Ann Barnes
Nechako Fraser Junction Metis
Prince George, British Columbia, 31 May 1993

One group of women from the west felt strongly enough about their exclusion from crucial aspects of the political process to voice their concerns at the Commission's special Métis Circle Consultation with representatives of eastern Métis in Ottawa in April 1994. Bernice Hammersmith, from the Metis Society of Saskatchewan, described the situation to that group:

How are Métis women involved in and presented in decision making at the community level? As far as I can tell, in our communities in Saskatchewan, the leaders are the women. They are the presidents of our locals, they are the secretaries of our locals, they are the treasurers of our locals, they are the community liaison people in our locals. The women are running the communities. However, their superiors are all males or their representatives for that area are males.

Youth

The position of Métis Nation youth was described to the Royal Commission, in part, by Métis spokeswomen. In several cases, however, youth spoke for themselves. From those presentations, three distinct but interconnected themes emerged: representation, healing and education.

Morgan McLeod stressed the inadequacy of political representation for Métis youth:

The main reason that I am here is to voice my concerns on youth views at the provincial Métis level. We, the Métis youth of Stanley Mission, feel that we are not represented in the provincial structure.

> We would [like to] have more impact on local issues in regards to the youth of our province.
>
> Morgan McLeod
> Stanley Mission Metis Youth Group
> La Ronge, Saskatchewan, 28 May 1992

Delbert Majer pressed the same point:

> Recommendation number three is to support organized national, provincial, regional and local youth councils, committees and groups....Often young people are looked at last after economic development, after self-government, after land issues. And it seems like non-youth politicians...have no energy or time left a lot of times to deal with the youth issue because often it's lost on the agenda – it's last.
>
> Delbert Majer
> Saskatchewan Metis Addictions Council
> Regina, Saskatchewan, 10 May 1993

Too often youth bear the brunt of community social problems. Raymond Laliberté called for local healing facilities designed for the needs of socially injured youth:

> On the issue of alcoholism and drug abuse, health in general, we require an adolescent healing lodge. We have to heal. To be more cost-effective, we don't require more in-patient treatment where we have to ship our people out of the north and get them treated in the south. We need some mobile treatment. We have to be more creative in that area.
>
> Raymond Laliberté
> Saskatchewan Metis Addictions Council
> La Ronge, Saskatchewan, 28 May 1992

Healing and improved representation of young people's viewpoint are bound up with education. Only through education and fuller political and social participation can Métis youth develop the knowledge and skills they will need, as adults, to make self-government work.

While education must equip students with the knowledge and skills they will need to participate fully in the twenty-first century, it is imperative that educational programs designed for Métis and other Aboriginal youth also enhance their knowledge of their ancestral culture. It is heartening that youth themselves consider a fuller understanding of their traditional culture vital to effective healing:

> The methods by which the centres could assist with healing could be history, customs, values, traditions, ceremonies and practices.
>
> Delbert Majer
> Saskatchewan Metis Addictions Council
> Regina, Saskatchewan, 10 May 1993

Métis youth's thirst for knowledge about their Aboriginal roots is evident. Freda Lundmark of Thompson, Manitoba, told the Commission:

> And how could we instill the Métis pride so that we can keep the children going? They asked that we invite them to any workshop or meeting that we have be it local, regional or provincial or even national. Always include youth in those workshops. They've asked for more information on Métis history and culture. They've asked to develop a Métis education program. They've asked that we get more involvement with the elders – youth-elder workshops, things like that. They've asked that we provide Métis days for them, cultural days. They asked that we have Saulteaux and Cree classes, Métis studies as part of an everyday part of our history. Instead of history learning about what Europe did, maybe learning about their own country and Métis. They've asked to have cultural type classes like jigging or square dance classes and overall more Métis awareness.
>
> Freda Lundmark
> Metis Women of Manitoba
> Thompson, Manitoba, 31 May 1993

Education

In Volume 3, Chapter 5 we emphasized the paramount importance of education to all Aboriginal people. To be effective, education looks in two directions at the same time: to the future for which it must equip the student; and to the past whose treasures it must preserve and make accessible. Education is a bridge between origins and destiny. The ability to cross and re-cross that bridge with ease is essential for every Aboriginal person. It allows one to preserve and enjoy one's cultural inheritance while participating fully as a citizen of the twentieth and twenty-first centuries. The bridge between past and future is as important for members of the Métis Nation as it is for other Aboriginal persons. Our observations and conclusions in Volume 3, Chapter 5 are applicable to Métis people and will not be repeated here. There are, however, a few educational matters in the Métis context that call for emphasis.

Métis children, who belong to a 'minority within a minority', find their formal education even more culturally arid than First Nations children. The little information about Aboriginal people they encounter in public schools is likely to have more to do with First Nations or Inuit cultures than their own. When material about Aboriginal people is developed for inclusion in school curricula, Métis educational authorities and elders should be consulted to ensure that the distinctiveness of Métis culture is not overlooked.

Another matter of importance is the issue of separate Aboriginal schools. Opportunities should exist, where practicable, for Métis parents to place their children in schools where the Métis culture is an integral component of their general education. The Canadian constitution already contributes to the preservation of the Catholic and Protestant religions and the French and English languages by guaranteeing public support for separate schools in parts of the country where the groups are in a minority position. Religious separate schools have existed in large parts of Canada since Confederation, under section 93 of the *Constitution Act, 1867* and subsequent constitutional provisions.[35] A guarantee of French and English minority language schools, where numbers warrant, was added more recently by section 23 of the *Constitution Act, 1982*.[36]

Some members of the Métis Nation who are either minority Roman Catholics or minority francophones are already beneficiaries of these separate school guarantees. Separate religious schools in the west, in fact, were intended originally for the benefit of the Métis population, which was predominantly Catholic. For that matter, the original constitutional guarantees (legal and legislative rather than educational) for the French language in the west were aimed mainly at the Métis, most of whom spoke French. French language educational rights under section 23 are very important to Métis people. But access to separate Catholic or French schools gives no assurance that children's education reflects the Aboriginal aspects of their Métis culture.

In our view, the establishment of Métis separate schools where the numbers of Métis parents desiring such facilities warrant, would contribute greatly to the protection and propagation of Métis culture. The case for such schools seems particularly strong in the case of the Métis Nation, many of whose members have had experience with separate schools since Manitoba entered Confederation in 1870.

Turning to post-secondary education, we reiterate a point noted earlier in this chapter, that the earlier refusal of the federal government to provide the same support for Métis people as it did for First Nations people and Inuit who sought advanced education has left some Métis at a serious educational disadvantage. We stated in Volume 3, Chapter 5 that negotiated measures to redress that imbalance are long overdue. In addition, although Aboriginal studies programs exist at many post-secondary institutions, few of them offer adequate Métis content.

Post-secondary educational institutions can be intimidating places: they are large, impersonal and remote from, if not alien to, the students' families. Their curricular and research priorities place relatively little emphasis on Aboriginal issues or related matters. Such institutional factors discourage Aboriginal participation in post-secondary education and contribute to an insufficiency of research information about Aboriginal concerns.

Problems of alienation and Aboriginal focus at the post-secondary level can be overcome, in part, by the establishment of Aboriginal institutions of higher learning. To this end, we proposed the establishment of an Aboriginal Peoples International University. In 1993, the Metis National Council presented a plan for an exclusively Métis university.[37] We doubt that an exclusively Métis university is feasible, but a separate Métis faculty or college might be an appropriate component of an Aboriginal Peoples International University.

There is, however, no reason to wait for the creation of an Aboriginal university before developing improved Métis post-secondary educational facilities. Giselle Marcotte of the Gabriel Dumont Institute (GDI) in Saskatoon told us about GDI's progress toward "federating with the universities of Regina and Saskatchewan to offer successful university education". The GDI and the University of Saskatchewan recently launched an important initiative in the form of an agreement for jointly operating Gabriel Dumont College. Discussions are under way concerning the possibility of transferring the GDI's teacher education program, Suntep, to the new college. These projects should be encouraged in every possible way.

Other post-secondary initiatives could also provide valuable support for Métis culture. Designating and funding university professorships and scholarships for Métis studies would be of great benefit. Universities should ensure that their Aboriginal studies programs include substantial Métis content. The governments from which public funding for such programs is received must be prepared to support such improvements. Because the collegial atmosphere is of great importance to the success of post-secondary studies, consideration should also be given to providing residences for Métis students.

RECOMMENDATION

The Commission recommends that

Education 4.5.5

When implementing this Commission's recommendations on education affecting Aboriginal persons, great care be exercised to ensure the preservation and propagation of distinct Métis cultures. Measures to achieve that goal might include, where appropriate,

(a) consultation with Métis elders when educational programs are being planned;

(b) establishment of and public funding support of separate Métis schools where numbers warrant;

(c) assisted access to post-secondary education for Métis persons;

(d) creation of a college or faculty of Métis studies and professorships, scholarships and programs of Métis studies; and

(e) provision of residential facilities in post-secondary educational institutions that will be congenial to Métis students.

Other recommendations relating to or having an impact on education are presented in connection with Métis culture, the subject to which we turn now.

Culture and language

Language is a major component of culture. A people and its language and culture are inseparable: if the language and culture die, the people ceases to exist as a people. Preservation of their culture and their contact with Aboriginal languages underlies and informs all other concerns of the Métis Nation. Many Métis have described the importance of Aboriginal languages to the Métis culture in the same terms as Jim Penton:

> I would argue, and argue very strongly, that all Aboriginals have a specific right to their own languages and to education in those languages. If people do not have language rights and cultural rights, they have no rights at all, and the law becomes absolutely meaningless. The Constitution of Canada becomes meaningless.
>
> Senator Jim Penton
> Metis Nation of Alberta
> Lethbridge, Alberta, 25 May 1993

Much of our discussion of Aboriginal cultures in general (see Volume 3, Chapter 6) applies equally to the Métis Nation, but a few Métis-specific observations must also be made. Our first observations relate to the language of Métis, Michif.[38]

The 1991 Aboriginal peoples survey found that Métis people use Aboriginal languages less than other Aboriginal people in Canada. Michif, which is unique to the Métis Nation, is today spoken by only one per cent of the Métis population over the age of 15. Alarmingly, the number of children between five and 14 who speak Michif was too small to be reported in the survey.[39] Many more Métis people speak Amerindian or Inuit languages than speak Michif (see Table 5.13). While it is not realistic to expect Michif to become the day-to-day language of the Métis Nation, it is possible for the other Aboriginal languages with which Métis people have been associated historically to play a more significant role in their everyday lives than is now the case.

It might be asked why anyone should be concerned about preserving and studying a form of communication now used by only a handful of people and unlikely ever again to be a vital language for a large population. Does anyone question the value of preserving ancient Greek or Sanskrit? Ancient languages tell us much about the people who created and used them: what their origins were, how they thought, what they valued, how they lived. They also tell us a lot about language itself, how it develops and evolves. How could we justify standing passively by as a unique component of the human story slipped away beyond recall?

TABLE 5.13
Aboriginal Identity Population Age 5-14 and 15+ Who Speak an Aboriginal Language, 1991

| | North American Indian | | | | Métis | | Inuit | | Total | |
| | On-reserve | | Non-reserve | | | | | | | |
	5-14	15+	5-14	15+	5-14	15+	5-14	15+	5-14	15+
Newfoundland and Labrador	—	—	35.8	27.6	—	—	14.7	25.8	18.7	20.0
Prince Edward Island	33.3	29.6	—	—	—	—	—	—	—	18.1
Nova Scotia	42.1	67.0	—	12.9	—	—	—	—	28.4	46.5
New Brunswick	42.4	63.7	—	30.5	—	—	—	—	22.5	47.8
Quebec	82.7	85.1	12.4	14.9	5.6	3.0	97.2	97.0	53.9	46.9
Ontario	52.0	62.1	3.2	12.2	—	4.6	—	—	12.6	24.8
Manitoba	53.4	81.6	8.0	36.1	3.7	15.7	—	—	23.3	43.8
Saskatchewan	36.6	69.6	15.2	43.0	6.5	31.6	—	—	19.8	48.0
Alberta	39.5	73.0	10.0	32.4	6.3	20.3	—	38.5	14.7	35.9
British Columbia	13.8	31.6	5.7	13.0	—	8.9	—	—	7.9	18.5
Yukon	—	27.9	9.2	18.5	—	—	—	—	9.2	19.4
Northwest Territories	30.0	76.9	38.7	70.5	12.9	24.7	76.8	86.2	60.8	74.3
Canada	44.3	65.4	9.0	23.1	4.9	17.5	67.0	74.6	21.4	35.8

Notes: Of the 14,725 Métis aged 15+ who reported (in the 1991 Aboriginal Peoples Survey) speaking an Aboriginal language, 10,340 said they spoke Cree; 2,295 spoke Ojibwa; 820 spoke Michif; 645 spoke an Athapaskan language; and 400 spoke Chipewyan.
— Figures suppressed because of small size; their coefficient of variation is higher than 33.3%.

Source: Statistics Canada, 1991 Aboriginal Peoples Survey, catalogue no. 89-533.

Michif is in an especially precarious position. The APS figures speak volumes about how difficult it will be to save this language. Such an effort will not be cheap, but surely the cost of preventing the obliteration of a unique part of human culture can be justified. There still may be time to rescue Michif from becoming obsolete, and there are good reasons for taking heroic measures to prevent its total extinction. Pieter Bakker, a Dutch expert on languages has warned "of the utmost importance of studying and describing and preserving this unique language".[40]

A unique problem affecting Métis Nation linguistic culture is the lack of a territorial base within which Métis people can use, develop and promote their languages. The APS found that the retention of language skills is strongly associated with a "place or territory where Aboriginal persons form a majority....Where such communities are absent...language skills have, by and large, been lost, a process...known as linguistic assimilation".[41] We return to this question in discussing the need for a Métis Nation land base.

The establishment of Métis or Aboriginal separate schools would help to address the problem of language loss. Separate schools would ensure not only that formal instruction in Aboriginal languages is given but also that the all-important 'playground influence' reinforces instruction.

The family also plays an important role in preserving languages. If a language is not spoken at home, its chances of survival are limited. Many Métis parents and grandparents themselves have lost Aboriginal languages and so cannot pass them on. Even where senior family members do know a language, they sometimes will not speak it because it is seen as irrelevant to modern life or as a badge that attracts racist discrimination. This attitude must change. Intergenerational transfer of language must occur for the language to survive and flourish. (For a more detailed discussion of language retention, preservation and renewal, see Volume 3, Chapter 6).

Métis attempts to save Michif can be seen in the creation of a Métis language lexicon by Father Guy Lavalee, OMI, a Métis priest, and such events as the Michif Language Conference, held in Yellowknife in January 1994 and sponsored by the Métis Heritage Association.

There is a clear need for recognition by Canadian educational institutions that Michif is an endangered Aboriginal language urgently in need of preservation measures. Without that recognition, the maintenance of the existing language base and the creation of educational opportunities to expand its use, Michif will become extinct. Only one educational institution in North America offers course work in Michif. Located on the Turtle Mountain Indian Reservation in North Dakota, it is not readily accessible to Métis students living in Canada. Valuable work is being done at Turtle Mountain. The radio station there has recorded stories of the 'Roogaroo' (similar to Aboriginal 'Windigo' legends), and a Michif dictionary produced there has been published in Canada.[42]

With the other endangered Aboriginal languages, Michif forms a significant portion of the human mosaic. The loss of these languages and their rich content would be tragic for human history.

The state of knowledge about Métis Nation history also requires attention. Every culture draws its nourishment from the past, and no medium of communication, popular or scholarly, can be expected to explain a culture if its history is not accurately known. Our earlier observation that one end of the educational bridge must be firmly anchored in the past is as true for informal sources of learning as it is for formal instruction.

Most Canadians know little of Métis history. They may know a bit about Louis Riel and may have heard of Gabriel Dumont. But many know nothing about Cuthbert Grant – fur trader, hero of the Battle of Seven Oaks, founder of a major Métis settlement, magistrate, and organizer of police protection for the Red River community. Who has heard of folk-poet Pierre Falcon? Frontier physician and judge John Bunn? Lawyer, political activist and philanthropist Alexander Isbister? How many know that John Norquay, one of the longest serving and most popular of Manitoba's early premiers, was Métis? Little has been published about these larger-than-life Métis pioneers, and even less about the countless other key figures and pivotal events of Métis history. What little has been published is not widely distributed and is too often subject to distortion and calumny.

Historical sites of great importance to the Métis Nation, such as Batoche on the North Saskatchewan River and the Forks in Winnipeg, are being developed by non-Métis authorities in ways to which Métis people sometimes object. Some historical artifacts are exhibited to the public in inappropriate locations and in disrespectful contexts, such as the moccasin and lock of hair, claimed to be from Louis Riel's corpse, which are displayed – along with the hood he was hanged in, handcuffs used to secure him, and the coroner's death certificate – at Casa Loma in Toronto. Riel's death rope is on show at the RCMP museum in Regina. This is demeaning to the memory of a hero of the Métis Nation and the founder of Manitoba.

The proposed institutional changes in post-secondary education will, if implemented, stimulate research and writing about Métis history, and that will ultimately result in more widespread and accurate knowledge of the Métis heritage by Métis people and other Canadians. By the same token, the sooner the Métis story is known, the sooner these changes will be considered. It is therefore desirable that early support be found for projects designed to bring Métis history out of the archives and into the Canadian consciousness. Such projects might include public financial support for research and publications (television, movies and other creative media as well as books) about Métis history and culture; the development, under Métis auspices, of historical sites significant to the Métis; and the restoration to Métis possession of artifacts pertinent to Métis history.

RECOMMENDATION

The Commission recommends that

Culture and **4.5.6**
Language When implementing the recommendations made in Volume 3, all governments and relevant agencies bear in mind the distinct circumstances of Métis culture and languages.

Governments and private authorities and agencies should collaborate with authorized Métis representatives on measures to preserve, cultivate and study elements of Métis culture, including the following:

(a) Aboriginal languages: to encourage and assist Métis people to learn and use the Aboriginal languages with which their Métis ancestors were historically associated;

(b) Michif language: to implement, with Métis collaboration and public funding, special measures to save Michif from extinction and to encourage and assist Michif research and instruction;

(c) research and publications about Métis history and culture: to provide financial support for research and publications to disseminate information about Métis Nation history and culture by means of print, radio, television, film, theatre and other modes of expression;

(d) historical sites: to establish major Métis cultural history centres at historically significant sites such as Batoche and the Forks in Winnipeg, to be owned and operated by Métis representatives; and

(e) repatriation of artifacts: to repatriate major Métis artifacts from public and private collections to appropriate Métis-run locations.

While these recommendations reflect those we made in Volume 3, Chapter 6 about Aboriginal cultures in general, we emphasize that cultural factors are intrinsically unique and must be addressed differently in each distinct culture.

Lands and resources

Although many Métis communities exist in Canada, the only ones comparable to reserves in terms of their associated land bases are the Metis Settlements of

Alberta, created and administered under the authority of the province's *Metis Settlements Act*. As discussed earlier, however, doubts about the constitutional validity of some parts of the legislation should be removed by constitutional amendment (see Recommendation 4.5.4).

Adequate land bases have always been essential to the collective material and spiritual well-being of Aboriginal peoples and central to their Aboriginal rights. Because they lack the reserves accessible to many First Nations, Métis people's need for land bases of their own is especially important. The Métis Nation's claim for satisfactory land bases for all its citizens has both legal and moral/political foundations, which are set out at some length in Appendices 5A, 5B and 5C. In this section we provide a brief overview.

The legal case for a Métis land and resource base

The legal arguments in support of the Métis Nation claim to have its land bases restored are complex in the extreme. Only the courts can decide such questions conclusively. Nevertheless, as a backdrop to our review of the moral and political claims, we outline the legal arguments.

Métis claims for Aboriginal rights – rights embedded in the common law and recognized and affirmed in section 35 of the *Constitution Act, 1982* – are based on their Aboriginal ancestry. One of the most fundamental of these rights is the right to a collective land base and associated resource use rights. The Métis Nation asserts that this includes a right of collective Métis ownership of appropriate land within its homeland upon which to maintain Métis communities, to hunt, fish and gather subject only to laws of Métis making, and to conduct culturally significant activities.

Those who deny the existence of a Métis legal right to a land and resource base point to the fact that section 35 of the *Constitution Act, 1982* recognizes and affirms "existing" rights only and contend that no such rights persist because they were extinguished in the past by voluntary relinquishment and statutory erasure. The Métis Nation's response is that there has been no effective extinguishment. They maintain that although both the *Manitoba Act, 1870* and the *Dominion Land Act, 1879* contained provisions that might be read as extinguishment measures, their legal efficacy is open to doubt owing to ambiguous wording and the massive irregularities involved in their negotiation and administration.

Fiduciary duty is the second important legal issue in claiming a Métis land and resource base. Even if the courts do not accept their contention that the many ambiguities and irregularities associated with the *Manitoba Act* and *Dominion Lands Act* invalidated any possible extinguishment of their Aboriginal rights, the Métis people assert that responsibility for the ambiguities and failure to prevent irregularities, of which federal and provincial authorities were well aware, violated the fiduciary duty owed to Métis people by those governments. This fiduciary duty is based on common law, the *Royal Proclamation of 1763* and, in the case of western "Aborigines", the *Rupert's Land and North-Western Territory Order* of 1870.[43] Métis people assert that the appropriate legal remedy for the alleged violation of fiduciary duty is compensation sufficient to establish an adequate land and resource base.

The position of federal and provincial governments on this issue seems to be that they did not owe a fiduciary duty to Métis people; that if they did, it was not violated by irregularities; that if there was a violation, the passage of time has eliminated any right to sue; and that if there still is a right to sue, the compensation claimed is excessive. Métis people have legal responses to each of these defences.

The *Manitoba Act* and *Dominion Lands Act*, pivotal to many of the claims advanced by the Métis Nation, give rise to two categories of legal issue. One category involves the extent to which the two laws support either Métis claims to title or the Crown's claim of extinguishment.

The other category involves the new rights created by those laws: the entitlement of Métis children to share in the 1.4 million acres of land and so on. Whether or not these new rights can be viewed as substitutes for Métis Nation Aboriginal rights, they were legally distinct entitlements, and their implementation gave rise to a host of difficult legal questions. Was every entitled Métis person given the chance to benefit? Was fraud or chicanery practised in particular cases? If so, to what extent were government officials involved? If not involved, were officials aware of the unfair dealings, or should they have been? What is the legal effect of the passage of time and the acquisition of competing rights by innocent third parties?

The prospect of large-scale litigation concerning individual claims of that sort is nightmarish. While we cannot predict the likely outcome of any particular piece of litigation, we are certain that it would be undesirable from every point of view to leave the resolution of individual Métis Nation claims to so haphazard, costly and time-consuming a process. A negotiated settlement would be infinitely preferable.

The *Constitution Act, 1930* gave status to the provisions of the *Natural Resource Transfer Agreements.* It is on these agreements that the Métis Nation's claim to exclusive land bases analogous to those of other Aboriginal peoples in Canada is based. In addition, its members also assert the right to hunt and fish for food in the three prairie provinces at all times of the year on unoccupied Crown land and other land to which they have a right of access.

When the ownership of natural resources, denied at their entry into Confederation, was finally bestowed on the prairie provinces by constitutional amendment in 1930, it was subject to certain Aboriginal rights of resource use:

> In order to secure to the Indians of the Province the continuance of
> the supply of game and fish for their support and subsistence, Canada

agrees that the laws respecting game in force in the Province from time to time shall apply to the Indians within the boundaries thereof, provided, however, that the said Indians shall have the right, which the Province hereby assures to them, of hunting, trapping and fishing game and fish for food at all seasons of the year on all unoccupied Crown lands and on any other lands to which the said Indians may have a right of access.[44]

It can plausibly be contended that prairie Métis enjoy the same or similar protections as First Nations with respect to hunting for food. Provincial authorities disagree and are currently attempting to enforce provincial wildlife laws against prairie Métis who hunt or fish for food on vacant Crown land. The 1930 guarantee has been raised as a defence, but the judicial decisions on the question are inconclusive so far. Litigation currently before the courts may eventually resolve the issue.

The moral and political case for a Métis land and resource base

Whatever the legal situation, it is clear to the Commission that the Métis Nation is entitled, both morally and politically, to have access to land bases and land use rights sufficient to fulfil its legitimate aspirations as an Aboriginal people.

The basis for the moral case depends to some extent on historical facts that are difficult to establish and that differ sharply from area to area (see Appendix 5C). It can be said with certainty that, as a result of governmental policies and their irregular implementation in years gone by, the people of the Métis Nation, through no fault of their own or of their ancestors, find themselves deprived of the collective land bases that once supported their ancestors.

The extent to which governments can be blamed for the result is a matter of opinion. Some argue that dispossession of the western Métis was an intended goal of federal land policies from 1870 onward;[45] others contend that the dispossession was brought about chiefly by the inexorable operation of market forces, to which many Métis people willingly submitted.[46]

Our conclusion is that even if the former view cannot be accepted with complete confidence, the latter must clearly be rejected. Putting aside all evidence on which there is no agreement, it is unquestionable that the governments of Canada and the prairie provinces must bear paramount responsibility for the lack of an adequate Métis land and resource base today. These are the indisputable facts:

- The verbal promises made to the Manitoba Métis in 1870 were never fulfilled.
- The benefits that were eventually bestowed under the *Manitoba Act* and *Dominion Lands Act* were so long delayed, for the most part, that their value was severely eroded by a huge influx of new settlers grabbing up much

of the choicest land and by the decision of many discouraged Métis to migrate further westward.

- The *Dominion Lands Act* provisions were imposed on Métis people without negotiation.
- Much of the land potentially available to Métis people under the *Dominion Lands Act* was located too far from where they lived to be of practical use to them, as were the government offices where the land transactions were processed.
- The 'market transactions' whereby many Métis were stripped of their land were marked by sharp dealing and fraud on the part of private land agents and occasionally of government officials.
- The government of Canada was aware that such sharp dealing and fraud was being practised on a large scale but failed to take effective steps to prevent it or to compensate for it.
- Métis people have been denied the right that 'Indians' have, under the *Natural Resource Transfer Agreements*, to hunt and fish for food on unoccupied Crown land.

Even if all debatable questions about the legal and moral rights of the western Métis were disregarded altogether, the foregoing undeniable facts, considered in light of governments' fiduciary obligations to Métis people, create an unanswerable moral entitlement for the Métis Nation to an exclusive land base as well as to fair harvesting rights on unoccupied public land.

The political case for restoring Métis land bases is even stronger than the moral one. As explained in Volume 2, Chapter 3, Aboriginal peoples' right of self-determination and self-government is well established. In our view, the Métis Nation has almost certainly reached the point of social and political development at which this right accrues. We would be astonished if its nationhood were denied by any reasonable recognition policy. Possession of a land base is vital to the full exercise of nationhood, especially Aboriginal nationhood, which has always been intimately connected with the land. For the Métis Nation to realize its aspirations – economic, governmental and cultural – a satisfactory land base is essential.

For the Métis Nation, the legal question of entitlement to its historical land base is of secondary importance since, even if legal extinguishment occurred, it was accomplished in such a fundamentally unjust and flawed manner that every principle of fairness demands the return of what was taken. In any case, they assert, a land base is a vital element of full nationhood. They regard the establishment of Alberta's Metis Settlements as a good but insufficient beginning to the restoration of their land base and demand that the process now be completed.

We agree. Full nationhood and the governmental autonomy it implies require a territorial anchor. This is not to say that the area governed needs to be coterminous with the territory over which exclusive land rights exist. Recognition that Métis Nation governmental authority extends to its citizens throughout its homeland would be compatible with the existence of a relatively small number of exclusive Métis land bases scattered throughout the homeland. Meaningful Métis self-government would not be possible, however, without some such exclusive territories, appropriately located and sufficient in size and resources to nurture the culture that makes self-government worthwhile; to enable citizens, wherever they live, to benefit from it; and to provide an adequate economic foundation for the nation. Although this land base would be primarily rural, an urban component would also be required. For those who reside in cities, as so many Métis do, appropriate urban land bases are also needed, as explained in our general discussion of lands and resources (see also Appendix 5C).

Not everyone is easily moved by arguments based on rights; some require hard-nosed practical reasons. Perhaps the best pragmatic reason to recommend a political solution to the land base question is that waiting for a complete legal solution would prolong the agony unacceptably and would require the expenditure of inordinate amounts of energy and money.

The number, size and location of Métis Nation land bases and the conditions and restrictions under which they would be established and operated are matters for negotiation, and the Commission accordingly has little to recommend in that regard. A few general guidelines may nonetheless be useful. Certainly, the land bases must be suitable in terms of size, location and type of land to accommodate both residential needs and reasonable resource uses of the Métis people of each area. It should not be expected that every Métis person with access to a particular land base would necessarily live on it. While exclusive Métis Nation proprietorship of the collective land base would be the general rule, the sharing of all or part of a land base with other Aboriginal groups and with non-Aboriginal persons might be agreed upon in some situations, and joint management arrangements for the exploitation of particular resources might sometimes also be desirable.

While the foregoing discussion has focused on the situation for the Métis Nation, it should not be forgotten that Métis people of the east, whose situation we examine more fully later, also have legitimate grounds upon which to base claims for land.

RECOMMENDATION

The Commission recommends that

Métis Land Bases   4.5.7

The governments of Canada and the relevant provinces and territories be prepared to make available, through negotiations

with each recognized nation of Métis people, land bases sufficient in number, size, location and quality to permit the fulfilment of the nation's legitimate social, cultural, political and
economic aspirations.

No one should suppose that this will be a rapid or easy process.
Negotiations will undoubtedly be prolonged, and many difficult snarls will
have to be unravelled. One thing can and should be done quickly, however, and
that is the constitutional confirmation of Alberta's Metis Settlements, a question
dealt with earlier (Recommendation 4.5.4).

Not all Aboriginal resource use rights are necessarily exercisable on exclusively Aboriginal lands. We have pointed out that "Indians" of the prairie
provinces have the right under the *Constitution Act, 1930* to hunt, trap and fish
"game for food on all unoccupied Crown lands, and on any other lands to which
the said Indians may have a right of access". Whether that right extends to Métis
persons is as yet uncertain legally, but in our view, from a moral and political perspective, it ought to. Métis people in the prairie provinces have the same need,
and in our view the same moral right as their First Nations counterparts to seek
sustenance from unoccupied public lands. We therefore call upon the governments of the three provinces to which the *Constitution Act, 1930* applies –
Manitoba, Saskatchewan and Alberta – to recognize the right of all Métis
Nation citizens to exercise the food exemption guaranteed by that act. While no
equivalent formal guarantee exists for areas outside the prairie provinces, it is our
view that Métis and other Aboriginal persons outside those provinces whose
Aboriginal rights have never been extinguished ought to have a similar entitlement and that it ought to extend, where appropriate, to salt-water fisheries in
public waters.

This issue is made especially urgent by the absence of a sufficient Métis land
base. With neither a territorial base of their own nor the same opportunity that
prairie First Nations members have to hunt for food at all times of the year on
unoccupied public property, the people of the Métis Nation risk losing their
ancestral links with the land. Therefore, although the food exemption provision
of the 1930 act may ultimately become an element of land claims negotiations,
its confirmation cannot wait for those negotiations to conclude. An immediate
response by the governments of the prairie provinces would terminate expensive
litigation now under way and would contribute to keeping Métis people in touch
with the land while land claims negotiations are in progress. In some cases, the
need for change in provincial policies concerning Métis food harvesting is especially urgent because the individuals affected need the food for sustenance. The

exclusion of Métis people from the food exemption has hit the poor the hardest. They should not have to await the outcome of prolonged political negotiations to feed their families.

RECOMMENDATION

The Commission recommends that

Métis Right to **4.5.8**
Hunt and Fish for The governments of Manitoba, Saskatchewan and Alberta
Food
  (a) recognize immediately that the right, under the *Constitution Act, 1930,* of "Indians" of those provinces to hunt, trap and fish for food in all seasons on unoccupied Crown land and other land to which they have a right of access applies to all Métis persons in those provinces;
  (b) consult with leaders of the Métis Nation when determining who qualifies as a Métis person for that purpose;
  (c) give the same right to non-status Indians residing in the prairie provinces after they have demonstrated their Aboriginal ancestry by some prescribed and fair method; and
  (d) give the same right to Aboriginal persons residing outside the prairie provinces unless it has been extinguished by a legally binding extinguishment measure, and extend the right, where appropriate, to public waters.

Other interim measures probably also will be needed. If Métis land claims negotiations prove as slow in reaching conclusions as we anticipate, the economic benefits associated with control of a land base will have to be found elsewhere in the meantime. While some support might be found in subsidies, it would be preferable from every point of view if most derived from land-related enterprises. We therefore urge that while negotiations for a permanent land base are under way, federal, provincial and territorial governments consider entering into temporary land use agreements with the Métis Nation. It might be mutually advantageous for land use agreements of more permanent duration to be negotiated, perhaps on a joint use basis and in conjunction with other Aboriginal interests, or with private interests.

RECOMMENDATION

The Commission recommends that

Interim and
Permanent Land
Use Agreements

4.5.9

Federal, provincial and territorial governments

(a) be prepared to enter into temporary land use agreements with Métis nations while land claims negotiations are pending or continuing; and

(b) be prepared, where appropriate, to consider longer-term land use agreements with Métis nations, perhaps in association with other interests, Aboriginal or private.

Self-government

We stated in our constitutional commentary, *Partners in Confederation*, and elaborated in Volume 2, Chapter 3 of this report, that every Aboriginal people has as a component of its Aboriginal rights the inherent right of self-government.[47] The right of the Métis Nation to govern itself is therefore undeniable.

We are aware that some Métis people, although proud of their Métis heritage and imbued with Métis culture, are satisfied with existing governmental arrangements and do not want the picture complicated by the addition of Métis governmental structures. It is, of course, their democratic right to reject self-government. Our position is that Métis people have the right to make that choice, and we believe that when they do, the majority will opt for self-government.

Historically, the Métis Nation exercised the power of self-government on many occasions and in many ways, the Riel provisional governments of 1869-1870 and 1884-1885 being the best-known instances. Today, the Métis Nation is demonstrating its capacity for self-government in the governmental structures of the Alberta Metis Settlements. Provincial and territorial Métis organizations are now making the transition from benevolent associations and lobby groups to quasi-governmental bodies. The Métis National Council has developed nation-wide governmental associations, and the Metis Nation of Saskatchewan has enacted wildlife conservation legislation to be observed by its citizens. The successful constitutional negotiations conducted by the Congress of Aboriginal Peoples (when it was the Native Council of Canada) and the Métis National Council with federal, provincial and territorial governments leave no doubt about the Métis Nation's ability to hold its own in intergovernmental diplomacy.

The ways in which the right of self-government is exercised, and through which it will be integrated with other governmental authorities, are subject to determination by each Aboriginal people and to intergovernmental negotiation. It would be inappropriate for the Commission to suggest the form or forms that Métis self-government should take. However, government structures must be capable of serving a citizenry spread across several provinces and territories, which could include

- a number of predominantly Métis communities with sizeable adjacent land bases;
- several predominantly Métis communities without adjacent land bases;
- several large urban areas with diverse populations; and
- numerous rural and smaller urban areas with diverse populations.

The structures are, to a considerable degree, already in place. They assume the establishment of adequate territorial and funding bases, recognition by other governmental authorities, and agreement on respective roles and integration. Negotiations on the missing elements are long overdue.

RECOMMENDATION

The Commission recommends that

Negotiations on Métis Self-Government

4.5.10

The governments of Canada and of relevant provinces and territories

(a) be prepared to negotiate immediately with appropriate Métis representatives (as well as, where appropriate, other Aboriginal governments) on the manner in which Métis self-government will be recognized by and integrated with other governments and assisted to become financially self-sufficient; and

(b) pursue independently and swiftly those aspects of self-government that are not dependent upon land base considerations, although it will be appropriate for part of these negotiations to take place in the context of negotiations concerning the nation's land base.

Métis access to Aboriginal benefits programs

Métis people have been disadvantaged over the years, along with non-status Indians, by being denied access to programs – from non-insured health benefits to post-secondary education – that have been available to other Aboriginal peoples. (For more detailed discussion, see Volume 3, Chapters 3 and 5.)

Some people demand both immediate and retrospective parity of access to the programs from which they have been excluded. While recognizing the very serious wrong done to Métis people by excluding them for more than a century from benefits provided under the authority of section 91(24) of the *Constitution Act, 1867*, the Commission is of the opinion that negotiated settlements are preferable to perpetuating the paternalism of the past and extending it to Métis people. In our view, the focus should be on negotiated arrangements that permit all Aboriginal nations, including Métis nations, to assume eventual responsibility for their own benefit programs. These should be coupled with appropriate interim measures such as the Aboriginal scholarship fund referred to in Volume 3, Chapter 5. We agree, however, that parity of access must apply to all new Aboriginal programs in future, assuming Métis consent. The sooner effective nation-to-nation negotiations on the future of the Métis Nation are completed, the fewer such interim measures will be required.

Conclusion

The people of the Métis Nation live diverse lives. They include both rural residents and city dwellers. They pursue livelihoods in just about every field of endeavour, from the traditional Aboriginal occupations of trapping and fishing, to agriculture, business and professions like medicine, engineering, architecture, journalism and law. They are found in every economic and educational stratum, although they are, on average, considerably less well off economically and educationally than other Canadians. More important than those differences is their common Métis heritage, forged in the fur-trade partnerships that opened the North American northwest to the rest of the world. That heritage is part of every Métis Nation citizen.

The Métis Nation is struggling for preservation of its culture and eradication of discrimination. The nation's determination has been tempered in the flames of much fiercer conflicts, and its leaders are confident of victory in several arenas. Important court cases concerning land and harvesting rights are working their way to the Supreme Court of Canada, and other litigation is in process. Although they are hopeful that their legal rights eventually will be confirmed by the courts, Métis leaders recognize that legal rights are less important than moral and political rights. They are therefore pursuing political initiatives, and it is our hope that other Canadian governments will be wise enough to explore those initiatives with them.

The twentieth century began with the people of the Métis Nation uprooted, fragmented and dispirited. They are determined that before it closes they will have

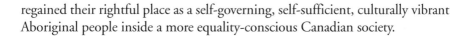

regained their rightful place as a self-governing, self-sufficient, culturally vibrant Aboriginal people inside a more equality-conscious Canadian society.

3. The Other Métis[48]

3.1 History

Several Métis communities came into existence, independently of the Métis Nation, in the eastern part of what we now call Canada, some of them predating the establishment of the Métis Nation.[49] The history of Métis people who are not part of the Métis Nation is not easy to relate. For one thing, their past has not been much studied by historians. If the Métis Nation's story is unfamiliar to most Canadians, the story of the 'other' Métis is almost untold. For another thing, their story is made up of several largely unconnected segments, each relating to a different geographic area. Here we can provide only the briefest of sketches for each of the areas involved. Each sketch represents a complex history that has yet to be studied in detail.

Because the recommendations made with respect to the Métis Nation seem applicable, with appropriate adjustments, to other Métis as well, no recommendations are made in this section.

Labrador

Even before Jacques Cartier's explorations in the 1530s, European fishermen were exploiting the fishery in the Strait of Belle Isle. Later, non-Aboriginal fishermen came from Newfoundland. Although many of these men stayed aboard their vessels most of the time (thereby acquiring the name 'floaters'), some established shore bases, either seasonal – 'stationers' – or permanent – 'livyers' or 'settlers'. Inevitably, relationships developed between the men who lived on shore and the women of the indigenous Inuit and Innu populations. The children and grandchildren of those unions formed communities with distinct ways of life. The first Métis communities appear to date from the late 1700s.[50] The Labrador Métis Association described the origins of its people this way:

> For many generations...before Newfoundland and Labrador joined with Canada, and even long before Canada itself existed as a nation, the Labrador Métis, who were then commonly referred to as the 'livyers', or 'settlers', lived on the coast, both north and south, in complete harmony with the land and the sea, much the same as their Inuit and Indian neighbours. The same can be said for those who ultimately settled in the Lake Melville region and became the celebrated trappers of central Labrador....

[T]he people in such places as Paradise River, Black Tickle and Pinsent's Arm on the south coast [who are now calling themselves Métis] are essentially no different than the Inuit of Rigolet, Postville, or Makkovik on the north coast. [I]t is only geography and the attitude of outsiders that separates them....

I say to you and to Canada we are not livyers. We are not settlers. We are Métis – the progeny of our Indian and/or our Inuit and European settlers who long ago settled this harsh and beautiful land when others considered Labrador to be the land God gave to Cain.

Bernard Heard
Labrador Métis Association
Happy Valley, Newfoundland and Labrador, 16 June 1992

The statement that the Labrador Métis are essentially no different from Inuit should not be misunderstood. It may be true that it is only geography and the attitude of outsiders that separates these two groups, but those two factors have been significant in isolating and shaping Métis cultures everywhere.

Although economic activities and resource use patterns of the Labrador Métis are similar to those of Inuit and Innu in neighbouring areas, social and geographic distinctions have always existed between these peoples. This sense of identity resulted in the development of about 20 primarily Métis communities in the area from upper Lake Melville south to the Strait of Belle Isle. To the north of the region, communities are chiefly Inuit; to the south and west, they are mainly Innu. A relatively well-defined geographic area has developed, therefore, of communities populated predominantly by Aboriginal people who have long considered themselves different from other Aboriginal and non-Aboriginal people in the area. Their livelihood depends heavily on seasonal harvesting of the sea and the land in patterns with ancient origins. The territory within which they have traditionally exercised harvesting rights overlaps with that of Innu inhabitants.

As the Labrador Métis Association brief suggests, communities of mixed-ancestry Labradorians did not always refer to themselves as Métis. That term has come into use relatively recently in Labrador, chiefly since the inclusion of the word "Métis" in section 35 of the *Constitution Act, 1982*. Some members of the Métis Nation think it is not appropriate for Labradorians to call themselves Métis now when they did not do so in the past. The position of the Labrador Métis Association and its members is that what counts is not the expression used – then or now – but the substance of their ancestry and their identity. Although they had no need in the past to call themselves anything but livyers or settlers or Labradorians, they always knew they were Aboriginal people of mixed ancestry who long had lived in distinct communities and pursued a distinctive way of life. That, they contend, is precisely what the word Métis means in section 35 of the *Constitution Act, 1982*. They are accordingly now claiming the Aboriginal entitlements that the constitution describes as being available to Métis people.

It seems clear that the Métis of Labrador are an Aboriginal people within the meaning of section 35. They display the social and geographic distinctiveness, the self-consciousness and the cohesiveness of a people, along with an unmistakably Aboriginal relationship to the natural environment. If their political institutions are not so fully developed as those of some other Aboriginal nations, it seems likely that they will be soon. It is likely that they would qualify as a nation under the recognition policy we have proposed. Since they are probably a people and are undeniably Aboriginal, we do not consider it legally crucial whether they are labelled Métis or Aboriginal for constitutional purposes. For social and political purposes, they are entitled to call themselves Métis if that is how they wish to identify themselves.

The Métis people of Labrador were never the subject of any Aboriginal treaty. On the other hand, until recently there was little or no governmental interference with their harvesting of the natural resources of their region. In short, they were largely ignored by governmental authorities. Recently, however, their harvesting activities are being interfered with by government to an extent they consider a violation of their Aboriginal rights. That contention is being examined by the courts. A collective land claim is also under study.[51]

The Maritimes

Métis people in the Maritime provinces can also trace their communities to early contacts between the Aboriginal populations (Mi'kmaq and Wuastukwiuk, or Maliseet) of the region and French or British newcomers. Rewards were offered by British authorities in the early eighteenth century to British subjects who married Indians.[52] The offspring of Aboriginal-European marriages often congregated, as in Labrador, in communities away from those of both ancestral peoples.[53]

Along with most of the rest of the early Maritime population, Métis people were profoundly affected by the British expulsion of Acadians between 1755 and 1763. Métis communities endured or regenerated, however, in parts of what are now Nova Scotia and New Brunswick. One of the earliest recorded uses of the word Métis ("Isle Mettise") occurs on a map drawn in 1758 of the area drained by the Saint John River.[54]

The New Brunswick Association of Métis and Non-Status Indians stated in a 1984 presentation to the Native Council of Canada that Métis people were, in the early years, generally included as Indians, in Wuastukwiuk and Mi'kmaq treaties.[55] They participated in the treaty process as *individuals*, however (although some maritime Métis people participated as Indians); they did not do so *as a people*, despite the fact that government negotiators seem to have been well aware of their distinct culture and identity. From the late 1870s onward, the governmental practice of treating Métis individuals as Indians for treaty purposes was abandoned, and a series of *Indian Act* amendments was adopted with a view to encouraging enfranchisement by Métis and other people previously treated as Indians. In short, the government of Canada consciously ignored the New Brunswick Métis as a separate people.

Quebec

Some of the earliest origins of the western Métis Nation can be traced to Quebec: the first francophone *coureurs de bois* to serve the western fur trade came from the lower St. Lawrence region. Their migration to the Great Lakes basin resulted in some of the first clearly identifiable Métis communities in North America, and their subsequent movement westward culminated in the evolution of the people who went to the barricades with Louis Riel and Gabriel Dumont. In talking about the French element of the Métis Nation, it may be useful to think of the Métis culture as having been conceived in Quebec, gestated in Ontario and born on the western plains.[56]

Whether or not the intermarriage of First Nations people with the early French settlers of Quebec was ever a significant element of official French colonial policy, as it apparently was for the British in Acadia, is a subject of some disagreement among historians. Champlain certainly supported establishing such a policy, but it does not seem to have been made official. The approach of later administrations is unclear.[57] With or without government stimulus, Aboriginal-French intermarriage on a large scale (especially when there were few female immigrants) was a reality of early Quebec society. Distinct communities resulted, perhaps because European people came to North America before European institutions arrived.

Collectively, too, Métis people have a presence in Quebec that cannot be ignored. Some 8,690 people in Quebec identified themselves as Métis in Statistics Canada's 1991 Aboriginal people's survey.[58] The Commission received several forceful and informative presentations on behalf of Quebec Métis from such organizations as the Association des Métis et des Indiens hors-réserve du Québec and the Métis Nation of Quebec. Some presenters referred to Quebec Métis as "the twelfth distinct Aboriginal nation in the province of Quebec and the fifty-fifth Aboriginal nation in Canada".[59] In explaining their distinctiveness as a nation, Métis people emphasized that they should not be considered "Indians living off reserves" any more than Québécois should be considered "francophones living outside France".[60] They pointed to the early origins, the number and the permanence of Métis communities in Quebec:

> We formed little by little our own communities in respect of our own reality. We were denied access to the communities...constituted by European settlers and those of the Native nations.
>
> Élizabeth LaMadeleine
> Métis Nation of Quebec
> Montreal, Quebec, 28 May 1993

Over the centuries our people have developed their own physical communities with a social, political and cultural community structure that is unique to us and that we, like other Aboriginal nations, wish to preserve. Île du Grand Calumet, Fort Coulonge, Saint Epiphane, Otter Lake, Quyon, Mont Laurier, Chicoutimi, Trois-Rivières, Les Escoumins are examples of these communities. [translation]

Sylvie Plouffe
Métis Nation of Quebec
Montreal, Quebec, 28 May 1993

[W]e do not live off the reserves; we have specific communities. Go to the Île du Grand Calumet, I invite you to come to the Île du Grand Calumet...You will see the Métis beauty of an island. [translation]

Claude Aubin
Métis Nation of Quebec
Montreal, Quebec, 28 May 1993

In 1992 the Native Alliance of Quebec presented a paper to a consultation forum on the Charlottetown Accord, which demonstrated the determination of Quebec Métis to take charge of their collective destiny:

We the Métis People of the province of Quebec are distinct Aboriginal People in the province of Quebec and in Canada. We will no longer remain in the back seat of First Nations dreams, hoping for their good will. We the Métis people have a right to the front seat and we are taking it.[61]

Ontario

There is a difference of opinion about how far east the homeland of the Métis Nation extends. There can be little doubt that the Great Lakes region was important for that part of Métis Nation culture that draws on Quebec antecedents. The difference of opinion concerns whether Métis people whose ancestors remained in Métis settlements in Ontario rather than emigrating to the prairies should be considered part of the Métis Nation. The answer to that question, in the Commission's view, is essentially political rather than historical or legal. If a community and the Métis Nation agree that the community is part of the Nation, then surely it is; otherwise, it is not. The fact that we have chosen, as a matter of convenience, to treat the Ontario Métis here rather than in the section devoted to the Métis Nation signifies nothing regarding the political question. Indeed, it may be worth noting that the political relationship between the Métis Nation and the Métis people of Ontario has changed during the term of the Commission's mandate.

It is indisputable that the distinct Métis communities of Ontario – in locations as widespread as Burleigh Falls (near Peterborough),[62] Moose Factory (on

James Bay), Sault Ste. Marie and Rainy River (in the north and west of Thunder Bay)[63] – have long and unique histories, as well as indisputable claims to recognition of their Aboriginal origins and entitlements. The Métis community at Sault Ste. Marie, a hub of early fur-trade activity, has a particularly long and eventful history. It would appear, in fact, that the area was largely under Métis control from the late seventeenth to the mid-nineteenth century. The pre-eminence of a Métis family called Langlade has been noted by historians.[64]

It is reported that in 1849 (the same year the Red River Métis organized to protest Guillaume Sayer's prosecution for free trading), Métis people of the Sault Ste. Marie area helped seize a mining operation of a Quebec-based company.[65] That event seems to have influenced the Canadian government the following year to appoint W.B. Robinson to negotiate Aboriginal treaties in the area. The Robinson treaties took some account of the Métis population, which was estimated, presumably in terms of families, to be 84 on Lake Superior and 200 on Lake Huron. Robinson commented on the matter in his official report:

> As the half-breeds at Sault Ste. Marie and other places may seek to be recognized by the Government in future payments, it may be well that I should state here the answer that I gave to their demands on the present occasion. I told them I came to treat with the chiefs who were present, that the money would be paid to them – and their receipt was sufficient for me – that when in their possession they might give as much or as little to that class of claimants as they pleased. To this no one, not even their advisers, could object, and I heard no more on the subject.[66]

There was considerably more to the question of Métis claims in the Huron and Superior area than this reference would suggest. For one thing, the claim had Indian support. Chief Shingwakance and Chief Nebenaigoching of the Ojibwa people, who led the Indian negotiating team at Sault Ste. Marie, gave commissioner Robinson a list of about 60 Métis, whose claims they submitted with the proposed text for a section of a treaty that would have provided 100-acre grants from the Ojibwa lands to the Métis individuals named. While acknowledging that the Indians could allocate some of their treaty land to the Métis, Robinson was unwilling to include such a provision in the treaty.[67] He may have feared that Indians might then claim a correspondingly larger share of public lands or that openly recognizing Métis entitlements would create a precedent.

The idea that Métis people had an Aboriginal entitlement distinct from that of their Indian relatives was not a novel concept to those who took part in the Robinson treaty negotiations in 1850. A treaty between the Ojibwa and the United States government, signed at Fond du Lac on Lake Superior in 1826, had called for 640-acre allocations to designated "halfbreeds". That treaty provision had been the model for the draft provision that Shingwakance and

Nebenaigoching had unsuccessfully urged Robinson to accept. In 1836 an American treaty with Ojibwa of northern Wisconsin and Michigan had provided for the distribution of $150,000 in cash among "halfbreed relatives" of the Indians covered by the treaty.

Although he rejected special treatment of "halfbreed" claims in the treaties, Robinson did agree that "Canadians resident on the lands just surrendered at Sault Ste. Marie" should be "liberally dealt with" in connection with "land on which they have long resided and have made improvements". These "Canadians", most of whom were Métis, were advised to petition the government with their claim, and when they did (stressing their Aboriginal connections rather than their old settler status), Robinson urged the government to give them favourable consideration. What came of the idea was an offer to allow them to buy back 50 acres of their own land for 1 shilling per acre, a fee intended to help the government recoup surveying and patenting costs.

Precisely how many Métis individuals acquired land under this buy-back scheme is not clear. A few certainly did, but a recent study of the question concludes: "It appears...that few Métis obtained patents". More Métis chose to be treated as Indians, live on reserves and accept treaty benefits, but that group is also difficult to quantify. By no means all Métis people in the areas covered by the Robinson treaties sought treaty status, and not all who did so were accepted. It depended, in part, on who was responsible for administering the treaties in particular areas. Those administered by Hudson's Bay Company officials seem more likely to have included Métis people, while those administered by the chiefs were less likely to include them, though some chiefs were willing to do so. After 1875, however, when the government took over distributing treaty benefits, it made a major effort to eliminate Métis people from the rolls.[68]

While an accurate reckoning of the proportion of Great Lakes Métis who received treaty benefits or land grants will never be possible, it seems likely that it is small. A recent study of the Robinson treaties states:

> One group of Aboriginal people...derived very little benefit from the treaties. These were the Métis, whose settlements in 1850 dotted the upper Great Lakes region. If it was better to be Ojibway in Canada than in the United States...it was far worse to be a Halfbreed.[69]

At Rainy River in 1873, an agreement was struck between government representatives and the Métis community, as a distinct collectivity, on a 'halfbreed adhesion' to Treaty 3.[70] However, the political fall-out from the Métis uprising at Red River contaminated Métis-government relations and spawned federal policies that increasingly deprived Métis people of their Aboriginal entitlements. The 'halfbreed adhesion' was repudiated by government, and the Métis of Rainy River found themselves, much as their compatriots elsewhere in Ontario, frozen out of treaty benefits .

In 1905, when Treaty 9 was being negotiated, the government's treaty commissioners encountered a major Métis presence in the Moose Factory area. By that time there was no longer any question of bargaining with the Métis as a group. Those who had been assimilated to the Indian way of life were generally given treaty status, but those who asserted Métis identity were offered scrip under the *Dominion Lands Act.*[71]

The Métis community at Burleigh Falls, which has deep historical roots, consists of persons whose forebears took treaty status in the early and mid-nineteenth century but who gradually lost their treaty rights by marrying non-status men or through other forms of enfranchisement. They have actively asserted their Métis identity and rights as a group since at least 1975.[72]

3.2 Looking at the Present, Looking Toward the Future

The 'other' Métis are better organized now than they have ever been. They have established democratic organizations that could in time evolve into full-fledged instruments of self-government. Although they are not so elaborately organized as the Métis Nation, they are nonetheless fully prepared to work for the best interests of their members, and they are anxious to take their rightful place at bargaining tables where those interests are being discussed. The Métis of Labrador may well have reached nationhood status, and other Métis soon will follow suit. In the meantime, all major communities of Métis seem well equipped to engage in interim discussions concerning their future.

Among the activities in which their organizations are engaged is the defence of their right, as Aboriginal people, to pursue resource harvesting. The Métis of Labrador, for instance, are currently engaged in litigation against fishing and hunting restrictions imposed by government authorities. They hope the courts will rule that they have the right to hunt and fish without restriction, because their Aboriginal right to do so was never lawfully extinguished.

As with the Métis Nation, other Métis are deeply concerned about their place in Canada's future. To a considerable extent, in fact, their present is preoccupied with their future. Generally speaking, other Métis share the goals of the Métis Nation, but their aspirations and approaches differ in significant ways from those of the Métis Nation. The following observations are brief because they focus primarily on those differences.

Nation-to-nation relations

Like their western counterparts, other Métis want to be fully responsible for their own fate. They want to be represented separately, as much as possible, in negotiations about their future relations with Canada. This is a natural consequence of recognition of nationhood.

With groupings of Métis communities whose nationhood may not be developed fully enough for recognition, complete independent representation may be put off. It is likely, however, that considerable immediate independence on certain issues would be appropriate and practicable for some communities.

Because their political structures are less well developed in some respects than those of the Métis Nation, and because they are labouring under stringent economic circumstances, other Métis need financial support to help them perfect their organizations and make preparations for effective negotiation and implementation of governance arrangements. Indeed, as we noted in the chapter on self-government (see Volume 2, Chapter 3), even fully emerged Aboriginal nations need interim funding to assist in nation building. Other Métis, like all Aboriginal people reconstructing their nations, should have access to such funds.

Sections 91(24) and 35

Other Métis concur that section 91(24) of the *Constitution Act, 1867* must be amended to confirm that it applies to all Aboriginal peoples, and they also seek assurance that section 35 of the *Constitution Act, 1982* applies to all Métis, not just to those who are part of the Métis Nation. In fact, they want confirmation that they are Métis within the meaning of section 35.

Education, culture and language

Other Métis feel as strongly as the members of the Métis Nation about the need for federal, provincial and territorial measures to preserve and enhance Métis cultures, Métis use of Aboriginal languages, and education for and about Métis people if they are to survive as a people. Unlike the Métis Nation, they have no distinct language to protect, but encouraging and assisting their use of Aboriginal languages is equally important to them. As to other aspects of their cultures, especially their history, other Métis have a greater need for assistance because their stories are not as well known as those of their western counterparts.

Land and resource base

Other Métis contend that the case for their having an existing, unextinguished Aboriginal entitlement to land and resource use is as strong as that of the Métis Nation. There were few, if any, attempts to extinguish their Aboriginal title to land as in the west under the *Manitoba Act* and *Dominion Lands Act*. The legal right of other Métis to negotiate land claims settlements is therefore difficult to dispute. In the case of the Labrador Métis people, there is no doubt they can negotiate directly, but for other eastern Métis communities the means of conducting negotiations must be given careful consideration.

Self-government

Like the representatives of the Métis Nation, organizations of other Métis are anxious to talk to federal, provincial, Aboriginal, territorial and municipal politicians about implementing the inherent Aboriginal right of self-government. This will be easier for the Labrador Métis than for less fully developed Métis communities of the east, but even there some progress toward eventual self-government may be possible.

Benefit program compensation and parity

Other Métis have been as much the victims of government discrimination as members of the Métis Nation, with the result that they too are in grave need of catch-up measures in almost every area. Because their level of organization is not as mature as that of the Métis Nation and therefore not as well equipped to take over their own benefit programs, they require more external assistance than the western Métis. They also require a guarantee against discrimination in new programs.

Conclusion

Even if they were looked upon as a homogeneous collectivity, other Métis would constitute a minority within a minority within a minority: they are a neglected fragment of Canada's Métis population, which is itself a small and too often overlooked part of the larger Aboriginal minority. Other Métis are not a homogeneous collectivity, of course. They include many discrete communities and groups. Few Canadians are more exposed by their ethnicity to the risks of isolation and alienation than other Métis.

Yet other Métis have made remarkable progress toward winning recognition as founding partners of Canadian society and securing the benefits to which that partnership entitles them. Their determination to finish the job is evident. We believe that the other Métis, with assistance of the type we have recommended, can create a future characterized by full participation in Canadian affairs as integral, though distinct, elements of the Aboriginal universe.

As mentioned at the beginning of this section, we have not made separate recommendations for other Métis. While their uniqueness is unquestionable, we believe their needs can be met by the application to them, with appropriate changes, of the general principles underlying the recommendations previously made.

NOTES

1. For an explanation of the plural word 'peoples', see the discussion of Métis cultures and communities below.

2. The Commission takes no position on which areas and communities should be considered part of the Métis Nation; that is a matter for the Métis Nation and the communities in question to determine for themselves. The population figures

mentioned in this chapter are cited for the sole purpose of indicating the relative sizes of the Métis populations of each province and territory.

3. See note 4 and accompanying text.

4. See Dale Gibson, "The Beneficiaries of Section 35" (forthcoming). Harry W. Daniels, who was instrumental as president of the Native Council of Canada, in negotiating the inclusion of section 35(2) in the *Constitution Act, 1982*, contends that it was intended to cover all Métis people and non-status Indians, regardless of where they lived in Canada. The government of Newfoundland and Labrador has taken the position, as expressed in its letter to the Commission on 18 March 1994, that while it "recognizes there are people of aboriginal descent in the province who identify themselves as 'métis', it does not agree that they are "Métis" within the meaning of section 35(1) of the *Constitution Act (1982)*". See Appendix 5F.

5. *Re the term 'Indians'*, [1939] S.C.R. 104; [1939] 2 D.L.R. 417 at 433 per J. Kerwin.

6. Peter W. Hogg, *Constitutional Law of Canada*, 3rd Edition, (supplemented) (Scarborough, Ontario: Carswell 1992); C. Chartier, "'Indian': An Analysis of the Term as Used in Section 91(24) of the B.N.A. Act" (1978) 43 Sask. L. Rev. (1978-79) 37; and Bradford W. Morse and John Giokas, "Do the Métis Fall Within Section 91(24) of the *Constitution Act, 1867?*", in *Aboriginal Self-Government: Legal and Constitutional Issues* (Ottawa: RCAP, 1995). A contrary view was expressed by Bryan Schwartz in *First Principles, Second Thoughts: Aboriginal Peoples, Constitutional Reform and Canadian Statecraft* (Montreal: Institute for Research on Public Policy, 1986), p. 245.

7. Public Inquiry into the Administration of Justice and Aboriginal People, *Report of the Aboriginal Justice Inquiry of Manitoba*, Volume 1: *The Justice System and Aboriginal People* (Winnipeg: Queen's Printer, 1991).

8. In her article, "Métis d'Oka condamnés à l'exode", *Recherches amérindiennes au Québec* 12/2 (1982), Michelle Sarrazin explains how some Métis were forced to leave their homes because of municipal housing policies.

9. See Appendix 5A. The inclusion of Sault Ste. Marie as part of the Métis Nation homeland is not intended to express a position on the extent of that homeland, a question that is subject to dispute. We refer to Sault Ste. Marie here only as a reminder that however far the homeland can be considered to extend, some of its inhabitants have historical links with Métis communities in the Great Lakes basin.

10. Pieter Jan Bakker, "'A Language of Our Own': The Genesis of Michif, the Mixed Cree-French Language of the Canadian Métis", PH.D. dissertation, Drukkerij Universiteit van Amsterdam, 1992, pp. 1-2.

11. See Roy St. George Stubbs, *Four Recorders of Rupert's Land: A Brief Survey of the Hudson's Bay Company Courts of Rupert's Land* (Winnipeg: Peguis Publishers, 1967), p. 30.

12. See Maggie Siggins, *Riel: A Life of Revolution* (Toronto: Harper Collins, 1994), p. 67; and W.L. Morton, *Manitoba: Birth of a Province* (Altona, Manitoba: Manitoba Record Society, 1965).

13. Legally, this is an open question. See discussion of surrender in Appendix 5A.

14. Siggins, *Riel* (cited in note 12), p. 191.

15. Thomas Flanagan, *Metis Lands in Manitoba* (Calgary: University of Calgary Press, 1991).

16. Dale Gibson and Lee Gibson, "Who was Gilbert McMicken?" (1986, unpublished).

17. D.N. Sprague, *Canada and the Métis, 1869-1885* (Waterloo, Ontario: Wilfrid Laurier University Press, 1988), p. 125.

18. See D.N. Sprague, "Government Lawlessness in the Administration of Manitoba Land Claims, 1870-1887" (1980) 10 Man. L.J. 415.

19. Paul L.A.H. Chartrand, *Manitoba's Métis Settlement Scheme of 1870* (Saskatoon: Native Law Centre, University of Saskatchewan, 1991), p. 32.

20. *An Act respecting the appropriation of certain Dominion Lands In Manitoba*, S.C. 1874, c. 20.

21. *House of Commons Debates*, 6 July 1885, p. 3114.

22. *An Act respecting the Public Lands of the Dominion [Dominion Lands Act]*, S.C. 1872, c. 23, s. 42.

23. *An Act to amend and consolidate the several Acts respecting the Public Lands of the Dominion [Dominion Lands Act 1879]*, S.C. 1879, c. 31, s. 125(e).

24. See, generally, Bob Beal and Rod Macleod, *Prairie Fire: The 1885 North-West Rebellion* (Edmonton: Hurtig Publishers, 1984); and Siggins, *Riel* (cited in note 12), p. 327. The war was not just a Métis affair. See also A. Blair Stonechild, "The Indian View of the 1885 Uprising", in F. Laurie Barron and James B. Waldram, eds., *1885 and After: Native Society in Transition* (Regina: Canadian Plains Research Centre, 1986), p. 166. Reference is made to the hanging of eight Cree people at Regina, apparently for their part in the war.

25. T.C. Pocklington, *The Government and Politics of the Alberta Metis Settlements* (Regina: Canadian Plains Research Centre, 1991), p. 7.

26. *Constitution Act, 1930*, S.C. 1930, reprinted in R.S.C. 1985, Appendix II, No. 26, Schedule (1) Manitoba, s. 13; schedule (2) Alberta, s. 12.

27. See Pocklington, *Alberta Metis Settlements* (cited in note 25); and Catherine E. Bell, *Alberta's Metis Settlements Legislation: An Overview of Ownership and Management of Settlement Lands* (Regina: Canadian Plains Research Centre, University of Regina, 1994). Professor Bell is currently engaged in a major study of dispute resolution in the settlements.

28. Pocklington, *Alberta Metis Settlements*, p. 27.

29. *Constitution of Alberta Amendment Act, 1990*, S.A. 1990, c. C-22.2. See Bell, *Alberta's Metis Settlements Legislation*.

30. Translated by Elizabeth Maguet and republished in 1982 as *Hold High Your Heads, History of the Métis Nation in Western Canada* (Winnipeg: Pemmican Publications, 1982). Other studies of Métis history include Marcel Giraud, *The Métis in the Canadian West*, trans. George Woodcock (Lincoln and London: University of Nebraska Press, 1986); and Antoine S. Lussier and D. Bruce Sealey, eds., *The Other Natives: Les Métis*, 2 vols. (Winnipeg: Manitoba Métis Federation Press and Éditions Bois-Brûlés, 1978). Most historians seem to agree, however, that the definitive history of the Métis has yet to be written.

31. Métis National Council, transcripts of the hearings of the Royal Commission on Aboriginal Peoples [hereafter RCAP transcripts], Ottawa, Ontario, 4 November 1993. See *A Note About Sources* at the beginning of this volume for information about transcripts and other Commission publications.

32. The Métis Nation Accord did not include all provinces. At that point, only five provinces joined federal representatives in agreeing to sign the accord. They were, however, the provinces within which the Métis Nation lies: the three prairie provinces, Ontario and British Columbia. The government of the Northwest Territories later entered into the agreement as well.

33. The asterisk meant that a political accord was to be used. For the proposed text of that accord, see Appendix 5E.

34. Pocklington, *Alberta Metis Settlements* (cited in note 25); and Bell, *Alberta's Metis Settlements Legislation* (cited in note 27).

35. The separate school guarantees in section 93 (*Constitution Act, 1867* (U.K.), 30 & 31 Vict., c. 3, reprinted in R.S.C. 1985, App II, No. 5) are too lengthy to quote in full. The central guarantee is found in section 93(1), which states that nothing in any provincial statute about education "shall prejudicially affect any Right or Privilege with respect to Denominational Schools which any Class of Persons have by Law in the Province at the Union". This protection has been held to extend to the right of members of the denomination in question to manage their own schools: *Roman Catholic Separate Schools of Ottawa* v. *Ottawa* [1917] A.C. 76. Because the only denominational schools whose supporters possessed rights or privileges "by law...at the union" in 1867 were Protestant and Roman Catholic, only schools of those faiths are protected by section 93.

36. This guarantee is also too long to quote in full. Among other things, it ensures that any Canadian citizen "whose first language learned and still understood" is English or French, or who "received their primary school instruction in Canada" in one of those languages, and who resides in a province where that first language or primary school language is "the language of the English or French linguistic minority population of the province", has the right to have his or her children "receive their primary and secondary school education in that language in that province" (section

23(1)). That right includes, where numbers warrant, receiving that instruction "in minority language educational facilities provided out of public funds", but applies only "wherever in the province the number of children of citizens who have such a right is sufficient to warrant the provision to them out of public funds of minority language instruction" (section 23(3)). As with separate school rights under section 93, this right extends to management of the minority language schools by members of the minority. That point was established, along with several others, by the Supreme Court of Canada in *Mahe* v. *Alberta*, [1990] 1 S.C.R. 342.

37. Giselle Marcotte, Gabriel Dumont Institute Research and Development Team, RCAP transcripts, Saskatoon, Saskatchewan, 28 October 1992; and Gerald Morin, President, Métis National Council, RCAP transcripts, Ottawa, Ontario, 4 November 1993.

38. Although Michif is often referred to as a single language, it is in fact a related group of Indian-French linguistic blends.

39. Statistics Canada, 1991 Aboriginal Peoples Survey, Catalogue No. 89-533 (hereafter APS).

40. Bakker, "'A Language of Our Own'" (cited in note 10), p. 2.

41. Statistics Canada, APS (cited in note 39).

42. Patline Laverdure and Ida Rose Allard, *The Michif Dictionary: Turtle Mountain Chippewa Cree*, ed. John C. Crawford (Winnipeg: Pemmican Publications, 1983).

43. Métis people claim to be 'Indians' within the meaning of the *Rupert's Land and North-Western Territory Order* of 23 June 1870. It probably does not matter whether the order in council applies to them since the fiduciary duty of the provincial and federal governments, in any event, is rooted in common law. See Appendix 5A.

44. *Constitution Act, 1930* (cited in note 26).

45. See Sprague, *Canada and the Métis* (cited in note 17).

46. See Flanagan, *Metis Lands in Manitoba* (cited in note 15).

47. RCAP, *Partners in Confederation: Aboriginal Peoples, Self-Government, and the Constitution* (Ottawa: Supply and Services, 1993).

48. This section draws on Martin F. Dunn, "All My Relations – The Other Métis", research study prepared for the Royal Commission on Aboriginal Peoples [RCAP] (1994). For information about research studies prepared for RCAP, see *A Note About Sources* at the beginning of this volume. The appropriateness of describing the people discussed in this section as 'Métis' is disputed by some. See our discussion earlier in the chapter on the differing uses of the term 'Métis'.

49. See Olive Patricia Dickason, "From 'One Nation' in the Northeast to 'New Nation' in the Northwest: A Look at the Emergence of the Métis", *American Indian Culture and Research Journal* 6/2 (1982). A revised version appears in Peterson and

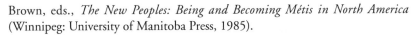

Brown, eds., *The New Peoples: Being and Becoming Métis in North America* (Winnipeg: University of Manitoba Press, 1985).

50. See J.C. Kennedy, *People of the Bays and Headlands: Anthropological History and the Fate of Communities in the Unknown Labrador* (Toronto: University of Toronto Press, 1995); and J.C. Kennedy, *Labrador Village* (Prospect Heights, Illinois: Waveland Press, 1996). The position of the government of Newfoundland and Labrador on the status of Métis people in that province is described in note 4 and in Appendix 5F.

51. Kirk Lethbridge, Labrador Métis Association, RCAP transcripts, Sheshatshiu, Newfoundland and Labrador, 17 June 1992.

52. See Jacqueline Louise Peterson, "The People in Between: Indian-White Marriage and the Genesis of a Metis Society and Culture in the Great Lakes Region, 1680-1830", PH.D. thesis, University of Illinois, 1981.

53. See Olive Patricia Dickason, *Louisbourg and the Indians: A Study in Imperial Race Relations, 1713-1760* (Ottawa: Supply and Services, 1976).

54. A photocopy of the 1758 map was provided to the Commission by the Skigin-Elnoog Housing Corporation of Fredericton, New Brunswick. Its provenance has not been confirmed, however. Of course, the presence of the word Métis on a map does not necessarily confirm the presence of a Métis population there.

55. "The Métis of New Brunswick", Report to Native Council of Canada, October 1984.

56. No metaphor can reflect a complex historical phenomenon accurately. In reality, the French elements of the Métis Nation culture were themselves conceived, gestated and born in many different locations.

57. See Dickason, *Louisbourg and the Indians* (cited in note 53); Dickason, "From 'One Nation' in the Northeast" (cited in note 49); Peterson, "The People in Between" (cited in note 52); Peterson, "Prelude to Red River: A Social Portrait of the Great Lakes Métis", *Ethnohistory* 25/1 (Winter 1978), p. 41; and Isabelle Perrault, "Traite et métissage: un aspect du peuplement de la Nouvelle France", *Recherches amérindiennes au Québec* 12/2 (1982), pp. 86-94.

58. The Laurentian alliance of Métis and non-status Indians has also commissioned research about their demographic situation in Quebec. See Danielle Gauvreau, Francine Bernèche and Juan A. Fernandez, "La Population des Métis et des Indiens sans statut: essai d'estimation et distribution spatiale", *Recherches amérindiennes au Québec* 12/2 (1982), pp. 95-103.

59. Sylvie Plouffe, Métis Nation of Quebec, RCAP transcripts, Montreal, Quebec, 28 May 1993 [translation].

60. Réjean Pilote, Métis Nation of Quebec, RCAP transcripts, Montreal, Quebec, 28 May 1993 [translation].

61. Native Alliance of Quebec, "Moratorium, The Métis People of the Province of Quebec", tabled at the consultation forum of the Native Alliance of Quebec on the Charlottetown Accord, Campbell's Bay, October 1992. The Native Alliance of Quebec appeared before the Commission at hearings in Montreal on 1 December 1993.

62. We understand that residents of Burleigh Falls have recently been restored to *Indian Act* status. While that development illustrates the political nature of many identity issues, it cannot obliterate the historical association of Burleigh Falls with Métis people.

63. Other early Métis settlements were formed at Penetanguishene on Georgian Bay, Shebandowan (Killarney) on Lake Huron east of Manitoulin Island, and Gachkiwang (Pembroke) on St. Joseph's Island. James Morrison, "The Robinson Treaties of 1850: A Case Study", research study prepared for RCAP (1993).

64. See Brad Morley, "Charles de Langlade, 'Riel' of the Lakes", *Invisible Natives, Dimensions* Special Editions 8/3 (June/July 1980), p. 19; Peterson, "The People in Between" (cited in note 52), Carolyn Harrington, "Sault: First Capital", *Invisible Natives*, p. 8; Ontario Metis and Non-Status Indian Association [OMNSIA], "The Development of a Halfbreed Community in the Upper Great Lakes", Ontario Métis and Non-Status Indian Association Report, 1979; "Historical Survey of the Relationship Between Half Breeds and the Wars which were Part of the Social Milieu of Eastern North America", in summary field report for OMNSIA, 1979; and "Métis Middlemen Heart of Frontier Community", *Invisible Natives*, p. 22. (OMNSIA is now the Ontario Metis and Aboriginal Association.)

65. See Harrington, "Sault: First Capital"; K. Noble, "Field Report on Robinson Treaties Area", summary field report for the Ontario Métis and Non-Status Indian Association, 1979, p. 48; and Morrison, "The Robinson Treaties" (cited in note 63).

66. Alexander Morris, *The Treaties of Canada with the Indians of Manitoba and the North-West Territories* (Toronto: Belfords, Clarke & Co., 1880), p. 20.

67. Morrison, "The Robinson Treaties" (cited in note 63), from which the following account is drawn.

68. Dunn, "All My Relations" (cited in note 48).

69. Morrison, "The Robinson Treaties" (cited in note 63).

70. W. Moss, "Métis Adhesion to Treaty 3", summary of field report for OMNSIA, 1979; E.B. Borron, "Report on Indian Claims Arising Out of the Northwest Angle Treaty #3", Archives of Ontario, F1027 Irving Papers, 30/36/6(2), 1893; and Gail Lem, "A Chronology of the Adhesion by the Half-Breeds of Rainy River and Lake", Native Council of Canada, 1977.

71. J. Long, "The Métis of Treaty #9", OMNSIA, 1979.

72. Kawartha Branch, OMNSIA, 1978.

Appendix 5A

General Sources of Métis Rights˙

The sources of Métis rights are diverse. While some are shared with all Aboriginal peoples, others are Métis-specific. Some rights are common to all Métis people, others attach to particular Métis groups. Many grow from Aboriginal roots, but some are of more recent origin. Some are widely accepted, others are controversial. Some are legal in nature, others are moral or political. The general sources of rights applicable to all Métis people are examined briefly here. Sources specific to the Métis Nation are dealt with in Appendices 5B and 5C. The present discussion of general sources begins with those that relate to legal rights, considered in roughly chronological order, and concludes with moral and political sources. Categories often overlap, and the lines between them sometimes blur. The gulf between legal and moral or political sources is crossed by several bridges.

It is hoped that this preliminary examination of general sources will facilitate an understanding of the more detailed discussions of particular rights in Appendices 5B and 5C. While those discussions focus on rights that are Métis-specific, it is important to appreciate the relationship between those rights and the entitlements that Métis people share with the other Aboriginal peoples of Canada. Therefore, although a full analysis of the rights of all Aboriginal peoples would not be appropriate here, the general principles involved are reviewed briefly as a backdrop to an overview of Métis rights.

1. Legal Sources

Legal systems are human constructs, shaped by politically organized societies to serve their particular ends. They have no application beyond the societies for which they were designed or to which they have been extended. The common law of England does not apply to France, for example, and the civil law of France does not apply to England or to countries that inherited English law (although Quebec's civil law is rooted in Quebec's French inheritance). A threshold question to be answered before launching a discussion of legal rights applicable to Métis and other Aboriginal peoples, therefore, is whether the legal system in question is European-based or Aboriginally based.

For purposes of this discussion, the viewpoint is that of Canada's formal European-rooted legal structure. This approach is not intended to deny the existence of an Aboriginal legal order independent of the European-based order or

---

˙ This appendix was prepared for the Commission by Dale Gibson, Belzberg Fellow of Constitutional Studies, University of Alberta.

to suggest that one is superior to the other. It is simply a recognition of the fact that 'legality' is an empty notion outside the context of a specific legal system and an indication that the European-rooted legal context has been chosen as the basis for this particular analysis. That choice was dictated by the fact that the Royal Commission on Aboriginal Peoples was created under and is subject to the governmental structure of Canada (which has European origins), of which legal systems are but a part. The Commission's recommendations will also be implemented in the setting of that governmental and legal system.

The argument is sometimes made that even from the perspective of Euro-Canadian legal systems, non-Aboriginal governments did not acquire the right to assert legislative control over Aboriginal people in some parts of what is now Canada until well after they began purporting to do so.[1] The basis for this argument is the principle that legal sovereignty over a territory cannot be acquired by mere assertion; the claim must be supported by 'effective occupation' of the territory. As to those parts of North America included in the Hudson's Bay Company (HBC) charter of 1670, by which Charles II of England ceded the entire Hudson Bay drainage area (known as Rupert's Land) to the company, the argument contends that the company never exerted 'effective control'.

Those who hold that view claim that neither French and British control over eastern Rupert's Land nor the Hudson's Bay Company's fur trade operations and occupation of trading posts in western Rupert's Land amounted to sufficient effective occupation to displace Aboriginal control (at least not beyond the immediate environs of trading posts and non-Aboriginal settlements). Thus, they conclude that early English and Canadian legislation that purported to affect Aboriginal peoples in the area covered by the HBC charter was not legally valid. They acknowledge that effective control was established in later years, but they argue that this was not until after significant post-Confederation legislation had been enacted. If they are right, it means, for example, that the *Dominion Lands Act* of the 1870s, which had a major impact on Métis people in the northwest, was a nullity. This is so, they say, because Canada's claim to jurisdiction over Rupert's Land was founded on the transfer of Rupert's Land in 1869 from the company to the British Crown and subsequently to the Canadian government. If the Hudson's Bay Company did not possess Rupert's Land in the first place, there was nothing to transfer to Britain or Canada.

There are some difficulties with that thesis. It may well overestimate the degree of control needed to establish effective occupation for legal purposes and underestimate the degree of control actually exercised in Rupert's Land. The effect of Lord Selkirk's colonizing efforts at Red River and of his 1817 treaty with Indian nations of the area deserves to be considered, for example, as does the significance of the *Canada Jurisdiction Act, 1803*, a statute setting out juridical arrangements for Rupert's Land.[2]

Assuming, however, that the historical analysis of these critics is correct, it does not alter the foregoing conclusions about the current state of the law concerning Aboriginal legal rights. This is so because of a legal principle known as the *de facto* doctrine, according to which acts done and rights acquired in good-faith reliance upon laws generally thought to be valid at the time will not be nullified by subsequent discovery that the laws in question were unconstitutional.[3] Legal rights will, therefore, be analyzed on the assumption that the Euro-Canadian legal system was fully applicable from the first.

The fact that the following legal analysis is based on the formal Euro-Canadian legal system is subject, however, to two very important qualifications. One is that Canadian law itself recognizes and incorporates Aboriginal rights.[4] The other is that not all rights are legal rights. The moral and political rights of the Métis peoples, which may well outweigh legal rights in certain respects, are considered at the conclusion of the legal analysis.

1.1 The Starting Point: Aboriginal Rights

Most legal rights of Métis peoples are rooted, directly or indirectly, in Aboriginal rights.[5] Since 1982, the strongest legal basis for making that connection to Aboriginal rights is section 35(1) of the *Constitution Act, 1982*, which states that "the existing Aboriginal and treaty rights of the Aboriginal peoples of Canada are hereby recognized and affirmed", and section 35(2) of the same instrument, which defines Aboriginal peoples to include "the Indian, Inuit and Métis peoples of Canada". It is important to understand, however, that section 35 does not grant Aboriginal rights in itself. Aboriginal rights existed before the 1982 constitution. They predate the existence of Canada, in fact, having their origins in the earliest indigenous societies of North America. As Chief Justice Dickson said on behalf of the Supreme Court of Canada in *Guerin* v. *The Queen*, Aboriginal rights are legal rights "derived from the Indian's historic occupation and possession of their tribal lands".[6]

Because the rights recognized and affirmed by section 35 are described as "existing", their extent is determined in part by the state of Aboriginal rights immediately before April 1982, when section 35(1) came into effect. The following analysis of Aboriginal rights begins with an examination of the extent to which they were embodied in principles of law inherited by Canada from the United Kingdom. We go on to consider the impact of Indian treaties and of legislation and constitutional provisions.

Aboriginal rights in general

Aboriginal rights are legal rights. The common law, which applies to all parts of Canada in matters relating to the Crown and its obligations, recognizes unextinguished Aboriginal rights as giving rise to enforceable legal obligations. The Supreme Court of Canada has so held in several rulings.[7]

This means, for example, that Aboriginal title to unsurrendered land (a right of occupancy that can be sold to no one except the Crown) is a common law right. The right to hunt, trap and fish, as well as to exploit natural resources in other ways, is another aspect of Aboriginal rights. Extending well beyond land and resources rights is the freedom to participate in and perpetuate Aboriginal cultures in all of their many aspects. One of the most fundamental of Aboriginal rights is the inherent right of self-government, described in our constitutional discussion paper, *Partners in Confederation*.[8] All peoples of the world have the right to create their own governmental arrangements, and at the point of first contact with Europeans, the Aboriginal peoples of North America were politically organized and effectively governed.

It must be understood, however, that although Aboriginal rights, including the right of Aboriginal self-government, were legally recognized, they were never considered to be either absolute or perpetual legal rights. They could be surrendered or modified by treaty, and they could be altered or abolished by statute. Extinguishment by statute was legally possible because it was always assumed by common law that the paramount government, with control over everybody, Aboriginal people and Europeans alike, was the one that derived its ultimate legal authority from the Parliament of England. As Chief Justice Dickson explained in *R. v. Sparrow*, the Supreme Court's celebrated first decision on section 35, "there was from the outset never any doubt that sovereignty and legislative power, and indeed the underlying title, to such lands vested in the Crown".[9] By Crown, he was undoubtedly referring to all organs of British government, including Parliament, where legislative matters were concerned.

Commentators have condemned the lack of ethical legitimacy of this approach, as well as the specious natural law reasoning by which early scholarly apologists of colonialism attempted to justify its morality. Some have even questioned its legality.[10] It seems unlikely, however, that Canadian courts will ever abandon this view as the historical foundation of their approach to Aboriginal legal rights.

However, as explained in *Partners in Confederation*, Aboriginal rights that were not fully extinguished before 1982, including the right of self-government, are no longer subject to being overridden by statute. Since the entrenchment of existing Aboriginal rights in section 35(1) of the *Constitution Act, 1982*, the only way to limit them is by agreement, by constitutional amendment, or by the limited legislative regulatory powers referred to in the *Sparrow* decision.

An important question, about which opinion is far from unanimous, concerns the extent to which the Aboriginal rights recognized and affirmed by section 35 are to be defined by history. The Canadian constitution has long been held by the highest judicial authorities to be a 'living tree', capable of growth over time.[11] This has led some to speculate that section 35, enacted in 1982, may have grafted onto the living tree a new kind of Aboriginal rights appropriate for the contemporary circumstances of Aboriginal peoples in Canada. They suggest that the word 'existing' in section 35 should be construed as referring to rights suitable for conditions in 1982 and the future, rather than for times gone by. If so, we would not need an historical analysis to show whether ancient rights have been extinguished, the only question being whether those rights are appropriate according to the contemporary values of Canadian society. While it is difficult to believe that Canadian courts will accept this approach completely, some of its elements assist an understanding of the constitutional guarantee of existing Aboriginal rights in section 35.

History cannot be ignored altogether. Aboriginality is an historical notion. The word itself derives from the Latin for 'from the beginning'. Although the word 'existing' in section 35 undoubtedly places the focus on contemporary circumstances, it must be remembered that it is only existing *Aboriginal* rights of Canada's Aboriginal peoples that are constitutionally recognized and affirmed, not *every* right they may hold. What evidence there is concerning the purpose of inserting the word existing in section 35 late in the drafting process suggests that it was intended to reassure provincial politicians, some of whom were reluctant to entrench the rights of Aboriginal peoples, that no new rights would be created and that rights previously extinguished would remain extinguished.[12]

On the other hand, the law does not require the rights of Aboriginal peoples to be locked forever in the grip of history's dead hand. Some early authorities did, it is true, take a 'frozen rights' approach to Aboriginal entitlements. There was, for example, a 1979 trial-level decision of the Federal Court of Canada, *Baker Lake* v. *Minister of Indian Affairs*, in which, while ruling that Inuit of the Baker Lake area of the Northwest Territories held unextinguished Aboriginal title to the area, Justice Mahoney stated that those who assert Aboriginal title must prove, among other things, that the claimants and their ancestors were members of an organized society that occupied the specific territory claimed, to the exclusion of other organized societies, before sovereignty was asserted by the Crown. Moreover, he said, the common law "can give effect only to those incidents of...enjoyment [of land] that were, themselves, given effect to by the [Aboriginal] regime that prevailed before".[13] Brian Slattery's widely respected study of Aboriginal rights in Canada takes issue with this frozen rights approach, pointing out that it "forces Aboriginal title into a mould familiar to English law, while disregarding the factors peculiar to its origins", and the Supreme Court of Canada eventually approved of his position, concluding: "Clearly, then, an approval to the constitutional guarantee embodied in section 35(1) which would incorporate 'frozen rights' must be rejected".[14] It is probably necessary for a group claiming Aboriginal title to show possession for "a substantial period", which Slattery explains as being sufficient to establish "an enduring relationship with the lands in question" and to "defeat the claims of previous native possessors and to resist newcomers".[15] As to the precise time required, however, he takes a flexible approach:

> The requisite length of time depends on the circumstances, but in most cases a period of twenty to fifty years would seem adequate.

> Time is less important for its own sake than for what it says about the nature of the group's relationship with the land and the overall merits of their claim.[16]

All that needs to be established is sufficient prior occupation to remove any doubt about the genuineness and intended permanence of possession by the claimants' Aboriginal ancestors.

In short, contemporary Aboriginal rights are nourished by both historical and modern factors. In attempting to understand the interaction of past and present, it may be helpful to note that section 35 applies the adjective 'Aboriginal' to two different nouns: rights and peoples. The interplay of historical and contemporary elements is probably different in those two contexts.

Identifying the Aboriginal peoples to whom the guarantees of section 35 belong may call for a more contemporary approach than determining the content of Aboriginal rights. Since constitutional guarantees exist for the benefit of present and future Canadians, not for those who have passed from the scene, it makes sense that the groups that constitute Canada's Aboriginal peoples should be groups with which *today's* Aboriginal peoples identify. If a new community of Aboriginal persons springs up somewhere, or an old one reorganizes, it is the new grouping upon whose membership the Aboriginal rights should devolve. As Catherine Bell has observed,

> traditional and contemporary cultures, customs and lifestyles become more important when defining entitlement to, and the content of, aboriginal rights rather than being determinative of whether a group is 'aboriginal.'[17]

It is unlikely that even the judge who decided the *Baker Lake* case would disagree with that assessment. He stated:

> While the existence of an organized society is a prerequisite to the existence of an aboriginal title, there appears no valid reason to demand proof of the existence of a society more elaborately structured than is necessary to demonstrate that there existed among the aborigines a recognition of the claimed rights, sufficiently defined to permit their recognition by the common law upon its advent in the territory.[18]

He added: "That their society has materially changed in recent years is of no relevance".[19]

History does have one important role in identifying Aboriginal peoples. Before a group can claim to be an Aboriginal people, it must be able to establish that it is composed, at least predominantly, of persons with Aboriginal ancestry (whether genetic or determined by marriage or adoption), in the sense that some of their forebears were living in North America before Europeans arrived. Beyond that requirement, it is probable that the term Aboriginal *peoples* in section 35 will be interpreted in a modern manner.

When we turn to the meaning of existing Aboriginal *rights* in section 35, the picture is somewhat more complex. History must play a larger role here because it is only 'existing' rights that are recognized and affirmed by section 35. If the Aboriginal rights of some Aboriginal peoples were extinguished, in whole or in part, by legitimate extinguishment mechanisms (discussed below), that extinguishment must be recognized for legal purposes, and history must be consulted to determine both its legitimacy and its extent.

History also places some broad limits on the nature of rights that can be claimed by particular peoples. It is only the *Aboriginal* rights of Aboriginal peoples that are protected by section 35, so rights that were not, as a general category, exercised by a people in pre-contact times would not be covered. To take an obvious example, no Aboriginal people could claim an Aboriginal right to form limited liability corporations, since no such entities existed in pre-contact Aboriginal societies. Nor could they claim an Aboriginal right to exemption from income tax. Probably, for the same reason, even some forms of resource exploitation would be excluded (such as diversion of a major river crossing the territory of an Aboriginal people if the result would be to interfere substantially with navigation or inflict massive deprivations on downstream users).

It is important to understand, however, that this historical restriction does not freeze Aboriginal rights in the precise shape they had before contact. As Brian Slattery has rightly said,

> [A]boriginal land rights are not confined to "traditional" uses of land. The doctrine of aboriginal title attributes to a native group a sphere of autonomy, whereby it can determine freely how to use its lands. Its decisions may be influenced, of course, by "traditional" notions, but the stronger influence in the end will likely be current needs and attitudes. For most native groups, land use is a matter of survival not nostalgia.[20]

Old rights and practices take new forms in modern times. Dog sleds are replaced by snowmobiles; Inuit art expands to embrace new media; Aboriginal religious practices are modified by new influences and changing circumstances; resource exploitation grows from hunting, fishing and trapping to include logging, mining, petroleum extraction and hydroelectric generation; education moves on from the training by parents and storytelling by elders to formal schooling at many levels. In all these respects and the many others that make up Aboriginal rights, it is important to understand that it is the contemporary versions of Aboriginal peoples' ancient prerogatives that are preserved by section 35.

Métis Aboriginal rights

Crucial to much of the discussion that follows is the question of whether Métis people are entitled to exercise existing Aboriginal rights. It can confidently be concluded that they are. The evidence from which that conclusion flows is plentiful and persuasive.

Historically, Métis people were closely linked to other Aboriginal peoples. Although the first progeny of Aboriginal mothers and European fathers were genetically both Aboriginal and European, for the most part they followed an Aboriginal lifestyle. Predominant kinship ties also tended to be with the Aboriginal community. In unions between Aboriginal women and Scottish employees of the Hudson's Bay Company, the husbands had a common tendency to treat their 'country families' as temporary, to be left behind when they retired to Scotland.[21] The French-Indian families tended to greater permanence, and their lifestyle, at least initially, was closer to Aboriginal patterns than to European ones.

Subsequently, distinctive Métis social patterns of predominantly Aboriginal character evolved in some areas, although not all persons of mixed Aboriginal and European ancestry chose to follow them. Some opted for European ways; others preferred to embrace Indian ways. Métis culture had developed most fully on the prairies, and the situation by the late nineteenth century was described by Alexander Morris thus:

> The Half-breeds in the territories are of three classes – 1st, those who, as at St. Laurent, near Prince Albert, the Qu'Appelle Lakes and Edmonton, have their farms and homes; 2nd, those who are entirely identified with the Indians, living with them and speaking their language; 3rd, those who do not farm, but live after the habits of the Indians, by the pursuit of the buffalo and the chase.[22]

Alexander Morris anticipated the complete assimilation of the first and second groups into the European and Aboriginal communities respectively. As for the third group, whom he styled "Métis",[23] he suggested that although they should not be "brought under the treaties", land should be assigned to them and assistance should be provided to them. Other evidence of acceptance that Métis persons could avail themselves of Indian status if they chose to do so is found in documents relating to early western treaties, such as the report of W.M. Simpson concerning Treaty 1:

> During the payment of the several bands, it was found that in some, and most notably in the Indian settlement and Broken Head River Band, a number of those residing among the Indians, and calling themselves Indians, are in reality half-breeds, and entitled to share in the land grant under the provisions of the Manitoba Act. I was most particular, therefore, in causing it to be explained, generally and to

individuals, that any person now electing to be classed with Indians, and receiving the Indian pay and gratuity, would, I believed, thereby forfeit his or her right to another grant as a half-breed; and in all cases where it was known that a man was a half-breed, the matter, as it affected himself and his children, was explained to him, and the choice given him to characterize himself. A very few only decided upon taking their grants as half-breeds. The explanation of this apparent sacrifice is found in the fact that the mass of these persons have lived all their lives on the Indian reserves (so called), and would rather receive such benefits as may accrue to them under the Indian treaty, than wait the realization of any value in their half-breed grant.[24]

Evidence is also found in the transcript of negotiations leading to Treaty 3:

CHIEF – I should not feel happy if I was not to mess with some of my children that are around me – those children that we call the Half-breed those that have been born of our women of Indian blood. We wish that they should be counted with us, and have their share of what you have promised. We wish you to accept our demands. It is the Half-breeds that are actually living amongst us – those that are married to our women.

GOVERNOR – I am sent here to treat with the Indians. In Red River, where I came from, and where there is a great body of Half-breeds, they must be either white or Indian. If Indians, they get treaty money; if the Half-breeds call themselves white, they get land. All I can do is to refer the matter to the Government at Ottawa, and to recommend what you wish to be granted.[25]

The significance of these observations to the present discussion is threefold:

- They indicate that Métis people were recognized, even at that relatively late date, as being entitled to assert Indian status (and thus entitled to Aboriginal rights).
- They show that the operative method of classifying persons for that purpose at the time was self-identification, regulated, presumably, by community confirmation.
- They confirm that Métis rights had not yet been brought under the treaties.

Until recently, the strongest legal evidence that Métis people were entitled to lay claim to Aboriginal rights, even after a distinctive Métis nation had evolved, was section 31 of the *Manitoba Act, 1870*, a statute of the Parliament of Canada that was subsequently accorded constitutional status by the *Constitution Act, 1871*:

And whereas it is expedient, *towards the extinguishment of the Indian Title* to the lands in the Province, to appropriate a portion of

ungranted lands, to the extent of 1,400,000 acres thereof, for the benefit of the families of the half-breed ["Métis" in the French version]
residents, it is hereby enacted that [such lands be selected and granted
to the children of half-breed heads of families residing in the Province
at the time the lands were transferred to Canada].[26] [emphasis added]

Section 31 will require extensive analysis later. In the present context, its
importance lies in the fact that it includes an acknowledgement by both Canadian
and British parliaments that the people of the Métis Nation were entitled to share
Indian title to the land and, it seems clear by implication, all other elements of
Aboriginal rights. Further acknowledgement of the existence of Métis Aboriginal
rights is found in subsequent legislation, such as the federal *Dominion Lands Act,*
1879, which referred in section 125(e) to Indian title and its extinguishment by
grants to Métis people living outside Manitoba on 15 July 1870.

The most recent and conclusive evidence that Aboriginal rights can be exercised by Métis peoples is section 35(2) of the *Constitution Act, 1982,* which
explicitly includes the Métis among the Aboriginal peoples whose existing
Aboriginal rights are recognized and affirmed by section 35(1). The constitution
of Canada, of which that provision is part, is the supreme law of Canada (as
stated in section 52(1) of the same act). Stronger legal confirmation than that
would be difficult to imagine.

As to the relationship of Métis to First Nation and Inuit Aboriginal rights,
there appear to be two fundamentally different views. The first traces Métis rights
to the ancient rights of the peoples from whom Métis peoples derive their
Aboriginal ancestry. From that point of view, these rights are older than Métis
peoples themselves. The other view is that Métis Aboriginal rights were not
derived from those of the ancestral Aboriginal nations but sprang into existence
when the Métis themselves were born as a distinct people.[27]

The first approach is more consistent with the meaning of the word
Aboriginal: from the beginning. It is also supported by some of the historical evidence referred to above, such as the linkage of Métis to Indian title in the
Manitoba Act, 1870; the *Dominion Lands Act;* and the revelation in the documents concerning the early western treaties that Métis people who chose to do
so were permitted (and presumably considered entitled) to associate themselves
with and exercise the rights of Indian peoples.

The other point of view – that an entirely distinct Aboriginal people came
into being as a result of contact between the Indigenous population and
Europeans and subsequent socio-economic developments – also finds strong support in history. It is unquestionable, for example, that a unique way of life was
forged by Métis people of the North American plains and by the mixed-ancestry communities of Labrador. Morris's book recognized the fact for the prairie
Métis and suggested that those Métis who chose to live the distinctive life associated with that culture should not be brought under the treaties. This second

approach would not do violence to the dictionary meaning of Aboriginal either, since the word could be read to mean 'from the beginning of significant European settlement'.

Which view is more valid probably depends upon context. For cultural and political purposes, such as the design of arrangements appropriate to the present and future needs and aspirations of Métis people, the second approach seems better suited. New peoples emerged from Aboriginal-European contact and the development of distinctive communities and folk-ways. That fact cannot be ignored by Canadians today or by those who are concerned about the shape of Métis life of tomorrow. For legal purposes, however, the first approach seems more likely to apply. The very notion of Aboriginal rights, in a legal sense, has to do with entitlements carried over from a pre-existing legal order into a newly established legal system. By the time the Métis communities came into being as cohesive socio-cultural entities, a European-derived legal and governmental system (albeit rudimentary in some regions) had been in place for some time. It seems unlikely that any Canadian courts would recognize, in addition to the Aboriginal rights possessed by First Nations citizens, an entirely distinct second order of Aboriginal rights held by new social entities that did not exist when the European-based order first asserted jurisdiction.

It is important to stress, however, that the fact that Métis Aboriginal rights spring from the same source as First Nation Aboriginal rights does not mean they are *subordinate* to those rights. Some people view the relationship as one of sub-ordination. It is sometimes said, for example, that treaties negotiated by Indian representatives without collective Métis participation can extinguish Métis Aboriginal rights. This appears to be a mistaken view. It is worth noting how similar this superior-subordinate model is to both the colonial process by which Great Britain dealt with Canadian affairs at one time and the paternalistic manner in which the government of Canada handled all Aboriginal matters until recently.

Colonialism has ended in British-Canadian relations; both countries are now independent members of the world community with equal footing under international law. Colonial attitudes are also disappearing, if slowly and grudgingly, from the relationship between the government of Canada and Aboriginal peoples. It is difficult to understand why anyone would consider a paternalistic model appropriate for dealing with Métis Aboriginal rights in the 1990s. It seems clear, at any rate, that the law does not subordinate Métis rights to First Nation or Inuit rights. Basic constitutional principles, as currently understood and applied in Canada and the rest of the democratic world, simply leave no room for doubt that Métis Aboriginal rights are independent from and equal in status to those of other Aboriginal peoples.

The most authoritative basis for that conclusion is section 35 of the *Constitution Act 1982*, the first two subsections of which state:

Recognition of Existing Aboriginal and Treaty Rights
35(1) The existing aboriginal and treaty rights of the Aboriginal peoples of Canada are hereby recognized and affirmed.
Definition of "Aboriginal Peoples of Canada"
(2) In this Act, "Aboriginal peoples of Canada" include the Indian, Inuit and Métis peoples of Canada.

The plural word "peoples" is especially important since it shows that Aboriginal and treaty rights apply to multiple Aboriginal collectivities rather than to a single Aboriginal universe.[28] The fact that the Métis are explicitly included among those peoples establishes conclusively that Métis Aboriginal and treaty rights are autonomous rights.

The inclusion of Métis people in the constitutionally recognized category of Aboriginal peoples also has major implications under international law. Articles 1 and 2 of the United Nations *International Covenant on Economic, Social and Cultural Rights* state:

1. All peoples have the right of self-determination. By virtue of that right they freely determine their political status and freely pursue their economic, social and cultural development.
2. All peoples may, for their own ends, freely dispose of their natural wealth and resources without prejudice to any obligations arising out of international economic co-operation based upon the principle of mutual benefit, and international law. In no case may a people be deprived of its own means of subsistence.[29]

The draft International Declaration on the Rights of Indigenous Peoples, which has been under discussion in the international community since the early 1980s, makes it clear that this right of self-determination has special significance for the Aboriginal peoples of the world:

Article 3. Indigenous peoples have the right of self determination. By virtue of that right they freely determine their political status and freely pursue their economic, social and cultural development;
Article 8. Indigenous peoples have the collective and individual right to maintain and develop their distinct identities and characteristics, including the right to identify themselves as indigenous and to be recognized as such;
Article 25. Indigenous peoples have the right to maintain and strengthen their distinctive spiritual and material relationship with the lands...which they have traditionally owned or otherwise occupied or used....
Article 27. Indigenous peoples have the right to the restitution of the lands, territories and resources which they have traditionally owned or otherwise occupied or used, and which have been confiscated,

occupied, used or damaged without their free and informed consent. Where this is not possible, they have the right to just and fair compensation. Unless otherwise freely agreed upon by the peoples concerned, compensation shall take the form of lands, territories and resources equal in quality, size and legal status.[30]

Perhaps the most fundamental feature of Aboriginal peoples' status under the Canadian constitution and the right that they and all other peoples of the world are accorded by international law is the autonomy of each people. The international instruments speak of *self*-determination, and the Aboriginal rights recognized and affirmed by section 35 of the *Constitution Act, 1982* include, as pointed out in *Partners in Confederation*, the inherent right of *self*-government. The idea that Métis Aboriginal rights are in some way subordinate to First Nation or Inuit Aboriginal rights, or dependent upon First Nation or Inuit leadership for their definition or implementation, is incompatible with the rights of self-determination and self-government that Métis people share equally with all other Aboriginal peoples.

Further evidence, both historical and current, of the independence of Métis Aboriginal rights can be found in sources as diverse as Alexander Morris's book about the early western Indian treaties and Métis involvement in the process and substance of the ill-fated Charlottetown Accord.[31]

How did the erroneous view that Métis rights are subordinate arise? There were probably several causes. One source of error appears to lie in the misapplication of an otherwise valid proposition concerning the legal basis of Aboriginal rights. That proposition is the previously mentioned principle that Aboriginal rights depend on "proof of possession of a territory by an organized society at the time of the Crown's assertion of sovereignty". Some observers appear to think that because a distinct Métis culture did not emerge until after the British and French Crowns had asserted sovereignty in North America, Métis title is not pre-existing and therefore not Aboriginal and is subject to Aboriginal title.

What this conclusion overlooks is that the Aboriginal ancestors of the Métis people *were* in possession of the land before European assertions of sovereignty and that they exercised that possession as members of organized societies. While it is true that the organized societies (or nations or peoples) existing before European-Aboriginal contact did not include the distinct collectivities we now know as the Métis peoples, they did include numerous other distinct groups whose composition, organization, culture and interrelations were in constant flux over time. New Aboriginal nations and alliances formed as old ones disintegrated, and mixed ancestry was common long before any Europeans arrived. The formation of new Aboriginal communities composed of Aboriginal persons with European ancestry was no different as a socio-political phenomenon from group reformulations that had been occurring since the dawn of human society in North America:

The rise of 'peoples', or the development of a collective political consciousness, ought to be recognized as a dynamic process not subject to 'cut-off' dates to conform to the preferences of other political societies.[32]

The idea that Aboriginal rights can be claimed only by groups that were organized as Aboriginal nations before European contact may have been strengthened by the misconception that Aboriginal title to land is equivalent to the European concept of exclusive ownership or possession. If that were true, it might follow that newly formed peoples like the Métis could not have claims concerning land already in the exclusive possession of other Aboriginal peoples. However, in most of the areas where Métis peoples evolved, land and resources were shared by *all* Aboriginal peoples inhabiting the particular area.[33] The Cree, the Sioux and other Aboriginal peoples all simultaneously exercised the right to exploit the resources of the northwestern plains of North America before Europeans arrived, for example. There appears to be no reason why the exercise of the same rights after contact by the new Aboriginal people who chose to call themselves Métis should be treated differently.

A third possible basis for the mistaken view that Métis rights are subordinate to First Nation rights is the use of the term Indian title in the *Manitoba Act, 1870* and the *Dominion Lands Act, 1879*. Both enactments stated that the distribution of land or scrip to Métis persons was aimed "towards the extinguishment of the *Indian title* to the lands" [emphasis added]. A modern reader, unaware of the way the word 'Indian' was used by government officials in the late nineteenth century, might think that Métis title in the west was merely a subset of Indian title.

The truth is that both Métis title and Indian title, as those terms are used today, are coequal subsets of Aboriginal title. The word Indian was used by nineteenth-century British and Canadian governmental authorities in the same way we now use Aboriginal.[34] The area west and north of Upper Canada was known officially as the Indian Territories, without differentiation among the various Aboriginal peoples who lived there.[35] By section 91(24) of the *Constitution Act, 1867*, the Parliament of Canada was given legislative jurisdiction over Indians, and the Supreme Court of Canada later ruled that the word includes Inuit.[36] Studies conducted for the Commission indicate that the courts will, when called upon to do so, find that Métis people are also Indians for purposes of section 91(24).[37] Because the same government officials who drafted section 91(24) also drafted the 1870 order in council that brought the vast north-central part of North America into Confederation, it is highly probable that even the reference to "Indian tribes" in that document meant Aboriginal peoples in general.

Read with a nineteenth-century vocabulary, therefore, the term Indian title in the *Manitoba Act* and the *Dominion Lands Act* means Aboriginal title, and the significance of the word towards in "towards the extinguishment of the Indian Title" becomes clear: it means that when the obligations to Métis persons imposed by the *Manitoba Act* and the *Dominion Lands Act* had been met, that portion of Aboriginal title would be void, leaving the non-Métis portion to be dealt with in other ways. Far from indicating the subordination of Métis title to Indian title, therefore, the *Manitoba Act* and the *Dominion Lands Act* provisions show that the land entitlements of all Aboriginal peoples, including the Métis, are independent and coequal in status.

To say that the Aboriginal rights of all Aboriginal peoples are independent and coequal in status does not imply that those rights are necessarily the same for all Aboriginal peoples. Traditional practices of the Siksika (Blackfoot) differed in significant respects from those of the Cree, for example. Those differences never prevented the Siksika, Cree and Métis peoples from simultaneously exercising their Aboriginal rights in the past in the same areas of the prairies, and there is no reason why it should do so now. The theoretical possibility that some aspects of Aboriginal land use by one group might interfere with the rights of other groups seldom materialized in the case of the western Métis; neither the Métis occupation of river lots nor their harvesting of buffalo and other wildlife was seriously incompatible with the simultaneous exercise of Aboriginal rights by the other Aboriginal inhabitants of the area. Nor is there evidence of significant incompatibility between the land use practices of the eastern Métis and those of the Inuit and First Nations peoples with whom they shared the land.

It makes no sense, therefore, to suggest that Métis Aboriginal rights can be extinguished by a treaty negotiated between the Crown and representatives of other Aboriginal peoples, or that they are in any other way inferior or subordinate to the rights of other Aboriginal peoples.

Although the content of Aboriginal rights is the same, in broad outline, for Métis as for First Nations and Inuit, the details may differ considerably in important ways. Just as the Cree and Mi'kmaq peoples, though equally possessed of Aboriginal rights, manifest some of those rights differently, so Métis peoples may exercise their Aboriginal rights differently from other Aboriginal peoples. Cultural customs of some Métis groups are certainly unique, and there were significant historical differences in resource uses as well as in forms of self-government.

Some historical forms of Métis self-government, such as the organization of the buffalo hunt, were undoubtedly distinctive. And while the provisional governments created under the leadership of Louis Riel to govern the Red River Settlement from 1869 to 1870 and the Saskatchewan Métis from 1884-1885 may have been of too temporary a nature to be considered valid models for permanent Métis Aboriginal government institutions, they provided striking illustrations of the principle, acknowledged by Prime Minister Sir John A. Macdonald in 1869, that where no other governmental system operates, "it is quite open for the inhabitants to form a government, ex necessitate".[38] Although that principle applies to more than Aboriginal peoples, it strongly reinforces the Métis Aboriginal right of self-government.

Group or individual rights?

There are differing views about whether Aboriginal entitlements are group rights or individual rights. Group rights, as the term signifies, are vested in and exercisable by groups on behalf of their individual members. Individuals have no legal means of enforcing them.

Aboriginal rights appear to have both group and individual aspects. They are undoubtedly group rights in certain important respects and probably in most respects. Land rights were not exercised individually on the prairies in Aboriginal times, at least not in the sense of individuals claiming exclusive long-term use of particular tracts of land.[39] In the case of nomadic Aboriginal peoples, land rights were collective in nature. Another long-recognized collective Aboriginal right is the legal authority of Aboriginal leaders to negotiate and enter legally binding treaties, including treaties that extinguish Aboriginal rights, on behalf of the entire membership of their nations. Sections 35(1) and 35(2) of the *Constitution Act, 1982* can also be seen as underlining a group approach to rights by their references to Aboriginal peoples, since peoples are collectivities.

On the other hand, certain aspects of Aboriginal rights (such as the right to hunt and fish for subsistence) were often exercised by individuals historically and are still seen as individual. In the *Sparrow* case, for example, the Supreme Court of Canada permitted a First Nation individual to invoke, under the authority of section 35(1), an Aboriginal right to fish as a defence to individual prosecution for fishing by a method prohibited by federal law. Section 35(4) of the *Constitution Act, 1982* states, moreover, that

> Notwithstanding any other provision of this Act, the aboriginal and treaty rights referred to in subsection (1) are guaranteed equally to male and female *persons*. [emphasis added]

It would appear, therefore, that Aboriginal rights are sometimes individual and sometimes collective, depending on the nature of the right in question and the circumstances in which it arises or is sought to be exercised. The link between individual and group rights seems to be that only those persons (like Mr. Sparrow) who are members of collective Aboriginal peoples have the ability to exercise individual Aboriginal rights.[40]

Extinguishment

Aboriginal legal rights remain operative only to the extent that they have not been lawfully extinguished. Three methods of legal extinguishment have been recognized in the past: voluntary surrender, legislation and constitutional amendment.[41]

Surrender

Aboriginal rights can be given up, although only to the Crown, only for consideration (something of value given in exchange for the surrender), and (at least where group rights are involved) only by a well-defined Aboriginal group whose leaders understand the legal significance of the situation. The surrender agreement is usually known as a treaty. Where the language of the treaty is unclear, the ambiguity is to be resolved in favour of the Aboriginal people.[42]

Much remains uncertain about extinguishment by surrender; there may be other requirements as well.[43] How thoroughly must the negotiators have understood the legal implications of the agreement? Do the benefits provided in consideration of the surrender have to be adequate, in the sense of being reasonably proportional to the value of the rights surrendered? In the case of ordinary contracts, the law does not concern itself with the adequacy of consideration, but the situation may well be different in the case of Aboriginal treaties because the Crown owes a special fiduciary responsibility to the Aboriginal peoples in question. What is the effect of a "failure of consideration", in the sense of substantial non-compliance by the government of Canada with its obligations under a treaty? Does the Crown's fiduciary obligation affect that matter as well? The answers to these and other questions are unclear.

Some things are clear. One is that treaties can result in the surrender of only the rights they deal with expressly or by unavoidable implication. Another is that treaties bind only those groups whose representatives were parties to the treaties. Both factors could affect existing Métis Aboriginal rights in important ways.

Treaties vary widely in their terms. Some deal with land rights, others do not; some deal explicitly with resource rights, others fail to do so; some touch on governance, others are silent on the subject. To determine what rights may have been surrendered by a particular treaty it is necessary to examine carefully the contents of that treaty. Thus, discovering Métis Aboriginal rights arising from Indian treaties, as for Indian rights arising from the same treaties, will depend on close document-by-document analysis.[44]

Some treaties were entered into with representatives of only some of the Aboriginal groups residing in the areas involved. The fact that excluded groups were sometimes persuaded to adhere to existing treaties at a later date suggests that those groups would not have been legally affected unless they did so.[45] In the case of Métis people, this is an important fact, because they were scrupulously excluded from most Indian treaties unless they chose as individuals to be considered Indians for that purpose.

Little evidence exists to indicate the involvement of Métis groups in the negotiated surrender of Aboriginal rights. For the Métis of the east, the far west, and the north, in fact, there is absolutely no evidence that such negotiations ever occurred until quite recently. For the Métis Nation, there are two possible exceptions to the rule that the federal government would not make treaties with Métis groups.

The first possible exception was an instance where a Métis group unquestionably did participate in treaty negotiations but where the aftermath seems to have turned the incident into an 'exception that proves the rule'. In 1875 a 'half-breed adhesion' to western Treaty 3 was negotiated, signed and partially implemented. It was subsequently repudiated by the federal government, however, and that government consistently thereafter denied treaty status to Métis groups, although it continued to allow Métis individuals to opt for Indian status.[46]

The other possible exception is somewhat more plausible. Manitoba's constitution, the *Manitoba Act, 1870*, was based largely on negotiations between representatives of the government of Canada and the residents of the Red River settlement and its provisional government. For many western Métis, the *Manitoba Act* constitutes a Métis treaty. Some academic commentators agree. Strong textual support for that point of view comes from section 31 of the *Manitoba Act*, which provided that land grants should be made to certain Métis persons" towards the extinguishment of Indian title to the lands of the Province". There are legal difficulties with the 'treaty' interpretation of the *Manitoba Act*, however.

One difficulty is that the *Manitoba Act*, at least on the face of it, does not contain all the terms agreed upon between the Red River delegation and the Canadian negotiators in 1870. There were important additional verbal promises, partially confirmed by a letter from Sir George-Étienne Cartier on behalf of Canada, to Abbé Ritchot, who headed the Red River contingent. Only if those promises could be incorporated inferentially into the text of section 31 (legally, a dubious possibility) would it be wise for the Métis to regard the *Manitoba Act* itself as a treaty.

Another difficulty is that the *Manitoba Act* derives its legal authority from the unilateral law-making powers of the parliaments of Canada and the United Kingdom and contains provisions that were never agreed to by the Red River representatives. If the *Manitoba Act* negotiations are to be regarded as having produced a Métis treaty, therefore, the treaty must have been a separate agreement, legally distinct from the *Manitoba Act* itself, comprising both some provisions of the *Manitoba Act* and the verbal agreements.[47]

Another obstacle to the idea of a Métis treaty is that it is doubtful that the Red River negotiators represented the Métis population exclusively. They appear to have been nominated, on behalf of the general populace of Red River, by a settlement-wide committee known as the Convention of Forty, as well as by the provisional government headed by Louis Riel (and even the provisional government had a small non-Métis component). The negotiators chosen to represent Red River were Abbé Ritchot, Judge John Black and Alfred Scott, a Winnipeg hotel keeper. None was Métis, and they were not even uniform in their Métis sympathies. It is true that Ritchot, the primary Red River negotiator, gave constant voice to Métis concerns and that the legislative assembly of the provisional government, which was predominantly Métis in its composition, ratified the act after being told by Ritchot about the accompanying verbal assurances.[48] Perhaps it is possible to consider the Red River negotiators as having had a dual mandate: to negotiate a land settlement for the Métis and to arrange province-hood on behalf of all residents of the area.

Politically speaking, it is certainly legitimate to refer to the *Manitoba Act* and attendant verbal promises as a Métis treaty, and no one can justifiably object when the Métis who trace their origins to the Red River Valley treat it as such in negotiations concerning their aspirations for the future. Legally, how-ever, the situation is far from clear.

But ultimately it does not matter, from a legal perspective, whether the *Manitoba Act* provisions constitute a treaty. Aboriginal rights were extinguish-able, according to common law, by legislative enactment or by constitutional amendment as well as by treaty. The provisions of section 31 of the *Manitoba Act* were part of a legislative enactment having constitutional force. The extin-guishment implications are therefore the same legally, whether or not the act was a treaty. (Treaties can be sources of Métis rights as well as instruments of extin-guishment. Later in this appendix, we discuss the possibility that the *Manitoba Act* and related promises could be considered a treaty for the meaning of the guar-antee contained in section 35 of the *Constitution Act, 1982.*)

More important than whether the *Manitoba Act* extinguishment provision was part of a treaty or a statute is whether, and to what extent, it resulted in the legal extinguishment of Métis Aboriginal rights in Manitoba. Subsumed in that question are several difficult legal puzzles. Was the vague phrase 'towards the extinguishment' sufficiently explicit to effect extinguishment in law? If so, was the extinguishment conditional upon full and fair distribution of the associated land grants to their intended recipients? Who were the intended recipients? If the intended recipients did not include all Manitoba Métis, did the Aboriginal title of the excluded group survive? To the extent that the Aboriginal title of Manitoba Métis was extinguished, how were other aspects of their Aboriginal rights, such as the inherent right of self-government, affected? These matters are addressed in Appendix 5C.

Legislation

Until 1982, when section 35 was enacted to give constitutional recognition to existing Aboriginal rights, such rights could be extinguished by simple legisla-tive enactment. The *Sparrow* case made it clear, however, that extinguishment by legislation had to be unmistakable in intent and that mere statutory regulation did not equate to extinguishment. The body competent to extinguish by statute is the Parliament of Canada, to which section 91(24) of the *Constitution Act, 1867* assigned authority to make laws concerning "Indians, and Lands reserved for the Indians". (This assumes, in the context of Métis rights, that section 91(24) applies to Métis people as well as to "Indians".) The *Indian Act* is the principal federal statute, but by no means the only one, that has encroached on Aboriginal auton-omy over the years. Powers of self-government exercised initially by Aboriginal communities on their own authority were eventually modified and controlled by statute; many other Aboriginal entitlements, such as the right to hunt and fish, were legislatively restricted in a variety of ways. Although legislative extinguishment of Aboriginal rights has not been possible since 1982, Parliament remains capable, according to the *Sparrow* decision, of a limited degree of regulation of those rights. To qualify for application under the *Sparrow* principles, however, legislative regulation must now meet a very stringent test.[49] The *Indian Act* does not apply to Métis people unless they are registered as Indians, but certain other federal legislation impinging on Aboriginal rights does affect them.

A number of provincial enactments have also encroached on Aboriginal rights. Although it is doubtful that the provincial legislatures have the constitutional jurisdiction to do so on their own authority, Parliament has delegated much authority to them by section 88 of the *Indian Act*, which subjects Indian people to provincial laws of general application. Section 88 is not applicable to Métis persons, however, since the *Indian Act* restricts its application to persons who are registered or entitled to be registered as Indians under the act.

An attempt to extinguish the Aboriginal title of the Métis of Manitoba was made in the *Manitoba Act, 1870*. Since that act had constitutional authority, its extinguishment provisions are examined in the next section. With respect to the Aboriginal title of western Métis outside the tiny original 'postage stamp' province of Manitoba, a key enactment was the *Dominion Lands Act, 1879* and subsequent amendments, which offered scrip, redeemable for Crown lands, in return for extinguishment of Indian title. Although a large quantity of prairie land was eventually distributed through that scrip system, almost none of it ended up in Métis hands, most scrip having been bought for ready cash by land speculators and redeemed by them or by people who purchased it from them. The process by which that came about is well illustrated in Frank Tough and Leah Dorion's study of Métis entitlements in the regions of western Treaties 5 and 10 and is examined more fully in Appendices 5B and 5C.[50] No attempt appears ever to have been made to extinguish Métis title by legislation outside the areas covered by the *Manitoba Act* and the *Dominion Lands Act*. The extent to which resource use rights and other Métis Aboriginal rights may have been extinguished is touched on later in this appendix.

Constitutional amendment

Since 17 April 1982, when proclamation of section 35 constitutionalized all unextinguished Aboriginal rights, Parliament has not had the power to extinguish Aboriginal rights by ordinary legislation. Aboriginal rights can now be extinguished only by surrender or by constitutional amendment.

The only constitutional provision purporting to extinguish Aboriginal rights is section 31 of the *Manitoba Act, 1870* (a federal statute confirmed and given constitutional status by the *Constitution Act, 1871*):[51]

31. And whereas, it is expedient, towards the extinguishment of the Indian Title to the lands in the Province, to appropriate a portion of such ungranted [Crown] lands, to the extent of one million four hundred thousand acres thereof, for the benefit of the families of the half-breed residents, it is hereby enacted, that, under regulations from time to time made by the Governor General in Council, the Lieutenant-Governor shall select such lots or tracts in such parts of the Province as he may deem expedient, to the extent aforesaid, and divide the same among the children of the half-breed heads of families residing in the Province at the time of the said transfer to Canada, and the same shall be granted to the said children respectively, in such mode and on such conditions as to settlement and otherwise, as the Governor General in Council may from time to time determine.

Implementation of the *Manitoba Act* was subject to considerable subsequent legislation, both federal and provincial, enacted with a view to clarifying, modifying and supplementing section 31 and other provisions of the *Manitoba Act*. The constitutional validity of some of that supplementary legislation is questionable and is the subject of litigation now before the courts. Administration of the *Manitoba Act*, so far as Métis people were concerned, has been the subject of intense controversy ever since 1870. The manner in which the *Manitoba Act* promises were carried out is examined in Appendix 5C.

Conclusion

The critical question remaining is what, if anything, was extinguished? The overall impact of the various attempts to extinguish Métis Aboriginal rights in the west is difficult to assess accurately, partly because the facts are not, and probably never will be, fully known, and partly because the law of extinguishment remains unclear in several crucial respects. A few observations, however, can be made with reasonable confidence.

Most explicit measures to extinguish Métis Aboriginal rights addressed only the Aboriginal title to land, leaving other Aboriginal rights, such as cultural and governmental rights, largely undisturbed. Section 31 of the *Manitoba Act*, for example, refers only to extinguishment of the Indian title to the lands in the province. This is not to say that other Aboriginal rights could not be extinguished by legislation, but the Supreme Court of Canada in *Sparrow* placed severe limits on Parliament's power to do that. The extent of remaining Métis Aboriginal resource-use rights depends on the answers to at least two controversial legal questions, examined later in this appendix: Are they distinct from title rights? and To what extent has legislation on the subject expressed an unequivocal intention to extinguish them?

Some Métis groups were never party to either treaties or legislation purporting to extinguish Aboriginal title to land. Where such groups possess sufficient cohesiveness and distinctiveness to be considered peoples, they would seem to retain Aboriginal title to the lands they historically possessed as a group. Identifying such groups and determining the degree of distinctiveness and cohesiveness required to qualify them as bearers of group rights will not be easy, of course, but some, such as the Métis Nation and perhaps the Labrador Métis, are easy to identify.

Where legislation (*Manitoba Act* and *Dominion Lands Act*) purported to extinguish Métis Aboriginal title in return for grants of land, large-scale irregularities (ranging from fraud and unconstitutional alteration of rights to negligence and breach of fiduciary duty) have been documented. These irregularities resulted in very little of the compensatory land grants ending up in Métis hands. This failure of consideration, if true, may well have nullified the extinguishment. The law of extinguishment is not clear enough on this question to permit a reliable conclusion until a high level court has ruled on it, but the question is currently before the courts.

Where Aboriginal rights were effectively extinguished for a group as a whole by some treaty or legislative provision, the fact that certain individual members of the group did not participate in the group decision or did not share in the compensatory benefits would probably not have nullified the extinguishment, although it might give those individuals or their successors a right to personal relief. Aboriginal title being a group right, it can be extinguished only by group action. If an otherwise valid extinguishment instrument created individual rights in return for extinguishment, those individual rights are probably enforceable individually, but non-compliance in a few specific cases would not affect the general efficacy of the extinguishment. Whether this was the case for the *Manitoba Act* and the *Dominion Lands Act* will depend on whether the courts find that the large-scale failure of consideration that is alleged to have occurred in those situations had the legal effect of nullifying the extinguishment process altogether.

While it is not possible to reach definitive conclusions about all of the aspects of the extinguishment of Métis Aboriginal rights in advance of judicial rulings on certain questions, it seems clear that some of those rights – perhaps most of them – have never been extinguished. Aboriginal rights, therefore, constitute a major source of Métis legal rights.

1.2 The *Royal Proclamation of 1763*

In 1763, following the conclusion of hostilities with France, George III of England issued a Royal Proclamation concerning his newly acquired North American territories. That proclamation contained several provisions relating to Aboriginal peoples. Underlying those provisions was an acknowledgement that lands "not having been ceded to or purchased by" the Crown were reserved to "the several Nations or Tribes of Indians...as their hunting grounds". This provided powerful early evidence of the existence of Aboriginal rights in English law.

Although this Royal Proclamation applied to much of what is now eastern Canada, it did not apply directly to the homeland of the Métis Nation (which fell within the vast area known as Rupert's Land covered by the 1670 Charter of the Hudson's Bay Company), since the proclamation expressly excluded "the Territory granted to the Hudson's Bay Company".[52] It also excluded settled parts of Quebec, Newfoundland, Florida and the 13 New England colonies. Whether it applied to what is now British Columbia is a matter of doubt, the Supreme Court of Canada having divided inconclusively on the issue in *Calder*.

These exclusions from the 1763 proclamation were not fatal to Aboriginal rights, however; the Supreme Court has made it clear on more than one occasion that Aboriginal rights never depended on the Royal Proclamation for their existence; it was evidentiary only.[53]

In any case, the omission of Hudson's Bay Company lands, which was the most serious exclusion affecting Métis people, was offset in part by an imperial order in council, dated 23 June 1870, that transferred those lands to Canada in accordance with section 146 of the *Constitution Act, 1867*, subject to an obligation to respect Aboriginal interests that was similar to that contained in the 1763 proclamation. The 1870 order in council is examined in Appendix 5C.

1.3 The Crown's Fiduciary and Other Obligations

A strong case can be made in support of the proposition that Canadian governments owe a legal duty of care to the Aboriginal peoples of Canada, including Métis people.[54]

This duty of care is a consequence of the fact that Aboriginal peoples, including Métis, hold Aboriginal rights. It is a legal axiom that rights and obligations are correlative. Thus, it would be meaningless, in a legal sense, to assert that someone had a right unless someone else had an obligation to do something that would permit that right to be realized or to refrain from doing anything that would prevent its realization. If I have a legal right to be paid by you, you must have a corresponding obligation to pay me; if you have the right to express yourself freely, governments must have a corresponding obligation to refrain from acting in ways that would suppress or interfere with your free expression. Section 35(1) of the *Constitution Act, 1982* recognizes and affirms existing Aboriginal rights. Since rights and obligations are correlative, section 35(1) must recognize and affirm an implicit obligation on someone's part to refrain from suppressing those rights and perhaps even to contribute positively to their realization. An obligation on whose part? Since constitutional responsibilities have been held to be exclusively governmental in nature, the obligation must lie with governments.[55]

Compelling authority for concluding that such an obligation exists is provided by the *Guerin* decision.[56] In that case, the Supreme Court of Canada held that the Crown was legally liable for damages to an Indian band for mismanaging the leasing of certain band lands to a golf club. The court found that the nature of Aboriginal title in land and the fact that it can be surrendered only to the Crown, coupled with the surrender provisions of the *Indian Act*, created a unique fiduciary relationship between the Crown and Indian peoples concerning surrendered Indian lands. That fiduciary relationship imposes trust-like responsibilities on the Crown, requiring it to act with the utmost good faith and care in the interests of the Indian people affected by its actions.

While the principle determined in the *Guerin* case was stated to apply to surrendered Indian lands, it seems to have broader application. Some of the conduct for which the Crown was held liable in that case occurred before the land in question was surrendered by the band. In any event, the Supreme Court of Canada subsequently stated the principle in much broader terms in *Sparrow*, a decision that dealt with legislative restrictions on the Aboriginal right to fish:

> In our opinion, *Guerin*, together with *R. v. Taylor and Williams* (1981), 62 C.C.C. (2d) 227, 34 O.R. (2d) 360 (C.A.), ground a general guiding principle for section 35(1). That is, the government has the responsibility to act in a fiduciary capacity in respect to Aboriginal peoples. The relationship is trust-like, rather than adversarial, and contemporary recognition and affirmation of Aboriginal rights must be defined in light of this historic relationship.[57]

Not only does this more recent articulation of the fiduciary duty appear to extend beyond Indian lands, surrendered or otherwise, but the court's use of the term Aboriginal peoples suggests that the duty is not restricted to Indian peoples. If it applies to Inuit and Métis people as well, the fact that the duty was found in *Guerin* to be based partially on the terms of the *Indian Act*, which does not encompass those groups, may lessen its significance. The Supreme Court seemed to be indicating in *Sparrow* that the federal government's fiduciary responsibility for Aboriginal peoples is rooted, independently of the *Indian Act*, in the historical relationship of the Crown to all those peoples.

While that historical relationship was originally with the British Crown, it was transferred to Canadian authorities in 1867 (and later dates for areas subsequently added to Canada).[58] Because section 91(24) of the *Constitution Act, 1867* confers on Parliament jurisdiction over "Indians, and Lands reserved for the Indians", it is the Crown expressed through Canada (the federal rather than provincial order of government) upon which this responsibility now primarily falls. However, there may also be matters within provincial jurisdiction for which, because of their impact on Aboriginal peoples, provincial governments have fiduciary responsibilities.[59]

Does the fiduciary obligation apply to Métis peoples? It appears that it does. It will be recalled, first, that the Supreme Court of Canada was careful in *Sparrow* to describe it as a duty owed to Aboriginal peoples, not just to Indian people, and the court did this with full knowledge that section 35(2) now defines Aboriginal peoples to include Métis. Moreover, it seems clear that although section 91(24), enacted in 1867, refers expressly only to Indians, that term embraces *all* Aboriginal peoples, including the Métis.

In *Re Eskimos* the Supreme Court, in determining that 'Eskimos' (Inuit) were 'Indians' under section 91(24) of the *Constitution Act, 1867*, stated that the decision was based upon how Eskimos were viewed at or around the time of Confederation. What is the evidence regarding use of the term Indian in relation to the Métis at or around the time of Confederation?

There is considerable evidence and legal scholarship to suggest that in 1867 the population of mixed Aboriginal and European ancestry was included under the broad generic term Indians in section 91(24) of the *Constitution Act, 1867*.[60] There are also interpretations of the evidence and legal argument that assert that the Métis were not considered Indians at the time of Canada's union.[61] The author of Canada's leading treatise on constitutional law has stated, however, that most of the evidence and argument favours the view that the Métis are Indians under section 91(24).[62] The Manitoba Aboriginal Justice Inquiry concluded in 1991 that "Métis people...fall within the constitutional definition of 'Indians' for the purposes of section 91(24)...and fall within primary federal jurisdiction".[63] Two research studies conducted for the Commission reached the same conclusion.[64] These conclusions have considerable though not unanimous support from Métis representatives. Some Métis people are offended to be characterized as 'Indians' because, in their view, the term undermines the distinct nature of Métis peoples. Some Inuit have similar concerns.

The key to resolving this difference of opinion appears to lie in the fact that legal terminology does not always correspond with everyday language. In a social sense, of course, it would be wrong to refer to Inuit or Métis persons as Indians. For the special legal purpose of determining who falls under the law-making jurisdiction and responsibility of Parliament, however, only the word Indian is available to us.[65] It was placed in the constitution in 1867 at a time when its drafters thought it a satisfactory general equivalent of Aboriginal. That being so, courts will probably have no difficulty concluding that Métis are Indians within the special legal meaning that word bears in section 91(24) of the *Constitution Act, 1867* while also acknowledging that Métis are socially, historically and culturally distinct from all other Aboriginal peoples.

This does not necessarily deprive provincial legislatures of constitutional jurisdiction to legislate on aspects of Métis rights that have provincial dimensions. It means, however, that Parliament has paramount jurisdiction and that the fiduciary obligation owed to Aboriginal persons, including Métis people, is owed primarily by the government of Canada.

What does that fiduciary obligation entail? It certainly means that governments must do nothing that would interfere with the free exercise of existing Aboriginal rights. That negative obligation clearly applies to both federal and provincial governments. There is good reason to believe that at least the federal government, in which section 91(24) vests authority over Aboriginal matters, also has a positive obligation to take steps necessary to the full realization of existing Aboriginal rights.

Courts have traditionally been more reluctant to impose positive duties (requiring someone to undertake a particular action) than negative ones (prohibiting someone from doing something). Positive obligations have always been imposed in some circumstances, however, and since fiduciary responsibilities have long been recognized to be positive as well as negative in some circumstances,[66] the fiduciary relationship referred to in *Guerin* and *Sparrow* would seem to include a duty to take positive measures. This conclusion is consistent with the nature of constitutional obligations generally. Although many constitutional obligations of governments are predominantly negative (not to prevent exercise of the fundamental freedoms of religion, expression, association and so on), some are unquestionably positive (to hold elections at least every five years, to convene Parliament and provincial legislatures at least once a year, to provide public support for minority denominational schools and minority language schools). There is no reason, therefore, to interpret the federal government's constitutional obligations concerning Aboriginal rights as entirely negative. At least one writer has concluded that the fiduciary duty to Aboriginal peoples involves both positive and negative obligations.[67] It is instructive to note that the Supreme Court of Canada has recently indicated that it is willing, in appropriate circumstances, to award positive remedies, such as reading into statutes unconstitutionally excluded legislative benefits rather than just striking down the deficient legislation.[68]

Although the full implications of the federal government's positive obligations respecting existing Aboriginal rights cannot be catalogued, it is possible to speculate about some of them. Where there are Métis groups with whom treaties or claim settlements were never completed, it seems clear that the government of Canada is obliged to initiate negotiations. If the exclusion of Métis groups from treaty or settlement negotiations in which they should have been included has resulted in harm to Métis interests, the government of Canada is probably obliged by its fiduciary duty to compensate the Métis groups for such harm. If the realization of a particular Métis Aboriginal right requires legislative enactment, Parliament may well have an obligation to enact suitable legislation.[69] While the courts may not be empowered to order Parliament to fulfil a legislative obligation, they clearly have the power to order compliance with the constitution by the Crown and its subordinates. Even Parliament may be subject to declaratory rulings of the courts, which can have a powerful political impact.

1.4 Treaty Rights

Treaties are major sources of rights for First Nations. This is not true, generally speaking, for Métis peoples because few treaties have been made with them as such. As explained earlier, some consider that section 31 of the *Manitoba Act, 1870* and attendant verbal promises constitute a treaty, but courts would probably not accept that interpretation.

This means that the *Manitoba Act, 1870* should be looked upon as a constitutional not a contractual guarantee, which could remove the possibility of direct enforcement by the courts of the verbal promises made to Abbé Ritchot by George-Étienne Cartier and John A. Macdonald. Nevertheless, the written constitutional guarantee remains capable of judicial enforcement and of interpretation in light of the verbal promises.

1.5 Section 35 of the *Constitution Act, 1982*

Section 35(1) of the *Constitution Act, 1982* recognizes and affirms the existing Aboriginal rights of the Aboriginal peoples of Canada. Although it is only existing rights to which section 35 applies, it is nevertheless appropriate to treat that provision as an independent source of rights in at least two respects. First, it constitutionalized the 1982 status quo, so far as Aboriginal and treaty rights are concerned, with the consequence that those rights can no longer be extinguished by ordinary legislation (or, arguably, even by consent unless the consent is confirmed by constitutional amendment). Second, by declaring, in section 35(2), that Aboriginal peoples include Métis for purposes of section 35(1), it has confirmed their independent existence and removed any possibility that their rights can be perceived as somehow subordinate to those of other Aboriginal peoples.

By focusing on the rights of peoples rather than individuals, section 35 emphasizes the collective side of Aboriginal and treaty rights. It will be recalled that collective rights (such as the right of self-government or of treaty negotiation) are enforceable only by the group and cannot be exercised by individuals on their own behalf. Although the *Sparrow* decision shows that section 35 has significance for individuals, it is likely that the only persons who can rely on section 35 as individuals are members of the Aboriginal people whose particular rights are in question. Even though he was of Aboriginal ancestry, Mr. Sparrow would probably not have been allowed to exercise Aboriginal fishing rights if he could not show that he was currently accepted as a member of his people (see our discussion on group and individual rights earlier in this appendix). The processes and criteria of group membership are, therefore, of great importance.

How is membership in an Aboriginal people determined?[70] Although various tests have been employed over the years, for various purposes in various jurisdictions (degrees of consanguinity, bureaucratic discretion, family status, individual choice and so on), the method that has won widest acceptance in recent years is a modified self-determination approach, consisting of three elements:

- some ancestral family connection (not necessarily genetic) with the particular Aboriginal people;

- self-identification of the individual with the particular Aboriginal people; and
- community acceptance of the individual by the particular Aboriginal people.

It is sometimes suggested that a fourth element is also required: a rational connection, consisting of sufficient objectively determinable points of contact between the individual and the particular Aboriginal people, including residence, past and present family connections, cultural ties, language, religion and so on, to ensure that the association is genuine and justified. The more common view, however, appears to be that while these criteria can be used to determine whether an individual should be accepted as a member, they are not primary components of the test.

It is important when considering section 35 to know something about the meaning of the word 'peoples'.[71] Unfortunately, no authoritative definition of its meaning in section 35 exists. Definitions from other sources, such as international law, can be helpful, bearing in mind that the meaning of any word is strongly influenced by the context in which it is used. Catherine Bell has suggested that a definition developed by the International Commission of Jurists might be applicable. In that definition, 'people' has the following elements:

- a common history;
- racial or ethnic ties;
- cultural or linguistic ties;
- religious or ideological ties;
- a common territory or geographical location;
- a common economic base; and
- a sufficient number of people.[72]

This definition is clearly not adequate for all purposes, since, for example, the elements of common geography and a common economy would be hard to apply to the Jewish people outside Israel or to some of the widely dispersed Aboriginal peoples of Canada, including many Métis. It nevertheless conveys a good general impression of the factors commonly considered to constitute a people, including the key requirement that members exhibit a sense of community and societal cohesiveness, a feature that other groups with common characteristics (women, for example, or people with disabilities) do not possess. This cohesiveness need not involve formal governmental structures. The International Court of Justice advised in 1975 that it is possible for a people (in that case, nomadic inhabitants of the Sahara desert) to exist for the purpose of exercising the right of self-determination under international law without possessing the governmental machinery of a nation-state.[73]

A definition of Indigenous peoples in an early draft of a proposed International Covenant on the Rights of Indigenous Nations was as follows:

The term Indigenous People refers to a people (a) who lived in a territory before the entry of a colonizing population, which colonizing population has created a new state or states to include the territory, and (b) who continue to live as a people in a territory and who do not control the national government of the state or states within which they live.

For Métis in Canada, the reference in this proposal to having lived in a territory before the arrival of the colonizing population is problematic, since Métis could not, by definition, have existed before contact. That difficulty is of little significance to Canadian constitutional law, however, since section 35(2) of the *Constitution Act, 1982*, which supersedes all international understandings so far as the law of Canada is concerned, explicitly includes the Métis among the Aboriginal peoples to whom section 35(1) applies.

It is significant that section 35 employs the plural word 'peoples' rather than the singular 'people'. The beneficiaries of section 35 are clearly considered to be grouped in several distinctive Aboriginal peoples, rather than to constitute a single Aboriginal people. What is not entirely clear from the bare text of section 35 is whether the phrase "Indian, Inuit and Métis peoples of Canada" was intended to refer to three peoples or whether some or all of the three categories encompass multiple peoples. Bell argues persuasively for the latter approach. Applying international standards to the Canadian situation, with due allowance for contextual differences, there can be little doubt that many distinct First Nations exist in Canada, from the Mi'kmaq Nation of the east to the diverse cultures of the prairies and west coast. Although fewer distinct peoples exist among Inuit and Métis than among First Nations, the cultural differences among various groups of Inuit and Métis mark them as multiple peoples too.

Some Aboriginal groups are referred to by themselves and others as nations. What is the relationship between a people and a nation? It appears that the terms have synonymous meanings. Webster's *International Dictionary of the English Language* explains that the word nation is derived from a Latin verb meaning to be born and defines it in part as follows:

> A people connected by supposed ties of blood generally manifested by community of language, religion and customs, and by a sense of common interest and interrelation; thus the Jews and the Gypsies are often called nations....
>
> Popularly, any group of people having like institutions and customs and a sense of social homogeneity and mutual interest. Most nations are formed of agglomerations of tribes or peoples either of a common ethnic stock or of different stocks fused by long intercourse. A single language or closely related dialects, a common religion, a common tradition and history, and a common sense of right and wrong, and a more or less compact territory, are typically characteristic; but one or more of these elements may be lacking and yet

leave a group that from its community of interest and desire to lead a common life is called a nation.

It seems reasonable to conclude that the meaning of section 35 would not have been altered significantly if its drafters had substituted the word nations for the word peoples.[74]

Can there be peoples within peoples? It seems so. The Hasidim, for example, can be considered a people within the much broader people comprising world Jewry. In the Canadian Aboriginal setting, the Cree people constitute a nation as, probably, do certain smaller Cree groupings. Whether subdivisions as small as bands can aptly be described as peoples is uncertain. Some bands do refer to themselves as nations, but that usage is not universally accepted. It is clear, however, that separate bands, even if not peoples in themselves, may exercise, as collectivities, at least some elements of their peoples' rights. The Supreme Court of Canada in *R. v. Sparrow* attributed Aboriginal rights to the Musqueam band, which had only 649 members. While the band was not described as a people or nation, its distinctive existence since pre-contact times was noted and relied upon as a basis for the decision that it is entitled to exercise Aboriginal rights. Such smaller peoples do not necessarily have the same characteristics and capacities as the larger ones, however, and a group may well be a people for one purpose but not for another. While the Musqueam band might be a people for the purpose of exercising Aboriginal fishing rights or the inherent right of self-government within the context of the Canadian state, it is highly unlikely that it would be considered by international law to be a people entitled to the degree of self-determination required to establish a separate nation-state.[75]

Problems could arise from overlapping concepts of nationhood or peopledom in situations where the larger and smaller groups both seek to exercise control over some aspect of nationhood. Since a common approach to problem solving among Aboriginal peoples tends to be 'bottom up' rather than 'top down', the general principle applicable to resolving such jurisdictional difficulties ought to be that the smaller nation has exclusive priority over local questions (such as membership in the smaller nation or the exercise of hunting rights within its territory), and the larger one is paramount with respect to issues that extend beyond local significance. Thus, while a Cree band may decide whom to admit or exclude from its own membership, it cannot decide who is or is not a member of another band, a Cree, an Indian or an Aboriginal person.

How do these observations about peoples and nations apply to Métis people?

It is clear, in the first place, that the historical Métis Nation of the west is a people within the meaning of section 35 and, accordingly, is a nation with which other orders of government in Canada must treat when dealing with the collective Aboriginal and treaty rights of those who form part of the nation. The Métis of Labrador appear at least close to being in an equivalent position. Other cohesive collectivities of Aboriginal people who refer to themselves as Métis may possibly be peoples and nations as well.

It remains a matter of dispute whether the Labrador Métis and other eastern Métis can be considered Métis peoples within the strict meaning of that expression in section 35. It probably does not matter, however, for legal purposes since they are unquestionably Aboriginal peoples, and section 35 applies to all Aboriginal peoples, regardless of whether they can be classified as Indian, Inuit, or Métis.[76]

1.6 The *Canadian Charter of Rights and Freedoms* and the *Canadian Bill of Rights*

The rights discussed thus far have, for the most part, been specific to Aboriginal peoples. Certain other general rights may also have peculiar application to Canadians of Métis inheritance. This is true of section 32 of the *Manitoba Act*, which, although applicable to *all* Red River residents in possession of settled lots before 1870, was especially important to the Métis since they were by far the most numerous of the pre-provincehood settlers. It may also be true of some rights conferred on all Canadians by the *Canadian Charter of Rights and Freedoms,* which came into force on the same day that Aboriginal rights were recognized and affirmed in section 35 of the *Constitution Act, 1982*. Similar rights, although lacking constitutional status, were created by the *Canadian Bill of Rights* of 1960.

Even if it is erroneous to believe that cultural and governmental rights constitute a part of the unextinguished Aboriginal inheritance of Métis people, alternative constitutional protection for those same rights might be found in the fundamental rights provision of the Charter. Section 2 guarantees freedom of conscience and religion, freedom of expression and freedom of association. The right to associate freely with others empowers Métis people to form groups, without governmental interference, composed of any others with whom they have an affinity. And, of course, freedom of religion and expression, read in light of the injunction in section 27 to interpret the Charter in a manner that preserves and enhances Canada's multicultural heritage, ensures that those who gather together will be able to manifest their cultures as they choose. An argument even could be made, perhaps, to the effect that freedom of expression includes the right to organize and participate in distinctive forms of self-government.

The guarantee of equality rights under section 15(1) of the Charter may be especially significant. That provision prohibits discrimination based on race or national or ethnic origin, among other factors. It is well established that this includes systemic discrimination – inequality that results unintentionally from the manner in which government conducts public affairs.[77] A powerful case can be made for the position that the Métis of Canada, both as individuals and as groups, have been the victims of systemic discrimination over the years and still are. Special federal government programs and grants designed to benefit persons with Indian status (and sometimes Inuit) have often been closed to Métis persons. Métis persons denied access to a program of financial assistance for post-secondary education that is available to other Aboriginal persons may well be able to persuade a court that they have been discriminated against unconstitutionally. Those who wished to defend the exclusion would have to establish that the situation and needs of Métis persons are so unlike those of other Aboriginal people in relevant respects that they cannot reasonably be expected to be treated comparably. It seems unlikely that a convincing case could be made. The comparison would have to be based on functional criteria, not on such arbitrary factors as whether a person's great-grandparents opted for or against taking Métis scrip.

1.7 International Law

Many international instruments to which Canada is a party enshrine basic human rights applicable to the situation of the Métis peoples of Canada. These include United Nations guarantees in a number of documents.[78] The *Universal Declaration of Human Rights* states, in part, that

> 7. All are equal before the law and are entitled without any discrimination to equal protection of the law....

> 8. Everyone has the right to an effective remedy by the competent national tribunals for acts violating the fundamental rights granted him by the constitution or by law.

The *International Covenant on Economic, Social and Cultural Rights* declares that

> 1. All peoples have the right of self-determination. By virtue of that right they freely determine their political status and freely pursue their economic, social and cultural development.

> 2. All peoples may, for their own ends, freely dispose of their natural wealth and resources without prejudice to any obligations arising out of international economic co-operation based upon the principle of mutual benefit, and international law. In no case may a people be deprived of its own means of subsistence.

The *International Covenant on Civil and Political Rights* guarantees the right of self-determination, identical to Article 1 of the cultural covenant. It further guarantees a right of resource use, identical to Article 2 of the cultural covenant. Finally, it states:

> 27. In those states in which ethnic, religious or linguistic minorities exist, persons belonging to such minorities shall not be denied the

right, in community with other members of their group, to enjoy their own culture, to profess and practise their own religion, or to use their own language.

In addition to these fully adopted international instruments, an International Declaration on the Rights of Indigenous Peoples is in the process of being enacted. Significant articles of that draft declaration read as follows:[79]

> Article 3. Indigenous peoples have the right of self-determination. By virtue of that right they freely determine their political status and freely pursue their economic, social and cultural development;
> Article 8. Indigenous peoples have the collective and individual right to maintain and develop their distinct identities and characteristics, including the right to identify themselves as indigenous and to be recognized as such;
> Article 25. Indigenous peoples have the right to maintain and strengthen their distinctive spiritual and material relationship with the lands...which they have traditionally owned or otherwise occupied or used....
> Article 27. Indigenous peoples have the right to the restitution of the lands, territories and resources which they have traditionally owned or otherwise occupied or used, and which have been confiscated, occupied, used or damaged without their free and informed consent. Where this is not possible, they have the right to *just and fair* compensation. Unless otherwise freely agreed upon by the peoples concerned, compensation shall take the form of lands, territories and resources equal in quality, size and legal status.[80] [emphasis added]

These international norms do not constitute a direct part of Canadian law. International conventions are binding on Canada as a country in international law, but they impose no direct legal obligations enforceable against Canadians in Canadian courts.[81] We do not, therefore, consider them further in the legal context. They do provide strong support, however, for the moral and political arguments covered later.

1.8 Remedial Rights

The ancient legal maxim, *ubi ius ibi remedium* – where there is a right, there is a remedy – reminds us that the law provides many types of remedy for the breach of legal wrongs, including an inherent power of superior courts, in some situations, to fashion novel remedies where existing ones are inadequate to redress particular violations of rights.[82] To those who work with the law, the maxim may sometimes seem misleading, since they know how many procedural impediments clutter the path between right and remedy and that legal remedies are not always ideal, even when available. It is nevertheless significant that the law starts from the assumption that every wrong has a remedy unless the contrary can be proved.

Questions concerning the legal redress of Métis rights can be divided into two categories: types of legal relief available, and time limitations.

Types of legal relief available

Self-help

To the extent that Aboriginal rights have not been extinguished, some of them can be exercisable without the help of legal institutions. A right to hunt, for instance, can be realized simply by hunting. A right to engage in Aboriginal religious practices can be fulfilled by just doing it, as can a right of self-government, to the extent that it causes no detriment to those who choose not to subject themselves to the government in question.

Whether this is true for all unextinguished Aboriginal rights is not certain. Could an Aboriginal group whose Aboriginal title to land remains intact physically exclude others from the land in question? Some would say they could, as long as they observed generally applicable laws concerning the use of force. Others would argue that this is not legally possible, because the concept of Aboriginal title often involves a sharing of the resource rather than an exclusive use of it by any one group. Self-help must be used with great caution.

Administrative adjudication

If it were considered advisable to engage in individualized adjudication of Métis claims for past denials of rights, a special claims tribunal with expertise in Métis matters and procedures tailor-made for such matters would probably be the most effective agency. Past inquiries into Métis affairs[83] have not succeeded in resolving these issues, however. If this were a desirable way to proceed, legislative authorization by Parliament would be required. No suitable tribunal exists, and much thought would be required to devise one. The government of Canada has refused to accept a Métis claims commission in the past.[84]

Litigation

It would be possible for those who contend that rights of their Métis predecessors were violated to seek judicial redress. Some such litigation is already in progress. Other actions against the Crown for breach of fiduciary duty are foreseeable. This approach would not always provide entirely satisfactory solutions, however. Courts do not generally have the specialized knowledge of and expertise in Aboriginal matters required to deal well with these kinds of disputes, and their procedures are not well suited to the task. Problems of proof are difficult. As will be seen, some serious time limitation problems arise in the context of litigation. The impact of even successful litigation is sporadic, because it usually focuses on particular narrow fact situations rather than on broad questions of social policy.

The easiest type of Métis rights litigation, from the procedural and evidentiary points of view, would be a challenge or challenges to the constitutional validity of questionable federal and provincial legislation or actions concerning those rights. The cases now before the courts include claims of that type. A claim or claims under the Charter, based, for example, on allegations of systemic discrimination, would be relatively simple to launch. Such litigation could seek a variety of appropriate specific remedies or a simple declaration of rights upon which subsequent political remedies might be based. Section 24(1) of the Charter offers a particularly wide range of remedial options, including, where appropriate, mandatory and structural injunctions. Constitutional references can be, and occasionally are, raised in criminal proceedings, such as in prosecutions of Métis persons for alleged violations of hunting and fishing laws.

Even in constitutional litigation, however, judicial solutions are far from ideal. The process is slow, unpredictable and often prohibitively expensive. The questions addressed depend on who happens to have commenced legal proceedings and for what purpose, and decisions are often all-or-nothing matters, lacking the balance and sophistication permitted by negotiated solutions.

Time limitations

The passage of time can sometimes provide a defence to even the strongest of legal claims. Section 32(1) of the federal *Crown Liability Act* stipulates that causes of action against the federal Crown within particular provinces are subject to the time limits imposed by the laws of the province in question.[85] In Manitoba, for example, the *Limitation of Actions Act* imposes the following time limits, among others:

- actions grounded on fraudulent misrepresentation, within six years from the discovery of the fraud;
- accident, mistake, or other equitable ground of relief, six years from the discovery of the cause of action;
- recovery of land, 10 years after the right accrued;
- any other action, within six years after the cause of action arose.

Section 53 states:

> At the determination of the period limited by this Act to any person for taking proceedings to recover any land...the right and title of that person to the land is extinguished.[86]

The *Public Officers Act* of Manitoba provides, in section 21(1), that actions against public officials must be brought within two years next after the act, neglect or default complained of, or, in case of continuance of injury or damage, within two years next after the ceasing thereof.[87]

By placing time limits on actions against public officers and on actions for fraud, breach of fiduciary duty (which relates to equitable relief), recovery of land, and any other action, these laws erect major obstacles to the ability of courts to remedy violations of Métis rights that are alleged to have occurred well over a century ago.

There are circumstances in which these time limits can sometimes be extended or avoided. Few of those circumstances would be applicable to litigation concerning Métis rights, however. Section 14 of the Manitoba *Limitations of Actions Act* permits actions to be brought late if the plaintiff was not aware of "all material facts of a decisive character upon which the action is based", but that provision ceases to be operative 30 years after the cause of action first arose (section 14(4)). Another extension device unlikely to be applicable is section 5, which delays the beginning of the limitation period for any cause of action concealed by the fraud of the person relying on the limitation period until the time when the fraud was first known or discovered. Even assuming that recently discovered fraud of that kind could be established, the perpetrator of the fraud would be long-since dead. Only if such fraud were practised on behalf of the Crown or some other existing corporate entity, therefore, could section 5 be invoked today, and the likelihood of those circumstances being established are not great.

There are, nevertheless, a few time extension possibilities that could be applied to modern claims for violations of Métis rights. One is built into certain of the provisions themselves. The Manitoba time limits respecting fraud and equitable relief both refer, for example, to a period commencing from the discovery of the fraud or cause of action. Frauds or breaches of fiduciary obligation *discovered* within the last six years would still be actionable, therefore, regardless of when the wrongdoing originally occurred. Another and even more important possibility arises from the fact that legal wrongs of a *continuing* nature always remain actionable, because each new day that the wrong continues brings with it a new cause of action. It is possible that the Crown's continuing failure to meet its positive fiduciary obligations to Métis people would, if established, involve a continuing wrong of that kind.

Undoubted instances of continuing wrongdoing incapable of being legalized by limitation laws are unconstitutional legislation and unconstitutional acts or omissions by government authorities. If the Parliament of Canada and/or the legislature of Manitoba enacted statutes that violated the constitutional rights of the western Métis, litigation to establish that fact cannot ever be limited by time.[88] Continuing systemic discrimination against Métis people will always be open to Charter challenge. And constitutional defences can always be raised to criminal prosecutions relating to matters affected by Aboriginal or treaty rights.

2. Sources of Moral and Political Rights

2.1 Entitlement

Whatever their legal rights might be, the Métis people of Canada appear to have an indisputable moral and political right to immediate political action by both federal and provincial governments to deal with Métis concerns.

It is not necessary to dwell at length on the sources of that entitlement, since they are obvious:

- the internationally recognized right of all distinct peoples or nations, including Aboriginal peoples or nations, to appropriate levels of political self-determination;
- the fact, previously explained, that many Canadians of Métis ancestry are members of Métis peoples or nations; and
- the fact, touched upon earlier and elaborated in succeeding appendices, that both Métis individuals and Métis people collectively have suffered severe injustices at the hands of Canadian governments, federal and provincial, in the past, with continuing detrimental consequences.

However strong or weak the legal arguments may be (and there is good reason to consider many of them strong), it would be difficult for any fair-minded Canadian aware of the facts to deny that Métis people have a moral entitlement to reparation for a century and a quarter of abuse and neglect.

In the international community, where opinion is shaped by the various UN instruments quoted earlier, it can be expected that observers aware of the situation of Métis people in Canada would strongly condemn inaction or weak action by Canadian authorities to ensure just and prompt redress for the many wrongs they have suffered.

2.2 Inadequacy of Legal Solutions

In foregoing discussion we examined a wide variety of legal rights to which Métis in all parts of Canada appear to be entitled. Many of these rights seem likely to be confirmed by the courts if their realization is left to litigation. Perhaps, therefore, Métis people could expect eventually to receive substantial redress through the courts.

Litigation seldom offers the best solutions, however, especially for complex socio-political problems. Leaving the determination of Métis claims entirely to the courts would be unsatisfactory for many reasons. The law is far from certain about several of the legal rights discussed. Some of the injustices complained about over the years may not have involved illegal behaviour in the first place or may have been rendered unactionable by the passage of time. The severe standards of proof demanded by litigation present major hurdles; what seems obvious to a historian or sociologist may not seem so to a judge. The off-the-shelf remedies available to the courts may be less suitable and less flexible than remedies that could be consensually or legislatively tailor-made for the particular problem. Litigation is not well suited to ensuring consultation with all affected parties and interests. It is sporadic and yields only hit-or-miss remedies, rather than solutions that are integrated with whatever else is going on in the community. It is maddeningly slow and inordinately costly, and litigation contributes to combative mind-sets that are inimical to rational, co-operative problem solving. In situations as complicated as the rectification of historical wrongs to whole segments of society, the courts can at best provide guidance about the legal rights involved and incentive for remedial action. At worst, they can fragment such remedial action and delay its implementation.

Political solutions are therefore to be preferred; however, the political process is difficult to harness. Demands on the time and attention of politicians, especially those in power, are incessant. To persuade politicians to deal effectively with a problem as massive and intractable as the quest for justice by Métis people requires convincing them that the problem is urgent, that it is capable of being solved on acceptable terms, and that there are good political reasons for doing so. A convincing case can nevertheless be made for immediate political action.

2.3 Timeliness of Political Action

Why is the time finally ripe for the redress of these long-standing Métis wrongs? Several reasons could be cited, including growing public awareness of the need, the pressure of current litigation, and the inclusion of Métis people in section 35(2) of the *Constitution Act, 1982*. The primary reason is that Métis people are now organized politically in ways that cannot be ignored. This is most obviously true in the case of the Métis Nation, where political awareness is very high and the quality of political leadership is impressive. In eastern Canada too, however, there is a new Métis self-awareness and a growing realization in the general community that the Métis must be reckoned with. The Métis of Labrador have leadership befitting the nation they claim to be, and other Métis organizations in eastern Canada are gathering strength. This new political effectiveness has enabled the Métis to tell their story to other Canadians more compellingly than ever before, and it has empowered them to put increasing pressure on federal and provincial politicians to do something material about their complaints. It has also given them skilled leaders who are ready and able to negotiate practical forms of redress and to monitor or administer those solutions to ensure their effective implementation.

Another reason for taking advantage of the political window now open goes back to the legal issues discussed earlier. If a political solution is not arrived at soon, the courts will be left to their own devices. Several legal actions are already in progress, and litigation will increase, with an unfortunate impact on rational decision making by governments, unless something stops it soon. Nothing is likely to stop the litigation process except agreed settlements of Métis grievances on terms more general and more sophisticated than courts can fashion.

2.4 The Process

Appropriate political solutions will be complex and much too situation-specific to speculate on here, but one general observation must be made: unilateral solutions, however well intentioned, will not be satisfactory. Canada's Métis peoples, especially the Métis Nation, have already had too many bad experiences with remedial measures imposed upon them by legislation and policies they had nothing to with shaping. What is needed is bilateral and multilateral negotiation between the government of Canada (in conjunction, where appropriate, with provincial, territorial and Aboriginal governments) and the Métis peoples in question.

3. Conclusions

3.1 Legal Rights

The legal rights of Métis people include the following:

- **Aboriginal rights** are recognized and affirmed by section 35 of the *Constitution Act, 1982.* They include title to land, resource exploitation, cultural rights and self-government. Although only existing rights are so protected, it seems clear that the Aboriginal rights of Métis people have never been fully extinguished. The precise extent to which they may have been extinguished will require careful situation-by-situation analysis. In many cases, however, the continued existence of Métis Aboriginal rights is obvious. Where they do continue to exist, Métis Aboriginal rights are independent of the rights of other Aboriginal peoples.
- The **fiduciary duty of the Crown** applies to the Métis people. The degree to which Canadian governments have met this obligation calls for detailed scrutiny.
- The *Canadian Charter of Rights and Freedoms* and the *Canadian Bill of Rights* add important guarantees of cultural expression and equality to the totality of Métis legal rights. The equality guarantee is especially significant given the benefits available to other Aboriginal peoples that have been denied Métis peoples.
- **Remedial rights** are available to provide appropriate legal redress for the violation of legal rights, although some procedural obstacles such as time limits may be difficult to overcome in some circumstances.

Other legal rights, specific to the Métis Nation, are discussed in Appendices 5B and 5C.

3.2 Moral and Political Rights

The fact that a strong case might be made for legal relief does not mean that Métis people would be wise to make litigation the primary route to restitution or that governments would be either wise or just to stand back and await the outcome of litigation. Lawsuits are slow, costly, unpredictable, piecemeal and clumsy. Negotiated political solutions to problems as complex as those of Métis rights are much to be preferred over judicial ones. One academic authority, who has expressed the view that a negotiated settlement is "without a doubt the most satisfactory way", has also warned that "where the prevailing political will or philosophy is one that favours the interests of the state against the interests of the Aboriginal peoples, then the outcome of a negotiated settlement can be easily predicted".[89] It appears, however, that the political climate is right for a negotiated settlement. Métis people are now represented by organizations that are both determined and equipped to engage in those negotiations, and their significance and political strength grows by the day.

The government of Canada and, where appropriate, the governments of the provinces and territories are obliged, politically as well as morally, to make arrangements for such negotiations as soon as possible. The political wisdom of doing so should be obvious. As to the moral obligation, even if Métis people had no legal entitlement to redress, their moral claim to justice would be overwhelming, whether measured by the standards of international law or by the even higher domestic standards of fair play in which Canadians have always taken pride.

Annex to Appendix 5A
Correspondence Concerning
a Métis Claims Commission

Minister of Justice and Attorney General of Canada
Ministre de la justice et procureur général du Canada

April 24, 1981

Mr. Harry Daniels
President
Native Council of Canada
170 Laurier Avenue West
Suite 500
Ottawa, Ontario
K1P 5V5

Dear Mr. Daniels:

Please find enclosed the Government's response to your land claim submission, as prepared by our legal advisors. You will note that it is their considered opinion that the claim as submitted does not support a valid claim in law nor would it justify the grant of funds to research the issue further.

Notwithstanding this opinion, let me state again that the Government is very concerned about the social and economic conditions experienced by many Metis and Non-Status Indians and that those problems will remain a focus of the Government's attention.

However, because of this position of our legal advisors, it is our view that the problems of MNSI are not to be resolved by land claim compensation and that we must now search for other means to address the unique problems of this group of native Canadians.

Yours sincerely,

Jean Chrétien
Ottawa, Canada

December 22, 1981

Mr. Jim Sinclair
Constitutional Spokesman
Native Council of Canada
170 Laurier Avenue West
5th Floor
Ottawa, Ontario
K1P 5V5

Dear Mr. Sinclair:

Thank you for your letters of November 24 and 25, 1981, in which you raised again the question of native land claims. I will try to clarify the government's position on this issue as it relates to the Constitutional process.

On the basis of the material which the native groups submitted, my officials concluded that there was no valid land claim in law. As I have told you in recent meetings, if you have other material which would cast further light on this matter and perhaps lead the government to revise its opinion, I will be very pleased to receive it and will ask my officials to review their findings.

I must hasten to point out, however, that it is the wording of the Constitutional resolution and not the opinion of government lawyers which will determine the protection afforded your people in the new Constitution. A legal opinion of the Minister of Justice does not have the force of law, and if the courts eventually maintain that your "existing rights" include land title, the government will be obliged to live with that decision.

I have, furthermore, stressed to you that the land title does not exhaust the list of aboriginal rights which you may claim. It is therefore mistaken to say that to deny the validity of land claims is to deny you any and all rights.

On the question of a consent clause and the extension of section 91(24) to cover Métis and non-status Indians, I would certainly be prepared to deal with these issues at the post-patriation First Ministers' Conference in which native leaders will participate. However, I cannot at present commit the federal government to supporting these propositions. Our final stance on these issues will be negotiated around the conference table.

On the establishment of a political process for the discussion of issues of concern to the Native Council of Canada, we already have the mechanism of joint Cabinet-NCC meetings. My officials are currently trying, in consultation with the NCC, to set up such a meeting for late January. I have also agreed to convey to the Prime Minister your desire to meet with him, although his heavy schedule will make it difficult to arrange a major meeting in the very near future. If you have a proposal to present for establishing a further mechanism for government/native consultation, I will study that proposal with great interest, but first I need to have the details before me.

Finally, I will be writing to you separately to discuss the extension of funding of national native organizations in preparation for your participation in the First Ministers' Conference.

Yours sincerely,

Jean Chrétien

NOTES

1. See Kent McNeil, "Aboriginal Nations and Québec's Boundaries: Canada Couldn't Give What It Didn't Have", in *Negotiating With A Sovereign Quebec*, ed. Daniel Drache and Roberto Perin (Toronto: James Lorimer & Company, 1992), p. 116.

2. *Canada Jurisdiction Act, 1803* (U.K.), 43 Geo. III, c. 138.

3. See Dale Gibson and Kristin Lercher, "Reliance on Unconstitutional Laws: The Saving Doctrines and Other Protections" (1986) 15 Man. L.J. 305.

4. See Brian Slattery, "Understanding Aboriginal Rights" (1987) 66 Can. Bar. Rev., p. 727.

5. Some may ask why so much emphasis should be given to the notion of Aboriginal rights – an alien notion imposed on Aboriginal peoples by an alien legal system and involving a form of what some consider racist arrogation that autonomous Indigenous peoples should not have to tolerate. Would it not be more appropriate, they ask, to approach Métis rights on a nation-to-nation basis? The answer is that while this may well be true from a moral and political standpoint, the present discussion concerns the norms of that 'alien' (that is, Canadian) legal system. Moral and political considerations are discussed later. A legal analysis is useful at this point because knowing what relief, if any, the legal system is capable of delivering will help us to determine what new political measures may be needed.

6. *Guerin* v. *R.*, [1984] 2 S.C.R. 335 at 376.

7. See Slattery "Understanding Aboriginal Rights" (cited in note 4); Peter W. Hogg, *Constitutional Law of Canada*, 3rd ed. (Toronto: Carswell, 1992), p. 679. The principal Supreme Court rulings on the subject are *Calder* v. *B.C. (A.G.)*, [1973] S.C.R. 313, 34 D.L.R. (3d) 145; *Guerin* v. *R.*, [1984] 2 S.C.R. 335, 13 D.L.R. (4th) 321; *R.* v. *Sparrow*, [1990] 1 S.C.R. 1075, 70 D.L.R. (4th) 385; and *Roberts* v. *Canada*, [1989] 1 S.C.R. 322 at 340.

8. RCAP, *Partners in Confederation: Aboriginal Peoples, Self-Government, and the Constitution* (Ottawa: 1993).

9. *Sparrow* (cited in note 7) at 1103.

10. See James Young Blood Henderson, "Land in British Legal Thought", research study prepared for the Royal Commission on Aboriginal Peoples [RCAP] (1994). For information about research studies prepared for RCAP, see *A Note About Sources* at the beginning of this volume.

11. The living tree approach was first articulated by Lord Sankey, on behalf of the judicial committee of the Privy Council, in *Edwards* v. *Canada (A.G.)*, [1930] A.C. 124 at 136, and has since been applied by the courts many times.

12. The word 'existing' was discussed by the Supreme Court of Canada in *Sparrow* (cited in note 7) at 1091.

13. *Baker Lake (Hamlet of)* v. *Minister of Indian Affairs and Northern Development* (1979), 107 D.L.R. (3d) 513 (F.C.T.D.) at 542 and 543. At a later point (at 546), Judge Mahoney refers to "time immemorial", which in English common law is sometimes taken to refer to the year 1189, the beginning of the reign of Richard. In this case, he stopped the clock at the time of early British assertions of authority over North America: the period from 1610 to 1670.

14. The Supreme Court's approval occurred in *Sparrow* (cited in note 7) at 1093. For Slattery's view, see "Understanding Aboriginal Rights" (cited in note 4) at 759.

15. Slattery, p. 758. As to the references to previous and new claimants, it should be borne in mind that Slattery acknowledges the possibility of Aboriginal groups *sharing* possession of land.

16. Slattery, p. 758. While Slattery offers scant supporting authority for these views, until the Supreme Court of Canada has spoken on the issue, every analyst is forced to speculate on the basis of general principle. Slattery's approach seems to be well attuned to general principles of Aboriginal law.

17. Catherine Bell, "Who Are the Metis People in Section 35(2)?" (1991) 29 Alta. L. Rev. 351 p. 369. See also Dale Gibson, "The Beneficiaries of Section 35" (forthcoming).

18. *Baker Lake* (cited in note 13) at 543.

19. *Baker Lake*, at 544.

20. Slattery, "Understanding Aboriginal Rights" (cited in note 4), p. 746.

21. See Jennifer S.H. Brown, *Strangers in Blood: Fur Trade Company Families in Indian Country* (Vancouver: University of British Columbia Press, 1980); and Sylvia Van Kirk, *"Many Tender Ties": Women in Fur-Trade Society in Western Canada, 1670-1870* (Winnipeg: Watson & Dwyer, n.d.).

22. Alexander Morris, *The Treaties of Canada With the Indians of Manitoba and the North-West Territories* (Toronto: Belfords, Clarke & Co., 1880), p. 294.

23. For a discussion of the complex labelling process to which the Métis, along with all other Aboriginal peoples, have been subjected over time, see Paul L.A.H. Chartrand, "'Terms of Division': Problems of 'Outside Naming' for Aboriginal People in Canada", *Journal of Indigenous Studies* 2/2 (Summer 1991), p. 1.

24. Morris, *Treaties of Canada* (cited in note 22) p. 41.

25. Morris, *Treaties of Canada*, p. 69.

26. *Constitution Act, 1871* (U.K.) 34-35 Vict., c. 28; *Manitoba Act, 1870* (U.K.), 33 Vict., c. 3, reprinted in R.S.C. 1985, App. II, No. 8.

27. See Catherine Bell, "Metis Aboriginal Title", LL.M. thesis, University of British Columbia, 1989.

28. See Gibson, "Beneficiaries of Section 35" (cited in note 17).

29. *United Nations Resolutions*, Series I: *Resolutions Adopted by the General Assembly*, vol. XI, 1966-1968, comp. and ed. Dusan J. Djonovich (Dobbs Ferry, New York: Oceana Publications, 1975), p. 165.

30. United Nations Economic and Social Council, Commission on Human Rights, Sub-Commission on Prevention of Discrimination and Protection of Minorities, 45th session, UN Document E/CN.4/Sub2./1993/29 (1993), pp. 52-57. The provisions quoted are qualified by other articles in the draft declaration that restrict the rights of peoples to establish new nation states. The articles cited demonstrate an emphasis in the draft declaration on self-reliance that is incompatible with the notion of subordinate rights.

31. Morris, *Treaties of Canada* (cited in note 22), p. 294-295.

32. Paul L.A.H. Chartrand, "Self-Determination Without a Discrete Territorial Base?", in *Self-Determination: International Perspectives*, ed. D. Turp.

33. *Delgamuukw* v. *R. (B.C.)* (1993), 104 D.L.R. (4th) 470; 30 B.C.C.A. 1; Slattery, "Understanding Aboriginal Rights" (cited in note 4), pp. 741, 758; David G. Mandelbaum, *The Plains Cree: An Ethnographic, Historical and Comparative Study* (Regina: Canadian Plains Research Centre, University of Regina, 1979), pp. 7-46; and Irene M. Spry, "The Tragedy of the Loss of the Commons in Western Canada", in *As Long as the Sun Shines and Water Flows: A Reader in Canadian Native Studies*, Ian A.L. Getty and Antoine S. Lussier, eds. (Vancouver: University of British Columbia Press, 1983).

34. See Chartrand, "Terms of Division" (cited in note 23), p. 5.

35. *Canada Jurisdiction Act, 1803* (U.K.), 43 Geo. III, c. 138.

36. *In the matter of a reference as to whether the term "Indians" in head 24 of section 91 of the British North America Act, 1867, includes Eskimo inhabitants of the province of Quebec*, [1939] S.C.R. 104, commonly referred to as *Re Eskimos*.

37. See Bradford W. Morse and John Giokas, "Do the Métis Fall Within Section 91(24) of the *Constitution Act, 1867?*", and Don S. McMahon, "The Métis and 91(24): Is Inclusion the Issue?", in *Aboriginal Self-Government: Legal and Constitutional Issues* (Ottawa: RCAP, 1995); see also Hogg, *Constitutional Law of Canada* (cited in note 7), p. 666; and Clem Chartier, "'Indian': An Analysis of the Term as Used in section 91(24) of the *BNA Act*" (1978-1979) 43 Sask. L. Rev. 37. Also see the discussion of this issue in the section on the Crown's fiduciary and other obligations later in this appendix. For contrary views, see Bryan Schwartz, *First Principles, Second Thoughts: Aboriginal Peoples, Constitutional Reform and Canadian Statecraft* (Montreal: Institute for Research on Public Policy, 1986), p. 245; and Thomas E. Flanagan, "The History of Metis Aboriginal Rights: Politics, Principle, and Policy" (1990) 5 Can. J. L. & Soc. 71. In 1991, the Aboriginal Justice Inquiry of Manitoba concluded that Métis do fall within section 94(24). See Manitoba, Public Inquiry into the Administration of Justice and Aboriginal People, *Report of the Aboriginal Justice Inquiry of Manitoba*, Volume 1: *The Justice System and Aboriginal People* (Winnipeg: Queen's Printer, 1991).

38. Letter from Sir John A. Macdonald to William McDougall, MP, 27 November 1869, quoted in George F.G. Stanley, *Louis Riel* (Toronto: Ryerson Press, 1963), p. 76.

39. Whether the customary use of permanent river lots by individual members of the Métis Nation from relatively early times could be considered an 'Aboriginal' practice goes back to the question, just discussed, about whether Métis rights are necessarily referable to the Aboriginal rights of other Aboriginal peoples.

40. See Bell, "Who Are the Metis People", pp. 353-381, and Gibson, "Beneficiaries of Section 35" (both cited in note 17).

41. See RCAP, *Treaty Making in the Spirit of Coexistence: An Alternative to Extinguishment* (Ottawa: Supply and Services, 1995).

42. Slattery, "Understanding Aboriginal Rights" (cited in note 4), p. 763, as to informed consent, and pp. 761-762, note 131, as to ambiguity.

43. See RCAP, *Treaty Making* (cited in note 41).

44. It is not just the documents themselves that require study, of course. Equally important are the oral understandings that accompanied the documents, such as the promises made to the Manitoba Métis at the time of the *Manitoba Act, 1870*. See Appendix 5B.

45. See Morris, *Treaties of Canada* (cited in note 22), p. 329; and Frank Tough and Leah Dorion, "'The claims of the Half-breeds...have been finally closed': A Study of Treaty Ten and Treaty Five Adhesion Scrip", research study prepared for RCAP (1993).

46. Martin F. Dunn, "All My Relations: The Other Métis", research study prepared for RCAP (1994).

47. See Paul L.A.H. Chartrand, *Manitoba's Métis Settlement Scheme of 1870* (Saskatoon: Native Law Centre, University of Saskatchewan, 1991), p. 127.

48. See Philippe R. Mailhot, "Ritchot's Resistance: Abbé Noël Joseph Ritchot and the Creation and Transformation of Manitoba", PH.D. dissertation, University of Manitoba, 1986.

49. *Sparrow* (cited in note 7) at 1111.

50. Tough and Dorion, "'The claims of the Half-breeds'" (cited in note 45).

51. *Constitution Act, 1871* and *Manitoba Act, 1870* (cited in note 26).

52. But see Kenneth M. Narvey, "The Royal Proclamation of 7 October 1763, the Common Law and Native Rights to Land Within the Territory Granted to the Hudson's Bay Company" (1973-1974) 38 Sask. L. Rev. 123.

53. See, for example, *Guerin* (cited in note 7) at 376.

54. See Slattery "Understanding Aboriginal Rights" (cited in note 4), p. 753; and Canadian Bar Association, *UFOs – Unidentified Fiduciary Obligations* (Winnipeg: Canadian Bar Association, 1994).

55. *R.W.D.S.U.* v. *Dolphin Delivery* (1986), 33 D.L.R. (4th) 174 (S.C.C.).

56. *Guerin* (cited in note 7).

57. *Sparrow* (cited in note 7) at 408.

58. *R.* v. *Secretary of State (U.K.)*, [1982] 2 All E.R. 118 (C.A.).

59. Slattery, "Understanding Aboriginal Rights" (cited in note 4), p. 755; and Gord Hannon, "Benefits and Burdens: A Number of Questions About Fiduciary Duties of the Provincial Crown to Aboriginal People", in Canadian Bar Association, *UFOs* (cited in note 54).

60. See authors and publications cited in note 37.

61. See, for example, Schwartz, *First Principles, Second Thoughts*, and Flanagan, "History of Metis Aboriginal Rights" (both cited in note 37).

62. Hogg, *Constitutional Law of Canada* (cited in note 7).

63. *Report of the Aboriginal Justice Inquiry of Manitoba* (cited in note 37).

64. Morse and Giokas, "Do the Métis fall Within Section 91(24)", and McMahon, "The Métis and 91(24)" (both cited in note 37).

65. It has sometimes been suggested that Parliament's jurisdiction over "peace, order and good government" provides an alternative basis for federal jurisdiction over Métis. For an assessment of the argument see Larry Chartrand, "The Métis Settlements Accord: A Modern Treaty", paper presented at an Indigenous Bar Association conference (unpublished, 1992). It seems an unnecessary complication, though, to treat federal jurisdiction over those Aboriginal persons who are Métis on a different basis than federal jurisdiction over those who are Inuit.

66. They include, for example, a long-established duty to make full disclosure of facts known to be of significance to the beneficiaries' interests: Mark Vincent Ellis, *Fiduciary Duties in Canada* (Don Mills, Ontario: Richard De Boo, 1993), pp. 1-5.

67. Peter W. Hutchins, "Benefits and Burdens: When Do Fiduciary Obligations Arise?", in Canadian Bar Association, *UFOs* (cited in note 54).

68. See *Schacter* v. *R.* (1992), 93 D.L.R. (4th) 1 (S.C.C.).

69. The Supreme Court of Canada recognized in the *Sparrow* decision (cited in note 7), that section 35 incorporates fiduciary obligation and that it imposes responsibilities with respect to legislative regulations affecting Aboriginal rights.

70. See Coopers & Lybrand, "Identification Process for Indigenous Peoples in Selected Countries and Options for the Registration of Métis Peoples in Canada", research

study prepared for RCAP (1993); and *Queensland, State of* v. *Wyvill* (1989), 90 A.L.R. 611 at 616.

71. See Chartrand, "Terms of Division" (cited in note 23) for a review of authorities on the meaning of 'peoples'. See also Bell's study, "Who Are the Metis People" (cited in note 17).

72. Bell, "Who Are the Metis People". A somewhat similar list of characteristics is found in *Greco-Bulgarian Communities,* a 1930 decision of the permanent Court of International Justice, quoted in L.C. Green, "Canada's Indians: Federal Policy, International and Constitutional Law" (1970) 4 Ottawa L. Rev. 101. See also Ian Brownlie, "The Rights of Peoples in Modern International Law", in *The Rights of Peoples,* ed. J. Crawford, p. 1; and Russel L. Barsh, "Indigenous Peoples and the Right to Self-Determination in International Law", in B. Hocking, ed. *International Law and Aboriginal Human Rights* (Sydney: The Law Book Company, 1988), p. 68.

73. *Western Sahara,* Advisory Opinion, [1975] I.C.J. Rep. 12 at 31-33. A similar question, put to the United Nations Human Rights Committee on behalf of the Lubicon Lake Indians of Alberta by Chief Bernard Ominayak, was put aside without decision because the Committee ruled that Chief Ominayak could not, as an individual, bring a question to it. United Nations document CCPR/C/38/D167/1984, 26 March 1990.

74. A contrary view is expressed in a research study prepared for RCAP by Harold Bhérer, "Canadian Governments and Aboriginal Peoples: Plan for A Project Under the Aboriginal Governance Research Program" (1993).

75. In "Terms of Division" (cited in note 23), p. 10, Chartrand points out that the government of Canada has taken the position internationally that the use of the word 'peoples' in section 35 does not signify peoples who, under international law, would be entitled to the right of self-determination: Canada, Privy Council Office, Observer Delegation of Canada, UN Working Group on Indigenous Populations, Fifth Session, August 1987, Geneva. "Review of Developments Pertaining to the Promotion and Protection of Human Rights and Fundamental Freedoms of Indigenous Populations", p. 2. Chartrand counters this view in "Self-Determination" (cited in note 32).

76. See Gibson, "The Beneficiaries of Section 35" (cited in note 17).

77. See Dale Gibson, *The Law of the Charter: Equality Rights* (Toronto: Carswell, 1990), p. 119 and following.

78. *The International Bill of Human Rights* (New York: United Nations, 1978) contains the Universal Declaration of Human Rights; the International Covenant on Economic, Social and Cultural Rights and the International Covenant on Civil and Political Rights; and Optional Protocol.

79. UN Document E/CN.4/Sub2/1993/29 (1993) (cited in note 30).

80. It must be acknowledged that other provisions of the draft declaration place important restrictions on the right of self-determination; it is not an unqualified right in all circumstances. The provisions quoted do provide powerful evidence, however, that cultural, social, economic and political autonomy of distinct peoples is a principle that has won wide acceptance across the world.

81. Hogg, *Constitutional Law* (cited in note 7), p. 285 and following.

82. *Ashby* v. *White* (1702), 2 Ld. Raym. 938; 3 Ld. Raym. 320.

83. See Chartrand, *Manitoba's Métis Settlement Scheme* (cited in note 47), pp. 6-8 and p. 1 concerning inquiries in 1881 and 1943, for example.

84. See Chartrand, *Manitoba's Métis Settlement Scheme*, p. 147, for a discussion of a possible claims commission approach. The government of Canada has rejected such an approach in the past. See the annex this appendix.

85. *Crown Liability Act*, R.S.C. 1985, c. C-50.

86. *Limitation of Actions Act*, R.S.M. 1987, c. L. 150, ss. 2(1) (j) (k) (n), 25.

87. *The Public Officers Act*, R.S.M. 1987, c. P230.

88. *Amax Potash* v. *Saskatchewan*, [1977] 2 S.C.R. 576 (S.C.C.).

89. Chartrand, *Manitoba's Métis Settlement Scheme* (cited in note 47), p. 145.

APPENDIX 5B

SPECIAL SOURCES OF MÉTIS NATION RIGHTS*

Appendix 5A described several general sources for the rights of all Métis: Aboriginal and treaty rights (confirmed by section 35 of the *Constitution Act, 1982*); the Crown's fiduciary obligation to Aboriginal peoples; the Charter and Bill of Rights and so on. The people of the Métis Nation are fully entitled to rely on all those sources. This appendix outlines three additional sources of Métis rights that are applicable exclusively to the Métis Nation.

The omission of Hudson's Bay Company (HBC) lands from the *Royal Proclamation of 1763* was offset by an imperial order in council dated 23 June 1870 that transferred those lands to Canada in accordance with section 146 of the *Constitution Act, 1867*. The order in council was known as the *Rupert's Land and North-Western Territory Order, 1870*. When HBC surrendered the territory to the British Crown, the Crown agreed to the terms by which Canada proposed to govern it and conveyed it to Canada subject to certain conditions. One condition of the conveyance stated in the order in council was that,

> upon the transference of the territories in question to the Canadian Government, the claims of the Indian tribes to compensation for lands required for purposes of settlement will be considered and settled in conformity with the equitable principles which have uniformly governed the British Crown in its dealings with the aborigines.[1]

Section 146 gives this obligation constitutional authority by stating that such conditions have the same effect as if enacted by the British Parliament. While much of the discussion concerning Métis Nation rights hinges on the interpretation and implementation of the provisions of the *Manitoba Act, 1870* and the *Dominion Lands Act*, it is also important to understand the legal underpinnings of those acts, and particularly the order in council that brought the territory of the Métis Nation into Confederation.

1. The *Rupert's Land and North-Western Territory Order*, 1870

It was pointed out in Appendix 5A that the *Royal Proclamation of 1763*, which contained one of the earliest formal acknowledgements of Aboriginal rights,

---

* This appendix was prepared for the Commission by Dale Gibson, Belzberg Fellow of Constitutional Studies, University of Alberta, and Clem Chartier, consultant, of Saskatoon.

probably did not apply directly to the Métis Nation homeland. That conclusion is not of great legal significance, however, because the common law also embodied such an acknowledgement, and an order in council issued by imperial authorities in 1870 concerning Rupert's Land was to similar effect. We examine that order in council in this section.

Section 146 of the *Constitution Act, 1867* provided for the admission of other colonies into the union:

> It shall be lawful...to admit those Colonies or Provinces, or any of them, into the Union, and on Address from the Houses of the Parliament of Canada, to admit Rupert's Land and the North-western Territory, or either of them, into the Union, on such Terms and Conditions in each Case as are in the Addresses expressed and as the Queen thinks fit to approve, subject to the Provisions of this Act...as if they had been enacted by the Parliament of the United Kingdom of Great Britain and Ireland.

The first piece of legislation enacted in the process of admitting Rupert's Land was *An Act for enabling Her Majesty to accept a Surrender upon Terms of the Lands, Privileges and Rights of The Governor and Company of Adventurers of England Trading Into Hudson's Bay, and for Admitting the same into the Dominion of Canada* of 31 July 1868, known by its short title as *Rupert's Land Act, 1868*.[2] By this act, the "whole of the Lands and Territories held or claimed to be held by the said Governor and Company" could be declared part of Canada by order in council as provided in section 146 of the *Constitution Act, 1867*.

The second piece of legislation, assented to on 22 June 1869, was *An Act for the temporary Government of Rupert's Land Act, 1869*.[3] This act provided for admitting Rupert's Land and the North-Western Territory into the Dominion of Canada and stated that when united and admitted they would be known as the North-West Territories. This act was expected to remain in force until the end of the next session of Parliament.

The third piece of legislation was the *Manitoba Act, 1870* assented to 12 May 1870. This act provided for the creation of the province of Manitoba upon the admission of Rupert's Land and the North-Western Territory into the Dominion of Canada as provided for by section 146. By section 30, all ungranted or waste lands in the province would be vested in the Crown and administered by the Government of Canada, subject to "the conditions and stipulations contained in the agreement for the surrender of Rupert's Land by the Hudson's Bay Company to Her Majesty". Section 31 of the act is the subject of detailed analysis later. Sections 35 and 36 are also relevant:

> 35. And with respect to such portion of Rupert's Land and the North-Western Territory, as is not included in the Province of

Manitoba, it is hereby enacted, that the Lieutenant-Governor of the said Province shall be appointed, by the Commission under the Great Seal of Canada, to be the Lieutenant-Governor of the same, under the name of the North-West Territories, and subject to the provisions of the Act in the next section mentioned.

36. Except as hereinbefore is enacted and provided, the Act of the Parliament of Canada, passed in the now last Session thereof, and entitled, "An Act for the Temporary Government of Rupert's Land, and the North-Western Territory when united with Canada," is hereby re-enacted, extended and continued in force until the first day of January, 1871, and until the end of the Session of Parliament then next succeeding.

In the following month, on 23 June 1870, the *Rupert's Land and North-Western Territory Order* was issued. By this order, the Northwest Territories was admitted and became part of the Dominion of Canada as of 15 July 1870. As provided in the *Manitoba Act*, the province of Manitoba was carved from the area on the same date.

As can be seen from section 146, quoted earlier, the order has constitutional status. It is now part of the constitution as a schedule to the *Constitution Act, 1982* entitled *Rupert's Land and North-Western Territory Order*. The order contains a reference to three schedules, the first being an address from the Senate and House of Commons to the Queen.[4] The second schedule contains resolutions, memos and a second address from the House of Commons and Senate to the Queen. The third schedule contains the deed of surrender from the Hudson's Bay Company to the Queen.

The first schedule provides the terms and conditions for the admission of the North-Western Territory:

And furthermore, that, upon the transference of the territories in question to the Canadian Government, the claims of the Indian tribes to compensation for lands required for purposes of settlement will be considered and settled in conformity with the equitable principles which have uniformly governed the British Crown in its dealings with the aborigines.

With respect to the admission of Rupert's Land, the following reference appears in the main body of the order, although the exact wording is contained in the third schedule, the surrender:

14. Any claims of Indians to compensation for lands required for purposes of settlement shall be disposed of by the Canadian Government in communication with the Imperial Government; and the Company shall be relieved of all responsibility in respect of them.

The second address, which provides for the admission of Rupert's Land, was adopted by the House of Commons on 29 May 1869 and the Senate on 31 May 1869. The following is an excerpt from a memorandum in that address:

> Upon the transference of the territories in question to the Canadian Government it will be our duty to make adequate provision for the protection of the Indian tribes whose interests and well-being are involved in the transfer, and we authorize and empower the Governor in Council to arrange any details that may be necessary to carry out the terms and conditions of the above agreement.

Because of the different provisions for admitting Rupert's Land and the North-Western Territory, it may be necessary to ascertain the exact borders of the respective territories. In any event, the order covered a vast expanse of territory and had direct application to substantially the whole of the Métis Nation territory.

The 1870 condition was somewhat less sweeping than the provisions concerning Aboriginal peoples in the *Royal Proclamation of 1763*, in that it did not directly acknowledge Aboriginal title to ungranted and unpurchased lands and stipulated only that compensation be considered and settled for lands required for purposes of settlement.[5] The condition was not insignificant, however, for it provided the impetus for the subsequent series of western treaty negotiation and made clear that the obligation it created to deal with compensation claims was a pressing one, taking effect *upon* the transference of the territories. Its acknowledgement that "equitable principles" govern the Crown's relations with "aborigines" was also important, as will be seen when the fiduciary duty of the Crown is discussed.

It is not absolutely clear whether the 1870 condition was intended to apply to Métis people, but it probably was. They were likely considered to be included in the term 'Indian tribes' by the British authorities who imposed the condition. Those same authorities simultaneously approved the draft *Manitoba Act*, which stated that the grant of 1.4 million acres for the benefit of the families of the half-breed residents was to be made toward the extinguishment of the Indian title. 'Half-breed' was rendered as 'Métis' in the French version of the act. That leaves little doubt that Métis people were considered to have a claim to Indian title. While the language of the condition in the order in council dates from 1867, when the original Canadian address to the Crown concerning western lands was made, the *Manitoba Act* had been drafted by the time the order in council was finally issued. Probably, therefore, Métis people were considered 'Indians' in both documents. This would mean that section 31 and the 'Indian tribes' condition in the order in council were considered to constitute two distinct parts of a package deal relating to Aboriginal rights. To put it another way, section 31 was likely regarded as only partial fulfilment of the more general obligation recognized by the order in council, leaving the Métis not covered by section 31 (those who lived outside the small area designated as Manitoba) to be dealt with in some other way (eventually by the *Dominion Lands Act*).[6]

The importance of these exclusions from and uncertainties about the Royal Proclamation and order in council is not very great, because the Supreme Court of Canada has confirmed the legal status of Aboriginal rights and has stated that they do not depend upon the royal ordinances. They derive primarily, as Chief Justice Dickson put it in *Guerin*, "from the Indians' historic occupation and possession of their tribal lands".[7] What is probably more important than the role of these ordinances in establishing the existence of Aboriginal rights is the fact that the 1763 proclamation and the 1870 order in council both confirm the obligation of the Crown to deal (as the order in council put it) uniformly with 'aborigines' (a term that was surely intended in an empire-wide context to apply to a wider group than Indians) "in conformity with equitable principles". The significance of this acknowledgement relates to the Crown's fiduciary duty to Aboriginal peoples.

2. The *Manitoba Act, 1870*

Manitoba's constitution, the *Manitoba Act, 1870* (enacted originally by the Parliament of Canada and later confirmed by the British Parliament in the *Constitution Act, 1871*), contains guarantees of Métis rights within the limited geographic area of the original 'postage stamp province' of Manitoba. Only section 31 deals explicitly with Métis ("half-breed" in the English version) people.[8]

> 31. And whereas, it is expedient, towards the extinguishment of the Indian title to the lands in the Province, to appropriate a portion of such ungranted lands, to the extent of one million four hundred thousand acres thereof, for the benefit of the families of the half-breed residents, it is hereby enacted, that, under regulations to be from time to time made by the Governor General in Council, the Lieutenant-Governor shall select such lots or tracts in such parts of the Province as he may deem expedient, to the extent aforesaid, and divide the same among the children of the half-breed heads of families residing in the Province at the time of the said transfer to Canada, and the same shall be granted to the said children respectively, in such mode and on such conditions as to settlement and otherwise, as the Governor General in Council may from time to time determine.

Section 32 also contains guarantees that were important to 1870 Métis residents of Manitoba and their descendants. It was designed to ensure that those who were already in possession of land before Manitoba became a province would continue to own that land, even if their rights had not been formally acknowledged by the rudimentary hit-or-miss landholding system maintained by the Hudson's Bay Company prior to 1870.[9]

32. For the quieting of titles, and assuring to the settlers in the Province the peaceable possession of the lands now held by them, it is enacted as follows:-

(1) All grants of land in freehold made by the Hudson's Bay Company up to the eighth day of March, in the year 1869, shall, if required by the owner, be confirmed by grant from the Crown.

(2) All grants of estates less than freehold in land made by the Hudson's Bay Company up to the eighth day of March aforesaid, shall, if required by the owner, be converted into an estate in freehold by grant from the Crown.

(3) All titles by occupancy with the sanction and under the license and authority of the Hudson's Bay Company up to the eighth day of March aforesaid, of land in that part of the Province in which the Indian Title has been extinguished, shall, if required by the owner, be converted into an estate in freehold by grant from the Crown.

(4) All persons in peaceable possession of tracts of land at the time of the transfer to Canada, in those parts of the Province in which the Indian Title has not been extinguished, shall have the right of pre-emption of the same, on such terms and conditions as may be determined by the Governor in Council.

(5) The Lieutenant-Governor is hereby authorized, under regulations to be made from time to time by the Governor General in Council, to make all such provisions for ascertaining and adjusting, on fair and equitable terms, the rights of Common, and the rights of cutting Hay held and enjoyed by the settlers in the Province, and for the commutation of the same by grants of land from the Crown.

Although these section 32 guarantees applied to all old settlers, regardless of ancestry, they played a major role in the saga of Métis rights in Manitoba for several reasons. In the first place, the settled population of Manitoba in 1870 (approximately 12,000) was predominantly Métis (approximately 10,000). Second, the land referred to in section 32 was the most valuable in the province, consisting as it did chiefly of river lots, which were valued for their wooded areas, the richness of their soil, their easy access to water, fish and transportation, and their proximity to other settlers. Finally, in the years following 1870, there appeared to be discrimination favouring non-Métis over Métis claimants by government lands administrators, the Métis claims being less successful.

The explicit words of sections 31 and 32 did not embody the complete agreement about land rights reached between the Red River and Canadian negotiators. Thomas Flanagan's 1991 book, *Metis Lands in Manitoba*, which generally defends the government of Canada's actions and is sceptical of claims that the Manitoba Métis were badly treated, acknowledges that fact.[10] When the Red River negotiators, headed by Abbé Ritchot, protested the fact that the language of the legislation did not encompass all the agreements reached with the Canadian negotiators, John A. Macdonald and George-Étienne Cartier, they were verbally assured that "it will be the same thing".

Although the latter quotation comes, along with numerous references to further assurances, from Ritchot's diary, which may not be a wholly objective source, the subsequent conduct of the Canadian negotiators, Cartier especially, provides strong corroboration of Ritchot's version. Cartier and other federal authorities held many meetings with Ritchot in an obvious attempt to win his confidence, and important verbal promises were made in the course of those meetings. On 18 May 1870, Ritchot wrote to Cartier reminding him of an unfulfilled promise by Macdonald and himself to have an order in council passed to supplement the *Manitoba Act* with verbal agreements not embodied in the act. The verbal agreements expressly mentioned in the Ritchot letter included (1) allowing Manitoba authorities to select and divide the children's allotment; (2) appointing a committee for that purpose "composed of men whom we ourselves were to propose", including, perhaps, the Catholic and Anglican bishops; and (3) confirming, free of charge, the land titles of settlers outside the compass of the Selkirk Treaty.

The next day Cartier and the governor general met with Ritchot and promised a letter confirming the verbal agreements. After further prompting by Ritchot, Cartier produced a letter a few days later with two postscripts insisted on by Ritchot who was not content with Cartier's vague initial wording. The letter and postscripts included the following assurances:

- No payment would be required for confirmation of the land titles of settlers outside the compass of the Selkirk Treaty.
- The governor general confirmed that "the liberal policy which the Government proposed to follow in relation to the persons for whom you are interesting yourself is correct, and is that which ought to be adopted".
- "You may at any time make use of this letter...in any explanation you may have to give connected with the object for which you were sent as delegates to the Canadian Government."
- "As to the [1.4 million] acres of land reserved...for the benefit of families of half-breed residents, the regulations to be established from time to time...respecting the reserve, will be of a nature to meet the wishes of the half-breed residents, and to guarantee, in the most effectual and equitable manner, the division of that extent of land amongst the children of heads of families of the half-breeds...".

It will be noted that of the three verbal assurances mentioned expressly in Ritchot's letter of 18 May, only the confirmation of land titles was stated explicitly. The acknowledgements that Ritchot was correct about the policy the Government proposed to follow, that the regulations would meet the wishes of the 'half-breed' residents, and that Ritchot could make use of the letter in any explanation he might have to give understandably led Ritchot to believe that *all* the verbal assurances would be honoured. As a result, he urged the legislative assembly of Assiniboia (the legislative arm of Riel's provisional government) to ratify the *Manitoba Act*, assuring members that "whenever there is a doubt as to the meaning of the Act...it is to be interpreted in our favour". Flanagan concludes:

> Thus, from the very beginning, the land provisions of the Manitoba Act as understood by the Metis differed from the wording of the statute as passed by Parliament....Ritchot returned to Red River and became the oracle through whom the Manitoba Act was interpreted there. Thus, his belief that the agreement with Canada included not only the act but also Cartier's letter and verbal reassurances, almost as if they were supplementary protocols of a treaty, exercised a powerful influence.

Flanagan emphasizes that Ritchot was only one of three negotiators from Red River and that another of the three, Judge John Black, seemed to consider the text of the *Manitoba Act* sufficient. Black did not play a prominent role in the negotiations, however, especially in the late stages. His detachment was hardly surprising given that he had ceased to reside at Red River and was in Ottawa on his way home to retirement in Scotland. It was Ritchot who constantly goaded Cartier for written confirmation of the verbal agreements, and it was Ritchot whom Cartier authorized to "make use of this letter...in any explanation you may have to give" to the people of Red River. Ritchot's belief that the agreement included both the words of the statute and the supplementary assurances made and alluded to in Cartier's letter was not a product of his imagination; it was a view the government of Canada had authorized him to transmit to the people of Red River.

The promises made to the Manitoba Métis in the *Manitoba Act* were never adequately fulfilled. The extent to which performance fell short of promise is examined in Appendix 5C.

Sections 31 and 32 of the *Manitoba Act* and the associated verbal promises were by no means the only concessions won from the government of Canada by the Red River negotiators in 1870. The entire act, granting full-fledged provincehood to an area on which federal authorities had initially wanted to bestow no more than territorial status for the foreseeable future, constituted a brilliant victory for the western emissaries. That general victory had relatively little special significance for Métis people as such, but they did value two guarantees very highly because of their importance to the preservation of the Métis culture: the right under section 22 to maintain denominational schools (most Manitoba Métis being Roman Catholics) and the right under section 23 to have the French language (which most Manitoba Métis spoke) used in the courts, the laws and the legislature. The subsequent erosion of these educational and linguistic rights was a far from minor component of what many consider to be the betrayal of Manitoba's Métis people.[11] Sections 22 and 23 are not dealt with here, however, because, like the act as a whole, they were enacted for the benefit of all denominational school supporters and all francophones; and, unlike section 32, they do not appear to have been applied in a manner that was discriminatory to Métis people.

3. The *Dominion Lands Act*

The *Dominion Lands Act*, providing for the administration of public lands in Manitoba and non-provincial territories, was first enacted in 1872 and was amended from time to time after that. The 1879 amendments were particularly important because they contained acknowledgements of Indian title and of claims to that title by 'half-breeds', as well as references to satisfying prior settlement claims. Although these references were couched more cautiously than the equivalent provisions in the *Manitoba Act* and never enjoyed the constitutional status bestowed on the Manitoba provisions by the *Constitution Act, 1871*, they were the basis for an important chapter in the story of Métis rights in western Canada.

The general recognition and protection of Aboriginal rights in the *Dominion Lands Act* was expressed in section 42:

> None of the provisions of this Act respecting the settlement of Agricultural lands, or the lease of Timber lands, or the purchase and sale of Mineral lands, shall be held to apply to territory the Indian title to which shall not at the time have been extinguished.

Assuming that Indian title included Métis title, as it did under the *Manitoba Act* as well as under a later provision of the *Dominion Lands Act* itself (section 125(e), added in 1879), this seems to have created a statutory obligation to postpone homesteading by newcomers to the west until Métis (and other Aboriginal) title was extinguished. That obligation was honoured more in the breach than in the observance.

As a method of extinguishing Métis title outside Manitoba, section 125(e) of the *Dominion Lands Act* established an approximation of section 31 of the *Manitoba Act*, but with major differences. Section 125(e) empowered (but did not directly obligate) the federal cabinet to

> satisfy any claims existing in connection with the extinguishment of the Indian title, preferred by half-breeds resident in the North-West Territories outside the limits of Manitoba, on the fifteenth day of July

[1870], by granting lands to such persons, to such extent and on such terms and conditions, as may be deemed expedient.

In addition to its lack of constitutional authority and obligatory language, this measure differed from section 31 in that no quantity of land was specified, and grants were not restricted to children as they were in section 31 but were available to any "half-breed" resident of the territory the cabinet found it "expedient" to favour.

The territorial equivalent of section 32 (confirming prior settlement rights) was section 125(f) of the *Dominion Lands Act, 1879*, which empowered the federal cabinet to

> investigate and adjust claims preferred to Dominion land situated outside of the Province of Manitoba, alleged to have been taken up and settled on previous to the fifteenth day of July [1870], and to grant to persons satisfactorily establishing undisturbed occupation of any such lands, prior to, and being by themselves or their servants, tenants or agents, or those through whom they claim, in actual peaceable possession thereof at the said date, so much land in connection with and in satisfaction of such claims, as may be considered fair and reasonable.

Again, there were important contrasts between this provision and its *Manitoba Act* counterpart. Besides those previously noted, this measure required both occupation before 15 July 1870 and actual possession on that date. It also vested absolute discretion in the cabinet to determine how much land was fair and reasonable to satisfy each claim.

Implementation of these Métis-oriented provisions of the *Dominion Lands Act* and related legislation was, like the *Manitoba Act* guarantees, the subject of considerable controversy (see Appendix 5C).

4. The *Constitution Act, 1930*

When Manitoba, Saskatchewan and Alberta became provinces, ownership of their ungranted public lands was retained by the Crown in right of Canada. This differed from other provinces, where the provincial Crown owned such lands from the beginning. The Red River delegates who negotiated Manitoba's entry into Confederation with Macdonald and Cartier in 1870 had argued for provincial ownership but had been unsuccessful. This anomaly remained a point of bitter contention between federal authorities and the prairie provinces until 1930, when the government of Canada finally agreed to transfer what remained of prairie public lands to the provinces. This agreement was recorded in three natural resource transfer agreements, one for each province, which were constitutionalized by the *Constitution Act, 1930*.

Sections 10, 11 and 12 of the Saskatchewan and Alberta agreements (11, 12 and 13 for Manitoba) – which form a distinct part of the agreements, entitled Indian Reserves – include important undertakings by the provinces concerning the rights of Aboriginal persons in relation to the public land surrendered to the provinces by the agreements.

The first of these commitments, set out in section 10 (section 11 for Manitoba), makes available from unoccupied Crown lands further areas as agreed by federal and provincial authorities to be "necessary to enable Canada to fulfil its obligations under the treaties with the Indians of the Province". This provision does not affect Métis people except to the extent that there are prairie treaties expressly involving Métis people. If the agreements reached by representatives of the government of Canada and residents of the Red River settlement in relation to the *Manitoba Act, 1870* are considered evidence of a treaty (a proposition discussed in Appendix 5A), there may be a basis for applying this section to Manitoba Métis to enable the federal government to meet unfulfilled obligations under the *Manitoba Act*. Otherwise, section 10 is not of relevance to the Métis Nation.

Of unquestionable significance to Métis rights, however, is section 12 (section 13 for Manitoba) of the agreements, which states:

> In order to secure to the Indians of the Province the continuance of the supply of game and fish for their support and subsistence, Canada agrees that the laws respecting game in force in the Province from time to time shall apply to the Indians within the boundaries thereof, provided, however, that the said Indians shall have the right, which the Province hereby assures to them, of hunting, trapping game and fish for food at all seasons of the year on all unoccupied Crown lands and on any other lands to which the said Indians may have a right of access.

Central to the impact on Métis rights of this assurance of the right to hunt, trap and fish for food is whether the word Indians was intended to include Métis persons. Regrettably, there is not yet any conclusive judicial answer to that question, and the few authorities available point in contradictory directions. There is strong reason to believe, however, that Métis people are included. Those authorities are examined more fully in Appendix 5C in the section on judicial decisions.

It is possible, too, that sections 1 and 2 of the agreements have some significance for Métis rights. Section 1 transfers the lands in question from the federal Crown to the provincial Crown, "subject to any trusts existing in respect thereof, and to any interest other than that of the Crown in the same". Section 2 obliges the provinces to carry out the terms of every existing contract of purchase or lease of Crown land or mineral interests and "any other arrangement whereby any person has become entitled to any interest therein as against the

Crown". Moreover, the provinces agreed in section 2 "not to affect or alter any term of any such contract or other arrangement by legislation or otherwise", except by consent or by laws of general application. Unextinguished Aboriginal rights in relation to Crown land might well be considered an interest in land, and the Crown's fiduciary responsibilities might be considered a trust (even though the Supreme Court of Canada held in *Guerin* that they do not create a trust in the strict sense of the term). If so, the *Constitution Act, 1930* imposed those responsibilities on the prairie provinces and gave them constitutional force long before section 35 came into existence.[12] Whether this relieved the government of Canada of its former responsibilities is not clear.

5. Conclusion

Métis entitlements do not end with legal rights. As observed earlier, politically negotiated solutions are generally preferable to judicially imposed ones, and it is clear that the Métis Nation is prepared organizationally to enter into immediate negotiations. Their moral entitlement to engage in that process stems from their inherent right of self-government as an autonomous Aboriginal people. Their entitlement to a fair settlement derives from both the multitude of sources already discussed and the fact that, as illustrated in Appendix 5C, grievous wrongs have been inflicted on the people of the Métis Nation since 1869, and satisfactory redress for those wrongs has never been provided.

NOTES

1. *Rupert's Land and North-Western Territory Order (1870)*, reprinted in R.S.C. 1985, Appendix II, No. 9.

2. S.C. 1868, c.105.

3. S.C. 1869, c.3.

4. Adopted by the House of Commons on 16 December 1867 and by the Senate on 17 December 1867.

5. But see the generous interpretation suggested in *Re Paulette* (1973), 42 D.L.R. (3d) 8 (N.W.T.S.C.).

6. For a discussion of who were considered residents of Manitoba in 1870, see Paul L.A.H. Chartrand, *Manitoba's Métis Settlement Scheme of 1870* (Saskatoon: Native Law Centre, University of Saskatchewan, 1991), p. 40 and following.

7. *Guerin* v. *The Queen*, [1984] 2 S.C.R. 335 at 376.

8. See Chartrand, *Manitoba's Métis Settlement Scheme* (cited in note 6); "Aboriginal Rights: The Dispossession of the Métis" (1991) 29 Osgoode Hall L.J. 457; and "The Obligation to Set Aside and Secure Lands for the Half-Breed Population

Pursuant to section 31 of the Manitoba Act, 1870", LL.M. thesis, University of Saskatchewan, 1988; D.N. Sprague, *Canada and the Métis, 1869-1885* (Waterloo, Ontario: Wilfrid Laurier University Press, 1988); and Thomas Flanagan, *Metis Lands in Manitoba* (Calgary: University of Calgary Press, 1991). See also D.N. Sprague, "Government Lawlessness in the Administration of Manitoba Land Claims, 1870-1887" (1980) 10 Man. L.J. 415.

9. See Archer Martin, *The Hudson's Bay Company's Land Tenures and the Occupation of Assiniboia by Lord Selkirk's Settlers, With a List of Grantees Under the Earl of the Company* (London: William Clowes and Sons, 1898).

10. Flanagan (cited in note 8), p. 40 and following. The account in the next few paragraphs relies on Flanagan, pp. 40-47. For a fuller discussion of Flanagan's book, see Appendix 5C.

11. See *Winnipeg, City of* v. *Barrett*, [1892] 10 A.C. 445 (Man. Q.B.); *Brophy* v. *Manitoba (A.G.)*, [1895] 11 A.C. 202 (S.C.C.); *Manitoba Language Reference*, [1985] 1 S.C.R. 721 (S.C.C.).

12. See the discussion in Chartrand, *Manitoba's Métis Settlement Scheme* (cited in note 6), pp. 9-10.

APPENDIX 5C
MÉTIS NATION LAND AND RESOURCE RIGHTS*

Métis Nation land and resource rights involve a complicated mixture of history, geography, politics and law. Because the historical facts differ sharply from one area to another, the following analysis is divided into three broad geographic categories: the part of Manitoba that includes the Red River Valley and that constituted the original province created by the *Manitoba Act, 1870*; the remaining (chiefly prairie) areas to which the *Dominion Lands Act* of 1872 was applied; and the rest of the Métis Nation homeland. A final section deals with resource use rights.

In all three areas, the legal starting point is the same: the Aboriginal title that Métis shared with all Aboriginal peoples. The reason for examining each area separately is that, until very recently, only two attempts to extinguish Métis Aboriginal title on a Métis-specific basis were ever made. These were made, on somewhat different terms, under the *Manitoba Act*, and the *Dominion Lands Act*. Because of their differences, those attempts must be considered independently. Then we must look at the situation of Métis Nation groups whose Aboriginal rights have never been extinguished.

Although our analysis of Métis rights must begin with law, it cannot end there. The discussion of Métis land rights in each geographic area therefore concludes with observations, as important as the legal ones, about the moral and political entitlement of the Métis Nation to a land base upon which their future as a people can be founded.

1. *Manitoba Act* Territory

The first attempt by the government of Canada to deal formally with Métis rights occurred in the *Manitoba Act, 1870*.[1] This was a statute of the Parliament of Canada that was given retroactive constitutional status by the British Parliament in the *Constitution Act, 1871*. The implementation of the *Manitoba Act*, so far as Métis rights were concerned, was a national disgrace. Maladministration was rampant, ranging from negligence to outright fraud. While there are differences of opinion about the legal consequences of that maladministration, few detached observers would doubt that the descendants of the Red River Métis are owed a huge moral debt. To assess the legal and moral/political ramifications, we must carefully examine the historical record.

---

* This appendix was prepared for the Commission by Dale Gibson, Belzberg Fellow of Constitutional Studies, University of Alberta; Clem Chartier, consultant, Saskatoon; and Larry Chartrand, professor, Faculty of Law, University of Alberta.

1.1 Maladministration of *Manitoba Act* Entitlements

Thomas Flanagan maintains in *Metis Lands In Manitoba*, a book based on research commissioned by the government of Canada, that "the federal government generally fulfilled, and in some ways overfulfilled, the land provisions of the *Manitoba Act*" and that Métis families profited from "a veritable cascade of benefits".[2] In our opinion, much of the evidence marshalled in Flanagan's book, far from supporting those conclusions, lends strong support to the opposite view, advanced by D.N. Sprague, Paul Chartrand and others, that promises made to the Métis population of Manitoba were broken in many important respects.

General

Flanagan's book adopts a bottom-line approach. Acknowledging that many errors and other irregularities were committed in the course of implementing sections 31 and 32 of the *Manitoba Act*, he concludes that at the end of the day, the government of Canada acted with "generosity towards the Métis" (p. 228).

Because justice delayed is justice denied and because justice denied requires redress, an effective assessment of promise fulfilment must consider more than the bottom line of how much was done over a period of time. The assessment must also evaluate how procrastination and maladministration may have eroded or nullified the promises before they were kept. Flanagan's assessment pays little heed to such issues. Delay and its impact, as well as fraud and deception, are major elements of the story of western Métis rights and are discussed below. It will be seen that even from a bottom-line perspective, Thomas Flanagan's assessment of the thoroughness with which Canada kept its promises to Métis people is open to serious question.

Land for children

Flanagan states that the 1.4 million acres promised by section 31 for children of Métis heads of families were eventually all distributed, although it took from 1877 until 1900 to complete the process and more than 90 per cent of the land was diverted by sales of entitlement to persons other than Métis children (pp. 86, 121). Because the number of persons entitled to claim under section 31 was miscalculated, however, the size of each grant (240 acres) exhausted the 1.4 million acres before the claims of all Métis children could be accommodated. The result was that 993 claims were dealt with by issuing scrip worth $240 each instead of by direct land grants (pp. 92-93). For at least those 993 surplus claims, then, Flanagan was clearly wrong to conclude that "the government complied exactly with the wording of section 31 of the *Manitoba Act*" (p. 94).

Allotment of children's grants

The Red River and Canadian negotiators agreed verbally that a committee whose members would be persons nominated locally, working under the supervision of the Manitoba legislature, would select the land from which the Métis children's grants would be made, and that the local people would also be in charge of the allotment of those grants.[3] When this promise was not reflected in the *Manitoba Act*, Abbé Ritchot and his colleagues complained and were assured by John A. Macdonald and George-Étienne Cartier that it would be "the same thing" in practice. Cartier's letter of May 1870, while not referring explicitly to these matters, was obviously designed, with other verbal undertakings, to reassure Ritchot about them and to encourage him to convey his satisfaction to the people of Red River. He did so, expecting the government's promises to be kept.

In actuality, however, the allocation of children's land grants under section 31 were determined, albeit with occasional local input, primarily by federal authorities. The constitutionally entrenched requirement of section 31 that the lieutenant governor play a personal role in the allocation was ignored. The distribution of allotments resulting from that broken promise created great dissatisfaction among the beneficiaries of the land grant. The most fundamental reason for dissatisfaction was that the grants were distributed in a way that resulted in a dispersal of Métis people throughout Manitoba. A homogenous Métis homeland would have been possible if the grants had been located closer to existing Métis river lots.

> Instead of selecting the lands in places where the families might be expected to survive in community, the government sponsored a scheme of dispersal. Instead of securing the families in locations selected by them according to local custom, and according to the promises that accompanied acceptance of the federal union, the government confirmed the usurpation by immigrant settlers from the established portions of Canada, who brought with them the political power to suppress the province's original inhabitants.[4]

Because its stated purpose was to benefit the families of the Métis, section 31 contained implied promises that the land granted would be appropriate to the social and economic circumstances ("reasonably fit to benefit the Métis") and suitable for the establishment of a permanent community (since "families" included future generations). The distribution did not observe the promise of either appropriateness or permanence; the consequence was to destroy the possibility of preserving a vibrant and cohesive Métis people on a coherent land base.

Scrip for parents

The extent to which section 31 of the *Manitoba Act* was intended to benefit and extinguish the Indian title of Métis heads of family has been a matter of controversy over the years. The language of section 31, read literally, appears to call for land grants only to children. But the statement that the 1.4 million acre allotment was "for the benefit of the families of the half-breed residents", coupled with the fact that parents are both members of families and children of their own parents, has led some to contend that section 31 was a guarantee of land benefits for *all* Métis residents.[5] Such evidence as exists concerning discussions between Canadian and Red River negotiators in 1870 may support the narrower interpretation as far as the grants were concerned.[6] The language used was far from clear, but the long-term benefit of all Manitoba Métis was certainly agreed to be the object of the grants.

The significance of excluding Métis parents from the ambit of section 31 (assuming that to have been the intent) was double-edged. If it denied them land grant benefits, it also left their Aboriginal title unextinguished. It was perhaps for that reason that the government decided, after much vacillation, that although Métis parents should not share in the 1.4 million acres, they should be issued scrip for 160 acres each toward extinguishment of their Indian title. A statute to that effect was enacted in 1874.[7] At the same time, however, an identical issue of scrip was authorized for long-time non-Métis settlers and their children in recognition of their contribution to the development of the area.[8] Explanations offered for the grants to non-Aboriginal settlers seldom claimed for them a unique contribution but rather that they were, in the words of John A. Macdonald, "as much pioneers of that country...as the half-breeds". That grant therefore appears either to have deprived the Métis parents of an equivalent reward for their equivalent role as "pioneers of that country" or, if the Métis parents' grant was intended to be such a reward, to have given them no compensation for extinguishment of their Indian title.

As far as grants to Manitoba Métis parents are concerned, then, the bottom line of promise fulfilment is that

- if they were entitled to share in section 31 benefits, the substitution of scrip for land and of 160 acres for 240 acres violated the *Manitoba Act*; and
- the fact that they received nothing more than other (non-Métis) long-time settlers either cheated them of an equivalent settlement award or meant that the extinguishment of their Indian title was without compensation.

Settled lands

Thomas Flanagan asserts that "the government did fulfil its obligations under section 32" (p. 157). D.N. Sprague strongly disagrees.[9] Regardless of whose interpretation one accepts, it is clear that the government of Canada did not altogether ignore its obligation under section 32 of the *Manitoba Act* to confirm the title of settlers (chiefly Métis because of their numerical predominance) who had "occupancy" or "peaceable possession" of Manitoba land before Manitoba was created. Nor, however, did it fulfil that promise completely.

Flanagan states (pp. 186-187) that within the inner parishes of the settlement belt at the junction of the Red and Assiniboine rivers, the areas closest to

Upper Fort Garry and Winnipeg, 96.5 per cent of the river lots (1,562 out of 1,619) were eventually made the subject of patents issued under section 32 of the *Manitoba Act*. Flanagan admits (pp. 188-189) that in the outer parishes of the settlement belt – areas further from the fork of the Red and Assiniboine and more heavily populated by Métis – and in other parts of the province, the section 32 patent rate was considerably lower (41 per cent and 54.8 per cent respectively) and that it was dramatically lower in some of the remoter areas (St. Malo, 27 per cent; Rat River, 7 per cent). He contends, however, that even in those parts of the province, patents were issued for most of the lots that had been settled substantially and that the rejected claims related to lots that had only been staked and not otherwise occupied. Flanagan says: "The very fact that patents were issued under the *Manitoba Act* demonstrates that the Dominion government recognized the occupancy of those who lived on the land prior to 1870." Furthermore, he writes (pp. 187, 189): "In all parishes *Manitoba Act* patents were granted where people really lived".

From these statistics, Flanagan concludes that Sprague is wrong to attribute the large post-1870 Métis migration westward from Manitoba to Métis dispossession or their inability to obtain land patents (pp. 189-190). Flanagan's own figures show, however, that very few patents were issued until after the Métis migration was well under way. The first patents were not issued until 1874, and only two were granted that year (p. 167). Although the number increased sharply the following year, only 336 titles (12 per cent of the eventual total) were confirmed before 1877, by which time, according to Sprague, the flow of emigration had become "remarkable" (p. 139). Section 32 patents continued to be issued at a roughly constant annual rate until 1886, the final one being granted in 1929 (p. 167). Flanagan admits that "many, perhaps even most" of the patents he has documented "were not made to the original occupants" because the occupants' claims to title had been sold and they had moved away (p. 187). He does not speculate about the motivation of those who left.

Nor does Flanagan dispute Sprague's evidence that many individuals lost all or part of their claims to lands they occupied because of unjustifiably restrictive bureaucratic interpretations of peaceable possession, subsequently softened, but not before many claims had been denied or abandoned. Those definitions were especially damaging to staked claims made by Métis (and others) in outlying areas. Abbé Ritchot later reminded Macdonald that he had displayed a map of these areas and explained the staking process to Macdonald and Cartier during the 1870 negotiations. In July 1870, Ritchot, armed with the verbal assurances and the reinforcing letter of George-Étienne Cartier, personally led a Métis expedition to Rat River to stake claims before the land transfer to Canada took place. This action demonstrated that he firmly believed, on the basis of what he had been promised in Ottawa, that such claims would be recognized under section 32(4) of the *Manitoba Act*. By his words and example, others were encouraged to do likewise. A high proportion of those last-minute claims were rejected by federal officials, who took the position that substantial improvements had to be made to the land to satisfy the requirement of peaceable possession. Although Flanagan describes the staked claims problem as a "marginal issue" (p. 157), he affirms that it was surrounded by "great controversy", which was examined eventually by a royal commission (p. 177). Overall, while patents were ultimately issued for the great bulk of river lots that had been occupied before 1870, the promise of section 32 was never completely kept, even in the fullness of time.

Hay and common lands

The controversy over hay lands, which usually lay contiguous to the rear of settled river lots, was rooted in long-standing patterns of land use that dominion authorities ignored, despite their recognition by section 32(5) of the *Manitoba Act*, until considerable harm had been done to the rights of Métis and other old settlers.

Flanagan's book devotes considerable attention to the question of hay lands and common lands. Because the problem was not Métis-specific (although more Métis than others were affected, because of their greater numbers), we will not dwell on it at length. We do, however, wish to make one observation about Flanagan's conclusion that "the government's commutation of the rights of hay and common produced reasonable satisfaction among the old settlers" (p. 219). While acknowledging the absence of evidence for that statement, he suggests that it is plausible to draw such a conclusion from the fact that by 1886 the "melancholy chorus of earlier years" had been reduced to "scattered complaints" (p. 220). In the face of Flanagan's own evidence about homestead claims pre-empting hay lands claims and about substitutions of scrip for land, it is difficult to credit his conclusion that the hay question had been settled satisfactorily by 1886 simply because the volume of complaints had subsided. The world was a very different place for the western Métis in 1886, after the Northwest rebellion, than it had been in 1870. The migration from Manitoba was largely over, and Métis dreams of a western homeland lay shattered in the ruins of Batoche.

Justice delayed

To look only at promise fulfilment, as Flanagan does, without regard to the effect of the passage of time, is to ignore an important aspect of Métis rights – the fact that many of the promises were spoiled by delay, like meat left out in the prairie sun. The accompanying time line, based on the dates provided in Flanagan's book, shows how long it took for the federal government to fulfil its *Manitoba Act* promises (Figure 5C.1).

Except for parental scrip, the bulk of which was issued in 1876, six years after the promises were first made, it took 11 years before even half the commitments

FIGURE 5C.1
Time Line for Government Fulfilment of Promises in the *Manitoba Act*

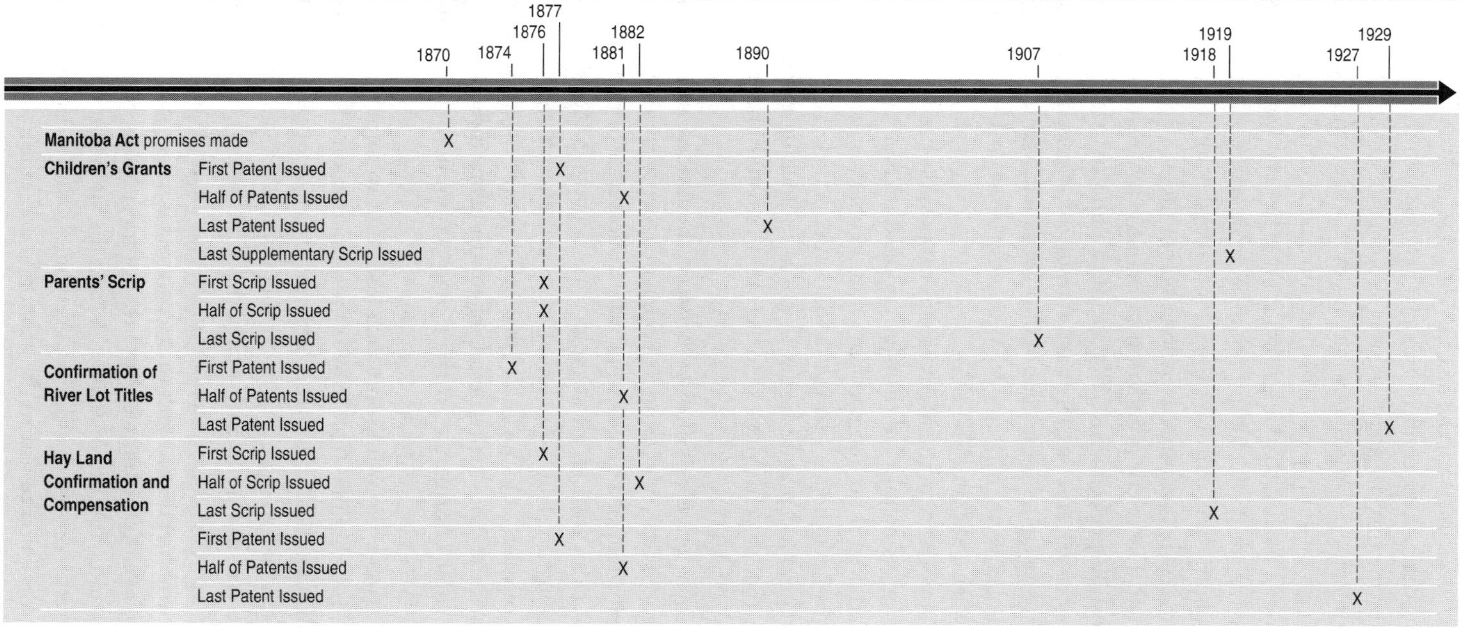

Note: This time line shows how long it took before the various promises made in the *Manitoba Act, 1870*, were fulfilled by the federal government. The median figures (date at which half the patents or scrip had been issued) were calculated on the assumption that rates of issue were uniform during 1876-1888 (for scrip) and 1877-1885 (for patents). Flanagan gives only totals for these.

Source: Based on dates in Thomas Flanagan, *Métis Lands in Manitoba* (Calgary: University of Calgary Press, 1991), pp. 85-86, 93, 140, 167, 214.

made in 1870 were met. For the first six years, absolutely nothing of value was provided to the Métis except confirmation of a handful of the least controvertible river lot titles. For the first decade, there was also uncertainty about the likelihood of promise fulfilment because of bewildering shifts in government policy.

During that long period of inaction and confusion, the demographic composition of Manitoba changed radically. The tidal wave of non-Aboriginal immigration, against which the *Manitoba Act* guarantees had been intended to provide economic and cultural protection, arrived before the safeguards were in place and overwhelmed the Métis long before these safeguards were even half implemented. The Métis population of Manitoba, which constituted a majority of almost 80 per cent in 1870, became a minority within a few years. The loss of majority status was in part a result of Métis migration westward. According to Sprague, more than 4,000 Métis left Manitoba: migration took place slowly between 1871 and 1876, rapidly between 1877 and 1880, and in a rush between 1881 and 1884.[10]

The importance of the Métis exodus has possibly been exaggerated by some commentators. A majority of the Métis population had remained in Manitoba, after all, and even if no one had left, Métis people would soon have been outnumbered by newcomers. The migration was nonetheless a major demographic and cultural event. Sprague argues that it is compelling evidence of the harsh impact on the western Métis of delays and non-fulfilment of *Manitoba Act* promises.

Flanagan rejects any linkage between the exodus and broken promises: "The evidence is overwhelming that Sprague's theory about Métis emigration – that they left Manitoba because they were dispossessed of their lands – is simply wrong" (p. 189). Instead, he suggests, "the departing Métis were drawn by a plains economy that had been moving westward since the 1850s" (p. 190). What he fails to consider is the possibility that Métis who left were drawn to the plains economy because more than a decade of governmental dithering and denials had destroyed their confidence in their own economic or cultural survival in Manitoba.

Flanagan's bottom-line approach leads him to some curious conclusions. He claims, for example, that delay in implementation of children's grants was "not wholly prejudicial", in that it "amounted to a compulsory savings program for the Métis children" (p. 225). At another point, after acknowledging that "perfect justice was not done", he writes that "in the end, almost everyone got something" (p. 179). The latter comment illuminates Flanagan's other conclusions and demonstrates the gulf that separates his understanding of the purpose of the *Manitoba Act* guarantees from that of most Métis people. For the Métis, sections 31 and 32 of the *Manitoba Act* and the attendant verbal promises were not measures to ensure that almost everyone would eventually get something. They were designed to assure the economic and cultural survival of a unique people. They recognized that Métis people were about to experience severe economic disruption and that their homeland would soon be inundated by people of an alien culture. Even if the government of Canada had ultimately complied with every one of the guarantees, the inexcusable delay ensured that compliance was too late to serve the guarantees' intended purpose.

Justice debauched

Incomplete and delayed compliance with promises was only part of the *Manitoba Act* tragedy.[11] Métis land entitlements and scrip quickly became the subject of speculative trading by land agents, many of whom were woefully short of scruples. The lengthy delays, far from creating the compulsory savings program Flanagan imagines, provided a strong incentive to sell out early and cheap.[12] Instances of sharp dealing and fraud were common, although the full extent of such practices will never be known. Children of tender years were particularly vulnerable targets, and constitutionally questionable legislation dissolving or weakening normal legal protections for children aided and abetted their exploitation.

While most of the fraudulent and predatory practices by which individual Métis were cheated of their constitutional legacy were perpetrated by private operators, there are documented instances of bribery and fraud even on the part of government employees. One of the most notorious involved a key department of the interior official named Robert Lang, who extracted bribes from *Manitoba Act* claimants in return for expediting the claims process. Lang's activities were known to government authorities, including Prime Minister Macdonald, as early as April 1883, but he was allowed to remain on the job until early 1885. His salary continued until April 1885, by which time he had fled, with his ill-gotten assets, to the United States. He was not formally dismissed until 1887, and he was never prosecuted or sued for his activities.[13]

The government of Canada owed a fiduciary duty to the Manitoba Métis as an Aboriginal people. While the government itself may not have been involved directly in commercial exploitation of their *Manitoba Act* benefits, it was aware of much of the exploitation and, as a fiduciary, should have taken effective steps to stop it.

Conclusion

A 1991 study of the implementation of section 31 of the *Manitoba Act* found the government of Canada to have breached its constitutional obligations in fourteen respects.[14] Merely listing the subject headings of that analysis indicates the sweeping nature of the indictment:

1. Delay
2. Failure to Attach Settlement Conditions
3. Failure to Enact Laws to Protect Section 31 Interests

4. Failure to Exercise a Crown Discretion in Each Case
5. Failure to Maintain Crown Supervision Over the Intended Regulated Scheme
6. Failure to Provide Lands by Giving Scrip as a Substitute
7. Failure to Select the Lands Ahead of Incoming Settlement
8. Failure to Consider the Choice of the Beneficiaries in Respect of Land Selection
9. Failure to Distribute Lands Fit for the Purposes of Section 31
10. Failure to Give Lands to All the Children of Heads of Families
11. Failure to Provide a Benefit to Heads of Families
12. Failure to Grant the Lands for Purposes of Settlement Only
13. Setting a Time Limit for Section 31 Claims
14. Appropriating for the Purposes of the Dominion a Portion of the Lands Selected for Section 31 Purposes.

This long list of governmental transgressions does not even attempt to address the breaches that occurred in relation to section 32 of the *Manitoba Act.*

The promises made to the Métis population of Manitoba in return for their concurrence in the creation of the new province in 1870 were violated or ignored (or their implementation delayed) on a massive scale. If the unfair treatment of Métis rights in the *Manitoba Act*, the *Dominion Lands Act*, and the *Constitution Act, 1930* were ever the subject of a play, it might appropriately be called a tragedy in three acts. It is certainly no exaggeration to describe it as a national disgrace.

1.2 Contemporary Consequences

The land allotments called for by section 31 of the *Manitoba Act* were made "towards the extinguishment of the Indian Title". The process by which that provision was implemented was so flawed, so drawn out, and so contaminated by sharp practice and fraud that its basic purpose – to give the Métis people of Manitoba a satisfactory land base upon which their community and culture could flourish – was frustrated. Although ultimately only the Supreme Court of Canada can determine the legal significance of that fact, a strong case can be made for the view that the process nullified the extinguishment of Indian title contemplated by section 31. If that view is correct, the remedy is obvious: the government of Canada has a legal obligation to begin land settlement negotiations as soon as possible with representatives of the descendants of the Métis people of that area.

It can also be argued persuasively that the government's informed tolerance of the widespread chicanery that accompanied implementation of section 31, along with its own incomplete and delayed compliance with section 31, constituted serious breaches of its fiduciary duty. Fiduciary breaches may also have occurred in the implementation of section 32, which, although designed to protect all old settlers, was expected to be of importance in preserving the Métis community in the Red River Valley. The government of Canada had a fiduciary duty in the administration of section 32 to the extent that it had an impact on the Métis population of Manitoba. That impact was considerable. If there were violations of fiduciary duty in the implementation of section 32, the remedial ramifications are again clear. Breaches of the Crown's fiduciary duty to protect Métis interests would create an entitlement to compensation, and if the breaches were as serious as they seem to have been, appropriate amount of the compensation would be high.

This assessment of legal issues is not authoritative. Only the Supreme Court of Canada can settle them conclusively. Important as they are to understanding the Métis Nation's historical situation, the answers to these legal questions are outside the scope of the Commission, which is to recommend measures by which the grave historical wrongs suffered by Aboriginal peoples, including Métis, can be put right. Whatever the ultimate judicial solutions to the legal puzzles we have examined, there is no room for reasonable doubt on the moral and political plane: the Métis residents of Manitoba did not receive anything resembling what they were promised in 1870 as compensation for the extinguishment of their Indian title, and the government of Canada fell inexcusably short of its moral obligation to treat Manitoba Métis equitably. Regardless of the legal case, the government of Canada is morally obliged to enter negotiations with Métis representatives to correct this injustice.

2. *Dominion Lands Act* Territory

The *Manitoba Act* did not purport to resolve the issue of Métis title completely. Although an agreement was reached between the Métis and the Canadian government regarding the territory of the original 'postage stamp' province of Manitoba, no such agreement was reached with Métis people from other parts of the Métis homeland.

We now examine how the *Dominion Lands Act 1879* affected Métis Aboriginal title in the rest of the area that now makes up most of the prairie provinces.[15] There is serious doubt about the capacity of the *Dominion Lands Act* to extinguish the Métis interest in land in the territory to which the act applied. If it did extinguish the Aboriginal title of the Métis, a second question concerns whether the Métis received fair and just compensation for such extinguishment. The evidence is conclusive that the Métis of the west were denied fair compensation.

2.1 Dubious Extinguishment

As noted earlier, section 31 of the *Manitoba Act* recognized the existence of the Indian title of the Métis. Section 125 of the *Dominion Lands Act 1879* extended this recognition to the rest of the Northwest Territories:[16]

125. The following powers are hereby delegated to the Governor in Council:...

(e) To satisfy any claims existing in connection with extinguishment of the Indian title, preferred by half-breeds resident in the North-West Territories outside of the limits of Manitoba, on the fifteenth day of July, one thousand eight hundred and seventy, by granting land to such persons, to such extent and on such terms and conditions, as may be deemed expedient.

Another provision, relating to the confirmation of title to settled lands outside Manitoba, was, like section 32 of the *Manitoba Act*, important for Métis settlers even though it did not apply exclusively to them:

f. To investigate and adjust claims preferred to Dominion land situate outside of the Province of Manitoba, alleged to have been taken up and settled on previous to the fifteenth day of July, eighteen hundred and seventy, and to grant to persons satisfactorily establishing undisturbed occupation of any such lands, prior to, and, being by themselves or their servants, tenants or agents, or those through whom they claim, in actual peaceable possession thereof at the said date, so much land in connection with and in satisfaction of such claims, as may be considered fair and reasonable.

Although section 125 of the *Dominion Lands Act* was enacted in 1879, it was not until an order in council of 31 March 1885 that it was finally implemented.[17] The order allowed for the issuance of either land scrip or money scrip:

1. To each halfbreed head of family resident in NWT...the lot or portion of land of which he is at present time in *bona fide* and undisputed occupation...to the extent of 160 acres; if said land he is in *bona fide* occupation of is less than 160 acres, the difference to be made up by an issue of scrip redeemable in land at the rate of $1 per acre; those halfbreeds not in *bona fide* occupation of any land shall be issued scrip for $160 redeemable in land.

2. To each child of a halfbreed head of family...the lands he is at present in *bona fide* and undisputed occupation...to the extent of 240 acres; any [difference] to be made up by an issue of scrip redeemable in land...if not in *bona fide* occupation of any land, such child to be issued scrip redeemable in land for $240.[18]

If Métis residents satisfied the requirements of occupation of land, (which were ethnocentric and unduly restrictive given the traditional nature of Métis land use patterns), they were entitled to land scrip; if not, they were entitled to money scrip redeemable for land.[19]

The implications of the *Dominion Lands Act* have been the focus of a number of legal studies.[20] The concern has stemmed from the fact that despite the statute's express provision of land grants to all Métis heads of family and children, only a small percentage of Métis ever received and retained land.[21]

The *Dominion Lands Act* was not, as the *Manitoba Act* had been, the product of a negotiated settlement. Although the *Dominion Lands Act* recognized the existence of Métis Indian title, Métis people had no opportunity to negotiate the terms of surrender of that title. By enacting the *Dominion Lands Act*, Parliament attempted to extinguish Métis title unilaterally and to deny Métis peoples any say in how they would be compensated for their title. This failure to deal with Métis people in the northwest as Aboriginal collectivities capable of deciding their own best interests was not only an insensitive and immoral act of disregard, it was arguably unconstitutional.

The Crown had promised, in the *Rupert's Land and North-Western Territory Order* of 1870, that its actions regarding Aboriginal interests in land would conform with "equitable principles which have uniformly governed the British Crown in its dealings with the aborigines". Similar protections were enunciated in the *Royal Proclamation of 1763*. Of particular importance was the requirement for Aboriginal consent to extinguish Aboriginal title, which was a necessary prerequisite for opening the Northwestern territory to general settlement because, according to Justice Morrow in *Re Paulette*, the *Rupert's Land Order* and attached schedules are part of the constitution of Canada.[22] The federal government was thus under a positive constitutional obligation to deal equitably with the Aboriginal peoples of Rupert's Land and the Northwest Territories. Thus, if one defines Métis as Indians or Aboriginal people under the *Rupert's Land Order*, then as a group they had a constitutional right to participate in negotiations concerning whether and on what terms their Aboriginal title should be extinguished.

The arguments applicable to the issue of whether Métis are Indians under section 91(24) of the *Constitution Act, 1867* are equally applicable to the interpretation that should be given the *Rupert's Land Order*. The order and the *Constitution Act, 1867* were drafted in the same period.

We have suggested elsewhere that the weight of the arguments strongly supports the conclusion that the term Indians in section 91(24) must be given a broad definition that includes Métis. It seems likely that if a court were asked the question directly, it would find that the Métis are Indians within the meaning of the *Rupert's Land and North-Western Territory Order* as well. In any event, the Supreme Court of Canada pointed out in *Guerin* that Aboriginal rights exist independently of royal ordinances.[23]

In unilaterally enacting section 125(e) of the *Dominion Lands Act* without acquiring the consent of the Métis, Parliament violated the equitable principles it was obligated to respect. As a result, the constitutional capacity of section 125 to extinguish Métis Aboriginal title may be in doubt. If the doubt is justified, Métis Aboriginal title persists in much of western Canada and has been constitutionally entrenched by section 35 of the *Constitution Act, 1982*.

Even if section 125 was within Parliament's constitutional jurisdiction, questions arise as to its effect. The phrase "in connection with the extinguishment" could be interpreted to mean that the grants are to be only a part of a larger extinguishment process and would not, in themselves, affect Aboriginal title until some more direct act of extinguishment occurred (which never happened). It is also possible that even if the grants were intended to bring about extinguishment directly, they had that effect only for Métis who actually became land owners under the scheme. Finally, the mere granting of scrip may not have constituted granting land under section 125.

2.2 Fiduciary Duty

Even if doubts about the constitutional validity and legal effect of section 125(e) are not justified, it is unquestionable that the equitable principles the government of Canada was obliged to respect in its relations with Indians included the fiduciary duty, described in Appendix 5A, to act in the best interests of Aboriginal people. One aspect of that duty required the government to proceed, where possible, by negotiation rather than by unilateral legislation when dealing with Aboriginal title. There were other obligations too; the government of Canada was duty-bound in everything it did affecting the Métis to act in the best interests of Métis people.

In assessing whether the Crown fulfilled that fiduciary duty, the following questions must be addressed:

- Was it in the best interests of Métis people for Parliament to substitute individual grants for the collective entitlements of Métis communities?
- Was it in the best interests of Métis people to be given compensation with no guarantees of hunting, fishing or other rights that would enable them to make a living and ensure the survival of their way of life?
- Was it in the best interests of Métis people to be given compensation in a form that benefitted speculators, not the Métis?
- Was it in the best interests of Métis people to be allotted scrip for homesteads in lands hundreds of miles from their home communities?
- Was it in the best interests of Métis people to have to deal with land title offices hundreds of miles away to acquire the land promised?
- Was it in the best interests of Métis people that dominion land agents interpreted 'occupation' of the land to require cultivation rather than traditional Métis activities of hunting, fishing and trapping?
- Was it in the best interests of Métis people for the federal government, when the failure of the scrip program became clear, to ignore the problem?

- Was it in the best interests of Métis people for the federal government to ignore and facilitate abuses by speculators and government officials?

The foregoing are only some of the issues that arise from the administration and implementation of the *Dominion Lands Act.* To answer some of these questions, Frank Tough and Leah Dorion conducted research on the scrip process in northern Saskatchewan and northern Manitoba, which paralleled the Treaty 5 and Treaty 10 commissions that occurred from 1906 to 1910. The researchers reconstructed the paper trail associated with scrip certificates: application, assessment of claim and transactions. They concluded that the scrip scheme program was based on "one of the most convoluted policies ever created by the Canadian nation state". Their description reveals that Métis people were largely irrelevant to the process:

> At a few points in the process, the Métis play a brief part. They stand before a Commissioner and provide some information. They assign their scrip to a scrip middleman...Some Xs are attached to paper, a power of attorney, a scrip receipt, a quit claim deed. If the case is complicated by guardianship of a minor or the estate of a deceased claimant, more papers are signed. A few may have entered a Dominion Lands Office and played a part in locating land in their name, after which the land was assigned to a scrip middleman or small purchaser. If the scrip needed to be redbacked, then perhaps more signatures and Xs were attached to another set of documents. Some of these documents are executed in blank.[24]

Tough and Dorion report that the department of the interior was aware of the lack of benefit accruing to the Métis in exchange for their Aboriginal title, in particular, the problem of Métis being forced to locate their entitlements in surveyed homestead lands. In northern Saskatchewan and Manitoba, for example, no Métis were able to claim land unless they relocated to the homestead belt, far from their communities. This meant moving hundreds of miles from their homes, their families and their economic pursuits.

Exploiting the Métis dilemma were the scrip speculators. Métis people who were not willing to leave their homes, identity and families had only to go to the scrip commissioner's tent to find ready buyers. In most cases, they had no choice but to sell the land they were entitled to at a fraction of its value. An official of the department of interior named Semmens complained about the failure of the scrip policies for Métis people in the northern and unsurveyed lands:

> The claim of half-breeds of Keewatin [northern Manitoba] is based upon adhesions made in that territory. Why not give them land on their own soil instead of allowing them to claim valuable Alberta or Saskatchewan lands which they will not improve. They sell to white

men as soon as they receive a settlement and these white men pay but little and gain much and grow wealthy quick on advantages intended for the half-breed only if it were determined that only Keewatin Lands would be given it would dampen the ardour of Buyers and lands good enough for the Halfbreed might be given for their use in their own territory. My experience goes to show that nine-tenths of these people will not settle on the land given to them.[25]

Despite these concerns, nothing was done to change the scrip program.

The government of Canada apparently did not want the Métis occupying large contiguous areas, analogous to Indian reserves, perhaps fearing that such occupation would discourage immigration to the west. In Manitoba, an order in council recommended "'in view of the great dissatisfaction which has been caused in Manitoba by the locking up of large and valuable tracts of land for distribution among Half-breeds' that *only* scrip be issued to satisfy the claims".[26]

The Crown's underlying policy of preventing the Manitoba Métis from getting land in large tracts was revealed by Adams George Archibald, lieutenant governor of Manitoba, in a memo to the secretary of state, Joseph Howe. After quoting the memo, a report prepared for the Metis Association of Alberta concludes:

> The government wanted to establish a situation where potential settlers and developers would have as much freedom as possible in choosing sites for development. It was felt that if the Métis lands were made inalienable, as the Indian reserves were, that this would completely block an orderly settlement of land. (p. 110)

Archibald's original plans were for a good faith implementation of section 31 of the *Manitoba Act*, which would have been much more direct, taking only two years. However, that policy was rejected by the secretary of state.

> Howe said that they could not condone 'giving countenance to the wholesale appropriation of large tracts of country by half-breeds.' Archibald was told to back away from his...recommendations, 'to leave the land department and the Dominion Government to carry out their policy without volunteering any interference'.

The policy appears to have been applied to the Northwest Territories as well as to Manitoba.

To further this policy, the lands promised to Métis people were to be administered under a system that would facilitate both non-Aboriginal settlement and the appropriation of Métis land. If this was the objective of the Crown, it conflicted with its fiduciary obligation to ensure that the best interests of the Métis were served. Métis provisions in the *Dominion Lands Act* were certainly contrary to the best interests of Métis people.

If the Crown did have a fiduciary duty to act in good faith in regard to Métis Nation lands – which seems likely, even if the courts have not yet expressly decided the issue – there can be little doubt that the duty was breached. Research shows that the scrip program benefitted speculators at the expense of the Métis with the Crown's knowledge and sometimes its assistance.[27] One of the most flagrant acts was the 1921 amendment to the *Criminal Code* that imposed a very short time limitation of three years on anyone wanting to press criminal charges regarding Métis scrip entitlements. The scheme employed to implement section 125 of the *Dominion Lands Act* almost completely prevented Métis from patenting land. The research conducted by Frank Tough and Leah Dorion illustrates the nature and extent of Métis frustration.

In the *Guerin* decision, the Supreme Court of Canada described the fiduciary duty owed to Aboriginal peoples by the Crown as follows:

> Equity will not countenance unconscionable behaviour in a fiduciary, whose duty is that of utmost loyalty to his principal.

The government of Canada claimed to be protecting the Métis by enactment and implementation of legislation, but the measures were, for the most part, protective only in theory. The Crown, aware that most Métis were not benefitting from the scrip program, should have taken remedial steps in the best interests of the Métis. In our opinion, its failure to do so constitutes a grave breach of fiduciary duty. If that failure did not nullify the extinguishment provisions of the *Dominion Lands Act* altogether, it at least entitled the victims of the breach to fair reparation.

2.3 Lack of Uniform Treatment

The Crown promised in the *Rupert's Land Order, 1870* that its actions regarding Aboriginal interests in land would conform with equitable principles that *uniformly* governed its dealings with Aboriginal people. In a research study conducted for the Commission, Joseph Magnet observed that

> in the North-West Territories, the federal government acted unilaterally to extinguish Métis Aboriginal title, contrary to the practice of negotiating treaties which had been used with Indian tribes since [early contact]. In doing so, the federal government discriminated against the Métis. Indian tribes negotiated the surrender of their Aboriginal title through treaty. In return, they received reserve lands, perpetual annuities, farm implements, livestock, schools, instructors, etc. Indians retained their hunting and fishing rights on surrendered lands. Indians came under the protection of the federal government. Their reserve lands, which became collective homelands,

were held in trust by the Crown until such time as they were voluntarily surrendered. In stark contrast, each Métis received at most a grant of 240 acres of land as a once-and-for-all settlement of his or her claim to Aboriginal title.[28]

Such discriminatory treatment does not comply with the policy of uniform treatment for the Aboriginal peoples of the west implied in the *Rupert's Land Order*.

Furthermore, the Métis did not have the same protection as First Nations had with the requirement that reserve land could be surrendered or sold only to the Crown. The Crown holds Indian lands in trust for their benefit and protects the lands from unscrupulous third-party purchasers. The Métis were not given equivalent protection. This discriminatory policy is hard to reconcile with the uniformity of treatment promised in the *Rupert's Land Order* and with the Crown's fiduciary duty to Métis people.

2.4 Conclusion

To a person unfamiliar with Métis rights and how they were dealt with under the *Dominion Lands Act*, the fact that huge tracts of prairie land were distributed in the name of Métis individuals outside Manitoba suggests that fair and just compensation was received for extinguishment of Métis Aboriginal title. The reality, however, was that the extinguishment process was fundamentally flawed:

- The Métis were neither consulted about nor given an opportunity to negotiate the terms under which their Aboriginal title was to be extinguished.
- Compensation to individuals was substituted for the collective right of Aboriginal title.
- The land allocated was usually located so far from their homes as to be useless to the Métis, except for the token sums offered by land speculators. In some cases, they received only cash grants.
- The compensation, far from reflecting equitable principles in dealings with Aboriginal people, was discriminatory. It did not treat Métis as well as Indian peoples, in that the land provided was unnegotiated, arbitrary, individualized, non-contiguous, far from the recipients' homes, without protection against non-Aboriginals, and without the other benefits accorded Indians. It did not treat the Métis affected as well as the Métis of Manitoba, since the latter had an opportunity to negotiate the terms of their compensation and were in some cases offered land grants in addition to the land on which they had already settled.
- Sharp dealing and fraud, to which the government of Canada usually turned a blind eye, robbed many Métis individuals of the compensation they were offered.

These flaws were so basic and so flagrant that they deprived the extinguishment process of all legitimacy. Even if that were not the case legally, it was most certainly the case morally. The attempted extinguishment of Métis Aboriginal rights under the *Dominion Lands Act* cannot be reconciled with the Crown's fiduciary obligations, the equitable principles referred to in the *Rupert's Land Order*, or the dictates of common decency.

3. Other Métis Nation Territory

This part of the appendix addresses some issues relating to the parts of the Métis Nation homeland not dealt with under the *Manitoba Act* or the *Dominion Lands Act* or by policies and orders in council under those acts.

3.1 British Columbia

The colony of British Columbia became a province of the Dominion of Canada on 20 July 1871. It was excluded from the purview of the *Dominion Lands Act*, which received assent on 14 April 1872. In the absence of separate legislation, orders in council, policy or treaties, the Métis in the province of British Columbia would not have been affected or involved in settling their Aboriginal title or other Aboriginal rights.

The only legislative provisions that might have bearing on Aboriginal rights are the terms and conditions embodied in the *Order of Her Majesty in Council Admitting British Columbia into the Union*, dated 16 May 1871. Term 13 provides:

> The charge of Indians, and the trusteeship and management of the lands reserved for their use and benefit, shall be assumed by the Dominion Government, and a policy as liberal as that hitherto pursued by the British Columbia Government shall be continued by the Dominion Government after the Union.[29]

Acting under this provision in 1889, the federal government entered into Treaty 8 with the Indian people of the Northwest Territories and northeastern British Columbia. The Métis in the Northwest Territories were dealt with through half-breed scrip commissions. The Métis within that portion of Treaty 8 that fell within British Columbia were not. A good example of this is the Métis community of Kelly Lake, close to the Alberta border.

As well, a number of Métis are believed to have moved to other parts of British Columbia prior to 1871. In the hearings of the Select Committee on the Hudson's Bay Company of 1857, Alexander Isbister, a Métis, testified that some Métis crossed the Rocky Mountains to Vancouver:

> There were a number of emigrants, amounting to about 200, who left Red River the very spring I left it myself to come to England; they went across the country from Red River with their cattle and carts, and went right down to Fort Vancouver with all their property.[30]

Although they are not referred to as Métis, it can be assumed that most of those persons were in fact Métis. There was certainly some migration by Métis people to B.C., but research is needed to determine how many of them did so prior to its becoming a province. The Aboriginal title of those Métis people, of course, could not be dealt with unless they returned to areas covered by the acts in question.

Some Métis people who were covered by the *Manitoba Act* and the *Dominion Lands Act* later moved to British Columbia. If those acts did not extinguish Métis Aboriginal title to land, then whether or not post-1870 Métis migrants to B.C. can claim title must be determined. If they do not have Aboriginal title to these lands, what accommodations are necessary to satisfy their moral and political rights to lands and resources?

3.2 The North and Ontario

Apart from the province of British Columbia, the traditional territories of the Métis Nation largely fell within the province of Manitoba and the Northwest Territories.[31] The Northwest Territories, which included the entire drainage basin of Hudson Bay, covered the majority of the land mass of Canada, including approximately three-quarters of what is now Ontario, two-thirds of what is now Quebec, and half of what is now Labrador. Although the provinces of Ontario and Quebec (like British Columbia) were excluded from coverage, much of the vast northern area that is now part of Ontario and Quebec at that time fell within the Northwest Territories, to which the *Dominion Lands Act* did apply.

In practice, however, the government of Canada made little effort to apply the *Dominion Lands Act* east of Manitoba. There appears to be no legal reason why the government limited the distribution of Métis scrip to what are now the three prairie provinces and the Mackenzie Valley of the Northwest Territories. The Métis of Rainy River, for example, who concluded the ill-fated adhesion to Treaty 3 in 1875, ought to have had their rights safeguarded by the 1870 order. Since the Rainy River area was still part of the Northwest Territories in 1883, they could have been dealt with by virtue of section 125. So could Métis people in Moose Factory and other portions of the Northwest Territories that became part of Ontario a few years later. Even after those parts of the Northwest Territories became part of Ontario, pre-existing Métis rights should have been dealt with by the federal and Ontario governments.

The same holds true for those parts of the Métis Nation homeland in Ontario that fell outside the purview of the *Dominion Lands Act*. In the absence of treaties by which their Aboriginal rights were surrendered, Métis people within the original boundaries of the province of Ontario, like their counterparts in British Columbia, possessed the same rights as Métis people covered by the *Manitoba Act* and the *Dominion Lands Act*. Those rights have never, however, been recognized, much less respected.

4. Resource Uses

The report of the Northern Fur Conservation Area Trappers Association describes the importance of resources to Métis people:

> For over two hundred years now, the Métis of Northern Saskatchewan have lived in harmony with our land and its resources. We have made use of the land, the trees, the wild plants, the waters, the fish and the game, taking what we needed for our livelihood. During this time we built strong values, strong families, and strong communities.
>
> These communities...were not just a small patch of land defined by some bureaucrat...it includes the trap lines of our families, it includes the lakes and the fish which support our people, it includes the wild game which feeds our people, it includes the wild fruits which we harvest, it includes the wild rice which we harvest both commercially and for our own use, it includes the trees which we use to build our homes and which we also harvest commercially, and most important, it included the people and that spirit of the Métis community that can't really be described in [the English] words we learn in school.
>
> The spirit, the community soul that probably can only really be described in Cree...is not past. It is true that in recent years the soul of [communities]...has dimmed and the spirit of some of our people has been covered over, covered but not lost.
>
> We are fortunate, you see, because we have not been removed from our traditions for several generations, as has happened to many of our people who have lived in the cities of the south for several generations. Many of us, who live in Northern Métis communities, still make our living in the traditional ways, and almost all of us remember the days when we used our resources for our needs and processed these resources in our own communities. Today most of us remember, today we understand.
>
> But in two or three generations who will understand, if we don't regain control over our own lives? What will become of our people and our way of life, if governments are allowed to continue to take control of our traditional sources of livelihood, then give control of these resources to the big companies and the mining companies?[32]

This passage captures the essence of the need to affirm and recognize the rights of Métis people to use natural resources. The presentation describes the daily connection of the Métis of Northern Saskatchewan with the resources of the area. The fact that urban Métis may not have this same relationship does not diminish their right to preserve their traditional links to the land.

This analysis must look beyond rights and traditions, however, to recognize the economic and social implications of resource ownership and use. A main foundational attribute of Métis society, indeed all Aboriginal societies, is the harvesting of natural resources. Hunting and trapping remain an important part of life for many Métis. Beyond that, there is a valid claim to other resource ownership and use on a scale sufficient to provide spiritual and material support for Métis aspirations.

4.1 Harvesting and Other Traditional Use Rights

In terms of traditional harvesting rights, the primary area of importance to many Métis is wildlife. Included here are the right to hunt game and fowl, to trap furbearing animals, and to take fish. This is important because many Métis are actively involved, to varying degrees, in these activities today. In addition, Métis also gather berries and other edible plant life, use plants and roots for medicines, use wood for cooking and warmth, and collect materials for handicrafts.

Resource harvesting is undertaken for both individual consumption and commercial purposes. Many Métis harvest big game and fowl in the autumn. Those living a subsistence or traditional lifestyle hunt and trap throughout the year. A large number of Canadian wild fur trappers are Métis. This continuing practice is based on the traditional way of life of the Métis throughout the Métis homelands. Historically, the Métis were an integral part of the fur trade and were directly connected to the buffalo hunt. This way of life has been recognized by governments in legislation, orders in council and policies.

Archival and court documents

On 27 May 1927 Special Fisheries Regulations for the Provinces of Saskatchewan and Alberta and The Territories North Thereof were adopted by order in council. Under the authority of the federal department of marine and fisheries the regulations provided that

> 3. Any Indian or half-breed resident in either of these provinces shall be eligible for an annual fishing permit, which shall entitle him or a member of his family to fish with not more than sixty yards of gill-net for domestic use, but not for sale or barter....Such permit shall be issued free.[33]

In the Northwest Territories, there has been a long-standing tradition of recognizing the Métis people's harvesting practices and reliance upon wildlife. This tradition was recognized in an order in council passed on 14 January 1931 concerning the permission granted to Indians and Métis to trap beaver during a three-year closed season:

> That because of a serious epidemic of influenza which broke out among the natives in 1928, making it difficult to secure food, Treaty

Indians and half-breeds were permitted under the authority of P.C. 2146, dated 28th November, 1928, to take a limited number of beaver;

That representations have now been made that because of the scarcity of fur-bearing animals in the Mackenzie District the natives have not been able to secure adequate returns from their trapping operations to enable them to purchase sufficient food for themselves and their families.

Therefore...the Royal Canadian Mounted Police as game officers...be empowered to issue a permit to one member of each Indian family or each half-breed family leading the life of Indians...where the needs of such family warrant such an exception being made.[34]

On 3 July 1947 an order in council was issued to deal with an unnecessary slaughter of caribou "upon which many of the native residents are dependent for food and clothing".[35] By this order in council, P.C. 786 of 10 May 1924 was revoked, and regulations for the protection of game in the Northwest Territories, established by P.C. 1925 of 22 July 1939, were amended. Section 14 of the regulations was revoked and replaced by the following:

14   (1) Subject to the provisions of these regulations, or of any ordinance of the Northwest Territories, the holder of a hunting and trapping licence may:
      (a) hunt, kill, take or trap game during the open season;
      (b) have in his possession at all times the pelts and skins of such game as he has legally trapped or killed;
      (c) sell, trade, ship or remove such pelts and skins.
  (2) The rights of a holder of a hunting and trapping licence, as specified in this section, may be exercised, without the issue of a licence, by the following: every native-born Indian or native-born half-breed leading the life of an Indian; every native-born Eskimo, or native-born half-breed leading the life of an Eskimo.[36]

More recently, the courts in the Northwest Territories were asked to decide whether the fisheries regulations violated the *Canadian Bill of Rights* on the basis of race since they exempted Indians, Inuit and persons of mixed blood from licensing that applied to the accused, who was not an Aboriginal person.[37] At trial, Justice Ayotte dismissed the preliminary objection on the basis that Parliament, by virtue of section 91(24) of the *Constitution Act, 1867*, had jurisdiction to pass the challenged regulatory scheme. On appeal, the Northwest Territories Supreme Court overturned the conviction. However, in the judgement, Justice de Weerdt stated that "persons of mixed blood" are "commonly called 'Métis' in the Mackenzie Valley area". He noted in regard to the regulations that the "federal objective presumably in mind when section 22 of the Regulations was enacted was the preservation of aboriginal rights and freedoms in relation to domestic fishing by 'Indians' in the widest sense of that term".

The Crown appealed, and the Court of Appeal reinstated the conviction on the basis that section 22 was a method by which "natives, or persons of native descent or native blood" are accorded priority for food purposes, for a restricted resource and for the objective of conservation. According to Justice Stevenson, the

> Governor in Council concluded that a limited priority was to be given to natives. The rationale for according native persons priority for food is clear. Their needs are a primary responsibility of Canada under the Constitution, a responsibility confirmed, in many cases, by treaty.[38]

In a 1936 presentation, "What Canada is Doing for the Hunting Indians", prepared for the North American Wildlife Conference in Washington, D.C., T.R.L. MacInnes of the department of Indian affairs outlined federal and provincial initiatives in setting aside Indian hunting areas in Ontario:

> As far as possible it is the object to retain the Northern Section for the Indians living in that area and other residents living north of the Grand Trunk Pacific Railway line that would be eligible for the same privileges as granted to Treaty Indians and half-breeds, with the understanding, however, that as far as the white trappers are concerned their trapping grounds will be limited to a certain given area in close proximity to their respective homes.[39]

In the 1930s, the government of Alberta established a royal commission to investigate the conditions of the 'half-breed' population of Alberta. Their report was released in 1936 by the department of lands and mines. That commission recommended a colonization scheme providing lands to 'half-breeds' that were conducive to hunting and fishing. In this regard, the commission was of the opinion that the Métis would get food from hunting and fishing:

> In the earlier stages the whole of their living would come from these sources. It is to be hoped that they would, in time, come to rely more and more on their farming and stock raising operations.[40]

The commissioners viewed the Métis as having a definite prior and valid claim to harvesting rights and as relying on traditional hunting and fishing practices to support themselves:

> The Commission is of opinion that as the Métis were the original inhabitants of these great unsettled areas and are dependent on wildlife and fish for their livelihood, they should be given the pref-

erence over non-residents in respect of fur, game and fish....They should, however, be given free permits under proper regulations, both for fishing and hunting, and if any area was in danger of depletion, that particular area should be protected for the Métis who should be given preferred rights. We are firmly of opinion that non-resident commercial operators have no right to deplete the fish, the game and fur-bearing animals in any district and leave the native inhabitants to be a charge on the country.

The perspective of the Saskatchewan government at the time is shown in a letter from T.C. Davis, attorney general for Saskatchewan, to T.A. Crerar, federal minister of the interior, mines, immigration and superintendent general of Indian Affairs, dated 11 December 1935. The letter followed a conversation between the two about "the problem of the half-breed in Saskatchewan". The problem and solution, according to Davis, were as follows:

> These non-treaty half-breeds constitute a considerable problem. The Indian strain predominates and they are to all intents and purposes Indians in their habits and their outlook upon life. They are unable to compete with the white man and therefore have to receive assistance from the state. They would be infinitely better off if they were under the direction of the Department of Indian Affairs and put on the Indian Reserves.
>
> We would therefore suggest that they be given the opportunity of becoming Treaty Indians, moving onto the Indian Reserves and coming under the jurisdiction of the Indian Department.

In discussing the proposed fur conservation blocks in Saskatchewan, Field Officer W.G. Tunstead of Ile-a-la-Crosse proposed:

> Since the treaty indian are already in bands, areas can be blocked off to accommodate the entire band. Believe that the halfbreed, or at least the great majority of them should likewise be handled in this way. They like the treaty indian have been nomads for so many generations that staying put in any one particular spot just can't be done. Having large areas where they would have ample room to move around within its boundaries should prove more to the point.[41]

Wildlife conservation and the welfare of the Métis remained important issues in Saskatchewan. In a 1961 letter to a lawyer dealing with the Métis people about compensation for the Primrose Air Weapons Range, Premier Tommy Douglas said: "My understanding has always been that the Métis had certain traditional rights in the matter of trapping and fishing".[42] Douglas's sentiments are in accord with the Métis view that they have an Aboriginal right under section

35 of the *Constitution Act, 1982* to harvest wildlife. In this connection, the issue of extinguishment will have a bearing on whether or not the rights have survived.

The *Natural Resources Transfer Agreements* of 1930 provide protection for the continuing right of 'Indians' to hunt, trap and fish for food in the provinces of Manitoba, Saskatchewan and Alberta. This legal issue has not been settled; it has, however, received some judicial attention, which we consider below.

Judicial decisions

The continuing right of Métis people to hunt and fish has not been settled by the courts at this time. The leading case in this area was *R. v. Laprise* in which the Saskatchewan Court of Appeal ruled in 1978 that non-treaty Indians were not covered by paragraph 12 of the *Natural Resources Transfer Agreement (Constitution Act, 1930).*[43] The court ruled that persons not entitled to registration under the *Indian Act* were also not covered. George Laprise stated in his testimony that his mother was a treaty Indian and his father a non-treaty Indian. (Since the passage of Bill C-31 in 1985, Laprise has gained Indian status.) He wasn't sure whether his father or his grandfather had received scrip. Review of records indicate that his paternal grandfather and grandmother did receive it.

Two recent cases, which have not proceeded past the Court of Queen's Bench, have given hope to the Métis that their rights will be recognized and protected by the courts. In Manitoba two Métis men were charged with hunting out of season. As a defence, they argued that they had a common law Aboriginal right to do so by virtue of section 35 of the *Constitution Act, 1982.*[44] They did not rely on the *Natural Resources Transfer Agreement.* In Alberta a Métis man was charged with hunting without a licence and with possessing wildlife contrary to the *Wildlife Act,* that is, he did not have a licence to kill moose. As a defence, he argued that he had the right to hunt moose because he was an Indian within the meaning of the *Natural Resources Transfer Agreement.*[45] He did not rely on section 35 of the *Constitution Act, 1982.* We address the Manitoba case first.

McPherson case

This case raises several issues, including extinguishment – that is, whether the right is an existing one – and whether the right is limited only to Métis living a subsistence lifestyle. On the issue of extinguishment, the trial judge concluded that

> some Metis historically may have given up their Aboriginal rights by the acceptance of [scrip] and their families and descendants may be bound by that decision of their ancestor. Other individuals, who consider themselves Metis people may have lost their Aboriginal right to hunt by reason of the fact that for an extended period of time, they have no longer participated actively in the traditional hunting, fish-

ing and gathering way of life but rather have become molded into the mainstream lifestyle. The evidence was that hunting should be firstly reserved for those who truly require hunting as a means of subsistence.... The court agrees with that proposition.[46]

While the decision supports Métis hunting rights in some ways, its suggestion that those rights may have been extinguished for some Métis because their ancestors accepted scrip or they had abandoned a traditional lifestyle is questionable. As the Supreme Court of Canada said in *Sparrow*, "the test of extinguishment to be adopted, in our opinion, is that the Sovereign's intention must be clear and plain if it is to extinguish an aboriginal right".[47]

In the case of the Métis, the legislation dealing with Métis land rights is set out earlier in this appendix. Even if the courts found that Métis Aboriginal title had been extinguished validly (which we believe is not the case), the extinguishment of Métis Aboriginal rights to hunt and fish is far from certain, since those rights were never mentioned in any document that claimed to extinguish Métis Aboriginal title.

Historically, when successive governments intended to effect extinguishment, clear and plain words to that effect were used. For example, in dealing with the surrender by the Hudson's Bay Company of its territory, the surrender was very explicit:

> 4. Upon the Acceptance by Her Majesty of such Surrender all Rights of Government and Proprietary Rights, and all other Privileges, Liberties, Franchises, Powers, and Authorities whatsoever, granted or purported to be granted by the said Letters Patent to the said Governor and Company within Rupert's Land, and which shall have been so surrendered, shall be absolutely extinguished.[48]

With respect to Indian peoples and treaties, there was specific language when extinguishment was being intended. Treaty No. 10, for example, states clearly:

> Now therefore the said Indians do hereby cede, release, surrender and yield up to the government of the Dominion of Canada for His Majesty the King and His successors for ever all their rights, titles and privileges whatsoever to the lands included within the following limits....[49]

The order in council authorizing Treaty 10 provided that the treaty would include the setting aside of reserves or land in severalty, the payment of monies to each Indian, educational provisions and assistance for farming or other work.[50] For Métis people, the order in council provided only for the issuing of money scrip in the amount of $240 for purchase of Crown land or land scrip for 240 acres of Crown land.

There was no mention in the order in council of hunting and fishing rights for either the Indian or Métis peoples. In fact, as a result of the negotiations, Treaty 10 provided for the continuation of the Indian right "to pursue their usual vocations of hunting, trapping and fishing throughout the territory surrendered". These rights were provided in other treaties, and there was no other way for most Indian people to survive.

There is evidence that the scrip commissioner, Mr. McKenna (who also happened to be the treaty commissioner) assured the Métis in the area covered by Treaty 10 that their way of life would not be affected by accepting scrip. Most Métis, like their Indian relations and neighbours, had no other way to survive, a point supported by the commissioner in his report:

> The Indians dealt with are in character, habit and manner of dress and mode of living similar to the Chipewyans and Crees of the Athabaska country. It is difficult to draw a line of demarcation between those who classed themselves as Indians and those who elected to be *treated with* as half-breeds. Both dress alike and follow the same mode of life. It struck me that the one group was on, the whole, as well able to provide for self-support as the other.[51] [emphasis added]

Ross Cummings, a Métis from Buffalo Narrows who was present at Ile-a-la-Crosse when scrip was distributed in 1906, confirmed in a recorded interview at Batoche in 1976 that dialogue between the scrip commissioner, McKenna, and the Métis assembled to receive him concerned the effect that accepting scrip would have on hunting, trapping and fishing rights. According to Cummings' recollection of the discussion, harvesting rights would not be affected:

> CLEM CHARTIER: [English] Ask if the people knew that they were giving up their rights?

> JACQUES CHARTIER: [interpreting in Cree] Did they know they were giving up their rights to hunt, fish and trap and the use of their land?

> ROSS CUMMINGS: [Cree] The Big Boss [Scrip Commissioner] said I won't tell you guys what to do as long as the sun moves. I won't tell you guys what to do, I'll look after you. We'll look after you. That's what I heard him say. There was a lot of people outside that heard him say that too. You'll be given money and the money man [Indian Agent] will give you money to use. If you're given money, the money man will give you equipment to use. As long as the sun is moving they will always look after you. That's when they took the land and they took the money. The treaties first and then the halfbreeds. That's when I became a non-treaty and took the scrip.

CLEM CHARTIER: Were the halfbreeds told that too or just the treaty Indians?

JACQUES CHARTIER: Was everybody told that or just the halfbreeds?

ROSS CUMMINGS: Yes, yes he told everybody there gathered at the assembly.

CLEM CHARTIER: Even if you still took land scrip you'd still get hunting and fishing rights?

JACQUES CHARTIER: Even if you took land scrip you'd still get hunting and fishing rights?

ROSS CUMMINGS: Yes, yes. Nobody was told anything until maybe twenty years later and then they started telling us. Twenty years…[English] after that scrip. [Cree] Everybody hunted, we hunted everywhere and then all of a sudden they started to come after us. Then we had to pay for everything we did. [English] We pay everything. Pay everything. Worse every year. Even now worse everything.[52]

The following year, in 1977, Mr. Cummings and another scrip recipient were at a meeting at Palmbere Lake in northwestern Saskatchewan and informed participants through an interpreter, Louis Morin, as follows:

Charlie Janvier from LaLoche and Ross Cummings from Buffalo, they said they were 16 years old at the time they first gave the scrip and they were promised everything. They said they were promised everything as long as the sun moves you'll get what you want and this scrip, it's going to be just for a while, your kids or your children, they're going to have another scrip and they're going to get some more money and your hunting rights of everybody will never be affected. Now they say everything is broken, there is nothing what we were promised, that is what these two old…chaps, said.[53]

At that same meeting, one of the guests, elder, spiritualist and healer William Joseph of the Whitefish Reserve (also known as the Big River Reserve) near Debden, Saskatchewan, addressed the audience. According to Mr. Joseph, the understanding of the signatories to Treaty 6 was as follows:

Regards about land scrip, the Government promised the Indians, Métis Society to have their land scrip every 25 years, free taxes; I learned that over 50 years ago, by the people that signed the treaties, 1876, I seen them in person; I am the interpreter in my days, back about 60 years ago. I studied, I compared with Métis Society, the same with our treaties. They are the same thing, you people have no reserve, but you have the free land every 25 years. But the promise is dying away; Why?!! You don't study enough, you don't inquire what happened.

You have the same right to kill meat, but you seems to be shivering, you're afraid to step over, don't be ashamed, God will help you....[54]

Another scrip recipient, in his testimony in the Laprise trial in 1976, related that

> Robbie Fontaine, 79 years of age, testified that he was a half-breed and that he had some recollection of the time when the Treaty and Scrip Commissioner attended the area. His evidence was that it had only been for the last twenty to thirty years that the Non-Treaty Indians have required licences to hunt. He said that Treaty and non-Treaty Indians always lived the same lifestyle in the area.
>
> Mr. Fontaine further gave evidence of an occasion many years before where he took a trip similar in duration to that taken by the accused to hunt caribou, although he was not a Treaty Indian, that hunting was considered lawful. He corroborated the evidence of the accused with respect to the tradition of sharing the fruits of hunting.[55]

Further support is given to this understanding that Métis people had continuing hunting rights by another scrip recipient, Marie Rose McCallum of Ile-a-la-Crosse, in a questionnaire filled out in 1976. Mrs. McCallum was born on 26 February 1890 and would have been 16 years old when commissioner McKenna distributed scrip in that community. According to her, she and her contemporaries understood that they would continue to have hunting and fishing rights. She declared that hunting and fishing were done openly all year 'round and that it was only later that they could not hunt and fish without a licence.[56]

While official government records or documents acknowledging that scrip commissioners guaranteed Métis people that their way of life would not be affected appear not to exist, corroboration for the statements made by the scrip recipients can be found in the 1911 final report of the Alberta and Saskatchewan fishery commission (known as the Prince Commission), presented to J.D. Hazen, minister of marine and fisheries by commissioners Prince, McGuire and Sisley.

The report contains accounts of witness presentations. At Lac la Loche, Saskatchewan, the report lists the following witnesses: Lamuel Janvier, Michel Lamerge, Angus McLean at the Hudson's Bay Company post and Reverend Père Pinard, Joseph Janvier, Pierre Maurice and J. Pickering at Revillon Company Post. According to available scrip records, Michel Lamerge, Joseph Janvier and Pierre Maurice received scrip. It is assumed that Angus McLean, Reverend

Pinard and J. Pickering were non-Aboriginal people. Lamuel Janvier was most likely Métis, as the records indicate his wife received scrip.

The following evidence was recorded:

> Fish are hung in October....It would be hard on the natives to stop fishing in spawning time. Only lake near this is Whitefish Lake – great mortality of whitefish there two years ago. Worms there destroy nets in the fall – about 250 Indian residents around La Loche. Scrip Commissioners told the Indians they would not be interfered with in fishing or hunting.[57]

It is clear that the commissioners are referring to the Métis of La Loche as Indians in a generic sense. It is also clear from Scrip Commissioner McKenna's report that the Aboriginal people at La Loche were Métis. Of his trip to La Loche, McKenna wrote:

> The people at this point were all half-breeds and were dealt with as such. On the 8th of the same month, I left for La Loche mission, across La Loche lake, a distance of nine miles, where more half-breeds had to be met and dealt with. There were at this point three aged Chipewyan women who desired to be attached to the Clear Lake band, and I entered them as members and paid them treaty.[58]

The following year, Scrip Commissioner Borthwick also travelled to La Loche and confirmed that the Aboriginal people living at La Loche Lake were Métis, although treaty Indians from Whitefish Lake (Garson Lake on the Saskatchewan-Alberta border) covered by Treaty 8 were also present:

> In addition to the half-breeds assembled here, I found a number of families of Indians from Whitefish Lake, who asked very earnestly that I should pay them their annuities....[59]

These scrip commissioners' reports certainly indicate that the majority of occupants of the La Loche Lake area were Métis.

The Prince Commission report also provides evidence that Ile-a-la-Crosse was populated by Métis. Some of the witnesses listed in its records had received scrip. According to their evidence,

> Indians cannot fish in winter – their trappings time. Mr. McKenna, Treaty Commissioner said they would not be interfered with....Thirty natives fish for the Commercial Company.[60]

Again, while this evidence is not crystal clear, Ile-a-la-Crosse was and remains a Métis community, and the 30 fishermen referred to must have been Métis. It should also be noted that the Prince Commission used the term Indian to encompass the Métis:

for the sake of brevity the term "Indian" is meant to include Halfbreed as well....The distinction is that the Halfbreed is a Canadian citizen while the Indian can be made so only with difficulty under our present Indian Act.[61]

That an Aboriginal right to hunt and fish or conduct other harvesting activities can exist independently of Aboriginal title to land is reflected in a letter written by Jean Chrétien as minister of justice and attorney general of Canada to the Native Council of Canada on 22 December 1981 (see annex to Appendix 5A):

I have, furthermore, stressed to you that land title does not exhaust the list of aboriginal rights which you may claim. It is therefore mistaken to say that to deny the validity of land claims is to deny you any and all rights.

Support for this proposition is given by the 1993 *Federal Policy for the Settlement of Native Claims*. Regarding the objectives of comprehensive claims settlements, the policy affirms:

The primary purpose...is to conclude agreements with Aboriginal groups that will resolve the debates and legal ambiguities associated with the common law concept of Aboriginal rights *and* title.[62][emphasis added]

The document goes on to address lands and resources, saying that Aboriginal groups are asked to relinquish undefined Aboriginal rights to lands *or* resources, in favour of rights in the settlement agreements (p. 5).

From this it is clear that even if extinguishment is a factor, some Aboriginal rights, including resource-use rights, can survive independently of title to land if not clearly referred to in the document that purported to extinguish title. Certainly, there is doubt about whether the government clearly and plainly intended to extinguish Métis people's Aboriginal right to hunt and fish, which was integral to their way of life and necessary for their survival. In this connection, one can take guidance from the words of Judge Goodson in the *Ferguson* case. After referring to the *Sparrow* decision, he stated:

The last quotation makes reference to holding the Crown to a "substantive promise." In the case of the "Métis" the question that comes to mind is, "what is that substantive promise?" Is it land? Is it scrip money? Is it the right to hunt for food? It is difficult to imagine a more basic Aboriginal right than the right to avoid starvation by feeding oneself by the traditional methods of the community.[63]

Such a fundamental and basic right can be determined by the principles of interpretation reaffirmed by the Supreme Court of Canada in *Sparrow*.

In *Nowegijick* v. *The Queen*...the following principle that should govern the interpretation of Indian treaties and statutes was set out: 'treaties and statutes relating to Indians should be liberally construed and doubtful expressions resolved in favour of the Indians'.[64]

Even if the term Indian is being used in its narrow meaning, it cannot be expected that the Supreme Court of Canada would fail to apply the same principle to all Aboriginal peoples, including the Métis.

The weight of evidence and developing case law would therefore support an interpretation that Métis Aboriginal rights to the harvesting of traditional resources are "existing" Aboriginal rights under section 35 of the *Constitution Act, 1982*. Whether the Manitoba trial judge deciding *McPherson* was correct in considering the rights to be restricted to Métis who have not abandoned a traditional hunter and gatherer lifestyle is very doubtful. Since that issue also arose in the Alberta case, we address it in that context.

Ferguson case

In the *Ferguson* case, noted earlier, a descendant of Métis scrip recipients based his defence on the *Natural Resources Transfer Agreement* between the federal government and the province of Alberta. The paragraph relied on is identical to paragraphs in the agreements with the provinces of Manitoba and Saskatchewan.

The main issue in this case was whether Métis are encompassed by the term Indian in those agreements. As seen earlier, the Saskatchewan Court of Appeal in *Laprise* ruled that non-treaty Indians and those not entitled to be registered under the *Indian Act* are not included. In Ferguson, however, the Alberta Court of Queen's Bench upheld the interpretation of provincial court Judge Goodson that non-treaty Indians *are* included. It should be noted that historical documentation aiding the interpretation of the paragraph was available in *Ferguson* but not in *Laprise*.

In *Ferguson* the analysis revolved around the 1927 *Indian Act* definitions of Indian and non-treaty Indian. The receiving of scrip was not seen as a factor; what was considered relevant was whether the Métis person involved would be characterized as a non-treaty Indian:

> 2(h) "non-treaty Indian" means any person of Indian blood who is reputed to belong to an irregular band, or who follows the Indian mode of life, even if such person is only a temporary resident in Canada.

Judge Goodson found on the facts of the case that Ferguson was "following the Indian mode of life" and was therefore a non-treaty Indian. While this ruling would cover a large number of Métis, particularly in the northern parts of the prairie provinces, it leaves open the question of whether it includes persons who do not appear to be following the Indian way of life. Assuming that it does not, the court's reliance on this definition raises the question of what defines the Indian mode of life. Many First Nations people no longer hunt. Does that mean that they no longer live the life of "Indians"? What about those who hunt only occasionally? Are modern hunting methods permitted, or must bows and arrows be used? Since the Canadian constitution has long been considered a "living tree" by the courts, it is probable that all such questions would be resolved in favour of a contemporary definition of the "Indian mode of life", unrestricted by old folkways. Another factor, however, appears to make mode-of-life questions irrelevant.

Why is the *Indian Act* definition so important? How can an *Indian Act* definition properly be the sole determinant of the meaning of words used in a *constitutional* guarantee like that contained in the transfer agreements? It is doubtful that it can, and if it cannot the whole question of mode of life becomes irrelevant. While the *Indian Act* in place in 1930 can be used as an aid in determining the definition of Indian in the transfer agreements, it cannot be the sole determining factor. The transfer agreements have constitutional status, which places them above the *Indian Act*. There are, moreover, other aids to assist in interpreting the agreements, including archival documents surrounding their enactment and legislative provisions with respect to hunting and fishing that were in place in 1930. Those aids suggest a broader meaning of Indian than the *Indian Act* definitions.

Shortly after the transfer agreements came into force, the government of Alberta requested from its legal advisers an interpretation of the terms 'game' and 'unoccupied Crown lands', mentioned in the section of the transfer agreements dealing with Aboriginal rights. They were concerned that Indians would be able to hunt in game preserves unless such areas could be classified as occupied lands.[65] They suggested that game should take the same meaning as that found in the provincial *Game Act*. In response, the assistant deputy attorney general of Alberta agreed that in the absence of a definition of game in the agreements, the term should be defined with reference to the Alberta *Game Act*.

The federal government was also asked for a legal interpretation on the question in a letter from the Alberta agriculture minister to Duncan Campbell Scott, deputy superintendent general of Indian affairs. W. Stuart Edwards, deputy minister of justice for Canada, provided the opinion in a letter dated 12 February 1931; it differed from the provincial interpretation in both respects. With respect to game, he stated,

> I apprehend that the intent of this proviso is to secure to the Indians a definite right or privilege and to except the Indians from the application of the Provincial Game Laws in respect of the exercise of that

right. The Assistant Deputy Attorney General of Alberta has expressed the opinion that the signification of the term "game" in this proviso is governed by the definition of "game" in the Provincial Game Laws, but, in my opinion, the more consistent and probable construction sanctions the view that the Indians are entitled to enjoy the right secured to them by the proviso without reference to any limitations upon the meaning of the term "game" which may exist under the Provincial Game Laws from time to time in force, and that the term "game" in the proviso is, therefore, to be understood in its ordinary sense, i.e., as meaning birds and beasts of a wild nature, fit for food, such as may be obtained by hunting and trapping. I am further of opinion that, while the Province may competently enact regulations to prevent and punish any abuse of the right, secured to the Indians by clause 12, the right to regulate the exercise of that right and to place any restrictions upon it resides exclusively in the Dominion Parliament by virtue of sec. 91, Head No. 24, of the British North America Act, 1867.

He then defined unoccupied lands:

> Secondly, with regard to the term "unoccupied Crown lands" in the proviso of clause 12, I am of opinion that this term may be taken to comprise all lands from time to time owned by the Crown within the Province (1) the title to, or right to the use and enjoyment of, which is not from time to time disposed of to any person, and (2) which are not, from time to time, *bona fide*, appropriated or set aside, by competent provincial authority, for a specific public purpose, (including, e.g., a park, a game preserve or a wild bird sanctuary) and in fact used and enjoyed for such purpose.

After internal discussion, that legal opinion was forwarded to the governments of the three prairie provinces.

The issue of interpretation arose again by way of a letter dated 5 August 1933 from W.S. Gray, of the Alberta attorney general's department, to the department of Indian affairs. Mr. Gray referred to the justice department's legal opinion with respect to game and unoccupied Crown lands and requested another legal opinion dealing with interpretation of the term Indians, suggesting the following interpretation:

> We take it that the proper interpretation is the definition of Indians in The Indian Act, as distinguished from the definition of Non-Treaty Indians, and therefore that the privileges given to the Indians under Section 12 of the Act are confined to Treaty Indians.

In his reply, dated 30 August 1933, Edwards referred to *R. v. Wesley*,[66] in which the interpretation of the term game was the same as that provided by Edwards in his earlier opinion. With respect to Gray's interpretation of the term Indians, he said, in a letter sent on 7 October 1933:

> With this opinion I do not agree. The terms "Indian" and "non-treaty Indian" are defined in section 2(d) and (h) of the Indian Act, R.S.C., 1927, c. 98, in and for the purposes only of that Act....There is nothing in the object of the clause or the context or in any other part of the *Agreement* to justify such a restriction of the primary and natural meaning of the expression "the Indians of the Province" in that clause, and I am of opinion that it embraces and was intended to embrace all the Indians of the Province, whether treaty or non-treaty Indians. This larger interpretation of the expression (which I regard as, in itself, the more proper and natural) also seems to be the most consistent with the object of this particular clause of the agreement.

Gray requested further views from the department of Indian affairs in a letter sent on 7 October 1933:

> With regard to the interpretation of the word "Indians" in this Section I think difficulties are liable to arise if the broad meaning put upon it by Mr. Edwards is to be followed. I think there is no doubt that the Natural Resources Agreement was intended to continue to the Indians the rights they formerly had under the various Treaties, and that it is a reasonable interpretation of the word "Indians" to construe it as being confined to the persons entitled to the benefit of the Treaties....Further, if a very general interpretation is put upon the word, no doubt half-breeds and all persons having any Indian blood would claim the benefits of the Agreement.

In response to this letter, Edwards wrote again on 7 November 1933 and concluded:

> If the connotation of these words be considered *simpliciter* its descriptive signification seems to require and to admit of no plainer exposition than the language itself affords: any person so resident who answers the description of Indian, whether a treaty or a non-treaty Indian, is within the scope of that phrase....what is there in the terms of cl. 12 to require a more restrictive signification to be given to the words used? Nothing in my opinion; on the contrary, if the phrase is to be understood in the sense which best harmonizes with the declared object of the clause, namely, "to secure to the Indians of the Province the continuance of the supply of game and fish for their support and subsistence", non-treaty, no less than treaty,

Indians, must be held to be within the scope of the phrase used, and, therefore entitled to the benefit of the clause. The assurance of the right to hunt and kill game for food on unoccupied Crown lands in a province surely cannot be said to be of less consequence to non-treaty than treaty Indians. Apart from these considerations, I desire to add that each of the two Governments, parties to this Agreement, were well aware of the distinction between treaty and non-treaty Indians; and I am satisfied that if they had intended to limit the benefit of this provision to treaty Indians, they would have taken care to express that intention unambiguously, as they might very easily have done, e.g., by using the words 'treaty Indians of the Province'.

With respect to the last point, Judge Goodson allowed into evidence in the 1993 *Ferguson* case a 9 January 1926 draft of the agreement between Canada and Alberta because it formed part of the legislative history leading to the agreement endorsed by both governments. That draft provided:

9. To all Indians who may be entitled to the benefit of any treaty between the Crown and any band or bands of Indians, whereby such Indians surrendered to the Crown any lands now included within the boundaries of the Province, the Province hereby assures the right to hunt and fish on all unoccupied Crown lands administered by the Province hereunder as fully and freely as such Indians might have been permitted to so hunt and fish if the said lands had continued to be administered by the Government of Canada.

Since the draft was eventually discarded in favour of one that dropped the reference to treaty, Judge Goodson concluded that the drafters clearly intended "Indians" to mean more than Indians with treaty status.

Another draft contained in the archival file dealing with the transfer agreements but that was not introduced in *Ferguson* is from the fall of 1929. This draft is between the governments of Canada and Manitoba, and it contains the same wording as the January 1926 Alberta draft. Like the Alberta draft, wording that excluded "treaty" replaced other text. These two drafts certainly support Edwards's legal opinion that if the parties to the agreements had intended to restrict the right expressed there only to treaty Indians, they could have retained the original wording.

While Edwards, the deputy minister of justice, did not directly address whether Métis were included in the term Indians, it is clear that he had them in mind as he prepared his second opinion in response to Gray's letter. Clearly, he was including Métis and all persons of Indian ancestry under the designation of non-treaty Indians.

Support for the view that the federal government knew about Métis reliance on wildlife was provided earlier in this appendix. This is evident from the special federal fisheries regulations for Saskatchewan, Alberta and the Northwest Territories, which were in force in 1930, and from federal orders in council for the N.W.T. in force in 1930.

A further argument that can be made as evidence of the inclusion of Métis in the *Constitution Act, 1930* is the fact that the term Indian or Indians has never been defined in any of Canada's constitutional documents. From the *Royal Proclamation of 1763* to the *Constitution Act, 1982*, there is strong support for the view that the term Indians was used generically to refer to Indigenous or Aboriginal peoples. In 1982, Aboriginal peoples replaced the term.

There does not appear to be any reason to believe that the term Indians had a different meaning in different constitutional documents as Canada's constitution evolved. Unless it can be shown otherwise, the appropriate approach is to give the same word in the same constitution the same meaning. In this connection, the Supreme Court of Canada held in 1939 that Inuit were encompassed by section 91(24); the same court also held that Inuit were covered by the Royal Proclamation.[67] It is highly probable that the courts would rule that Inuit in northern Manitoba are covered by the term Indians in the transfer agreement. And it is equally probable that Métis (who are expressly included in the term Aboriginal peoples in section 35 of the *Constitution Act, 1982*) will also be held to be Indians under the transfer agreements and other constitutional provisions, whatever their mode of life might be.

4.2 Commercial Uses

Being Aboriginal is not inconsistent with being modern. While traditional forms of resource use – hunting, fishing and trapping – continue to be of primary economic importance to some Métis, and are central to the cultural values of all Métis, the economic survival of the Métis Nation in the modern world depends on its ability to exploit natural resources commercially, as peoples do the world over.

Forestry, mining, oil and gas extraction, commercial fishing, game farming, wild rice farming, tourism and outfitting and hydro-electric generation, and the manufacturing enterprises that spring from such activities must be available to the people of the Métis Nation. A substantial land base and the authority to develop are prerequisites of commercial use of the land.

To ensure the permanent existence of a resource base upon which these activities can depend, it goes without saying that development has to be on a sustainable basis. The resource-use record of Aboriginal peoples in general and the Métis Nation in particular over the centuries offers assurance that the environment would be no less safe under Métis management than it has been in non-Aboriginal hands.

4.3 Urban Lands

Terms like Aboriginal land bases and resource uses conjure up images of wilderness or agricultural landscapes. These types of land bases are required by Canada's

Métis, but as the statistics presented in Chapter 5 show, a high proportion of Métis are urban dwellers. Métis who live in cities retain a cultural need for connections with non-urban Métis land bases; but they also have need, as do all urban-dwelling Aboriginal persons, for easily accessible communal land bases, for cultural, social, recreational, governmental and commercial purposes, in the cities where they live. Satisfactory settlement of Métis land claims must therefore include provision for adequate Métis-owned urban community facilities to serve the needs of Métis persons living in urban areas in numbers large enough to warrant such facilities.

4.4 Implementation

Implementing resource use policies that permit sustainable modern commercial development alongside traditional harvesting practices will require sophisticated management strategies. Among the co-operative approaches required are co-jurisdiction arrangements with other governments; inter-governmental agreements to share rents, royalties and other resource revenues; resource-use licences granted to Métis Nation enterprises; and joint venture agreements with other (private and public) enterprises. Fundamental to all such arrangements will be a land claims agreement or agreements establishing viable land bases for the Métis Nation.

NOTES

1. See Paul L.A.H. Chartrand, *Manitoba's Métis Settlement Scheme of 1870* (Saskatoon: Native Law Centre, University of Saskatchewan, 1991); "Aboriginal Rights: The Dispossession of the Métis" (1991), 29 Osgoode Hall L.J. 457; "The Obligation to Set Aside and Secure Lands for the "Half-breed" Population Pursuant to section 31 of the Manitoba Act, 1870", LL.M. thesis, University of Saskatchewan, 1988; D.N. Sprague, *Canada and the Métis, 1869-1885* (Waterloo, Ontario: Wilfrid Laurier University Press, 1988); "Government Lawlessness in the Administration of Manitoba Land Claims, 1870-1887" (1980), 10 Man. L.J. 415; Thomas Flanagan, *Metis Lands in Manitoba* (Calgary: University of Calgary Press, 1991); and Gerhard Ens, "Métis Lands in Manitoba", *Manitoba History* 5 (Spring 1983), p. 2.

2. Flanagan, *Metis Lands*, pp. 225 and 227.

3. Chartrand, *Manitoba's Métis* (cited in note 1), p. 22.

4. Chartrand, *Manitoba's Metis*, p. 76.

5. Chartrand says, for example,

> Comparing the meaning of 'benefit' with the technical meaning of 'grant' reveals the intention to provide a benefit to all members of the families by way of licence of occupation, whereas the children only

obtain grants of estates in the land in accordance with the objects of a regulated land settlement scheme. (p. 32)

6. See Flanagan, *Metis Lands* (cited in note 1), pp. 34-35 and p. 78 and following.

7. *An Act respecting the appropriation of certain Dominion Lands in Manitoba*, S.C. 1874, c. 20.

8. In fact, the grant to non-Métis "old settlers" had been authorized the previous year (*An Act to authorize Free Grants of land to certain Original Settlers and their descendants, in the territory now forming the Province of Manitoba*, S.C. 1873, c. 37) in a statute displaced before its implementation by the 1874 legislation: Dale Gibson, "Was Section 31 Really Aimed at Extinguishing Métis Title?", discussion paper prepared for the Royal Commission on Aboriginal Peoples [RCAP] (1994).

9. Sprague, *Canada and the Métis* (cited in note 1).

10. Sprague, *Canada and the Métis*, p. 139.

11. See generally, Sprague, "Government Lawlessness" (cited in note 1).

12. Even Sir John A. Macdonald acknowledged to the House of Commons in 1885 that "despairing of ever receiving patents for their lands, the majority of the claimants had disposed of their rights for a mere song to speculative friends of the Government" (House of Commons, *Debates*, 6 July 1885, p. 3117).

13. Flanagan, *Metis Lands* (cited in note 1), pp. 168-171.

14. Chartrand, *Manitoba's Métis* (cited in note 1), p. 138-144.

15. The *Dominion Lands Act* was first enacted in 1872, but it did not refer directly to Métis until it was amended in 1879. The 1872 act did, however, acknowledge Indian title in section 42: "None of the provisions of this Act respecting the settlement of Agricultural lands, or the lease of Timber lands, or the purchase and sale of Mineral lands, shall be held to apply to territory the Indian title to which shall not at the time have been extinguished."

16. Douglas Sanders, "A Legal Analysis of the Ewing Commission and the Métis Colony System in Alberta" (Saskatoon: University of Saskatchewan Native Law Centre, 1978), p. 3. The Northwest Territories at the time included all the current prairie provinces, other than the 'postage stamp' province of Manitoba.

17. Metis Association of Alberta and Joe Sawchuck, Patricia Sawchuck and Theresa Ferguson, *Metis Land Rights in Alberta: A Political History* (Edmonton: Metis Association of Alberta, 1981), pp. 38, 118. The authors state that the order was made in response to the growing unrest that culminated in the North-West Rebellion in the spring of 1885.

18. Quoted in Richard I. Hardy, "Metis Rights in the Mackenzie River District of the Northwest Territories" (1980) 1 C. N. L. R. at 13.

19. See Hardy, "Metis Rights", for a discussion of the procedures that had to be followed in applying for land grants.

20. See, for example, Hardy, "Metis Rights"; Sanders, "A Legal Analysis" (cited in note 16); Metis Association et al., *Metis Land Rights* (cited in note 17); and Frank Tough and Leah Dorion, "'The claims of the Half-breeds...have been finally closed': A Study of Treaty Ten and Treaty Five Adhesion Scrip", research study prepared for RCAP (1993).

21. Tough and Dorion, "'The claims of the Half-breeds'", estimate that for the Treaty 10 and Treaty 5 areas, only 1 per cent of the Métis land scrip was ever patented by Métis grantees.

22. *Re Paulette*, [1973] 6 W.W.R. 97 at 136 (N.W.T.S.C.).

23. For discussion of Métis as 'Indians' under section 91(24) of the *Constitution Act, 1867*, see Chapter 5 and Appendix 5A. For discussion of whether Métis are within the *Rupert's Land Order, 1870*, see Appendix 5B. The Supreme Court's observations are found in *Guerin* v. *R.*, [1984] 2 S.C.R. 335 at 376.

24. Redbacking allowed a scrip buyer/middleman to take possession of land without the Métis claimant being present. This was essential given that the Métis scrip claimant might live in York Factory, Manitoba, while the lands were located in Peace River territory in Alberta. See Tough and Dorion, "'The claims of the Half-breeds'" (cited in note 20).

25. National Archives of Canada [NAC], Record Group [RG] 10, Vol. 4009, File 249, p. 462, pt. 1A, 24 October 1910.

26. Quoted in Metis Association et al., *Metis Land Rights* (cited in note 17), p. 92, from which the following account is drawn.

27. See, for example, L. Heinemann, Association of Metis and Non-Status Indians of Saskatchewan, "A Research Report: An Investigation into the Origins and Development of the Metis Nation, the Rights of the Metis as an Aboriginal People, and their Relationship and Dealings with the Government of Canada", 31 March 1984, Métis Nation of Saskatchewan Archives. See also Metis Association et al., *Metis Land Rights* (cited in note 17), pp. 146-151, for other examples of scrip injustices.

28. Joseph E. Magnet, "Métis Land Rights in Canada", research study prepared for RCAP (1993).

29. M. Ollivier, *British North America Acts and Selected Statutes, 1867-1962* (Ottawa: Queen's Printer, 1962), p. 178. This order is part of the constitution, being contained in a schedule to the *Constitution Act, 1982* under the title *British Columbia Terms of Union.*

30. *Report From the Select Committee on the Hudson's Bay Company*, ordered by the House of Commons to be printed 31 July and 11 August 1857; Saskatchewan Archives Board [SAB], Government Publications Section, Shortt, F, 1060.43, G 78, C.1., p. 356. Isbister left for England in 1841 or 1842, as indicated in his response to question 2402, p. 121.

31. We are referring here only to that portion of the Métis Nation lying north of the boundary between Canada and the United States. The traditional Métis Nation homeland includes a considerable portion of the north-central United States.

32. Excerpt from a presentation made by a delegation of mayors from northwestern Saskatchewan to the General Assembly of the Métis National Council, September 1986.

33. Order in council P.C. 1927-1034, NAC RG2, Vol. 1404.

34. Order in council P.C. 1931-51.

35. Order in council P.C. 1947-2567.

36. Order in council P.C. 1939-1925.

37. *R. v. Rocher*, [1982] 3 C.N.L.R. 122 (N.W.T. Terr. Ct.); [1983] 3 C.N.L.R. 136 (N.W.T.S.C.); [1985] 2 C.N.L.R. 151 (N.W.T.C.A.).

38. *R. v. Rocher*, [1985] 2 C.N.L.R. 155.

39. NAC RG10, MR C-8535.

40. Alberta, *Enquiry into and Concerning the Problems of Health, Education and General Welfare of the Half-Breed Population of the Province of Alberta: Report* (Edmonton: 1936).

41. SAB, NR 1/2 120.

42. SAB R 33.1,372 (999-16).

43. *R. v. Laprise*, [1978] 1 C.N.L.B. (No. 4) 118; [1978] 6 W.W.R. 85 (Sask. C.A.).

44. *R. v. McPherson*, [1992] 4 C.N.L.R. 144 (Man. Prov. Ct.); *R. v. Fiddler*, [1994] 4 C.N.L.R. 137 (Man. Q.B.).

45. *R. v. Ferguson*, [1993] 2 C.N.L.R. 148 (Alta. Prov. Ct.); [1994] 1 C.N.L.R. 117 (Alta. Q.B.).

46. *R. v. McPherson*, (cited in note 44), p. 156.

47. *R. v. Sparrow* (1990), 70 D.L.R. (4th) 385 at 401.

48. *Rupert's Land Act, 1868* (U.K.), c. 105, reprinted in R.S.C. 1985, App. II, No. 6.

49. *Treaty No. 10 and Reports of Commissioners* [1907]. Reprint. (Ottawa: Queen's Printer, 1966).

50. Order in council P.C. 1906-1459, in *Treaty No. 10*.

51. *Treaty No. 10*.

52. Tape recording made at Batoche in September 1976. Mr. Ross was 18 years old when he witnessed the assembly with the scrip commissioner at Ile-a-la-Crosse.

53. Metis Family and Community Justice Services [Saskatchewan], "Governance Study: Metis Self-Government in Saskatchewan", research study prepared for RCAP (1993) [note omitted].

54. William Joseph lived in the area covered by Treaty 6. He was 82 years of age in 1977; he passed over to the spirit world in 1978. At the time Mr. Joseph was a senator of the Federation of Saskatchewan Indians and had been a founder and president of the Queen Victoria Treaty Protection Association, which later merged to form the FSI. The passage is quoted in Clem Chartier, "British North America Act, 1930: The Legal Right to Hunt, Trap and Fish", 13 March 1978, paper for Law 390B.

55. *R. v. Laprise* (cited in note 43).

56. Association of Métis and Non-Status Indians of Saskatchewan, Aboriginal Rights research questionnaire, 13 July 1976. Métis Nation of Saskatchewan Archives.

57. NAC RG23, vol. 366, file 3216, pt. 3.

58. *Treaty No. 10* (cited in note 49), p. 5.

59. *Treaty No. 10,* p. 14.

60. NAC RG23 (cited in note 57), p. 17.

61. NAC RG23, p. 62.

62. Department of Indian Affairs and Northern Development [DIAND] *Federal Policy for the Settlement of Native Claims* (Ottawa: DIAND, 1993).

63. *R. v. Ferguson* (cited in note 45), p. 156.

64. *R. v. Sparrow* (cited in note 47), p. 407.

65. Memorandum from Benj. Lawton, Game Commissioner, to H.A. Craig, Deputy Minister of Agriculture, 1 October 1930, NAC RG10, vol. 6820, file 492-4-2. The rest of this account is drawn from documents in this archival file.

66. (1932), 2 W.W.R. 377 at 344-345.

67. *Sigeareak E1-53* v. *R.*, [1966] S.C.R. 645 at 650.

Appendix 5D

Proposed
Métis Nation Accord*

Métis Nation Accord

Between

Her Majesty the Queen in Right of Canada
as Represented by the Prime Minister

and

Her Majesty the Queen in Right of the Provinces of
British Columbia, Alberta, Saskatchewan,
Manitoba and Ontario

and

The Government of the Northwest Territories
as Represented by Their Respective First Ministers

and

The Métis Nation of Canada as Represented
Nationally by The Métis National Council
and Provincially by
The Pacific Métis Federation
The Métis Nation Of Alberta
The Métis Society of Saskatchewan
The Manitoba Métis Federation
The Ontario Métis Aboriginal Association
The Métis Nation-Northwest Territories

as Represented by Their Respective Presidents

---

* This document is the best efforts draft of the Métis Nation Accord, dated 7 October 1992, prepared
for final review by first ministers and Aboriginal leaders.

Whereas in the Northwest of Canada the Métis Nation emerged as a unique Nation with its own language, culture and forms of self-government;

And whereas historically the Métis Nation has sought agreements with Canada to protect its land and other rights;

And whereas Métis were formally recognized in the *Manitoba Act, 1870* and the *Dominion Lands Act*;

And whereas the existing aboriginal and treaty rights of Aboriginal peoples including the Métis are recognized and affirmed in the *Constitution Act, 1982*;

And whereas the Métis Nation, Canada and the Provinces agree that it is just and desirable to recognize the contribution made by the Métis to the Canadian federation and further agree that measures are necessary to strengthen their place within the Canadian federation;

And whereas the Métis people of Canada have contributed and continue to contribute to the development and prosperity of Canada;

And whereas the Métis Nation, Canada and the Provinces agree that it is necessary and desirable to set out their respective roles and obligations to each other;

NOW THEREFORE the representatives of the Métis Nation, Canada and the Provinces hereby agree to enter into an Accord with the following terms:[1]

1. Definitions

For the purposes of the Métis Nation and this Accord,

(a) "Métis" means an Aboriginal person who self-identifies as Métis, who is distinct from Indian and Inuit and is a descendant of those Métis who received or were entitled to receive land grants and/or scrip under the provisions of the *Manitoba Act, 1870*, or the *Dominion Lands Act*, as enacted from time to time.

(b) "Métis Nation" means the community of Métis persons in subsection a) and persons of Aboriginal descent who are accepted by that community.

(c) "Incremental program delivery costs" means those costs for the new or enhanced programs intended exclusively for Métis and delivered by Métis self-governing institutions, additional to the costs of programs which are replaced by those new or enhanced programs.

(d) "Transfer payments" means financial transfers provided to Métis self-governing institutions by Canada or the Provinces, whether in the form of block grants, cost-sharing, formula finance or like methods and intended to help defray the costs of Métis self-governing institutions.

(e) "Direct costs of Métis self-governing institutions established as a result of self-government agreements" means the start-up and operating costs of structures established to direct Métis self-government, including boards and

---

1. Provisions referring to the proposed constitutional amendments are under consideration pending finalization of the legal text and the general Political Accord.

legislative bodies, but excluding the operating costs of organizations intended to deliver programs.

(f) "Provinces" means the provinces of British Columbia, Alberta, Saskatchewan, Manitoba and Alberta and the Northwest Territories.

(g) "Métis self-governing institution" means an institution established pursuant to a self-government agreement.

(h) "Self-government negotiations" means negotiations within the context of section 35.2(1) of the *Constitution Act, 1982.*

2. Enumeration and Métis Registry

Canada and the Provinces will contribute resources to the Métis Nation to conduct an enumeration of the Métis Nation including the costs of administering and maintaining a Métis Nation controlled national registry. This process, which will include a right of appeal, will be determined through multilateral negotiations among the parties to this Accord.

3. Self-Government Negotiations

(a) Without altering the obligations of the Government of Canada and the Provinces under section 35.2 of the *Constitution Act, 1982,* the Government of Canada, the representatives of the Métis Nation and the Provinces agree to negotiate in good faith the implementation of the right of self-government, including issues of

    (i) jurisdiction; and

    (ii) economic and fiscal arrangements,

with the objective of concluding tripartite self-government agreements elaborating the relationship among the Métis Nation, Canada and the Provinces.

(b) For the purposes of the Northwest Territories, negotiations will be conducted through comprehensive land claims, treaty or self-government negotiations and will include both Métis and Indians as parties.

(c) Notwithstanding subsection b), subsection a) shall apply in the Northwest Territories

    (i) in geographic areas where an Indian band proceeds to treaty land entitlement negotiations and where Métis in that geographic area are ineligible or decide not to be participants in said negotiations; and,

    (ii) one year following the effective date of this Accord, except for those parts of the Northwest Territories covered by comprehensive land claims, treaty or self-government agreements that include both Métis and Indians as parties or where such negotiations are in progress.

4. Lands and Resources

Within the context of self-government negotiations,

(a) Canada and the Provinces agree, where appropriate, to provide access to lands and resources to Métis and Métis self-governing institutions;

(b) Where land is to be provided, Canada and the Provinces, except Alberta, agree to make available their fair share of Crown lands for transfer to Métis self-governing institutions;

(c) The value of the transfers and access referred to in this section shall be taken into account in self-government negotiations; and

(d) Canada and the Provinces agree to enter into discussion with representatives of the Métis Nation on the establishment of a land negotiation process.

Consistent with the above, it is acknowledged that Alberta has negotiated and transferred the fee simple in 1.28 million acres of land to the Métis in Alberta and has committed to spending $310 million over 17 years, pursuant to the Alberta-Métis Settlements Accord.

5. Resourcing of Negotiations

Canada and the Provinces agree to contribute adequate resources to enable representatives of the Métis Nation to participate in tripartite self-government negotiations.

6. Devolution

In self-government negotiations, Canada and the Provinces will negotiate the transfer to Métis self-governing institutions the portion of aboriginal programs and services currently available to Métis.

7. Cost of Institutions

Canada agrees to provide a substantial portion of the direct costs of Métis self-governing institutions established as a result of self-government agreements. The Provinces and the Métis Nation will provide the remaining portion of the costs. The Métis Nation share of the remaining portion of the cost will be determined in self-government negotiations taking into account the capacity of Métis governments to raise revenue from their own sources.

8. Net Incremental Program and Delivery Costs

Canada agrees to provide its share of the net incremental program and delivery costs deriving from self-government agreements. The Provinces and the Métis Nation will provide the remaining portion of the costs. The Métis Nation share of the remaining portion of the cost will be determined in self-government negotiations taking into account the capacity of Métis governments to raise revenue from their own sources.

9. Transfer Payments

Within the context of self-government negotiations,

(a) Canada and the Provinces agree to provide Métis self-governing institutions with transfer payments to enable them to establish and deliver programs and services to Métis.

(b) These transfer payments shall assist Métis self-governing institutions to establish similar types of programs and services as those enjoyed by other Aboriginal peoples.

10. Preservation of Existing Commitments

(a) Canada will not reduce funding or services to the Aboriginal peoples of Canada as a result of the signing of this Accord or the coming into force of section 91A of the *Constitution Act, 1867*.

(b) Canada and the Provinces will not reduce funding or services to Métis as a result of the signing of this Accord or the coming into force of section 91A of the *Constitution Act, 1867*.

11. Alberta Métis Settlements

Without derogating from the Métis Nation's right of representation on general matters, this Accord recognizes that the Alberta Métis Settlements' General Council has the sole right to negotiate, conclude and implement intergovernmental agreements respecting the lands, members, and self-government of the Métis Settlements in Alberta.

12. Gender Equality

The rights and benefits referred to in this Accord are guaranteed equally to female and male persons.

13. Non-Derogation

(a) Nothing in this Accord shall be construed so as to abrogate from any aboriginal, treaty, or other rights or freedoms that pertain to the Aboriginal people of Canada.

(b) Nothing in this Accord is intended to apply to any other Aboriginal people who are not within the ambit of this Accord.

14. Nature of Instrument and Legal Certainty[2]

Upon a proclamation issued by the Governor General under the Great Seal of Canada of amendments to the Constitution of Canada, which include an amendment to the *Constitution Act, 1982* recognizing the inherent right of self-government of the Aboriginal peoples of Canada and the coming into force of section 91A of the *Constitution Act, 1867*, clarifying that all of the Aboriginal peoples of Canada are included in section 91(24), the Government of Canada shall recommend to Parliament and the Governments of the Provinces shall rec-

---

2. Canada and British Columbia have indicated that legislation will be introduced.

ommend to their Legislative Assemblies legislation or take such other steps as are necessary to confirm that this Accord is approved, is legally binding on Her Majesty and is both enforceable and justiciable. The Accord shall be included as a schedule to the legislation.

15. Application of Political Accord Relating to Aboriginal Constitutional Matters

The provisions of the Political Accord Relating to Aboriginal Constitutional Matters and the proposed "Negotiations Processes Accord" shall apply to the Métis Nation. Where the provisions of the Métis Nation Accord are more specific or relate to matters not addressed in the Political Accord Relating to Aboriginal Constitutional Matters and the proposed "Negotiations Processes Accord," the provisions of the Métis Nation Accord shall prevail.

16. Representation of the Métis Nation

(a) The Métis Nation is represented nationally by the Métis National Council. Provincial and territorial representation of the Métis Nation includes the Pacific Métis Federation, Métis Nation of Alberta, Métis Society of Saskatchewan, Manitoba Métis Federation, Ontario Métis Aboriginal Association and the Métis Nation-Northwest Territories, acting either collectively or in their individual capacity, as the context requires, or their successor Métis organizations, legislative bodies or governments.

(b) The parties agree that:

   (i) self-government agreements referred to in this Accord shall be negotiated only by duly mandated representatives of the Métis Nation directly concerned including, for greater certainty, duly mandated representatives of Métis Nation communities;

   (ii) the preferred means for resolving issues with respect to the representation of Métis for the purposes of participation in self-government negotiations, is to use procedures internal to the Métis Nation; and

   (iii) if requested by a group of Métis, the federal and provincial governments concerned may participate in an informal, mutually agreed upon process with the Métis Nation to resolve a representation issue that is not resolved internally.

17. Ratification Procedure

This Accord shall be considered adopted by the Métis Nation upon the passage of a duly authorized motion by a special assembly of elected Métis representatives of the Métis Nation as defined herein.

Yvon Dumont, President Métis National Council Manitoba Métis Federation	Norm Evans, President Pacific Métis Federation
Larry Desmeules, President Métis Nation of Alberta	Gerald Morin, President Métis Society of Saskatchewan
Gary Bohnet, President Métis Nation-Northwest Territories	Ron Swain, President Ontario Métis Aboriginal Association
British Columbia	Alberta
Saskatchewan	Manitoba
Ontario	Canada
Northwest Territories	

EXCERPTS FROM THE DRAFT LEGAL TEXT OF THE CHARLOTTETOWN ACCORD 9 OCTOBER 1992

Proposed Amendment to the *Constitution Act, 1867*

12. The said Act is further amended by adding thereto, immediately after section 95 thereof, the following...[section]:...

95E. In the context of section 91A, the legislature of Alberta may make laws, and the Parliament of Canada may make laws, in relation to the Métis in Alberta and to Métis settlement lands in Alberta and, where such a law of Alberta and a law of Parliament conflict, the law of Parliament prevails to the extent of the conflict.

Proposed Amendment to the *Alberta Act*

23. The *Alberta Act* is amended by adding thereto, immediately after section 24 thereof, the following section:

Definitions

24.1 (1) In this section,

"Métis Settlements General Council"

"Métis Settlements General Council" means the Métis Settlements General Council incorporated by the Métis Settlements Act (Alberta);

"Métis settlement land"

"Métis settlement land" means land held in fee simple by the Métis Settlements General Council under letters patent from Her Majesty in right of Alberta.

Expropriation

(2) The fee simple estate in Métis land, or any interest in it less than fee simple, may not be acquired through expropriation by

(a) any person,

(b) Her Majesty in right of Alberta, or

(c) Her Majesty in right of Canada, except with the consent of the Governor in Council after consultation between the Government of Canada and the Métis Settlements General Council,

but an interest less than fee simple may be acquired in that land in a manner permitted by the *Métis Settlements Land Protection Act* (Alberta).

Exemption from seizure

(3) The fee simple estate in Métis settlement land is exempt from seizure and sale under court order, writ of execution or any other process whether judicial or extra-judicial.

Restriction on Legislature

(4) No Act of the Legislature may

(a) amend or repeal the *Métis Settlements Land Protection Act* (Alberta),

(b) alter or revoke letters patent granting Métis settlement land to the Métis Settlements General Council, or

(c) dissolve the Métis Settlements General Council or result in its being composed of persons who are not settlement members,

without the agreement of the Métis Settlements General Council.

Restriction on Parliament of Canada

(5) No Act of the Parliament of Canada may dissolve the Métis Settlements General Council or result in its being composed of members who are not settlement members without the agreement of the Métis Settlements General Council.

Application of laws

(6) Nothing in this section shall be construed as limiting

(a) the application of the laws of Alberta or Canada to, or

(b) the jurisdiction of the Legislature of Alberta or the Parliament of Canada to enact laws in and for Alberta applicable to,

Métis settlement land and any activities on or in respect of that land, except to the extent necessary to give effect to this section.

Non-derogation

(7) Nothing in this section shall be construed so as to abrogate or derogate from any rights referred to in Part II of the *Constitution Act, 1982*.

Appendix 5F

Correspondence Concerning the Métis of Labrador

Letter dated 17 February 1994 from Harry W. Daniels, former president, Native Council of Canada, to Kirby Lethbridge, president of the Labrador Métis Association, concerning the application of section 35 of the Constitution Act, 1982 to Métis people who are not part of the Métis Nation.

In response to your question "What did the term "Metis" mean when inserted into the Constitution of Canada?" I am providing the following for your information.

Firstly, let me state that at the time I was President of the Native Council of Canada which was a Federation of Metis and Non-Status Indian Organizations representing Metis and Non-Status Indians from the Yukon to Newfoundland. As the President, I was responsible for negotiating constitutional change on behalf of the constituents of the Native Council of Canada.

On the 30th of January, 1981 when the agreement was reached that Indians, Inuit and Metis be specifically identified as Aboriginal People, in what is now Section 35(2) of the Constitution Act, 1982, it was at my insistence that the above-mentioned were included.

With specific reference to the term "Metis" it was understood at the time that it (Metis) included the member organizations and their constituents who self-identified as a Metis person. The notion being that self-identity is a right that cannot be usurped by any means. It was also understood that the term Metis was not tied to any particular geographic area, keeping in mind that Aboriginal people from coast to coast identified with the term Metis as their way of relating to the world.

The then Minister of Justice and now Prime Minister of Canada, the Rt. Hon. Jean Chrétien made the final deal and I distinctly remember stating that all our people were included whether they identified as Metis or the erroneous term Non-Status Indians. At that time we held a more accommodating view of what a Metis person was and is, contrary to the views of revisionist historians and lawyers who were not involved in the process.

In my view, the people of Labrador who identify as Metis are expressing their right to self-identify as an Aboriginal person and are included in the people who I negotiated into the Constitution in 1981, and should enjoy all the rights that inhere in them as Aboriginal people.

I trust that this short letter answers your question and is of some assistance. If necessary I am prepared to testify under oath that the above is a true statement. Please do not hesitate to call me if a further clarification or additional information is required.

In Brotherhood,

Harry W. Daniels
Honourary President, Native Council of Canada
Board Member, Metis Society of Saskatchewan

GOVERNMENT OF
NEWFOUNDLAND AND LABRADOR

Executive Council
Intergovernmental Affairs Secretariat

March 18, 1994

Ms. Linda Jordan
Commission Secretary
Royal Commission on Aboriginal Peoples
P.O. Box 1993
Station "B"
Ottawa
K1P 1B2

Dear Ms. Jordan:

Thank you for your invitation to attend the forthcoming Métis Circle Special Consultation, April 5-6, 1994.

While the Government of Newfoundland and Labrador recognizes there are people of aboriginal descent in the province who identify themselves as "métis", it does not agree they are "Métis" within the meaning of S. 35 (1) of the <u>Constitution Act (1982)</u>. Accordingly, I do not think it appropriate to accept your kind invitation. We would appreciate receiving, however, copies of any discussion papers distributed to the participants.

May I wish you a successful conference.

Ray Hawco

RAY HAWCO
Assistant Secretary to Cabinet
(Native Policy)

P.O. Box 8700, St.John's, Newfoundland, Canada, A1B 4J6

6

THE NORTH

In the north we found a paradox. On one hand, the North is the part of Canada in which Aboriginal peoples have achieved the most in terms of political influence and institutions appropriate to their cultures and needs. On the other, the North itself is a region with little influence over its own destiny. Most of the levers of political and economic power continue to be held outside the North and, in some cases, outside Canada.[1]

Within this northern paradox, however, there have been great opportunities. In some parts of the North, a unique process of democratic reform of public institutions has been under way for some years. During the life of this Commission, the efforts of many came to fruition. In 1991, Inuit of the eastern Northwest Territories (N.W.T.) concluded a comprehensive claims agreement with the federal government and, simultaneously, began the process of establishing a new territory in their homeland.[2] Through a variety of means, Inuit and government representatives are now planning the shape and structure of Nunavut, which will be created by division of the N.W.T. in 1999. As Nunavut was being planned and negotiated, residents of the western N.W.T. were also engaged in a process of public discussion and research to define future political arrangements in that region. (A new name has not been chosen for the new territory that will be created in the west, but the region is commonly referred to as Denendeh, which in the Dene languages means 'land of the people'.) Inuvialuit and Dene, Métis and non-Aboriginal, the peoples of the west are culturally much more diverse than their eastern neighbours, but in Denendeh as well, residents are approaching consensus on key constitutional issues.[3]

In the Yukon, the First Nations communities represented by the Council for Yukon Indians have negotiated a new form of highly decentralized comprehensive claims agreement. Labrador Inuit have been pioneers in securing transfer of the administration of social expenditures from the province, while

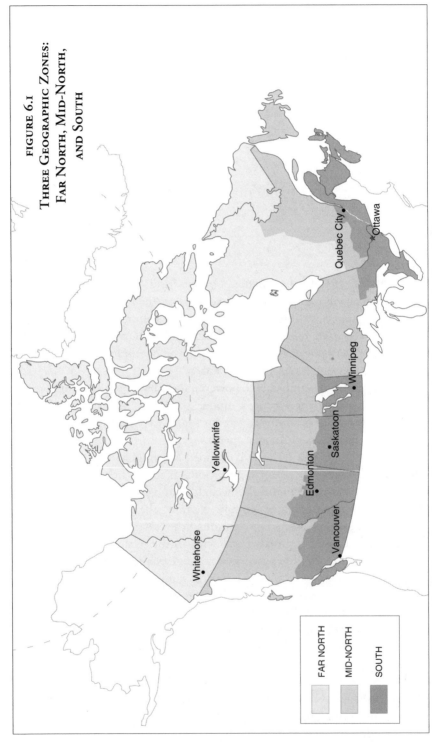

FIGURE 6.1
THREE GEOGRAPHIC ZONES:
FAR NORTH, MID-NORTH,
AND SOUTH

FAR NORTH

MID-NORTH

SOUTH

Note: The geographical zones identified here reflect demographic, climatic, economic   *Source:* See note 1 at the end of the chapter.
and social factors.

continuing claims negotiations. In northern Quebec, Inuit and Crees negotiated the first modern comprehensive claims agreement in Canada and have now completed nearly 20 years of innovation, research and political development. Other nations – the Innu people of Labrador and the Aboriginal peoples of the northern parts of many provinces – have not yet achieved new regional or provincial political arrangements. In many places, though, detailed work has been under way on these matters and in the areas of social and economic development.

The political development achieved in the last 20 years in parts of northern Canada is striking. A framework for the future is beginning to emerge. As far as the economic and social future of northern communities is concerned, however, complacency would be ill-advised.

As discussed in Volume 2, Chapter 5, self-government in the absence of economic viability is hollow. Economic development and self-government without social well-being in Aboriginal communities are equally unacceptable. Northerners explained these connections to us repeatedly, and we accept their views. We recognize the work being undertaken by Aboriginal and non-Aboriginal northerners in co-operative constitutional development and the resolution of outstanding disputes. With them, we understand economic development and environmental stewardship to be essential complements to political development.

The most enduring economic base in northern Canada is the mixed economy – also called the traditional economy, the traditional-mixed economy, the domestic economy and the informal economy. In the mixed economy, households combine cash income from a variety of sources (wages, social transfers, arts and crafts production) with income in kind from the land, shifting their efforts from one sector to another as conditions dictate. Cash income is sometimes shared; food is shared often.[4] The mixed economy is the dominant economic form of most Aboriginal communities, and it is by far the most stable. The stability of the mixed economy is evident in its persistence since the earliest days of cash economy opportunities in the North, beginning with the fur trade. The central reason for this stability is its flexibility and adaptability, allowing producers to take advantage of a variety of economic opportunities. (See Volume 2, Chapter 5 on economic development and later sections of this chapter.) We believe that support of the traditional-mixed economy is the most effective way to promote the economic vitality of northern communities.

Cash income, and therefore wage employment, is essential to the operation of the mixed economy. Wage employment in the North is provided, generally, by three sectors: (1) federal/territorial/local public administrations; (2) the small business (mainly service) sector, including tourism; and (3) mining.[5] For the mixed economy to continue to flourish, it is imperative that Aboriginal people find wage employment in all of these sectors and that these wage-earning activities continue in a way that does not interfere with harvesting and other land-based activities. An important aspect of realizing this is a comprehensive and international approach to environmental stewardship in the North that ensures that the mixed economy will continue to be viable for generations to come.

Finally, we want to emphasize the importance of sustained attention to human resources development. Unemployment rates for northern Aboriginal people are much higher than those of their non-Aboriginal neighbours. The northern Aboriginal population is young, and so the number of Aboriginal people in the North who are unemployed or under-employed can be expected to grow. Economic development strategies based on the traditional-mixed economy provide the most likely basis for improved employment prospects for young people in the North. To ensure that those who will run the new governments, participate in economic development, and take care of the environment are prepared for what lies ahead, we recommend a number of measures designed to create maximum opportunities for individual human development while these major processes are under way.

1. LIVING IN THE NORTH

The North is the homeland of many peoples, among them Inuit, Inuvialuit, and the Northern and Southern Tutchone, Han, Kaska, Tlingit, Tagish, Gwich'in, Cree and Innu peoples, as well as the Sahtu Dene, Deh Cho Dene, Tlii Cho Dene (Dogrib), Sayisi Dene and Métis peoples. About 36 per cent of all Aboriginal people in Canada live in the territorial North and the northern parts of the provinces (Table 6.1). In many regions, Aboriginal people outnumber non-Aboriginal people, and almost everywhere in the North, Aboriginal people are numerous enough to influence the way of life of people who migrate to the North

TABLE 6.1
Aboriginal Identity Population by Region, 1991

	Aboriginal Identity Population	
	#	%
Canada	720,600	100.0
Total North	260,400	36.1
Far North	70,100	9.7
Mid-North	190,300	26.4
South	460,200	63.9

Note: Aboriginal identity population is adjusted for undercoverage in the 1991 Aboriginal Peoples Survey (APS).

Source: M.J. Norris, D. Kerr and F. Nault, "Projections of the Aboriginal Identity Population in Canada, 1991-2016", research study prepared by Statistics Canada for RCAP (February 1995).

TABLE 6.2

Aboriginal Identity Population as a Percentage of the Total Population, 1991

	Total Population	Aboriginal Identity Population[1] as a % of Total Population
Total North	1,691,120	13.4
Far North	152,130	39.9
Yukon	27,800	16.3
N.W.T.[2]	57,650	60.0
Quebec	36,310	41.1
Labrador	30,375	22.1
Mid-North	1,538,990	10.7
Quebec	557,635	3.3
Ontario	461,740	9.1
Manitoba	64,165	44.9
Saskatchewan	26,735	93.8
Alberta	173,305	16.1
British Columbia	255,410	9.1

Notes:

Far North = Yukon, N.W.T., northern Quebec and Labrador.

Mid-North = roughly the northern half of the western provinces, northern Ontario, and that portion of Quebec north of southern urban Quebec and south of the part of Quebec defined as Far North in Quebec (see Figure 6.1).

1. For comparison purposes, population data for the Aboriginal identity population are unadjusted for undercoverage in the APS because adjustments to the total population from the 1991 census have not been made. The percentages would not change significantly if adjustments were made to both populations.

2. Includes Nunavut: total population, 21,245; total Aboriginal identity population, 17,795 (83.8 per cent).

Source: Statistics Canada, 1991 Aboriginal Peoples Survey, custom tabulations; and 1991 Census, catalogue no. 93-304.

and to form an influential plurality of voters. As Table 6.2 shows, Aboriginal people form the majority in the N.W.T. – including and excluding Nunavut – and northern Saskatchewan. They form significant pluralities of voters in the northern regions of Quebec, Manitoba, Labrador, the Yukon and Alberta.

Most northern communities are small. Of the 928 communities in northern Canada, 584 have fewer than 1,000 people and 288 have under 300 (see Tables 6.3, 6.4 and 6.5). As a general rule, the smaller the community, the greater the proportion of Aboriginal residents.

TABLE 6.3
Total Population: Number of Communities by Population Size and Geographic Region, 1991

| | Number of Communities by Population Size Group | | | | |
	Exclusions*	1-299	300-999	1000+	Total
Far North					
Labrador	0	6	16	4	26
Quebec	9	7	11	11	38
Yukon	2	26	7	1	36
Northwest Territories	2	29	27	13	71
Total Far North (%)	13 (7.6)	68 (39.8)	61 (35.7)	29 (17.0)	171 (100)
Mid-North					
Quebec	15	49	102	88	254
Ontario	27	52	49	56	184
Manitoba	5	13	16	18	52
Saskatchewan	10	21	22	7	60
Alberta	4	27	17	28	76
British Columbia	14	58	29	30	131
Total Mid-North (%)	75 (9.9)	220 (29.1)	235 (31.0)	227 (30.0)	757 (100)
Total North (%)	88 (9.5)	288 (31.0)	296 (31.9)	256 (27.6)	928 (100)

Note:
* Community population sizes of zero or 'not applicable' and incompletely enumerated reserves in Ontario (18), Alberta (3), and the Yukon (1).

Source: Statistics Canada, 1991 Census, catalogue no. 93-304.

Even in the larger centres, there are distinctively Aboriginal features to almost every aspect of life. Many of the non-Aboriginal people who have moved to the North have been strongly influenced by Aboriginal realities. Some have chosen to live in predominantly Aboriginal communities, often becoming part of Aboriginal families. Even newcomers living in larger centres are in a position analogous to that of immigrants who come to Canada and adapt to local customs. There are many outward signs of a 'blended' northern identity: in clothing; in the characteristically friendly and frank demeanour of northerners toward each other and toward strangers; and in the conventions and more formal rules of political life, which emphasize accessibility and accountability of leaders. The ability of northerners to negotiate political compromises and to work on

TABLE 6.4

Aboriginal Origin Population: Number of Communities, by Population Size and Geographic Region, 1991

	Number of Communities by Population Size Group*			
	40-299	300-999	1000+	Total
Far North				
Labrador	11	4	1	16
Quebec	10	15	3	28
Yukon	18	1	1	20
Northwest Territories	22	28	10	60
Total Far North (%)	61 (49.2)	48 (38.7)	15 (12.1)	124 (100)
Mid-North				
Quebec	54	23	4	81
Ontario	71	31	8	110
Manitoba	12	11	11	44
Saskatchewan	21	18	4	43
Alberta	33	17	5	55
British Columbia	49	33	6	88
Total Mid-North (%)	240 (58.4)	133 (32.4)	38 (9.2)	411 (100)
Total North (%)	**301 (56.3)**	**181 (33.8)**	**53 (9.9)**	**535 (100)**

Note:
* Excludes incompletely enumerated Indian reserves and settlements, as well as census subdivisions with fewer than 40 persons with Aboriginal origins and/or Indian status.

Source: Statistics Canada, 1991 Census, catalogue no. 94-326.

constitutional principles has been demonstrated many times in the last decade. Certainly, there are varied interests and political conflict in the North, but in their negotiations with the federal government and in their relations with the rest of Canada, northerners have increasingly presented a common face. This in turn has begun to be reflected in federal northern policy.[6]

One source of the distinctive northern perspective is simply demographic: the most striking aspects of northern life draw upon the indigenous cultures of the North. These have been reinforced by other factors. Although there are still major differences between Aboriginal and non-Aboriginal northerners in income and access to senior level jobs, they share a common economic base and, increasingly, common economic interests. Outside a few larger centres, the mixed

TABLE 6.5
Census Subdivisions[1] with a Majority Aboriginal Origin Population, 1991

	Aboriginal Majority Communities	Number of Communities	Communities With Aboriginal Majority
	#		%
Far North[2]			
Labrador	7	25	28.0
Territoire nordique (Census Division 99, Quebec)	21	28	75.0
Yukon[3]	11	23	47.8
Northwest Territories	57	63	90.5
Total Far North	96	139	69.1
Mid-North[2]			
Quebec	19	227	8.4
Ontario[3]	46	149	30.9
Manitoba	36	45	80.0
Saskatchewan	38	48	79.2
Alberta	26	66	39.4
British Columbia	51	94	54.3
Total Mid-North	216	629	34.3
Total North	312	768	40.6

Notes:

1. Census subdivision is the general term applying to municipalities (as determined by provincial legislation) or their equivalent, e.g., Indian reserves, settlements and unorganized territories.

2. The 1991 census population by Aboriginal origin was used to obtain community-level data for all communities in the Far and Mid-North zones. The 1991 APS data were not used because they did not survey all communities in sufficient numbers to produce community-level data for each.

3. The Mid-North zone in Ontario excludes 18 Indian reserves that were incompletely enumerated in the 1991 Census; one such community in the Yukon is also excluded. Assuming they have majority Aboriginal populations, the percentage of communities with an Aboriginal majority would rise to 38.3% in Ontario and 50% in the Yukon.

Source: Statistics Canada, Canada's Aboriginal Population by Census Subdivisions and Census Metropolitan Areas, catalogue no. 94-326; and Census Divisions and Census Subdivisions: Population and Dwelling Counts, catalogue no. 93-304.

economy of occasional wage employment and land-based food and fur production, complemented by high public expenditures, forms the backbone of the economy. Wage employment is found most commonly in the public sector, with occasional pockets of tourism, mining and mineral development. Healthy development in all sectors requires a high degree of co-operation, which is reflected in joint venture corporations and various environmental management boards.

Many Aboriginal languages still flourish in the North, particularly compared to southern Canada. In 1991, in the far north, 70.2 per cent of Aboriginal adults (aged 15 and over) and 63.7 per cent of children (aged 5 to 14) were reported to speak an Aboriginal language. In the mid-north, 54.9 per cent of adults and 35.9 per cent of children were speakers of an Aboriginal language. In the south in 1991, 23.1 per cent of Aboriginal adults and only 8.6 per cent of children spoke an Aboriginal language.[7] (See Figure 6.1 for the locations of the far north, the mid-north and the south. For a further look at the situation concerning Aboriginal languages, see Volume 3, Chapters 5 and 6.) A similar situation prevails with Aboriginal traditions and science and technology. The strength of the mixed economy, with its hunting, fishing and gathering components, is probably a major reason for the survival of indigenous knowledge in the North. The technology for on-the-land production has changed: people use rifles, motorboats, snowmobiles and radios instead of harpoons, bows, kayaks, canoes, and *inuksuit* and other markers. Bone and ivory needles and stone cutting tools have been replaced by metal needles and steel knives. But hunters and fishers still need detailed knowledge of the habits of the wildlife upon which they depend, a detailed understanding of the weather and the seasons, and specialized techniques for observing and catching animals and fish. The assembly of clothing and footwear still relies on techniques refined over centuries.

While the fruits of the land are bountiful, northern Aboriginal people face severe economic hardships: there are the very high costs of travel, transportation and consumer goods and scant and very constrained wage-economy opportunities.[8] Aboriginal people live in communities still reeling from several decades of massive change. Over the last century and a half, most northern Aboriginal peoples have experienced the devastation wrought by epidemics of influenza, tuberculosis and other diseases. Almost all were disrupted by centralization and relocation programs and subsequently by federal social welfare programs. The move to analyze systematically what are generally acknowledged to be the substantial, far-reaching and cumulative effects of such changes has barely begun.[9] (The disruption of families and communities caused by resettlement is discussed in Volume 1, Chapter 11.) Despite all that has happened, many northern Aboriginal communities remain good places to live and raise families.

2. THE COMMISSION'S APPROACH TO THE NORTH

While all aspects of the Commission's mandate are relevant to northern Aboriginal people, the mandate also mentions the North specifically:

> The Commission may investigate the difficulties and cost of communications and transport, issues of environmental protection, sustainable economic and social development, access to natural resources, and any differential treatment of northern Aboriginal people by the Canadian and Territorial Governments.

The special difficulties of living in the North do affect Aboriginal people's economic, political, social and cultural prospects. The North is sparsely populated and far from markets and manufacturing centres. For several decades, political and economic control have been held outside the North. Legally and constitutionally, the Yukon and Northwest Territories are under federal administration, although in practice they are approaching quasi-provincial status. The northern area of each province has a different history, but in no case is there much local control over the regional political economy or much regional retention of capital.

Aside from these special difficulties, northern Aboriginal peoples can count some achievements and innovations that may be of interest to all Canadians. Northern Aboriginal and non-Aboriginal people have devised new forms of political negotiation and new constitutional frameworks that promise to meet some of their goals. Although the process is incomplete and by no means entirely satisfactory, in many places northerners have come a significant distance toward defining a new relationship between Aboriginal and non-Aboriginal people.

From 1992 to 1994, the Commission visited 50 communities in the North. In developing our approach, we considered social and economic information about how people actually live. Political boundaries are certainly important for policy development and political innovation, and our discussion of these matters takes this into account. But we have drawn no conclusions and offer no suggestions about where northern political boundaries should lie. Our North is primarily a social and economic reality.

In the next section of this chapter, we offer our understanding of what northerners – Aboriginal and non-Aboriginal – told us during the hearings, in other discussions we attended, and in briefs and letters. Building on that understanding, we then discuss the source of the current problems experienced by Aboriginal people in the North. In this we were assisted greatly by the testimony of elders and by the work of historians and other scholars. We want to explain the past in order to expose the practices, traditions, assumptions and material conditions that create the present, for it is action in the present and future that concerns us most.

This chapter also offers a brief overview of the political jurisdictions and regions that constitute the far north. For reasons of space, we have included the Northwest Territories and the Yukon in this discussion, as well as the Labrador and Nunavik (northern Quebec) jurisdictions inhabited by Inuit. This section provides a brief introduction to the varieties of northern life and circumstances, and it shows why local development of many policies and programs is essential.

General principles must apply equally to all, but specific measures will work best when they are designed and shaped by the people of each nation or region. Although space prevents detailed discussion here, the northern parts of Ontario, Manitoba, Saskatchewan, Alberta and British Columbia share many of the political, cultural and economic circumstances that we describe for Labrador, Nunavik, the Yukon and the Northwest Territories.

In the final sections of this chapter, we analyze several important issues and propose solutions. Environmental stewardship is an essential element of all future northern policies and programs, whether these be the policies of Aboriginal governments, other governments or private corporations. Healthy northern communities depend directly and indirectly on a healthy environment. The health of the northern economy depends on a viable environmental strategy and practical policies based on the real long-term northern economy. In economic development and in the rapid political development that many northern regions have faced, there is enormous potential for contributions to individual and family well-being. The ways this opportunity can be realized are explored at the end of the chapter.

3. What Northerners Told the Commission

One of our most difficult tasks in preparing this report was to report to the government and to Canadians in language faithful to both Aboriginal and non-Aboriginal ways of seeing the world. From the beginning we were acutely aware of the difficulties inherent in interpretation and understanding. We designed our public hearings to permit people to speak in their own languages and to allow us to hear people's views and confirm our interpretation of what they said. We were also assisted by our experience and knowledge as Commissioners: of the four Aboriginal Commissioners, two are from the North. As well, we relied on an extensive research program that involved several northern communities and some of the best scholars in this field.

We followed the advice of northerners who offered to share their experiences with us. Aboriginal people said that they did not want to be studied again but to be listened to and to have their words taken seriously. They emphasized the enduring strength of Aboriginal traditions and the importance of these traditions for communities seeking to find their way back to a healthy way of life. Continuity with the past and opportunities for cultural development are essential. Aboriginal people urged the Commission to remember the connections between all areas of life. Martha Flaherty, president of Pauktuutit, the Inuit Women's Association of Canada, explained:

> The overall health and well-being of our people are intrinsically tied to the social, political and economic development of our communities. We

can no longer afford to pay the price of dividing issues into manageable portfolios, programs and services. A holistic, integrated approach is necessary at every level and in relation to every issue or problem.

Martha Flaherty
President, Pauktuutit
Ottawa, Ontario, 2 November 1993[*]

This chapter was inspired in part by these words.

3.1 The Four Themes: Land, Community, Making a Living, Governance

Northern Aboriginal people spoke to the Commission on a wide range of issues. Some had very specific concerns, and where possible we have tried to respond. It has not been possible, however, to investigate and propose solutions for every matter raised.

As we thought about and discussed the testimony from the 50 northern communities we visited, we found a fair degree of consensus about what is important. Four related themes emerged: the importance of the land; the centrality of 'community' for individual well-being; the need for viable ways for individuals to make a living; and the changing face of governance, the political forms and traditions through which social and public decisions are made. These themes are helpful in organizing our discussion of northern Aboriginal peoples' concerns.

Land

Dene Chief Gabe Hardisty spoke for many northern Aboriginal people when he told us about his people's goals:

> I don't have anything written down. The way I was taught is to take your memories and speak your mind and speak from your heart, and that is how I was taught. Up until today, I am still living the way I was taught....Being Dene, we learn from our past and this is how we got this far....
>
> We live by the lakes and the rivers. We learn when to fish. At certain times of the season, we learned how to fish, and we used willows to make fish nets. This is how we fished for fish. These are the people we are from....
>
> We had our own government in the past. If we didn't have our own government, we wouldn't be here today....Since the coming of the white people, a lot of things have changed. When the Europeans

---

[*] Transcripts of the Commission's hearings are cited with the speaker's name and affiliation, if any, and the location and date of the hearing. See *A Note About Sources* at the beginning of this volume for information about transcripts and other Commission publications.

came here, we had done a lot of hunting to help them supplement food that was brought in from down south. At the time, if we had abandoned a lot of the European people here, they would have probably frozen....The way the European culture thinks is that they figure the Dene were too stupid to have a government. They figure we are too stupid to do things on our own. I don't think so. If we were stupid, we would probably not have survived. We had Dene government before the coming. That is why we are still here. Since the European government was started, there is nothing that has gone right for us. That is why we want our own government....

We want to do better for our land. This is what we were talking about. There have been a lot of meetings since the beginning. Twenty years ago, if we brought everything that we wanted to the government, if they looked at it, when Dene people say something, they don't think we are telling the truth. [translation]

Chief Gabe Hardisty
Fort Simpson, Northwest Territories
26 May 1992

Chief Hardisty's assertion that one of his people's goals is "to do better for our land" is a statement of profound importance. It is also one of the most difficult to translate into Commission recommendations, for it is grounded in an ethical system of closely linked personal and collective responsibilities in which responsibility to Creation, including the other beings that are part of Creation, is central. On several occasions, Aboriginal people explained the importance of 'land' and 'place' to their current well-being and to their plans for the future. For other Canadians, who may lack intimate experience with the land, the deep sense of responsibility that northern gathering and hunting peoples have to the land requires considerable effort to understand.[10]

Decisions about land rights and land management regimes will affect every aspect of the North's future, from cultural health to economic development, from the distribution of resources to people's ability to participate in Canada's political institutions. What is at stake is far more than legal title, jurisdiction or authority, but these are the instruments Aboriginal peoples have come to recognize as important to achieving their goals. In this regard there are still many open questions, some of which we address in this chapter but others that will be resolved only in practice.[11]

Community

The Aboriginal people are, by tradition, a people of the land. Their very nature is tied strongly to the land, and any answer to the economic problems must include their remaining on the land. We have many today that do not live in Old Crow because they have been faced with a need to make a living, but if we were to ask them, they would tell you that they would come back if it was possible to live.

Rae Stephensen
Old Crow, Yukon
17 November 1992

In the North, most Indigenous people still live in small communities among relatives and long-term friends for at least part of their lives. While some wage centres in the North are growing as people move there searching for employment and other opportunities, there are many viable small communities. Most northern Aboriginal people still call such places home, wherever they might live.

Their languages, histories and experiences may be different, but the small, predominantly Aboriginal communities of the North share a number of features. Typically, there are few permanent wage-earning opportunities, except in the public service and a few small service businesses. There is extensive use of the surrounding lands and resources and a high degree of dependence on the fruits of the land. Most individuals know a great deal about the strengths, weaknesses, talents and foibles of their neighbours, and they share a common history and heritage stretching back through generations.

Thus, the northern Aboriginal community is not just a collection of buildings. It extends beyond dwelling places to include land for fishing, gathering, visiting, trapping and hunting, and memorable places where important events occurred. Northern Aboriginal peoples' tenure in the settled communities of today is relatively recent; they have lived in more mobile, family-centred communities for centuries. In modern times, the attachment to the land and the strong sense of collectivity remains.

It is primarily in Aboriginal communities that their languages are preserved and language-specific knowledge is retained and transmitted. What is sometimes referred to generically as 'culture' is sustained and developed in these communities – flourishing Aboriginal communities where there is a strong commitment to cultural continuity and a co-operative spirit to build toward the future, bringing strength to the relatives, friends and other Aboriginal communities in their orbit. The presence of lively, diverse human settlements is also a treasure for all humanity.

Making a living

I want to give you an idea of the confusion that exists in our communities. A recent survey conducted in one of our communities was asking a question and the question was, "What is most important to you in your lives right now in this community?" The response that was most important to the majority of the people who responded to that questionnaire was that, number one, employment was the most important thing in our communities because the fact is in our communities, at this time, we have upwards of 85 to 95 per cent unemployment and the welfare rate is high.

Herb George
Gitksan-Wet'suwet'en Government
Commission on Social Development
Kispiox, British Columbia, 16 June 1992

Probably the most important challenge for the future of northern Aboriginal peoples is economic. Some northern communities today enjoy an adequate standard of living, with relatively good housing and other services and reasonable, if not ample, means for people to make a living. Other communities are in deep distress, suffering from poor infrastructure, inadequate cash flow and a general shortage of opportunity. Still other northern communities, and probably the largest group, are poised somewhere between these extremes. They have a deep appreciation for the many positive aspects of community life and a keen awareness that population and other pressures might lead to a deterioration in community health in the near future.

Aboriginal peoples are generally 'young' peoples; they are experiencing a more rapid increase in the proportion of young adults than is occurring in the general population. At the same time, through television and other media, northern communities are becoming less isolated, and northern youth are being drawn into ways of life more appropriate to wage-earning societies than to societies living primarily off the land. The most important issue for the growing population of young Aboriginal adults in the North is how they will make a living.

New and forceful measures are necessary. Large, non-renewable resource-based projects and heavy infrastructure investment have failed to create a dynamic regional wage economy. Given the importance of public sector employment and the likelihood that this sector will not continue to grow at previous

[T]he expertise of Inuit women in dealing with social issues is being recognized, but how can social issues be separated from economic issues? Where is unemployment, poverty and dependence separate from physical and emotional well-being or from the problems of youth suicide, alcohol and drug abuse, and ill-nourished children? Economic development cannot be isolated in a category of its own; all policies and programs must be designed, or redesigned, to include a more holistic perspective.

Simona Barnes
Pauktuutit
Ottawa, Ontario, 2 November 1993

rates, and considering the huge number of young people about to enter adulthood, it is clear that a new era is beginning. Responsibility to the land and sustaining vital communities will be important considerations in creating new opportunities for the current generation to earn a living. Taking these factors into account will help develop realistic strategies for northern economic development.

Our approach to northern economic development is based on a recognition that local knowledge and community innovations hold the key to developing northern economies, which are now cash-poor and high-cost. Later in this chapter we discuss economic policies based on the entire economic base, drawing the best from sectors such as mining, mineral exploration, transportation, renewable resources development and tourism, as well as from the more stable public sector and the long-standing hunting and fishing economies. The policies must also take into account the relationship between healthy social and family relationships and a viable economy.

Governance in the North

> Today we are in a time of healing for our children, our families, our communities and Mother Earth. While we struggled to reach a just and fair settlement for our land claims, our elders have held on to the past and have kept our languages, stories, histories and songs alive. They have been patiently waiting for the day when our people would reclaim what is rightfully ours. That day is upon us. We are putting into practice our own forms of self-government using our own regimes that have been passed down from generation to generation, as well as creating new structures to move us into the future.
>
> Judy Gingell
> Teslin, Yukon
> 27 May 1992

Northern Aboriginal people stress that economic and social development are not separable from political progress; each requires and complements the other. People in many parts of the North have been engaged in a process of rejecting and then rechannelling the frequently intrusive hand of federal, territorial and provincial administrations, particularly since the 1960s. The territorial North and the northern parts of most provinces still do not exercise control over most aspects of life. Control is exercised elsewhere by non-residents, and resources and capital tend to be exported, with little benefit remaining in the region. For the Aboriginal people in the North, there is the additional difficulty that these patterns were set by an alien culture to which they have few points of entry.

Some progress has been made in reversing these patterns, but as yet few of the changes are fully entrenched in institutions and practices. There are three areas of central concern:

- securing sufficient control over lands and resources so that the new governing institutions can take action to benefit the people they serve, which includes ensuring that governments have sufficient revenue to continue to provide existing services and to undertake new ventures;
- developing governing structures that are recognizably democratic and efficient, while at the same time reflecting indigenous traditions; and
- affirming and updating treaties so that the original agreements between northern Aboriginal people and newcomers can be respected. This includes new negotiations by nations and peoples that have not yet negotiated treaties or similar agreements.

These matters are discussed at length in Volume 2. In this chapter, we outline aspects of each question that are specific to the North.

3.2 How the Four Themes are Related

The four themes – land, community well-being, making a living and governance – are intimately related. Individual well-being depends upon community well-being, particularly for northern Aboriginal people. Community well-being relies on an adequate regime for sharing the use of the land and mediating among competing and potentially conflicting forms of resource development. An adequate land regime, in turn, depends on practical and effective arrangements for self-government, especially with respect to relations with other governments and authorities.

Turned another way, self-government requires adequate resources to finance administration, regulation and services. In the North, access to resources requires access to land. Adequate stewardship depends upon informal social controls and training systems that teach people the proper way to use the land. These customs and systems are developed, preserved and elaborated in healthy communities.

In light of the diversity of Aboriginal peoples, solutions are more likely to be regional, nation-based or local than pan-northern. Yet the root and ultimate objectives of many First Peoples are the same, and the impediments they encounter in their political, economic and cultural development are broadly similar. For this reason, the experience of northern Aboriginal people in negotiating future arrangements may well be useful to other Aboriginal people living in quite different climatic and demographic circumstances.

For example, Crees and Inuit in northern Quebec have nearly 20 years' experience of "negotiating a way of life" by way of a comprehensive claims agreement.[12] Aboriginal and non-Aboriginal residents of the Northwest Territories are specialists in developing processes for effective public discussion of constitutional development. Over the last 15 years, several initiatives have permitted wide-ranging, community-based, regionally defined discussion of the most fundamental issues; in some areas, consensus has been achieved. As

Aboriginal self-government is implemented across Canada, these experiences are bound to be useful to those making plans for other areas.

Beyond specific cases, there is the matter of coping with rapid, fundamental change in general. There will be a prolonged period of negotiation and discussion in many parts of the country. Northerners have experienced more recent change than most people. To anticipate what it might mean to implement the inherent right of self-government in a thorough manner across Canada, it is useful to study the northern transition.

4. THE SOURCE OF
CURRENT PROBLEMS

Many Aboriginal people who spoke to the Commission offered explanations of the great transformations their societies have experienced as a way of highlighting the source of their current concerns. Many of these concerns arise from the impact of colonization. Very few people who spoke to us of these matters merely laid blame; rather, they sought acknowledgement of what had occurred and a better relationship in the future.

The Commission published a detailed study of one sad episode in Canadian history, when Inuit from Inukjuak, northern Quebec, and Pond Inlet, Baffin Island, were relocated to Resolute Bay and Grise Fiord in the high Arctic.[13] In special hearings and later examinations, we had an opportunity to understand the impact of this relocation in great detail. We recognize the similarities between the high Arctic relocation and so many other cases of relocation – and other kinds of outside intervention – in Aboriginal communities across Canada (see Volume 1, Chapter 11). We recommended that the government acknowledge the wrongs done to the relocated Inuit, apologize to them, compensate them for the relocation, and acknowledge the Inuit contribution to maintenance of Canadian sovereignty in the high Arctic.

In Kangiqsujuaq, Quebec, on 29 March 1995, federal Indian affairs minister, Ronald A. Irwin, declared:

> No matter what the reasons for mounting a major undertaking like the relocation, no matter how well intentioned, such a major undertaking involving the movement of people would not be done in the same way today. Also, there may be differences in opinion as to the motivation behind the relocation, recognition has to be given to the significant contribution made by the residents of Grise Fiord and Resolute Bay to the establishment and maintenance of a Canadian presence in the high Arctic. It is my intention to discuss the matter in full with my government colleagues very soon. As you know, before any decision can be made it must have the support of the cabinet and government as a whole.[14]

Inuit who were relocated from Quebec and Baffin Island to the high Arctic islands share with many other Aboriginal people across Canada the need to understand and reshape their relations with the newcomers to their land. Aboriginal northerners offered us their analysis of the history of contact between non-Aboriginal and Aboriginal societies and of the changes that contact brought.

Kenneth Spence spoke to us about the effects of the flooding of his people's traditional land in northern Manitoba:

> We, the people, formerly of South Indian Lake are very frustrated and hurt by the ignorance of Manitoba Hydro. We are also victims of the flood that destroyed our beautiful community. We have been affected in a lot of different ways. We once had a very quiet, peaceful, pretty and prosperous community. We lived, like our forefathers, surviving on fishing and trapping which was plentiful before the flood. You would hardly ever find anybody living on welfare. The flood changed it all. [translation]
>
> Kenneth Spence
> Leaf Rapids Relocation Group
> The Pas, Manitoba, 20 May 1992

Clara Schinkel, a member of the Tagish Governance Society, told us:

> Over the last century a number of events occurred which began to undermine the Tagish people as a distinct nation. The gold rush and the building of the railway and the residential school at Carcross had a devastating effect on the Tagish culture. Many moved to Carcross and other places to obtain work. The Tagish people were fractional-ized. The missionaries taught only English in the schools and this, together with inter-marriage between Tagish and Tlingit, almost annihilated the Tagish language. The Tagish language has survived many centuries; however, it has become closer to extinction in the last century.
>
> Clara Schinkel
> Tagish Aboriginal Governance Society
> Whitehorse, Yukon, 18 November 1992

In another context, an Inuit elder, Annie Okalik, outlined the changes in work and family relations that occurred when the old way of life was left behind. She explained the sources of many of the problems facing Aboriginal communities today:

> My way of living is very different now than the way it used to be. And though we are provided with some comforts from modern culture, it isn't the same kind of comfort and peace that we had. While we still lived our traditional life I bore some children, and after we

moved to the settlement of Pangnirtung, I bore more. My two sets of children were raised in completely different ways. My eldest ones lived like I did; my younger children were born having to enter school. So my younger children are inclined more to modern living and my older ones to the traditional Inuit way of life.

In those days, there was no other place but our homes and parents. We honoured our parents then, and no one else. If we were told to do something, we did not refuse or talk back, nor were we to be lazy....My grandmother was really in charge of the children then, compared with today. She would tell me stories about her life when she was growing up and she'd tell me that our life now is so easy because there are no shamans to govern the lives of Inuit. But looking back, it really wasn't any easier, though our lives were made easier then by heeding the traditional laws....

Our life seems to have been completely turned over. An example of how life has changed for Inuit is that most of the young men do not know anything about hunting. Because I was the eldest child in our family, I would accompany my father during his hunting trips. We'd hunt by dog-team during the winter and on foot in the summertime; we'd also trap for fox. My father was a very quiet man; he never scolded me....What helped was the fact that I knew my limits and respected the rules. We would share all the tasks at hand. I remember I would get so sleepy after everything we needed was inside our little igloo and our *qulliq* [oil lamp stove] was turned on. He would say his prayers both at bedtime and morning. I have benefitted by the way my father lived his life....

Compared with our life now, we did not use drugs or alcohol, and I have seen how much these things have wrecked the lives of Inuit, especially the young people. I remember that when the supply ship came during the summer months, two of the Inuit employees of the Hudson's Bay Company store would consume alcohol, but they were moderate in their intake. Today, along with new things being introduced to the North, it seems that people will drink too much, with no limits at all.

I am not trying to say that all of the old ways of life were better, but in regard to alcohol intake now, it does seem that life was a lot better than it is today.[15]

Many of the older generation of northern Aboriginal people grew up on the land. The seasonal rhythm of the land and the cycles of game and fish shaped their existence. They lived in relationship with the birds, the mammals, the plant life, in harmony with the land, sea and air, and attuned to the movements of the moon, sun and stars. They moved from camp to camp to where the animals, fish and plant life were plentiful. Men and women each had roles and responsibilities; one was not more important than the other. Elders and children received most of the attention.

The generation following that older generation – people now between 30 and 50 – were caught in a massive transition. Many of this generation were born and raised on the land but spent their young adulthood living in a settlement or town. Their children in turn experienced a similar change: few young people were born in the outpost camps; many have only brief summertime experience of the land. Schooling in English has led to the loss of Aboriginal languages and alienation from Aboriginal culture. Like many other Canadian young people, northern Aboriginal youth prefer fashionable clothing and popular music and culture.

Thus, during the last two or three generations, there have been fundamental changes in the way northern Aboriginal people live. They have moved from living freely on the land to living in houses in settlements or towns.[16] Where they once had independence and control over their own lives, many now depend on wage employment, subsidized housing, social assistance or unemployment insurance. In various ways, government structures many aspects of their lives.[17]

Annie Okalik and many others trace the extensive abuse of alcohol and drugs to these changes. Okalik emphasizes the disintegration of the traditional laws that supported proper social behaviour and the stresses on individuals arising from the transformation of Aboriginal society in the last several decades. Although Aboriginal people have lived with non-Aboriginal people, sometimes closely, for the last 200 years, it has been mainly since the creation of year-round communities that traditional authority has been undermined.

Apphia Awa shares this view. Awa was born in 1931 in Ammitturmiut (Igloolik) on north Baffin Island, Northwest Territories. She was brought up on the land, married and had children, moved from camp to trading post to camp on north Baffin Island, and finally left the land to live in the community of Pond Inlet in 1972. She lived the traditional life, but her children are living a modern life. Several went away to residential school in Churchill, Manitoba, and now have successful southern-style careers. Others stayed closer to home. Awa describes the loss of authority in her life:

> When I was growing up, the elders were treated with a lot of respect. They would sit around and we would serve them. We would prepare their tea for them, we would do what they told us to do. At that time, our only jobs were serving the elders. The elders organized all the important work. They organized the skin preparations. They distributed the meat and told us how to prepare it. The younger children were always serving them with tea, bringing them things, getting the ice for water, doing all the menial tasks....

I'm not treated like an elder today. I'm not treated the way that we treated elders when we were growing up. Inuit now have to go to work all the time. The children, they are always in school. Elders today, we know that the younger generation have full-time jobs. We know that when they get home they have even more work to do, taking care of their children, their houses. The elders today realize this situation, that is why we don't ask to be waited on. That is why we tend to do things ourselves.

Also, things are different because of the alcohol. The elders today are just as knowledgeable but we don't talk or instruct the young people as much any more. If an elder tells a young person not to do something, when that person gets drunk he might get mad at the elder for having said that. He might go over to the elder's house and start yelling. He might scream at the elder when he is drunk, tell him what to do and say things like "I won't take it any more". The alcohol, that is why the elders don't want to talk any more. It is because when young people get drunk, they can get abusive towards the elders.[18]

The effect of this undermining of traditional authority has been to splinter Aboriginal society even further.[19] Young people have tended to break away from the traditional way of obeying their parents and grandparents and other authorities. They have been drawn increasingly into the wage economy, which rewards individual effort and pays no heed to the use that wage earners make of their incomes. Where there is no employment, people must rely on social assistance and other transfers; these can have a similarly individualizing effect. In a study prepared for the Commission, Peter Kulchyski found that state funding (in the form of social assistance and unemployment insurance, for example) "strongly encourages people to think and act as individuals, to marshall their resources for themselves, to define their interests separately from other members of the community".[20] These changes have weakened the bonds that previously held families together and are creating new norms that are still in flux.

As Okalik and Awa noted, traditionally young people went to the elders for guidance and advice. The advice was often in the form of a directive, the meaning and effect of which were rooted in tradition. Although today there are still elders who give advice and young people who require advice, to some the elders' directives seem ineffective or irrelevant (see Chapter 3 in this volume).

The drift away from traditional values and the imposition non-Aboriginal institutions and policies have produced many ill effects: alcoholism, crime, sexual abuse of children, spousal assault and elder abuse. Young people confront these problems and a central dilemma: they must succeed in the wage economy for their society to remain viable, but their psychological well-being rests on a reconnection with traditional values.

Lyla Andrew, who lives in Sheshatshiu, Labrador, offered her views about how these difficulties might be approached:

I think country living needs to be given a high priority. The impediments to country life, such as low-level flying and wildlife regulations, have to be eliminated. I'm not talking about the Innu going backwards. I'm talking about trying to find a way to promote today the need for Innu to live in the country, to educate their children in the country, to practise their spirituality in the country. Euro-Canadians treat the country experience as a holiday. They say the Innu are just going off on expensive camping trips. What this tells me is that there is an incredible lack of knowledge that Euro-Canadians have about the Innu. There are only a handful of non-Innu who have ever lived with Innu in the country. The Innu's most vocal critics, certainly locally, have never lived with Innu in the country, and they have no idea what country life is.... [translation]

Lyla Andrew
Sheshatshiu, Newfoundland and Labrador
18 June 1992

Mary Andrew, an Innu from the same community, agreed:

The country is more home to us than here, because that is where we are more traditional, that's where we have more control over our lives. [translation]

Mary Andrew
Sheshatshiu, Newfoundland and Labrador
18 June 1992

The psychological gap between old and young and the tensions experienced by almost everyone are made worse by problems related to education and language. According to many Aboriginal people, one of the strongest forces breaking Aboriginal societies apart has been the education system. It did so literally, by removing some children from their families to attend school (see Volume 1, Chapter 10). As schools were built in newly established communities, the education system affected the lives of all Aboriginal people. School attendance became compulsory. Teachers recruited in southern Canada taught an unmodified curriculum imported from the south. Children learned foreign words, foreign ways, foreign values.

Rhoda Katsak was one of those children. She was born at her family's winter camp near Amitturmiut (Igloolik), Northwest Territories, and spent her first few years living the traditional Inuit hunting life. She left the land to go to school when she was eight years old:

That first day of school in Igloolik, when I was eight, I started doing everything in English. English was all around us. It wasn't so much that we were punished when we spoke our Native language. It might have been that way in earlier years but there didn't seem to be that pressure for us. It was just that all there was at school was English so we were more or less forced to learn it. The teachers were brand new in town, they were all from the south and they didn't know any Inuktitut. We had to communicate with them. Also, all of the material was in English – "Fun with Dick and Jane", "Dick, Jane and Spot the Dog", those books were what we were learning from so we had to learn English pretty quick.

We had to learn to act according to *Qallunaat* [non-Aboriginal] standards and code of ethics too, "thank-you, excuse me, pardon me", that sort of thing. You say a sentence and then you say "please". I could never remember "please"....

We grew up thinking that we should try to be *Qallunaat* and that is why we had *Qallunaat* idols, idols like the Supremes, like Elvis, like Frobisher. That was the whole idea when we went to school. We didn't have Inuit idols, people like the woman Atagutaluk who almost starved to death in this area. The woman they named the new school in Igloolik after. Our heroes were all *Qallunaat*. It is even difficult today to change that mentality, even to change to a point where you think "I am an Inuk, I am a good enough person as I am". When we were growing up the *Qallunaat* were the better people. They were the people who had the authority, we were supposed to look up to them.[21]

Marius Tungilik of Repulse Bay, Northwest Territories, was one of the children taken away to a mission school in Chesterfield Inlet:

Obviously, my parents did not know what lay in store for us in school, or they did not have a say. While our command of the English language would develop, we were not taught anything about our language, our heritage, our culture, our governing systems, our spiritual background, our strengths. Any lessons pertaining to our people taught us that we were Eskimos, that we lived in igloos, that we rubbed noses, that Indians called us "Eaters of Raw Meat". Would our parents have consented to that sort of treatment if they knew? No, they could not have known, nor could they have had any say on the matter....

I am presently a regional director with the government of the Northwest Territories, a position I would never have dreamed of filling when I was younger. Not exactly, anyways. I had often taken long walks out into the tundra back home when I was about four or five and sang hymns out loud and daydreamed of helping people by leading others. I practised making speeches that the winds of changes were coming and of our need to be prepared.

Equipped with these dreams, coupled with the top-notch English education that I received in Chesterfield Inlet, I was able to grow into who I am today. Everyone has a dream. We should all learn to tap into them and strive to realize those dreams.

This top-notch education had a price. I had neglected my heritage for a very long period of time. It was not until I met my lovely wife, Johanne, in 1977 that my appreciation for the land and our culture developed and blossomed. The land was always there, it was always beautiful. The distaste that I had developed for my own culture and my own people in school had a very profound impact. It had taken me a very long time to become free of the brainwashing notion that our traditional ways were undesirable and obsolete. I was also blinded by work, ambition and the need to explore the world.

> Marius Tungilik
> Rankin Inlet, Northwest Territories
> 19 November 1992

Not every Aboriginal person has had the same experience as Marius Tungilik, but there are similarities in Aboriginal people's experiences in the education system. When elementary schools were built in every community, the teachings did not change. Children were still taught in English or French. What they were taught came from the south. They were taught nothing about being Aboriginal, nothing about the importance of the language or heritage; and no pride in being an Aboriginal person was instilled. They did not learn about the history of Aboriginal people or the history of contact with non-Aboriginal people:

> I was taught by the white society, by understanding the white people. I was taught how great Joey Smallwood is, and how great John Macdonald is. I was taught how to sing "O Canada" and "Ode to Newfoundland". One thing I was never taught is the history, the rich history that we have, the people here in Utshimasits [Davis Inlet]. I wasn't taught how great my people were, how great my ancestors were, how far the distances were they travelled from the Quebec border to everywhere in Nitassinan. I wasn't taught that there are other Native people in Canada. As I was growing up, I was learning things in my own way. My father showed me how to fish, hunt, and do things that they had been doing for generations.

> George Rich
> Vice-President, Innu Nation
> Utshimasits, Newfoundland and Labrador
> 1 December 1992

Since Rhoda Katsak, Marius Tungilik and George Rich were in school, there have been some important changes. The drift away from Aboriginal values and culture has continued, but not without resistance. Across the North, parents, teachers and education officials have been working to change the system to reflect the ways of life and values of Aboriginal peoples. In the 1970s, educators started revising southern curricula to include more northern material. Teacher education programs were created to train Aboriginal teachers. By the early 1990s, many schools in predominantly Aboriginal communities were able to teach children in their own language for at least the early primary grades (see Volume 3, Chapter 5).

The current problems in Aboriginal communities are not only the result of bad practices in the past. Sharon Venne explained how oil exploration on Lubicon lands during the 1980s destroyed the economy of the Lubicon Cree by driving away the moose and other game on which the Lubicon depended:

> In 1978-1979, the Lubicon Cree had a traditional economy based upon the produce of their lands. Within a four-year period, the Lubicon went from sustaining themselves to the welfare rolls.
>
> Sharon Venne
> Lubicon Cree First Nation
> Fort Chipewyan, Alberta, 18 June 1992

At the heart of this situation is an unresolved conflict over land and unfulfilled treaty obligations. Improvement will require, at minimum, that these two problems be addressed with energy and dispatch.[22]

In summary, many people who testified concerning the sources of current problems identified a lack of adequate control over their own political, cultural and economic lives – the inability to exercise self-determination. Aboriginal communities were relocated, traditional economic activities were disturbed, and systems for educating the young were changed – all without the informed consent of the people most affected. The legacy of these changes is found in disorganized and damaged communities.

None of these effects occurred in a few years. On the contrary, the transformation of northern Aboriginal societies has a long history. Only recently has dialogue between Aboriginal and non-Aboriginal people begun about the meaning and consequences of their shared history. To put the present in context, it is helpful to know something of the history of northern administration, discussed in the next section.

4.1 Early Northern Administration

Responsibility for much of northwestern Canada passed from the Hudson's Bay Company to the government of Canada in 1870; in 1880, Great Britain transferred the jurisdiction it had exercised over the Arctic Islands. The Aboriginal landholders, whose land was the object of these distant transactions, knew nothing at the time of the European disposition of their territories. The northern Aboriginal societies were not consulted; if they had been, the European transfers of vast lands would likely have appeared strangely ineffectual. None of the northern Aboriginal nations had a concept of commercial value in land or private property, and few had yet experienced the hierarchical and abstract power embodied in trading companies or monarchies. Except for the flurry of activity that attended the formation of the Yukon Territory in response to the gold rush, and the dispatch of the Royal North-West Mounted Police to the Yukon and other locations, there was scant indication in the North that changes of much importance had transpired.[23] Most of the contact between Aboriginal and non-Aboriginal people continued to be commercial or economic, through whaling, the fur trade and fishing.[24]

For decades after assuming jurisdiction over the North, the federal government was preoccupied with national consolidation and economic development in southern Canada. Relations with Aboriginal people and other northerners were conducted almost absent-mindedly, when mineral discoveries and sudden migrations of non-Aboriginal people threatened sovereignty or international peace. Such threats prompted the signing of Treaty 8 (in 1898) and Treaty 11 (1921), when gold seekers, in the first case, and oil developers, in the second, suddenly flooded into Aboriginal peoples' territories.

Provincial boundaries were altered and extended in stages through the late nineteenth and early twentieth centuries. The sixtieth parallel became the northern boundary of the four western provinces, dividing the Sayisi Dene, Slavey, Kaska, Tagish and Inland Tlingit peoples. South of the parallel, Crown lands and natural resources were assigned to provincial control, while the federal government retained jurisdiction in the territorial North.

4.2 Wartime and After: A Problem of Development?

The relative isolation of the North was broken permanently during the Second World War. The war in Europe created a need for aircraft staging and resupply. After Japan's attack on Pearl Harbour, the northwest (including Alaska, the Yukon and coastal British Columbia) became a potential battleground.

During most of the war, American military personnel in the North outnumbered the Canadian population (Aboriginal and non-Aboriginal) three to one.[25] They rapidly built the Alaska Highway, a winter road from the Mackenzie Valley to Alberta, the Canol pipeline (running from Norman Wells to Whitehorse), and an oil refinery in Whitehorse, all in anticipation of the need to defend against an invasion from the Pacific. Air fields were constructed and maintained across the Canadian North, from Goose Bay, Labrador, to

Whitehorse, Yukon. Late in the war, a mine was reopened at Port Radium on Great Bear Lake, Northwest Territories, to provide uranium for weapons research.

These events had a dramatic impact on the Aboriginal peoples whose lands were suddenly invaded, especially in the Yukon, where the military presence was both large and sustained.[26] Large numbers of military personnel, enormous quantities of materiel, and rapid construction all had a major and lasting impact on neighbouring communities.

The development of the Cold War after the Second World War prolonged northern military activity. Some military personnel remained stationed in the Arctic, and during the 1950s, a weather, radar and communications network was constructed.[27]

Both wartime and post-war military activity in the Canadian North was initiated and controlled largely by the United States, creating concern among federal government leaders. As one team of observers noted:

> Canadian interest in the North grew greatly after the Second World War, and the stimulus for this, it must be confessed, was not only fear of what the Russians might do, but concern at what the Americans were already doing.[28]

If the American presence in the Canadian North drew federal attention, it was the expanding post-war welfare state that led to intervention. In the new post-war terms, it was impossible to ignore northern Aboriginal people's living conditions, which in most places were difficult: diseases introduced by European visitors, a relative decline in fur prices, and the high cost of basic commodities had created hardships.

In very short order, northern Aboriginal people received the full array of programs and services being provided to Canadians in the south, including low-rent housing, schooling, medical care and social services. By the early 1960s, all northerners were receiving the full panoply of social welfare payments. Between 1949 and 1953, individual and group trapline registration was introduced in both territories to regulate game harvesting, and programs were begun to induce northern Aboriginal people to take up agriculture (where possible), home and handicraft industries, and wage labour.

Underlying all these measures was a new federal interpretation of the situation of Aboriginal people. Hardships became understood as a consequence of 'disadvantage' rather than, as in the past, an unremarkable feature of Aboriginal peoples' chosen way of life. Rather than being poor, they were seen as unemployed – or likely to be unemployed, as the old hunting way of life inevitably died out. The remedy for this was the introduction of programs to draw northern Aboriginal people into the new wage economy being created by opening the North to non-renewable resource development. A more or less similar shift in the attitudes of provincial administrations also occurred, although in most cases the changes were felt more gradually.[29]

In retrospect, there were two striking features of the new federal approach. First, it was developed with very little consultation with the people to whom it was directed. Second, it virtually ignored the terms of the numbered treaties, save for the payment of treaty annuities. Later, when other forms of funding began to flow to the band administrations of treaty nations in the North, the funds were channelled to the territorial governments. This controversial system, while convenient, created an asymmetry between federal treatment of treaty rights in northern and southern Canada.

Unlike provinces, territorial governments are established by acts of Parliament that define the governments' powers and areas of jurisdiction. This division of powers does not have constitutional protection.[30] Typically, ministers of the Department of Indian Affairs and Northern Development have retained responsibility for the territories.[31] Today the political balance is such that the territories are, in practice, treated much like provinces, although they lack control over Crown lands and natural resources and they are funded not through equalization but a system of transfers known as formula funding.[32] As the territories behave more and more like provinces, the system of diverting treaty entitlements to the territorial governments grows more questionable.[33]

4.3 The Changing Balance of Power in the 1970s

During the 1970s, all over the North and indeed all over Canada, Aboriginal peoples found the means to express their views on the development and aid initiatives directed to them. Between 1969 and 1973, northern Aboriginal peoples formed several organizations to represent their collective interests. The Council for Yukon Indians (CYI) was created by status and non-status Indians in the Yukon Territory.[34] The Committee for Original Peoples' Entitlement (COPE), the Indian Brotherhood of the Northwest Territories (later the Dene Nation), and the Métis Association of the N.W.T. (later the Metis Nation of the N.W.T.) represented Aboriginal peoples in the western Northwest Territories. Inuit Tapirisat of Canada was established in 1971 to provide a national voice for Inuit from Labrador, northern Quebec and the Northwest Territories. The 1970s were a period of dramatic confrontation and radical realignment of the balance of political forces in the North. Aboriginal peoples found a permanent place at the centre of political life.

Federal policy on northern development has been stated infrequently. In 1972, in response to the growing effectiveness and importance of northern Aboriginal peoples and increased sensitivity concerning federal actions in the North, the federal government published *Canada's North 1970-1980: Statement of the Government of Canada on Northern Development in the '70s*. The government listed its first objective as to "provide a higher standard of living, quality of life and equality of opportunity for northern residents by methods which are compatible with their own preferences and aspirations".[35] A new policy statement was not issued until 16 years later, in 1988. By this time, federal aspirations were led by a desire to "transfer all remaining provincial-type programs to the territorial governments, including responsibility for managing the North's natural resources".[36]

The new objectives implicitly recognized the impossibility of continuing quasi-colonial administration but offered little in the way of guidance for overcoming what were recognized explicitly as the greatest problems for the future: a growing population with little formal education and little education in land-based production; and the absence of a viable strategy for expanding the number of jobs available in the North. There has been no response to the persistent objections of treaty nations concerning the manner in which federal funds for education and health programs are disbursed.

The territorial governments are being redefined. In some provinces, such as Quebec, quite rapid development of regional governing institutions is under way. Proposals for new regional governing institutions are under active discussion in virtually all the other provinces. Some proposals are based on the development of institutions to be shared with non-Aboriginal residents, while others envision a base in an Aboriginal nation (see Volume 2, Chapter 3). It seems likely that the next round of institutional change and political development in Canada will be led by northerners, both Aboriginal and non-Aboriginal, working together to develop local, regional and nation-based governments that reflect the demographic reality of the North. We explore the implications of some of these political developments below.

5. REGIONAL DIMENSIONS
OF POLITICAL DEVELOPMENT

Most of this chapter focuses on issues common to most northern Aboriginal people. In this section, we review briefly some of the different situations of the nations and peoples living in the North.[37] Our attention here is on the key matters of land tenure and political jurisdiction. Our general conclusions and recommendations about such matters as treaties and land redistribution can be acted upon only in the specific circumstances of particular regions by the people most affected by them.

Regional differences were always a feature of northern Aboriginal societies. There are several Aboriginal nations and peoples in the North today, and many more local groups and communities. Each has a particular history, stretching far back before contact with Europeans.[38] In the pre-contact period, the northern Aboriginal peoples hunted, gathered and fished over large territories. They lived in relatively small family groups, which in turn were part of a larger association of people who spoke a common language and who would assemble in larger numbers, at least annually. Although the overall northern population was quite small and the areas they shared were vast, there was considerable contact between peoples of different language groups. We know from Aboriginal peoples' oral traditions that travel, trade and diplomacy were common among the independent Aboriginal peoples and nations. Archaeologists have documented a wide trade in such valuable items as obsidian, copper, silica, marine shells, amber and meteoric iron across the northern part of North America and into the south, and further afield with the peoples of Siberia, Greenland and perhaps beyond (see Figure 6.2).

Today, the language groups, regional identifications and specific oral histories still exist, but for many purposes the internal political boundaries of Canada shape the political organization and activities of northern Aboriginal people.

5.1 Yukon First Nations

The Aboriginal people of the Yukon speak seven distinct languages (Gwich'in, Northern Tutchone, Southern Tutchone, Tagish, Kaska, Han and Tlingit). Some members of these language groups also live in Alaska, northern British Columbia and the Northwest Territories. There are 17 First Nations communities in the Yukon, and together they will negotiate 14 comprehensive claims agreements under a single umbrella final agreement.[39] In 1991 an estimated 5,100 people reported Aboriginal identity, about 18 per cent of a total Yukon population of approximately 27,800.[40] Aboriginal people are the majority in smaller communities such as Pelly Crossing and Old Crow, but non-Aboriginal people are the majority in towns such as Haines Junction, Dawson and Watson Lake and in the capital, Whitehorse.

Probably the pivotal contact events for Yukon First Nations were the 1898 Klondike gold rush and the construction of the Alaska Highway during the Second World War. The Gold Rush brought thousands of outsiders to the region over a very short period. Many of the migrants came from the United States. For the distant federal government in Ottawa, the gold rush presented an immediate problem of sovereignty and a secondary problem of preserving local order. To establish a federal presence in this remote area, the Yukon Territory was quickly formed and a legislature established, and police were dispatched to the area.

By the early 1900s the gold rush was ebbing, and many non-Aboriginal migrants left the area. Those newcomers who chose to make the Yukon their home changed the demographic balance in the territory, but the territory was large and resources were plentiful.[41] Aboriginal people continued to hunt, trap and fish, moving across the land as was their custom. While gold mining had

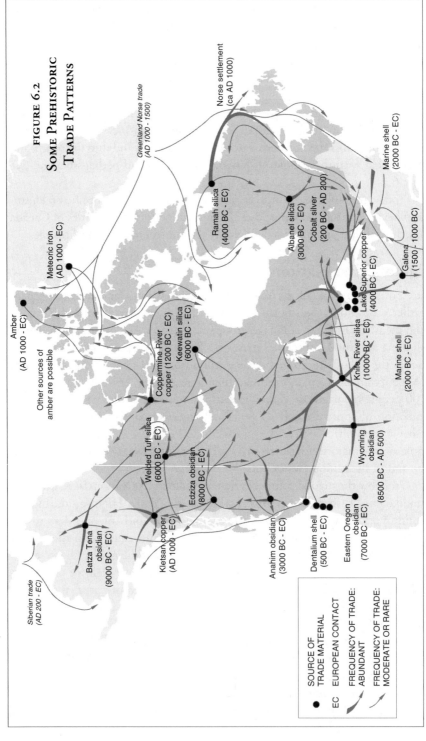

FIGURE 6.2
SOME PREHISTORIC
TRADE PATTERNS

Source: Adapted, with permission, from R. Cole Harris, ed. *Historical Atlas of Canada,* volume 1, *From the Beginning to 1800* (Toronto: University of Toronto Press, 1987), plate 14.

been environmentally destructive, the damage was confined to a few river valleys in the Klondike region. The gold rush nevertheless began the process of land alienation, which was exacerbated by the fact that while a territorial administration was being created, no treaties were negotiated.

The construction of the Alaska Highway in 1942 brought even greater and far-reaching changes to the lives of the Aboriginal people living in the regions through which the highway passed. During the construction phase, 34,000 construction workers and military personnel came to the Yukon, bringing with them opportunities for wage employment but also alcohol, infectious diseases, and social disruption. The highway itself became a major instrument for social change. It brought tourists and some small business development and facilitated the introduction of education, health and social programs.

All of these changes occurred without reference to the land rights of Yukon First Nations, despite residents' persistent objections. Nearly a century of frustration was articulated in 1968 by a Whitehorse chief, Elijah Smith, speaking to the Indian affairs minister of the day, Jean Chrétien:

> We, the Indians of the Yukon, object to the treatment of being treated like squatters in our own country. We accepted the white man in this country, fed him, looked after him when he was sick, showed him the way of the North, helped him to find the gold; helped him build and respected him in his own rights. For this we have received very little in return. We feel the people of the North owe us a great deal and we would like the Government of Canada to see that we get a fair settlement for the use of the land. There was no treaty signed in this Country and they tell me the land still belongs to the Indians. There were no battles fought between the white and the Indians for this land.[42]

Land claims

The Council for Yukon Indians (CYI) was formed in 1973 to represent everyone with "Indian ancestry" in the Yukon, irrespective of status under the *Indian Act*.[43] CYI advanced its claim on the basis of Aboriginal rights to lands that had never been surrendered.[44] Aboriginal people saw their claim as a means to close economic, social and communication gaps between Aboriginal and non-Aboriginal people in the Yukon.

Initially, the federal government refused to admit the existence of Aboriginal rights and would consider only claims to land and financial compensation.[45] Limited federal recognition of the dimensions of the problem created long delays. While the CYI claim was certainly about land, much of the public debate concerned self-government. As the debate unfolded in the Yukon, it posed alternative arrangements: under a proposed one-government system,

First Nations communities would share most institutions, services and programs with non-Aboriginal people; by contrast, a two-government system would involve some co-operation and shared institutions, but First Nations communities would establish their own school boards, health systems and local self-government institutions. This choice was particularly important in the Yukon, where many favoured independent institutions but where Aboriginal people constituted only about one-fifth of a small population and where Aboriginal and non-Aboriginal people lived in close proximity in many places.

These alternatives remained on the table for over a decade while – with some interruptions – negotiations proceeded. Finally, in 1988, an agreement in principle was reached that led to the signing of the Umbrella Final Agreement (UFA) in 1993.[46] The UFA broke new ground, providing constitutional protection for wildlife, creating a constitutional obligation to negotiate self-government agreements, and finding language for the agreement that avoided complete extinguishment of Aboriginal title.

Among its other provisions are title to 44,000 square kilometres of land, compensation of $260 million to be divided among the First Nations communities, the creation of a Yukon-wide land-use planning council and regional planning commissions and joint wildlife management boards. Under the terms of the UFA, First Nations communities will negotiate their own final agreements. Enabling legislation for these as well as for the Umbrella Final Agreement and Model Self-Government Agreement (which provide a framework for individual self-government agreements) was passed by Parliament in 1994.[47]

Issues for the future

The land and self-government agreements launch a new stage in the political and constitutional development of the Yukon. While the Yukon government's jurisdiction and authority are expanding through a process of devolution from the federal government,[48] the comprehensive claims agreements ensure that Aboriginal people will have a major influence on the political evolution of the territory. Under the terms of the agreements, Yukon Aboriginal peoples are guaranteed participation in public bodies dealing with everything from land use and development assessment to the management of wildlife and other resources. They also control significant pools of capital.

The UFA ensures that the developing government systems will incorporate, to varying degrees, traditional elements of leadership and decision making. For example,

> the preamble of the Champagne and Aishihik First Nations Self-Government Agreement asserts that "the Champagne and Aishihik First Nations have traditional decision-making structures based on a moiety system and are desirous of maintaining these structures...".

The Teslin Tlingit have already developed a form of government based on their five clans.[49]

To date, the development of political institutions in the Yukon has followed conventional lines. Although some policies and programs such as heritage programming, community justice and health care delivery draw somewhat on traditional Yukon Aboriginal knowledge, the way the Yukon government operates would be familiar to any Canadian. Decision-making and policy-development processes owe very little to Aboriginal political traditions.[50]

The creation of First Nations governments will have a major effect on the way the Yukon territorial government carries out its responsibilities, and there might be an opportunity for institutional change to harmonize public decision making with Aboriginal traditions. There is also a significant risk of inefficiency and policy gridlock, however. Under the self-government agreements, First Nations communities will be able to choose which programs and services they will run on their own. In other cases, there may be agreements for service delivery between a First Nation community (or several communities) and the territorial government. There may ultimately be as many as 15 separate governments sharing jurisdiction: the Yukon territorial government and the governments developed on the basis of the 14 final agreements being negotiated by First Nations communities. Considering the small size of the population and the limited revenue base, co-operation and simplification of the mechanisms for joint undertakings are urgent:

> The effectiveness of the territorial-First Nations relationship will be critical in minimizing these inefficiencies [resulting from the ability of First Nation communities to negotiate separate and different arrangements]. In managing this relationship and in relating to the agreement-based boards with their guaranteed Aboriginal participation, the territorial government will be highly motivated to respond to Aboriginal concerns rather than risk the high costs of difficult relations. The territorial government will particularly want to avoid relations becoming so difficult that frustrated First Nations decide to turn their backs on the usually more cost-effective joint activities and develop their own programs.[51]

Once the resources are transferred, First Nations communities will have a greater degree of administrative control over activities in the territory than ever before.[52] But there will continue to be a role, albeit a changed one, for the territorial government. A conventional political system is having to make room for Aboriginal governments.[53]

There are some outstanding and pressing issues. The long period of uncertainty over land claims and self-government negotiations has been replaced by another period of uncertainty as the agreements are implemented. Some of the problems the CYI representatives see themselves facing in the near future include the continuing inequality of bargaining power between the federal government and First Nations communities; the continuing need to secure constitutional protection for Yukon First Nation community self-government agreements; a demand by the federal government that the CYI repay a loan that funded its participation in land claims negotiations; and ensuring that the money is there to plan implementation of the claim.

Repayment of loans issued for purposes of claims negotiations is an irritant for most of the Aboriginal groups that have concluded final agreements or are now in negotiations. Federal policy still states that

> Aboriginal groups that wish to prepare a comprehensive claims submission can apply to the Research Funding Division for a research grant. Such requests are evaluated and a decision is made on the merits of each individual case. Once a comprehensive claim is accepted and active negotiations begin, the Aboriginal party is provided with loan funding to support the negotiation process. The loans are repaid after settlement through deductions from the Aboriginal party's financial compensation payments.

Only in the Quebec agreements, which were negotiated in the 1970s, were costs incurred by Aboriginal claimant groups paid by the federal government. In the case of the CYI, the federal government requires First Nations communities to repay $63 million in loans spent on the negotiations. Yukon First Nations told us of their opposition to this demand:

> We believe Canada's policy requiring the loan repayment should be reconsidered for the following reasons:
>
> *One*, the fiduciary that is in breach of his obligation should not penalize the beneficiary for the required funding to correct that same breach. The current policy would seem to be in direct conflict with the trust responsibility as set out in the *Sparrow* decision of the Supreme Court of Canada.
>
> *Two*, the decision to repay the funding for negotiations is the current policy of the government of Canada and may be challenged by the Yukon First Nation.
>
> *Three*, the delays in the negotiation process are due to changes within government, including ministers, negotiators and policy. Each delay has a time factor for re-educating the players about the issues. These delays have been very costly to CYI and the First Nations.
>
> *Four*, we recommend the loan payment be converted into a grant and not be repaid. As such, the loan should not be part of the land claims settlement and does not require constitutional protection.

> We strongly believe the loan funding issue may be dealt with through a contractual relationship between Canada and the First Nation.
>
> Judy Gingell
> Chairperson, Council for Yukon Indians
> Teslin, Yukon, 27 May 1992

5.2 Dene

Dene occupy a vast portion of north central Canada and parts of the United States. Their homeland includes the Mackenzie Valley south of the Inuvialuit homeland and west of Nunavut. These lands are shared by the Gwich'in, Sahtu Dene, Deh Cho Dene, Tlii Cho Dene (Dogrib), Sayisi Dene, Métis people and a growing number of non-Aboriginal residents. Dene also live in parts of the western Yukon, northern British Columbia, Alberta, Saskatchewan, Manitoba, Alaska and the lower United States. As with many traditional territories, there are sizeable areas of joint or overlapping historical and contemporary use of the lands of Dene, Inuvialuit and Inuit. Dene are part of a large Athapaskan family of nations whose roots extend as far south as the Navajo territories in the southern United States.

Although there had been sporadic contact with explorers, missionaries and traders since at least the late eighteenth century, more intense contact with outsiders began in Denendeh, as it did in the Yukon, with the Klondike Gold Rush.[54] Of the several routes to the gold fields, one began in Edmonton and took would-be prospectors down the Mackenzie River and then overland into the Yukon. This influx had a great impact on Dene of the region and led to treaty negotiations. Charles Mair, who was a member of the Half-Breed Commission of 1899, stated that rampages by miners led the government to recognize "the native's title" in the negotiation of Treaty 8.[55]

The protection and welfare of Dene were not the only reason for sending treaty commissions into the region, as is clear in an official statement by the deputy minister of Indian affairs:

> While under ordinary circumstances the prospect of any considerable influx might have remained indefinitely remote, the discovery of gold in the Klondike region quickly changed the aspect of the situation. Parties of white men in quest of a road to the gold fields began to traverse the country, and there was not only the possibility ahead of such travel being greatly increased, but that the district itself would soon become the field of prospectors who might at any time make some discovery which would be followed by a rush of miners to the spot. In any case the knowledge of the country obtained and diffused, if only by people passing through it, could hardly fail to attract attention to it as a field for settlement.

For the successful pursuance of that humane and generous policy which has always characterized the Dominion in its dealings with the aboriginal inhabitants, it is of vital importance to gain their confidence at the outset, for the Indian character is such that, if suspicion or distrust once be aroused, the task of eradication is extremely difficult.

For these reasons it was considered that the time was ripe for entering into treaty relations with the Indians of the district, and so setting at rest the feeling of uneasiness which was beginning to take hold of them, and laying the foundation for permanent friendly and profitable relations between the races.[56]

As René Fumoleau explains, there was good reason for this measured and understated approach:

In addition to extinguishing Indian title to the land, the Government was looking for tighter control over both Indians and whites, to insure peaceful settlement and development of the land, and to promote the harmonious co-existence of Indians and whites. In the North, as everywhere else, economic considerations far out-weighed all others in the formulation of Indian policy.[57]

For Dene, Treaty 8 was the means to a political relationship with non-Dene authorities and a way to encourage them to control their migrating citizens. Treaty 8 covered a relatively small portion of Dene lands; periodically, Dene sought an extension of the boundaries of Treaty 8, but their proposal was not to be accepted by federal negotiators.[58]

Economic considerations prompted the federal government to seek a treaty covering the rest of Denendeh some 20 years later. Non-Aboriginal people learned of quantities of producible oil at Norman Wells in 1920. Announced at a time when an expanding economy made the opening of the rich northwestern hinterland of Canada an attractive prospect, the news was greeted with great enthusiasm by the government, media and industry. Treaty 11 was signed in 1921.

The subsequent development of the oil production facility at Norman Wells, followed by the opening of mines at Yellowknife (1935) and in a few other isolated areas, reinforced the emerging pattern of enclave development that was to shape territorial development for the rest of the twentieth century. While most of the vast area of Denendeh remained occupied almost exclusively by Aboriginal people, there were a few trading centres, usually home to missionaries as well, and very few small centres of wage employment. The Mackenzie River and attendant lake and river systems formed the major transportation corridors for goods and territorial residents.

Restrictions on hunting and trapping started in 1917 with the closing of seasons on moose, caribou and other animals. In 1918, the *Migratory Birds Convention Act* further reduced hunting. Dene with treaties considered these regulations to be "breaches of the promise [in the treaties] that they would be free to hunt, fish and trap...".[59] (Dene without treaty believed they governed their traditional territories and objected to others making laws for them.) With the exception of this and other policing functions, the federal presence in the Northwest Territories was to remain relatively light until the Second World War and the subsequent Cold War, when large numbers of military personnel were stationed in the North. In the immediate post-war period, education, health and other social programs were introduced, bringing a few public servants into the territories. Finally, in 1967, the seat of territorial government was moved to Yellowknife, an event that led to the rapid expansion of the N.W.T. public service and a massive influx of staff from the south.

The transfer of administration of the territorial government from Ottawa to the North in 1967 affected matters such as treaty entitlements. For example, in most parts of Canada, funding for health and education for status Indians has been administered by the department of Indian affairs and is now available for devolution to bands that choose to take over this responsibility. In the Northwest Territories, funds for such purposes are administered by the territorial government; funding for treaty Dene education is 'blended' with general education funding. This has made it difficult to keep track of the extent to which treaty commitments are being met. It has also made it impossible for Dene bands to gain control over funding in these areas, as bands have in the south. Michael J. Prince and Gary Juniper note that

> in terms of public finance allocation and reporting at an aggregate level, Aboriginal peoples are dealt with in the same manner as non-natives in territorial expenditures. We should note, however, that Aboriginal people in the N.W.T. have long argued that the government of the N.W.T. (GNWT) is merely acting in the capacity of an 'agent' under management agreements for the delivery of the federal obligations to the North's Aboriginal peoples in such areas as education, health and social welfare. In the context of Aboriginal self-government, a critical public finance question is: what proportion of the territorial government's budget should be transferred directly to Aboriginal governments from the federal government, thereby bypassing the GNWT's consolidated revenue fund?[60]

Land claims

The discovery of oil in Prudhoe Bay, Alaska, in 1968 led to another round of negotiations concerning Dene lands. Soon after the Prudhoe Bay discovery, the federal government proposed construction of a pipeline along the Mackenzie Valley to carry oil from Prudhoe Bay to southern markets. Fearing the impact of the transportation corridor on their lands, Dene filed a caveat to stop the development.[61] The

Supreme Court of the Northwest Territories agreed with Dene that the project represented "an infringement upon their Treaty rights".[62] Justice Morrow ruled:

> I am satisfied that those same indigenous people...are prima facie owners of the lands covered by the caveat [filed by Dene to stop pipeline construction] – that they have what is known as Aboriginal rights...[and that] there exists a clear constitutional obligation on the part of the Canadian Government to protect the legal rights of the indigenous peoples in the area covered by the caveat.[63]

In the Northwest Territories, comprehensive claims negotiations began with the written assurance of the prime minister of Canada that negotiations were to be the modern fulfilment of Treaties 8 and 11. Dene and Métis people first began negotiating a single claim in 1974, following a joint assembly of Dene and Métis at Fort Good Hope, Northwest Territories.[64] The following year, at the second joint general assembly in Fort Simpson, the Indian Brotherhood of the N.W.T. (now Dene Nation) and the Métis Association of the N.W.T. (now the Metis Nation of the N.W.T.) passed the Dene Declaration.

Separate Dene and Métis comprehensive claims negotiations were conducted for a time, with single negotiations resuming in 1984. A draft final agreement was reached in 1990. This agreement, covering all Dene and Métis in Denendeh, was not in the end accepted by Dene and Métis people. The two groups had reservations about the agreement, including its requirement that outstanding Aboriginal rights be extinguished, its failure to deal adequately with treaty provisions, and its lack of an explicit provision for self-government, among other problems. Dene and Métis people anticipated that these matters would be addressed in subsequent negotiations, but the federal government was unwilling to continue Denendeh-wide negotiations.

Since 1990 two regional claims agreements have been concluded in Denendeh: one between the federal government and the Gwich'in of the Mackenzie Delta, the other between the federal government and the Sahtu Dene and Métis.[65] The Gwich'in negotiated title to 22,332 square kilometres of land, subsurface rights to 93 square kilometres, compensation of $75 million, and a share of resource royalties. The Sahtu Dene and Métis secured title to 41,437 square kilometres of land, subsurface rights to 1,813 square kilometres, compensation of $75 million, and a share of resource royalties. Provision was also made for joint management of wildlife and land-use planning. Dogrib are currently negotiating their own regional claim. Dene in the rest of Denendeh want to pursue land and government issues in relation to implementation of the treaties.

Issues for the future

The negotiation of regional claims revived old concerns about the best way to secure recognition of land rights and about the contemporary role of Treaties 8 and 11.[66]

In the western Northwest Territories, there continue to be simultaneous debates concerning implementation of Treaties 8 and 11 and the new form of public government that should be established after the division of the territory in 1999.

Some Dene communities have chosen treaty implementation as their path to self-government. For example, the Deh Cho Dene have declined to negotiate a regional claims agreement because they have concluded that they have no right to agree to extinguishment of title to the land. They explain, "Our laws from the Creator do not allow us to cede, release, surrender or extinguish our inherent rights."[67] Deh Cho Dene seek recognition of their version of Treaty 11 as the original accord between the Dene Nation and the Crown. They hold that the treaty is the primary document governing their relations with Canada, and – interpreted in the spirit in which it was negotiated – Treaty 11 is the document that will form the basis of all future interactions. (For further discussion, see Volume 2, Chapter 2.)

Deh Cho Dene have encountered significant difficulties in negotiating with the federal and territorial governments on this basis. The federal response has been, in the view of Deh Cho Dene, prohibitively narrow, allowing only segmented and incomplete consideration of important questions of land and jurisdiction.

Signatories of Treaties 8 and 11 that are not involved in regional claims expect to deal with the full range of their relations with the Crown in a coherent fashion; to date, they have lacked a process through which to do this. As 1999 and the formation of a new territorial government for the western Northwest Territories approach, the issue grows ever more urgent.

Full implementation of Treaties 8 and 11 will have consequences for such varied areas as territorial wildlife management, health and education spending, land use regulation and governmental arrangements. Implementation of the Gwich'in and Sahtu regional claims will have similar effects. These changes create a need for all northerners to work together to develop forms of territorial government that respect the various political choices of the northern Aboriginal nations.

We recognize the achievements to date of the residents of the western part of the Northwest Territories in finding consensus among many differing perspectives and interests and in working to create government institutions for the future territory that combine public government with the wishes of those who seek a nation form of self-government.

RECOMMENDATIONS

The Commission recommends that

Nations and Public Territorial Government

4.6.1

Dene of Denendeh (Northwest Territories) be given the opportunity to come to future negotiations on new political arrangements in Denendeh as a nation.

4.6.2

A treaty commission be established at the request of Dene communities seeking a treaty process.

4.6.3

The treaty commission's deliberations be the means by which the governing authorities for Dene are determined within the new western territory in addition to the framework of public government for that territory as a whole.

4.6.4

Those charged with developing institutions for Denendeh recognize the leading role Aboriginal nation government will play across the territory and design a form of territorial government that exercises lead responsibility in relatively few areas and plays a co-ordinating role with other governments' activities where appropriate.

4.6.5

Communities that want to participate in a treaty implementation process rather than regional land claims be given the same range of flexibility in terms of subject matter and quantity of land as if they were participating in a land claims process.

5.3 Métis People of the Northwest Territories

Most of the events in Dene history just reviewed are part of Métis history as well. But it is important to note at least some of the distinctive circumstances facing Métis people in the Northwest Territories who, for historical reasons, find themselves in a somewhat unusual position and whose fate is inextricably linked to Dene, who are their relatives and neighbours. (For a discussion of issues pertinent to Métis in each part of Canada, see Chapter 5 of this volume.)

Métis people are not signatories of Treaties 8 and 11, although at the time the treaties were signed, as today, Dene and Métis people lived together, often as members of the same extended families. The 'halfbreed commissions' offered scrip – either cash or small land allotments – to Métis people of the N.W.T. as a means of clarifying federal jurisdiction over the northern territories. By accepting scrip, Métis people opted out of the treaties.

In 1899, the federal cabinet stated: "It is obvious that while differing in degree, Indian *and Halfbreed rights* in an unceded territory must be co-existent, and should properly be extinguished at the same time".[68] As 1999 approaches, bringing division of the Northwest Territories, Métis people who live in

Denendeh seek to restore and protect their rights, in a similarly 'co-existent' process of constitutional development and land claims.

In 1972 the Métis Association of the Northwest Territories was formed. During the following two decades, sometimes in concert with Dene political organizations and sometimes separately, Métis people sought control of a land base and political self-determination. Gary Bohnet, president of the Métis Nation of the N.W.T., told us about what Métis people see as their most fundamental right:

> There has to be a land and resource base for Métis. It's fundamental. We have to be able to have control. We have to be able to work in partnership with co-management agreements with different jurisdictions.
>
> There is this myth out there that when you talk land and resources that the Métis may have less rights than some other Aboriginal people in this country. Well, that is [not true]. Our rights coexist along with the other Aboriginal peoples' in this country.
>
> Gary Bohnet
> President, Metis Nation of the Northwest Territories
> Ottawa, Ontario, 4 November 1993

After the draft comprehensive claims agreement negotiated by Dene and Métis people was rejected by the Aboriginal parties in 1990, federal policy changed to promote negotiation of so-called 'regional claims' with groups in the western N.W.T. formerly represented by the territory-wide organizations. The first regional claims agreement was concluded between the federal government and the Gwich'in of the Mackenzie Delta. Métis people were included in the agreement as 'Gwich'in'. The second regional claim was negotiated in 1993 by Dene and Métis people of the Sahtu region, an area immediately to the south of the Gwich'in lands. The Sahtu agreement refers explicitly to Dene and Métis people. In addition, separate management bodies have been established to manage money and investments for Dene and Métis people, giving both groups decision-making autonomy. Dene and Métis people in the area have established a joint Dene-Métis tribal council to co-ordinate their affairs in the settlement region.

In two regions, Métis people have opted to be part of federal negotiations with First Nations (the Gwich'in and the Sahtu Dene) under federal comprehensive claims policy. Furthermore, the government of Canada has recognized a responsibility to negotiate with Métis people in areas where Dene have decided to rely entirely on treaties. In areas where Métis people are not signatories to comprehensive claims agreements, exploratory discussions between Métis people and federal representatives have begun.

One of the main issues facing Métis people is how to structure self-government provisions so that they accord with the path of constitutional development in the Northwest Territories. In addition, complex problems of structure and implementation will come up in the dovetailing of Métis and Dene agreements, which will inevitably overlap in many areas and will need to be co-ordinated with territorial government arrangements.

5.4 Inuit

Inuit have lived in the Arctic north of the tree line for thousands of years. Their homeland encompasses the western and central Arctic, the Keewatin region of the barren lands, and the coasts of Hudson Bay, northern Quebec and Labrador, Baffin Island, and the high Arctic as far north as Ellesmere Island. Inuit are part of a circumpolar people who live in parts of Alaska, Greenland and Siberia. Today there are between 115,000 and 128,000 Inuit in the circumpolar North, of whom about 38,000 live in Canada.[69]

For two decades Inuit have been negotiating land claims agreements and self-government with Canadian governments. In most of the Inuit territories, Inuit are the large majority of the population. This has meant that dialects of Inuktitut, the common language of the Inuit, are still relatively strong, and that Inuit have considerable confidence in their ability to maintain cultural coherence as they work with and through the institutions of the larger Canadian society. Nevertheless, like other Aboriginal peoples in Canada, they have sought constitutional protection and legal guarantees of self-governing institutions. As the Inuit Tapirisat of Canada explained to us:

> [O]ur existence as a people also requires legal protection and guarantees. After all, it is our identity as a people that makes us "Inuit". Our concept of human rights recognizes the inseverable connection between the rights of peoples and the rights of individuals and recognizes the inseverable connection between Inuit and the land.[70]

This philosophy underlies both international and domestic initiatives of Inuit. Internationally, they have developed models of public government (with differing forms in Alaska, Greenland and Canada) and sought through various means to protect their way of life. For example, through the Inuit Circumpolar Conference (a federation of Inuit living in the circumpolar countries), they have developed the Arctic Policy, which makes recommendations to the nation-states in which Inuit live concerning virtually all aspects of social life.[71]

Within Canada, Inuit have exercised their right of self-determination by choosing various public government forms of self-government. As noted in Volume 2, Chapter 3, in the public government model, eligibility to participate as a citizen in governing institutions is based on long-term residency rather than membership or Aboriginal ancestry. Reflecting on the reasons for this choice, Wendy Moss explains the genesis of the public government model:

> Non-ethnic forms of government are attractive for their potential to ensure control and management over Crown lands in Inuit tradi-

tional territory as well as Inuit settlement lands. Inuit control through non-ethnic forms of government is premised upon the existence of an Inuit majority in the territories concerned (for example, Nunavut) or alternatively, structures of government that will ensure a strong Inuit voice even in a minority situation (proposals for a Western Arctic Regional Government have addressed this situation). [Nevertheless] there is a desire to leave open the option for so-called ethnic forms of self-government.[72]

Public government has certain definite advantages. It permits Inuit (in concert with other residents of the jurisdiction) to control land use and wildlife management over large land areas. For example, Nunavut, the new territory to be established in what is now the eastern Northwest Territories, covers about one-sixth the land area of Canada – far more land than a comprehensive claims settlement would place under the beneficiaries' direct control. Because Inuit form the large majority of voters in Nunavut, as a collectivity they will likely exercise the dominant influence in territorial politics for the foreseeable future.

But public government forms also carry certain risks. By choosing a form of public government now, Inuit have not ceded the right to choose a different form of self-government (on the nation-based model) at some time in the future. As Rosemarie Kuptana, president of the Inuit Tapirisat of Canada pointed out, her organization's goal remains to exercise self-determination within Canada and to adjust

> the essence of the relationship between Inuit and Canada [which] is an unequal power relationship in which Inuit rights have often been ignored and Inuit powers have been usurped by governments not of our making. The Inuit self-government and land claims agenda hopes to correct this by negotiating new government bodies in our territories, and asserting our rightful status as a people while respecting the human rights of other people.
>
> Rosemarie Kuptana
> President, Inuit Tapirisat of Canada
> Ottawa, Ontario, 3 November 1993

In all the Inuit territories with land claim settlements – Nunavik, the lands of Inuvialuit and Nunavut – comprehensive claims agreements complement plans for self-government. We turn now to a brief look at how the land claims process unfolded in these three Inuit homelands and to the situation of the Labrador Inuit.

Inuit of Nunavik and the James Bay and Northern Quebec Agreement

The Inuit experience with land claims and self-government began with plans to build the James Bay hydroelectric complex. Announced in 1971, the project was one of the largest of its kind in the world; plans called for the creation of a series of dams and reservoirs and the flooding of large tracts of land.

The Northern Quebec Inuit Association (later to become Makivik Corporation) promptly began negotiations with the Quebec government, the federal government, and the three companies involved in the project (the James Bay Energy Corporation, the James Bay Development Corporation and the Quebec Hydro-Electric Commission). In 1975, the parties signed the James Bay and Northern Quebec Agreement (JBNQA), which recognized Inuit title to 8,400 square kilometres of land and gave them $90 million in compensation for loss of the use of certain traditional lands.[73] It also included some provisions for regional government, a school board, and regimes for environmental protection and wildlife management. The agreement created a hunter income support program, which supports country food production by purchasing harvested wildlife and distributing it in Inuit communities and in the south.[74]

JBNQA was ratified by Quebec Inuit in a referendum in February 1976, after considerable internal debate.[75] Following ratification, the Northern Quebec Inuit Association was reorganized and renamed Makivik Corporation. Makivik was given responsibility for managing the compensation fund and fostering economic, social, political and cultural development of Inuit in Nunavik.[76]

There were many issues, but among the most important was the question of the form and philosophy of the political and administrative institutions that JBNQA would bring and the extent to which these were appropriate to the continued development of Inuit traditions.

Two decades after JBNQA was signed, major developments have occurred in Inuit institutions and in their relations with the governments of Quebec and Canada.[77] Negotiations between the provincial government and Makivik on implementation of some aspects of the agreement have been virtually continuous throughout the last 20 years. The form of self-government most suitable to Inuit circumstances has been a source of vigorous debate among Inuit and between Inuit and the government of Quebec. Recently, negotiations for a Nunavik government in the northern part of the province appear to be approaching a conclusion.

JBNQA provides for a regional administration under the auspices of the Kativik regional government (KRG) and also for a Kativik school board, both of which have been established. KRG has an elected council made up of members from the 14 Inuit communities and has powers over various matters of local administration.[78] Inuit have continued to work toward a greater degree of self-government in negotiations with the province of Quebec.

In 1991, the Nunavik constitutional committee presented the Quebec government with a draft constitution.[79] Negotiations were suspended during the Charlottetown constitutional reform discussions. Inuit tabled a draft political accord to provide Nunavik self-government in February 1993. In July 1994, a framework agreement was reached between the Quebec government and Inuit.[80]

The parties agreed to negotiate a form of self-government for the residents of Nunavik, including the establishment of a legislative assembly and adminstration.

The next step will be an agreement in principle on Nunavik government, envisioned by Inuit as a non-ethnic public government with jurisdiction over a variety of subjects exercised over the entire territory in Quebec north of the 55th parallel. There is agreement from Quebec and Inuit negotiators that the Nunavik government would receive block funding from the province, as well as a share of taxes collected within its boundaries. There is a possibility of sharing revenue from development of non-renewable resources as well.

Besides engendering and shaping self-government negotiations between the province of Quebec and Inuit of Nunavik, JBNQA also made possible a number of Inuit-initiated economic development ventures.[81] Investment revenue from the agreement's original pool of compensation capital has funded considerable applied research into economic development prospects and the creation of strategically positioned, Inuit-owned companies. For example, most recently Nunavik Arctic Foods (NAF) was incorporated as a subsidiary of Makivik Corporation. NAF harvests, processes and sells northern meat products, creating jobs in at least four communities and providing cash income to harvesters.

JBNQA was the first comprehensive claims agreement. Not only was it negotiated rather speedily, compared to other agreements,[82] but it was negotiated by individuals who had no experience with agreements of this type. Thus, it is not surprising that various matters of interpretation and implementation have emerged in the 20 years since the parties reached initial agreement.

Those implementing JBNQA have gained considerable experience in organizational development and training. As Makivik has worked to fulfil its mandate, means have been sought to involve the people living in the communities of Nunavik in the business of the corporation. As the Nunavik government is established, questions about even greater challenges arise: How will the government maintain meaningful contact with citizens, at a reasonable cost? What fiscal arrangements with the government of Quebec will ensure real autonomy? Will there be a financial or policy relationship between Makivik and the new government institutions?

Inuvialuit and self-government in the western Arctic

In 1984, Inuvialuit became the first Aboriginal people in the territorial North to sign a comprehensive land claims agreement.[83] The Inuvialuit Final Agreement recognized Inuvialuit title to 91,000 square kilometres of land in the western Arctic and provided compensation of $152 million for the surrender of other land and $17.5 million for economic development and social programs. There was also provision for a joint wildlife management regime. Although the 1984 agreement included a clause extinguishing the Aboriginal land rights of Inuvialuit in the territory,[84] Inuvialuit were successful in negotiating one provision related to self-government. This provision of the Inuvialuit Final Agreement (IFA) guarantees that Inuvialuit will not be treated less favourably than any other Aboriginal group with respect to governmental powers and authority. Section 4(3) of IFA states that "Canada agrees that where restructuring of the public institutions of government is considered for the Western Arctic Region, the Inuvialuit shall not be treated less favourably than any other native groups or native people with respect to the governmental powers and authority conferred on them."[85]

To complement the provisions of IFA, Inuvialuit have proposed a form of regional public government to be created by devolution of authority from the Northwest Territories government. The proposed western Arctic regional government would include all people living in the Inuvialuit settlement region (Inuvialuit, Dene, Métis people and non-Aboriginal people), and perhaps those of the neighbouring Gwich'in settlement area as well.[86]

Experience with implementation of IFA has been mixed. The economic institutions have generally functioned well, with the Inuvialuit Development Corporation playing a key part in the regional economy through investment of land claim compensation funds and developing various subsidiaries to market Inuvialuit products.

An area of critical concern to Inuvialuit has been implementation of land, resource and wildlife management regimes. These IFA provisions are being implemented at present, and Inuvialuit hunters have been able to control hunting and harvesting activities in a way that was not possible before the agreement. However, according to a review of these regimes, success in implementation depends somewhat precariously on government goodwill and co-operation, which have not always been forthcoming:

> The commitment of government to IFA implementation has been uneven at best, hollow at worst. Achieving a coherent level of corporate commitment to claim implementation across government remains a significant challenge for all government, notwithstanding the dedicated support that has been shown by some agencies.[87]

Governments have not enacted all the appropriate enabling legislation or made many necessary policy changes to ensure the full effect of IFA. A research study prepared for the Commission suggests that future claims should contain a list of enabling legislation that must be passed by a certain date following the agreement.[88]

Inuit of Nunavut

The creation of Nunavut will change the face of the North. Given the publicity it has received nationally and internationally, it will be watched closely as an example of Aboriginal self-government through public government – the first such model to be instituted since the establishment of Greenlandic Home Rule in 1979.

A number of features will mark the development of Nunavut:

- The government of Nunavut will have province-type powers that are important to the social, cultural and economic well-being of Inuit.
- The government will be able to manage wildlife and resources effectively because it will have jurisdiction over a large territory. Inuit will have strong and usually dominant representation on the relevant boards.
- Representatives will be elected by and accountable to a predominantly Aboriginal electorate.
- It is likely that Aboriginal people will continue to form a majority of the population for the foreseeable future and so will continue to have a major influence in economic, political and cultural life, whatever institutional changes are made.
- Fiscal relations with the federal government will take into account the cost of providing existing levels of government services.[89]

Nunavut was first proposed in 1976.[90] Since then, in response to federal unwillingness to negotiate self-government arrangements as part of the comprehensive claims process, Inuit have pursued a two-track strategy. They have negotiated comprehensive claims agreements with an eye to realizing all possible progress toward self-government, including securing an adequate resource base. At the same time, they have participated in available political forums, including the process to patriate and amend the Canadian constitution and the legislative assembly of the Northwest Territories.

In the N.W.T. legislative assembly, elected Inuit representatives worked co-operatively with other members to create the conditions under which Nunavut could be brought into being. In April 1982, a plebiscite asked voters in the N.W.T. whether they favoured the creation of a new territory in the eastern N.W.T., and 57 per cent of voters agreed to division. Fifty-three per cent of eligible voters cast a ballot. Voter turnout and affirmative votes were much higher in the eastern Northwest Territories than in the west although support for division tended to be stronger in predominantly Aboriginal communities (whether Dene, Métis or Inuit) than in the larger centres where more non-Aboriginal people – and more public servants – lived.[91]

The federal government accepted the verdict of the plebiscite but placed a number of conditions on federal action to divide the territory: that the outstanding land claims in the affected area be settled first; that there be continued support for division from residents of the N.W.T.; that all parties affected by division be required to agree on a new boundary; and that there be agreement on the division of powers among local, regional and territorial governments.[92]

In the end, the conditions were met. In 1990, the government of the Northwest Territories signed an agreement in principle with Tungavik Federation of Nunavut (now Nunavut Tungavik Inc.), entrenching their joint commitment to division of the Northwest Territories. Agreement on a boundary was achieved after a special commission proposal was accepted by the minister of Indian affairs in 1991, and the proposed division line was supported in a second plebiscite, held on 4 May 1992.

Through the 1980s, while these political events unfolded, comprehensive claims negotiations continued, ultimately producing an agreement that made direct reference to the creation of Nunavut. In November 1992, Inuit of Nunavut ratified the land claims agreement. With 69 per cent of eligible voters participating, 85 per cent approved the agreement. The Nunavut Agreement was signed by both parties in Iqaluit on 25 May 1993.

In June 1993, Parliament passed the *Nunavut Land Claims Agreement Act* and the *Nunavut Act*.[93] These two laws provide the framework for establishing Nunavut by dividing the Northwest Territories in 1999 and for the development of governing institutions, beginning immediately.

The land claims agreement recognizes Inuit title to 350,000 square kilometres of land and provides compensation of $580 million and a $13 million training trust fund; it also includes provisions for joint management and resource revenue sharing.[94] New agencies include the Nunavut Wildlife Management Board, the Nunavut Planning Commission, the Nunavut Impact Review Board and the Nunavut Water Board. These agencies will be composed of an equal number of federal, territorial and Inuit representatives. Since these bodies were created through the comprehensive claims agreement, they will have constitutional protection.

The composition of the boards and the planning commission has the potential to place a great deal of control in Inuit hands. With one-third representation from Inuit organizations and one-third from the Inuit-dominated territorial government, Inuit will have two-thirds representation on these crucial agencies.

Pursuant to the *Nunavut Act*, the Nunavut Implementation Commission (NIC) was established in December 1993. NIC includes representatives of the federal and territorial governments and of Nunavut Tungavik Inc., the body that represents Inuit of Nunavut and is responsible for implementing the land claims agreement. The mandate of NIC is to advise the three parties (federal, territorial and Inuit) on implementation questions, and it is likely the forum in which the stickier issues of implementation will be decided.

The immediate task is to plan for a new government and bureaucracy that will reflect the aspirations of the majority of Nunavut citizens and respond to their needs. In this respect, there are at least two important aspects of bureaucratic development: staff training and administrative development.

Staff training

An important goal is to ensure that the majority population of Inuit can staff their own governing institutions. The importance of education and training to self-determination cannot be overestimated. As a Commission research study noted:

The most obvious, but nevertheless critical, role was for the systems to educate and train Inuit in such a way that would permit their full participation in the policy making, management and operation of the administrative, cultural, economic, and other institutions developed as a result of agreements negotiated on land claims and self-government....

[T]he education and training system is seen as having a key role to play in producing a society of self-empowered individuals who have the skills necessary to participate fully in both the wage and/or traditional economy as they so choose. Such individuals must, in addition, attain the skills necessary to meet their civic responsibilities as well as those skills necessary to lead a satisfactory cultural, economic and social life.[95]

Estimates vary widely on the amount of money required for training, depending on assumptions about the duration and type of training required.[96] Given the current levels of education and training in the resident population, a major and sustained effort will be required. Aboriginal people in the North have lower levels of formal education than other Aboriginal people in Canada and than the general population. In 1991, 37 per cent of Aboriginal adults in the North had reached only Grade 8 or less, while fewer than 20 per cent had ever attended a post-secondary institution, and only 11 per cent had received a degree or other certification.[97] The situation is even worse in the far north (which includes the territories of the Yukon and the future Denendeh and Nunavut, as well as northern Quebec and Labrador; see Figure 6.1). In 1991, nearly half (45 per cent) of Aboriginal adults in the far north had achieved Grade 8 or less; just nine per cent had graduated from high school; and less than one per cent had a university degree (for an overview, see Figures 6.3, 6.4 and 6.5).

This situation is particularly alarming in light of the fact that most of the new jobs to be created as self-government is implemented will require some form of post-secondary training, in such areas as accounting, financial management, organizational development, planning and business development. The challenge for all new public governments of the North will be to undertake human development and training in a way that makes it possible for northern Aboriginal people to staff their own institutions.

It will be important for the new bureaucracies to emphasize skills and the capacity to acquire skills in their hiring practices, rather than relying entirely upon formal credentials to select employees. For employees hired on the basis of their potential to acquire skills, it will be essential to develop on-the-job training systems that permit learning while work is performed. Fortunately, Inuit have considerable experience with this form of training, developed over the years through the Arctic co-operatives system and the Inuit Broadcasting Corporation.[98]

Consideration might also be given to the development of an extensive high school and college co-operative learning system, similar to that of universities in southern Canada, in fields as diverse as engineering and public administration.

FIGURE 6.3

Unemployment Rate in the Aboriginal Identity Population Age 15+, 1991

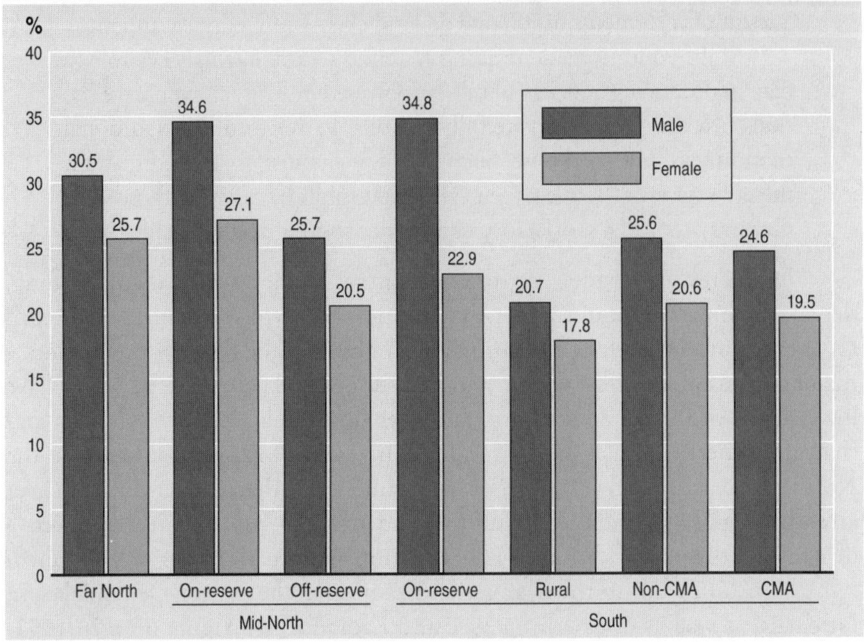

Notes:

Showing unemployment rate for the Aboriginal identity population age 15 and older no longer attending school full-time.

CMA = census metropolitan area.

Source: S. Clatworthy, J. Hull and N. Loughran, "Patterns of Employment, Unemployment and Poverty", research study prepared for RCAP (January 1995).

Under the co-op system, students interrupt their classroom studies to work for wages in settings similar to those for which they are being trained.

Administrative training

Creating a trained administration is only part of the equation. How that administration operates is another important question. In the formation of Nunavut, there is an opportunity for the institutions of government to be shaped by the culture of territorial residents. The challenge is to see how the majority culture of Nunavut can be knit together with the culture of the minority population, whose traditions currently pervade the structure of territorial administration.

R.G. Williamson has written about the roots of authority in Inuit society, where "good intellect and wisdom are paramount human qualities".[99] He says the quality of intelligence derives not from the rational ordering and under-

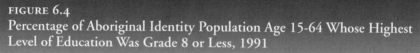

FIGURE 6.4
Percentage of Aboriginal Identity Population Age 15-64 Whose Highest Level of Education Was Grade 8 or Less, 1991

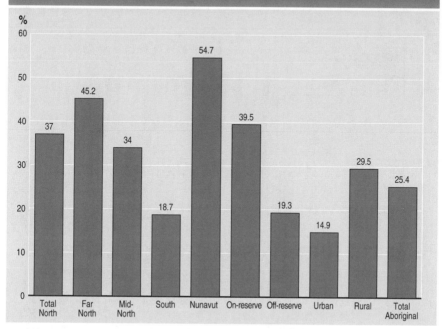

Note: Showing percentage of the Aboriginal identity population age 15-64 no longer attending school.

Source: Statistics Canada, 1991 Aboriginal Peoples Survey, custom tabulations.

standing of the universe but from a deeper understanding of one's place in the world and one's connection to the natural environment and to kin. In a similar vein, Gurston Dacks comments on the distinctive Aboriginal approach to social problem solving:

> Among Aboriginal peoples, the value attributed to the community and its unity and the faith in laws of nature provided by the Creator have defined the task of traditional Native politics as working together to understand how the laws of nature apply to a particular question. It is assumed that an answer to a question already exists and can be found if all participants in the decision to be taken work collectively to discern that correct answer.[100]

This leads to a key question about what is needed to ensure that these new political entities evolve in a direction responsive to the needs of their constituents and at the same time operate within the context of the Canadian federation.[101] Regimes of financing, styles of negotiation, the requirements for strategic planning, and the imperatives of probity, accountability and fiscal

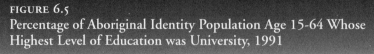

FIGURE 6.5
Percentage of Aboriginal Identity Population Age 15-64 Whose
Highest Level of Education was University, 1991

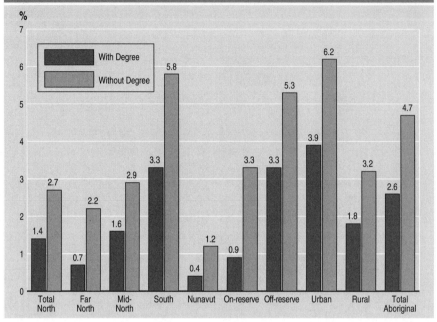

Note: Showing percentage of the Aboriginal identity population age 15-64 no longer attending school.

Source: Statistics Canada, 1991 Aboriginal Peoples Survey, custom tabulations.

responsibility – all must be present in a form that fits well with general Canadian practice. Making these arrangements in a manner that permits the culture of the original peoples of the region to grow and flourish is not a unique challenge but is common to all Aboriginal peoples who seek self-determination within Canada. We return to this matter in our later discussion of human development.

Finally, as is the case for all governments in Canada, Nunavut will be created in the shadow of fiscal restraint and the desire of governments to cut public spending. While the governments of Canada and the Northwest Territories have "committed themselves unequivocally to the creation of Nunavut",[102] fulfilment of this commitment is likely to require some additional expenditure, as well as artful planning, imagination and ingenuity.

The Labrador Inuit

The Labrador Inuit Association (LIA), founded in 1971, represents Inuit and Kablunangajuit in the northern Labrador communities of Nain, Hopedale, Makkovik, Postville and Rigolet.[103] Several of the Kablunangajuit descend from the European and Newfoundland men who came to settle on the north coast of Labrador during the nineteenth century. They came to fish, trap and trade. Some brought their wives from Europe or Newfoundland, and some married Inuit women. They settled in the wooded inlets on the coast and made their livelihood from trade, agriculture, trapping, fishing and hunting. They adopted many Inuit ways and skills, such as skin-boot making, seal hunting methods, and knowledge of the land, sea, and environment. Because they lived with Inuit, many of these settlers and their descendants eventually learned to speak Inuktitut.

Labrador is the only Inuit region without a completed land claims settlement. In part, this is because Labrador Inuit were the last Inuit region to submit a comprehensive claim proposal (in 1977), and in part it is because a willingness to negotiate on the part of both the federal and the Newfoundland government was required.[104] Federal acceptance of the claims proposal came in 1978, but the province did not join the process until 1980.

For various reasons, formal negotiations were not opened until January 1988. A framework agreement was reached in March 1990, with the condition that an intergovernmental memorandum of understanding be signed by the end of May 1992. The minister of Indian affairs was supposed to have reached an agreement with the province on cost-sharing arrangements. When a memorandum of understanding was not reached before the deadline, negotiations were suspended.

Today, Labrador Inuit are in the same constitutional position as all other Aboriginal peoples in Canada, but the history of relations between Inuit and non-Inuit is distinctive. The colonial history of Newfoundland and Labrador underlies some differences in contemporary attitudes and institutional circumstances.

The Labrador coast, where most Labrador Inuit have always lived, had been visited by Europeans for at least 700 years when European sovereigns began claiming the right to determine its governance. In 1713, the Treaty of Utrecht assigned the island of Newfoundland to Britain, while most of Labrador was assigned to France. In 1763, by virtue of the Treaty of Paris, France ceded to Great Britain almost all possessions and rights in North America, including Labrador. King George III immediately placed Labrador under the authority of the governor of Newfoundland. The Ungava Peninsula (containing what are now northern Quebec and Labrador) was divided into three parts. The east coast of Labrador and the north shore of the St. Lawrence were considered part of Newfoundland. The west coast and all the lands draining into Hudson Bay were part of Rupert's Land. The lands in between were considered 'Indian' territory, part of an enormous north-south corridor of unceded lands stretching from the north Atlantic coast almost to the Gulf of Mexico.

In 1765, the governor of Newfoundland issued an "Order for Establishing Communication and Trade with the Esquimaux Savages on the coast of Labrador", requiring in part that the Inuit population be treated "in the most civil and friendly manner".[105] He also offered land in Labrador to Moravian missionaries, who were already established in Greenland, believing that the missionaries would maintain the European presence while limiting destructive contact between Inuit and Europeans.

There followed a period of extraordinary jurisdictional fluidity, most of which was not apparent to the Aboriginal residents of the area.[106] The borders of Quebec were extended to include Labrador by the *Quebec Act, 1774*. Labrador was returned to Newfoundland in 1809, and then a portion of Labrador was transferred back to Quebec in 1825. The boundary was moved again in 1898.

A final dispute between Canada and Newfoundland over the location of the boundary was eventually decided by the judicial committee of the privy council in 1927.[107] The boundary of Labrador has not changed since then.[108] These changes made relatively little difference on the Labrador coast, where economic regulation and social services were managed by the Moravian church.[109] However, since 1927, Quebec has claimed that the privy council decision did not reflect Quebec's claims to Labrador. As part of its mandate, the Commission d'étude sur l'intégrité du territoire du Québec (the Dorion Commission) analyzed the validity of the decision and identified several alternative boundaries that would have been more favourable to Quebec while keeping with the historical and juridical interpretation available to the privy council. Nevertheless, the commission's general conclusion was that, contrary to what many in Quebec felt, no gross legal error had been made by the privy council in its decision and thus no legal option was available to reverse the decision, particularly when successive governments effectively accepted the boundary as the border between the two provinces.[110]

In discussions between Canada and Newfoundland leading to Confederation in 1949, the matter of governmental responsibility for Inuit (and the Innu people) was considered by the negotiators. It is some indication of the state of local politics that neither Inuit nor the Innu were consulted about their disposition. A joint Canada-Newfoundland special committee concluded that both Aboriginal peoples should become a direct federal responsibility, as in the rest of Canada. The special committee identified 11 conditions that would apply to Aboriginal people if union occurred.[111] In the end, however, the 1949 Terms of Union with Canada contained no reference to Aboriginal people.[112]

After some discussion of the legal dimensions of this arrangement, a 1954 agreement, outside the Terms of Union, provided for federal funding to be transferred to the Newfoundland government for administration of programs for the Aboriginal peoples of Newfoundland and Labrador. Under the agreement, the federal government would

> assume 66⅔% of costs in respect of Eskimos and 100% of costs in respect of Indians relating to "agreed capital expenditures...in the fields of welfare, health and education" and would assume the full

costs of hospital treatment for Indians and Eskimos of northern Labrador during a 10-year period and "to undertake an aggressive anti-tuberculosis program" during the same period. For its part, the government of Newfoundland was to assume all other "financial and administrative responsibilities for the Indian and Eskimo population of Labrador" excluding such federal benefits as family allowances and old-age pensions.[113]

In practice, funding provided under the federal-provincial agreements has not been directed specifically to Aboriginal people but to 'designated communities': the agreements fund persons according to where they live, not on the basis of whether they are Aboriginal or non-Aboriginal. This arrangement avoids the necessity of deciding who is an Aboriginal person and who is not.[114]

The government of Newfoundland and Labrador found this system of federal funding inadequate for communities' needs and periodically through the last three decades sought more funding and even more direct involvement of the federal government in providing services to Inuit and Innu communities. Successive federal governments declined to do this, although after the 1974 report of the Royal Commission on Labrador noted that the level of funding in these agreements was much lower than that received by Aboriginal peoples in similar regions of northern Canada, funding levels increased significantly.[115]

In 1984 the federal cabinet agreed to direct funding contribution agreements between the federal department of health and Aboriginal organizations of Newfoundland and Labrador:

> The Non-Insured Health Benefits (NIHBs) operates from our head office in Northwest River with the help of the CHRs and the Health Liaison Team. LIHC is extremely proud of this program as we are one of only two Aboriginal groups in the country to administer a comprehensive program ourselves rather than having MSB do it. MSB has recently commissioned a report on our program and that of Conne River with positive results.[116]

The province has also reached agreement with the Labrador Inuit Association (LIA), which administers some educational funding:

> [Y]ou have to realize that we've only been administering the program for five years, so it takes a while for us to change the program where we can to make it fit our needs or to fit the students' needs. When we were starting to administer this program, there was just between 15 and 20 students, and the program, by the way, was under the Canada and Newfoundland Inuit agreement. And the budget was about $150,000....Now we have up to as high as 180 students and

we have a budget of $1.6 million, so obviously we have been doing something right.

Tim McNeill
Education (Regional), Labrador Inuit Association
Makkovik, Newfoundland and Labrador, 15 June 1992

Since federal funding is provided under agreements that have to be renewed periodically, there has been regular conflict over levels of funding and concern on the part of the provincial government that the federal government will try to offload its responsibilities. This circumstance has complicated the negotiation of a comprehensive claims agreement, as there have always been three parties to this discussion, with varying interests. The province has tended to view Inuit as provincial residents like any others and to see self-government as a sort of extension of municipal government.[117]

It is possible, nevertheless, to see the shape Inuit public government could take in Labrador. Institutions such as the OkalaKatiget Communications Society, the Labrador Inuit Development Corporation, and LIA already fulfil some of the functions of governments. As in Quebec, it may be that a regional government within the provincial framework will be developed.

One important area to be resolved concerns the legal system. LIA has consistently argued for the importance of recognizing Inuit customary law as part of any land settlement in northern Labrador:

> Labrador Inuit customary law was the underpinning of Labrador society and even today Labrador Inuit customs and traditions are fundamental to the identity and self-esteem of Labrador Inuit, and a primary means through which the Inuit have traditionally exercised their rights of self-government.[118]

> Within the context of self-government LIA is examining a range of questions about how customary law should be applied and through what institutions or authorities.[119]

Negotiation and implementation of the land claim will occupy the resources of the Labrador Inuit for the coming years. As negotiations proceed, they are overshadowed by the difficult problems of who is entitled to participate in the claim and whether benefits obtained under that claim might create dangerous political tensions in Newfoundland and Labrador society.

LIA has allowed Kablunangajuit to become members in the association. This has raised the expectations of those outside the settlement area, who maintain that they share a culture, lifestyle and ethnicity with claim members. As benefits negotiated outside the land claim (for example, non-insured health benefits and post-secondary student support) accrued to Inuit, members joined from outside the land claims area to receive the benefits. LIA now has to decide whether those members outside the land claim area should participate in the claim and, if not, how to remove them from the lists.[120]

The question of funding continues to plague progress in Labrador, just as it does in other Inuit regions. The Newfoundland government has also been cutting spending. This attempt to control budget deficits could have a direct impact on Inuit, since the federal government gives the province what is essentially block funding for Aboriginal services (in education and health), and the province determines how to spend it. There is nothing to guarantee that this money will not be diverted to other priorities. Both LIA and ITC have called for direct negotiations between the federal government and Aboriginal organizations, followed by a bilateral funding agreement between the two parties, as a means of resolving this concern. Armed with these tools, northerners may well break new ground in coping with some of the common problems of industrialized countries today: increased pressure on public expenditures, global competition that is having a general levelling effect on incomes, and the reduced capacity of states to regulate or borrow to create full employment.[121]

5.5 Conclusion

The pace of political and institutional change in the territories and in the northern parts of some provinces is remarkable. Inevitably, unresolved disputes and outstanding issues remain. We hope that northerners will continue their progress toward new institutions that reflect the demographic and cultural balance in the northlands. We support co-operative political development and innovation along the lines now being pursued by northerners, and we urge the federal, provincial and territorial governments to act decisively to resolve outstanding disputes. We urge that every effort be made by all parties to achieve consensus.

RECOMMENDATION

The Commission recommends that

High Cost of Government in the North

4.6.6

In Nunavut and in the remaining part of the Northwest Territories, future arrangements allocate clear responsibilities between Aboriginal nation governments and territorial institutions and be kept simple and focused, given the high cost of government across a widely dispersed population.

Individuals at the community level should understand the institutional and political changes taking place. A continuing public education campaign is needed to ensure that people in these communities are fully aware of the new developments and their effects. Care must be taken to explain as simply and transparently as possible the eventual division of powers among the various governments in each of the new territories, whether they be at the level of the community, nation or territory. Public education initiatives could use print and broadcast media (including community radio stations), as well as public education kits for workshops with community organizations (community councils, school boards, etc.).

RECOMMENDATION

The Commission recommends that

Public Education   **4.6.7**
Public education materials be developed in co-operation with Aboriginal communications groups to explain the institutional changes taking place in Nunavut and the remaining part of the Northwest Territories.

6. ENVIRONMENTAL STEWARDSHIP

Culture is not only hunting, fishing and trapping. Even white people do that. The Chinese people do that. People all over the world do that. There is more than that. There is the spiritual side of culture. The mental side. The physical side. The social side. The economical side.

Randall Tetlichi
Old Crow, Yukon
17 November 1992

We want to do better for our land. This is what we were talking about. [translation]

Chief Gabe Hardisty
Fort Simpson, Northwest Territories
26 May 1992

6.1 Background

Environmental stewardship is an essential element of all future northern policies and programs, whether these are developed by Aboriginal, territorial, provincial or federal governments. Stewardship goes beyond establishing sustainable harvesting practices, mediating land-use conflicts, protecting the environment,

After Skookum Jim found gold, everything changed.
White people came to this country.
White people learned everything from Indians.
Now they want the whole thing, the land!
I've got sixty-four grandchildren in this Yukon.
I worry about them, what's going to happen?
White people, where's their grandpa? their grandma?
Indians should have their own land.

Source: Annie Ned, interviewed and quoted in Julie Cruikshank, *Life Lived Like a Story* (Vancouver: University of British Columbia Press, 1990), p. 338.

stopping or cleaning up pollution – although it includes all of these. Stewardship also means a revival and entrenchment of certain older ways of seeing the relationship between human beings and the environment. It consistently recognizes the utter dependence of humanity on the natural world. It involves the recognition that all resources, exploited past a certain point, are non-renewable. Central to stewardship is the realistic appreciation that all natural processes and systems are interrelated, that they know no domestic or international boundaries, and that responsible development requires co-operation among human beings and between human beings and the natural world.

Protecting the northern environment is essential for the physical, emotional and spiritual health of individuals and communities. It is also a matter of economic rationality.

Elsewhere in this chapter we recommend that economic development planning in the North be built on the mixed economy model. Most families in the North (except those living in a very few wage centres) draw their income from a combination of wage employment, the sale of handmade commodities, and hunting, gathering and fishing. Individuals, or more commonly families, may engage in all of these activities, making the best use of all the opportunities available to them. Virtually no one lives by traditional pursuits alone; likewise, few Aboriginal people in the North live entirely by wages, and there is little prospect that everyone will be able to do so in the future. The vitality of the mixed economy depends on both wage employment and the harvest of renewable resources.

Conflict over land use and over control and regulation of land use has been at the centre of the political relationship between northern Aboriginal nations and non-Aboriginal institutions and governments for many decades. Treaties 8 and 11 were in large measure attempts to regulate joint land use and occupancy in the face of disorderly and unpredictable incursions of gold-seekers and oil developers. The treaties were somewhat successful in this original purpose, but

When non-Aboriginal Canadians use categories such as 'wilderness' and 'natural resources' to refer to the land and the 'wealth' that it contains, they are not employing categories that transcend cultural boundaries. Rather, as they are used to describe Canadian landscapes, they embody a whole series of inferences concerning human relationships to this 'undeveloped' land that have historically been the cultural domain of Euro-Canadians. By now this should go without saying. In fact, however, it has done little to alert the tendency of the relevant state institutions to assume that the Euro-Canadian technical paradigm of resource management possesses a superior intrinsic rationality and predictive capacity. Such power is assumed to endow this paradigm with a universal applicability that should transcend cultural boundaries.

Source: Andrew Chapeskie, "Land, Landscape, Culturescape: Aboriginal Relationship to Land and the Co-Management of Natural Resources", research study prepared RCAP (1995).

less so in stopping or slowing the erosion of Aboriginal access to the land in later years. Where no treaties existed, there was essentially no regulation of joint land use at all until very recently.

In retrospect, it is clear that the Second World War and the years immediately following were particularly important ones for northern land use and for what has come to be called environmental impact. The wartime arrival of thousands of military personnel and their equipment, followed by construction of the DEW line and the establishment of a military presence at various northern locations, left many permanent legacies, including localized pollution caused by industrial waste that was not safely discarded. The most troubling of these have been polychlorinated biphenols (PCBs).

Forty-two DEW line stations were built in the Canadian North during the 1950s; by 1963, half the stations were no longer needed. In the 1980s, the active DEW line sites were converted for use in the North Warning System. PCBs were used at all locations,[122] and discarded PCBs were stored in barrels and left at the sites. A clean-up plan has been developed, and removal of the PCBs began in the summer of 1995.

The post-war period also saw the opening of mines and the development of hydroelectric projects, especially in the mid-north. In the 1950s and '60s, there were relatively few checks on any environmental effects these projects might have. There was also scant attention to local consultation, so most of the projects were implemented before the Aboriginal peoples using the land had a chance to appreciate their impact. For example, the construction of the Nonacho Dam on the Taltson River in the Northwest Territories was completed with no consultation with Dene Sonline living in the area. Dene Sonline came upon blasting and construction crews when they went out on the land for late winter trapping. The Nonacho Dam flooded an area Dene Sonline call Nánúlá Kúé. The flooding damaged the land, trees, animals, fish, birds and their habitat. It flooded gravesites, cabins and traplines. It altered caribou crossing routes and affected the quality of the water. All the knowledge that had been passed on from generation to generation about Nánúlá Kúé was lost when the land was flooded. Dene Sonline saw it as a "breaking of trust between the people and the land and water". This had a profound psychological effect on Dene Sonline that is still felt today.[123]

Similar situations have occurred in other parts of northern Canada as well. Partly as a result of such experiences, Aboriginal peoples began to organize politically to halt potentially dangerous developments and, in the longer term, to influence land-use decisions and mitigate environmental damage. The large project proposals of the 1970s, such as the James Bay hydroelectric power development and the Mackenzie Valley pipeline, galvanized Aboriginal peoples across the North. They organized to pressure governments to halt or regulate the projects. One result of this activity was the establishment of the comprehensive claims negotiation process, which was intended to achieve in modern times what the treaties had achieved (at least in part) in the past: secure and peaceful access to northern resources by those interested in developing them, and the regulation of land and water use so that Aboriginal hunters, trappers and fishers, and industrial developers, could coexist. A second result of land-use conflicts in the 1970s was the introduction of regulatory and review processes, such as the Federal Environmental Assessment Review Process.[124]

Through the 1980s, the range of environmental issues being addressed in open political debate expanded to include land, sea and air pollution and the impacts of military tests and exercises.[125] The focus of government policy shifted from understanding environmental issues at the local or regional level to seeing the environmental consequences of development from a transboundary (international and circumpolar) perspective.[126]

Besides efforts to halt developments that directly affected the viability of the hunting, trapping and fishing economies, Aboriginal people and their allies across the North also tried to influence the scale and rate of industrial economic development. Recognizing that this form of development has benefitted Aboriginal communities only marginally,[127] Aboriginal people in the North pressed for better-paid jobs, effective training programs and local benefits in the form of small business opportunities. There has been some success in this regard, so that it is now unlikely that any major project would be developed in the North without such measures to benefit the local population. The challenge remains finding ways to limit negative impacts on the renewable resources in the North and extending training and employment benefits past the peak phase of projects.[128]

The evolution of environmental policies and programs since the 1970s has involved the creation of a complex set of organizations and legislative provisions designed to assess and monitor environmental impacts of development projects, minimize negative consequences and, more generally, shift the focus of development from the approach of the 1960s – development for development's sake – to the approach of the '90s – creating sustainable forms of development.[129]

If oil and gas exploration or forestry disrupt hunting and trapping areas, if mines pollute streams and rivers, and if offshore petroleum production and transportation drive away marine mammals, the mixed economy of the North cannot survive. Northern Aboriginal peoples, moreover, will be forced away from the life that sustains them and ensures the survival of their cultures. This reality has long been recognized by northern Aboriginal people. In many parts of the North, they have been working to develop regimes of environmental stewardship appropriate to their areas. We consulted people about their experience in developing these regimes, and we offer some recommendations concerning the difficulties that are now becoming apparent. In this area, however, it is obvious that the Aboriginal and non-Aboriginal people who live in the North are taking the lead in finding solutions.

Three particularly important matters were raised in our public hearings:

- pollution control, prevention and clean-up;
- co-ordination and enhancement of existing regulatory regimes; and
- more thorough and effective integration of traditional knowledge in the regimes established to ensure sustainable use.

6.2 Pollution Control

Mercury contamination, radiation, PCBs, airborne particulates and other substances may have a severe long-term impact on the health of all northern residents. There is not the space here to address the effects of all these pollutants, but we can provide some sense of the potential problems. (See also Volume 3, Chapter 3.)

Although a comprehensive overview of pollution in northern Canada has not yet been developed, research indicates some serious problems on the horizon.[130] From 1985 to 1987, Health and Welfare Canada supported studies at Broughton Island, N.W.T., to assess the risks to the health of Arctic residents of consuming country foods containing PCBs. Seal, caribou, narwhal, fish and walrus accounted for 90 per cent or more of the country foods consumed. Human blood, breast milk and various foods were measured for concentrations of PCBs. The study found that 15.4 per cent of males and 8.8 per cent of females ingested more than the tolerable daily intake of PCBs set by Health and Welfare Canada. PCB concentrations in blood samples exceeded tolerable amounts in 63 per cent of children under 15 years of age, 39 per cent of females aged 15 to 44, six per cent of males 15 years and older, and 29 per cent of women 45 years and older. All samples of the breast milk contained PCBs, and one-quarter exceeded the established tolerable PCB level. Santé Québec reports similar findings in northern Quebec.[131]

While these studies give cause for concern, it is important to recognize that there is no general conclusion yet that country foods are unsafe. Rather, the findings are a warning that the people who consume country foods should monitor contaminant levels where they live, through information provided by the health and environment departments of the federal, provincial or territorial government.[132]

6.3 Environmental Management Regimes

Federal, provincial and territorial governments share responsibility for administering environmental regimes in the North. The Federal Environmental Assessment Review Office (FEARO) is responsible for conducting environmental impact assessments of development projects. On 19 January 1995 the *Canadian Environmental Assessment Act* was proclaimed. Among other provisions, the act enshrines the right to intervener funding and gives FEARO the power to subpoena witnesses and to assess the cumulative impact of development projects.[133] At provincial and territorial levels, responsibility for environmental management rests with various departments, such as the Ministère des Ressources naturelles (Quebec), the Ministry of Natural Resources (Ontario and Manitoba), the Ministry of Parks and Natural Resources (Saskatchewan), and the Department of Renewable Resources (Northwest Territories).[134] These ministries (and in some provinces, rural municipalities) manage the day-to-day regulatory process, including land-use permits, local development planning and water-use regulation.

Environmental management structures and policies differ throughout the North. Structures and policies depend on the situation of the Aboriginal people who live in a particular region, whether the group is subject to the *Indian Act*, and whether the group has entered into a comprehensive claims agreement. Where a group remains subject to the act, environmental management remains in the control of the federal government. Environmental management agreements with band councils are usually classified as 'interim' agreements; that is, they are of a temporary nature and subject to periodic re-evaluation.[135] These agreements exist as a result of policy, not legislation, and so are less stable than cases where Aboriginal groups have ratified comprehensive claims agreements, which make provision for similar functions.

Since the inception of the James Bay and Northern Quebec Agreement (JBNQA) in 1975 and the Northeastern Quebec Agreement in 1978, federal and provincial authorities have shared responsibility for environmental management with Aboriginal organizations created by comprehensive land claims agreements. This has involved the creation of co-management boards and councils, typically with 50 per cent Aboriginal membership and 50 per cent federal and provincial/territorial appointees.[136]

Assessments of the effectiveness of these co-management boards have revealed mixed results. In the JBNQA case, Alan Penn concludes that

> in the administration of public lands and natural resources...it has become apparent that the mechanisms in the Agreement have done very little to expand the economic and social prospects for the Cree communities. To many...the consultative mechanisms are impractical as a means of influencing government policy; instead, they can serve too readily as a pretext for inaction or containment.[137]

The problems experienced by co-management boards established through the JBNQA stem from the fact that the Aboriginal groups (Crees and Inuit) and the government continue to have very different understandings and expectations about what environmental assessment regimes are intended to achieve. In the James Bay case, these differences originate in the positions taken by Aboriginal groups and the Quebec government during and since negotiation of JBNQA.[138] The major failure of the regimes is that they provide insufficient direction regarding standards and criteria for approving or rejecting proposed development projects. In particular, the Kativik environmental quality commission, together with the Kativik regional government, lacks clear authority to act on environmental issues.[139] This is because of several problems, including lack of baseline data on environmental impact, the absence of independent data (from Aboriginal and government sources), and the lack of intervener funding.[140]

The Inuvialuit Final Agreement (1984) resulted in the elaboration of five management principles:

- the protection and preservation of Arctic wildlife, environment and biological productivity through the application of conservation principles and practices;
- the integration of wildlife and land management regimes and the co-ordination of legislative authorities;
- the application of special protective measures to lands determined to be important for wildlife, research or harvesting;
- the effective integration of the Inuvialuit into all bodies, functions and decisions pertaining to wildlife management and land management in the Inuvialuit Settlement Region; and
- the application of the relevant knowledge and experience of both the Inuvialuit and the scientific communities.

Under the agreement, the Inuvialuit Land Administration (ILA) is responsible for environmental management and will be directly accountable to the future Inuvialuit regional government. Co-management boards established through ILA have achieved some measure of effectiveness, mainly because of the flexibility of management options and processes set up in the agreement. However, Lindsay Staples criticizes governments for their lack of commitment to the IFA implementation process and points to the inconsistency between government departments in co-ordinating policies and interpreting IFA legislation.[141]

According to provisions in the Nunavut Agreement (1993), environmental management regimes will be introduced with the creation of the Nunavut government in 1999. Article 5, part 2 of the agreement creates the Nunavut Wildlife Management Board (NWMB), composed of equal numbers of nominees from government and Inuit organizations.[142] The board's jurisdiction includes participation in research, establishment of levels of total allowable harvest, assessment of basic-needs levels for communities, establishment or removal of non-quota limitations, and identification of wildlife management zones. NWMB held its first meeting in Iqaluit, N.W.T., in January 1994.

The co-management boards established by comprehensive claims agreements benefit from their association with these constitutionally entrenched agreements. They still face the task of establishing themselves early as effective organizations with the capacity to develop relationships with other institutions, such as provincial and territorial departments.

While there are still limitations on the effectiveness of environmental co-management boards, there is consensus that they represent an important improvement over the one-sided situation that existed before the signing of JBNQA. Aboriginal organizations may still be subject ultimately to government control in environmental management, but co-management boards increasingly allow Aboriginal groups to participate in and influence policy making.

One of the more successful examples of co-management in the North is the Beverly and Qamanirjuaq Caribou Management Board (BQCMB). (For details, see Volume 2, Chapter 4, Appendix 4B.) Established in 1982 as part of a 10-year intergovernmental agreement, BQCMB was created in response to a widely perceived crisis in the management of the Beverly and Qamanirjuaq barren-ground caribou herds, whose migratory routes cross jurisdictional and harvester-group boundaries in the north-west of Canada (see Figure 6.6).[143] A basic problem in the management of these herds involved a disagreement between caribou harvesters and government biologists over the number of animals that constituted the herds. This conflict, in a context where hunters and trappers were accustomed to exercising some authority and considerable discretion in collective harvesting decisions,[144] led to the development of the management board.

The board's mandate is to advise the federal government and the ministries of renewable resources of the Northwest Territories, Saskatchewan and Manitoba on the management of the two herds. A secondary function involves promoting conservation through education and communication.[145]

BQCMB consists of 13 members, of which eight are caribou users and five are government representatives appointed by DIAND, the Manitoba ministry of natural resources, the Saskatchewan ministry of parks and renewable resources, and the N.W.T. department of renewable resources. The government of the Northwest Territories appoints four of the user members, while Manitoba and Saskatchewan each appoint two.[146]

A recent review of its operations acknowledges that management effectiveness is limited by the board's advisory status. Nonetheless, BQCMB is considered a positive example of co-management, particularly in comparison to the situation before it was set up. It has provided a forum for resolution of disputes and for the development of consensus on key questions of herd size and quotas.[147] In 1992, the board's mandate was extended by a further 10 years.

BQCMB and other co-management boards face difficulties arising from language and cultural differences. The language of work is English, a provision that systematically restricts who can be appointed a user representative; that is, appointees must come from the bilingual Aboriginal population. This means that older unilingual hunters, who generally have the most extensive traditional environmental knowledge, are effectively prevented from being appointed to the board.

Furthermore, terminology such as 'wildlife management', 'census' and 'population' are central concepts that guide decision making. It is questionable whether all co-management board members share the same understanding of these basic concepts. For example, the term 'wildlife' reflects a perspective on the relationship between people and animals that is rooted in agrarian and urban ways of life. The term cannot be translated directly into Aboriginal languages.[148] Hence, there is a need to negotiate the meanings of these concepts so that harvesters and the scientific community can communicate and manage more effectively.[149] The integration of scientific knowledge and traditional environmental knowledge should be at the core of co-management. Negotiation and integration are beginning to occur only now, however.

6.4 Traditional Knowledge

By traditional knowledge we mean

> a cumulative body of knowledge and beliefs, handed down through generations by cultural transmission, about the relationship of living beings (including humans) with one another and with their environment....[It] is an attribute of societies with historical continuity in resource use practices; by and large, these are non-industrial or less technologically advanced societies, many of them indigenous or tribal.[150]

The traditional knowledge of Indigenous peoples encompasses vast and diverse elements in the common human heritage of understanding. Traditional knowl-

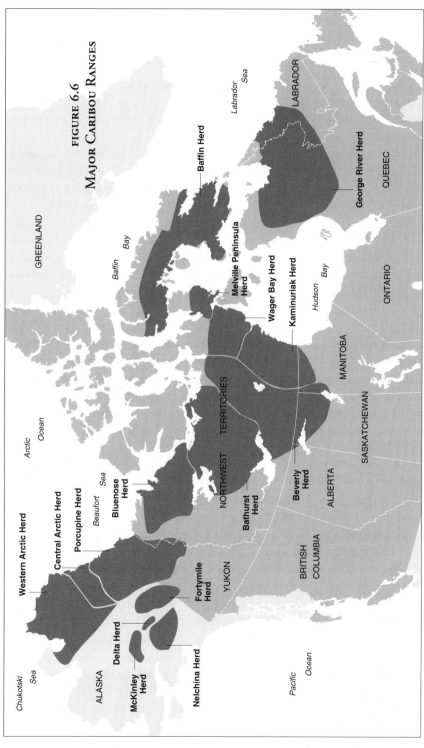

FIGURE 6.6
MAJOR CARIBOU RANGES

Source: Adapted, with permission, from George Calef, *Caribou and the barren-lands* (Ottawa and Willowdale: Canadian Arctic Resources Committee and Firefly Books, 1995); and from *Canadian Geographic* 105/3 (June/July 1985).

edge was threatened by colonization and has been made less accessible because – in North America at least – it is preserved almost entirely by oral means. While a great deal has no doubt been lost, traditional knowledge is now being recovered and recorded. Researchers are documenting bodies of knowledge in virtually every aspect of human life, including knowledge about physical, mental and spiritual health, science and technology, navigation, and all forms of production from the land and waters. A particularly rich vein of knowledge is available on matters of environmental stewardship.

The traditional knowledge of Aboriginal people in northern Canada about environmental matters comprises observations about all the interacting aspects of the local environment. These observations are based on experience and experimentation. They guide a set of protocols and a system of self-management that governs resource use.[151] The observations are classified, interpreted and understood through spiritual (that is, non-empirical) belief systems.[152] The spiritual aspect of traditional knowledge acts as a moral code that governs human-animal-environmental relations and is expressed through customary rules and laws rooted in the values and norms of the community to which it belongs.

Traditional knowledge can be seen to have two aspects. The spiritual aspect is integral to the cosmological and ethical beliefs of indigenous societies. While the validity or truth value of the spiritual aspects of traditional knowledge cannot be assessed scientifically, its social existence and transmission can be measured, as can effects on the environment (in, for example, the conservation of resources). The second feature of traditional knowledge is its practical base: traditional explanations of environmental phenomena are based on cumulative, collective experience, tested over centuries by people who required a sophisticated and practical knowledge of the land on which they depended for every aspect of life.

As with other components of culture, traditional knowledge is reproduced, validated and revised daily and seasonally through the annual cycle of social activities. It is elaborated and transmitted in Aboriginal languages and passed from elders to youth in each generation.[153]

Traditional knowledge is generally recorded and transmitted through an oral tradition, often in the form of stories, and it is learned through observation and experience on the land in the company of those who are knowledgeable. A general characteristic of traditional knowledge is the understanding that all parts of the environment – animal, vegetable and mineral – have a life force. Human life is not superior to other parts of creation. For example, Inuit traditionally believe that animals have souls and that certain places are considered sacred by virtue of having spirits. A fundamental consequence of traditional knowledge is the belief that human beings can use – but do not have the right to control or exploit – other animate or inanimate elements of the environment.

There is increasing interest in integrating traditional knowledge with the knowledge of biologists, botanists, climatologists and others in deliberations about environmental regulation. There is growing legitimacy for these ideas.[154] Just what is involved in integrating the two forms of knowledge is still a matter of some uncertainty, although various attempts have been made. Milton Freeman, for example, notes that the Berger inquiry (1977) was the first environmental and social impact assessment that took into consideration the views and knowledge of the Inuvialuit, Dene and Métis peoples of the northwest corner of Canada. Freeman emphasizes that, over the last two decades, "the credibility of native hunters as accurate interpreters of nature has become more widely accepted".[155]

Traditional ecological knowledge, along with scientific data, is used in the Hudson Bay Research Program. This program examines the various approaches to assessing cumulative effects in the Hudson Bay bio-region. The program is a three-year collaborative research initiative involving the Canadian Arctic Resources Committee, the Environmental Committee of Sanikiluaq, and the Rawson Academy of Aquatic Science.

John Sallenave has identified three barriers to the integration of traditional ecological knowledge:

- **Different perspectives:** Sallenave observes that there is frequently a distinct difference between what Aboriginal people think are significant impacts and what policy makers and those in favour of development projects think are significant impacts. These differences are probably rooted in both the habits of mind and the practical priorities of each group.
- **Scientific scepticism:** Scientists are sceptical about the credibility or reliability of Aboriginal information gathered through interviews, preferring 'hard' data such as biophysical data. Some may dismiss Aboriginal knowledge as subjective, anecdotal and unscientific.
- **Politics:** Policy makers may resist altering established decision-making processes to accommodate the use of traditional ecological knowledge, for reasons having to do with an interest in controlling the process.[156]

While these barriers are real, there is growing interest in overcoming them among scientists and policy makers, as well as Aboriginal people engaged in economic development planning, environmental protection and wildlife management. Work to integrate traditional environmental knowledge is probably most advanced in the Northwest Territories, where the government has adopted a traditional knowledge policy with far-reaching implications for the entire public service and regulatory process. The policy recognizes that

Aboriginal traditional knowledge is a valid and essential source of information about the natural environment and its resources, the use of natural resources, and the relationship of people to the land and to each other....[The Government of the Northwest Territories] will incorporate traditional knowledge into Government decisions and actions where appropriate.[157]

Among other measures, the policy obliges public servants to administer all programs and services "in a manner consistent with the beliefs, customs, knowledge, values and languages of the people being served".

6.5 The International Agenda on the Environment

Northern Aboriginal peoples and their non-Aboriginal neighbours have recognized the dangers inherent in the current jurisdictional division of the circumpolar Arctic basin, which is a single ecological and cultural area. For this reason and others, they have undertaken policy and organizational initiatives in the international arena.[158]

One of the earliest initiatives was launched in 1984 by the Inuit Circumpolar Conference (ICC), an organization representing Inuit from Greenland, Canada, the United States and Russia. ICC has developed an Arctic policy that covers virtually all aspects of circumpolar life and applies to all nation-states in the circumpolar basin. ICC invites these nation-states to adopt and implement the Arctic policy, whose main provisions are as follows:

- affirmation and protection of Inuit rights at the national and international level. This includes the right to self-government, as well as issues of global security, peace and development in the Arctic and circumpolar co-operation;
- protection of the circumpolar environment. Included here are provisions for the protection and management of Arctic resources, as well as Arctic marine transportation and transboundary nuclear pollution;
- social development, including health and social well-being, equality between women and men, and the role of Inuit youth and elders;
- cultural development, such as Inuit culture and language, communications, archaeological and cultural property and religious freedom;
- economic development, including employment and training, air transportation and international trade; and
- educational issues and northern scientific research.[159]

These principles are designed to influence and guide the decisions of policy makers in each of the eight nation-states with a presence in the Arctic. Political self-determination of each Arctic Aboriginal people is vulnerable to the economic, environmental and social change brought about by developments in the south.[160] By working together across international boundaries, Inuit hope to exercise more influence. Thus, the ICC Arctic policy states:

Public policies and programs of government, and international agreements, must reflect the ICC principles. Formal mechanisms should
be devised to ensure timely and effective Inuit input into policy and
decision-making. Governments must devolve responsibilities and
authorities, with the necessary financial assistance, upon Inuit
regional and community groups to develop and implement programs that affect Inuit.[161]

There have been other circumpolar environmental initiatives; Aboriginal
peoples from Canada have been involved in the development of each of them.
The Finnish government proposed an international co-operative body to monitor the quality of Arctic waters, in response to concern about contaminants in
the Arctic food chain, suspected to come from pollutants in Arctic waters but
originating outside the Arctic.

The Arctic Environmental Protection Strategy (AEPS) is another important
model. In June 1991, representatives of the governments of Canada, Denmark,
Finland, Iceland, Norway, Sweden, the former USSR and the United States
signed an accord in Rovaniemi, Finland, committing themselves to a multi-phase
strategy to protect the circumpolar environment. The AEPS commits these
nations to taking specific steps to protect the Arctic environment and establishes
an Arctic monitoring and assessment program. The strategy is important because
"it represents a collective, circumpolar approach toward environmental issues,
many of which do not respect political boundaries".[162]

Another case is the Porcupine Caribou Management Board. The caribou
migrate from calving grounds on the north slope of Alaska, through the northern Yukon, into the delta of the Mackenzie River, providing a vital source of food
for Inuvialuit, Gwich'in and Inupiat people of 13 communities (see Figure
6.6). They are also hunted by non-Aboriginal people. The Inuvialuit Final
Agreement created an opportunity for international agreements involving the
governments of Canada and the United States, as well as Alaska, the Yukon and
the Northwest Territories, to protect the herd's habitat and ensure the continuation of subsistence hunting on both sides of the international border.

A second step was the establishment of the Alaska and Inuvialuit Beluga
Whale Committee in 1988 "to facilitate and promote the wise conservation [and]
management of beluga whales in Alaska and the western Canadian Arctic".[163]
The committee, which operates on a consensus basis, is working to establish an
international agreement.

6.6 Conclusion

For Aboriginal people, environmental stewardship is more than a question of politics, it is a matter of cultural and economic survival. The long-term effects of
global pollution on the residents of the entire circumpolar region present a
challenge for the affected nation-states, as well as the communities and people

who live within their borders. Concerted multilateral efforts will be required. Environmental management regimes offer a different kind of challenge, and the promise – just beginning to be realized – of effective systems that make the best use of the knowledge and skills of Aboriginal and non-Aboriginal science.

RECOMMENDATIONS

The Commission recommends that

Aboriginal People
in Environmental
Stewardship

4.6.8

The government of Canada recognize the contribution of Aboriginal traditional knowledge to environmental stewardship and support its development.

4.6.9

The government of Canada make provisions for the participation of Aboriginal governments and organizations in future international agreements concerning environmental stewardship.

4.6.10

The federal department of health continue the close monitoring of contamination of northern country food by atmospheric and other pollution and, given the importance of these foods to northern people, communicate the results of this work quickly and effectively to users of these renewable northern resources.

4.6.11

All governments in Canada support the development of co-management regimes along the lines of those already established in the North.

7. SUPPORT FOR THE NORTHERN ECONOMY

If Toronto had 80 per cent unemployment, as is the case in most of our reserves, would you address the social or economic problems first? I think if you had 80 per cent unemployment in Toronto, you would have rioting in the streets.

Chief Frank Beardy
Muskrat Dam First Nation
Big Trout Lake, Ontario, 3 December 1992

> The economic circumstances in which LIA [Labrador Inuit Association] operates are best characterized as extreme poverty and heavy dependence on government support programs. The short, ten-week, commercial fishery is seen as the economic mainstay of the Labrador Inuit economy. This fishery has declined steadily and more rapidly over the years. Catches of all the traditional and principal commercial species, cod, salmon and char, keep getting smaller and smaller. The only "fish" which are plentiful are seals but there is no market for pelts as a result of the successes of the animal rights movement. The resulting decline in income is devastating the Labrador Inuit economy. They no longer have the income necessary to qualify for unemployment insurance benefits or to finance subsistence activities on the land.[164]

We turn now to a question we heard everywhere during our hearings in the North: How are the Aboriginal people who choose to remain in the North going to make a living in the future?

Over the next decade or so, the adult population of Aboriginal people in the North will continue to grow significantly (Table 6.6).[165] Nothing close to a sufficient number of jobs is likely to be created, especially in the smaller communities and more remote areas. Compared to southern Canada, per capita public expenditures in the North (particularly the territorial North) have been high, primarily a result of the climate, the sparse population distribution, and the need to subsidize virtually every form of economic activity.[166] As the population grows, the absolute amount of public expenditures is expected to grow. Yet public funds are expected to remain tight and probably to get much tighter, at least in the short term. The effects of federal and provincial fiscal restraint are not likely to be sufficiently offset by northern-generated revenues.[167] Taken together, these factors point to the need for careful rethinking in the area of economic and social spending. In a time of restraint, how are positive programs to be put in place to give young people reasonable choices for earning a living in the future?

We believe that the policies for northern economic development that are most likely to succeed are those that complement and build on the strengths of the traditional-mixed economy. The Berger inquiry into the construction of the Mackenzie Valley pipeline concluded nearly 20 years ago:

> In the North today, the lives of many native families are based on an intricate economic mix. At certain times of the year, they hunt and fish; at other times they work for wages....There are, in reality, four sectors in the northern economy: subsistence, trading of renewable resource produce, local wage employment, and industrial wage employment. We can trace the history of the native economy along

a spectrum that has subsistence activities at one end and industrial wage labour at the other. But we must bear in mind that overlapping or mixed economic forms are now integral to the native economy.[168]

The four sectors identified by Berger are still important in the North: subsistence hunting, fishing and gathering, the sale of renewable resources products, local (or small business) wage employment, and industrial wage employment. However, we would add to the "intricate economic mix" some other sources of income – public service employment, subsidies to the harvesting sector, and social welfare transfers.[169] It is by combining income from these sources that most northern Aboriginal people have made a living for several decades and that they still make a living today.

The traditional-mixed economy has been given many names. At one time, analysts referred to 'traditional pursuits'; later they identified the traditional, mixed, domestic, informal or renewable resources economies. We have chosen the term 'traditional-mixed' because it captures two of the most important features of this economic sphere. The reference to tradition recognizes that hunting, gathering and fishing are how northern Aboriginal peoples have traditionally made their living; the term also honours the fact that traditional knowledge and skills are important to success on the land and the reality that traditional spiritual values – a way of seeing the world – influence the activities of the land. This point was explained to us repeatedly at our public hearings. One of the plainest statements was made by Mark Wedge:

> What drove the economy prior to the contact with the European culture, the European people? Some of the stories that some of the elders had brought out was that prior to the contact it was spiritual values that drove this economy.
>
> Mark Wedge
> Whitehorse, Yukon
> 18 November 1992

The economy is mixed because it blends what were once considered incompatible practices: wage employment, transfer payments, and traditional participation in fishing, hunting and gathering.[170]

Extended families share income in kind (from hunting, fishing and gathering) and cash income (from wage employment, the sale of arts and crafts, and social welfare transfers). Sharing occurs within households and between them. Frequently, cash income from various sources is used to support land-based production. For example, wages from short-term employment or social assistance payments may be used to purchase the supplies necessary for a hunting trip; the food harvested on such trips will be shared and used to sustain families and other community members. In addition, by-products of the hunting trip – fur and hides – are often used along with imported materials such as cloth and wool in

Text continues on page 468.

TABLE 6.6
Projections of Aboriginal Identity Population by Age Groups, 1991, 2001 and 2016

		Both Sexes				Males				Females			
		0-14	15-54	55+	Total	0-14	15-54	55+	Total	0-14	15-54	55+	Total
		(thousands)											
Total Aboriginal													
Far North	1991	26.3	38.1	5.6	70.1	13.5	19.5	2.9	35.9	12.8	18.6	2.8	34.2
	2001	27.5	49.8	8.8	86.1	14.1	25.8	4.2	44.1	13.4	23.9	4.6	41.9
	2016	26.7	60.6	18.7	106.0	13.8	31.7	8.8	54.4	12.9	28.9	9.9	51.6
Mid-North	1991	71.4	103.6	15.3	190.3	35.9	51.5	7.5	95.0	35.5	52.1	7.7	95.3
	2001	74.7	136.1	23.7	234.5	37.6	68.5	10.9	117.0	37.1	67.6	12.8	117.5
	2016	72.5	166.6	50.2	289.2	36.8	84.6	22.7	144.2	35.7	81.9	27.5	145.1
South	1991	165.1	263.5	31.7	460.2	84.0	123.6	14.7	222.4	81.1	139.8	17.0	237.9
	2001	173.1	347.0	49.8	569.9	88.2	164.6	21.6	274.5	84.9	182.4	28.2	295.4
	2016	167.7	424.2	106.3	698.2	86.2	203.8	45.7	335.6	81.5	220.4	60.6	362.5
Total	1991	262.8	405.2	52.6	720.6	133.4	194.6	25.2	353.2	129.4	210.6	27.5	367.4
	2001	275.3	532.8	82.4	890.5	140.0	258.9	36.8	435.6	135.4	273.9	45.6	454.9
	2016	266.8	651.4	175.1	1,093.4	136.8	320.2	77.2	534.2	130.1	331.3	97.9	559.3

TABLE 6.6 (continued)
Projections of Aboriginal Identity Population by Age Groups, 1991, 2001 and 2016

		Both Sexes (thousands)				Males				Females			
		0-14	15-54	55+	Total	0-14	15-54	55+	Total	0-14	15-54	55+	Total
Status Indians													
Far North	1991	8.8	14.7	2.5	26.0	4.5	7.6	1.3	13.3	4.4	7.1	1.2	12.7
	2001	9.6	20.0	3.9	33.4	4.9	10.4	1.8	17.1	4.7	9.6	2.1	16.4
	2016	8.3	24.0	8.0	40.2	4.2	12.6	3.8	20.6	4.0	11.4	4.2	19.7
Mid-North	1991	51.4	77.8	11.9	141.1	26.0	38.8	5.8	70.7	25.3	39.0	6.1	70.4
	2001	55.8	105.8	18.4	180.1	28.4	53.2	8.3	89.9	27.4	52.6	10.2	90.2
	2016	48.2	127.0	38.1	213.2	24.7	64.4	17.2	106.3	23.5	62.5	20.9	106.9
South	1991	90.9	159.1	21.0	271.0	46.1	75.1	9.5	130.8	44.8	84.0	11.4	140.2
	2001	98.8	216.4	32.6	347.8	50.3	103.0	13.6	166.9	48.5	113.3	19.1	180.9
	2016	85.3	259.4	67.4	412.1	43.7	124.7	28.2	196.7	41.6	134.6	39.2	215.4
Total	1991	151.1	251.6	35.4	438.0	76.6	121.5	16.6	214.8	74.4	130.1	18.7	223.2
	2001	164.2	342.2	54.9	561.4	83.6	166.7	23.7	273.9	80.7	175.5	31.3	287.4
	2016	141.8	410.3	113.5	665.6	72.6	201.8	49.2	323.5	69.2	208.5	64.3	342.0

TABLE 6.6 (continued)
Projections of Aboriginal Identity Population by Age Groups, 1991, 2001 and 2016

	Both Sexes (thousands)				Males				Females			
	0-14	15-54	55+	Total	0-14	15-54	55+	Total	0-14	15-54	55+	Total
Non-status Indians												
Far North 1991	1.1	0.9	—	2.1	0.6	0.4	0.0	1.0	0.5	0.5	—	1.1
2001	1.1	1.1	0.1	2.3	0.6	0.5	0.0	1.1	0.5	0.6	0.1	1.2
2016	1.5	1.4	0.2	3.1	0.8	0.7	0.0	1.5	0.7	0.7	0.2	1.6
Mid-North 1991	8.8	9.8	1.2	19.7	4.4	4.8	0.7	9.9	4.3	5.0	0.5	9.8
2001	8.6	11.6	1.9	22.0	4.4	5.8	1.0	11.2	4.2	5.7	0.9	10.8
2016	11.8	15.1	4.5	31.5	6.1	7.8	2.3	16.2	5.7	7.3	2.2	15.2
South 1991	36.9	49.2	4.7	90.8	18.5	22.7	2.2	43.5	18.4	26.5	2.5	47.3
2001	36.1	58.2	7.5	101.8	18.3	27.7	3.3	49.3	17.8	30.6	4.2	52.5
2016	49.7	75.9	18.2	143.8	25.5	37.2	7.7	70.4	24.2	38.7	10.5	73.4
Total 1991	46.8	59.9	6.0	112.6	23.5	28.0	2.9	54.4	23.3	31.9	3.0	58.2
2001	45.7	70.9	9.4	126.1	23.2	34.0	4.3	61.5	22.5	36.9	5.1	64.5
2016	63.0	92.5	22.9	178.4	32.4	45.8	10.0	88.1	30.7	46.7	12.9	90.2

TABLE 6.6 (continued)
Projections of Aboriginal Identity Population by Age Groups, 1991, 2001 and 2016

		Both Sexes				Males				Females			
		0-14	15-54	55+	Total	0-14	15-54	55+	Total	0-14	15-54	55+	Total
		(thousands)											
Métis													
Far North	1991	2.1	3.7	0.3	6.2	1.1	1.9	0.2	3.2	1.0	1.9	0.1	3.0
	2001	2.1	4.7	0.5	7.3	1.1	2.4	0.3	3.7	1.0	2.4	0.2	3.6
	2016	1.9	5.7	1.1	8.7	1.0	2.9	0.6	4.5	0.9	2.8	0.5	4.2
Mid-North	1991	13.2	18.7	2.5	34.3	6.2	9.6	1.3	17.1	6.9	9.1	1.2	17.2
	2001	12.8	23.7	4.1	40.6	6.1	12.2	2.2	20.4	6.7	11.6	2.0	20.2
	2016	11.6	28.5	9.1	49.3	5.6	14.8	4.6	25.0	6.0	13.7	4.5	24.3
South	1991	36.7	55.6	6.6	98.9	18.8	26.1	3.1	48.0	17.9	29.5	3.5	50.9
	2001	35.6	70.6	10.9	117.0	18.4	33.1	5.3	56.7	17.2	37.5	5.6	60.3
	2016	32.5	84.8	24.1	141.4	17.0	40.2	11.1	68.3	15.5	44.6	13.1	73.2
Total	1991	52.0	78.0	9.4	139.4	26.2	37.5	4.6	68.3	25.8	40.5	4.9	71.1
	2001	50.4	99.0	15.5	165.0	25.6	47.6	7.7	80.9	24.8	51.4	7.8	84.0
	2016	46.1	119.0	34.3	199.4	23.6	57.9	16.2	97.8	22.4	61.1	18.1	101.7

TABLE 6.6 (continued)
Projections of Aboriginal Identity Population by Age Groups, 1991, 2001 and 2016

		Both Sexes				Males				Females			
		0-14	15-54	55+	Total	0-14	15-54	55+	Total	0-14	15-54	55+	Total
		(thousands)											
Inuit													
Far North	1991	13.8	17.8	2.3	34.0	7.5	8.9	1.3	17.6	6.4	8.9	1.1	16.4
	2001	15.3	23.5	3.2	42.0	7.8	12.2	1.5	21.5	7.5	11.3	1.7	20.5
	2016	16.0	32.6	6.1	54.7	8.2	16.7	2.6	27.5	7.8	15.9	3.5	27.2
Mid-North	1991	0.1	0.1	0.0	0.2	0.0	0.0	0.0	0.0	0.1	0.1	0.0	0.2
	2001	0.1	0.1	0.0	0.2	0.0	0.0	0.0	0.0	0.1	0.1	0.0	0.2
	2016	0.1	0.1	0.0	0.2	0.0	0.0	0.0	0.0	0.1	0.1	0.0	0.2
South	1991	1.9	1.7	0.0	3.7	1.1	0.6	0.0	1.7	0.9	1.1	0.0	2.0
	2001	2.1	2.2	0.0	4.4	1.1	0.8	0.0	1.9	1.0	1.4	0.0	2.5
	2016	2.2	3.1	0.0	5.4	1.2	1.1	0.0	2.3	1.1	2.0	0.0	3.1
Total	1991	15.9	19.6	2.3	37.8	8.5	9.5	1.3	19.3	7.3	10.1	1.1	18.5
	2001	17.5	25.8	3.2	46.6	8.9	13.0	1.5	23.4	8.6	12.8	1.7	23.2
	2016	18.3	35.8	6.1	60.3	9.3	17.7	2.6	29.7	9.0	18.1	3.5	30.6

Note:
— non-zero values of less than 50.
Because of multiple identities reported in the individual Aboriginal groups, the sum of the four groups is greater than the count for the total Aboriginal population.

Source: Statistics Canada, Demography Division, Population Projections Section.

fine-craft items such as hats, mittens, slippers and coats. Bone, antlers or soap-stone (depending on the region of the North) are used for art carvings and other items made for sale.

Far from being incompatible with wage employment, the traditional-mixed economy is healthier when there are opportunities for people to earn cash wages. Wages can be used to buy the necessary items for going out on the land; in turn, the land provides food and other necessities of a much higher quality than could ever be purchased in the North by cash alone. In this sense, land-based production in the typical northern economy 'subsidizes' both the wage economy and the social welfare system.

What is essential is that the enterprises that generate wage employment be conducted in a manner that does not damage the environment (and thus the basis of the traditional-mixed economy) and that the jobs provided by enterprises be structured in a way that permits hunting, fishing and trapping to continue.

Part of the reason for our support of the traditional-mixed economy lies in our assessment of previous approaches to northern economic development. Development approaches based on very high levels of infrastructure construction and other forms of subsidy for major non-renewable and capital-intensive resource projects have not drawn many northern Aboriginal people into full-time wage employment; few such programs will likely be affordable in any case.

Yet we do not dismiss the wage economy. The traditional-mixed economy is not an isolated sphere of activity. Rather, it is the vital core of regional economies that include wage employment, small business development and various forms of investment and public expenditure. For many northern Aboriginal people, therefore, seasonal, part-time or permanent wage employment is an important aspect of their participation in the mixed economy. In light of this, we recognize the continuing importance of public and private sector wage employment. We also endorse a variety of measures, identified by many northern Aboriginal organizations and governments, to enhance opportunities for employment and business development. (See Volume 2, Chapter 5 for a discussion of most of these measures.) There is a high degree of consensus about the merits of such measures and an increasing amount of independent research that demonstrates their relevance.[171] They include

- import substitution;
- long-term strategically planned labour force training;
- promotion of internal trade;
- development of the small business sector;
- selective commercialization of the wildlife harvest;
- specialized export development;
- eco-tourism;
- creation of job opportunities in the public service for local Aboriginal people to reduce the expense of importing and training public servants;

- job sharing; and
- flexibility in work schedules.

These solutions are based on the experience of the last several decades with other approaches to economic development. Since that experience is important to understanding the applicability of the measures just listed, we now consider some approaches used in the past.

7.1 Past Approaches to Northern Economic Development

During this century, two broad approaches to public spending for northern development have been tried: *laissez-faire* (where government abstains from involvement) and infrastructure development.

From Confederation to the Second World War, the federal purse was mainly closed to northern Aboriginal peoples. Some small amounts were paid to northern residents as a result of treaty obligations, policing was provided, and very occasionally, charitable expenditures were made. This laissez-faire period is captured in the phrase 'best left as Indians' – Ottawa's earlier belief that northern Aboriginal peoples should make their own living, as they had always done. To some extent the federal government's attitude applied to all citizens across Canada, Aboriginal or non-Aboriginal, until the changes that came with and followed the Second World War. However, a minority viewpoint, even during the Depression, was that the state had a responsibility to mitigate the effects of the major changes Aboriginal societies were experiencing.[172]

Laissez-faire disappeared as a new spirit of interventionism began to inform federal economic development policy and practice during the 1950s and early 1960s. In the immediate post-war period, the general view in Ottawa was that publicly funded infrastructure development would stimulate the development of regional economies by providing mainly construction jobs in the short run and by creating an attractive environment for private developers in the longer term. This view underlay regional development policy generally and the northern development approaches of prime ministers Louis St. Laurent and John Diefenbaker in particular and embraced this vision of economic development: build a railway or a road to a mine, subsidize the establishment of the mine, and in the natural course of things, Aboriginal people will be drawn into the new jobs created. However, despite federally sponsored training programs for northern Aboriginal people, relatively few of them have found permanent employment in these industries.[173]

The culmination of the northern development policy was a wave of major non-renewable resource development projects in the 1970s. These included, for example, the Syncrude oil sands development, hydroelectric development in northern Quebec, the lead-zinc mine at Nanisivik, Northwest Territories, and the Nelson River hydroelectric projects in Manitoba. Governments were typically involved not only in the provision of infrastructure support but also in various types of direct subsidies. These included tax incentives, informal regulatory sponsorship by certain government agencies, research and development assistance, direct subsidies to encourage local employment and training, and some regulatory measures designed to ensure that socio-economic benefits such as training and small business development would accrue to the region.

Neither the 1950s nor the 1970s version of development contributed greatly to Aboriginal community development. Creation of wage employment opportunities benefitted only a few Aboriginal individuals. Furthermore, despite some small business stimulation, large projects have had almost exclusively negative short-term effects in neighbouring communities. There are various reasons for this, including the necessarily rapid pace of such large projects; the finite duration of the projects; and the extent to which it is feasible for corporations to operate 'contained' operations in the North, using centralized purchasing and a fly-in labour force. Regulation can mitigate the last factor but would consume some of the leverage local people and their governments have. It is difficult to get much of lasting local value out of megaprojects.[174] The cost in public funds of each job created (whether the person who finds employment is Aboriginal or non-Aboriginal) is very high. Many of the new positions tend to be filled by workers from elsewhere, as even under regulatory constraints companies have found it cheaper to fly in trained workers than to recruit, train and retain local employees. Furthermore, and most decisively, considering the current emphasis on deficit reduction and public spending restraint, it is difficult to imagine support in the 1990s for massive public subsidies of private industry on the scale of the 1970s and 1980s, when drilling for dollars under the old National Energy Program was routine. The range of options has narrowed dramatically.

7.2 The Contemporary Northern Economy

We believe that the 1990s are the beginning of a more realistic and more creative phase in planning economic development in the North. Both territorial governments, for example, have recently studied the problems of their economies and have reached broadly similar conclusions.[175]

The 1990s witnessed the convergence of a number of factors in the North that pose tremendous challenges to Aboriginal people and to Canada as a whole. These challenges include

- unemployment and underemployment in certain key areas of the North, particularly in small, predominantly Aboriginal communities;
- continued limited prospects for non-renewable resource-based economic development and employment;
- government fiscal restraint, resulting in declines in direct expenditures and investment as well as reduced employment opportunities by the largest employer – the government;

- per capita costs for delivering public programs in housing, health, education and social services that are the highest in Canada;
- a young and rapidly growing population and its need to be engaged in productive activity;
- recognition of environmental issues in the North and the need for sustainable development based on both scientific and indigenous knowledge;
- recognition of the under-utilized renewable resources potential in some parts of the traditional economy;
- a gradual shift of political power to northern regions and the development of new public institutions based in the North; and
- with political development and Aboriginal self-government, stabilization of the regime for resource regulation.

We favour a policy response rooted in sustaining viable communities and promoting a diversified economy that encompasses both wage employment and harvesting renewable resources. Through comprehensive land claims settlements and emerging systems of self-government, Aboriginal peoples in the North have an opportunity to re-establish the traditional-mixed economy in a land where direct use of natural resources is a vital dimension of making a living.

Northerners may well break new ground in coping with common problems of industrialized countries today: increased pressure on public expenditures, global competition creating downward pressures on incomes, and the reduced capacity of states to regulate or borrow to create full employment.

7.3 The Value of Country Food

> To interpret the value of hunting solely as a means of subsistence and to give it a cash value would be objectionable to most Cree, as hunting is a way of life. It involves a religious sense of being in harmony with the forest and the animals....Hunting also provided employment and a sense of dignity and independence to the hunter. Nonetheless a cash income can be imputed....[176]

There are several fundamental reasons for the deep commitment of Aboriginal people in the North to country food and to the domestic system that underlies its production and consumption, and these extend beyond traditional eating habits and preferences. The first has to do with the nutritional value of country food (see Volume 3, Chapter 3).

In general, country food is much richer in protein than the meats imported from southern Canada and has a lower fat content. For example, seal meat consists of 32 per cent protein and two per cent fat, and caribou is 27 per cent protein and one per cent fat. In contrast, beef is 17 per cent protein and as much as 23 per cent fat. Also, country foods tend to contain less saturated fat than beef and other southern meats. This applies not only to sea mammals and fish but also to beaver, muskrat, polar bear and caribou. Country foods are also much higher in iron and calcium, as well as other essential nutrients such as vitamin A, vitamin C, thiamine and riboflavin. Changes in the diets of Inuit, Métis and First Nations people to include more southern foods have significantly increased the incidence of tooth decay, obesity, iron deficiency, vitamin A deficiency and diabetes.[177]

Harvested country food is usually the more economical alternative to store-bought imported foods, especially if nutritional value is taken into account.[178] Country food and its harvesting also have a very high cultural value. The social relations underlying the production of food in the traditional economy are critical to the functioning of that economy, and the sharing of food within the household and through the extended family and community are the primary means of reinforcing those social relations.

Finally, there is a growing body of evidence to show the importance of food gathered by hunting, gathering and fishing to household income. In the Northwest Territories, for example, more than half the Aboriginal population reported that all or most of its food came from this source (see Figure 6.7).

As noted earlier, Aboriginal harvesters require a relatively small but steady source of cash income to continue to harvest. This has been true for decades, although the situation has become more acute as fur prices decline (or vacillate wildly) and as the equipment and supplies necessary for harvesting increase in cost. In this area, some positive policy steps need to be taken, with additional public expenditures (or reallocation) and careful attention to program development.

7.4 Supporting the Traditional-Mixed Economy

Some portion of the cash needed in a mixed economy is available from wages and small business income, but there is also a need for subsidy from governments. In our discussion of Aboriginal economies (Volume 2, Chapter 5), we argue that income support funds such as social assistance and unemployment insurance can be used more actively and constructively in contributing to the economic development of Aboriginal communities. We recommend a new holistic approach to the development of innovative uses of social assistance, which must be controlled by Aboriginal communities.

One approach we suggest is to incorporate social assistance with income support programs for harvesting activities. An essential focus of social security reform in the North is to enable Aboriginal people to hunt for food, process it, transform it and export it to create jobs for Aboriginal people. This point is especially relevant to communities where, in the Northwest Territories for example, harvesters continue to make up a large portion of the social assistance caseload.[179]

Some northern regions are more advanced in this area than others – in northern Quebec, hunter and trapper income support programs are well-established – but in all parts of the North there are many ways to improve support

FIGURE 6.7
Amount of Food Obtained Through Hunting and Fishing, 1991

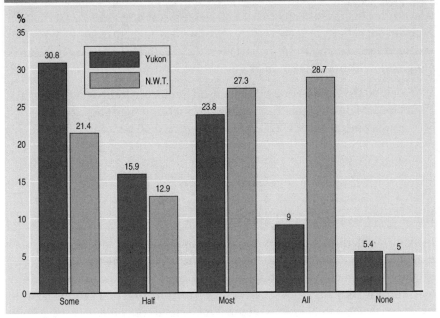

Note: Showing percentage of the Aboriginal identity population age 15+ living in the territories that obtains food (meat, fish, game birds) through hunting and fishing.

Source: Statistics Canada, 1991 Aboriginal Peoples Survey, catalogue no. 89-533 (1993).

for the traditional-mixed economy. Northerners explained to us that this issue has several dimensions.

High costs exacerbated by regressive taxation

The price of goods and services in the North ranges from 25 to 100 per cent higher than the Canadian average. The figure varies with geographical location and transportation costs, with the lower number referring to centres accessible by roads, such as Whitehorse and Yellowknife, and the higher applying to fly-in communities farther north. Northerners in some communities do not receive the basic dietary requirements of life. In such cases, it is strong ties to the land and access to country food that supply low-income families with essential dietary staples.

However, flat taxes, such as the federal goods and services tax, do not take the variation in consumer prices into account at the point of purchase. This situation applies not only to immediate supplies such as fuel and ammunition but also to the price of capital equipment used for harvesting, such as snowmobiles and outboard motors.

Low-income taxpayers may eventually apply for and receive a rebate on taxes paid, but this is generally only a fraction of the actual tax paid and is not adjusted for the tax difference based on the real cost of goods. Provincial sales taxes are not subject to such a rebate. Northerners' higher cost of living is thus increased again by point-of-purchase taxes. As a result of this situation, Makivik Corporation identifies taxation as

> one of the most serious development problems Inuit in Quebec face...[Makivik argues that, taking] into account high costs and real purchasing power, the real tax rate can exceed 30 per cent.
>
> Makivik Corporation
> Montreal, Quebec
> 29 November 1993

Innovative uses of social assistance

In many northern communities, social assistance payments and unemployment insurance are an important source of cash in the traditional-mixed economy, particularly in the rural North. Social assistance supplements the value of country food and also in many cases subsidizes the gathering of food from the land. In fact, people who can harvest traditional foods tend to require less social assistance.[180] Because of the positive effects associated with harvesting, there is a need for programming that encourages a greater measure of self-reliance rather than continuing dependency.

Social assistance programs are poorly suited to the needs of wildlife harvesting because they are designed as a support for consumption rather than for investment in production.[181] For example, in Fort Resolution, N.W.T., social assistance does not provide sufficient income to support extended periods out on the land, and hunters state that increasingly they must limit their expeditions to day trips and weekend trips.[182] Hence, a lack of cash-paying jobs combined with subsistence levels of social assistance have limited the ability of many northern Aboriginal families to participate fully in traditional harvesting pursuits.

The James Bay Crees of northern Quebec noted during the development of their income support program, that

> an incentive is needed to promote the maintenance of subsistence production. Fur production and sales, which are a by-product of subsistence activity, provided a strong incentive in the past when the fur market was viable.[183]

Since the European ban on seal furs and the sharp decline in fur sales generally, this income source has shrunk to the point of insignificance. Disincentives to harvesting, inherent in the current welfare system, include regulation against earning income from the products of the harvest, and the monthly payment system that works against spending prolonged periods in the bush.

Members of the Omushkegowuk First Nation, located on the Ontario side of James Bay, have responded to the serious threats to their harvesting economy by proposing a detailed modification of the social assistance system.[184] Unlike the Crees in Quebec, the northern Ontario Cree do not have a land claims agreement through which a self-supported hunter and trapper income support program could be funded. Hence, the Omushkegowuk Harvesters' Association aims to achieve similar goals by reversing the current negative relationship between welfare and harvesting. Their harvesters income security program proposes using social assistance funds to provide supplementary income to families and individuals engaged in full-time harvesting (a minimum of 120 days a year). These funds would be disbursed in the form of grants to enable the capitalization of the harvesting process and seasonal payments in recognition of extended periods spent in the bush. The Omushkegowuk Harvesters' Association suggests that this program be integrated with other programs involving product marketing, resource management, transportation support, and bush schooling for the children of the harvesters. (The Hunter and Trapper Income Support Program of James Bay and Northern Quebec and the Nunavut Wildlife Harvesters Income Support Program are discussed in greater detail later in this chapter.)

In the Arctic, the Baffin Region Inuit Association (BRIA) has developed a different, more comprehensive approach.[185] BRIA has devised an economic development plan and strategy leading up to 1999, when Nunavut will come into being. Working closely with governments and other Inuit organizations to redirect and restructure available programming, including social assistance, BRIA proposes an arrangement whereby these funds are used as seed money to leverage self-help projects that will in turn lead to increased self-sufficiency. This plan addresses the many social ills that arise from the decline of the self-sufficient hunting society. It is based on goals of self-sufficiency in the basic needs of life and relies on hunting and the production of country food to generate at least 20 per cent of the region's economic activity.

BRIA's objective is to achieve 80 per cent participation in the labour force, including both the wage economy and traditional activities. The five-year plan proposes to replace the current 60 per cent social assistance dependency rate with a 60 per cent participation rate, through creation of a private sector consisting mainly of Inuit family-owned micro- and small businesses, together with activities derived from the traditional harvesting sector (hunting, country food processing, a seal fur garment industry, sewing and handicraft production, carving and various art forms). Combined with the use of the compensation fund under the Nunavut Final Agreement, these public funds should be accessible in ways that give Inuit a chance to build a strong, modern, but culturally vibrant society.

We support the suggestion made by several Aboriginal organizations that such innovative uses of social assistance funds be explored vigorously.[186] We offer a number of recommendations in this area in the chapter on economic development (Volume 2, Chapter 5). The potential of such programs would be to increase the number of Aboriginal northerners able to hunt, fish and trap while they actively contribute to the economic (and nutritional) well-being of the community.

Alternative approaches to unemployment insurance

Unemployment insurance is also an important element in the traditional-mixed economy. For instance, to a limited extent, unemployment insurance has been used to sustain the ocean fisheries. In the fishery, people who have been able to work for the required time can receive unemployment insurance.[187] However, for a significant number of northern Aboriginal people engaged in the fishery, this has not been possible. Toby Andersen, chief land claims negotiator for the Labrador Inuit Association, explained the situation in this way:

> You look out through the window and why are our fishermen not fishing? It's ice, right? They can't put out nets. All our fishermen here in Makkovik, their unemployment insurance benefits expired the 15th day of May. Every year that happens. Why? Because you're supposed to be fishing. We're tied to an unemployment insurance policy that's standard or mandatory right across Canada. And there's no exception for a unique area known as northern Labrador where there is an Aboriginal society.
>
> Past experience is when the ice travels up the coast and hits the extreme southern Labrador and the northern part of the island in Newfoundland and fishermen can't put their gear in the water because the ice is into the bays and the boats, Ottawa extends the unemployment insurance benefits to those fishermen because they can't fish because of ice conditions. Our fishermen can't get it. Now, isn't that discrimination?
>
> Toby Andersen
> Chief Negotiator, Labrador Inuit Association
> Makkovik, Newfoundland and Labrador, 15 June 1992

With unemployment rates as high as 70 per cent in some communities, many northerners never had the opportunity to work enough weeks to become eligible. There is widespread support among Aboriginal representatives for proposals to extend unemployment insurance to non-standard employment, including self-employed Aboriginal trappers and resource harvesters. For example, Inuit Tapirisat of Canada, the Labrador Inuit Association, the Métis National Council, the Native Women's Association of Canada, and the Congress of

Aboriginal Peoples have come out in public support of proposals to include Aboriginally defined non-standard employment in the UI scheme.

Parliament recently enacted legislation amending the unemployment insurance system.[188] The new Employment Insurance (EI) program benefits Aboriginal northerners in some ways but falls short in others. Recipients will be allowed to earn up to $50 weekly without reducing their benefits otherwise payable. The eligibility period will be measured in hours rather than weeks. Northern seasonal workers, multiple-job holders and part-time workers will therefore become eligible more quickly than before.

Flexible measures such as these are relevant to Aboriginal communities in the North that depend to a large extent on cottage industries, short intermittent work periods, and resource-based seasonal work that, for geographic and climatic reasons, often has not extended to the previously required 12-week eligibility period. Indeed, seasonal work is seen by many Aboriginal northerners as an invaluable contribution to their local and regional economies, providing the potential for expanded economic activity in the future (tourism, for example).

However, benefits have been reduced under the new legislation. Consideration has not been given to higher northern living costs. The requirement that new entrants to the labour force work longer hours to qualify will hinder young northerners. We believe the uniquely high cost of living in the North needs to be factored into EI benefits. The North is an area of high unemployment, and people should not be doubly penalized by the region's high living costs. The Commission believes that the Employment Insurance Commission should consider recommending appropriate cost-of-living allowances in its report to Parliament (due by December 1998) on the phased implementation of the reforms.

We believe there is also scope to integrate the federal government's planned job creation partnerships – enabling groups of EI claimants to work in concert with community organizations – and its three-year, $300-million transitional jobs fund for high unemployment regions with our recommendations on innovative community uses of social assistance funds. Both approaches favour strong local input, including private organizations. We note as well that the jobs fund could be used to support the federal economic development initiative in northern Ontario and strategic sectors such as tourism. (See Volume 2, Chapter 5, particularly the discussion of income support alternatives.)

Many people spoke to us of the apparent unfairness of federal and provincial practices with respect to various industries. While agriculture, for example, is heavily subsidized with a sensitive array of measures, little has been done to support the traditional-mixed economy when it has been threatened.

Inuit noted that when the sealing industry collapsed as a result of international reaction to the Newfoundland seal pup harvest, seal hunters received no compensation for their losses. Inuit had used the money made from selling pelts to purchase equipment to go out onto to the land for all kinds of hunting. When they could no longer earn cash from the sale of pelts, they could no longer afford to buy equipment to go out onto the land as often as they wished.[189]

Another problem arose in the implementation of the cod moratorium package, a program instituted in 1993 to compensate fishers affected by the ban on cod fishing. The Commission was told that Inuit of Nain, Newfoundland and Labrador, felt the impact of the depletion of cod stocks before anyone else in the province but that they were excluded from the compensation package.

Aboriginal peoples in northern Quebec, where claims agreements have established hunter income support programs, are in the most stable position. Those in the Northwest Territories have had access for many years to various measures in support of the traditional-mixed economy, including fur-purchasing programs and public subsidies for hunting and trapping distributed through community-level associations of hunters and trappers. But there are no programs comparable to those in Quebec anywhere in Canada.

The moment has arrived to deal constructively with the disparate problems facing northern Aboriginal peoples trying to earn a living in the traditional sector. Unemployment insurance has been used for many years throughout Canada as a flexible subsidy for workers in industries with seasonal variations in labour force demand. This role for the unemployment insurance system has come into question. However, unemployment insurance must be examined along with social assistance to design ways to support increased self-reliance in areas of the country where income supplements of some kind will be a permanent fixture of the economy for a significant portion of the workforce. Such a restructuring will have a far better economic and social impact than continuation of social assistance.

Hunter and trapper income support programs

At present, there are two hunter and trapper income support programs operating in northern Canada and another in the planning phase.

The James Bay and Northern Quebec Agreement, negotiated by the Crees and Inuit, created the first programs designed to support harvesting in a direct and systematic fashion. The Crees and Inuit have developed somewhat different programs; both appear to be operating to the benefit of the claims agreements beneficiaries.[190]

Such programs provide a better solution to the shortage of cash than social assistance, which can erode individual self-esteem. Hunter and trapper income support programs

> provide a strong income multiplier through the production of food, are a spur to economic development of communities by placing money directly in the hands of those in the community who are in need and are in turn most likely to spend it in the community, and are likely to be cheaper than alternative programs when all are taken into account.[191]

[The traditional economy] has the capacity to absorb relatively large amounts of labour at relatively high wage levels, provided that the long-term carrying capacity of the environment is not exceeded. Moreover, no other sector of the economy appears to hold the potential to expand employment over the next decade at the rate necessary to provide jobs for the rapidly increasing population....

Source: N.C. Quigley and N.J. McBride, "The Structure of an Arctic Microeconomy: The Traditional Sector in Community Economic Development", *Arctic* 40/3 (September 1987), p. 209.

The Cree Income Security Program

The income support program of the Crees of northern Quebec is a production support program for hunters and trappers that funds individuals according to the time they spend out on the land.[192] This program forms part of the James Bay and Northern Quebec Agreement. It recognizes the importance of the mixed economy and attempts to offer financial support through a structure similar to a negative income tax, guaranteeing a minimum level of income based on family needs. In addition, cash income is provided to harvesters depending on the number of days spent harvesting, in the form of a per diem rate. To be eligible for the program the harvester must work no fewer than 120 days harvesting, spend more time harvesting than working for a wage income, and earn less from harvesting than from wage labour.[193]

In 1992-1993, the guaranteed income was $3,240 for the head of the 'beneficiary unit' (family, defined in broad terms) and an additional $3,240 for the 'consort' (partner). There is also a per diem portion that can be collected to a maximum of 240 days, at $38.27 per day. Any wage earnings over the guaranteed annual income reduce the guaranteed income by 40 per cent of the wages earned. For example, a harvester earning $5,000 in the wage economy would receive a reduction in guaranteed annual income of $2,000 (40 per cent of $5,000). Payments are made in advance to allow harvesters to prepare and purchase the equipment needed to harvest. Program costs in 1992 were $14.8 million, according to the Cree Hunters and Trappers Income Security Board. There were 1,214 beneficiary units, representing 3,018 individuals, in 1992. The benefit per unit in 1991-1992 was $11,719.[194]

The basic income levels, per diem rates and offset percentages can all be adjusted for different situations. Important attributes of the Cree Income Security Program are that the program involves the Crees directly in program design, recognizes and supports economic activity that provides meaningful work, and contributes to a diversified economy that is in harmony with the land, the seasons and the people who live and work in these communities.

The Northern Quebec Hunter Income Support Program

This program was developed by Inuit and is administered by the Kativik regional government and participating Inuit communities and funded by the Quebec environment and wildlife ministry. It provides for the purchase of harvested food that is then distributed, free of charge, to Inuit living in the North who cannot hunt and to those living in the south. The Inuit-designed program also invests in capital equipment for harvesting, such as boats for communal use. The 1992 annual report showed a budget of $3 million. Clearly more limited than the program established by the Crees, the program for Inuit "affects relatively few people in the eligible communities", but it does benefit "those who are most in need and those who have surplus produce to sell".[195]

The contrast between the programs designed by the Crees and Inuit is interesting. Essentially, the Cree program compensates people for going out on the land, regardless of what they do with the products of their efforts, while the Inuit program encourages hunters to bring food into the communities and ensures that it is shared with those who want it. One commentator noted:

> The two...models described above are very different from one another, reflecting differences in culture and heritage of the two Aboriginal peoples. One programme is no better than the other, for they each serve a purpose particularly suited to the group for which they were developed.[196]

The Nunavut Hunter Support Program

Compared with the northern Quebec programs, the Nunavut Hunter Support Program is recent. It is just beginning operations and hence is in an experimental phase. The Nunavut program was not included in the comprehensive claims agreement and so has a much less secure future than the Cree and northern Quebec Inuit programs. Paul Okalik, director of implementation of Nunavut Tungavik Incorporated (NTI), told us at our public hearings that

> in [NTI's] initial negotiations on the land claim, we were trying to get a program similar to the Cree of James Bay, but we weren't able to convince the government on that. However, we decided to spend our own money and set up our own program....The federal government committed absolutely nothing.

Paul Okalik
Director, Nunavut Tungavik Incorporated
Montreal, Quebec, 29 November 1993

The Nunavut program is cost-shared by Nunavut Tungavik Incorporated and the government of the Northwest Territories in the first five years of operation. It provides annual lump-sum payments (up to $15,000) to a limited number of full-time hunters to help cover costs of equipment, fuel and supplies. To distribute the funds as broadly as possible, a hunter is eligible for support only once during this initial five-year period. At present, the program has little leeway to develop into more than a capital and operating fund for full-time hunters and as such does not have the long-term features of income support programs for Cree and Inuit in Northern Quebec.[197] The Nunavut Harvesting Program will replace the various programs now administered by the territorial government.

We should emphasize that while Canada appears to lead the world in developing effective hunter and trapper support programs,[198] there is still much to be learned about the best approaches for particular situations. Particular peoples, nations and residents of specific regions must have a say in the design of programs to ensure that they are suited to local economic conditions; although all programs may involve some combination of income support, incentive and regulation, many variations are possible.

Given the realities of living and working in the North, we conclude that it is time to review the structure, fit and fundamental goals of social assistance and income supplement programs in the North. Our discussion of economic development (Volume 2, Chapter 5) includes an examination of the linkages between social assistance and community and individual entitlements.

RECOMMENDATIONS

The Commission recommends that

Redesign of
Income Programs
4.6.12
Federal and territorial governments establish a task force with strong Aboriginal representation to review all social assistance and income supplement programs across the territorial North with the goal of restructuring these programs to make them effective instruments in promoting a mixed economy and sustain viable, largely self-reliant communities.

4.6.13
Based on the work of the task force recommended in 4.6.12 and recognizing the fundamental changes under way in the structure and administration of social assistance programs across Canada, territorial governments take the initiative, in consultation with federal and provincial governments, to create a northern social policy framework with sufficient flexibility to allow existing levels of social assistance spending to be used to fund community work creation and provide income supplements related to community employment or traditional production and harvesting.

4.6.14
Employment insurance and social assistance legislation be amended to take into account the specific differences in employment patterns, the high cost of living, the administrative delays that result from great distances between communities, and other factors unique to the northern economy.

The importance of the wage sector

There is a tendency to overestimate the importance of the wage sector in a traditional-mixed economy, because economic activity in the wage sector is more directly and routinely quantifiable than traditional activity is.[199] But there is no doubt that the provision of adequate wage employment opportunities must proceed with as much vigour as the development of programs to support Aboriginal people who go out on the land. The traditional-mixed economy flourishes when participants have opportunities for wage employment that are compatible with going out on the land.

In most parts of the North today, the major sources of employment are the public service sector, small (generally service) businesses, mining, and jobs arising from the development of renewable resources. Following is a discussion of opportunities and challenges in the mining and renewable resource-based sectors. Later in the chapter, we discuss public service employment. We discussed small business in Volume 2, Chapter 5.

Mining

After public service employment, the most important source of wage employment for northerners is mining. (We discussed ways to improve Aboriginal participation in this sector in Volume 2, Chapter 5.) Mining is also the single largest private sector, goods-producing, export dollar activity in the North.[200] Mining has not been, however, a major source of employment for northern Aboriginal people. For example, in the Northwest Territories, the Royal Oak Giant mine, near Yellowknife and the Dene village of Dettah (which has a steady rate of 90 per cent unemployment), has just three per cent Aboriginal labour force participation; Ptarmigan gold mine, operated by Treminco Resources, has a four per cent Aboriginal participation rate; and Nerco Con, near Yellowknife, has never exceeded six per cent Aboriginal participation.[201]

Aboriginal people in the North have been extracting minerals for centuries. Inuit, for example, collected, traded and used soapstone, which was made into cooking pots, lamps and beads; and copper, which was hammered into knives, ornaments and other implements.[202] Europeans became interested in northern mineral wealth as they moved through the region over the centuries. Often their 'discoveries' were already well known and used by Aboriginal people. In this century, interest in northern mineral wealth has increased, but production in the North has remained vulnerable to international market forces, high operating costs and competition from more accessible sources.

Despite its vulnerability, mining is a vital source of revenue in the territories and is also important to the northern provincial economies. The territories produce nearly six per cent of the country's metallic minerals. The Yukon, where mining has been the main industry since the discovery of gold in 1896, accounts for a little over three per cent of national production.

Aboriginal workers have participated in all sectors of the mining industry – from working on exploration crews to working underground – yet they are not represented in the workforce in proportion to the overall Aboriginal population. While a number of efforts have been made to increase Aboriginal involvement in the industry (through joint ventures, for example), there remain a number of impediments.

A survey conducted by the sub-committee of the Intergovernmental Working Group on the Mineral Industry found – and mining companies and Aboriginal people agree – that the barriers to increased Aboriginal participation are "lack of experience, education and training, and the lack of desire to work in a mine".[203] While the latter factor is a personal choice, public policy could address the first three factors.

The low levels of formal education of Aboriginal people in the North and the increased mechanization of mining operations combine to form a major obstacle. The development of partnerships between the companies and Aboriginal communities is seen by many community members as a means to learn more about the industry, develop dialogue on managing the environment, and gain income and equity positions in operations.

Aboriginal peoples' attempts in the last several decades to develop employment opportunities in the mining industry are reflected in the arrangements negotiated by Makivik Corporation on behalf of Inuit in northern Quebec and the Raglan Mining Company, a wholly owned subsidiary of Falconbridge.[204] Under the terms of the agreement, a nickel mine to be located near Katinniq, 100 kilometres southeast of the community of Salluit, in northern Quebec, will produce nickel concentrate, which will be processed in Sudbury, Ontario, and Nikkelverk, Norway. Inuit will have preference for employment at the mine, and their participation will be aided by special training programs to be delivered locally. An Inuit employment and training officer will be hired. In addition, measures will be instituted to promote the development of local businesses in the sectors supporting the new mine.

Evidence that the mining sector will continue to offer some opportunities in specific areas of the North comes with the recent discovery of important quantities of base metal mineralization containing nickel, copper and cobalt at

Voisey's Bay, 35 kilometres southwest of Nain, Labrador. This area is claimed by both the Labrador Inuit Association (LIA) and the Innu Nation. The Voisey's Bay deposit may become one of the largest nickel mines in Canada.

There are a number of ways Aboriginal people could benefit from mining developments, provided appropriate arrangements are made and environmental protection standards are maintained. In no situation has mining been a panacea, but it may be that enough has been learned so that regulated mineral development can be undertaken in a manner that does not damage and perhaps even enhances the traditional-mixed economy.[205] Some possible benefits are:

1. Aboriginal people can participate and benefit as direct employees of mining operations. In this case, short-term rotational schemes seem to be the most attractive and successful. Both the volatility of the mineral sector, and the reality that not all available Aboriginal workers will choose to work underground or on oil well derricks, temper optimism about the potential benefits of this sector.

2. Aboriginal people can participate through the service industry. An enhanced local service industry has the additional benefit of improving services to local communities. Opportunities exist in the service sector for both employment and ownership. For example, there are a growing number of expediting, catering and accommodation companies servicing exploration and development activity.

3. Entering into joint ventures with mining companies to explore and/or develop mineral properties. The investment arms of Aboriginal organizations are now being funded through federal economic development assistance and, where possible, by funds coming from the settlement of land claims.

4. Aboriginal people can benefit through the implementation of socio-economic agreements with mining companies. For example, the Nunavut land claim agreement includes provisions requiring the negotiation of Inuit impact and benefit agreements for most mining developments on Inuit-owned land.

5. In some areas, Aboriginal people can participate as owners of the resource, receiving royalties and other benefits from development of their land. For example, some of the land received by Inuit of Nunavut in their settlement agreement includes title to subsurface mineral rights. The land with subsurface rights was selected by the Inuit with the object of maximizing mineral potential. Nunavut Tungavik is now developing policies in consultation with the mining industry as to how these lands should be explored and developed.[206]

The World Bank and the natural resources committee of the United Nations Economic and Social Council have begun to examine the international potential of small-scale mining. In 1993, the UN established international guidelines for the development of small- and medium-scale mining, attesting to the growing level of interest from the international community in the sector.[207]

These guidelines are the product of hard lessons learned internationally and may also provide an option for Aboriginal northerners:

> Failure to realize real social and economic welfare gains, coupled with the depressed state of many mineral markets, the lack of investment in exploration and new development, as well as structural adjustment programmes, have resulted in a radical re-think of both macro-investment policies and the role of the mineral sector in national development....This re-evaluation of options has included formal recognition of the positive potential of local autonomous mineral development at a smaller scale, and a number of countries have begun to take concrete steps towards establishing a more viable commercial basis for small-scale entrepreneurship in mining and mineral processing. In Canada, Aboriginal communities are increasingly being put in the position of having to consider the prospect of major mineral developments within their traditional territories.[208]

From a policy and management perspective, a rational framework for both small- and large-scale mining opportunities has the potential to offer Aboriginal communities substantial advantages, including creating jobs; stabilizing revenue streams; developing managerial, technical and trade skills at the community level; improving integration with the existing economy; and increasing participation in decision making and in managing and controlling potentially adverse environmental and social repercussions.[209]

Employment in renewable resource-based industries

Many see a significant opportunity for growth in the number of jobs created by expansion of industries based on renewable resources in many parts of the North.[210]

Business opportunities include specialized uses of renewable resources, such as northern-grown wood to build distinctive northern-designed furniture; leather and fur from seals and other species that are hunted for food; and certain northern foods for a southern or international market. Except where such items are by-products of current subsistence activities (seal leather, for example), there are clear limits on how much development the northern environment will sustain.[211]

Eco-tourism represents a relatively low-impact use of what is perhaps the North's greatest resource, its natural beauty. Guiding for big-game hunting has long been established in most parts of the North as a source of income to some northern residents. Eco-tourist businesses are joining these traditional establishments. The newer businesses cater to photographers, sightseers, wilderness adventure travellers (those who enjoy activities such as whitewater rafting and mountaineering) and people seeking the natural beauty and tranquility of the North.

Aboriginal art from the North is recognized and valued internationally. Sculptures, paintings and wall-hangings, distinctive clothing and jewellery, using a mix of renewable and non-renewable resources, provide many families and some communities with an important cash income. Many of these activities involve single artists. Those in the eastern Arctic market their output through the Arctic co-operatives and obtain immediate cash payment for their products as well as ready access to supplies and tools. Others, such as the weaving centre in Pangnirtung, have organized on a community basis. The centre helps local artists with design and technical assistance, training, supplies and marketing expertise. Many, particularly in Denendeh, operate as individual artists who sell their products on the open market or through private dealers.

Commercial harvesting of fish and wildlife has also assumed significant importance in some areas of the North. A fishery based on harvesting through the ice near Pangnirtung has provided fresh turbot in the winter months for Montreal and New York markets at premium prices for Inuit fishers. The Inuit in Nunavik have operated a highly successful shrimp fishery in Ungava Bay and along the northern Labrador coast for a number of years. They are now sharing their expertise with developing countries through the Canadian International Development Agency. The Inuit in Labrador operate a commercial caribou hunt using a modern packing plant in Nain. They marketed meat in Europe when the reindeer herds there were affected by the Chernobyl nuclear accident. Inuvialuit in the western Arctic operate a commercial muskox harvest in the winter months and sell their products in Japanese markets.

A common challenge facing many of these activities is access to management and business skills to turn a subsistence activity that supports a few families into a larger undertaking that could provide cash incomes and create a mixed economy that can support many families. Often, an operation such as a local fishery or a handicraft operation would benefit greatly from professional management but cannot, at its current level of activity, support the salary and related costs of a manager. The operation is then caught in a no-growth situation, unable to take advantage of the skills or resources at hand and often unaware of its own growth potential.

Aboriginal, provincial and territorial governments must find innovative ways of bringing skilled management to small operations, perhaps employing individuals with excellent professional skills who can provide timely management assistance to several enterprises in a specific area at the same time. Such professionals could use communications and computer technology to supplement their presence.

Economic activity is highly rationed in the North, and those opportunities that are available need innovative and skilled support measures to maximize their potential. It is no longer justified to fill development roles with generalists whose main activities have been to advise clients on government programs or hand out program funding. Resources would be better spent attracting highly skilled manager-consultants who combine management experience with the ability to relate to local entrepreneurs. These people can develop a pool of trained local managers within the communities. All the economic development challenges that face Aboriginal people elsewhere in Canada are accentuated in the North, and the analysis and recommendations in our chapter on economic development (Volume 2, Chapter 5) are directly relevant, but the question of access to management expertise has particular importance.

RECOMMENDATION

The Commission recommends that

Skilled Management Supports

4.6.15

Aboriginal, federal, provincial and territorial governments encourage innovative means of delivering skilled management support – including operations, financial and marketing expertise – to small enterprises through Aboriginal economic development corporations.

All these forms of economic activity based on renewable resources appear to be compatible with support for the mixed economy and are likely to appeal to Aboriginal people who have chosen to make part of their living on the land. What is not yet clear is the extent to which these newer vehicles of economic development are mutually compatible and sustainable over the longer term. One study noted examples of potential conflict:

> There is potential for a conflict between the development of wildlife as a tourism resource and its development as a marketable food or fur product....[T]here may also be potential for conflict between [Aboriginal] non-renewable resource harvesters and renewable resource harvesters. [I]t is time...to recognize that the economy cannot develop without impacting the environment. The challenge for the future is the creation of sustainable development – development that meets the needs of the present without compromising the ability of future generations to meet their own needs.[212]

7.5 Conclusion

Demographic and economic realities highlight the need for concerted efforts to expand the number and kind of opportunities available to Aboriginal young people and adults to earn a living. It is clear that an important tool of northern economic development will continue to be public expenditures, whether through direct employment or promoting the development of other sectors. We believe that the safest and most promising direction for such expenditures, as well as for regulation of land use, is one that strengthens the traditional-mixed economy of areas of the North where Aboriginal people predominate. There is scope to support both the older, more traditional sources of cash and employment and new ventures in areas as yet not fully exploited. In all cases, development must be undertaken in the context of environmental stewardship.

RECOMMENDATION

The Commission recommends that

Research Program   **4.6.16**

Faculties of agriculture, forestry and business administration in Canadian universities, in collaboration with the proposed Aboriginal Peoples International University, develop a northern research program focused on the creation of employment and business opportunities through the use of the renewable resources sector, the exportation of traditional foods and food products, and the development of expertise to manage these resources at sustainable levels.

8. INVESTING IN PEOPLE

Promoting the well-being of people and their communities should be at the heart of any program of economic or political development. Having explored political change, environmental stewardship and economic development, we turn now to consider some opportunities for investing in people – making it possible for the Aboriginal people of the North to benefit from the economic and political changes occurring around them.

We begin with the principle that the goal of political and economic development is to create the maximum security and potential for individual human development. In the North, this will require continued efforts to ensure the full participation of Aboriginal people – as well as their non-Aboriginal neighbours – in the institutions of economic and political development. A great deal of political progress has occurred in the last decade or two, and there are many vibrant communities and healthy people in the North, but there are also significant problems. It is important to recognize these in developing plans for the future.

8.1 The Need to Heal

Many of the people who spoke to us in northern communities emphasized the deep social problems facing their communities.[213] They saw little point in hur-

Commissioner Starts Healing Circle
in his Community

Juusipi Kakutuk, community worker and Commissioner* from Akulivik, urged the people in his community to start talking about their problems, to begin healing the pain that was causing trouble within peoples' homes and was spreading to the community at large. When Juusipi first tried to begin these healing circles, he was met with resistance. Nobody wanted to talk about their personal pain. Juusipi proceeded slowly, talking first with women's groups, and then with drug and alcohol abuse committees and health committees. Now he meets regularly with parents, teenagers and younger children.

Juusipi used the video on healing sessions that was produced in Inukjuak to sensitize people on the concept and the positive power of these sessions. He has found parents to be the most receptive group. They get together once a week to talk about their problems and in the process, they help one another. Teenagers have also begun meeting weekly, and sometimes they meet together with the parents group. Juusipi has also started talking regularly with younger students, discussing such issues as substance abuse, sexual abuse and suicide prevention. Juusipi says, "now everybody's talking...Elders, teens, children...everybody!"

Juusipi knows that it's very difficult to start the process of talking about one's deep-rooted pain. But it's only when the talking starts that the healing can begin. Juusipi feels that these healing sessions should be encouraged in all the communities. He stresses that the people must take the initiative locally to deal with their problems, and not wait for outside agencies to step in to try to solve their problems.

---

* Commissioner in this context refers to members of the Council of Commissioners of the Kativik School Board.

Source: Anngutivik [Kativik School Board periodical] 8/2 (Spring 1993), p. 91.

rying economic or political development in the absence of complementary measures to deal with personal trauma, addictions, the scars of abuse, family breakdown, and the very common experiences of violence and death. We agree.

We recognize that the massive changes and major disruptions of the recent past have caused real and deep problems in the present. These problems will not disappear automatically when Aboriginal people achieve political self-determination and economic vitality – although in the long run, these two conditions will contribute a great deal to promoting well-being for future generations.

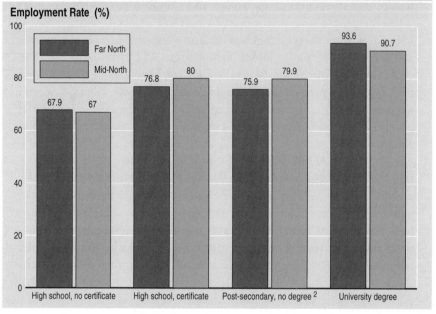

FIGURE 6.8

Employment Rates in the Aboriginal Identity Population Age 15+, by Highest Level of Education, 1991

Notes:

1. Showing Aboriginal identity population age 15 or older not attending school full-time.

2. Post-secondary, no degree includes persons who attended non-university schools (whether or not they received a certificate), as well as persons who attended university but did not receive a degree.

Source: Statistics Canada, 1991 Aboriginal Peoples Survey, custom tabulations.

In Volume 3 of this report, we outlined specific measures to address social problems in Aboriginal communities. Our proposals in the present chapter are meant to supplement those measures and to link the process of healing and individual development with political and economic development.

8.2 Opportunities Presented by Political Development

As the regional review presented earlier in this chapter suggests, the North has been home to an unusual number and variety of constitutional and political innovations. In the last decade and a half, northerners have reformed legislative and administrative practices in the Northwest Territories and launched a process that will lead to its division into two territories. In the Yukon, the comprehensive claims process is gradually but inexorably changing the face of local and territorial government, and in Nunavik and the traditional territory of the James Bay Crees, unique public and quasi-public institutions are under constant development.

FIGURE 6.9
Unemployment Rates in the Aboriginal Identity Population Age 15+, by Highest Level of Education, 1991

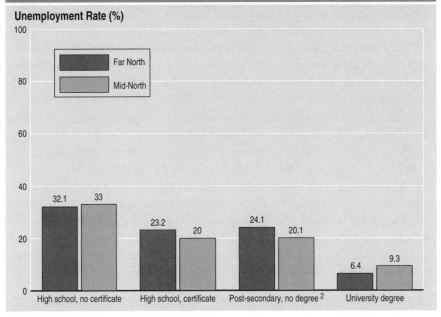

Unemployment Rate (%)

Legend: Far North / Mid-North

High school, no certificate: 32.1 / 33
High school, certificate: 23.2 / 20
Post-secondary, no degree [2]: 24.1 / 20.1
University degree: 6.4 / 9.3

Notes:
1. Showing Aboriginal identity population age 15 or older not attending school full-time.
2. Post-secondary, no degree includes persons who attended non-university schools (whether or not they received a certificate), as well as persons who attended university but did not receive a degree.

Source: Statistics Canada, 1991 Aboriginal Peoples Survey, custom tabulations.

There is no indication that the rate of innovation will decline. The resolution of the issues underlying existing treaties and comprehensive claims agreements, as well as settlement of the remaining outstanding claims, will lead to the creation of other new governing institutions and special-purpose organizations. These might include community-based organizations for social services and economic development, nation governments, new community-level structures, co-ordinating bodies for regulating land and wildlife use, and innovations in the public government forms being pioneered in Nunavut, Nunavik, the Yukon and the northern parts of provinces. The opportunities are manifold.

Wage employment

One immediate by-product of Aboriginal institutional development has been and will continue to be a sharp increase in the overall number of jobs. For example, one estimate suggests that approximately 2,300 new jobs will be created directly by the establishment of Nunavut and the government of Nunavut; the estimate does not include new employment as a result of federal government restructuring, or any indirect job creation resulting from business development.[214] Most of the new employees in the new Aboriginal institutions will have to be well educated: for example, about 85 per cent of the new jobs in Nunavut will require between two and four years of post-secondary education.

Unfortunately, the educational requirements of the new positions will bar many people from employment, as only a minority of northern Aboriginal people of working age have completed high school (see Figures 6.3, 6.4 and 6.5, pp. 438-440). Throughout the North (as elsewhere), employment is connected to education, and the higher the level of formal education people have, the more likely they are to be employed (see Figures 6.8 and 6.9). It is particularly alarming, then, that the trend in recent years in some parts of the North has been a decline in the number of students graduating from high school.

Our chapters on economic development (Volume 2, Chapter 5) and education (Volume 3, Chapter 5) offer comprehensive recommendations to address the educational needs of Aboriginal peoples. The Commission also recognizes the value of education gained through direct experience. Learning by doing is fundamental to education in many Aboriginal cultures, and Aboriginal institutions grounded in Aboriginal values can reflect this concept.

RECOMMENDATION

The Commission recommends that

Hiring Criteria **4.6.17**

All governments hiring personnel for northern and remote communities take into account skills acquired through life experience and the demonstrated capacity to develop new skills along with, and at times in place of, formal educational credentials.

We also offer some supplementary suggestions, keeping in mind the needs of the new Aboriginal institutions and the adult labour force.

Culturally appropriate administration

The institutional face of political self-determination for Aboriginal peoples has the potential to yield a new type of Aboriginal-influenced public service. The new northern public service would certainly have some similarities with the traditional public services of federal, territorial and provincial administrations, as well as with existing Aboriginal political and service delivery organizations. The new public services will likely require division of labour, accountability, probity, transparent reporting relationships, and measures to ensure responsiveness to elected officials. Within these parameters, however, the shape and processes of the new bureaucracies could vary considerably from current practices.

The new public services will be Aboriginally controlled, in ways that have not been possible to date. Beyond setting the policy direction, Aboriginal peoples developing their own governing institutions in the North may experiment with different bureaucratic styles. There may be a new approach to the standard bureaucratic division of labour, featuring widely institutionalized job sharing or team approaches to accomplishing tasks. Job sharing in its simplest form involves two individuals sharing equal responsibility for a single job. Time on the job may be divided by day (morning and afternoon), week, or two-week rotations. Labour pools train several more workers than are actually needed for a given number of positions, so that at any one time, some workers from the pool will be employed while others are free to hunt, trap, fish or gather wood.

RECOMMENDATION

The Commission recommends that

Accommodating the Traditional Economy

4.6.18

Government employment policies accommodate the demands of traditional economic activities by increasing opportunities for job sharing, periodic leave and shift work.

Different aspects of accountability to the public may be more important in Aboriginal bureaucracies. In the governments of most democratic countries today, political accountability flows through elected representatives; for example, federal and provincial public servants are accountable to Canadians through the minister responsible for the department in which they work and by way of the department's internal chain of command. Aboriginal governments may choose to alter this system somewhat, for example, by extensive use of elders to guide committees for particular service units. Aboriginal governments may choose 'flattened' or 'de-layered' hierarchies, various forms of decentralized decision-making committees, and variations on the decentralized administrations already tried by the Inuit Broadcasting Corporation and many existing political organizations.[215]

We do not intend to prescribe any particular measures here but only to note that standard bureaucratic operating procedures are far from immutable. They embody practices developed in a particular cultural context and in response to certain economic and sociological needs. While certain basic functions are necessary in any public institution existing today, those functions can be performed in various ways.

The public bureaucracies now established in the North reflect their origins in industrial, fairly densely populated, complex societies in which impersonal relations between public servants and the public have long been seen as desirable. None of these conditions necessarily prevails in the North, and some of the distinctive features of existing northern public institutions reflect attempts to adapt the institutions to northern conditions.

Northern Aboriginal peoples may well choose to reshape the practices they have inherited so that these enhance rather than obstruct the evolution of modern Aboriginal cultures.[216] They may also conclude that the inherited bureaucratic forms are suitable to their needs. Either way, northern Aboriginal peoples are not likely to be able to choose the form of their new institutions if they lack the educational attainment and entry-level skills for public service employment. It is necessary, then, to create opportunities for individuals who have already left school to gain the necessary skills and to ensure that young people have a reasonable chance of acquiring the type of education they will require to find employment in the new institutions of self-government.

Sustained human resource development planning

Before contemplating any adventurous innovation, it is necessary to ensure that the new organizations are staffed, as much as possible, by the Aboriginal peoples by whom and for whom they are being created. Yet in the new institutions established as a result of public government innovations and the implementation of comprehensive claims, a large proportion of the skilled workforce is still coming from the south.[217]

One feature of the new public institutions being established as a result of political self-determination is helpful in addressing this problem. By and large, the new institutions should have relatively stable funding levels and the capacity for long-range planning. This circumstance will make it possible to develop sophisticated human resource development plans in which institutions make a long-term commitment to individual development.

RECOMMENDATION

The Commission recommends that

Stable Funding for Education and Training

4.6.19

Governments provide stable multi-year funding to northern educational institutions that have the capacity to deliver the education and training needed for self-government and a diversified economy.

The difficulties with most existing training programs for Aboriginal people are well known, as are the measures most likely to train people successfully for employment opportunities.[218] These measures include

- individual assessment of candidates, leading to individually tailored training plans;
- a long-standing commitment from the employing organization to provide periodic work experience;
- assignment of a counsellor or mentor to each person in training;
- periodic reassessment of the training plan and adjustment, if necessary; and
- arrangement for training in the candidates' home communities, with adequate provision for child care.

Arctic Co-operatives Limited and the Inuit Broadcasting Corporation, which have developed particularly effective on-the-job training for adults in the 1970s and '80s, followed these guidelines and should be considered program models in this area.

RECOMMENDATION

The Commission recommends that

Education and Institutional Development

4.6.20

The education and training of Aboriginal adults and young people form an integral part of all plans for institutional development in the North.

Considering that the population of people who could be candidates for the new positions is relatively small and concentrated in communities where a great deal is known about each individual, and since the number and types of available jobs are reasonably predictable, there is a good chance of education and training plans succeeding over the long term.

The role of traditional knowledge

The first principle guiding the activities of the Nunavut Planning Commission states that "people are a functional part of a dynamic biophysical environment, and land use cannot be planned and managed without reference to the human community; accordingly, social, cultural and economic endeavours of the human community must be central to land use planning and implementation".[219] Everything we have heard suggests that this principle is widely shared by the Aboriginal nations and peoples of the North. Traditional knowledge is strikingly appropriate to the fulfilment of this purpose, in a way that the fragmented forms of knowledge and understanding typical of modern non-Aboriginal societies are not.

Yet it is not evident *how* traditional knowledge can be applied to modern problems of individual psychological well-being and of bureaucratic process and decision making.[220] As discussed earlier in the chapter, research on the activities of the new co-management boards suggests that even where experts in Aboriginal traditional knowledge and experts in the traditions of western science meet with a common interest in regulating, for example, the harvest of a single species, communication and co-operation can be difficult.

How might traditional knowledge be brought to bear on other, less concrete problems? There is no single, simple answer to this question. But all over the North, interesting experiments are under way.[221] The Dene Cultural Institute is an independent research institute and archive with a growing track record in participatory community-based research on topics of social significance. For example, studies have been completed on the Gwich'in language, traditional justice systems of the Dogrib, and concepts of traditional governance. Working with community elders and language experts, researchers from within and outside the community seek a modern, English-language representation of concepts from each Aboriginal nation's store of traditional knowledge. There are other cultural institutes elsewhere in the North. In Arviat, Northwest Territories, the Inuit Cultural Institute has been operating for 15 years, primarily as a research base, archive and museum, while the Okalakatiget Society, based in Nain, Labrador, maintains a prominent position in local communications, translation and public education.

At all of these institutions, traditional knowledge is gathered, valued, preserved, transmitted and, in subtle ways, *developed* as the knowledge held by elders is applied to modern problems. The Commission supports this approach.[222]

RECOMMENDATIONS

The Commission recommends that

Support for
Traditional
Knowledge
4.6.21

Governments provide continuing support for the development of institutes that gather and research traditional knowledge and apply it to contemporary issues.

4.6.22

Traditional knowledge be incorporated in all appropriate institutions, including cultural and research institutes, regulatory boards and the education and training system.

A related area concerns the development of Aboriginal languages as modern languages. Aboriginal language development is necessarily a community-based process and one that will rely on elders, as they are currently the most fluent speakers. It will also involve inventing new words to express concepts for which there may be no equivalent in some Aboriginal languages.

Work with traditional Aboriginal knowledge goes far beyond research and documentation; it improves the self-esteem and cultural understanding of the people engaged in the process.

8.3 Conclusion

For Aboriginal people to participate fully in the development of their communities, they must have opportunities to contribute to the well-being of their society. For this reason, we have recommended specific measures in this chapter to maximize opportunities for individual human development and ensure the full participation of Aboriginal people in their own economic and political development. There is already considerable experience in the North with employment training and bicultural education. It remains to build on this experience and to make its lessons known throughout the North – and indeed wherever Aboriginal peoples are assuming responsibility for their political and economic institutions.

NOTES

1. While there is no absolute geographical definition of what constitutes the North, a number of authors have developed boundary lines, usually based on such determinants as geography, climate, population density, economic structure and the proportion of the population made up of Aboriginal people. For purposes of the Commission's work, we established a set of boundaries for examining the demographic and socio-economic conditions of the Aboriginal peoples in three major zones across Canada: the far North, the mid-north and the south. These zones, which were not designed or defined with political boundaries in mind, are shown in Figure 6.1. To establish the boundaries, we relied on research by L.-E. Hamelin, *Canada: A Geographical Perspective* (Toronto: Wiley Publishers of Canada Limited, 1973); R.M. Bone, *The Geography of the Canadian North* (Toronto: Oxford University Press, 1992); and A.M. Maslove and D.C. Hawkes, *Canada's North, A Profile* (Ottawa: Industry, Science and Technology, 1990).

2. The *Nunavut Land Claims Agreement Act*, S.C. 1993, c. 29; pursuant to the agreement Parliament passed legislation (*Nunavut Act*, S.C. 1993, c. 28) to establish the new territory of Nunavut in 1999.

3. For example, there is a high degree of support for relatively decentralized territorial public administration and for various measures to promote strong popular influence in politics. See Mark O. Dickerson and Robert Shotton, "Northern Self-Government and Subsidiarity: Centralization versus Community Empowerment", research study prepared for the Royal Commission on Aboriginal Peoples [RCAP] (1993); and Gurston Dacks, "The Adaptation of Public Governing Institutions in the Territorial North", research study prepared for RCAP (1993). For information about research studies prepared for RCAP, see *A Note About Sources* at the beginning of this volume. See also Dene Nation and Métis Association of the Northwest Territories, *Public Government for the People of the North*, Discussion Paper (Yellowknife: November 9, 1981); Special Representative for Constitutional Development in the Northwest Territories, *Constitutional Development in the Northwest Territories: Report of the Special Representative* (Ottawa: Supply and Services, 1980); and Northwest Territories, *Working Toward a Common Future* (Yellowknife: Commission for Constitutional Development, 1992).

4. See Jill Oakes and Rick Riewe, "Informal Economy: Baffin Regional Profile: Report to the Royal Commission on Aboriginal Peoples", brief submitted to RCAP (1994). For information about briefs submitted to RCAP, see *A Note About Sources* at the beginning of this volume. Lynda Lange, "Fractured Vision: Frustration and Hope in Fort Resolution, N.W.T.", research study prepared for RCAP (1993); and Peter Kulchyski, "Solutions from Fort Simpson", research study prepared for RCAP (1994).

5. Information derived from Statistics Canada, 1991 Census, custom tabulations. While these are the most important sources of employment, Aboriginal people are not represented proportionately in these employment sectors; for example, few are employed in mining. See also Northwest Territories, Bureau of Statistics, *Labour Force Survey, Preliminary Report* (Yellowknife: 1985).

6. We saw some evidence of a similar process in the northern parts of the provinces, although the lack of North-specific political institutions everywhere except Quebec makes the northern perspective difficult to recognize. The territories have an obvious institutional interest in presenting a united front and since the late 1970s have been generally able to do so. Federal northern policy (as in the June 1988 statement, *A Northern Political and Economic Framework*, by the Department of Indian Affairs and Northern Development [Ottawa: Supply and Services]) has begun to reflect northerners' identified priorities in economic and political development.

7. Statistics Canada, 1991 Aboriginal Peoples Survey, custom tabulations. All of these statistics refer to people who reported Aboriginal identity.

8. The federal government subsidizes the cost of transporting goods, mainly food, to isolated, northern communities that do not have year-round road access. In 1995-1996, federal support totalled $17.1 million to operate the Northern Air Stage

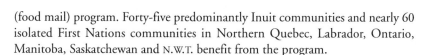

(food mail) program. Forty-five predominantly Inuit communities and nearly 60 isolated First Nations communities in Northern Quebec, Labrador, Ontario, Manitoba, Saskatchewan and N.W.T. benefit from the program.

9. In *Best Left as Indians: Native-White Relations in the Yukon Territory, 1840-1973*, K.S. Coates analyzed the impact of massive changes on Aboriginal peoples living in what is now the Yukon (Montreal & Kingston: McGill-Queen's University Press, 1991). With reference to Alaska, Yupik Harold Napoleon has drawn a powerful analogy between these effects and post-traumatic stress syndrome, first identified in the aftermath of the war in Vietnam. See Harold Napoleon, *Yuuyaraq: The Way of the Human Being*, ed. Eric Madsen (Fairbanks: Center for Cross-Cultural Studies, University of Alaska, 1991).

10. R.G. Williamson has documented the central importance of place in Inuit history and well-being. As he explains, the land is home: it includes the soil, rocks, water, ice and all the living creatures. R.G. Williamson, "Significant Aspects of Acculturation History in the Canadian Arctic: Analysis of the Forces of Inuit and Southern White Interaction until Mid-Century", research study prepared for RCAP (1994). Similar views are reflected in our report, *Treaty Making in the Spirit of Co-Existence: An Alternative to Extinguishment* (Ottawa: Supply and Services, 1995); and Rene Lamothe, "Statement to the Mackenzie Valley Pipeline Inquiry, Fort Simpson, 9 September 1975", in *Dene Nation: The Colony Within*, ed. Mel Watkins (Toronto: University of Toronto Press, 1977).

11. Thierry Rodon, "Pratiques de cogestion au Nunavut", paper presented at the 67th annual meeting of the Canadian Political Science Association, University of Quebec at Montreal, June 1995. Some of the outstanding issues are discussed later in this chapter, in the section on traditional knowledge, and in Volume 2, Chapters 4 and 5.

12. The phrase is from Ignatius E. La Rusic, "Negotiating a Way of Life: Initial Cree Experience with the Administrative Structure Arising From the James Bay Agreement", paper prepared for Research Division, Policy, Research and Evaluation Group, Department of Indian Affairs and Northern Development (Ottawa: October 1979).

13. RCAP, *The High Arctic Relocation: A Report on the 1953-55 Relocation* (Ottawa: Supply and Services, 1994).

14. DIAND, "Speaking Notes for the Honourable Ronald A. Irwin, Minister of Indian Affairs and Northern Development, to the Makivik Annual General Meeting", Kangiqsujuaq, Quebec, 29 March 1995, p. 3. On 28 March 1996 the minister announced that a reconciliation agreement had been reached with Inuit relocated from northern Quebec and Baffin Island to the High Arctic in the early 1950s.

15. Annie Okalik, "A Good Life", in *"Gossip": A Spoken History of Women in the North*, ed. Mary Crnkovich (Ottawa: Canadian Arctic Resources Committee, 1990), pp. 3-5.

16. With respect to the Innu of Quebec, see the testimony given by An Antane Kapesh in Anne André, *Je suis une maudite sauvagesse* (Ottawa: Éditions Leméac, 1976).

17. A similar explanation is provided by Charlie Snowshoe, "A Trapper's Life", in *Dene Nation: The Colony Within*, ed. Mel Watkins (Toronto: University of Toronto Press, 1977).

18. Interviewed and quoted in Nancy Wachowich, Apphia Awa, Rhoda Katsak and Sandra Katsak, "Unikaavut: Our Lives: Stories from the Lives of Three Generations of North Baffin Inuit Women", research study prepared for RCAP (1994).

19. Marc G. Stevenson, "Traditional Inuit Decision-Making Structures and the Administration of Nunavut", research study prepared for RCAP (1993).

20. Kulchyski, "Solutions from Fort Simpson" (cited in note 4).

21. Interviewed and quoted in Wachowich et al., "Unikaavut: Our Lives" (cited in note 18).

22. More information on this case is available in John Goddard, *Last Stand of the Lubicon Cree* (Vancouver: Douglas & McIntyre, 1991). See also E. Davie Fulton, *Lubicon Lake Indian Band Inquiry: Discussion Paper* (Ottawa: Government of Canada, 1986).

23. See K.J. Rea, *The Political Economy of The Canadian North: An Interpretation of the Course of Development in the Northern Territories of Canada to the Early 1960s* (Toronto: University of Toronto Press, 1968); and Peter Clancy, "Contours of the Modern State in the Territorial North: Policies, Institutions and Philosophies", research study prepared for RCAP (1994).

24. See, for example, Philip Goldring, "Inuit Economic Responses to Euro-American Contacts: Southeast Baffin Island, 1824-1940", in *Historical Papers*, ed. Dana Johnson and Louise Ouellette (Ottawa: Canadian Historical Association, 1986), p. 146.

25. David Judd, "Seventy-five Years of Resource Administration in Northern Canada", *The Polar Record* 14/93 (1969), pp. 791-806; and David Judd, "Canada's Northern Policy: Retrospect and Prospect", *The Polar Record* 14/92 (1969), pp. 593-602.

26. Judd, "Canada's Northern Policy".

27. The network included the Distant Early Warning (DEW) Line and other stations. See K.J. Rea, *The Political Economy* (cited in note 23).

28. T. Armstrong, G. Rogers and G. Rowley, *The Circumpolar North: A Political and Economic Geography of the Arctic and Sub-Arctic* (London: Methuen & Co., 1978). Part of the federal response to the American presence was the 1944 dispatch of a research survey team to the North. The multidisciplinary Arctic Survey, funded only in part by Canadian sources, published the results of their research in the *Canadian Journal of Economics and Political Science* and in C. A. Dawson, ed., *The New North-West* (Toronto: University of Toronto Press, 1947). Prefiguring what was to become the centre of federal northern development policy in the 1950s and 1960s, many

of the authors urge state intervention to develop the northern economy and to provide services to the people living there.

29. The analysis of federal northern development policy here draws substantially on Frances Abele, "Canadian Contradictions: Forty Years of Northern Political Development", *Arctic* 40/4 (December 1987), pp. 310-320; reprinted in K.S. Coates and William R. Morrison, ed., *Interpreting Canada's North: Selected Readings* (Toronto: Copp Clark Pitman, 1989). See also Mark O. Dickerson, *Whose North?: Political Change, Political Development and Self-Government in the Northwest Territories* (Vancouver: University of British Columbia Press and Arctic Institute of North America, 1992); Gurston Dacks, *A Choice of Futures: Politics in the Canadian North* (Toronto: Methuen, 1981); and Michael S. Whittington, ed., *The North* (Toronto: University of Toronto Press in co-operation with the Royal Commission on the Economic Union and Development Prospects for Canada, 1985). Some of the consequences of the post-war changes are discussed in Volume 1, Chapter 11 on the relocation of Aboriginal communities. Others have studied certain aspects of provincial northern development initiatives: John Loxley, "The 'Great Northern' Plan", *Studies in Political Economy: A Socialist Review* 6 (Autumn 1981); Murray Dobbin, "Prairie Colonialism: The CCF in Northern Saskatchewan, 1944-1964", *Studies in Political Economy* 16 (Spring 1985); and Carol Brice-Bennett, "Renewable Resource Use and Wage Employment in the Economy of Northern Labrador", background report prepared for the Royal Commission on Employment and Unemployment, St. John's, Newfoundland, September 1986.

30. *Northwest Territories Act*, R.S.C. 1985, c. N-27; and *Yukon Act*, R.S.C. 1985, c. Y-2.

31. Responsibility for northern administration and Indian affairs was lodged originally in the department of the interior, passing through several administrative arrangements before the Department of Indian Affairs and Northern Development (DIAND) was established in 1966.

32. See Rebecca Aird, ed., *Running the North: The Getting and Spending of Public Finances by Canada's Territorial Governments* (Ottawa: Canadian Arctic Resources Committee, 1989); and Michael J. Prince and Gary Juniper, "Public Power and the Public Purse: Governments, Budgets and Aboriginal Peoples in the Canadian North", research study prepared for RCAP (1995).

33. The 1969 white paper (*Statement of the Government of Canada on Indian Policy, 1969*) proposed transferring responsibility for many services provided to Indian people to the provinces – an attempt to off-load the federal responsibility that was widely opposed by treaty nations. Today, responsibilities in such areas as education are being transferred from the department of Indian affairs to First Nations governments, along with funding, but such transfers are not available to bands in the territorial North.

34. The CYI amalgamated the Yukon Native Brotherhood (YNB) and the Yukon Association of Non-Status Indians (YANSI), creating a single organization to represent Aboriginal people who had status under the *Indian Act* and those who did

not. Thereafter, no distinction between the two groups was made in negotiations about the territory's political future.

35. DIAND, *Canada's North 1970-1980: Statement of the Government of Canada on Northern Development in the '70s* (Ottawa: Information Canada, 1972).

36. DIAND, *A Northern Political and Economic Framework* (Ottawa: Supply and Services, 1988), p. 5.

37. One chapter cannot deal adequately with all the Aboriginal nations present in the vast area of northern Canada. We discuss a representative selection here and refer readers to other chapters of this report where the circumstances of many others are discussed.

38. First contacts between Europeans and Aboriginal peoples took place over a very long period. As Olive Patricia Dickason notes: "In what is now Canada, first meetings for which there is a reasonably acceptable record began with the Norse about 1000 A.D. and continued as late as the second decade of the twentieth century, when members of the Canadian Arctic Expedition met isolated bands of Copper and Netsilik Inuit. Not only that, these people were completely unknown to the Canadian government; these Inuit knew of whites, however, as their ancestors had encounters with them. Three years later, in 1918, Royal North-West Mounted Police, while on a search for Inuit wanted for murder, were still meeting people who had never seen a white. In other words, first meetings with Inuit occurred, off and on, over a period of more than 900 years. The Amerindian time span for such encounters was about 400 years, with some Athapaskans of the far Northwest being among the last to meet the white man early in the twentieth century." O.P. Dickason, *Canada's First Nations: A History of the Founding Peoples from Earliest Times* (Toronto: McClelland and Stewart, 1992), p. 86. See also Dorothy Harley Eber, *When the Whalers Were Up North: Inuit Memories from the Eastern Arctic* (Montreal & Kingston: McGill-Queen's University Press, 1989); James R. Gibson, *Otter Skins, Boston Ships, and China Goods: The Maritime Fur Trade of the Northwest Coast, 1785-1841* (Montreal & Kingston: McGill-Queen's University Press, 1992); and Pat Sandiford Grygier, *A Long Way from Home: The Tuberculosis Epidemic Among the Inuit* (Montreal & Kingston: McGill-Queen's University Press, 1994).

39. The 14 nations that are party to the agreement are Carcross/Tagish First Nation, Champagne/Aishihik First Nations, Dawson First Nation, Kluane First Nation, Kwanlin Dunn First Nation, Liard First Nation, Little Salmon/Carmacks First Nation, First Nation of Na-cho Ny'a'k Dun, Ross River Dena Council, Selkirk First Nation, Ta'an Kwach'an Council, Teslin Tlingit Council, Vuntut Gwich'in First Nation, and White River First Nation.

40. Mary Jane Norris, Don Kerr and François Nault, "Projections of the Population with Aboriginal Identity in Canada, 1991-2016", research study prepared for RCAP by the Demography Division, Statistics Canada (1995). The Aboriginal population is adjusted for undercoverage in the 1991 Aboriginal Peoples Survey (APS).

41. In 1901, the total population of the Yukon was 27,219, 3,322 of whom were Aboriginal people (12.2 per cent). A decade later, the declining non-Aboriginal population increased the Aboriginal proportion to 17.5 per cent. The highest recorded Aboriginal proportion was in 1931 (38.7 per cent), when the non-Aboriginal population reached its lowest post-gold-rush numbers. By 1971, the construction of the Alaska Highway and other industrial developments had reversed the trend once again, so that Aboriginal people accounted for 14 per cent of the overall population. Census data from Coates, *Best Left as Indians* (cited in note 7), p. 74.

   In 1991, the total population of the Yukon was 27,800, 5,100 of whom were Aboriginal (18.3 per cent). Statistics Canada, 1991 Census, Cat. No. 94-327, 1993.

42. Quoted in Jonathan L. Pierce, "Indian Claims in the Yukon, 1968-1984: Aboriginal Rights as Human Rights", M.A. thesis, Carleton University, Ottawa, 1988, pp. 45-46.

43. Pierce, "Indian Claims in the Yukon", pp. 56-57.

44. Council for Yukon Indians, "Together Today for Our Children Tomorrow: A Statement of Grievances and an Approach to Settlement by the Yukon Indian People", report prepared for the Commissioner of Indian Claims and the Government of Canada (Whitehorse: 1973).

45. See RCAP, *Treaty Making* (cited in note 10) and Volume 2, Chapter 4.

46. "Umbrella Final Agreement between the Government of Canada, the Council for Yukon Indians and the Government of the Yukon. Agreement made this 29th day of May, 1993", in DIAND, *Umbrella Final Agreement* (Ottawa: Supply and Services, 1993).

47. See Tony Penikett, "Land Claims and Self Government Agreements in Yukon", in *Canadian Parliamentary Review* (Autumn 1993), p. 14. The CYI Umbrella Final Agreement adopted the option of "partial extinguishment" under the 1986 Comprehensive Land Claims Policy. See RCAP, *Treaty Making* (cited in note 10), pp. 43-44. Four *Yukon First Nations Final Agreements* (1993) and corresponding self-government agreements have been concluded. They are the Vuntut Gwich'in First Nation Final Agreement, First Nation of Na-cho Ny'a'k Dun Final Agreement, Teslin Tlingit Council Final Agreement, and Champagne and Aishihik First Nations Final Agreement, all approved and given effect by the *Yukon First Nations Land Claims Settlement Act*, S.C. 1994, c. 34 (proclaimed 14 February 1995). Negotiations for five other self-government agreements are in progress.

48. See Gurston Dacks, ed., *Devolution and Constitutional Development in the Canadian North* (Ottawa: Carleton University Press, 1990).

49. Dacks, "Adaptation of Public Governing Institutions" (cited in note 3).

50. Dacks, "Adaptation of Public Governing Institutions".

51. Dacks, "Adaptation of Public Governing Institutions".

52. K.S. Coates, "First Nations and the Yukon Territorial Government: Toward a New Relationship", research study prepared for RCAP (1994).

53. Dacks, "Adaptation of Public Governing Institutions".

54. See, generally, Kerry Abel, *Drum Songs: Glimpses of Dene History* (Montreal and Kingston: McGill-Queen's University Press, 1993).

55. Charles Mair, member of the Half-Breed Commission of 1899, quoted in René Fumoleau, *As Long As This Land Shall Last: A History of Treaty 8 and Treaty 11, 1870-1939* (Toronto: McClelland and Stewart, 1974), p. 48.

56. Quoted in Fumoleau, *As Long As This Land Shall Last*, pp. 49-50 [note omitted].

57. Fumoleau, *As Long As This Land Shall Last*, p. 50. See also Dickerson, *Whose North?* (cited in note 29); and Rea, *The Political Economy* (cited in note 23).

58. Fumoleau, *As Long As This Land Shall Last*, Chapter III: The Years Between The Treaties, 1900-1920.

59. *Northern Frontier, Northern Homeland: The Report of the Mackenzie Valley Pipeline Inquiry: Volume One* (Ottawa: Supply and Services, 1977), p. 167.

60. Prince and Juniper, "Public Power" (cited in note 32). See also Andrew Webster, "They are Impossible People, Really: Social Administration and Aboriginal Social Welfare in the Territorial North, 1927-1993", research study prepared for RCAP (1993).

61. The story is told in detail in Edgar J. Dosman, *The National Interest: The Politics of Northern Development, 1968-75* (Toronto: McClelland and Stewart, 1975).

62. Eileen Sasakamoose, Sharon Venne and Rene Lamothe, "Northern Treaty Research for Royal Commission on Aboriginal Peoples", research study prepared for RCAP (1994).

63. *Re Paulette's Application* (1973) 6 W.W.R. 97 (N.W.T.S.C.).

64. The Dene Declaration is reprinted in Watkins, *Dene Nation* (cited in note 10).

65. The Gwich'in Agreement (1992) approved and given effect by the *Gwich'in Land Claim Settlement Act*, S.C. 1992, c. 53; and the Sahtu Dene and Metis Agreement (1993) approved and given effect by the *Sahtu Dene and Metis Land Claim Settlement Act*, S.C. 1994, c. 27.

66. Susan Quirk and Antoine Mountain, "Dene Nation: An Analysis", research study prepared for RCAP (1993).

67. Deh Cho First Nation, Declaration of Rights, p. 1 (1993).

68. National Archives of Canada, Records of the Privy Council Office, Privy Council Minutes, Record Group (RG) 2, series 1, volume 796 (also available in records of the Department of the Interior, RG15), Order in Council 918, 6 May 1899 [emphasis added].

69. In its 1993-94 Annual Report, Inuit Tapirisat of Canada puts the world Inuit population at 115,000, while the Inuit Circumpolar Conference estimates it at 120,000, divided as follows: Canada, 30,000; Alaska, 35,000; Greenland, 50,000;

and Russia, 5,000. According to the 1991 Aboriginal Peoples Survey, there are about 38,000 Inuit in Canada (adjusted data).

70. Inuit Tapirisat of Canada, "Submission of the Inuit Tapirisat of Canada to the Royal Commission on Aboriginal Peoples" (1994), p. 6. For information on briefs submitted to RCAP, see *A Note About Sources* at the beginning of this volume.

71. Inuit Circumpolar Conference [hereafter ICC], *Principles and Elements for a Comprehensive Arctic Policy* (Montreal: McGill University, Centre for Northern Studies and Research, 1992).

72. Wendy Moss, "Inuit Perspectives on Treaty Rights and Governance Issues", in *Aboriginal Self-Government: Legal and Constitutional Issues* (Ottawa: RCAP, 1995), p. 104.

73. The agreement was enacted by *James Bay and Northern Quebec Native Claims Settlement Act*, S.C. 1976-77, c. 32; and *An Act approving the Agreement concerning James Bay and Northern Quebec*, S.Q. 1976, c. 46.

74. Canadian Arctic Resource Committee, "Aboriginal Peoples, Comprehensive Land Claims, and Sustainable Development in the Territorial North", brief submitted to RCAP (1993), Appendix E, pp. 11-16.

75. Norbert Rouland, *Les Inuit du Nouveau-Québec et la Convention de la Baie James* (Quebec City: Association Inuksiutiit Katimajiit and Centre d'études nordiques, Université Laval, 1978), pp. 134-142.

76. Norbert Rouland, "Les Inuit du Nouveau-Québec et l'entrée en vigueur de la Convention de la baie James (avril 1977-octobre 1978)", *Études Inuit Studies* 3/1 (1979), p. 83.

77. Gérard Duhaime, "Le chasseur et le minotaure: itinéraire de l'autonomie politique au Nunavik", *Études Inuit Studies* 16/1-2 (1992), pp. 149-178; Paul Bussières, "Droits collectifs et pouvoirs chez les Inuit du Nunavik", *Études Inuit Studies* 16/1-2 (1992), pp. 143-148. For an assessment of many facets of the agreement, see Sylvie Vincent and Gary Bowers, eds., *James Bay and Northern Quebec: Ten Years After* (Montreal: Recherches amérindiennes au Québec, 1988).

78. M. Malone, "Study of Current Practice in Financing Aboriginal Governments: Kativik Regional Government Case Study", research study prepared for RCAP (1993).

79. See "Document: Constitution du Nunavik", *Recherches amérindiennes au Québec* 19/4 (Winter 1989), pp. 74-77.

80. *Nunavik Assembly and Government: Negotiation Framework Agreement between the Special Negotiator for the Gouvernement du Québec and the Chief Negotiator for the Nunavik Constitutional Committee*, signed 21 July 1994.

81. Stephen Hendrie, "Makivik 1995 AGM: Referendum Year", in *Makivik News* (Spring 1995), pp. 5-13.

82. Letha J. MacLachlan, "Northern Comprehensive Aboriginal Claims Agreements", research study prepared for RCAP (1993).

83. Until 1976, Inuvialuit had been negotiating a comprehensive claims agreement in concert with other Inuit of the N.W.T., through the Inuit Tapirisat of Canada. When the Inuit Tapirisat of Canada withdrew its proposed comprehensive claim in 1976, the Committee for Original Peoples' Entitlement (COPE), representing Inuvialuit, sought and received a mandate from its membership to proceed with the North's first regional claim negotiations. The Inuvialuit Final Agreement (1984) (IFA) was approved and given effect by the *Western Arctic (Inuvialuit) Claims Settlement Act*, S.C. 1984, c. 24, as amended by S.C. 1988, c. 16.

84. *Inuvialuit Claims Settlement Act*, chapter 24, section 3, subsection 3. The IFA Aboriginal claimant groups not only released their Aboriginal title, rights and interests to the land in their territory, they also agreed that legislation giving effect to the Agreement would "extinguish all native claims, rights, title and interests of all [Indians, Inuit and Inuvialuit] in and to the [Traditional Territory]...whatever that may be". MacLachlan, "Northern Comprehensive Claims Agreements" (cited in note 82).

85. Cited in Janet M. Keeping, *The Inuvialuit Final Agreement* (Calgary: Faculty of Law, University of Calgary, 1989).

86. RCAP transcripts, Montreal, Quebec, 29 November 1993. The proposed arrangements are discussed in Volume 2, Chapter 3.

87. Lindsay Staples, "The Inuvialuit Final Agreement: Implementing its Land, Resource and Environmental Regimes", research study prepared for RCAP (1994).

88. Staples, "Implementing Land, Resource and Environmental Regimes".

89. Gurston Dacks, "Nunavut: Aboriginal Self-Determination Through Public Government", research study prepared for RCAP (1994).

90. For a more detailed discussion, see R. Quinn Duffy, *The Road to Nunavut: The Progress of the Eastern Arctic Inuit Since the Second World War* (Montreal and Kingston: McGill-Queen's University Press, 1988); and Nunavut Constitutional Forum, *Building Nunavut: Today and Tomorrow* (Ottawa: Nunavut Constitutional Forum, 1983).

91. Frances Abele and M.O. Dickerson, "The 1982 Plebiscite on Division of the Northwest Territories: Regional Government and Federal Policy", *Canadian Public Policy* 11/1 (March 1985), pp. 1-15; and Government of the Northwest Territories, *Report of the Chief Plebiscite Officer on the Plebiscite on Division of the Northwest Territories* (Yellowknife: 1982). Despite general support among Aboriginal people of the Northwest Territories, there was considerable concern about the location of the boundary, especially in communities near its possible location. The unilateral imposition of the boundary between the Yukon and N.W.T. and between the N.W.T. and neighbouring provinces had separated Dene and Métis people into several jurisdictions. Voters were wary of repeating this experience. It is probable that both turnout and support for division in the west would have been stronger had a boundary acceptable to Dene and Métis people been proposed in the plebiscite question.

92. DIAND, *Notes for an Address by the Honourable John Munro, P.C., M.P., Minister of Indian Affairs and Northern Development*, Legislative Assembly, Yellowknife, N.W.T., 26 November 1982.

93. The Nunavut Land Claims Agreement (1993) approved and given effect by the *Nunavut Land Claims Agreement Act*, S.C. 1993, c. 29; and *Nunavut Act*, S.C. 1993, c. 28.

94. Under the terms of the land claims agreement (article 29), Inuit agreed to repay almost $40 million in loans received from the federal government to cover their negotiating costs.

95. ATII Training Inc., "Northern Education and Training Systems for Inuit: A Strategic Analysis", research study prepared for RCAP (1993).

96. Estimates range from $50 million, according to the department of Indian affairs, to $174 million according to ATII Training Inc., "Northern Education and Training Systems". The variation is a result of differences in assumptions about the duration of training and types of attendant measures. Also see Dacks, "Nunavut" (cited in note 89). Issues associated with training are discussed later in this chapter.

97. In Canada as a whole, 14 per cent of Aboriginal adults had post-secondary degrees or certificates, 32 per cent had completed high school and 25 per cent had Grade 8 or less. 'Adult' here means individuals between 15 and 64 years of age and no longer attending school in 1991. See Statistics Canada, 1991 Aboriginal Peoples Survey, custom tabulations.

98. Frances Abele, *Gathering Strength: A Study of Native Employment Training Programs in the Northwest Territories* (Calgary: Arctic Institute of North America, 1989).

99. Williamson, "Significant Aspects" (cited in note 10).

100. Dacks, "Adaptation" (cited in note 3).

101. For a detailed discussion of approaches to 'appropriate' decision making, see Stevenson, "Traditional Inuit Decision-Making" (cited in note 19).

102. Dacks, "Nunavut" (cited in note 89).

103. The non-Inuit members of the Labrador Inuit Association (LIA) are Kablunangajuit. They include individuals who have some Inuit ancestry as well as individuals who do not have Inuit ancestry but were born before 30 November 1990, permanently settled in the land claim area before 1940, or are descendants of persons who settled in the land claim area before 1940 (information from the 1995 LIA membership forms).

104. To support the Labrador Inuit claim, a land use and occupancy study was initiated in 1975. In 1977, LIA documentation of their claim was submitted to the federal government. See Carol Brice-Bennett, ed., *Our Footprints are Everywhere: Inuit Land Use and Occupancy in Labrador* (Nain, Newfoundland and Labrador: Labrador Inuit Association, 1977).

105. Adrian Tanner et al., "Aboriginal Peoples and Governance in Newfoundland and Labrador", research study prepared for RCAP (1994) [note omitted].

106. Most of the information in this section is drawn from W.J. Eccles and Susan L. Laskin, "The Seven Years' War", in *Historical Atlas of Canada*, Volume 1, *From the Beginning to 1800*, R. Cole Harris, ed. (Toronto: University of Toronto Press, 1987), plate 42.

107. *Re Labrador Boundary* (1927), 2 D.L.R. 401. See also *Encyclopedia of Newfoundland and Labrador*, Volume 3 (St. John's: Harry Cuff Publications, 1991), pp. 216-221.

108. In 1924, while Newfoundland and Quebec were preparing their case for review by the judicial committee of the Privy Council, Newfoundland offered to sell Labrador to Quebec for $30 million. It was put up for sale to Canada in 1931 for $110 million, but Canada declined. David Lough, "Transition from Traditional to Wage Economy – The Labrador Experience", draft paper prepared for the third annual Interprovincial Conference of Ministers with Responsibility for Northern Development, Thompson, Manitoba, 9 to 11 September 1980, p. 3.

109. Occasionally, the Newfoundland government passed legislation in response to serious problems. For example, legislation was passed in 1882 prohibiting Aboriginal persons from possessing alcohol (*An Act respecting the Sale of Intoxicating Liquors on the Coast of Labrador*, S.N. 1882, c. 8). In 1911, legislation prohibited anyone from taking an Aboriginal person out of Labrador. This law came as a result of the transportation of a group of 57 Labrador Inuit to Chicago in 1893, where they were placed on display at the World's Columbian Exposition and then left stranded (*An Act respecting the Esquimaux and Indians resident in Labrador*, S.N. 1911, c. 9); see Tanner et al., "Aboriginal Peoples" (cited in note 105).

110. "Il n'est donc pas possible...de souscrire à l'appréciation que d'aucuns ont faite de la décision et du tracé de 1927: une 'grossière erreur de droit et de fait.'" *Rapport de la Commission d'étude sur l'intégrité du territoire du Québec: 3. La Frontière du Labrador, 3.1 Rapport des commissaires, Tome 1* (Quebec City: 1971), p. 417; and "L'argument le plus fort, en 1971, qui fait que la 'cause' du Québec dans l'affaire du Labrador est irrémédiablement compromise, c'est le fait, peu connu semble-t-il de ceux qui préconisent le 'retour du Labrador au Québec', que les gouvernements successifs du Québec ont, à divers titres et de plusieurs manières, reconnu le tracé de 1927 comme la frontière effective entre les deux provinces." *Rapport de la Commission d'étude, 3.2 Synthèse*, p. 14.

111. Tanner et al., "Aboriginal Peoples" (cited in note 105).

112. The reasons for this are not entirely clear. Future Newfoundland premier J.R. Smallwood and at least some public servants apparently were convinced that it would be a retrograde step in terms of political rights for Aboriginal peoples living in Newfoundland and Labrador to fall under the administration of the federal department of Indian affairs. On the federal side, there was some reluctance to assume the additional burden, particularly at a time when the policy was to reduce dependency on the department of Indian affairs. Another concern was that there were too few Aboriginal people to justify creating a separate administration. Also,

the Newfoundland government may have feared the political consequences of being unable to provide for its non-Aboriginal citizens the level of services that would have been provided by the federal government in the Aboriginal communities. Tanner et al., "Aboriginal Peoples" (cited in note 105).

113. Donald M. McRae, *Report on the Complaints of the Innu of Labrador to the Canadian Human Rights Commission* (Ottawa: Canadian Human Rights Commission, 1993), p. 7.

114. Tanner et al., "Aboriginal Peoples" (cited in note 105).

115. See Tanner et al., "Aboriginal Peoples"; McRae, *Report on the Complaints of the Innu* (cited in note 113); and Newfoundland, *Report of the Royal Commission on Labrador* (St. John's: Queen's Printer, 1974).

116. Iris Allen, Labrador Inuit Health Commission, "Aboriginal People Living in Remote and Northern Areas", in RCAP, *The Path to Healing*, Report of the National Round Table on Aboriginal Health and Social Issues (Ottawa: Supply and Services, 1993), p. 132.

117. Tanner et al., "Aboriginal Peoples" (cited in note 105).

118. Inuit Tapirisat of Canada, "Submission of the Inuit Tapirisat" (cited in note 70), p. 92.

119. Moss, "Inuit Perspectives" (cited in note 72), p. 111, quoting the Inuit Tapirisat of Canada.

120. Tony Williamson, "Angojokok-AngojukKauKatiget-Labrador-imi Inuit katutjikate-genninga: Labrador Inuit Politics from Household to Community to Nation", research study prepared for RCAP (1994).

121. Some of the international and domestic dimensions of this problem are explored in Benoît Lévesque, André Joyal and Omer Chouinard, eds., *L'autre économie: Une économie alternative?* (Sillery, Quebec: Presses de l'Université du Québec, 1989). See also Volume 2, Chapter 5.

122. Royal Roads Military College, *The Environmental Impact of the DEW Line on the Canadian Arctic* (Victoria: Department of National Defence, 1993).

123. Ellen Bielawski, "The Desecration of Nánúlá Kúé: Impact of the Taltson Hydroelectric Development on Dene Sonline", research study prepared for RCAP (1994).

124. Other examples in northern Canada included the Lancaster Sound Green Paper exercise and the Land Use Planning Program, run jointly by the Department of Indian Affairs and Northern Development, the territorial governments, and Aboriginal organizations. The Federal Environmental Assessment Review Process remains the most frequently used and elaborate mechanism for making decisions in advance of projects that are anticipated to have a significant environmental impact. The three-year Beaufort Sea Environmental Review assessed development of offshore oil production facilities on the western Arctic coast. In Labrador, an

Environmental Assessment Panel took six years to decide that military training activities could continue under certain conditions.

125. See A. Saunders, "Banking on the Big Fix: Circumpolar Nations Pool their Expertise to Tackle Pollution", *Arctic Circle* 1/2 (September/October 1990), pp. 52-53; S. Hazell, "Where the Caribou and the Cruise Missiles Play: When will DND Start Really Listening to the Concerns of Northerners?", *Arctic Circle* 1/6 (May/June 1991), pp. 34-35; and Peter Tyson, "Tracking Acid Rain in the Arctic", *Arctic Circle* 2/2 (September/October 1991), pp. 32-34.

126. Peter J. Usher, "The Beverly-Kaminuriak Management Board: An Evaluation of the First Ten Years and Recommendations for the Future", unpublished report prepared for the Beverly and Kaminuriak Caribou Management Board (1991).

127. David DesBrisay, "The Impact of Major Resource Development Projects on Aboriginal Communities: A Review of the Literature", research study prepared for RCAP (1994).

128. George Wenzel, *Animal Rights, Human Rights: Ecology, Economy and Ideology in the Canadian Arctic* (Toronto: University of Toronto Press, 1991).

129. Terry Fenge, "Environmental Clean-up and Sustainable Development in the Circumpolar Region", *Northern Perspectives* 21/4 (Winter 1993-94), pp. 1-3.

130. Several overviews and considerations of remedies appear in John M. Lamb, ed., *Proceedings of a Conference on 'A Northern Foreign Policy for Canada'* (Ottawa: Canadian Polar Commission and Canadian Centre for Global Security, 1994).

131. Santé Québec, *Report of the Santé Québec Health Survey Among the Inuit of Nunavik, 1992*, Volume I: *Health Determining Factors*, ed. Mireille Jetté.

132. Environment Canada, A State of the Environment Fact Sheet, No. 94-1 (Ottawa: Supply and Services, 1994).

133. Marina Devine, "Panel will Probe BHP Diamond Mine Plans: Ottawa Foots $250,000 for Review", *Nunatsiaq News* (16 December 1994), p. 10.

134. Andrew Chapeskie, "Land, Landscape, Culturescape: Aboriginal Relationships to Land and the Co-Management of Natural Resources", research study prepared for RCAP (1995).

135. Laurie K. Montour, "Natural Resource Management Agreements in First Nations' Territories", research study prepared for RCAP (1994).

136. MacLachlan, "Northern Comprehensive Aboriginal Claims Agreements" (cited in note 82).

137. Alan Penn, "The James Bay and Northern Quebec Agreement: Natural Resources, Public Lands, and the Implementation of a Native Land Claim Settlement", research study prepared for RCAP (1995).

138. Paul F. Wilkinson and Maria Vincelli, "An Evaluation of the Implementation of the Environmental Regimes Established by Comprehensive Claims Settlements in Canada", research study prepared for RCAP (1995).

139. Lorraine Brooke, "Experiences of the Inuit of Nunavik with Wildlife Management and the James Bay and Northern Quebec Agreement (1975-1995)", research study prepared for RCAP (1995).

140. Wilkinson and Vincelli, "An Evaluation" (cited in note 138).

141. Staples, "Inuvialuit Final Agreement" (cited in note 87).

142. MacLachlan, "Northern" (cited in note 82). See also *Nunavut Land Claims Agreement Act*, S.C. 1993, c. 29, s. 10.

143. Studies conducted by the Government of the Northwest Territories (GNWT) indicated a much lower caribou population than harvesters believed to exist. Based on the data collected by biologists, the GNWT Department of Renewable Resources imposed strict bag-limits on harvesters. Subsequently, it became clear that more caribou were indeed available than the initial government studies had suggested. Peter Usher, "The Beverly-Kaminuriak Management Board: An Experience in Co-Management", in *Traditional Ecological Knowledge: Concepts and Cases*, ed. Julian T. Inglis (Ottawa: International Program on Traditional Ecological Knowledge and International Development Research Centre, 1993), p. 111.

144. See Peter Clancy, "Political Devolution and Wildlife Management", in *Devolution and Constitutional Development in the Canadian North*, ed. Gurston Dacks (Ottawa: Carleton University Press, 1990).

145. Usher, "Beverly-Kaminuriak: An Experience" (cited in note 143); and P. Cizek, "The Beverly-Kaminuriak Caribou Management Board: A Case Study of Aboriginal Participation in Resource Management" (Ottawa: Canadian Arctic Resources Committee, 1990), p. 1.

146. Usher, "Beverly-Kaminuriak: An Experience", p. 112; and Cizek, "A Case Study", pp. 4-5.

147. See Usher, "Beverly-Kaminuriak: An Evaluation" (cited in note 126); Usher, "Beverly-Kaminuriak: An Experience"; Cizek, "Beverly-Kaminuriak: A Case Study"; and Gail Osherenko, "Sharing Power with Native Users: Co-Management Regimes for Native Wildlife" (Ottawa: Canadian Arctic Resources Committee, 1988).

148. Peter J. Usher, "Lands, Resources and Environment Regimes Research Project: Summary of Case Study Findings and Recommendations", research study prepared for RCAP (1994); and Bielawski, "The Desecration of Nánúlá Kúé" (cited in note 123).

149. Phyllis Morrow and Chase Hensel, "Hidden Dissention: Minority-Majority Relationships and the Use of Contested Terminology", *Arctic Anthropology* 29/1 (1992), pp. 38-53; and Usher, "Beverly-Kaminuriak: An Experience" (cited in note 143).

150. As defined by Fikret Berkes, "Traditional Ecological Knowledge in Perspective", in *Traditional Ecological Knowledge: Concepts and Cases* (cited in note 143), p. 3; and Milton M.R. Freeman, "Graphs and Gaffs: A Cautionary Tale in the Common-Property Resources Debate", in *Common Property Resources: Ecology and*

Community-Based Sustainable Development, ed. Fikret Berkes (London: Belhaven Press, 1989), pp. 92-109. The ideas in this section are discussed more fully in Volume 3, Chapter 5.

151. Martha Johnson, ed., *Lore: Capturing Traditional Environmental Knowledge* (Ottawa: Dene Cultural Institute and the International Development Research Centre, 1992), p. 4.

152. Wenzel, *Animal Rights, Human Rights* (cited in note 128).

153. Johnson, *Lore* (cited in note 151), p. 8.

154. R.R. de Cotret, letter to the editor, *Arctic Circle* 1/41 (January/February 1991), p. 8, cited in Ellen Bielawski, "Inuit Indigenous Knowledge and Science in the Arctic", *Northern Perspectives* 20/1 (Summer 1992), pp. 5-8. This and other articles in this issue of *Northern Perspectives* illustrate the growing support for this viewpoint. In fact, the main objective of the Inuit Circumpolar Conference at the Earth Summit in Rio de Janeiro in 1992 was to "have the role and value of the traditional knowledge of indigenous peoples clearly recognized in the decisions of UNCED [United Nations Conference on Environment and Development]". Mary Simon, "Environment, Sustainable Development and Self-Government", *Études Inuit Studies* 16/1-2 (1992), p. 24.

155. Quoted in *Northern Perspectives* 22/1 (Spring 1994), p. 18.

156. John Sallenave, "Giving Traditional Ecological Knowledge Its Rightful Place in Environmental Impact Assessment", *Northern Perspectives* (cited in note 155), p. 19.

157. *Response by the Government of the Northwest Territories to the Report of the Traditional Knowledge Working Group* (Yellowknife: N.W.T. Department of Renewable Resources, 1994), p. 13.

158. Pierre-Gerlier Forest and Thierry Rodon, "Les activités internationales des autochtones du Canada", *Études internationales* 26/1 (March 1995), pp. 35-57; and Peter Jull, *The Politics of Northern Frontiers in Australia, Canada and Other 'First World' Countries* (Darwin: Australian National University, North Australia Research Unit, 1991).

159. ICC, *Principles and Elements* (cited in note 71).

160. Franklyn Griffiths and Justin Peffer, "Turning Point in Canadian Policy Towards the Circumpolar North: Implications for Aboriginal Peoples", research study prepared for RCAP (1993), p. 4.

161. ICC, *Principles and Elements*, (cited in note 71) p. 147.

162. Canadian Arctic Resources Committee, "The Arctic Environmental Protection Strategy", *Northern Perspectives* 21/4 (Winter 1993-94), p. 4.

163. Staples, "Inuvialuit Final Agreement" (cited in note 87) [note omitted].

164. Veryan Haysom, "The Struggle for Recognition: Labrador Inuit Negotiations for Land Rights and Self-Government", *Études Inuit Studies* 16/1-2 (1992), p. 188.

165. Norris, Kerr and Nault, "Projections of the Population" (cited in note 40).

166. Gordon Robertson, *Northern Provinces: A Mistaken Goal* (Montreal: Institute for Research on Public Policy, 1985); Aird, *Running the North* (cited in note 32); Prince and Juniper, "Public Power" (cited in note 32); and L. Wade Locke and Peter G.C. Townley, "An Inventory of Provincial Expenditures for the Benefit of the Innu and Inuit of Labrador", research study prepared for RCAP (1994).

167. Transfers from the federal government made up 83.5 per cent of the total revenues of the government of the Northwest Territories in 1980-81 and an estimated 77.8 per cent in 1990-91. For the Yukon territorial government, federal transfers made up 61.8 per cent of total revenues in 1980-81 and an estimated 77.6 per cent in 1990-91. See Table 5.7 ("Government of the Northwest Territories Revenue 1980/81 to 1990/91") and Table 6.5 ("Yukon Territorial Government Revenues by Source, 1980-1981 to 1990-1991") in Prince and Juniper, "Public Power" (cited in note 32). Separate data are not available for the northern parts of the provinces. Inuit have chosen to open some lands in Nunavut for mineral exploration, in anticipation of the looming shortage of public funds. Whether there will be significant long-term income in the form of royalties depends on what is found and on the economics of production. Overall, northern mineral taxation revenues have usually not exceeded the public subsidies necessary to launch mining ventures.

168. Mackenzie Valley Pipeline Inquiry (cited in note 59), pp. 121 and 122.

169. Some significant subsidies have been available to develop and support the art and crafts industries; in the Northwest Territories there have also been programs to support hunting, trapping and fishing for many years.

170. For a quantitative analysis of one traditional-mixed economy, see N.C. Quigley and N.J. McBride, "The Structure of an Arctic Microeconomy: The Traditional Sector in Community Economic Development", *Arctic* 40/3 (September 1987), p. 204.

171. Heather M. Myers, "An Evaluation of Renewable Resource Development Experience in the Northwest Territories, Canada", PH.D. dissertation, Cambridge University, Scott Polar Research Institute, 1994; Peter Douglas Elias, *Development of Aboriginal People's Communities* (Toronto: Centre for Aboriginal Management (CAMET) and Captus Press, 1993); Katherine A. Graham et al., *A Climate for Change: Alternatives for the Central and Eastern Arctic* (Kingston: Queen's University, Centre for Resource Studies, 1984), p. 157 and Appendices; and Frederick H. Weihs Consulting and Sinaaq Enterprises, "A Review and Assessment of the Economic Utilization and Potential of Country Food in the Northern Economy", research study prepared for RCAP (1993).

172. Public servants who were inspired by the more protective and social democratic approach in Greenland attempted to mitigate the laissez-faire philosophy, but they were not successful. See Clancy, "Contours of the Modern State" (cited in note 23).

173. Jon Pierce and Robert Hornal, "Aboriginal People and Mining in Nunavut, Nunavik and Northern Labrador", research study prepared for RCAP (1994); Price Waterhouse, "Aboriginal Participation in the Minerals Industry", research study prepared for RCAP (1993); and K.J. Rea, *The Political Economy of Northern*

Development, Background Paper No. 36 (Ottawa: Science Council of Canada, 1976).

174. Abele, *Gathering Strength* (cited in note 98); Wanda Wuttunee, "On Our Own Terms, Aboriginal Peoples and the Minerals Industry: Yukon and Denendeh", research study prepared for RCAP (1993); DesBrisay, "The Impact" (cited in note 127).

175. Yukon 2000 was a broadly participatory process of consultation and analysis that informed the Yukon government's decision to invest strategically in territorially based industries, such as furniture manufacturing and fish farming, as a form of import substitution, and to support the development of service and tourism industries. With the long-term goal of reducing the territory's reliance on the unpredictable and highly subsidized private mining sector, the strategy requires sustained political commitment and continuing expenditure of public funds. It is not a quick fix. The government of the Northwest Territories also endorsed a strategy of import substitution and proposed means to increase local participation in and control over the direction of economic development. Removing the barriers to internal trade received special attention. See *The SCONE Report: Building Our Economic Future* (Yellowknife: Legislative Assembly of the Northwest Territories, 1989); C.E.S. Franks, "The Public Service in the North", *Canadian Public Administration* 27/2 (Summer 1984), pp. 210-241; and Myers, "An Evaluation" (cited in note 171).

176. Ignatius E. La Rusic, "Subsidies for Subsistence: The Place of Income Security Programs in Supporting Hunting, Fishing, and Trapping as a Way of Life in Canada's Aboriginal Communities", research study prepared for RCAP (1993) [note omitted]. See also Peter Usher and Frederick H. Weihs, *Towards a Strategy for Supporting the Domestic Economy of the Northwest Territories*, prepared for the Legislative Assembly of the Northwest Territories Special Committee on the Northern Economy (Ottawa: P.J. Usher Consulting Services, 1989).

177. Weihs Consulting and Sinaaq Enterprises, "Review and Assessment" (cited in note 171).

178. Wenzel, *Animal Rights, Human Rights* (cited in note 128); La Rusic, "Subsidies for Subsistence" (cited in note 176); and Hugh Brody, *Living Arctic: Hunters of the Canadian North* (Toronto: Douglas & McIntyre, 1987).

179. P. Reichert and M. Spigelman (SP Research Associates), "Time on Assistance: A Study of the Patterns of Welfare Use in the Northwest Territories", report prepared for the Deputies Steering Committee on Income Support Reform, Government of the Northwest Territories (1991).

180. Research in the Northwest Territories shows that where the primary food economy is strong, social assistance payments are lower. Prince and Juniper, "Public Power" (cited in note 32).

181. Weihs Consulting and Sinaaq Enterprises, "Review and Assessment" (cited in note 171).

182. Lange, "Fractured Vision" (cited in note 4).

183. La Rusic, "Subsidies for Subsistence" (cited in note 176).

184. Ontario, Community and Social Services, *First Nations' Project Team Report: Social Assistance Legislation Review* (Toronto: Queen's Printer for Ontario, 1992).

185. Baffin Region Inuit Association, "Case Study #3 - Inuit Hunters in Nunavut", in "Inuit and Social Security Review" (cited in note 186).

186. For example, as suggested by the Labrador Inuit Association and the Baffin Region Inuit Association, in "Inuit and Social Security Review: Four Case Studies", prepared by Inuit Tapirisat of Canada for Human Resources Development Canada (3 February 1995).

187. For example, in Pangnirtung (on Baffin Island) most women working in the fish processing plant felt the seasonal nature of the fishery was positive since it allowed them to qualify for unemployment insurance benefits. Several noted this cycle allowed them to engage in traditional pursuits, with strong social or cultural returns during the rest of the year, despite these activities having small or negative economic returns. Bruce D. Ashley, "Community Economic Impact of Commercial Fisheries Development in Canada's Eastern Arctic: The Pangnirtung Winter Turbot Fishery", M.A. thesis, School of Resource and Environmental Management, Simon Fraser University (1993).

188. *An Act respecting employment insurance in Canada*, S.C. 1996, chapter 23; and *Budget Implementation Act 1996*, S.C. 1996, chapter 18.

189. Gwen Reimer, "A Case Study of an Inuit Economy: Pangnirtung, Northwest Territories", research study prepared for RCAP (1993).

190. See *An Act respecting income security for Cree hunters and trappers who are beneficiaries under the agreement concerning James Bay and Northern Quebec*, R.S.Q. c. S-3.2.; and *An Act respecting the support program for Inuit beneficiaries of the James Bay and Northern Quebec Agreement for their hunting, fishing and trapping activities*, R.S.Q. c. P-30.2.

191. Weihs and Sinaaq, "Review and Assessment" (cited in note 171). Also see Jo Ann Gagnon, *Le régime de chasse, de pêche et de trappage et les conventions du Québec nordique*, Nordicana Series, No. 45 (Quebec City: Centre d'études nordiques, Université Laval, 1982).

192. Weihs and Sinaaq "Review and Assessment"; see also Gagnon, *Le régime de chasse*.

193. La Rusic, "Subsidies for Subsistence" (cited in note 176). Also see Lorraine F. Brooke, "The James Bay and Northern Quebec Agreement: Experiences of the Nunavik Inuit with Wildlife Management", research study prepared for RCAP (1995).

194. Canadian Arctic Resources Committee, "Aboriginal Peoples, Comprehensive Land Claims" (cited in note 74).

195. Canadian Arctic Resources Committee, "Aboriginal Peoples, Comprehensive Land Claims", Appendix E, p. 12.

196. Canadian Arctic Resources Committee, "Aboriginal Peoples, Comprehensive Land Claims", Appendix E, p. 13.

197. RT and Associates, "Nunavut Harvest Support Program Background Document", December 1993.

198. La Rusic, "Subsidies for Subsistence" (cited in note 176).

199. For a discussion, see Eugene Swimmer and David Hennis, "Inuit Statistics: An Analysis of the Categories Used in Government Data Collections", research study prepared for RCAP (1993); and Jack C. Stabler, "Development Planning North of 60: Requirements and Prospects", William G. Watson, "A Southern Perspective on Northern Economic Development", and Michael S. Whittington, "Introduction: Northern Studies", all in Whittington, ed., *The North* (cited in note 29).

200. Wuttunee, "On Our Own Terms" (cited in note 174).

201. GNWT, Department of Energy, Mines and Petroleum Resources, 1992, quoted in Wuttunee, "On Our Own Terms".

202. Pierce and Hornal, "Aboriginal People and Mining" (cited in note 173).

203. Pierce and Hornal, "Aboriginal People and Mining"; and DesBrisay, "The Impact" (cited in note 127).

204. An agreement was signed on 25 February 1995 between Makivik Corporation and Qarqalik Landholding Corporation of Salluit, Northern Village Corporation of Salluit, Nunaturlik Landholding Corporation of Kangiqsujuaq, Northern Village Corporation of Kangiqsujuaq and Société minière Raglan du Québec.

205. Claudia Notzke, *Aboriginal Peoples and Natural Resources in Canada* (North York: Captus Press, 1994); Pierce and Hornal, "Aboriginal People and Mining" (cited in note 173).

206. Pierce and Hornal, "Aboriginal People and Mining".

207. United Nations, *Seminar Report (United Nations Interregional Seminar on Guidelines for the Development of Small/Medium Scale Mining, 15-19 February 1993* Harare, Zimbabwe (New York: 1993). See also Australia, *Report of the Committee of Review of Aboriginal Employment and Training Programs* (Canberra: 1985).

208. Jeffrey Davidson, "Rethinking Aboriginal Participation in the Minerals Industry: An Exploration of Alternative Modes", research study prepared for RCAP (1994).

209. Davidson, "Rethinking Aboriginal Participation".

210. See for example, Mike Robinson et al., "Coping with the Cash: A Financial Review of Four Northern Land Claims Settlements with a view to Maximizing Economic Opportunities from the Next Generation of Claims Settlements in the Northwest Territories", study prepared for the N.W.T. Legislative Assembly Special Committee on the Northern Economy (Yellowknife: 1989); *The SCONE Report* (cited in note 175); and Myers, "An Evaluation" (cited in note 171).

211. Weihs and Sinaaq, "A Review" (cited in note 171).

212. Robinson et al., "Coping with the Cash" (cited in note 210), p. 131 [note omitted].

213. See RCAP, *Choosing Life: Special Report on Suicide Among Aboriginal People* (Ottawa: Supply and Services, 1995); *Focusing the Dialogue*, Discussion Paper 2 (Ottawa: Supply and Services, 1993), pp. 51-62; and Volume 3 of this report.

214. ATII Training Inc., "Northern Education and Training" (cited in note 95).

215. See Dacks, ed., *Devolution and Constitutional Development* (cited in note 48); and D.A. Rondinelli, *Development Projects as Policy Experiments: An Adaptive Approach to Development Administration* (London: Methuen, 1983) and "Government Decentralization in Comparative Perspective: Theory and Practice in Developing Countries", *International Review of Administrative Science* 47/2 (1981), pp. 135-136.

216. See Stevenson, "Traditional Inuit Decision-Making Structures" (cited in note 19); Dacks, "Adaptation" (cited in note 3); and Dickerson and Shotton, "Northern Self-Government" (cited in note 3).

217. See ATII Training, "Northern Education and Training" (cited in note 95); and Mary Easterson, "First Nation Education in Yukon and Northwest Territories: A Historical Perspective and Contemporary Perspective", research study prepared for RCAP (1994).

218. There is a large body of scholarly and applied literature on this topic. See Abele, *Gathering Strength* (cited in note 98); Joseph E. Couture, "Native Training and Political Change: A Personal Reflection", *The Canadian Journal of Native Studies* 2/1 (1982), pp. 12-24; A.R. Hoyle, "Evaluation of Training: A Review of the Literature", *Public Administration and Development* 4 (1984), pp. 275-282; J. Mark Stiles, *Developing the Potential From Within: A Report on Management Training for the Inuit Broadcasting Corporation and Taqramiut Nipingat Inc.* (1983); and R.A. Young and P. McDermott, "Employment Training Programs and Acculturation of Native Peoples in Canada's Northwest Territories", *Arctic* 41/3 (1988), pp. 195-202.

219. *Agreement Between the Inuit of the Nunavut Settlement Area and Her Majesty in Right of Canada* (signed in Iqaluit, 25 May 1993), article 11, Part 2 (11.2.1) (Ottawa: DIAND and Tungavik, 1993).

220. Bielawski, "The Desecration" (cited in note 123).

221. José Mailhot, *Traditional Ecological Knowledge: The Diversity of Knowledge Systems and Their Study* (Montreal: Great Whale Public Review Support Office, 1993), pp. 34-36.

222. Details on the application of Aboriginal traditional knowledge in a variety of institutions can be found throughout this report. In particular, see the chapters on lands and resources and economic development (Volume 2, Chapters 4 and 5), much of Volume 3, and the chapter on elders' perspectives (Chapter 3 in this volume).

7

URBAN PERSPECTIVES

We continue as two worlds, the Indians and the other city-people; we/they. We are frightened and suspicious of one another....[F]ew human movements so confront our history; so confront our private fears and stereotypes; so confront our myths; and so leave us confused and paralyzed.[1]

There is a strong, sometimes racist, perception that being Aboriginal and being urban are mutually exclusive.[2]

MANY CANADIANS THINK OF Aboriginal people as living on reserves or at least in rural areas. This perception is deeply rooted and persistently reinforced. Yet almost half of Aboriginal people in Canada live in cities and towns. As many Aboriginal people live in Winnipeg as in the entire Northwest Territories. Before the Commission began its work, however, little attention had been given to identifying and meeting the needs, interests and aspirations of urban Aboriginal people. Little thought had been given to improving their circumstances, even though their lives were often desperate, and relations between Aboriginal people and the remainder of the urban population were fragile, if not hostile.

The information and policy vacuum can be traced at least in part to long-standing ideas in non-Aboriginal culture about where Aboriginal people 'belong'. There is a history in Canada of putting Aboriginal people 'in their place' on reserves and in rural communities. Aboriginal cultures and mores have been perceived as incompatible with the demands of industrialized urban society.[3] This leads all too easily to the assumption that Aboriginal people living in urban areas must deny their culture and heritage in order to succeed – that they must assimilate into this other world. The corollary is that once Aboriginal people migrate to urban areas, their identity as Aboriginal people becomes irrelevant.

Research undertaken for the Commission, however, contradicts the idea that Aboriginal people consider their cultures and traditions irrelevant to urban life. They emphasize that to cope in the urban milieu, support for enhancing and maintaining their culture and identity is essential. Whenever that support is absent, the urban experience is profoundly unhappy for Aboriginal people.

Item 6 of the Commission's terms of reference, "The constitutional and legal position of the Métis and off-reserve Indians", states that we may "examine legislative jurisdictions concerning the Métis and non-status Indians, and investigate the economic base of, and the provision of government services to, these people and to off-reserve Indians".

Many Aboriginal people made submissions to the Commission on urban issues. Critical issues included the challenges to their cultural identity, exclusion from opportunities for self-determination, discrimination, and the difficulty of finding culturally appropriate services. As one intervener told us:

> Urban Aboriginal residents are tired and cynical. They have been pushed first by white-skinned and now by brown-skinned leaders. Such residents show their resistance by not showing up in numbers to political events. This allows the return of...elite leaders. Overall, urban Aboriginal people are not empowered to the point where they can govern themselves or hold their leaders accountable.
>
> What worked for our ancestors may not work today. Harsh realities for the urban Aboriginal underclass such as drug addiction and enforced unemployment are not like the harsh realities of weather and poor trapping.[4]

Through four rounds of public hearings, Commissioners received 322 submissions on topics of concern to urban Aboriginal people. Briefs, research papers and policy papers were received from nearly 30 organizations with a significant interest in urban issues. In June 1992 we held a national round table on urban issues. We also commissioned studies on self-government, institutional and economic development, cultural identity, housing and Aboriginal youth in the urban context.

Aboriginal people living in urban areas number about 320,000, or 45 per cent of the total Aboriginal population. By the year 2016, they will number about 455,000. A comprehensive demographic and socio-economic profile of urban Aboriginal people is presented later in this chapter. Some features stand out.

Historically, Aboriginal women have significantly outnumbered Aboriginal men in urban areas and continue to do so, having dominated recent migration into urban areas. Urban Aboriginal people are considerably younger than the urban population in general. They are also generally less well educated: only four per cent hold a university degree, compared to 13 per cent of non-Aboriginal urban residents.

Aboriginal people in urban areas are also economically disadvantaged relative to their non-Aboriginal neighbours. Although labour force participation rates for urban Aboriginal residents approach those of other Canadians, their unemployment rate is two and a half times greater. Those working for 40 or more weeks a year had average incomes more than 36 per cent lower than non-Aboriginal people in the same circumstances. Average annual income from all sources for Aboriginal people in urban areas lagged 33 per cent behind that of non-Aboriginal residents.

The incidence of poverty is high. In Winnipeg, Regina and Saskatoon, the 1991 census found that more than 60 per cent of Aboriginal households were below the low income cut-off – the poverty line defined by Statistics Canada.[5] For single-parent households headed by women, the situation was disastrous – between 80 and 90 per cent were below the line. Moreover, the situation was almost as bad in nearly every major city in Canada.

This chapter focuses on the situation of Aboriginal people living in Canada's urban areas and the issues the Commission was told are most critical. We have been guided in our work by the goal of making urban environments places where Aboriginal people can experience a satisfying quality of life, both in their dealings with the non-Aboriginal community and in affirming Aboriginal cultures and rights. We believe that this will lead to healthier, more vibrant cities and towns for Aboriginal and non-Aboriginal people alike.

1. Cultural Identity

Throughout the Commission's hearings, Aboriginal people stressed the fundamental importance of retaining and enhancing their cultural identity while living in urban areas. Aboriginal identity lies at the heart of Aboriginal peoples' existence; maintaining that identity is an essential and self-validating pursuit for Aboriginal people in cities. Commissioners heard that there is a strong trend toward reacquisition of cultural identity throughout the Canadian Aboriginal population. Contemporary urban Aboriginal people, in particular, are more positive about their Aboriginal identity today than at any time in the past.[6]

The Commission undertook a major research study to examine cultural identity as experienced by Aboriginal people living in urban settings. The study involved a series of 10 two-day learning circles (discussion or focus groups) held in six cities across Canada. A total of 114 participants attended from all Aboriginal groups, including Métis, Inuit and First Nations. Participants included artists, youth, inmates, and elders, both women and men.[7] The project's purpose was to understand the essential elements of cultural identity and the factors that strengthen and enhance it in urban areas (together with those that diminish or extinguish it), and to pinpoint the events and experiences that define cultural identity in individual lives.

Participants indicated that their Aboriginal cultural identity is of paramount importance to them. Many had experienced identity confusion but had been able, over time, to build a more positive identity for themselves. Others continued to carry a heavy burden of pain and self-doubt that undermines their cultural identity.

Constant interaction with non-Aboriginal society in the urban environment presents particular challenges to cultural identity. Aboriginal people want to achieve an adequate standard of living and participate in the general life of the dominant society, while at the same time honouring and protecting their own heritage, institutions, values and world view. Sustaining a positive cultural identity is particularly important for Aboriginal people in urban areas because of the negative impact of their often troubled contacts with the institutions of the dominant society. Maintaining identity is more difficult because many of the sources of traditional Aboriginal culture, including contact with the land, elders, Aboriginal languages and spiritual ceremonies, are not easily accessible.

This chapter focuses on the survival and maintenance of Aboriginal cultural identities in urban society. Since a large percentage of Aboriginal people today live in urban settings, the extent to which they are able to sustain a positive cultural identity will significantly affect the survival of Aboriginal peoples as distinct peoples.

1.1 The Essence of Cultural Identity

Most Aboriginal people are raised in an environment characterized by Aboriginal beliefs, values and behaviour. The identity instilled by that upbringing tends to persist. Testimony to the Commission emphasized its resilience, even in the face of intensive contact with urban culture. But the immediate environment necessarily shapes the expression of cultural values. The requirements of survival in the city frequently force Aboriginal people to change their way of life and reshape the way they express their beliefs and values. The resulting adaptations run a complete range, from maintenance of a strong Aboriginal identity based on traditional Aboriginal culture to assimilation into the pervasive non-Aboriginal culture. In integrating themselves into an urban environment, most Aboriginal people fall between these two extremes. Some remain trapped between worlds, unable to find their place in either culture; this often creates tension, alienation and identity confusion. Others successfully adapt to urban life by blending aspects of both cultures and becoming bicultural; they maintain a strong Aboriginal identity into which they integrate elements of non-Aboriginal culture. A small but growing number of Aboriginal people have created positive new identities in response to the challenges and opportunities of urban life. In the words of one presenter:

> The fundamental change of the past 20 years has been, I think, the acceptance of both Aboriginal people and mainstream Canadians of the way in which traditional Aboriginal people have viewed themselves and the resultant construction of new identities, not as victims, or as noble savages, or primitive beings but as for example Cree,

Ojibwa, Inuit with dignity and knowledge and deserving of respect and a place in contemporary society. The ability to construct an identity for the self, either as an individual or as a collective, lies at the heart of modernity. I now see a group of people who are constructing a positive identity for themselves: who now see themselves as an integral part of and contributors to society around them.

David Newhouse
Associate Professor, Trent University
Toronto, Ontario, 3 November 1992*

Understanding another culture is difficult because it requires us to appreciate, without having lived the same experiences, another people's way of comprehending the world. It demands openness and sensitivity. We have to set aside assumptions, beliefs and cultural ethnocentricity in order to try and see the world as others see it. If we are successful, we may be able to perceive how other people, in very different circumstances, conceive of their environment and their place, both physical and spiritual, within it. We may even achieve an understanding of their shared meanings and ideas, including the intellectual, moral and aesthetic standards that guide them.

For most Canadians, understanding the practice of traditional Aboriginal cultures in cities is particularly difficult because we have been taught to 'understand' narrow and inaccurate stereotypes of Aboriginal culture. The images of Aboriginal culture for many people are totem poles, stone carving, pow-wow dancing, canoes, moccasins and feather head-dresses. These are among the images of Aboriginal people that are presented in schools and in popular culture. Viewed this way, culture is no more than a collection of objects and rituals, observed in isolation from their vitality and meaning within a particular cultural context. This view also emphasizes the past and leaves the impression that Aboriginal cultures are static rather than dynamic and contemporary. But the artistic and material aspects of Aboriginal culture, though important, are only a small part of its reality and need to be understood within the larger context of Aboriginal peoples' world views, belief systems and changing ways of life.

In its broadest sense, culture is everything – tangible and intangible – that people learn and share in coming to terms with their environment. It includes a community's entire world view, together with the beliefs, values, attitudes and perceptions of life that may be reflected in its material objects. It is the community's common understanding of the everyday world, with its meanings, symbols and standards of conduct, and it is communal acceptance of appropriate behaviour in that world.

---

*Transcripts of the Commission's hearings are cited with the speaker's name and affiliation, if any, and the location and date of the hearing. See *A Note About Sources* at the beginning of this volume for information about transcripts and other Commission publications.

So Aboriginal cultural identity is not a single element. It is a complex of features that together shape how a person thinks about herself or himself as an Aboriginal person. It is a contemporary feeling about oneself, a state of emotional and spiritual being, rooted in Aboriginal experiences. In the words of Etah, a 17-year-old Aboriginal youth:

> There is something my uncle said, you know, "You're not a true Indian unless you...follow the culture, then you are an Indian." It's not a status thing. It's not a piece of paper. It's a spiritual thing, an emotional thing, a mental thing, a physical thing.[8]

Cultural identity is a state of being that involves being wanted, being comfortable, being a part of something bigger than oneself. Among urban Aboriginal people, there are many cultural identities, representing many Aboriginal cultures. One thing urban Aboriginal people from all parts of the country speak of, however, is "the spiritual bond, the common thread" that unites all Aboriginal peoples.[9]

Urban Aboriginal people also consistently identify a number of elements of their respective cultures as an integral part of their cultural identity: spirituality, language, a land base or ancestral territory, elders, traditional values, family and ceremonial life. First and foremost, Aboriginal people speak of their spirituality:

> All life is given by the Creator; all aspects of life are spiritual. All of creation is an interrelated whole. The land and all of life are intergenerational. A legacy we leave to our unborn children is a clean and healthy environment. The Creator has given all peoples their own cultural identity, which we hold as sacred and which will be preserved for all time. The identity of Aboriginal women/people embraces traditional laws and institutions, languages, beliefs, values, oral and written histories.
>
> Evelyn Webster
> Vice-President, Indigenous Women's Collective
> Winnipeg, Manitoba, 22 April 1992

Language, itself viewed as a gift of the Creator, is almost universally considered a central part of the experience of identity. Sustaining their Aboriginal cultural identity means, for most urban Aboriginal people, maintaining their Aboriginal language:

> To quote Verna Kirkness, language is the principal means by which culture is accumulated, shared and transmitted from generation to generation. The key to identity and retention of culture is one's ancestral language.
>
> Dawna LeBlanc
> North Shore Tribal Council,
> Anishnabe Language Teachers Association
> Sault Ste. Marie, Ontario, 11 June 1992

Cultural identity for urban Aboriginal people is also tied to a land base or ancestral territory. For many, the two concepts are inseparable. As an Inuvialuit living in Inuvik expressed it:

> It is on the land that important lessons are learned, lessons that are central to the Inuvialuit world view. It is also on the land that families grow together, where children learn the language and traditions of their ancestors – 'Driving my four dogs'. And it is on the land that people of the Inuvialuit community come together to celebrate and to grieve. Their ancient songs, dances and stories are about their relationship to each other, to the land and animals.[10]

Identification with an ancestral place is important to urban people because of the associated ritual, ceremony and traditions, as well as the people who remain there, the sense of belonging, the bond to an ancestral community, and the accessibility of family, community and elders. Participants in the Quebec learning circle stressed that land is key to the renewal of cultural identity and that relationship with the land and territories – and occupation and use of the land – are essential components of Aboriginal identity.

Elders are essential to cultural identity for urban Aboriginal people. They are seen as forces in urban Aboriginal peoples' lives that enabled them to endure or see beyond the pain and the turmoil they experienced in their families, communities and within themselves regarding their Aboriginal identity.[11] Inuvialuit youth living in Inuvik show a "genuine hunger to listen to the elders' stories in order to learn about themselves and their ancestors".[12] Urban Aboriginal people respect the elders' capacity to remind them of traditional values intrinsic to their cultural identity.

Responsibility, reciprocity, sharing, respect, kindness, honesty and strength were particularly mentioned by urban people as values they associate with their cultural identity. Urban Aboriginal people believe that these values were practised in traditional communities. They were reinforced by legends, cultural teachings of all kinds, rituals and ceremonies. Family members and individuals in the community instructed children in the importance of maintaining these values in their relationships with the natural and human worlds. For many urban Aboriginal people, these values remain as important to their cultural identity today as at any time. As Commissioners were told in Vancouver:

> Today we live in the modern world and we find that a lot of our people who come into the urban setting are unable to live in the modern world without their traditional values.

> Nancy van Heest
> Urban Images for First Nations
> Vancouver, British Columbia, 2 June 1993

Family plays a significant role in urban Aboriginal cultural identity. Within the Métis community, for example, family defines who one is:

> They [community people] know instantly...your whole biography. They know where you came from, who you are, how you've been raised and who actually did all that....When you go back or if you go to another community they won't ask you so much who you are but who are your parents, your grandparents...that whole identity thing of family. It's a very big thing in the Métis community, because it carries a lot of weight. The respect that is given you is again the family...it's like you're carrying more than just a name, it's a whole history of your family, its accomplishments, respectability, background history....And you can't get away from that. The individuality is completely dismantled at that point.[13]

Family is also regarded as the natural setting for cultural teaching. Although some urban Aboriginal people may no longer have contact with their immediate families, they remember the lessons of grandmothers, aunts or parents. Aboriginal cultures place great emphasis on family life and obligations within the family. Thus, for many urban Aboriginal individuals, the birth of children provides an impetus to reclaim their cultural identity, because they recognize that the obligation to teach their children the lessons of the culture is a key element of that identity.

For many urban Aboriginal people, cultural identity is intimately tied to celebrating the ceremonial life of their culture. Taking part in a pipe ceremony, lighting sweetgrass, dancing in pow-wows, fiddling and jigging, drum dancing, and going through a naming ceremony were identified as significant events through which Aboriginal people internalize the values of their cultures into their identity, reinforcing knowledge of who they are as members of the group and establishing their place in the world of the culture.

1.2 Racism

One of the most difficult aspects of urban life for Aboriginal people is dealing with the personal impact of racism. In the words of an Aboriginal woman living in Saskatoon:

> I think the most terrible experience for an Indian person in the urban setting is racism in the community. That diminishes your self-esteem, confidence and everything else. You experience racism every day in the stores and everywhere else on the street. All the other groups discriminate against you.[14]

Commissioners also heard that racism is systemic:

To me, it is clear that the racism so evident in Canada will not be easily eradicated. Elements of racism are intertwined in history, in the history books, in library books. It is found in school curriculum. Elements of racism are found in administration of justice, in law enforcement, and often within church groups. It is little wonder that the First Nations communities are in culture shock, that the youth are so often disoriented.

William Tooshkeniq
Association of Iroquois & Allied Nations
Toronto, Ontario, 3 June 1993

Racism is experienced through discrimination, bias, exclusion, stereotypes, lack of support and recognition, negative attitudes, alienation in the workplace and lack of role models in management positions. Racism is exclusion...racism is manifested in many ways. It is unconscious, direct, individual, systemic and institutional.

Louise Chippeway
Chairperson, Aboriginal Advisory Council
Roseau River, Manitoba, 8 December 1992

Many presenters and participants in the learning circles felt that acts of racism, prejudice and discrimination directed against them as Aboriginal people had a negative effect on their cultural identification. The development of an individual's identity is a social process guided by interaction with others. It begins with a child's interaction with family members and members of the community. The child adopts the world of those providing care and direction. Even under intense pressure to assimilate, Aboriginal people tend to socialize their children into an Aboriginal identity by teaching them the core values of Aboriginal culture – caring, honesty, sharing and strength. As they grow older, the children become aware that these values reflect a larger Aboriginal belief system and support a particular way of behaving. They realize that these core values are the key to defining who Aboriginal people are and what distinguishes them from others, and seek to maintain those values.

A healthy identity is promoted when others communicate a positive image, validating the individual's view of him- or herself. This reinforces self-image and self-esteem. As individuals extend their participation beyond their primary group and interact with members of the larger society, the image communicated back to them carries important implications for their identity. A Mi'kmaq woman recognized as an elder and leader described what she faced when she moved to Halifax:

When I was growing up there was so much discrimination that you didn't dare mention the word Mi'kmaq. That is why I came to Nova

Scotia and never told a soul....I even changed my name so nobody would know. I can understand my children because I thought they would go through the same thing I did....It would never have happened if it were not for the people saying mean things and discriminating against us....I cried many times because I did this. I felt guilty.[15]

Many Aboriginal people face a contradiction between the image presented to them by their families and Aboriginal communities and the image reflected to them by the dominant society. The stereotypes and negative images attached to them by mainstream society are superimposed on the identity internalized while growing up, often leading to identity confusion and low self-esteem. As one young man from Saskatchewan put it:

I'm a really confused young person....I was confused for a long time, I didn't even know my own strength....I had a lot of anger and a lot of unresolved issues in my life...just feeling like I couldn't go nowhere cause I was ashamed of being Indian....All my life I wanted to be White...because they have the money, they have the nice cars. I thought that was the way they live. Until... every time I tried to be White I'd fall short. Then I would become really frustrated and angry....I used to be ashamed of my people cause I thought... we're all on welfare, we're all in the jail systems – we're oppressed!...You know I couldn't understand it. I was ashamed like that for a long time.[16]

1.3 Urbanization

She remembers that she's Native, and is suddenly sad that her identity is defined by her colour....She thinks of her sacred stones in her pocket, and stroking them, she asks for protection as she sees one of her people getting thrown out of the Barry Hotel. Her heart aches as she sees children hanging around the streets. She thinks of her daughter in the next generation, walking down the same street. Will she have to go through the same degradation, humiliation, because of her colour?

Robin Bellamy
Executive Director, Friendship Inn
Saskatoon, Saskatchewan, 13 May 1993

Aboriginal people in cities interact closely with members of the larger society. For many migrants, this results in culture shock. The stress of the unwelcoming city, confusion, the experience of racism and the inability to find employment push some into crime. Others are provoked by their relationship with non-Aboriginal society to think about their identity and recognize their difference, their distinctiveness. For some, confronting other cultures engenders pride in their own:

> You're not only learning there are differences but you are building your identity on who you are and what you are. And either you turn against your culture and deny that you're Indian and try to assimilate or you can accept that you're Indian and you can still live in the city and...be a stronger person for it.[17]

Urban institutions often conflict with Aboriginal cultural values. The welfare system, for example, has substituted institutional dependency and familial division for reliance on extended family and community. The Commission was told how non-Aboriginal agencies can strip people of their identity:

> Almost all Métis children in the care of non-Aboriginal agencies are in the care of non-Métis families. The children are raised without contact or access to their language and culture. They are raised in a society that devalues their identity as Métis people and they learn to hide and be ashamed of their cultural distinctiveness. Most are forever lost to the Métis Nation.

> Yvon Dumont
> President, Manitoba Metis Federation
> Winnipeg, Manitoba, 22 April 1992

In the urban schools attended by Aboriginal children, there is little opportunity to learn, study or even play with classmates in Aboriginal languages. Statistics on language loss among the current generation of Aboriginal children attest to the relentless eradication of Aboriginal languages. Curricula seldom include the history of Aboriginal peoples. Urban Aboriginal people comment negatively on their public school experience:

> In public schools we could not learn about our heritage, culture or history. Also public schools direct us to take the French language instead of our own languages. We disagree with that because without our languages our identity as Native peoples is at risk of becoming extinct instead of distinct.

> Charmane Sheena
> Student, Shackan Band School
> Merritt, British Columbia, 5 November 1992

Urbanization itself can easily undermine a positive cultural identity. The main expression of traditional culture for Inuvialuit, for example, is to work and live on the land. Hunting, fishing, trapping, whaling, harvesting and preparing traditional foods support their culture. We heard first-hand about the devastating cultural impact of urbanization on families and communities during the early 1970s.

Many young Inuvialuit today have never lived on the land. Over the last generation, families settled in towns so children could attend school. This movement disrupted life on the land even before the anti-fur lobby devastated the economy of the fur trade. The oil boom brought high wages and a cash economy. That economy has now disappeared, but families still live in towns and live on the land only on weekends. Young Inuvialuit speak of the boredom of town life and the opportunities and experiences they feel they are missing on the land. Balancing this tension between town life and trips on the land is at the centre of their attempts to define who they are and how they will live their lives.

It is just as difficult for other Aboriginal people to find their cultures reflected in the urban environment. Many speak of the homogenizing effect that results:

> In short the experience for many [urban people] is that they pick up pieces of Aboriginal culture wherever they can; at times this includes using cultural elements from other nations that may be more immediately accessible or adapted to their needs.[18]

Métis people are particularly aware of the lack of Métis-specific cultural institutions and agencies in most urban centres. They speak bitterly of attempts to minimize their uniqueness, or to group them into a melting-pot of Aboriginal cultures:

> At the moment we are looking at strictly Métis institutions for Métis people. We feel that by agreeing to being lumped in with all other Aboriginal people, we run the chance of losing our identity as an Aboriginal people.
>
> Yvon Dumont
> President, Manitoba Metis Federation
> Winnipeg, Manitoba, 22 April 1992

As these concerns illustrate, there are no easy solutions to designing institutions and agencies to serve the discrete needs of different Aboriginal peoples.

1.4 Enhancing Cultural Identities in Urban Areas

> The most effective way to catch these problems before they start is through strengthening an individual's identity and awareness of the community that exists in the city.
>
> David Chartrand
> President, National Association of Friendship Centres
> Toronto, Ontario, 26 June 1992

Commissioners heard testimony across Canada that urban Aboriginal people are engaged in a major revitalization of culture. This does not mean turning the clock back, but rather selecting aspects of the old ways and blending them with the new. Presenters reported that many elements of traditional Aboriginal cultures are being renewed. Sun dances, sweat-lodge ceremonies, fasting, potlatches, traditional healing rituals and other spiritual ceremonies are all enjoying a revival. The psychological and spiritual wisdom of elders who kept their teachings alive is being recognized. Elders are being restored to their former place of respect in communities, and Aboriginal people are turning to them for guidance as they search in increasing numbers for a meaningful identity.

For the majority of urban Aboriginal people, the result of cultural revitalization is the development of a bicultural identity. Individuals enjoy an identity firmly rooted in the cultural world of their own people, while also possessing the skills and knowledge required to succeed in non-Aboriginal society. This identity includes the core values learned in the family that have remained resilient. Putting those values into practice in the city requires adapting and developing links with the sources of the culture – the land and spiritual world view. This was expressed by a Saskatoon resident:

> I think I've learned to maintain a sense of balance. Because I've adjusted to the European way of doing things in terms of working for money but at the same time maintaining my heritage. Even though it is difficult because in the urban setting we don't practise a lot of our ceremonial part of our heritage. So my job helps me get back home to do that.[19]

Maintaining cultural identity often requires creating an Aboriginal community in the city. Following three decades of urbanization, development of a strong community still remains largely incomplete. Many urban Aboriginal people are impoverished and unorganized. No coherent or co-ordinated policies to meet their needs are in place, despite the fact that they make up almost half of Canada's Aboriginal population. They have been largely excluded from discussions about self-government and institutional development. Aboriginal people in urban areas have little collective visibility or power. It is clear that they urgently require resources and assistance to support existing organizations and create new institutions to enhance their cultural identity.

A number of Aboriginal organizations are attempting to meet the needs of Aboriginal people in cities, including the strengthening of cultural identity. Winnipeg and Toronto both have more than 40 Aboriginal organizations. Many of these are developing culturally based approaches to their structures and program delivery. Friendship centres have a long history of providing cultural programming and have been the most effective urban resource in this regard. They were singled out by presenters and participants in the learning circles as places where one can "feel good about being Native" and find "support and acceptance".[20] They provide access to social contacts, information and services.

Individuals can meet elders and create a "synthetic family"[21] to fulfil the role of an extended family. For many urban Aboriginal people, a friendship centre is the heart of their urban Aboriginal community. (The programs and services offered by friendship centres are discussed later in the chapter in the section on service delivery.)

The Ontario Federation of Friendship Centres is one example of an urban Aboriginal organization that has incorporated traditional culture, through use of the Medicine Wheel, into its management style, board functions and delivery of programs and services. Decisions are reached by consensus rather than majority vote; the federation plays the traditional peacekeeper role of the Bear Clan; elders are involved in all training events; major elders' gatherings are held every few years to provide direction for the organization; meetings are opened and closed in a traditional manner with thanksgiving, greetings and sweetgrass; traditional feasts, socials and spiritual ceremonies are held; and hiring policies emphasize experience, individual characteristics and an understanding of the culture rather than academic or professional qualifications.[22]

The cultural survival schools that exist in a number of major cities are another example of institutions that address the identity needs of urban Aboriginal people. Schools such as the Ben Calfrobe School Society in Edmonton, the Prairie Indian Cultural Survival School in Calgary, Joe Duquette High School in Saskatoon and the First Nations School in Toronto are alternatives to the public school system for Aboriginal students. In addition to conventional academic subjects, traditional culture and language are a major part of the curriculum. Aboriginal material is also integrated into academic subjects. For example, Aboriginal authors are studied in English literature courses, First Nations arts and crafts in art courses, Aboriginal knowledge of the land in environmental studies, traditional Aboriginal games in physical education, and Aboriginal issues in history and social studies. Students also have the opportunity to attend cultural camps run by elders in rural settings. Elders and people who maintain a traditional way of life, as well as parents, are extensively involved in the schools' operation, and the schools are often overseen by parent councils.

A number of Aboriginal child and family service agencies that incorporate cultural considerations in developing and delivering services have been established in cities across Canada. Native Child and Family Services of Toronto, for example, has a service model based on traditional Aboriginal culture and reflecting Aboriginal beliefs. But whether an Aboriginal individual moving to the city finds thriving Aboriginal-controlled institutions and services depends entirely on the city in question. Urban communities offer an uneven checkerboard of programs and services, usually funded on a short-term pilot basis and directed to only a few aspects of Aboriginal life, such as housing and child care.

Urban Aboriginal people know what they need to support their personal and collective cultural development. Many told Commissioners that there is a need for urban institutions that serve as meeting places and resource centres for information and services. They also need greater access to resources – information, people, events and activities – that are culturally significant. Urban cultural education centres, discussed later in this chapter, could be one means of providing access to elders, resource materials and support. They could build links between Aboriginal and non-Aboriginal communities and foster a vibrant new relationship. Cultural programming and cross-cultural education, two broad areas of activity badly needed in urban areas, could form the basis of a wider mandate for urban cultural education centres.

Urban Aboriginal people also told Commissioners of the critical importance of a strong cultural foundation for the healing of the urban Aboriginal community. Speaking on behalf of Janet Yorke, director of a substance abuse treatment centre, Harold Orton told us,

> Throughout our work in addressing family violence we strive to return our people to a time where everyone had a place in the circle and was valued. Recovering our identity will contribute to healing ourselves. Our healing will require us to rediscover who we are. We cannot look outside for our self-image, we need to rededicate ourselves to understanding our traditional ways. In our songs, ceremony, language and relationships lie the instructions and directions for recovery. We must avoid a pan-Indian approach. The issues of violence in our communities are diverse and so are our own cultural ways.
>
> Harold Orton
> Counsellor, Barrie Community Care Centre for Substance Abuse
> Orillia, Ontario, 13 May 1993

The key to the healing process lies in protecting and supporting all the elements that urban Aboriginal people consider an integral part of their cultural identity: spirituality, language, a land base, elders, values and traditions, family and ceremonial life.

It is important that Aboriginal spirituality be recognized and affirmed by both Aboriginal and non-Aboriginal institutions. Ceremonial practices must be given appropriate support in urban centres. This may range from specific exemptions from anti-smoking by-laws and fire regulations, so that sweetgrass can be burned for ceremonial purposes, to recognition of Aboriginal healing ceremonies in hospitals. Land, together with the ritual, ceremony and traditions associated with it, is particularly important to the renewal of cultural identity. Support therefore may mean setting aside a parcel of land in urban areas as a sacred place for the city's Aboriginal population.

Supporting and promoting the use of Aboriginal languages is seen by urban Aboriginal people as critical to their cultural identity. It is now difficult for them to retrieve or reinforce their languages within English- and French-speaking institutions. Children are most vulnerable to the negative effects of the urban experience on Aboriginal languages, and programs to support language must begin with children.

Learning an Aboriginal language is important because language is an essential vehicle for the expression of culture, including core values and beliefs. Language also opens the door to many other facets of the Aboriginal community. It is used in spiritual ceremonies, songs and stories; understanding and speaking the language enriches the experience of these events. A member of the Anishnabe Language Teachers Association stressed the importance of language in her presentation to the Commission:

> Languages reflect fundamental differences in culture in ways that specific language groups perceive their world, their family relationships, kinship structure, relationship to other cultures, and to the land. Language impacts on our cultural, educational, social, economic, and political life, therefore language has a direct bearing on how we see ourselves as a people and our role in self-government, on land claims and our claim to a distinct society.
>
> Dawna LeBlanc
> Anishnabe Language Teachers Association
> Sault Ste. Marie, Ontario, 11 June 1992

In response to the pressing need to support Aboriginal languages in urban environments, a number of initiatives have begun in cities across Canada. Friendship centres have instituted language classes for adults. Cultural survival schools teach Aboriginal languages as part of their core curriculum. Other avenues are being explored. A presenter from Toronto described the development of an Aboriginal language immersion program in a child care centre as part of an effort to strengthen children's identity and self-esteem:

> It was and is the vision of the parents and community members to have a child care centre in this urban setting that helped their children retain their Native languages and cultural identity....In order to realize our goal of full immersion it was necessary to create a team of language specialists who, we are proud to say, are First Nations grandmothers. They deliver a language and cultural program for the children, the staff, and the families that encompasses the emotional, mental, spiritual and physical development of all individuals.
>
> Jackie Esquimox-Hamelin
> Gazhaadaawgamik Native School
> Toronto, Ontario, 2 June 1993

These initiatives should be strengthened and expanded. We therefore recommended in Volume 3, Chapter 5 that school boards and all levels of government support the development of Aboriginal-controlled early-childhood programming delivered in Aboriginal languages.

For a large number of Aboriginal people living in cities, maintaining a connection to the land is critical to their cultural identity. For many, it represents involvement with the source of traditional culture. For others, such as a Saskatoon woman who participated in one of our learning circles, it is simply a feeling of being part of something larger and good:

> [W]e went way up north and it was so beautiful just sitting out there in the open....Just being out there, there was a sense of something that comes over you....Just everything that was there, and you seem to relate to everything that was around you – the trees, the rocks, the water and all that. Everyone had a good feeling just being there...whereas in the city you don't have that.[23]

Urbanization among Aboriginal people tends to include frequent returns to their home communities. The continuing links to the community also serve to reinforce family ties and a sense of group cohesion. People return to visit family, attend social events such as weddings, participate in cultural happenings such as pow-wows and feasts, and take part in ceremonies such as sweat lodges.

But not all urban Aboriginal people have the option of visiting or returning to a home community. For an increasing number, the city has become a permanent home, and some have no links to a rural community. The ancestral lands of others may be distant. Yet Aboriginal cultural identity remains, even for these people, very closely tied to a relationship with the land and the environment. Access to land in or near the urban area for spiritual and cultural purposes is extremely important.

Urban Aboriginal youth express a real thirst for knowledge about their culture (see Chapter 4 in this volume). It is youth who are the least well served by current programs to revive and support cultural identity. Yet they are asking for an opportunity to hear the elders. Urban Aboriginal youth need cultural programs that help develop and sustain Aboriginal identity. These could bring youth and elders together in various ways, such as in a teaching-learning environment or in mutually supportive roles where, for example, Aboriginal youth provide services for elders in return for the opportunity to learn about their cultural heritage. Other activities might include Aboriginal games, organized together by urban youth and elders.

In fact, access to elders is generally an important need of urban people. It is elders who speak the language, who know about ritual, spirituality, stories, songs and dances – all fundamental expressions of Aboriginal identity. By sharing their knowledge and experience, elders play a significant role in strengthening the identity of individuals and the community as a whole. One of many individuals who related how important elders are in their understanding of themselves was Sonny, a member of the Nuu-chah-nulth Nation in British Columbia, now living in Victoria:

> At one treatment centre they had elders. They talked about balance...about drinking, how it tore their family apart. I guess that's when I really started to accept me. I became aware of who I am....Another time, they lectured or something...I find out where I come from...like the culture, and some of them said that made them feel good. And I know every time I was at home and they're having ceremonies and the potlatch – I always felt good. Especially the elders that came....[24]

Development of a positive cultural identity for urban Aboriginal people will benefit non-Aboriginal people as well. Non-Aboriginal institutions and agencies should recognize this by taking an active part in supporting and strengthening Aboriginal cultural identities. Urban Aboriginal people singled out education as one of the most significant factors affecting their cultural identity. Their educational experiences in urban centres have had both the most negative and the most positive effects on their cultural identity.

Participants in the urban learning circles recommended a public education program to educate Aboriginal and non-Aboriginal people in urban areas about Aboriginal cultures. The program's objective should be to promote greater mutual understanding between the Aboriginal and non-Aboriginal urban populations and to help eradicate the ignorance that some urban Aboriginal people say is the root cause of racism and discrimination directed against them. As we were told in Edmonton:

> Without knowledge of and access to these cultures and without public understanding of what these cultures are, we will lose our identity. Canadians must be educated....

Denis Tardiff
Association canadienne-française
Edmonton, Alberta, 11 June 1992

Supporting Aboriginal cultural identity in urban areas involves concerted efforts on the part of many organizations and institutions: developing curricula that include Aboriginal history, languages, cultural values and spirituality; publishing directories of Aboriginal urban services and networks for the information of Aboriginal and non-Aboriginal urban populations; remedying historical and present-day distortions of Aboriginal identity by presenting authentic portrayals of Aboriginal peoples, cultures and history.

1.5 Conclusion

Many urban Aboriginal people see their Aboriginal identity as the core of their existence. They derive substantial self-esteem from being Aboriginal, but they also face difficulties because of isolation from the home community, lack of family support, the constant barrage of non-Aboriginal values and experiences, and the need to deal with non-Aboriginal agencies and institutions with different value bases. While urban Aboriginal people want Aboriginal-controlled cultural institutions that will foster and reinforce their cultural identities, non-Aboriginal institutions must also become a source of positive support for Aboriginal cultural identities.

Recent years have seen significant efforts to rekindle the flame of Aboriginal cultural identity. Aboriginal culture is being revitalized in cities across Canada. Many urban Aboriginal people are creating bicultural identities for themselves, participating successfully in non-Aboriginal society while developing an identity firmly rooted in Aboriginal culture. They are creating adaptive strategies to cope with a changing environment by choosing alternatives that do not require them to give up their identity and that may contribute to maintaining or reviving their traditional culture.

Aboriginal people believe their presence strengthens the fabric of Canada. Canada's culture is enriched by their cultures. Canada's cities, too, have an obligation to recognize and embrace the cultural identities of urban Aboriginal people and their connections to the cities' historical and contemporary roles. Sustaining positive Aboriginal cultural identities in urban Canada is the responsibility of all Canadians, our governments and our institutions.

RECOMMENDATION

The Commission recommends that

Cultural Identity   4.7.1

Aboriginal cultural identity be supported and enhanced in urban areas by

(a) Aboriginal, municipal, territorial, provincial and federal governments initiating programs to increase opportunities to promote Aboriginal culture in urban communities, including means to increase access to Aboriginal elders;

(b) municipal governments and institutions and Aboriginal elders co-operating to find ways of facilitating Aboriginal spiritual practices in the urban environment; and

(c) all governments co-operating to set aside land in urban areas dedicated to Aboriginal cultural and spiritual needs.

2. FINANCING OF SOCIAL PROGRAMS
FOR PEOPLE OFF ABORIGINAL TERRITORY

We learned from many who testified at the Commission's hearings that wrangling between governments over jurisdiction with regard to Aboriginal people has resulted in inequities in the provision of services to Aboriginal people living on- and off-reserve. Many called this the most critical issue facing urban Aboriginal people. The issue has three facets.

First, urban Aboriginal people do not receive the same level of services and benefits that First Nations people living on-reserve or Inuit living in their communities obtain from the federal government. Many status people who have moved to the city believe they are disadvantaged because they are not eligible to receive all the services to which they had access on-reserve. Métis people have little access to federal programs because the federal government has been unwilling to acknowledge its constitutional responsibility for them.

Second, urban Aboriginal people often have difficulty gaining access to provincial programs available to other residents. Some provincial authorities operate on the principle that the federal government should take responsibility for all status Indians, regardless of where they live. Many individual service providers simply do not know what programs – federal, provincial, territorial or municipal – are available to Aboriginal people.

Third, although urban Aboriginal people are eligible for federal and provincial services and programs that are available to all citizens, they would like access to culturally appropriate programs that would meet their needs more effectively.

Jurisdiction with regard to urban Aboriginal people is confused at best. Intergovernmental and inter-agency squabbling is common. All levels of government and many Aboriginal organizations and service agencies are involved in urban Aboriginal initiatives. All too often the result is uncoordinated and inconsistent service delivery. The frustration of attempting to deliver services while struggling to obtain adequate program funding and deal with fractured jurisdiction is evident in the words of one participant in the Commission's round table on urban issues:

> Most of us are always fighting over dollars, to keep our administration going, to house ourselves, and look after our administration costs, whether we're Métis, Treaty, whatever....[W]e give people the runaround now when they come into the city. Well, you're Treaty and you've not been here one year so you go to this place. But, oh no, you've been here a year already so you go to this place. Well, you're Métis, you have to go somewhere else. It's too confusing for people.[25]

This section examines issues surrounding federal and provincial responsibilities for social programs (health, social assistance and education) as these concern Aboriginal people living off-reserve. First, we outline the jurisdiction of federal and provincial governments regarding Aboriginal peoples. We then review federal and provincial roles in the financing of social programs. We also identify some of the repercussions of current restraint efforts, including the Canada health and social transfer. We go on to summarize the Commission's proposals for sharing financial responsibility and examine the provincial role in financing social services to non-reserve Aboriginal people. Finally, we argue that the federal government should continue to be responsible for financing benefits derived from treaty obligations or policy measures benefiting status Indians living off-reserve when these exceed provincial benefits available to all residents.

The federal government currently finances a number of programs for people with Indian status living on-reserve. Some of these also apply to people with Indian status living off-reserve. Many of these programs arise from obligations undertaken in the historical treaties (see Volume 2, Chapter 2). Some of these obligations relate to individuals (post-secondary education, uninsured health benefits); others are clearly collective (the inherent right of self-government). Treaty beneficiaries regard the former and perhaps aspects of the latter not only as treaty rights but as portable rights, that is, as applying regardless of where beneficiaries live. The federal government takes the position that many of these benefits are extended to people with Indian status on the basis of policy rather than treaty right. The Commission's view is that there are strong grounds to believe that, based on the oral exchanges and understandings arrived at during negotiation of the historical treaties, the beneficiaries of at least the numbered treaties should enjoy many of these benefits as a matter of treaty right.

2.1 Jurisdiction

Federal role

Under the *Constitution Act, 1867*, section 91(24), jurisdiction over "Indians, and Lands reserved for the Indians" is assigned exclusively to the federal government. This federal jurisdiction applies to persons registered under the *Indian Act* and, as a result of judicial interpretation, to Inuit.[26] The federal government, however, has continued to resist arguments that Métis people are included within the scope of section 91(24), despite their inclusion in section 35 of the *Constitution Act, 1982*.[27] The relationship established by the treaties between Aboriginal peoples and the Crown, in addition to the traditional role assumed by the federal government to provide for the housing and education needs of Aboriginal people living on-reserve, has confirmed federal primacy over Aboriginal concerns.

The federal government also asserts that section 91(24) of the *Constitution Act, 1867* allows it to exercise jurisdiction over Aboriginal people, but does not require it to take responsibility for them. In other words, the federal government maintains that it can choose to exercise its jurisdiction or not.[28] It has generally taken the position that it is responsible for status Indians living on-reserve. In its view, obligations owed to all other Aboriginal people, including status Indians living permanently off-reserve, are the responsibility of the provinces:

> The federal government...believed that its obligations were generally limited to reserve borders. Any federal activities beyond these territorial limits were defined as *ex gratia* and restricted to band members still residing on reserve and those temporarily absent or in the process of changing their domicile. Thus, all expenditures and responsibilities for off-reserve residents (other than for specified time periods, or in the context of specific programs such as post-secondary education, or those with physical or mental handicaps requiring specialized assistance) were left to the provinces.[29]

The federal government, primarily through the Department of Indian Affairs and Northern Development (DIAND), funds a wide range of services for status Indians living on-reserve and some services for Inuit. Other federal departments and agencies, such as Health Canada and the Canada Mortgage and Housing Corporation, also fund on-reserve programs. Bands (and in some cases tribal councils or provincial or territorial Aboriginal organizations) may, depending on the size of the reserve and other factors, provide a range of services: education, health, policing, housing, economic development, alcohol rehabilitation, libraries, cultural education centres, daycare, child and family services, justice, senior citizens' programs, recreation, social assistance, counselling, natural resource management, infrastructure development and municipal services. Many programs have been developed and are delivered in a culturally appropriate manner that differs markedly from general non-Aboriginal social service programs. Many bands operate their own schools, for example, exercising administrative and fiscal control. Some have developed innovative Aboriginal language and cultural curricula. Funding for the schools is provided by DIAND on a per-student basis.

A number of culturally based services and programs are available to First Nations people on-reserve and to Inuit in their own communities. DIAND funds a cultural/educational centres program under which more than 70 centres, located mainly on reserves, offer cultural services such as museums, cultural research, elders' programs, curriculum development and cultural events.

A few federally funded programs are available to people with Indian status (whether residing on- or off-reserve) and Inuit. The most important are non-insured health benefits and post-secondary educational assistance. The medical services branch of Health Canada pays for non-insured health benefits, including dental services, eyeglasses, prescription drugs, medical devices and medical transportation. DIAND provides financial support for status Indians and Inuit enroled in post-secondary educational institutions (see Volume 3, Chapters 3 and 5).

Provincial role

Section 92 of the *Constitution Act, 1867* reserves to provincial legislatures the exclusive competence to make laws in relation to a number of matters. The most significant in the present context are public lands, health care and hospitals, social services, municipal institutions and government, property and civil rights, the administration of justice, and education. The relationship between federal jurisdiction over "Indians, and Lands reserved for the Indians" and many aspects of provincial jurisdiction, such as education and health, lies at the root of the confusion over responsibility in urban and off-reserve areas. The federal government's position – that it may choose whether to exercise its jurisdiction – has been a continuing source of conflict with the provinces:

> Thus the federal government believes it is *legally* entitled to say to the provinces: "We're not going to spend money on Aboriginal people any more; it's up to you." Saskatchewan disagrees with that statement of the law. We argue that jurisdiction and responsibility go together. The federal government has the jurisdiction and responsibility to regulate banking in Canada. Provinces have the jurisdiction and responsibility in relation to matters of a local and private nature. So, too, the federal government has jurisdiction and responsibility in relation to Aboriginal peoples.[30]

Constitutionally, provincial government jurisdiction with regard to Aboriginal people has been confined to non-reserve activities, particularly in instances where people lost their Indian status, or when land was surrendered to the Crown. Symbolically, provincial jurisdiction too often signalled a loss of rights and status for Aboriginal people.

Nevertheless, provincial governments have played a significant role in the lives of Aboriginal people. Provincial laws of general application that do not touch on 'Indianness' apply to Aboriginal people.[31] In addition, section 88 of the *Indian Act* authorizes the application of provincial laws that affect the status or capacity of Indians so long as they are not inconsistent with treaties or federal law.[32] Consequently, a variety of provincial laws apply to on-reserve activities, including provincial adoption and labour-relations laws.[33] On-reserve Indian people also have access to provincially insured medical services. Between the federal and provincial governments, as former Chief Justice Dickson described it, there is a "fluidity of responsibility across lines of jurisdiction" regarding Aboriginal peoples.[34]

Provincial governments, therefore, play a major role in providing services and programs to Aboriginal people. For the most part, the services and programs are those provided to all citizens of the province, such as education and health and social services. All Aboriginal people, including urban residents, are eligible. For example, income maintenance programs such as general welfare assistance and family benefits are provided to Aboriginal people in the same way as to any provincial resident; the benefits are paid by the province and the cost is shared by the provincial and federal governments (formerly under the Canada Assistance Plan and now under the Canada Health and Social Transfer, which came into effect on 1 April 1996).

In recent years, some provinces have begun to develop and fund Aboriginal-specific services to meet the needs of Aboriginal people in areas such as child and family services, health, justice, recreation, training and natural resource management. Most are directed to people living on reserves and are not available to urban Aboriginal people. The programs and services are administered by bands, tribal councils or provincial and territorial Aboriginal associations and are seen in some cases as part of a move to support self-government. They are generally more limited than comparable federally funded programs.

Provinces have also funded a limited number of Aboriginal-specific programs in urban areas. For example, urban friendship centres receive project money from the provincial government in most provinces (although their core funding is provided by the federal government). Some provinces have recently begun to include urban Aboriginal people in more significant policy and program initiatives. In 1994, the government of Ontario announced the Aboriginal health and wellness strategy – a five-year, $33-million program that involves four ministries and includes services for Aboriginal people living both on- and off-reserve.[35]

2.2 Fiscal Offloading

Both the federal and provincial governments, however, have occasionally used divided jurisdiction to limit their own responsibility for Aboriginal peoples.[36] For example, the *Indian Act* is silent regarding the provision of social services to Indian people living on-reserve. Provincial governments traditionally have declined to take financial responsibility for providing social assistance and child welfare services on-reserve. Some of the policy vacuum has been filled by federal-provincial agreements, such as the Indian Welfare Agreement of 1965, under which the federal government agreed to reimburse the Ontario government for about 92 per cent of the cost of delivering certain social services on-reserve. This has hampered devolution of social services to First Nations; provincial devolution has been limited until recently to services that the federal government has agreed to cost-share.[37]

The jurisdictional difficulties in providing social programs have been compounded by provincial reluctance to provide social assistance to Aboriginal people who have lived away from a reserve for less than a year. The federal government has shown a corresponding reluctance to provide support to individuals no longer living on-reserve. Recently, for example, the federal government ceased to provide full reimbursement to provinces for social assistance delivered to status Indians during the first year after they leave a reserve.

The resulting jurisdictional impasse has led to confusion among urban Aboriginal people about responsibility for social services and to their distrust and disillusionment with both levels of government. This has taken the form of profound resistance to devolution of responsibility from the federal to the provincial governments, particularly for treaty entitlements. According to a recent Alberta health ministry report: "First Nations people are afraid that if the province takes on the service responsibilities that they consider to be treaty rights, the Canadian government will be in a stronger position to argue that these health services are not rights".[38] Instead, Aboriginal organizations have called for the expansion of federal responsibility for Aboriginal people living both on- and off-reserve.[39]

Federal responsibility under the treaties and jurisdiction under section 91(24), together with provincial reluctance to assume financial responsibility for Aboriginal people, has contributed to Aboriginal people's desire to forestall any transfer of responsibility to provincial governments. Aboriginal people fear that the federal government will attempt to avoid its fiduciary duty and cut costs by transferring responsibility to provincial governments.[40] Indeed, some interveners suggested that the federal government was deliberately encouraging Aboriginal people to move away from reserves in order to reduce its financial obligations.[41]

In its efforts to manage its fiscal position, the federal government has limited the growth of expenditures related to a number of existing Aboriginal programs by capping them. It has also cut funding for some programs and has generally been reluctant to implement new programs. This has resulted in pressure on the provinces to assume responsibility for some essential programs. In some cases, this pressure has been redirected to municipal governments. In all cases, this development has given rise to considerable tension between the federal government and the provinces.

In Manitoba, for example, the 1992 throne speech stressed the need for more intergovernmental co-operation and noted that all provinces have opposed the "persistent pattern of federal government offloading of costs and responsibilities onto provincial and local governments. Federal offloading has affected virtually the entire range of public services, including training, off-reserve social services and agricultural support".[42] Offloading has, in turn, been a source of frustration in relations between provincial governments and Aboriginal people. Federal program cuts and reluctance to consider new programs push Aboriginal people to seek financial support from provincial governments, only to be met with the response that the provinces are themselves squeezed by federal reluctance to accept responsibility for Aboriginal people.

The federal government has historically covered all or at least part of the cost of some services (for example, child and family services and general welfare) for status Indians living off-reserve. People applied to the appropriate provincial or municipal agency, which delivered the service and was reimbursed by the federal government, usually through DIAND. The eligibility period was often limited, usually to one year after leaving the reserve. DIAND consistently took the position that funding services for people living off-reserve was a matter of policy, not a treaty right. In fact, application of the policy varied considerably from province to province.

The federal government's recent termination of full reimbursement of provinces for social assistance payments to off-reserve status Indians has been a particular source of tension between the provinces and the federal government, especially in the west. In Saskatchewan, for example, it has imposed a significant strain on the provincial budget and could adversely affect the development of Aboriginal programs in the future:

> Unilateral off-loading by the federal government has already cost Saskatchewan hundreds of millions of dollars. We have been warned to expect the federal government to announce further off-loading of social assistance payments to status Indians during the first year that they move off the reserve. This move would increase social services costs to the province by almost $20 million annually leaving the province of Saskatchewan with no options or hope for the future, given our reality. Increased costs in one area dictate reductions somewhere else.[43]

As a result of the confusion surrounding jurisdiction, policies have evolved ad hoc, with a great deal of variation between provinces. Most provinces have been reluctant to begin providing services directed specifically to urban Aboriginal people, given their views on the federal government's responsibilities. Indeed, some provinces have reduced funding for Aboriginal urban programs. Given the evident and serious need, however, all provinces have had to provide some services for Aboriginal people in addition to general programs available to all urban residents.

One example of the vacuum resulting from disputes over jurisdiction is found in Manitoba. Since the 1960s, DIAND had been funding social services provided to off-reserve status Indians in accordance with the terms of the Manitoba *Municipalities Act* for a 'transition' period of one year after leaving the reserve. To be eligible for services under the act, an individual must have lived in an urban area consecutively for one year and be self-supporting. In practice, many First Nations people never qualified because of frequent migration back and forth between the city and the reserve. A large percentage were also unable to meet the definition of 'self-supporting'. The federal government therefore continued to pay for social services for many individuals for more than one year. In 1991, it announced that it would no longer pay the full cost of social assistance for off-reserve status Indians. The funding arrangement would be replaced by the 50 per cent reimbursement available under the Canada Assistance Plan. The saving was to be reinvested in on-reserve child and family service agencies, mostly outside Manitoba.

When full reimbursement ceased, the province transferred funding responsibility to municipalities. It continued to bill the federal government, without success, and for a period municipalities provided services without full compensation. Municipalities then announced they would stop providing services. For a short time, off-reserve status Indians were denied social assistance. DIAND relented slightly, indicating that it would temporarily reimburse First Nations for assistance provided to off-reserve people who had been refused provincial and municipal assistance. In 1992, Manitoba announced that it would provide full reimbursement for off-reserve status Indians as an interim measure until another arrangement could be worked out among the federal government, the province and First Nations. But no discussions have taken place, and the issue remains unresolved.

Although provincial governments continue to insist that the federal government must assume its full constitutional responsibility for all Aboriginal people under section 91(24) of the *Constitution Act, 1867*, it is important to recognize that provincial governments have been major policy players in Aboriginal affairs in the past, especially in urban areas, and do in fact have some financial responsibility for Aboriginal matters. There is a critical need for the federal and provincial governments to clarify their respective legal and fiscal responsibilities.

2.3 Federal-Provincial Fiscal Arrangements

Following the Second World War, economic growth and higher government revenues brought with them an opportunity to develop new social programs to deal with some of the adverse effects of a market economy.[44] As provincial governments expanded health, education, income maintenance, and social services their interactions with Aboriginal people multiplied. The federal government entered the social services field by helping provinces with the cost of post-secondary education, health services and welfare. Although these matters were beyond federal legislative control, the federal government could help shape social policy through use of its spending power.

Aboriginal people experience the social and economic conditions that give rise to a need for social assistance in disproportionate numbers.[45] As many Aboriginal people face barriers to participation in the mainstream economy, for example, they experience a greater incidence of poverty and higher rates of dependency on social services.[46]

At the same time, many Aboriginal people contribute productively to economic life, regionally and nationally. As systemic barriers to Aboriginal participation in the economy are removed, dependence on social assistance will diminish and economic productivity increase. Aboriginal individuals' socio-economic fortunes are linked to the fortunes of all provincial and territorial residents. Provincial governments therefore have an incentive to promote the development of Aboriginal residents' health and productivity.

Until recently, the federal government helped finance provincial programs through three major transfer programs: equalization grants, Established Program Financing (EPF) and cost-sharing under the Canada Assistance Plan (CAP).[47]

Equalization grants are unconditional transfers paid to 'have-not' provinces to raise their capacity to deliver public services to a representative provincial standard. Their underlying principle, recognized in section 36 of the *Constitution Act, 1982*, is "to ensure that provincial governments have sufficient revenues to provide reasonably comparable levels of public services at reasonably comparable levels of taxation".

EPF cash transfers, payable to all provinces, were equal to the difference between an annually calculated 'entitlement' and the revenue provinces derive from tax transfers. This entitlement, representing a federal share in provincial health and post-secondary education expenditures, has been subject to varying annual adjustments related to population and economic growth. EPF cash transfers were unconditional block grants until 1984. In that year, the *Canada Health Act* rendered EPF cash transfers conditional on provincial health insurance plans meeting five standards: that they be comprehensive, universal, portable, accessible and publicly administered.[48]

The Canada Assistance Plan was an open-ended cost-sharing program under which the federal government financed 50 per cent of provincial expenditures on welfare allowances and social services provided to persons in need. The enabling federal legislation specified 'need', but left the definition of this criterion to the individual provinces.[49] Interprovincial variations in welfare allowances are substantial: in 1991, for example, the allowance for a single-parent, one-child family in Ontario was 23 per cent higher than that of the second most generous province, British Columbia, and 63 per cent higher than the allowance in New Brunswick.[50]

Since the mid-1980s, fiscal restraint measures have been instituted to slow the annual rate of growth in equalization grants and EPF entitlements. Ontario, British Columbia and Alberta challenged the ability of the federal government to limit payments under CAP. The ensuing court challenge was unsuccessful; the Supreme Court of Canada confirmed the principle of parliamentary supremacy – federal-provincial agreements between governments bind governments but not Parliament.[51]

The latest federal initiative affecting intergovernmental transfers will generate further downward pressures. In 1996-97 EPF and CAP are being amalgamated into a single block transfer called the Canada Health and Social Transfer (CHST).[52] The transfer is bound only by the continuing provisions of the *Canada Health Act* and does not discriminate based on residency. It will be allocated to provinces in accordance with their combined EPF and CAP allocation in 1995-96. Federal spending on CHST in 1996-97 will be $3.5 billion less than the amount spent on EPF and CAP in 1995-96. In 1997-98, CHST spending is scheduled to fall by another $2.5 billion.

2.4 The Commission's Proposals

It is in this climate of fiscal restraint that the Commission proposes clarification of federal and provincial responsibility for financing treaty entitlements and social programs.

We propose that the federal government assume the full cost of establishing self-government for Aboriginal nations on the extended territories that result from treaty negotiations (see Volume 2, Chapter 2), as well as off a land base, including whatever treaty rights are currently in place or arise from those negotiations. This would mean that the cost of existing social programs on reserves or in Inuit communities would continue to be the responsibility of the federal government until the programs were assumed by Aboriginal governments; at that time, the cost would be covered through fiscal arrangements. The federal government would also continue to cover the cost of treaty entitlements for Aboriginal people living off Aboriginal territory where these costs relate to benefits not ordinarily available or in excess of those available to other provincial or territorial residents.

In addition, we propose that the federal government cover the cost of these programs for Métis people living on Métis lands when these are established through treaty negotiations. Once self-government and an appropriate land base have been negotiated with Métis people, financing these services would be the subject of fiscal arrangements similar to those of other Aboriginal nations, including any additional payments to Métis people living off their territory to cover benefits in excess of those available to other provincial residents that had been agreed to in treaty negotiations. (Arrangements for financing self-government are detailed in Volume 2, Chapter 3.)

We recommend that provincial and territorial governments be responsible for financing social services to Aboriginal people living off Aboriginal territory that are ordinarily available to other provincial or territorial residents (such as secondary education and insured health services).

Aboriginal people living on-reserve generally benefit from social services delivered in a more culturally sensitive manner. Not only do Aboriginal people elect to be served by Aboriginal agencies if given the choice, but there are also "encouraging signs that programs delivered by Aboriginal Peoples are more effective in attaining their objectives than are programs designed and delivered by non-Aboriginal people for Aboriginal people".[53] We propose that the development of culturally appropriate services for Aboriginal people living off

Aboriginal territories where numbers warrant, and the continuing provision of those services, be the responsibility of provincial governments.

We believe the proposed division of responsibility for financing social services for Aboriginal people on and off Aboriginal territories has merit for several reasons. First, this division establishes clear lines of accountability, reinforcing the precepts of democratic government.[54] The governments (whether Aboriginal or provincial) responsible for entitlements or services are accountable to the individuals who are eligible to receive them. As Aboriginal people become financially independent, they will become a source of tax revenue for the government that delivers services to them.

Second, the proposal has the merit of respecting traditional lines of constitutional responsibility. The provinces continue to have financial responsibility for services such as health, welfare and education, assigned to them by the *Constitution Act, 1867*. While provinces are not entitled constitutionally to legislate in regard to matters affecting Aboriginal or treaty rights, there is nothing to prevent provincial laws that do not "abrogate or qualify treaty rights"[55] or that "*preferentially* single out Aboriginal persons or institutions" for purposes of affirmative action.[56] The federal government continues to bear responsibility for entitlements that arise out of the treaties over and above services normally provided by provincial governments. These are continuing obligations that have distinguished the federal government's relationship with Aboriginal peoples from that of most provincial governments.

2.5 Rationale for Provincial Role: The Right to Equality of Treatment

Aboriginal people have expressed concern about provincial governments assuming responsibility for financing social services for Aboriginal people off Aboriginal territory to the level of benefits available to other provincial residents. Some see this as tantamount to a limitation on existing Aboriginal and treaty rights, offending section 35 of the *Constitution Act, 1982*.

Aboriginal people see their relationship with the Crown as being primarily with the Crown in right of Canada.[57] Jurisdiction over "Indians, and Lands reserved for the Indians" was assigned constitutionally to the federal government. Conceptions about the superior constitutional and fiscal power of the federal government lend support to Aboriginal peoples' view. At the same time, the doctrine of parliamentary supremacy empowers Parliament to make or unmake any law within its jurisdiction, subject to the application of the *Canadian Charter of Rights and Freedoms* and the rights of the Aboriginal peoples of Canada. In addition, the doctrine of paramountcy, a principle of Canadian constitutional interpretation, provides that in the event of an operational conflict between federal and provincial laws, the federal law will take precedence.

Judicial interpretation has held that, by virtue of the *Constitution Act, 1867*, as well as custom and usage, the relationship between the British Crown and Aboriginal peoples in British North America devolved to the Crown in right of Canada and to the Crown in right of the individual provinces.[58] This is because Canada, unlike Great Britain, is a federation in which Parliament and the provincial legislatures are sovereign only in the areas of jurisdiction assigned to them by the constitution.[59] This has led to many of the jurisdictional disputes between the federal and provincial governments that have had such a detrimental effect on Aboriginal peoples. While the federal government has responsibility for First Nations and their lands under section 91(24) and hence is the appropriate party to all treaties with them, the provincial governments have exclusive jurisdiction over areas such as education, health and property, and civil rights within the province. The potential for conflict regarding which level of government should honour obligations to Aboriginal peoples in these areas is thus built into the constitution and must be resolved in a way that represents an equitable sharing of responsibility between governments. However – and this is our paramount concern – the sharing must be done in a way that ensures that all obligations to all Aboriginal people are fully honoured and respected.

Section 35 of the *Constitution Act, 1982*, which recognizes and affirms Aboriginal and treaty rights, is binding on both orders of government and requires them to end their jurisdictional wrangling and reach an accommodation regarding how Canada's obligations to Aboriginal people are to be fully and effectively discharged.

As pointed out by the Supreme Court of Canada in *Guerin* and *Sparrow*, Canada's relationship with Aboriginal peoples is a fiduciary one, trust-like in nature. Both orders of government must act in ways that honour this historical relationship between Canada and Aboriginal peoples.[60]

Provinces cannot discriminate in the treatment of their residents on grounds of personal characteristics that are irrelevant to the nature of the benefit or service being provided. Section 15(1) of the *Canadian Charter of Rights and Freedoms*, the equality section, forbids such discrimination.

This does not mean, however, that services provided to residents can ignore significant cultural differences in the intended recipients. For example, health services delivered to Aboriginal people must reflect a holistic approach to health, and educational curricula and programs should include an Aboriginal perspective on the history of Canada. An obligation to provide services is an obligation to provide them in ways culturally appropriate to those entitled to receive them.

Section 15(2) goes further, however, making it clear that the right to equality addresses more than just the manner in which benefits or services made available to all are to be provided. It also addresses the nature and extent of the services to disadvantaged individuals or groups in order to ameliorate their disadvantage. It authorizes affirmative action programs by specifying that these do not constitute violations of section 15(1). Under section 15(2), it is equality of outcomes that is important. Treating individuals or groups who are already disadvantaged or unequal in the same way as those who are not will not ameliorate the first group's disadvantage; it will build upon and perpetuate it.

The purpose of section 15(2) is remedial. It answers the question, "How does one remedy an existing disadvantage?", not by providing the same treatment to a disadvantaged group as to others, but by making sure they are treated in a way that removes their disadvantage and brings them to a position of equality with others.

Those opposed to remedying disadvantage in our society call this 'reverse discrimination', refusing to acknowledge the clear intent of the charter that remedying existing disadvantage or inequality by affirmative action under section 15(2) does not constitute discrimination for purposes of section 15(1).

The affirmative action exception appears in almost all provincial human rights codes, as well as in the *Canadian Charter of Rights and Freedoms*, and applies to the provision of benefits and services to Aboriginal people by the federal, provincial and territorial governments and also through provincial governments to municipal governments.[61]

Although provinces are barred under section 88 of the *Indian Act* from legislating in ways that impair the "status or capacity" of Aboriginal people,[62] they are perfectly free to deliver programs that improve the social conditions of Aboriginal people – as, indeed, they ought to do in the case of manifest disadvantage.[63]

In the Commission's view, therefore, provinces are obliged to provide services to all their residents, Aboriginal and non-Aboriginal alike, without discrimination; this includes making sure that such services are provided in a culturally appropriate manner. In addition, provinces faced with glaring inequalities in the living conditions of their Aboriginal and non-Aboriginal residents should in the interests of equality institute special programs designed to remedy these inequities. Moreover, no distinction should be made in the delivery of services between Aboriginal residents who have recently moved from a reserve and those who have been living off-reserve for some time.

A reasonable division of the financial burden between the federal and provincial governments would be for the federal government to assume the cost of culturally appropriate services for Aboriginal people on-reserve and provincial governments to assume their cost for Aboriginal residents in their province, where numbers warrant. The cost of special programs and services for Aboriginal residents required by human rights policy – over and above those ordinarily provided to other provincial residents – should be shared by the federal and provincial governments based on an agreed formula. This would include benefits and services required to remedy the long-standing disadvantage of

Aboriginal people and to bring their standard of living up to the level enjoyed by other Canadians.

2.6 Conclusion

Wrangling over jurisdiction has impeded urban Aboriginal people's access to services. Intergovernmental disputes, federal and provincial offloading, lack of program co-ordination, exclusion of municipal governments and urban Aboriginal groups from discussions and negotiations on policy and jurisdictional issues, and confusion regarding the political representation of Aboriginal people in cities have all contributed to a situation that has had serious adverse effects on the ability of Aboriginal people to gain access to appropriate services in urban centres. Seen in the light of the fiduciary duties owed to Aboriginal people by the federal and provincial Crowns; the obligation of provincial governments to provide services to off-reserve Indian people to achieve equality with other provincial residents; and the federal government's continuing financial role in supplementing, where appropriate, benefits provided by the provinces, inter-jurisdictional wrangling cannot be allowed to stand in the way of improvements in the social and economic conditions of urban Aboriginal people.

The issues are complex and multi-layered. Ultimately, their successful resolution will depend on the goodwill of all governments to find fair and workable solutions despite fiscal constraints. Aboriginal governments, no less than other governments, will be expected to devise self-government arrangements in this context of economic restructuring and fiscal constraint. It would be preferable for non-Aboriginal governments to adopt an approach to fiscal responsibility that enhances Aboriginal governmental autonomy while at the same time respecting the equal citizenship rights of all Canadians.

RECOMMENDATIONS

The Commission recommends that

Financing Social Programs

4.7.2

The federal government be responsible for

(a) the costs associated with developing, implementing and operating Aboriginal self-government initiatives on and off a land base through program funding and fiscal arrangements;

(b) programs, services and treaty entitlements for Aboriginal people living on reserves or extended Aboriginal territories;

(c) treaty entitlements or agreed upon social programs such as financial assistance for post-secondary education and uninsured health benefits for Indian people living off-reserve, to the extent that these exceed the programs or services provided to other residents by the province or territory in which they reside; and

(d) the cost of services for Métis people agreed to in treaty negotiations, once they have achieved self-government and a land base, including additional payments to Métis people living off their land base to cover benefits agreed to by treaty where those exceed benefits normally available to other provincial residents.

4.7.3
Provincial and territorial governments be responsible for

(a) providing and financing the programs and services that are available to residents in general, to all Aboriginal people residing in the province or territory, except those resident on-reserve, in Inuit communities or on extended Aboriginal territory; and

(b) providing programs and services for Aboriginal people that are culturally appropriate where numbers warrant.

Given the economically and socially disadvantaged situation of many Aboriginal people living in urban centres, some programs and services will require enrichment so that Aboriginal people can begin to enjoy the same quality of life as other Canadians. Responsibility for funding these enhancements should be shared between the federal and provincial/territorial governments. (For greater detail, see Volume 2, Chapter 3.)

RECOMMENDATION

The Commission recommends that

Financing 4.7.4
Affirmative Action   The cost of affirmative action programs and services to address
Programs   economic and social disadvantage affecting urban Aboriginal
people be shared by the federal, provincial and territorial governments on the basis of a formula basis that reflects provincial/territorial fiscal capacity.

3. Service Delivery

This section looks at some of the important issues in the delivery of health and social services, education and cultural policy to urban Aboriginal people, from the perspective of both users and providers. Among the services that may play a part in the daily lives of many urban Aboriginal people and families are child and family services, counselling of various types, community health, training and employment, referrals, social assistance, alcohol and drug rehabilitation, and low-cost housing. These services are delivered variously by Aboriginal organizations (either specific to a particular Aboriginal group or 'status-blind') and by non-Aboriginal agencies also serving non-Aboriginal clients. The number, range and nature of these organizations vary considerably from place to place in Canada.

3.1 The Current Situation: Issues, Needs and Problems

In many urban areas, there are significant numbers of programs and services for Aboriginal people delivered by federal, provincial and municipal governments, non-government organizations and Aboriginal agencies. Despite this extensive infra-structure, service delivery is hampered by difficulties and weaknesses. Many Aboriginal people who testified at Commission hearings described services as inadequate, not culturally relevant and sometimes even hostile. For many, services are not accessible because Aboriginal people cannot afford them or do not qualify. Many services required to make a successful transition to urban centres – or simply to enjoy a quality of life similar to that of non-Aboriginal people – are not available or are in very short supply. Housing is one example: Aboriginal housing corporations in urban areas have waiting lists of 100 or more.[64] As reported by an Ontario task force on urban Aboriginal people as long ago as 1981, respondents' access to housing is limited by the shortage of housing, discrimination by land-lords, limited finances, and limited information about housing availability. The situation has not changed substantially since then; shortages of housing are real, and the consequences for Aboriginal people in all parts of the province are painful.[65]

Métis senator Thelma Chalifoux told the Commission of the difficulty that seniors and veterans have obtaining housing and other basic services in urban areas:

> There are no homes for our Métis seniors or Indian seniors living off-reserve. There are no services for them. They are totally isolated because the existing services do not have Aboriginal people that could look in on them and counsel them....Our veterans are in the same boat. I visit veterans that live in one little shack, one little room, and they have nothing, and they're too proud to ask.
>
> Senator Thelma Chalifoux
> Metis Nation of Alberta
> Winnipeg, Manitoba, 21 April 1992

3.2 Cultural Appropriateness

Many urban services designed for the general population are not culturally relevant to Aboriginal people. As a result, cultural and spiritual needs go largely unmet. Aboriginal people made a strong case for holistic services that recognize and work to heal the whole person. But most social and human services are designed to address specific problems, such as unemployment or child neglect, and as such focus on symptoms rather than the underlying causes. Aboriginal people need and should have culturally appropriate services, designed by Aboriginal people, that promote healing through a holistic approach to individuals and communities.

Many services and programs are delivered by non-Aboriginal people and agencies that lack cultural training and awareness of Aboriginal reality. As a result, they tend to view conditions as isolated problems and to see the individual as being deficient or unable to fit into predetermined categories. Participants in the Commission's round table talks on urban issues described the traumatic consequences of this approach. For example, many Aboriginal women are reluctant to report sexual abuse or to enter substance abuse programs for fear that non-Aboriginal child welfare agencies will take their children away and place them in foster care, almost always in non-Aboriginal homes. As one participant said,

> Culturally appropriate counselling and care facilities with trained staff
> are required to deal with child abuse and incest. It won't work to place
> survivors in a non-Aboriginal environment. The whole family needs
> training, not just the victim. Aboriginal counsellors should be trained,
> and Aboriginal communities must take control of child and family
> services.[66]

Programs developed by mainstream service agencies do little to protect and enhance Aboriginal cultural identity because they are not designed to do so. They tend to have a very specific, one-dimensional focus. Their cultural unsuitability flows from the lack of direct Aboriginal involvement in their design, development and delivery. Aboriginal people and organizations are sharply under-utilized in all phases of programming, including monitoring and evaluation.

Some mainstream agencies and municipal governments have begun to realize that they cannot adequately meet the needs of urban Aboriginal people and are turning more frequently to Aboriginal agencies to provide services. But Aboriginal organizations and service agencies are severely underfunded, often operating on an ad hoc or short-term project-funding basis (see detailed examples in Volume 3, Chapter 3).[67] Unstable and fragmented funding arrangements make it impossible to plan and deliver quality services at an adequate level, and programs are often understaffed and overly dependent on unpaid and untrained volunteers. Burn-out of staff and volunteers is a constant problem as well. Administrators spend much of their time and energy seeking funding instead of delivering services.

Government funding for urban Aboriginal services has not kept pace with the growth of the urban Aboriginal population. Although 45 per cent of all Aboriginal people now live in urban areas, funding does not reflect this reality. Federal funding for programs such as the Aboriginal health program apply only to First Nations people living on reserves and Inuit living in their home communities. Aboriginal people living in urban areas are generally ineligible for these programs.

It is obvious that the current delivery system is seriously deficient in meeting the needs of urban Aboriginal people. They are being served by a system that is essentially foreign to them. Clearly, it must change.

3.3 Reform

The delivery of services to urban Aboriginal people must be improved in at least two important ways. First, in urban areas with a sufficiently large Aboriginal population, service delivery by Aboriginal institutions should be promoted by continuing to develop existing institutions and by supporting new initiatives. Second, services provided by non-Aboriginal institutions must be changed to improve access and cultural relevance. In addition, the question of whether service delivery should be 'status-blind' or be provided to each Aboriginal group by a separate institution must be addressed.

Aboriginal institutions

In many urban areas with large Aboriginal populations, service agencies and programs have evolved in the past two decades. By the fall of 1993, there were 35 to 40 Aboriginal agencies and organizations in Toronto providing services in education, health, community development and training, child and family services, housing, social services, legal services, and arts and cultural development. In Regina, approximately 25 Aboriginal agencies and non-government organizations were delivering services. As of the spring of 1994, Winnipeg had about 55 such agencies and organizations.

In cities such as Toronto, Winnipeg, Regina, Saskatoon and Edmonton, where Aboriginal residents number in the thousands, the need for and viability of Aboriginally controlled institutions seems clear. In urban centres where Aboriginal people are present in large numbers or make up an important proportion of the overall population, Aboriginal service institutions should be seen as fundamental to service delivery, not as discretionary initiatives. In addition to providing greatly needed services, they are also important vehicles for supporting Aboriginal identity. Moreover, since they are directed and administered by Aboriginal people, service institutions are also working examples of the community of interest model of self-government in urban centres. (See the discussion later in this chapter on governance for Aboriginal people in urban areas and, more generally, Volume 2, Chapter 3.)

In their presentations to the Commission, many Aboriginal people argued for urban Aboriginal service institutions that would, in addition to providing services, help to co-ordinate policy and planning for Aboriginal people in cities and provide a valuable link between reserve- or land-based service agencies and political entities in urban centres:

> Some of our recommendations are: the need for a provincial network of Aboriginal service providers established to function as a co-ordinating body for policy and planning; a restructuring of current service delivery institutions such as child welfare services to provide for the development of Aboriginal-controlled institutions that will deliver programming and services to Aboriginal clients; and processes to be established to provide for co-operative working relationships between urban- and reserve-based service agencies and political organizations.
>
> Marilyn Fontaine
> Aboriginal Women's Unity Coalition
> Winnipeg, Manitoba, 23 April 1992

A network of service institutions, especially in large urban areas, would promote consistent program delivery by developing and maintaining effective co-ordination with reserve- and rural-based agencies to ensure there are no gaps in the services provided to clients. For Aboriginal people new to urban life, an Aboriginal service agency can often make the difference between a relatively smooth transition and one marked by confusion and frustration.

Establishing an efficient and cohesive network of Aboriginal service delivery institutions does not necessarily require the creation of large numbers of new agencies and vast increases in funding. Many Aboriginal agencies already exist. In some cases, they are 'competing' for Aboriginal clients (and for funding based on the number of clients they attract) with non-Aboriginal agencies. Potential users are often unaware of their existence. Aboriginal people should not be expected to use only Aboriginal agencies. Where a qualified Aboriginal agency exists, however, non-Aboriginal agencies should inform Aboriginal people seeking services of its existence and, when requested, make appropriate referrals. Aboriginal and non-Aboriginal agencies providing services in the same area might also explore joint case-management arrangements.

Current expenditures could also be made much more effective. Most funding for urban services is channelled through non-Aboriginal agencies. It is not at all clear that the Aboriginal community benefits as much as it might from these expenditures, especially given the likely absence of Aboriginal representatives on many agency boards. To begin relieving chronic underfunding and ensure that benefits are better targeted, we believe priority should be given to redirecting an appropriate share of existing expenditures to Aboriginal service agencies.

Aboriginal service institutions should be seen as long-term responses to the needs of urban Aboriginal people. For struggling service institutions to develop effective institutional capacity, funding arrangements must become more predictable. Fragmented and ad hoc arrangements promote waste and dependency on the state. They undermine efforts to be accountable to the Aboriginal community and detract from long-term planning and human resources development.

RECOMMENDATIONS

The Commission recommends that

Aboriginal Service Institutions

4.7.5
Provincial, territorial and municipal governments give priority to making the existing Aboriginal service delivery system more comprehensive as the most effective means of meeting the immediate needs of urban Aboriginal people.

4.7.6
Federal, provincial and territorial governments ensure that existing and new Aboriginal service institutions have a stable and secure funding base by
(a) making contribution and grant agreements with Aboriginal service institutions for periods of at least five years; and
(b) adjusting funding for existing and new Aboriginal and non-Aboriginal agencies to reflect actual services provided and caseloads.

Non-Aboriginal institutions

Non-Aboriginal service agencies will continue to provide many services to Aboriginal people. Changes are urgently required to improve access, to involve Aboriginal people in the design, development and delivery of services, and to establish or enhance cross-cultural training. Aboriginal people should be closely involved in reviewing the cultural content of mainstream service delivery and recommending appropriate changes. Government employees working in Aboriginal policy and program development and service delivery should be among those who receive cross-cultural training. We were told that this should include immersion in Aboriginal communities and neighbourhoods.[68]

RECOMMENDATIONS

The Commission recommends that

Non-Aboriginal **4.7.7**
Service Agencies
Aboriginal people and organizations be directly involved in
the design, development, delivery and evaluation of all services
provided to Aboriginal clients by non-Aboriginal agencies.

4.7.8
Staff of non-Aboriginal service agencies directly involved in
Aboriginal service delivery be given cross-cultural training delivered by Aboriginal people and organizations and that government funding agreements reflect this obligation.

Status-blind versus separate institutions

There is debate in the Aboriginal community regarding how services should be provided, in particular whether an agency's services should be directed only to one
Aboriginal group or whether all groups should be served ('status-blind' services).

With regard to separate services, should Aboriginal service institutions be
autonomous and be an expression of self-government? Should they be accountable to an Aboriginal government? Some of the issues were outlined in a presentation to the Commission on behalf of the Métis National Council (MNC):

> While the MNC provincial affiliates have developed an extensive net-
> work of program and service delivery institutions, further work is
> required to determine what the most appropriate political structures
> would be required in a larger program and service delivery setting....
>
> Self-governing institutions would be similar, would be politically
> accountable, and may have a network of service delivery institutions
> not unlike what the anglophones have in Quebec. They have a very
> extensive network of program and service delivery.

> Marc LeClair
> Spokesperson, Métis National Council
> Toronto, Ontario, 26 June 1992

Many Métis and treaty people and organizations, particularly in the prairie
provinces, feel strongly that services should be provided on a 'Métis-only' or
'treaty-only' basis. Yvon Dumont, former president of the Métis National

Council, favoured separate services for Métis people in his remarks to the
Commission in Winnipeg:

> At the moment we are looking at strictly Métis institutions for Métis
> people. We feel that by agreeing to be lumped in with all other
> Aboriginal people, we run the chance of losing our identity as an
> Aboriginal people. So we feel that it is important that we concentrate
> right now on developing and protecting Métis culture and heritage.
>
> Yvon Dumont
> President, Manitoba Metis Federation
> Winnipeg, Manitoba, 22 April 1992

Many treaty people and organizations are also vehemently opposed to 'status-
blind' service delivery. Instead, they favour services developed by treaty people
for treaty people:

> As an assembly we...will strive to empower our people through the
> development of culturally appropriate programs and services for
> treaty people by treaty people.
>
> We feel that the responsibility to ensure that future generations
> will benefit from our treaty rights rests with the involvement of our
> people at all levels of government, particularly in the policy and deci-
> sion-making processes. There has to be a process that respects the
> aspirations of urban treaty peoples in the full and free exercise of our
> inherent rights to representation regardless of residency.
>
> Margaret King
> Saskatoon Treaty and First Nations Assembly
> Saskatoon, Saskatchewan, 28 October 1992

Other Aboriginal people and organizations maintain, however, that separate service delivery only reinforces 'divide and conquer' attitudes, and that services should therefore be delivered on a status-blind basis – all Aboriginal people
would qualify for a service, regardless of legal status or cultural heritage.

Some service providers maintain that establishing separate services in
urban centres would lead to services being run without sufficient control by the
clientele they serve and possibly by administrations that are out of touch with
urban needs. Status-blind services would help to overcome this difficulty. This
view was put forward to Commissioners in Winnipeg:

> The artificial division of Aboriginal people is inappropriate in the
> urban area. The urban Aboriginal community is committed to the
> development and delivery of services on a status-blind basis. Urban
> Aboriginal people must be self-determining. The urban Aboriginal
> community does not want to be annexed without any basic demo-

cratic rights, into a reserve/rural-based political system controlled by
an unresponsive leadership.

Marilyn Fontaine
Spokesperson, Aboriginal Women's Unity Coalition
Winnipeg, Manitoba, 23 April 1992

It has also been argued that status-blind delivery systems are more cost-effective
because they avoid duplication of services.[69]

It is clear that treaty and Métis people in the prairie provinces, especially
those closely associated with political organizations, are firmly in favour of separate service institutions. This is not surprising, given their long history of separate institutional development and the different paths they have taken in
seeking recognition. Currently, both have institutions or programs in education,
training, culture, housing, economic development, and child and family services.
Separate institutions have characterized the historical and practical experience
of Métis and treaty people in Manitoba, Saskatchewan and Alberta. Distinct
delivery structures are most common in Edmonton, Calgary, Regina, Saskatoon
and, to a slightly lesser degree, Winnipeg.

There is no such history in British Columbia, Ontario, Quebec, the
Atlantic provinces and the northern territories. In these areas generally, and
notably in the large urban centres of Vancouver, Victoria, Toronto, Montreal,
Quebec City, Halifax and Fredericton, service delivery is status-blind. For example, Métis Child and Family Services in Edmonton has been developed specifically for Métis people, while similar services provided through Ma Mawi Wi Chi
Itata Centre in Winnipeg and Native Child and Family Services in Toronto are
available to all Aboriginal people residing in those cities. Friendship centre services are delivered throughout Canada on a status-blind basis. There does not
seem to be strong support for introducing status-blind delivery for some types
of services and separate delivery for others.

We are persuaded by the success of friendship centres that status-blind service delivery is generally advantageous in urban areas, because it fosters development of an urban Aboriginal community and promotes efficient use of scarce
resources. However, policy development and implementation should also recognize the historical and geographic realities that have motivated the establishment of distinct institutions in some areas.

Service delivery options vary with the size of the client base and local cultural and political conditions. Aboriginal people, their leaders and service
providers will ultimately determine the most appropriate systems of urban service delivery. Three fundamental objectives should, however, inform these decisions: first, urban-based strategies and delivery methods must ultimately be
broad-based and inclusive; second, retaining and enhancing Aboriginal identity
and culture should be cornerstones of urban service delivery; and third, the
manner of service delivery must reflect the size of the client base.

RECOMMENDATIONS

The Commission recommends that

Status-Blind versus Separate Institutions **4.7.9**
Services to Aboriginal people in urban areas generally be delivered without regard to legal or treaty status.

4.7.10
Government policies on service delivery take into account the history and tradition of separate institutional development for Métis and treaty people in Manitoba, Saskatchewan and Alberta as well as local cultural, political and economic conditions.

3.4 Special Perspectives

Many people told the Commission that the delivery of services in urban areas must be reformed to respond more appropriately to their cultural and spiritual needs. In this section we look at the problem from the perspective of youth and people with disabilities.

Youth

The issues confronting urban youth attracted considerable attention at the Commission's round table on urban issues. According to participants, Aboriginal street youth are exposed to tremendous difficulties. A high percentage of the people using needle exchange programs in cities such as Edmonton and Vancouver are Aboriginal youth, and many young people are homeless, live on the streets from day to day, and are involved in prostitution, drugs and violence. Participants spoke in terms of surviving on the streets rather than living.

Many Aboriginal young people are facing the same situations as their older counterparts: cultural confusion, lost identity, high unemployment, violence, racism and substance abuse. Participants also described Aboriginal youth as experiencing much higher rates of pregnancy and sexually transmitted disease than other young Canadians. Young people often wind up living on the streets in urban centres because of abusive situations at home. One participant has seen people as young as 14 dying with needles in their arms. Others said Aboriginal youth need immediate help but that the kinds of services they need are rare and already overburdened.

As part of its research program, the Commission heard from Aboriginal street youth about their situation and experiences. Karen (not her real name) told researchers about the boredom and aimlessness of her life on the streets of Vancouver:

> I just kill time, I'd walk around. I'd go to Carnegie and all that. I'd go on Hastings and then I'd go to Granville and walk around there...and see all my friends around Granville. That's about it! I've been on the streets for two years. I'd go home, I'd stay on...I'd go to the streets for a week or so, then I'd go home...for food, I went down to ASU [Adolescent Street Unit] and got meal tickets, and when I didn't have a place to stay, my friends would offer me a place to stay, so I went with my friends. That's it.[70]

The special needs of Aboriginal youth are often overlooked or underestimated by service agencies developing and delivering programs. Boredom is an ever-present problem. Ways must be found to involve Aboriginal youth in developing programs that they will find relevant. In some cases, it might be sufficient to modify existing programs to ensure that Aboriginal cultural perspectives are accommodated. In other areas, particularly leadership development, programs designed specifically for Aboriginal youth are essential.

Commissioners heard that the future of Aboriginal communities rests with youth as advocates of social change.[71] Building leadership development programs that will instil a vision of what the future requires will be a long-term process, as Linda Clarkson emphasized in her study of the Aboriginal Council of Winnipeg:

> Mobilizing young people to become involved in learning approaches that are aimed at serving others will be a natural extension of the traditional indigenous sense of collective responsibility. At the same time, learning through providing service to others can be a significant step towards breaking the cycle of dependence in which many indigenous people feel themselves trapped....
>
> Mobilizing the direct involvement of youth is a unique and time-consuming process requiring definite skills and resources....Centring youth activities and learning in communities requires a commitment to, and a capacity for, mutual learning, patient listening and a tolerance for contrary views.[72]

The majority of the Aboriginal population is under 25 years of age. Population projections indicate that the age composition of the Aboriginal population will remain young, compared to the non-Aboriginal population, for at least another 25 years. This demographic reality, coupled with the current shortage of meaningful programming for Aboriginal youth, highlights the need for urgent and aggressive measures in urban centres.

RECOMMENDATIONS

The Commission recommends that

Youth Services **4.7.11**

Aboriginal governments and organizations accord higher priority to youth programming, particularly leadership development, sport and recreation.

4.7.12

Municipal, provincial, territorial and federal governments support, fund and actively provide services and programs for urban Aboriginal youth.

4.7.13

Aboriginal youth be closely involved in the design, development and delivery of youth services.

Persons with disabilities

The 1991 Aboriginal peoples survey indicated that there were just over 117,000 Aboriginal adults (aged 15 and over) with disabilities.[73] Many have had little choice but to leave their reserves or home communities and relocate in urban centres in search of appropriate services. In 1991, more than 83,000 Aboriginal adults with a disability were living in non-reserve areas. Of that number, 57,000 lived in urban areas. All too often, however, people with disabilities move to the city only to find jurisdictional disputes and an unsympathetic bureaucracy:

> The biggest problem disabled people face is government bureaucracy and jurisdictional problems.
>
> Ian Hinksman
> President, B.C. Aboriginal Network on Disability Society
> Vancouver, British Columbia, 15 November 1993

To the Aboriginal person with a disability, jurisdictional obstacles are often almost insurmountable. Unfortunately, in too many cases even those in charge do not know how to find a solution. It is easy to blame the caregiver, but the caregiver may not necessarily be at fault. In many instances he or she has a crushing caseload and insufficient information about available options.

In addition to jurisdictional bickering between federal, provincial and municipal governments, Aboriginal people with disabilities face a service delivery system that is generally unresponsive to their cultural and spiritual needs, as well as chronic underfunding of the services and programs upon which they rely. They must also deal with inadequate and inaccessible housing; emotional trauma; discrimination because they have a disability and are Aboriginal; barriers to training, employment and economic integration; and a general lack of respect and understanding from the larger society.

We heard from Aboriginal people with disabilities living in urban areas that society in general lacks an appreciation of their everyday struggles and experiences. Most people do not understand what it really means to have a disability and be Aboriginal. As we were told:

> Dignity and self-worth will only be achieved when ignorance is replaced by understanding and discrimination is replaced by acceptance.
>
> James 'Smokey' Tomkins
> President, National Aboriginal Network on Disability
> Ottawa, Ontario, 17 November 1993

As it is for other people with disabilities, finding adequate and accessible housing is a major problem for urban Aboriginal people with disabilities. Improved access is still required to many buildings in urban areas, especially for people with visual and hearing impairments. Aboriginal people with disabilities also need a national voice to raise their issues and to press for change in policies and programs in both the public and the private sector.

RECOMMENDATION

The Commission recommends that

Support for
Disabilities
Organization

4.7.14
The federal government provide funding for a national organization to represent and speak on behalf of Aboriginal people with disabilities.

Support for a national organization should not, however, absolve Aboriginal political organizations of their responsibility to take into account the needs and concerns of people with disabilities.

3.5 Friendship Centres

The first friendship centres were established more than 30 years ago. Since then, they have been the most stable and viable urban Aboriginal organizations.

Initially created to provide services to urban newcomers, their information and referral services are designed to help urban Aboriginal people and migrating Aboriginal people gain access to the range of services and resources available in urban areas. There are currently 113 friendship centres across Canada, 99 of which receive core funding from the federal government.

Throughout their history, friendship centres have played two fundamental roles in meeting the needs of urban Aboriginal people: a referral service and a gathering place. The first is a social service function, the second a community development role that has consistently characterized the centres' operations.

Friendship centres have generally been more successful than other Aboriginal institutions in meeting the needs of Aboriginal people in urban areas. Their programs have helped Aboriginal people to maintain their cultural identity and group solidarity. In most urban areas, the friendship centre is the only major voluntary association available to Aboriginal people to fulfil their social, recreational and cultural development needs. Friendship centres have played an important role in the revitalization of Aboriginal cultures currently under way in Aboriginal communities across Canada and have helped Aboriginal people assume a place in the Canadian cultural mosaic.

The centres have produced a wide range of positive achievements for Aboriginal people, including increased pride and self-esteem, and improved access to services, employment, training, housing and other benefits. Their activities have contributed to the development of stable and active urban Aboriginal communities, particularly their efforts to develop other Aboriginal agencies and organizations, hundreds of which grew out of friendship centre activities. The centres have created greater awareness of Aboriginal issues in urban communities, encouraged non-Aboriginal agencies to be more responsive to the needs of Aboriginal people, and created a positive image of Aboriginal people. They have also, by reflecting Aboriginal values in their structure and operations, provided a useful model for other community agencies.

Friendship centres have taken a lead in developing holistic services based on Aboriginal values, beliefs and practices such as caring, sharing, respect for others, acceptance, equality, individual responsibility for behaviour, non-interference and an emphasis on experience as a way of knowing. Evaluations of friendship centres consistently conclude that Aboriginal people feel more comfortable participating in centre activities than in activities of non-Aboriginal agencies.[74] Indeed, the success of the centres in addressing the needs of Aboriginal people has led to a situation where non-Aboriginal agencies increasingly refer Aboriginal clients to friendship centres.

One of the most important activities of the centres is the promotion of Aboriginal culture. This is particularly important for Aboriginal people in cities because many individuals have lost aspects of their culture, such as languages, and because it is often difficult to practise traditional Aboriginal culture without cultural resources such as elders, places to carry out ceremonies, and cultural education opportunities. Many centres conduct Aboriginal language classes; many more host cultural events such as elders' gatherings, pow-wows, square dances and feasts. These functions will become increasingly important as Aboriginal young people continue to search for ways to strengthen their culture. Friendship centres are ideally placed to expand their role in this regard through education, training, recreation and social programs. However, there is currently no specific funding for cultural education activities outside First Nations territories.

A related public education function assumed by friendship centres is providing a bridge between the Aboriginal and non-Aboriginal communities. Centres often act as a resource, providing information to non-Aboriginal people on the history, cultures and contemporary situation of Aboriginal people. Many centres maintain speakers bureaus of individuals available to address schools and organizations about Aboriginal people and issues. They also regularly conduct cultural awareness workshops and seminars to sensitize the personnel of non-Aboriginal organizations. They are also consulted by municipal governments and institutions on such issues as delivering appropriate services to Aboriginal clients and developing employment equity policies. The demand for expansion of this community development role will likely increase as urban Aboriginal communities become more complex and more insistent on the need to design and deliver appropriate services. The federal government should recognize the important role of friendship centres and provide sufficient resources to enable them to fulfil this community development function.

Friendship centres are the first place many Aboriginal people visit when facing a problem, trying to find out about a particular service, or generally seeking information about urban living. A study carried out in six Canadian cities on behalf of the Commission found that, after education and health institutions, friendship centres were the institutions most frequently used by Aboriginal people.[75] Fully 83 per cent of users were satisfied with their experience.

Although "friendship centres are ready to take a lead role in the co-ordination and/or delivery of services to urban Aboriginal peoples under self-government arrangements",[76] the National Association of Friendship Centres (NAFC) emphasized in its brief to the Commission that the centres are service providers, not political organizations:

> Urban Aboriginal communities are composed of an ever-changing population of status, non-status, Métis people and Inuit. All of these people are represented politically in one form or another by one of the four national groups. The NAFC looks after their service needs – the needs of the entire community for programs to deal with their common problems. Aboriginal people in the cities, regardless of

where they come from, are faced with the same issues. Friendship centres exist to address these concerns, not to speak for the people we service.

David Chartrand
President, National Association of Friendship Centres
Toronto, Ontario, 26 June 1992

NAFC believes that the National Aboriginal Friendship Centre program, currently administered by Canadian Heritage, should be devolved to NAFC.[77] We share this view, as devolution would support greater Aboriginal self-determination. It would also help ensure that funding allocations to individual friendship centres reflect the needs and aspirations of the urban Aboriginal people who use their programs. NAFC, with the advice, guidance and cumulative experience of its member friendship centres, is best able to respond to funding and policy issues related to the urban services provided by friendship centres.

RECOMMENDATION

The Commission recommends that

National
Friendship Centre
Program

4.7.15

The federal government devolve the administration of the National Aboriginal Friendship Centre program to the National Association of Friendship Centres.

3.6 The Urban Aboriginal Cultural Education Program

One of the most important community development activities of friendship centres is the promotion of Aboriginal culture. The promotion and maintenance of a strong cultural identity is critical to the well-being of urban Aboriginal residents. As David Chartrand, president of the National Association of Friendship Centres, told us:

Aboriginal culture in the cities is threatened in much the same way as Canadian culture is threatened by American culture, and it therefore requires a similar commitment to its protection. Our culture is at the heart of our people, and without awareness of Aboriginal history, traditions and ceremonies, we are not whole people, and our communities lose their strength. Cultural education also works against the alienation that the cities hold for our people. Social activities bring us together and strengthen the relationships between people in areas where those relationships are an important safety net for people who feel left out by the mainstream.

David Chartrand
President, National Association of Friendship Centres
Toronto, Ontario, 26 June 1992

We believe that friendship centres could become more involved in cultural education activities, particularly in large urban centres.

A related function is the centres' role in promoting cross-cultural sensitivity and understanding among non-Aboriginal individuals and organizations. Given the growing interest of schools and other institutions in Aboriginal peoples, friendship centres are often asked to participate in events, suggest resource persons, provide display material, give talks on Aboriginal culture, and so on. Although these activities are positive and constructive, friendship centre budgets simply do not enable them to meet all demands.

DIAND administers a cultural/educational centres program. Established in the early 1970s, its mandate is to carry out a wide variety of cultural and educational activities, including cultural research, language research and teaching; curriculum development; cultural sensitivity training for teachers; cultural events such as powwows and feasts; support and development of artists and craftspersons; library services; museums and art galleries; theatre, dance and music performances; programs involving elders; youth programs such as summer camps; and cultural ceremonies. There are about 75 cultural/education centres across Canada, with a total budget of $8 million administered from Ottawa.[78] Most of the centres are run by First Nations governments and are located on reserves or in towns near reserves. Although a small number are situated in large cities, such as Winnipeg and Saskatoon, the program is not generally accessible to those living in urban centres.

We believe that Canadian Heritage should establish a new urban Aboriginal cultural education program, to be administered and operated by friendship centres in larger urban centres across Canada. Friendship centres are the logical base for the program, which would complement the work centres are already doing. But the cultural outreach work currently carried out by the centres is chronically underfunded, too limited, often ad hoc in nature, and heavily dependent on volunteers. There is a need for substantial new institutional support. Although centres could provide some program services on a fee-for-service basis and generate revenue from the sale of Aboriginal products, capital and administrative core funding would be required.

The goal of the program would be community development through cultural education and programs designed for Aboriginal and non-Aboriginal people. Its creation would respond to public demand, cross-cultural interest in encouraging such initiatives, and the desire on the part of Aboriginal people to participate in educating the wider society about Aboriginal culture. The program would also serve Aboriginal people by establishing their own learning centres to help them renew their languages and cultures, as well as acquire some of the academic training needed to earn a living in today's society. It would support living traditions and contribute to maintaining essential bridges between urban and non-urban Aboriginal people and between those living in different cities. Centres offering the program could also be involved in developing curriculum materials for schools. Perhaps most important, they could be a major cultural, social and recreational resource for Aboriginal youth in the cities and could help meet the urgent need for institutional support for young people seeking to rekindle the fire of their Aboriginal cultural identity. (See Volume 1, Chapter 15 for a more detailed discussion.)

RECOMMENDATION

The Commission recommends that

Urban Cultural Education Program

4.7.16
The federal government establish and fund a national urban Aboriginal cultural education program designed for Aboriginal and non-Aboriginal people in large urban centres across Canada, to be generally administered by friendship centres.

3.7 Conclusion

The existing service delivery system in urban areas is not working well for Aboriginal people. For the most part its cultural values are not those of Aboriginal people, and it does not respond appropriately to their cultural, spiritual and socio-economic needs. Fundamental reform should begin immediately. First, Aboriginal people should, wherever possible, receive services from Aboriginal institutions. These institutions must have adequate, stable funding. The expansion and creation of Aboriginal service institutions in major urban centres, whether as agencies of Aboriginal governments or as autonomous entities, is the most effective and systematic method of responding to the needs of urban Aboriginal people over the long term and should be supported by municipal, provincial, territorial and federal governments. Second, Aboriginal people should be involved directly in the design, development and delivery of services provided by governments and mainstream agencies. Intensive and field-oriented cross-cultural training for non-Aboriginal service providers is essential.

We are particularly encouraged by the role friendship centres have played in urban service delivery, despite their limited resources, and we believe that the National Association of Friendship Centres should be given authority and responsibility for friendship centre programs currently administered by the federal government. We also recommend that the federal government establish a national urban Aboriginal cultural education program, to be operated by friend-ship centres in major urban centres.

4. ABORIGINAL WOMEN IN URBAN AREAS

Although their roles in formal and informal institutions are crucial to the day-to-day survival of urban Aboriginal people, the needs of urban Aboriginal women are virtually invisible, and the reality of their lives often remains unrec-ognized and unvalidated. In their submissions to Commissioners, they called for their presence to be recognized and their needs acknowledged:

> We urge the Commission to take into account in its proceedings the specific needs of Aboriginal women and their families in the urban setting. More than others, they are often ill-equipped and the victims of segregation and discrimination. [translation]
>
> Éléonor Huff
> Quebec Native Women's Association
> Montreal, Quebec, 27 May 1993

> Indian country is not [just] a man's world. Women will continue to be resident as long as man will exist and inhabit these same territo-ries, and so will our children and their children always. Status women resident off-reserve are too often a forgotten minority. Many become urbanized due to family abuse, separations and deaths, others, for per-sonal reasons. These women and their children are the abused, per-sonally and mentally.
>
> Shirley Gamble
> Brandon, Manitoba
> 10 December 1992

4.1 Who Are Urban Aboriginal Women?

First Nations, Métis and Inuit are all represented among urban Aboriginal women. They outnumber men in each group (see Table 7.1). They are also young; more than half (53.9 per cent) are 24 years of age or under, compared to less than one-third of non-Aboriginal women living in urban centres. Only one urban Aboriginal woman in 20 is over 55 years of age; the figure for the com-parable non-Aboriginal population is one in five.

Urban Aboriginal women have higher levels of education than the female Aboriginal population in general. But this does not necessarily lead to employ-ment. The unemployment rate for urban Aboriginal women is 21 per cent, com-pared to just under 10 per cent for non-Aboriginal urban women (Table 7.1).

TABLE 7.1
Comparison of Aboriginal Identity and Non-Aboriginal Populations in Urban Off-Reserve Areas, 1991

	Non-Aboriginal	Total Aboriginal	Registered NAI	Non-Registered NAI	Métis	Inuit[1]
Demography[2]						
Total Adjusted Population (#)	20,060,875	320,000	148,500	77,800	90,100	8,400
Male (%)	48.9	46.0	43.9	47.6	48.0	51.0
Female (%)	51.1	54.0	56.1	52.4	52.0	49.0
0-14 years (%)	19.7	36.6	33.4	41.0	37.5	42.0
15-24 years (%)	14.3	20.0	21.2	18.3	19.0	20.9
25-34 years (%)	18.5	19.7	20.6	18.5	19.6	17.1
35-54 years (%)	27.2	18.3	19.2	17.5	18.1	14.0
55+ years (%)	20.3	5.4	5.6	4.7	5.8	6.0
Lone parents[3] (%)	3.8	8.2	10.1	6.1	7.2	5.2
Language[3]						
Speak an Aboriginal language (age 5-14)	—	5.2	7.8	—	2.6	29.3
Speak an Aboriginal language (age 15+)	—	17.6	25.3	5.6	11.3	42.0
Would like to learn to speak an Aboriginal language (age 15+)	—	73.6	77.2	68.7	73.6	69.8

TABLE 7.1 (continued)
Comparison of Aboriginal Identity and Non-Aboriginal Populations in Urban Off-Reserve Areas, 1991

	Non-Aboriginal	Total Aboriginal	Registered NAI	Non-Registered NAI	Métis	Inuit[1]
Education[3] (age 15+)						
Less than high school certificate (%)	35.6	49.7	48.5	43.0	52.2	58.3
High school or trade certificate (%)	18.7	13.1	11.9	16.6	12.9	10.7
Non-university certificate (%)	15.8	14.8	13.9	18.0	14.7	14.6
University degree (%)	13.0	3.8	3.1	5.8	3.6	—
Labour Force Activity[3]						
Participation rate (%)	68.1	62.7	58.4	68.8	65.3	66.9
Unemployment rate (%)	9.7	22.9	27.4	27.4	20.0	25.9
Average total income ($)	24,876	16,560	15,392	18,772	16,853	17,045
% with total income less than $10,000	26.2	35.3	37.3	31.7	34.5	35.9
% receiving government transfer income	19.0	18.2	21.6	13.9	17.5	13.5

Notes:

NAI = North American Indian.

— Not available or not applicable.

1. Adjusted Inuit demographic counts were derived by applying the percentage of urban Inuit from the Aboriginal Peoples Survey (APS) actual counts to the total adjusted urban Inuit count.

2. Approximately 10,000 was added to the APS count to adjust for undercoverage of the population in participating urban off-reserve areas.

3. Percentages are based on actual (non-adjusted) 1991 APS counts.

Source: M.J. Norris et al., "Projections of the Aboriginal Identity Population in Canada, 1991-2016", research study prepared by Statistics Canada for RCAP (February 1995); and 1991 Aboriginal Peoples Survey, custom tabulations.

TABLE 7.2
Aboriginal Migrants by Sex and Destination, 1991

Destination	Men	Women	Women as a % of all migrants
On-reserve	6,000	6,635	52.5
Rural, off-reserve	7,165	9,285	56.4
Urban, non-CMA	10,020	13,970	58.2
Urban, CMA	13,465	18,395	57.7
Total	36,650	48,285	56.8

Note: Includes migrants age 15 years and older.
CMA = Census Metropolitan Area.

Source: S.J. Clatworthy, "Migration and Mobility Patterns of Canada's Aboriginal Population", research study prepared for RCAP (February 1995).

4.2 Migration

The majority of Aboriginal migrants to urban areas are women (Table 7.2). Women are considerably more likely than men to move to the city because of community factors (Table 7.3). Some leave their home communities to escape physical and sexual abuse. All too typical was the woman who told of leaving home at 13 and growing up on the streets. For her, the choice was either living in a small rural community and being sexually abused and silenced by her family, or leaving the community and living on the streets of the city which, though violent, felt safer.[79] Women told Commissioners:

> Strong networks of families exist in a community. When abuse is exposed, those networks are disrupted. People feel powerless. Women leave Native communities and go to the city to escape abuse.[80]

Other women described how their needs were not taken seriously by the people in power on their reserves and how they had no control over the issues that directly affected them:

> Presently the women in our communities are suffering from dictatorship governments that have been imposed on us by the *Indian Act*. We are oppressed in our communities. Our women have no voice, nowhere to go for appeal processes. If we are being discriminated against within our community or when we are being abused in our communities, where do the women go?...The Royal Commission to date has not heard the true story of Aboriginal women's oppression. The women are afraid to come out and speak in a public forum such

TABLE 7.3
Reasons for Migration to Off-Reserve Locations, 1991

	Men	%	Women	%
Family-related	1,490	32.0	1,930	28.6
Housing	1,025	22.0	1,515	22.5
Access to employment	1,065	22.9	1,175	17.4
Community factors	100	2.2	765	11.4
Access to school	540	11.6	755	11.2
Forced to move	220	4.7	380	5.6
Health-related	165	3.5	120	1.8
Total	**4,605**	**100.0**	**6,640**	**100.0**

Note: Includes migrants age 15 years and older.

Source: S.J. Clatworthy, "The Migration and Mobility Patterns of Canada's Aboriginal Population", research study prepared for RCAP (February 1995).

as this. We are penalized if we say anything about the oppression that we have to undergo in our community.

> Joyce Courchene
> President, Nongom Ikkwe
> Indigenous Women's Collective
> Winnipeg, Manitoba, 3 June 1992

Many Aboriginal women moved away from reserve communities because they lost status (usually by marrying a non-Indian) and the legal right to reside there under paragraph 12(1)(b) of the *Indian Act*. Since 1985 and the passage of Bill C-31, which amended the act, many have regained their status. Women who have regained status are more likely than men to live in urban areas, as are women who have applied for reinstatement. Many Aboriginal women have no option, therefore, but to live in urban areas, even though they would prefer to live in their community of origin. Their options are circumscribed by abuse, loss of status or the fact that their needs and perspectives are not taken into account by decision makers in their communities:

> While some women with Bill C-31 status prefer to live in urban areas, others want to return to their reserve community but cannot, because there are no resources to accommodate them, or band membership codes exclude them.

> Vicki English-Currie
> Calgary Native Women's Shelter
> Calgary, Alberta, 26 May 1992

4.3 The Urban Experience

We cannot present a complete picture of the lives of urban Aboriginal women. Too many voices are missing. But some common concerns did emerge from the testimony we heard. Urban Aboriginal women made it very clear that moving to an urban centre was not a rejection of Aboriginal cultures and values:

> Just because we reside in urban centres we did not give up as an Indian; we did not give up our status; we did not give up our treaties; we did not give up our band membership; we did not give up our tribal affiliations; we did not give up our linguistic affiliations; and we never gave up our right to live. We have never given up maintaining our rights as members of our bands. We are not non-Native. We continue to live Indian.
>
> Shirley Gamble
> Brandon, Manitoba
> 10 December 1992

For many Aboriginal women, however, migration to the city distances them from community support networks and makes it very difficult for them to enhance their connections to their cultures. Access to their teachers, grand-mothers and clan mothers is limited. There are few elders in urban centres, and finding guidance and training in traditional ways is not easy.

In addition to being isolated from extended families and communities, urban women are too often isolated from each other:

> We do know that, in many instances, life for Aboriginal women off-reserve can be even more problematic especially if they are lacking the prospects for employment. These women have less support systems and services available to them and they are often very much alone, without the physical or emotional support of family members (which in some cases they enjoyed on the reserve). Unemployed and left to their own devices, they often feel alienated and alone, help-less, powerless, and "without a voice".[81]

Women spoke of their desire to find their roles as urban Aboriginal women, to make connections and build networks in the urban Aboriginal com-munities.[82] They spoke of establishing their own organizations in urban centres to meet their distinct needs.[83]

Political organizations and leadership were also a focus of women's submissions to the Commission. Women from all Aboriginal groups documented their exclusion from existing decision-making bodies.[84] Urban Aboriginal women want to be involved in self-government negotiations, and they want to play political, social, economic and spiritual roles in self-governing structures. The roles Aboriginal women have played traditionally in governance and their responsibilities with regard to family, children and the elderly reinforce the importance of key roles for them in decision-making processes. In their submission to Commissioners, the Indian Homemakers' Association of British Columbia stated:

> The involvement of women in the political process can mean more action on issues that have been the root of our oppression as Aboriginal women. Such issues as family violence, sexual abuse, substance abuse, child care and housing can then be recognized as serious issues and put onto the agenda of priorities.[85]

Aboriginal women also described the racism and discrimination they encounter in urban life:

> Our women face racism and systemic stereotyping at every turn. For Aboriginal women, this racism and stereotyping is rampant right through the system, from the police to the courts, child welfare agencies to income security. Although the law is supposed to treat everyone equally, we all know this is not an Aboriginal reality.
>
> Darlene Hall
> Ikwe Widdjiitiwin
> Winnipeg, Manitoba, 23 April 1992

4.4 Housing

Discrimination in obtaining housing was mentioned often by women appearing at the Commission's public hearings:

> I have been denied housing because of my skin colour. I have been denied housing because I am a single mom. Being a Native and being a single mom really is discouraging because you can't get anywhere; you have that double-whammy put on you.
>
> Lisa Maracle
> Brantford, Ontario, 14 May 1993

Providing and sharing shelter is one of the most important ways Aboriginal women maintain family and community ties in urban centres.[86] Interviews with tenants of Aboriginal urban housing corporations highlighted two benefits of such housing for urban Aboriginal women:

> Family stability....For many [Aboriginal families] it meant that they did not have to constantly move from one place to another or to live with friends or relatives in an overcrowded setting. It meant a sense of permanence, or establishing some roots in the city while maintaining ties with reserve or rural communities....
>
> Growing sense of Aboriginal community in the urban setting....For the first time people's basic needs for affordable shelter were being addressed, allowing them to begin to address other needs such as

employment, education and cultural retention. The community became more identifiable and could be contacted more readily to participate in various social, cultural, and recreational activities.[87]

Suitable housing is key to improving the situation of Aboriginal women and families in urban areas. As our discussion of urban demographics later in this chapter demonstrates, affordable housing is badly needed. Our recommendations in this regard are contained in Volume 3, Chapter 4.

4.5 Services

Aboriginal women told Commissioners that their need for services is not being met by existing agencies and institutions. They said that most urban institutions are not equipped to provide culturally sensitive services to Aboriginal women and their families. They appealed for more input on the design and implementation of service delivery.

We heard of negative experiences women have had with a variety of service institutions and the consequences of these experiences.[88] Many no longer even call the police for urgent assistance, for example, because they do not expect to get any service:

> [I]f an Aboriginal woman calls the police because she is being assaulted, she is not always treated in the same manner as a non-Aboriginal woman making the same call. When we talk to women about calling the police for assistance, very often their response is, "Why bother, they will probably just ask me if I was drinking". Our women get this treatment from all aspects of the system.
>
> Darlene Hall
> Ikwe Widdjiitiwin
> Winnipeg, Manitoba, 23 April 1992

Some Aboriginal women living in urban areas have learned to fear and distrust the very agencies that are supposed to be helping them. They have found, for example, that when they are victims of family violence and seek support in non-Aboriginal women's shelters, they are not received the same way as other women:

> But when a non-native woman goes in they don't even bother to take her children away. They are there to comfort her and give her counselling. When people like me or someone else goes in, right away they take their children. You really have to fight to hang on to them. You really have to prove yourself as a mother, and the other non-native women do not have to do so.
>
> Kula Ellison
> Aboriginal Women's Council of Saskatchewan
> Saskatoon, Saskatchewan, 28 October 1992

For some women, the circumstances precipitating a move to an urban area mean that they arrive seeking healing. But they usually find that the kind of support they need is not available. Rarely do urban support services offer traditional spiritual practices, healing medicines or women's teachings that reflect Aboriginal values. Access to elders is limited, if available at all. Aboriginal women also find, when dealing with non-Aboriginal agencies and institutions, that the staff is untrained to deal with issues critical to Aboriginal women such as cultural expectations with regard to family roles and the effects of long-term colonization on individuals and families.

First Nations women believe that programs and funding available to women living on reserves should also be made available to women living in cities:

> As a recourse, I personally would like to see urban Indian women given the same status and treatment as our Bill C-31 sisters and their families on reserves, only I want to stay off-reserve. I want my home paid for by my band so that I too can live successfully on- or off-reserve. As band members anywhere in Canada, I think the time is right for reversing certain policies drawn up by non-Natives for Natives.
>
> Shirley Gamble
> Brandon, Manitoba
> 10 December 1992

These comments were echoed in other centres. In Saskatoon, Commissioners were told that treaty Indian women are organizing to ensure that governments in their communities of origin acknowledge their existence and take some responsibility for them.[89] Commissioners were urged to affirm "the mobility of our rights as treaty Indian women".[90]

Commissioners also heard that Aboriginal women have shown leadership in developing Aboriginal urban institutions and that "through their contribution we have been able to develop a network of services geared to the essential needs of Aboriginal people living in or passing through urban centres".[91] Now, many urban Aboriginal women are appealing for services that meet the specific needs of women. They are seeking a major role in the design and delivery of services, particularly in the area of child welfare. Commissioners were told of their desire to establish their own institutions in urban centres:

> We want Native centres and organizations which will deal strictly in Native women's issues. We want Native women's transition homes and a safe house locally, a Native women's drug and alcohol treatment centre, a Native women's resource centre to provide counselling services and all abuse prevention measures. Native women need liaison workers between the Native community and the Ministry of Social Services and Housing because many Native women fear and dislike

dealing with the white middle class social workers. Native women need a centre to help mothers deal with feelings of loss and anger, to learn how to empower ourselves and to redevelop our traditional Native parenting skills. Native women need daycare resources to enable them to further their education, develop life skills and seek employment. Urban Native women want recreational funding for their children, in order to develop self-esteem and healthy lifestyles.

Jackie Adams
Port Alberni, British Columbia
20 May 1992

4.6 Conclusion

Women form the majority of urban Aboriginal populations, as well as the majority of migrants to urban areas. Aboriginal women play a critical role and assume much of the responsibility for the well-being of Aboriginal people in urban communities; their initiatives have been essential in ensuring the day-to-day survival of Aboriginal people and cultures in cities. Their presence and roles must be recognized and their needs met. Aboriginal women must be involved in shaping the evolving relationship between Aboriginal people and urban authorities. There is overwhelming evidence that urban service delivery institutions are not meeting the specific needs of urban Aboriginal women. Action to correct this situation is urgently required.

RECOMMENDATIONS

The Commission recommends that

Aboriginal Women in Urban Areas

4.7.17

Aboriginal women give Aboriginal and non-Aboriginal service agencies direction and guidance in formulating policy and developing services that may be used by Aboriginal women and children and participate fully in the delivery of programs and services established specifically to meet the needs of urban Aboriginal women.

4.7.18

In addition to cross-cultural training, non-Aboriginal individuals and organizations whose work or responsibilities directly affect urban Aboriginal women's lives receive comprehensive information and education on the situation of urban Aboriginal women.

5. GOVERNANCE FOR ABORIGINAL PEOPLE IN URBAN AREAS

Commissioners found that self-government in urban areas raises a host of conceptual and practical questions that are difficult to resolve. Self-government off a land base requires a different approach than the land-based models most often associated with Aboriginal self-government.

Representations to the Commission and our own research highlight a pressing need to address governance issues in urban centres. In the words of Dan Smith, president of the United Native Nations of British Columbia:

> I want to emphasize that there is an urgent need for non-reserve Aboriginal people to be treated equally and fairly. After all, we are working toward the same end...whether [we] reside on- or off-reserve. The majority of bands, tribal councils and treaty areas do not have the capacity or infrastructure to address off-reserve Aboriginal issues and concerns....Historically, off-reserve Aboriginal people have had to look after themselves individually, and then over a period of time to organize into groups for mutual support. Self-determination for individuals and families is the foundation of Aboriginal people both on- and off-reserve.
>
> Dan Smith
> President, United Native Nations of B.C.
> Vancouver, British Columbia, 2 June 1993

The Federation of Canadian Municipalities emphasized in its brief to the Commission that municipalities have not been consulted regarding the potential effect on local responsibilities of negotiations and agreements between Aboriginal people and other orders of government:

> During consultations across the country, it became evident that both municipalities and Aboriginal peoples are frequently not knowledgeable of each other's difficulties and concerns. To some degree, the aspirations of both local governments and Aboriginal peoples have been marginalized and compromised by federal and provincial governments. As a result, the interface of municipal/Aboriginal interests, important to Aboriginal self-government, has been rendered all but completely invisible.[92]

Although the federation acknowledged the view that self-government is an inherent right, it said that Aboriginal governments should exercise delegated authority similar to municipal governments. At the same time, it recognized the need for Aboriginal-controlled organizations to deliver services in a culturally appropriate manner. While emphasizing the need for all orders of government to co-operate in defining appropriate areas of jurisdiction, the federation was also concerned that the federal government continue to assume some degree of responsibility for Aboriginal people in urban areas:

> For its part, the federal government cannot draw a line separating Aboriginal people on reserves and Aboriginal people in urban areas....The needs of urban Aboriginal people must be met through a distinct process separate from agreements with reserves. In this context, municipalities must be included in discussion among governments with respect to changes in their relations with Aboriginal peoples. Municipalities should not be left responsible for services previously provided by federal or provincial governments without consultation and an appropriate transfer of funds.[93]

In this section we consider various pathways to governance for Aboriginal people living in urban areas. First we consider reforms to existing public institutions to accommodate urban Aboriginal peoples' aspirations for greater participation in governance where they live and work. These reforms would not constitute Aboriginal self-government as such. Next, we consider how the objectives of self-government could be achieved through an urban Aboriginal community of interest approach, involving members with diverse Aboriginal origins. Finally, we explore approaches premised on the Aboriginal nation.

These three approaches are points along a spectrum of possibilities for urban governance. The reform of mainstream public institutions is a relatively integrated form of governance, while governance based on the nation would be a more autonomous form of self-government. We have concluded that the first two approaches, the reform of public institutions and community of interest government, can be implemented now as a priority in urban areas. Approaches that take the nation as their starting point are more likely to unfold over the longer term, as the process of rebuilding nations takes place. Urban Aboriginal people should be active participants in such processes.

5.1 Reform of Urban Governments and Public Authorities

While urban Aboriginal people express interest in self-government, there is also potential, especially in the short term, for greater involvement of urban Aboriginal people in mainstream urban governments. Even if self-government is established in cities and towns, the relationship between urban Aboriginal people and mainstream governments and institutions will not disappear. Various aspects of the legislation and services of local, provincial, territorial and federal governments will still extend to urban Aboriginal people. For these reasons we believe that urban governments and public authorities can be reformed to take better account of Aboriginal perspectives and interests.

Possibilities at the local government level include

- guaranteeing Aboriginal representation on school boards, boards of health, hospital boards, police commissions and other institutions whose work especially affects the lives of urban Aboriginal people;
- establishing permanent Aboriginal affairs committees by municipal councils, school boards and other agencies, boards and commissions; and
- potentially co-managing urban initiatives, particularly in areas where federal, provincial or territorial legislation has recognized a role for Aboriginal governments.

Guaranteed representation on appointed local bodies

Local government includes many agencies, boards and commissions. Unlike municipal councils and school boards, which are generally elected, police commissions, library boards, public health boards, recreation boards, hospital boards and many others are composed of appointees or a mix of elected representatives and appointees. Appointments are made by municipal councils, provincial or territorial governments, or sometimes both. Candidates for positions are sought in a variety of ways.

At the Commission's urban round table, participants noted that Aboriginal people are not generally represented on local boards and commissions, even when they have a clearly demonstrable interest. Aboriginal people may have a particular interest in the work of police boards, hospital boards and historical boards in many Canadian centres, to name a few obvious examples. As in the case of non-Aboriginal appointees, Aboriginal people on local boards and commissions should enjoy appropriate standing in their community, in addition to being suited to the requirements of board membership.

Aboriginal affairs committees

Another possibility for enhancing understanding between Aboriginal people and local governments is to establish Aboriginal affairs committees of municipal councils, school boards, and other boards and commissions to advise on issues in which the Aboriginal population has a particular interest. One example is Calgary's Aboriginal Urban Affairs Committee, an advisory committee with a majority of members drawn from the Aboriginal community. Committees of this kind help to foster understanding of the situation and priorities of Aboriginal residents. Two elements are essential to their success. First, the appointed Aboriginal members must have strong roots in the community and must reflect its composition. Second, the committee's relationship to the council or board must be well-defined and direct. The link between many urban issues and the situation of Aboriginal people living in cities and towns requires regular meetings between an Aboriginal affairs committee and the body to which it reports. Furthermore, the parent body must have substantial, not just token, representation on the committee. This will encourage the development of mutual understanding in sufficient depth to deal with issues and to avoid an 'us/them' relationship.

Co-management

Co-management arrangements are a way of bridging relations between Aboriginal governments representing urban residents and local, provincial, territorial and federal governments. At the most practical level, co-management ensures access to common services by all urban residents, while recognizing the essential aspects of Aboriginal culture that are the foundation of self-government.

Co-management does not necessarily imply creating separate Aboriginal institutions. Institutions and services could be established by a provincial, territorial, federal and in some cases local government to serve the general population, with specific provisions for Aboriginal people. Co-management of the institution or service, and the nature of Aboriginal participation, would be established in most cases through enabling legislation or negotiated agreements. For example, a provincial minister of education might mandate the establishment of an Aboriginal education authority in an urban centre. A co-management board might be established, providing for significant Aboriginal participation but also the participation of provincial and municipal representatives. The co-management framework might include provisions to safeguard provincial interests, as well as affirm the education authority's primary role in determining and meeting the educational needs and interests of Aboriginal residents.

Local governments exercise authority delegated by provincial and territorial governments. This limits their ability to delegate further. Co-management arrangements would therefore generally be implemented by federal, provincial or territorial legislation, even though they involve local services or functions. In fields such as culture and recreation, however, local agreements could be the foundation for co-management. However, municipal governments, officials and representatives should be involved in establishing and operating co-management arrangements where appropriate, or where municipal interests are affected.

These approaches do not represent self-government as such for urban Aboriginal people. All involve Aboriginal people working within the legislative, policy and administrative frameworks of mainstream Canadian governments. While this reality may afford urban Aboriginal people only limited opportunity to influence governance in urban centres, there are still important benefits. These include having a voice in local government decision making and promoting greater understanding and good relations between non-Aboriginal and Aboriginal people in urban centres.

RECOMMENDATIONS

The Commission recommends that

Representation of
Urban Aboriginal
People

4.7.19

Positions be designated for Aboriginal representatives on local boards and commissions responsible for services and the boards of institutions in which Aboriginal people have a significant interest.

4.7.20

Municipal councils and school boards in municipalities with a large Aboriginal population establish Aboriginal affairs committees to provide advice and guidance on Aboriginal issues.

4.7.21

Municipal, provincial, territorial and federal governments seek opportunities for co-management arrangements that would involve Aboriginal people in establishing, managing and operating urban institutions, programs and services in which they have an interest.

5.2 Urban Communities of Interest

On its own, reform of mainstream urban governance structures will not meet the aspirations of urban Aboriginal people for governance arrangements based on autonomy and self-government. A survey by the Congress of Aboriginal Peoples of more than 1,300 Aboriginal people living in six major metropolitan centres found that "virtually all Aboriginal respondents (92 per cent) either strongly (66 per cent) or somewhat (26 per cent) support this effort to have Aboriginal people in urban areas run their own affairs".[94] One option is for urban Aboriginal communities to take steps to govern themselves.

In describing these approaches, we use the term 'urban community of interest' to designate a collectivity that emerges in an urban setting, includes people of diverse Aboriginal origins,[95] and 'creates itself' through voluntary association. The approach encompasses two possibilities. One involves the urban community of interest in multiple government functions and activities. The second is a more simplified form in which the community of interest acts through a single-function institution and is organized for limited government purposes. (The urban community of interest model is also developed in Volume 2, Chapter 3.)

Multiple-function community of interest governments

Under the multiple-function community of interest model, the urban community of interest could form a self-governing, city-wide body with political and administrative functions, exercising self-government in a range of sectors and through a variety of institutions. In many cases, existing urban Aboriginal institutions would play an essential role in developing this form of governance because of their extensive experience in providing services to the urban Aboriginal population.[96] A study of the Aboriginal Council of Winnipeg, for example, proposes an approach to urban self-government based on co-operation among, and further development of, existing institutions.[97] An urban community of interest government would act through an array of agencies and institutions, establish an umbrella political structure to oversee and co-ordinate activities, and be recognized as a self-governing entity within the city.

In most cases the geographic reach of this form of governance would correspond to the municipal boundaries of a city or town. The jurisdiction of the community of interest government would have more of a communal orientation, however, relating to persons who participate voluntarily rather than to territory. Its jurisdiction in most instances would be delegated by provincial or federal governments as appropriate. A community of interest government could also operate on the basis of delegated authority from an Aboriginal nation, but probably only when members of the community of interest are predominantly from that nation.

It may also be possible for community of interest governments in different cities to co-operate with each other, or for urban communities of interest and nation-based Aboriginal governments to make agreements. The Native Council of Canada noted that "a supra-urban structure could play a vital role....[I]t could form a further level of pan-Aboriginality binding together all of the urban communities in Canada or within a specific region".[98] Community of interest governments could enter into agreements with other Aboriginal governments, including other urban governments, to co-operate in delivering some services. These agreements could play an important role in the efficient delivery of services to urban Aboriginal people.

A major strength of the urban community of interest approach is the opportunity it offers Aboriginal people in urban areas who have no other access to self-government. In many cases, these are the people who have the greatest need to affirm and enhance their cultural identity. Another strength is the likelihood that urban community of interest governments would be highly responsive to the particular needs of local communities. The approach would also provide a vehicle for immediate action on the part of non-Aboriginal governments to improve the situation of Aboriginal people in urban areas. Steps could be taken to support consensus and community building and to improve urban Aboriginal people's access to and control of institutions providing services.

Possibly the greatest challenge underlying this approach to self-government lies in the need to build many urban communities of interest from scratch. The potential difficulties have been described by scholar Bradford W. Morse:

> In the urban setting, asking the individual members of the potentially very diverse urban group, each with their own unique identity, traditions, language and culture, to put aside their differences and build a new community is a formidable task. It requires the rejection of the long history of federal intervention, and for the urban Aboriginal population to come to terms with their diversity in a way which can foster Aboriginal government with a diverse non-homogeneous population.[99]

A process of healing, consensus building and education about the options may be necessary to create a basis for meaningful participation by urban residents in decisions about governance.[100]

A final challenge for urban communities is the limited range of services that can be supported, especially where population numbers are low. However, co-operating with other Aboriginal and non-Aboriginal governments to deliver particular services may provide a mechanism for urban Aboriginal people to ensure that a broad range of needs can be met.

Single-function urban institutions

As discussed earlier in this chapter, many urban Aboriginal service institutions exist or are emerging in areas such as education, health, social services, housing and cultural affairs. We anticipate that in some cases urban communities of interest will want to act in a self-governing capacity through such institutions and in selected service sectors. For example, a community of interest's self-government objectives may be limited to establishing an Aboriginal-controlled education facility, such as a high school, or an Aboriginal health services clinic.

Implementation of such approaches to governance should not disrupt the delivery of existing services to urban residents through these institutions or the continued development and emergence of Aboriginal-controlled, single-function institutions. Speaking at a workshop on urban self-government, Terry Mountjoy, manager of Regina's social development unit, identified some of the city's concerns regarding the future of urban institutions not affiliated with either the Metis Nation of Saskatchewan or the Federation of Saskatchewan Indian Nations:

> For years, these local, non-affiliated groups have delivered many services to a large number of Aboriginal people in the city....As the political environment changes, it is important that these services not be disrupted. These groups also "represent" a number of Aboriginal residents of the city who support culturally appropriate but integrated

services. This Aboriginal constituency currently lacks a voice at the main national and provincial negotiating tables.[101]

Existing service institutions can contribute greatly to the community building required to develop urban community of interest governments. They provide opportunities for self-determination to relatively small, diverse Aboriginal populations that are too few in number to form urban governments. They could also continue to meet the immediate needs of urban Aboriginal people, and they might eventually be incorporated into Aboriginal governments with multiple functions.

Supporting and enhancing the work of existing urban institutions does present certain challenges. Autonomous service institutions might fragment urban communities and encourage the creation of competing organizations. Federal, provincial, territorial and municipal governments could see them as substitutes for other initiatives. Therefore, it is important that all governments recognize these challenges and work to minimize their negative impact.

In our view, whether they choose to be self-governing through single-function institutions or through governments that serve a variety of purposes and needs, urban communities of interest represent a viable pathway to self-government. Moreover, they have the added advantage that they can be implemented almost immediately, with the co-operation of federal, provincial and municipal governments.

RECOMMENDATION

The Commission recommends that

Urban Community of Interest Approaches

4.7.22

Where urban Aboriginal residents wish to pursue self-government based on an urban community of interest, whether involved in multiple government functions or acting through a single institution,

(a) municipal, provincial, territorial and federal governments foster and support community building, including, where appropriate, developing the community of interest's governance initiative; and

(b) municipal, provincial, territorial and federal governments participate in negotiations to establish urban community of interest governments and assist them in operating institutions and services for members of the community of interest.

5.3 Nation-Based Approaches to Urban Self-Government

The relationship to their traditional land remains fundamental for many urban Aboriginal people. The New Brunswick Aboriginal Peoples Council, which represents of off-reserve Aboriginal people in New Brunswick, made the point clearly:

> The cultural basis of Aboriginal peoples in the Province of New Brunswick is in their special relationship with the land and, in essence, they are defined by the land on which they have subsisted and lived....
>
> While the off-reserve Aboriginal people of New Brunswick do not have a specific land base, the Province of New Brunswick has always been viewed as Aboriginal land in its entirety. The Aboriginal communities of New Brunswick have always felt that the lands outside the reserves are traditional lands, and have continued to use them for harvesting and spiritual practices, as was promised in all the Treaties signed in the past.[102]

Many Aboriginal people living in urban areas also maintain strong ties to their nations of origin and look to them for participation in self-governing arrangements. For example, some participants at the Commission's round table on urban issues insisted that their identity is tied to their homelands:

> They said their cultural identities as First Nations people are tied to their communities, just as the identities of Métis flow from their settlements. The answer was for each group to extend jurisdiction from these home territories over the Aboriginal urban population.[103]

Several approaches have been suggested that take as their starting point urban Aboriginal peoples' nations of origin. These include the extra-territorial jurisdiction model; the host nation model; approaches proposed by the Metis Nation for institutions and distinct urban political communities; and the urban treaty nation governance model. All of these nation-based approaches to urban government must be based on the voluntary participation of individual urban citizens.

Under these approaches, the accountability of a nation government to its urban citizens will continue to present some challenges. In submissions to the Commission, many urban Aboriginal people said that their nations of origin did not take responsibility for their needs or well-being. While nation-based models of government may not resolve all problems of representation and government responsiveness, we believe the nation-based approaches outlined here are potential routes to self-government for urban Aboriginal people who wish to retain political and other ties with a nation of origin.

Extra-territorial jurisdiction

Under this approach, an Aboriginal nation with jurisdiction over a land base might exercise extra-territorial jurisdiction over its citizens living outside its exclusive land base, including in urban areas. The nation of origin could establish service agencies and other institutions to serve those of its urban citizens who chose to participate. It might also establish structures for their political representation – for example, a designated position on the governing council of the nation or a separate urban council with advisory or decision-making powers.

An example of this approach is provided by the Siksika Nation in Alberta, which has included the Siksika population of Calgary in its long-term self-government planning and its strategy for self-government negotiations. In these negotiations, the Siksika Nation proposes that its reserve-based government have jurisdiction over all Siksika citizens, on- or off-reserve, and that the nation take full responsibility for providing programs and services for them. In Calgary, where a significant number of nation members live, exercise of this responsibility would presumably take the form of service agencies and institutions for Siksika people. The Siksika Nation has signed a protocol agreement with the Siksika Urban Association in Calgary that affirms the inclusion of all Siksika in the Siksika Nation, regardless of place of residence, and their representation by the Siksika Nation chief and council.[104]

This approach would help dissolve distinctions between on- and off-reserve residents and would reinforce links to urban Aboriginal people's nations of origin; it has considerable support among First Nations.[105] Current initiatives are already addressing issues of design and implementation, and the results will be available to guide other First Nations.

This approach also has its share of challenges, however. Urban residents say they have frequently been ignored by their nations of origin. Adopting this approach, therefore, would require a reorientation of priorities and changes in decision-making structures. Also, the exercise of extra-territorial jurisdiction by individual Aboriginal nations might not be possible in urban areas that are home to Aboriginal people from a large number of nations. Serious inequalities could emerge among Aboriginal residents in a particular city if there were differences in the range and quality of programs and services provided by different Aboriginal nations. Finally, this approach potentially excludes a large number of urban Aboriginal people, because some nations would find it difficult to provide services in an urban area where their members are sparsely represented or far from the nation's land base.

Host nation

Many Canadian cities and towns are located on the traditional lands of Aboriginal nations, raising the possibility of linking urban Aboriginal governance with the traditional territories of Aboriginal nations. Under the host nation approach, an Aboriginal nation's jurisdiction could be extended to Aboriginal people living in urban centres in its traditional territory. The nation would act as a 'host' to Aboriginal residents from various nations and recognize them as forming one of its communities. This would require both a nation and an urban Aboriginal population willing to co-operate. The extent of governance exercised by the host nation would vary, but in most instances it would begin with program and service delivery. The host nation's authority would extend only to people who agreed to participate – those who chose to use programs and services offered by the host nation. Thus, the host nation would act in a governance capacity in relation to its own citizens as well as to the citizens of other Aboriginal nations who chose to associate with it for these purposes.

In terms of political representation, the host nation's government structure could allow for representation of urban Aboriginal people. Alternatively, the nation could establish a separate board, agency or council for the urban Aboriginal community to advise the nation government on its activities as host or to organize and operate urban programs, services and institutions directly.

The host nation concept could be implemented in various ways. For example, the host nation might have a prominent and central role in program and service delivery, with institutions and agencies bearing the stamp of that nation, its culture and traditions. Alternatively, as with other communities of the nation, the urban community could affirm its distinctiveness through programs and services that reflect the diversity of its membership.

The extent of the host nation's activities in urban areas would most likely be determined by the composition of the urban community. If a significant component of the community's membership were also citizens of the host nation, it might play an active role in providing services to these citizens and other Aboriginal people in the urban area. For example, as is evident in Table 7.4, a clear majority (79 per cent) of Aboriginal residents in Halifax are Mi'kmaq, and this city is within the traditional homeland of Mi'kma'ki. These figures suggest there are incentives for the Mi'kmaq Nation to be active in Halifax as a host nation and to accept the Aboriginal community in Halifax as one of its communities. This community could then be recognized as having the same inherent governmental authority as any other Mi'kmaq community. The urban community could elect its own leaders, send representatives to Mi'kmaq Nation meetings and deliver its own programs and services, as in any other recognized Mi'kmaq community.

In situations where few urban residents are affiliated with the host nation, or the community of interest is diverse but has a strong commitment to a form of self-government that accommodates all traditions, there may still be an incentive for a host nation to be active in the urban area. (Vancouver, for example, is home to members of at least 35 nations – Table 7.4).

The host nation concept is relatively new and underdeveloped. Implementing governance through a host nation could be lengthy and complex. Also, members of other Aboriginal nations living in the host nation's territory might not feel that their aspirations, cultures or values are reflected in the host nation's approach to governance. Further, the host nation approach could increase competition for limited resources between urban Aboriginal people pursuing self-government in different ways and existing urban initiatives in institution building and program and service delivery.

Given these concerns, the host nation approach to self-government should be considered as only one of many ways to include all urban Aboriginal people in a self-government project.

Urban Métis Nation governance

The need for Métis-specific governance institutions, including initiatives in urban areas, was a consistent theme of Métis people's presentations to the Commission. According to the Métis National Council:

> The Métis Nation feels strongly that institutions of Métis self-government should be established solely for Métis and categorically rejects approaches to urban self-government which lump Métis into institutions that serve both Indians and Métis.[106]

The urban Métis Nation governance approach would be a component of a broader vision of Métis Nation governance in urban and non-urban areas: a multi-layered system of inter-locking decision-making bodies at local, regional, provincial and national levels. Urban areas would be represented in Métis governments through urban Métis 'locals'. These locals would have authority in defined areas. As a community-level government, they would tailor their governance activities to the priorities and needs of their residents. Thus, urban locals might undertake functions different from those undertaken by their non-urban counterparts.

Urban local presidents would be members of and have voting privileges in the provincial Métis legislatures that have been proposed. This political structure would give urban locals considerable input in Métis government decision making. The Métis approach bodes well for strong local governments, including in urban areas.

Provincial Métis organizations have also developed an extensive network of institutions for program and service delivery in housing, economic development, education, and child and family services. These institutions would likely continue to serve urban Métis communities. Because of their representation in provincial-level Métis government structures, urban (and other) locals would have direct input into the overall management of these affiliated institutions.

In summary, Métis local self-governing bodies, both on and off a land base, would have a broad area of responsibility, including education, training and employment, housing, social services, justice, health and economic development. They would either deliver programs and services organized at the provincial or regional level of Métis government, working through existing or emerging institutions, or would develop their own programs and services.

Métis Nation governance in urban areas has at least two strengths: first, to a group of Aboriginal people who have been dispossessed historically, it would give access to self-government in a way that ensures their culture and goals will not be overwhelmed by Aboriginal groups with other agendas and histories;

Text continues on page 598.

TABLE 7.4
Aboriginal Population by Nation of Origin, Selected Census Metropolitan Areas, 1991

First Nation	Halifax		Montreal		Quebec City		Ottawa-Hull		Toronto		St. Catharines/ Niagara		Sudbury	
	#	%	#	%	#	%	#	%	#	%	#	%	#	%
Abenaki			190	5.9			30	1.1	25	0.5			60	3.1
Algonquian														
Algonquin			205	6.4			775	29.0	80	1.7	55	5.2	115	6.0
Attikamek					30	2.5								
Beaver			35	1.1										
Bella Coola														
Carrier									50	1.1				
Chippewyan														
Coast Tsimshian														
Comox														
Cree			155	4.8			315	12.0	460	9.7	25	2.4	140	7.3
Dakota			35	1.1					45	1.0				
Delaware									25	0.5				
Dog Rib Rae														
Gitksan														
Haida							45	1.7						
Haisla														

TABLE 7.4 (continued)
Aboriginal Population by Nation of Origin, Selected Census Metropolitan Areas, 1991

First Nation	Halifax		Montreal		Quebec City		Ottawa-Hull		Toronto		St. Catharines/ Niagara		Sudbury	
	#	%	#	%	#	%	#	%	#	%	#	%	#	%
Halkomelem														
Han									40	0.8				
Heilshuk														
Huron-Wendat			370	11.5	590	49.2	120	4.5	25	0.5				
Kutchin														
Kwakwa ka'wakw (Kwakiutl)														
Lillooet														
Mi'kmaq	590	79.0	485	15.0	95	7.9	265	9.9	245	5.2				
Mohawk	50	6.7	1,095	33.9	25	2.1	385	14.4	850	17.9	560	52.8	65	3.4
Montagnais			465	14.4	425	35.4	45	1.7						
Nisga'a									40	0.8				
Nootka														
Ojibwa	35	4.7	125	3.9			460	17.0	2,615	55.0	305	28.8	1,479	76.8
Okanagan														
Oneida									105	2.2	55	5.2		
Potawatomi									250	5.3				
Sarcee														
Sechelt														

TABLE 7.4 (continued)
Aboriginal Population by Nation of Origin, Selected Census Metropolitan Areas, 1991

First Nation	Halifax		Montreal		Quebec City		Ottawa-Hull		Toronto		St. Catharines/ Niagara		Sudbury	
	#	%	#	%	#	%	#	%	#	%	#	%	#	%
Sekani														
Shuswap														
Siksika (Blackfoot)			25	0.8					30	0.6				
Slavey														
Straits														
Squamish														
Tahltan														
Thompson														
Tlingit														
Tsilhqot'n (Chilcotin)														
Tutchone														
Wuastukwiuk (Maliseet)							75	2.8	45	1.0				
Other[1]	90	12.0	75	2.3	45	3.8	140	5.2	80	1.7	60	5.7	10	0.5
Total[2]	745	100.0	3,230	100.0	1,200	100.0	2,675	100.0	4,755	100.0	1,065	100.0	1,925	100.0

Notes:

1. Unenumerated reserves located in census metropolitan areas are excluded. First Nations with 20 or fewer persons are counted in the 'other' category.

2. Because of rounding, totals may not equal the sum of the figures in the column.

Source: Statistics Canada, 1991 Census, Custom Tabulations; Department of Indian Affairs and Northern Development, List of Bands by Nation, unpublished, 1991.

TABLE 7.4 (continued)
Aboriginal Population by Nation of Origin, Selected Census Metropolitan Areas, 1991

First Nation	Thunder Bay		Winnipeg		Regina		Edmonton		Calgary		Prince Albert		Victoria		Vancouver	
	#	%	#	%	#	%	#	%	#	%	#	%	#	%	#	%
Abenaki																
Algonquian							155	1.5							30	0.3
Algonquin															30	0.3
Attikamek																
Beaver							75	0.7								
Bella Coola															70	0.7
Carrier							70	0.7					60	1.8	340	3.2
Chippewyan			75	0.5	45	0.8	360	3.5	40	0.8	290	9.1			35	0.3
Coast Tsimshian							45	0.4	030	0.6			60	1.8	400	3.8
Comox													30	0.9	170	1.6
Cree	620	18.0	3,400	25.0	3,935	67.3	6,395	63.0	1,270	24.9	2,505	78.0	65	2.0	1,050	9.8
Dakota			280	2.0	830	14.2	1,060	10.0	240	4.7	210	6.6			35	0.3
Delaware																
Dog Rib Rae							30	0.3							30	0.3
Gitksan							35	0.3	35	0.7			25	0.8	440	4.1
Haida							40	0.4					45	1.4	435	4.1
Haisla															60	0.6

TABLE 7.4 (continued)
Aboriginal Population by Nation of Origin, Selected Census Metropolitan Areas , 1991

First Nation	Thunder Bay #	%	Winnipeg #	%	Regina #	%	Edmonton #	%	Calgary #	%	Prince Albert #	%	Victoria #	%	Vancouver #	%
Halkomelem					30	0.5			55	1.1			340	10.0	1,465	13.7
Han							30	0.3	50	1.0						
Heilshuk															420	3.9
Huron-Wendat																
Kutchin							105	1.0							30	0.3
Kwakwaka ̓ wakw (Kwakiutl)													240	7.4	610	5.7
Lillooet															270	2.5
Mi'kmaq			30	0.2			50	0.5	80	1.6					25	0.2
Mohawk			60	0.4			60	0.6	95	1.9			35	1.1	210	2.0
Montagnais																
Nisga ̓ a													35	1.1	420	3.9
Nootka													370	11.0	295	2.8
Ojibwa	2,850	81.0	9,780	70.0	845	14.5	985	9.7	820	16.1	180	5.6	155	4.8	900	8.4
Okanagan															170	1.6
Oneida																
Potawatomi																
Sarcee									730	14.3						
Sechelt															65	0.6

TABLE 7.4 (continued)
Aboriginal Population by Nation of Origin, Selected Census Metropolitan Areas, 1991

First Nation	Thunder Bay #	%	Winnipeg #	%	Regina #	%	Edmonton #	%	Calgary #	%	Prince Albert #	%	Victoria #	%	Vancouver #	%
Sekani															35	0.3
Shuswap							30	0.3	65	1.3			70	2.2	305	2.9
Siksika (Blackfoot)							305	3.0	1,335	26.2					150	1.4
Slavey							175	1.7							25	0.2
Straits													1,460	45.0	130	1.2
Squamish													80	2.5	1,300	12.2
Tahltan									25	0.5					60	5.6
Thompson									25	0.5			45	1.4	330	3.1
Tlingit															25	0.2
Tsilhqot'n (Chilcotin)															45	0.4
Tutchone															60	0.6
Wuastukwiuk (Maliseet)																
Other[1]	40	1.1	105	0.8	45	0.8	175	1.7	140	2.8	15	0.5	180	5.5	30	0.3
Total[2]	3,500	100.0	13,790	100.0	5,845	100.0	10,165	100.0	5,100	100.0	3,200	100.0	3,260	100.0	10,680	100.0

Notes:

1. Unenumerated reserves located in census metropolitan areas are excluded. First Nations with 20 or fewer persons are counted in the 'other' category.

2. Because of rounding, totals may not equal the sum of the figures in the column.

Source: Statistics Canada, 1991 Census, Custom Tabulations; Department of Indian Affairs and Northern Development, List of Bands by Nation, unpublished, 1991.

second, it has considerable support among Métis organizations already. However, like other nation-based approaches to urban governance, Métis initiatives must also meet the particular needs and interests of urban residents and ensure that they are adequately represented in provincial and national governance structures.

Urban treaty nation governance

Under the urban treaty nation governance approach, treaty entitlements or services would be provided through administration centres to citizens of treaty nations living in urban areas. These centres would provide a range of programs and services under one roof. They would likely have an associated governance structure – for example, an executive body or board of directors, including representation from participating treaty nations.

Treaty service administration centres could be organized and operated by several nations that are party to the same treaty or by nations party to different treaties. The precise nature of these arrangements could be determined by urban demographics and the representation of different treaty groups in urban centres. For example, as is evident in Table 7.5, in Regina, 68.4 per cent of the registered Indian population are beneficiaries of Treaty 4. The nations of origin of these treaty beneficiaries might join together to establish a Treaty 4 administration centre. In Winnipeg, where almost 25 per cent of the population are beneficiaries of Treaty 1 and the rest of the treaty population are beneficiaries of other treaties, it might make more sense to establish a centre operating under the auspices of several treaty nations. These treaty centres would operate under the joint authority of participating treaty nations.

This approach recognizes the portability of treaty rights and the connection that many urban treaty people wish to maintain with their nations of origin. Concentrating program and service delivery arrangements in one agency could potentially eliminate inefficiencies associated with fragmented and uncoordinated service delivery. It would also expose patterns in how the federal government meets its responsibilities to urban treaty people. The shortcomings of the urban treaty centres approach are similar to those for other nation-based approaches: accountability of nation governments to urban citizens and administrative complexity where several nations are involved.

Approaches to governance based on nations of origin may not meet the needs of Aboriginal people in urban areas for a variety of reasons. Some urban Aboriginal people have become estranged from their nations of origin. This was strongly emphasized in submissions from Aboriginal women. Participants at the Commission's round table stated, for example, that "Aboriginal organizations claim to represent Aboriginal urban people but involve little accountability and almost no voice for Aboriginal urban people".[107] Urban Aboriginal residents may identify with their city or town rather than with a nation of origin. This was particularly clear in submissions from Aboriginal youth living in cities.

The Commission is concerned that implementing nation-based urban governments could cause division in these communities or displace the efforts of many urban Aboriginal people to create communities that respect and accommodate all Aboriginal identities, cultures, values and priorities. Moreover, reconstitution of the nations on which these models rest may itself be a long and challenging process. Some nations will require time and resources to reorganize themselves and to heal divisions between urban and non-urban citizens. Therefore, nation-based approaches should be seen as a longer-term objective. It is nevertheless clear that urban governance initiatives such as those of the Métis Nation and the Siksika Nation are well on the road to implementation and should be fully supported by governments. We also recognize that many Aboriginal nations strongly reject approaches to governance that are pan-Aboriginal. In these situations, nation-based approaches may represent the only acceptable option for urban self-government.

RECOMMENDATIONS

The Commission recommends that

Nation-Based Approaches

4.7.23
Nation-based urban governance initiatives be pursued by nations when they have sufficient capacity to assume governance responsibility for the needs and interests of urban Aboriginal citizens.

4.7.24
The urban citizens of Aboriginal nations be fully consulted and participate in decisions concerning urban governance initiatives pursued by nations.

4.7.25
Aboriginal nations ensure that their urban citizens' needs and interests are recognized and that mechanisms are instituted to ensure they are represented in the political structures and decision-making processes of the nation.

4.7.26
Federal, provincial, territorial and municipal governments give full support to Aboriginal nations when they develop and implement urban governance initiatives.

TABLE 7-5
Registered Indian Population by Treaty Status, Selected Census Metropolitan Areas, 1991

Treaty Status[1]	Halifax #	Halifax %	Toronto #	Toronto %	Winnipeg #	Winnipeg %	Regina #	Regina %	Edmonton #	Edmonton %	Calgary #	Calgary %	Vancouver #	Vancouver %
Mi'kmaq[2]	590	71.0												
Williams[3]			545	9.5										
Robinson-Huron														
Robinson-Superior														
Treaty 1					3,885	24.8								
Treaty 4							4,470	68.4						
Treaty 6									4,065	34.2				
Treaty 7											2,140	38.5		
Other treaty[4]	160	19.0	3,885	68.2	9,465	60.4	950	14.5	5,535	46.6	2,380	42.8	2,610	21.3
Non-treaty[5]	15	1.8	330	5.8	380	2.4	310	4.7	580	5.0	515	9.3	7,890	64.2
Band membership not stated[6]	70	8.3	940	16.5	1,945	12.4	810	12.4	1,685	14.2	530	9.5	1,780	14.5
Total	835	100.0	5,700	100.0	15,675	100.0	6,540	100.0	11,865	100.0	5,565	100.0	12,280	100.0

Notes: Persons reporting a band/First Nation that falls within a census metropolitan treaty area were included in counts for Mi'kmaq, Williams treaties, etc., as appropriate.

1. People who reported a band/First Nation, but who were not registered: Halifax, 15; Toronto, 255; Winnipeg, 65; Regina, 25; Edmonton, 135; Calgary, 25; Vancouver, 210.

2. Mi'kmaq = Pre-Confederation treaty.

3. Includes persons in Toronto from the Beausoleil Band and the Mississaugas of the New Credit.

4. 'Other treaty' refers to persons who reported a band/First Nation whose treaty lies outside the census metropolitan area in question.

5. 'Non-treaty' refers to bands/First Nations that do not have a treaty.

6. Persons who stated that they were registered under the *Indian Act* but who did not report a band/First Nation on the census questionnaire.

Source: Statistics Canada, 1991 Census, catalogue no. 94-327, 1991 Aboriginal Data Users' Guide, and custom tabulations; Department of Indian Affairs and Northern Development, List of Bands by Treaty, unpublished, 1991.

5.4 Conclusion

There are many ways to improve the circumstances of urban Aboriginal people through urban governance arrangements. Recognizing and responding to self-government aspirations and improving the approach of Canadian governments and institutions to matters of primary concern to urban Aboriginal people will substantially improve the vitality and future of Canadian cities and towns.

Urban self-government arrangements are also essential tools for formulating new relationships between Aboriginal and non-Aboriginal people. As Aboriginal people living in cities become more involved in government decision making, acquire a greater ability to effect change in areas with a direct impact on their lives, and gain the capacity to institute fundamental, forward looking reforms, old stereotypes will disappear. Whatever form urban self-government takes, we are confident that it will go forward in an orderly and reasonable manner while meeting the needs and expectations of urban Aboriginal people. A vital part of this process will be for Aboriginal and non-Aboriginal governments to support education and healing among urban residents to ensure their meaningful participation in governance initiatives and to provide information about choices, options and decisions on governance. We address the issue of public education in greater depth in Volume 5, Chapter 4.

6. URBAN DEMOGRAPHICS AND SOCIO-ECONOMIC CONDITIONS

Until recently, information on Aboriginal people living in cities has been scarce. Census counts of Aboriginal populations have been based on questions about ethnic origins and ancestry, with varying definitions of origin and instructions for Aboriginal respondents.[108] Even these data are of limited use in establishing needs and planning services and self-government for Aboriginal peoples, because origin and ancestry provide little information about the potential demand for culturally adapted services and the desire to participate in Aboriginal institutions; the real key is how individuals identify themselves.

6.1 Aboriginal Peoples Survey

In 1991, Statistics Canada conducted a national post-census survey of Aboriginal people. The Aboriginal Peoples Survey (APS) was based on self-identification rather than ancestry,[109] but continued to reflect the urban/rural/reserve distinction traditionally employed in official statistics. This distinction was created and reinforced by policies of non-Aboriginal governments and ignores the fact that many Aboriginal people living in urban areas retain strong ties to their communities of origin.[110] These ties are important in exploring the demographic framework for self-government approaches based on citizenship or governance of traditional territories. Ultimately, data collected to support research in this area should not be organized in a way that perpetuates culturally inappropriate distinctions. Although some information on the diversity of urban Aboriginal residents can be gleaned from the 1991 census, the geography used in this chapter is of necessity based on Statistics Canada's standard urban/rural/reserve categorization.

6.2 Population Size and Dynamics

Current urban population size

The APS estimated the total 1991 Aboriginal population (First Nations, Inuit and Métis people) at 720,000. Almost two-thirds, or 466,100, resided off-reserve. Approximately 320,000 people, 44.4 per cent of the total Aboriginal population, lived in urban areas (Table 7.6).

Among the major Aboriginal groups, registered (status) Indians are the most numerous urban residents (148,500), followed by Métis people (90,100), non-status Indians (77,800) and Inuit (7,900). As a proportion of each group, however, non-status Indians are most heavily urban-based (69 per cent), followed closely by Métis people (65 per cent), then registered Indians (34 per cent) and Inuit (22 per cent) (see Table 7.6).

Migration

The APS collected data that enable migration patterns to be measured over the five-year period 1986-1991 for four geographic locations: reserves; rural non-reserve areas; census metropolitan areas (CMAs), urban areas with populations over 100,000; and urban non-CMAs, with populations between 1,000 and 100,000.[111]

Urban CMAs were net gainers of migrants between 1986 and 1991, while urban non-CMAs and rural non-reserve areas were net losers. Reserves also showed a net migration gain that was higher in absolute numbers than the urban CMAs. Analysis of migration flows between each type of location shows that urban CMAs gained Aboriginal population from smaller urban centres and from rural non-reserve areas, but experienced a net loss to reserves. However, a significant percentage (20 per cent) of the flow to reserves was composed of new registrants under Bill C-31. Winnipeg, Regina and Saskatoon had a higher percentage of in-migration from reserves and rural areas (combined) than eastern and western CMAs, including Calgary and Edmonton, whose major source of new arrivals was other CMAs.

Net migration patterns differed from one Aboriginal group to another. Registered Indians constituted the largest net gain for reserves, with CMAs following at the expense of smaller urban centres and rural areas. Although non-status Indians accounted for the majority of Aboriginal migrants to Vancouver,

Victoria and eastern CMAs, there was also a significant movement of non-registered Indians from CMAs to rural areas, resulting in a large net increase in the non-registered Indian population in rural areas and a small increase on reserves and in large urban areas. Among Métis people, CMAs showed the largest net gain, mostly from smaller urban centres. Métis people constituted between nearly one-quarter and one-third of migrants into every CMA from Winnipeg to Edmonton. Rural areas also experienced a net Métis migration originating from CMAs and from smaller urban centres. Finally, there was a very small outflow of Inuit from rural areas, largely northern communities, to small urban centres and CMAs.

Overall, urban centres with populations over 100,000 experienced a net migration gain from every Aboriginal group, while smaller urban centres had a net outflow from every group except Inuit, who had a small net inflow. Although rural areas showed a net loss of migrants, there was significant urban to rural migration among Métis people and non-registered Indians.

Finally, even though net migration to urban areas is relatively small in absolute numbers, 29 per cent of the total urban Aboriginal population in 1991 were recent in-migrants from other urban and rural areas and from reserves. This has important implications for housing, education, employment, training, and the types of services available to deliver appropriate assistance.

Projections

Except for the five-year migration pattern data derived from the APS, there is very little information on historical urbanization trends among Aboriginal people. However, data derived from a study prepared for the Commission indicate that the Aboriginal population residing in urban areas grew by 55 per cent over those 10 years. The non-Aboriginal urban population grew by approximately 11 per cent over the same period.[112]

Given migration patterns in urban areas between 1986 and 1991, it seems likely that natural increase has become a more important component of growth in the number of urban Aboriginal people than net migration. Another source of increase may be people who never identified themselves as Aboriginal before 1985 but who began to do so following passage of Bill C-31. Many of the 80,000 to 90,000 C-31 registrants were living in urban areas.

The total Aboriginal population can be expected to grow from about 720,000 in 1991 to more than a million by the year 2016, assuming that mortality rates will decline slowly and fertility rates continue a more rapid decline over the projection period. Taking into account recent trends in migration patterns and natural increase, the Aboriginal population in urban areas can be expected to grow by 43 per cent, reaching almost 457,000 by 2016. As a relative share of the total Aboriginal population, however, it is expected to decline slightly, from 44 per cent in 1991 to 42 per cent in 2016.

TABLE 7.6
Residence of Adjusted Aboriginal Identity Population, 1991

	Total Aboriginal		Registered NAI		Non-Registered NAI		Métis		Inuit[1]	
	#	%	#	%	#	%	#	%	#	%
On-reserve	254,600	35	254,600	58	—[2]		—		—	
Off-reserve	466,100	65	183,500	42	112,600	100	139,400	100	35,600	100
Total[3]	720,600	100	438,000	100	112,600	100	139,400	100	37,800	100
Urban	320,000	44	148,500	34	77,800	69	90,100	65	7,900	22
Rural	146,100	20	35,000	8	34,900	31	49,300	35	27,700	78

Notes:

NAI = North American Indian.

As a result of multiple Aboriginal group identity responses, the sum of on-reserve and off-reserve populations may be greater than the number in the total column.

Urban is defined as a population of at least 1,000 with a density of at least 400 persons per square kilometre.

The urban and rural counts do not include reserves.

Because of rounding, the totals may not equal the sum of the column figures.

1. 95,000 added to the APS count to compensate for the population on unenumerated reserves and undercoverage in participating reserve and non-reserve areas.

2. Actual APS counts for non-status Indians, Métis people and Inuit living on reserves were 3,600 (3.5%), 4,535 (3.4%) and 620 (1.7%) respectively. Because of the small numbers, these were added to non-reserve counts.

3. Non-reserve, urban and rural, adjusted counts for Inuit were derived by applying the percentage of urban and rural Inuit from the APS actual counts to the total adjusted Inuit count.

Source: M.J. Norris et al., "Projections of Canada's Aboriginal Identity Population in Canada, 1991-2016", research study prepared for RCAP (February 1995).

6.3 Composition of Urban Aboriginal Populations

The scope of institutional development in a particular location will necessarily be affected by the size of local Aboriginal populations. It will also reflect the diverse situation of urban Aboriginal residents with regard to current access to government funding and programs and aspirations for self-government.

Ancestry and identity

Ancestry and self-identification are not coincident among Aboriginal people in urban areas. In 11 CMAs studied, the percentage of people with Aboriginal ancestry who also identified with an Aboriginal group varied from 15.2 per cent in Montreal to 86.3 per cent in Regina (see Table 7.7). The size of the 'identity' population reflects changes in patterns of self-identification. Among the CMAs studied, Montreal, Halifax, Ottawa-Hull, Toronto and Victoria all contain a relatively high proportion of people with Aboriginal ancestry who do not currently identify themselves as Aboriginal people.

North American Indians

To pursue Aboriginal governance, social and economic development, and service delivery in an urban environment, the composition of First Nations populations must be understood in the context of their legal status, band membership, and treaty and nation affiliations. Band membership, for example, entails certain rights and privileges such as voting in band elections, voting on issues within the jurisdiction of the band council, and voting on the right to reside on the reserve.

North American Indians who are registered (status) Indians under the *Indian Act* are the largest group of Aboriginal urban residents (see Table 7.6). The 50,490 Indians living in urban areas who were reinstated under Bill C-31 make up more than one-third of this group.

In many CMAs, the vast majority of the registered Indian population are band members. Some, however, did not report a band or First Nation membership. The highest number of these was in Winnipeg (1,945), followed by Vancouver, Edmonton and Ottawa-Hull.

The distribution of treaty and nation affiliation in urban areas could have a significant impact on approaches to self-government. The treaty affiliations of First Nations residents of 10 selected urban areas showed no consistent pattern (see Table 7.5). In four areas (Halifax, Sudbury, Regina and Prince Albert), a majority of First Nations residents belonged to the bands whose treaty territory included the city. In four other areas (Thunder Bay, Winnipeg, Edmonton and Calgary), the percentage ranged between 25 and 43. In Vancouver, at the other extreme, 64 per cent of First Nations residents reported non-treaty band or First Nation affiliation, reflecting the general absence of treaties in British Columbia.

The distribution of nations of origin also varied considerably among urban areas (see Table 7.4). First Nations residents of Halifax are predominantly Mi'kmaq. Regina and Edmonton have a majority of Cree Nation people. Sudbury, Thunder Bay, Winnipeg and Toronto are mostly Ojibwa. Other large cities, such as Montreal, Vancouver and Calgary, have a greater mix of nations of origin.

Métis people

Métis people represent 28 per cent (about 90,000) of urban Aboriginal residents. The proportion of Aboriginal people identifying themselves as Métis people ranges from 10.1 per cent in Toronto to 46.9 per cent in Saskatoon, with actual numbers ranging from 345 in Victoria to 13,515 in Edmonton. Although prairie cities report the highest numbers and proportion of Métis residents, there are a significant number in eastern cities and in British Columbia.

Non-status Indians

The estimated 78,000 North American Indians not registered under the *Indian Act* residing in urban areas in 1991 (see Table 7.6) made up about 24 per cent of the total urban Aboriginal population. Little is known about their affiliation with a community of origin; in the 1991 census, few non-status Indians reported band or First Nation membership or affiliation. Although the impact of this substantial group on self-government issues, economic and social development, and service delivery may not be evident, it clearly constitutes yet another heterogeneous element in the composition of Aboriginal peoples in urban areas.

Inuit

About 8,400 Inuit were estimated to be living in urban areas in 1991, representing 2.6 per cent of the total urban Aboriginal population. Only 1,850 were reported residing in CMAs, with the remainder in northern centres such as Yellowknife, Iqaluit and Happy Valley-Goose Bay.

6.4 Demographic, Social and Economic Conditions

The 1991 APS collected data on a variety of demographic and socio-economic characteristics. While the data highlight the poverty of much of the urban Aboriginal population, this population is not homogeneous, and Aboriginal people are represented at all socio-economic levels. The plight of many, however, is serious. (Unless otherwise specified, the socio-economic data presented here are based on the APS counts, without adjustment for undercoverage, because information is not available on the socio-economic characteristics of the unenumerated population.)

TABLE 7.7

Aboriginal Ancestry and Aboriginal Identity in Selected Census Metropolitan Areas, 1991

	Population With Aboriginal Ancestry[1]	Ancestry Population Identifying as Aboriginal	% of CMA Population Identifying as Aboriginal
	#	%	%
Halifax	6,710	17.7	0.4
Montreal	44,645	15.2	0.2
Ottawa-Hull	30,890	22.4	0.8
Toronto	40,040	35.5	0.4
Winnipeg	44,970	78.2	5.4
Regina	12,765	86.3	5.8
Saskatoon	14,225	83.8	5.7
Calgary	24,375	57.7	1.9
Edmonton	42,695	68.5	3.5
Vancouver	42,795	58.5	1.6
Victoria	10,215	43.4	1.6

Notes:

CMA = Census Metropolitan Area.

1. Includes people who identified single and multiple ethnic or cultural origins.

Source: Statistics Canada, 1991 Census, Aboriginal Peoples Survey, catalogue no. 94-327.

Sex

The over-representation of women among urban Aboriginal residents has been a long-standing pattern. By 1991, 56 per cent of registered North American Indians in urban areas were women; among non-status Indians and Métis people in urban areas, 52 per cent were women (see Table 7.1). Only Inuit had more men than women in urban areas.

Part of the reason for the predominance of women among urban Aboriginal residents lies in their reasons for moving to non-reserve locations, which tend to be related to housing and family considerations rather than economic factors. Other research suggests that women are more likely to move to urban areas as heads of families and require different kinds of services than men, who are more likely to migrate as 'unattached' individuals.[113]

Age

Aboriginal people residing in urban areas are considerably younger than the general urban population (see Table 7.1). Thirty-seven per cent of women are under 15, compared to 20 per cent in the non-Aboriginal population. The difference continues into the 15-24 age group, which constitutes 20 per cent of urban female Aboriginal residents but only 14 per cent of non-Aboriginal women. And only five per cent of female Aboriginal residents are over 55, compared to 20 per cent of the non-Aboriginal urban population.

Use of Aboriginal languages

Many participants in the Commission's hearings expressed strong concern about the loss of Aboriginal cultures and languages. These concerns are borne out by data gathered for the APS (see Table 7.1, as well as Volume 3, Chapters 5 and 6). Only about 18 per cent of urban Aboriginal people aged 15 and over reported being able to speak an Aboriginal language; for Métis people and non-status Indians, this number fell to 11 per cent and 5.6 per cent respectively. Almost three-quarters of urban residents who had never spoken an Aboriginal language expressed a desire to learn one.

Education

APS data show that the urban Aboriginal population is generally less well educated than non-Aboriginal residents (see Table 7.1). Even though the percentage of the urban Aboriginal population holding a university degree is two to four times higher than the reserve and rural population, it amounts to only about four per cent, compared to 13 per cent of non-Aboriginal urban residents. A significant gap remains with regard to high school or trades certificates, which are held by 13 per cent of the urban Aboriginal population and almost 19 per cent of non-Aboriginal residents. Only among holders of post-secondary non-university certificates and diplomas does the difference narrow, to 15 per cent of Aboriginal residents and 16 per cent of non-Aboriginal residents.

Labour force characteristics

Early research on urban Aboriginal people assumed that over time they would be integrated into the labour force and benefit from economic mobility. These assumptions were challenged by studies in the 1970s and 1980s demonstrating the difficulty of achieving economic success in urban environments and undermining the notion that time and increasing familiarity with the city would facilitate urban Aboriginal residents' integration into the labour market.[114]

By 1991, Aboriginal labour force participation rates were approaching those of non-Aboriginal people in urban areas. However, unemployment rates were more than twice as high for Aboriginal people (see Table 7.1).

There is considerable variation between CMAs and between different aboriginal groups in particular CMAs regarding both participation and unemployment rates. Nevertheless, the aggregate figures suggest there is little reason to be optimistic about the employment situation of Aboriginal people in urban areas. The substantial variations between urban areas and Aboriginal groups also suggest that employment initiatives should be locally targeted.

Income

In light of the labour force situation of many urban Aboriginal residents, it is not surprising that their average annual incomes (from all sources) lagged fully 33 per cent behind those of their non-Aboriginal counterparts (see Table 7.1). The average total annual income for Aboriginal people was $16,560, compared to $24,876 for non-Aboriginal residents.

Aboriginal people no longer attending school and working for 40 or more weeks a year fare considerably better in urban areas than on reserves or in rural areas. Aboriginal CMA residents earned on average $25,375 per year, while reserve residents earned $20,109. Nevertheless, the income gap with comparable non-Aboriginal urban residents persisted; the latter had an average annual income of $34,602, more than 36 per cent higher than their Aboriginal counterparts.

Poverty

The incidence of poverty is very high among Aboriginal people residing in urban areas. Thirty-five per cent received less than $10,000 per year in income from all sources, compared to 26 per cent of the non-Aboriginal population (see Table 7.1).

The picture becomes worse when measured against the 'poverty line', or low income cut-off, defined by Statistics Canada. On the basis of 1991 census data for Aboriginal household incomes in selected CMAs, Winnipeg, Regina and Saskatoon reported more than 60 per cent of Aboriginal households below the low income cut-off. The situation was even more serious among female single-parent households in these cities, where between 80 and 90 per cent were below the poverty line. In other CMAs, between 40 and 76 per cent of these households fell below the poverty line.[115]

Housing

A study conducted for the Canada Mortgage and Housing Corporation (CMHC) to determine whether urban Aboriginal households were in 'core need' developed an index to measure the adequacy, suitability and affordability of housing units.[116] It found that in 1991, 33 per cent of urban area Aboriginal households were in core need, compared to 17 per cent of non-Aboriginal households.

The most prevalent problem was shelter affordability, with all CMAs from Winnipeg to Victoria reporting shelter costs exceeding 30 per cent of household income in about four of 10 Aboriginal households. At least eight of 11 CMAs reported that 60 per cent or more of female single-parent households had shelter costs exceeding this affordability index. In fact, single-parent families represented almost one-third of Aboriginal households with an affordability problem, with single-person households also accounting for one-third, and two-parent households with children constituting a further 18 per cent.

Comparative characteristics of migrants and non-migrants

Sex

Women dominated the 1986-1991 migration streams into all areas, especially urban areas where they represented about 58 per cent of all migrants (see Table 7.2). The APS also found that one woman in five living in urban areas had moved during the 12 months before the survey.

Reasons for moving

While the Clatworthy study did not explore reasons for moving to urban areas specifically, it did examine reasons for migrating to non-reserve areas generally (see Table 7.3). More than 30 per cent of migrants said they moved for family-related reasons. Access to employment and improved housing were each cited by 20 per cent. Eight per cent cited 'community factors', and five per cent said they were forced to move.

The percentage of women citing community factors was far higher than men, while the proportion citing access to employment was significantly lower. More women than men apparently moved for non-economic reasons. This finding is consistent with the economic condition of Aboriginal women who migrated to CMAs.

Family status

Spouses and single parents constituted more than 48 per cent of all migrants, with children making up another 35 per cent.[117] Single-parent families accounted for 12 per cent of the population migrating to CMAs from 1986 to 1991. 'Unattached' individuals constituted 16 per cent of all migrants and 19 per cent of those migrating into CMAs. The proportion of children was smaller among migrants than among non-migrants, suggesting that migrant families tend to move at an earlier stage of the family formation cycle.

Socio-economic characteristics

Sixty-two per cent of migrants to CMAs had a secondary school certificate or post-secondary schooling, compared to 50 per cent of non-migrants and 66 per cent of the non-Aboriginal population.[118] In smaller urban areas, only about 55 per cent of migrants and 35 per cent of non-migrants had a secondary school certificate or more.

Both male and female migrants to urban areas tend to be more active participants in the labour force than their non-migrant counterparts. In CMAs, non-migrants and female migrants participated in the labour force at the same rate as non-Aboriginal residents, while male Aboriginal migrants had a higher participation rate. Migrants, however, did not fare as well as non-migrants: both male and female migrants had higher unemployment rates. Moreover, the unemployment rates of urban Aboriginal residents were generally two and a half times higher than those of the non-Aboriginal population.

Aboriginal migrants who were out of school and working full-time in CMAs had slightly higher average employment income than non-migrants, but it was still more than 26 per cent lower than that of their non-Aboriginal counterparts.

The desperate economic conditions facing single-parent Aboriginal women were even worse among migrants to CMAs. In nine of 11 CMAs, more than 60 per cent of migrant female single-parent families were living below the poverty line. The situation was scarcely better for two-parent migrant families in Regina and Saskatoon, as many as 50 per cent of whom were below Statistics Canada's low income cut-off.

6.5 Conclusion

In this section we have used the available data to describe the key demographic, social and economic conditions of Aboriginal people living in urban areas, with particular emphasis on metropolitan areas.

Demographically, the urban Aboriginal population experienced very rapid growth between 1981 and 1991, increasing by 55 per cent (compared to an 11 per cent increase in urban non-Aboriginal residents). Although the future rate of growth is expected to be slower than in 1981-1991, the urban Aboriginal population is still expected to grow by 43 per cent in the next 25 years, from 320,000 in 1991 to 457,000 in 2016. It is vital for policy and programming purposes to remember that urban residents constituted 44 per cent of the total Aboriginal population in 1991.

Another major feature of the urban Aboriginal population is its diversity. This will have a significant impact on forms of urban self-government, institutions and service delivery vehicles. In particular, it is not clear how urban Aboriginal residents will identify themselves in the future and how they will organize for self-government purposes. The Commission is concerned that relevant information be collected and made a number of recommendations in this regard in Volume 2, Chapter 3.

Finally, the information presented in this section highlights the poverty, high dependency ratios and disadvantaged labour market position of urban Aboriginal residents and the particular plight of Aboriginal women living in urban areas. At the same time, socio-economic characteristics do vary widely between urban areas, so that Aboriginal people in different areas have distinct needs and priorities. Their aspirations and capacity to consider and implement self-government will also differ.

These factors suggest that while some initiatives should focus on providing immediate relief, others require more long-term planning and implementation strategies. The varying capacity of urban Aboriginal populations also suggests that information, strategies and experience relating to governance should be shared so that each community is not required to bear the entire burden of developing its own approaches to self-government and the provision of services.

7. Conclusion

Aboriginal people living in urban areas face many challenges, not the least of which is maintaining their cultural identity as Aboriginal people. Some become trapped between two worlds – unable to find a place in either their Aboriginal culture or the culture of the dominant society. Others find ways to bridge the gap, to remain firmly grounded in traditional values while living and working in an urban milieu. In this chapter we examined ways to maintain and strengthen Aboriginal identity in urban areas.

The influx of Aboriginal people into Canadian cities is a relatively recent phenomenon. Government policy, which was originally developed mainly to deal with Aboriginal people living in Aboriginal communities, has not kept pace. Policy has developed in a piecemeal, uncoordinated fashion, leaving gaps and disputes over jurisdiction and responsibility. Urban Aboriginal people have felt the effects socially – through unemployment, low wages and the like – and culturally, through systemic racism and a weakening or erasing of Aboriginal identity. The combination can be deadly. We have proposed a number of recommendations aimed at resolving jurisdictional confusion and fostering a sound, co-ordinated approach to urban Aboriginal policy. We have done so largely by listening to the testimony and ideas of urban Aboriginal people.

Aboriginal people want urban institutions that reflect Aboriginal values. As we have seen, this often means creating or strengthening Aboriginally controlled institutions. Urban Aboriginal people also want to be able to practise their culture and traditions in the urban setting. And like Aboriginal people everywhere, urban Aboriginal people are seeking self-determination. We have detailed a number of ways self-governance can operate in urban areas.

Territory, land and home have always been important to Aboriginal people. Those living in urban Canada are no different. For some, the land that lies beneath the concrete is their territory. Others choose to leave their homeland for a variety of reasons, be it education, employment or opportunity. Whatever the case, there is no need for Aboriginal people to shed their identity at the city limits. Identity is more than skin deep. It is in the blood, the heart and the mind, Aboriginal people told us; you carry it with you wherever you go.

NOTES

1. Larry Krotz, *Urban Indians: The Strangers in Canada's Cities* (Edmonton: Hurtig Publishers, 1980), pp. 10-11.

2. Native Council of Canada, *Decision 1992: Background and Discussion Points for the First Peoples Forums* (Ottawa: 1992), p. 10.

3. See, in general, Terry Goldie, *Fear and Temptation: The Image of the Indigene in Canadian, Australian and New Zealand Literatures* (Kingston and Montreal: McGill-Queen's University Press, 1989).

4. Debi Spence, "Rebuilding the Spirit of the Urban Aboriginal Under Class: Leading Aboriginal People to Self-Government", brief submitted to the Royal Commission on Aboriginal Peoples [RCAP] (1993), p. 9. For information about briefs submitted to RCAP, see *A Note About Sources* at the beginning of this volume.

5. A low income cut-off (LICO) represents the amount of income needed for basic necessities (and all other income is disposable). LICOs vary by family size, degree of urbanization and geographic location. The figures are updated yearly based on changes in the consumer price index.

6. John W. Berry, "Aboriginal Cultural Identity", research study prepared for the Royal Commission on Aboriginal Peoples (1993). For information about research studies prepared for RCAP, see *A Note About Sources* at the beginning of this volume.

7. Two-day learning circles were held in Victoria (two sessions); Inuvik, Northwest Territories (two sessions); Saskatoon; Winnipeg (two sessions); Quebec City; and Halifax (two sessions). The results are summarized in Kathleen E. Absolon and R. Anthony Winchester, "Cultural Identity for Urban Aboriginal Peoples: Learning Circles Synthesis Report", research study prepared for RCAP (1994).

8. Etah, a 17-year-old street youth in Vancouver, quoted in Lauri Gilchrist and R. Anthony Winchester, "Kāptī tipis ē-pimohteyahk (Urban Perspectives: Aboriginal Street Youth Study): Vancouver, Winnipeg and Montreal", research study prepared for RCAP (1995).

9. Absolon and Winchester, "Cultural Identity" (cited in note 7).

10. Absolon and Winchester, "Cultural Identity" (Inuvik).

11. Absolon and Winchester, "Cultural Identity" (Quebec City).

12. Absolon and Winchester, "Cultural Identity" (Inuvik).

13. Absolon and Winchester, "Cultural Identity" (Winnipeg).

14. Aboriginal Youth Council of Canada, "Aboriginal Youth in Crisis", brief submitted to RCAP (1993), p. 24.

15. Absolon and Winchester, "Cultural Identity" (Halifax) (cited in note 7).

16. Absolon and Winchester, "Cultural Identity" (Saskatoon).

17. Absolon and Winchester, "Cultural Identity" (Halifax).

18. Absolon and Winchester, "Cultural Identity" (Victoria).

19. Absolon and Winchester, "Cultural Identity" (Saskatoon).

20. Absolon and Winchester, "Cultural Identity" (Victoria and Winnipeg).

21. Kathleen E. Absolon and R. Anthony Winchester, "Urban Perspectives Cultural Identity Project, Victoria Report: Case Studies of 'Sonny' and 'Emma'", research study prepared for RCAP (1994).

22. Ian Chapman and Don McCaskill, *The Ontario Federation of Friendship Centres: Case Studies on Native Management* (Peterborough: Native Management and Economic Development Program, Trent University, 1990).

23. Absolon and Winchester, "Cultural Identity" (cited in note 7) (Saskatoon).

24. Absolon and Winchester, "Urban Perspectives" (cited in note 21).

25. RCAP, *Aboriginal Peoples in Urban Centres*, Report of the National Round Table on Aboriginal Urban Issues (Ottawa: Supply and Services, 1993), p. 17.

26. *Re Term "Indians"*, [1939] 1 S.C.R. 104 at 121; and [1939] 2 D.L.R. 417 at 433.

27. See Bradford W. Morse and John Giokas, "Do the Métis Fall Within Section 91(24) of the *Constitution Act, 1867*?", in *Aboriginal Self-Government: Legal and Constitutional Issues* (Ottawa: RCAP, 1995), p. 140.

28. Robert Mitchell, attorney general and minister responsible for Saskatchewan's Indian and Métis affairs secretariat, "Submission of the Province of Saskatchewan to the Royal Commission on Aboriginal Peoples" (11 May 1993), p. 5.

29. Bradford W. Morse, "Government Obligations, Aboriginal Peoples and Section 91(24)", in David Hawkes, ed., *Aboriginal Peoples and Government Responsibility: Exploring Federal and Provincial Roles* (Ottawa: Carleton University Press, 1989), p. 71.

30. Mitchell, "Submission of the Province of Saskatchewan" (cited in note 28), pp. 5-6.

31. See *R. v. Dick*, [1985] 2 S.C.R. 309 at 326-28; *R. v. Kruger*, [1978] 1 S.C.R. 104 at 115; and *R. v. Alphonse*, [1993] 5 W.W.R. 401 at 415-417 (B.C.C.A.).

32. See the cases cited in note 31. See also *Four B Manufacturing* v. *United Garment Workers of America and Ontario Labour Relations Board*, [1980] 1 S.C.R. 1031 at 1048; Douglas Sanders, "The Constitution, the Provinces and Aboriginal Peoples", in J. Anthony Long, Menno Boldt, Leroy Little Bear, eds., *Governments in Conflict? Provinces and Indian Nations in Canada* (Toronto: University of Toronto Press, 1988), pp. 155-156; and Patrick Macklem, "First Nations Self-Government and the Borders of the Canadian Legal Imagination" (1991) 36 McGill L.J. 382.

33. *Natural Parents* v. *Superintendent of Child Welfare* (1975), 60 D.L.R. (3rd series) 148; and *Four B Manufacturing* (cited in note 32).

34. *Mitchell* v. *Peguis Indian Band*, [1990] 2 S.C.R. 85 per Dickson C.J.C. at 109; see also RCAP, *Partners in Confederation: Aboriginal Peoples, Self-Government, and the Constitution* (Ottawa: Supply and Services, 1993), p. 33.

35. The Ontario government strategy is based on the final report of the Aboriginal Family Healing Joint Steering Committee, *For Generations to Come: The Time is Now* (September 1993); and Ontario Ministry of Health, *New Directions: Aboriginal Health Policy for Ontario* (Toronto: Queen's Printer for Ontario, 1994).

36. See Morse, "Government Obligations" (cited in note 29), pp. 71-72. One significant exception to this general rule was the establishment in 1938 of 12 Métis settlements in Alberta, which provided a land base and mechanisms for local self-government to many Métis and non-status Indians residing in Alberta. See *The Metis Population Betterment Act, 1940*, S.A. 1940, c. 6. Currently, there are eight Métis settlements.

37. See Report of the [Ontario] Social Assistance Review Committee, *Transitions* (Toronto: Queen's Printer, 1988); First Nations' Project Team Report, *Social Assistance Legislation Review* (Toronto: Queen's Printer, 1992); K.A. (Kim) Scott, "Funding Policy for Indigenous Human Services", in RCAP, *The Path to Healing: Report of the National Round Table on Aboriginal Health and Social Issues* (Ottawa: Supply and Services, 1993), pp. 90-107.

38. Alberta Health, *Strengthening the Circle: What Aboriginal Albertans Say About Their Health* (Edmonton: 1995), p. 5.

39. Sanders, "The Constitution, the Provinces and Aboriginal Peoples" (cited in note 32), pp. 160-162.

40. See First Nations Circle on the Constitution, Commissioners' Report, *To The Source* (Ottawa: Assembly of First Nations, 1992).

41. See RCAP, *Aboriginal Peoples in Urban Centres* (cited in note 25).

42. Manitoba, Legislative Assembly, *Debates and Proceedings*, No. 1 (26 November 1992) at 5.

43. Mitchell, "Submission of the Province of Saskatchewan" (cited in note 28), p. 5.

44. See Glenn Drover and Allan Moscovitch, "Inequality and Social Welfare", in Allan Moscovitch and Glenn Drover, eds., *Inequality: Essays on the Political Economy of Social Welfare* (Toronto: University of Toronto Press, 1981).

45. John H. Hylton, "The Case for Aboriginal Self-Government: A Social Policy Perspective", in John H. Hylton, ed., *Aboriginal Self-Government in Canada: Current Trends and Issues* (Saskatoon: Purich Publishing, 1994), p. 36; and John D. O'Neil, "Aboriginal Health Policy for the Next Century", in RCAP, *The Path to Healing* (cited in note 37), pp. 30-34.

46. For example, "67 per cent of First Nations in Ontario (representing 54 per cent of the reserve population) have persistently experienced social assistance dependency rates above 20 per cent...for the past twenty years." See First Nations' Project Team Report, *Social Assistance Legislation Review* (cited in note 37).

47. See, generally, David C. Hawkes and Allan M. Maslove, "Fiscal Arrangements for Aboriginal Self-Government", in D.C. Hawkes, ed., *Aboriginal Peoples and Government Responsibility: Exploring Federal and Provincial Roles* (Ottawa: Carleton

University Press, 1989), pp. 93-138; and Robin Boadway, *The Constitutional Division of Powers: An Economic Perspective*, study prepared for the Economic Council of Canada (Ottawa: Supply and Services, 1992).

48. R.S.C. 1985, c. 6, ss. 8-13.

49. See *Finlay* v. *Canada (Minister of Finance)*, [1993] 1 S.C.R. 1080; and Margot E. Young, "Starving in the Shadow of the Law: A Comment on *Finlay* v. *Canada (Minister of Finance)*", *Constitutional Forum* 5/2 (Winter 1994), p. 31.

50. Calculated from data in Thomas J. Courchene, *Social Canada in the Millennium: Reform Imperatives and Restructuring Principles* (Toronto: C.D. Howe Institute, 1994), p. 153.

51. *Reference Re Canada Assistance Plan (B.C.)*, [1991] 2 S.C.R. 525.

52. See the *Budget Implementation Act, 1995*, S.C. 1994-95, c. 17, Parts IV and V, ss. 31, 48.

53. Hylton, "The Case for Aboriginal Self-Government" (cited in note 45), p. 39. See RCAP, *Aboriginal Peoples in Urban Centres* (cited in note 25), pp. 7-8.

54. Ontario Fair Tax Commission, *Fair Taxation in a Changing World* (Toronto: University of Toronto Press, 1993), p. 66.

55. Brian Slattery, "Understanding Aboriginal Rights" (1987) 66 Can. Bar Rev. 727 at 776 [notes omitted].

56. Hawkes and Maslove, "Fiscal Arrangements" (cited in note 47), p. 101.

57. Aboriginal groups argued unsuccessfully before the English courts that the obligations imposed by pre- and post-Confederation treaties remained with the Imperial Crown. See *R.* v. *Secretary of State (Foreign and Commonwealth Affairs)*, [1982] 2 All E.R. 118 (C.A.).

58. See *R.* v. *Secretary of State*, at 135, Kerr L.J.; and at 142, May L.J.; and, generally, Alan Pratt, "The Fiduciary Relationship and Aboriginal Governance: Protection and Non-Interference", discussion paper prepared for RCAP (1995).

59. See *Liquidators of the Maritime Bank of Canada* v. *New Brunswick (Receiver-General)*, [1892] A.C. and Privy Council 437 at 441-42; and *Hodge* v. *R.*, [1883] 9 A.C. and Privy Council 117 at 132.

60. See Morse, "Government Obligations" (cited in note 29), p. 83; and Pratt, "The Fiduciary Relationship" (cited in note 58).

61. Affirmative action programs provide differential treatment in order to promote the idea of equality. See *Report of the Commission on Equality in Employment* (Ottawa: Supply and Services, 1984), pp. 2-3.

62. See *Dick* at 326; and *Kruger* at 110 (both cited in note 31).

63. See Morse, "Government Obligations" (cited in note 29), p. 88; and Bryan Schwartz, *First Principles, Second Thoughts: Aboriginal Peoples, Constitutional Reform and Canadian Statecraft* (Montreal: Institute for Research on Public Policy, 1986).

64. This was the situation in three of the four case studies of urban Aboriginal housing corporations undertaken by the Commission. The four case studies are MEWS Corporation (Stan Wilcox), "Urban Aboriginal Housing Project, Case Study: Gabriel Housing Corporation" (1993); H.P. Consultants, "Skigin-Elnoog Housing Corporation: Case Study" (1993); George W. Miller, "Inuit Non-Profit Housing Corporation of Ottawa: A Case Study" (1993); and Obonsawin-Irwin Consulting, "A Case Study of Urban Native Homes Inc. of Hamilton" (1993).

65. See RCAP, *Aboriginal Peoples in Urban Centres* (cited in note 25), p. 85.

66. RCAP, *Aboriginal Peoples in Urban Centres.*

67. See also our special report, RCAP, *Bridging the Cultural Divide: A Report on Aboriginal People and Criminal Justice in Canada* (Ottawa: Supply and Services, 1996).

68. Louis Bordeleau, Vice-President, Regroupement des centres d'amitié autochtones du Québec, transcripts of the hearings of the Royal Commission on Aboriginal Peoples [hereafter RCAP transcripts], Montreal, Quebec, 27 May 1993.

69. RCAP, *Aboriginal Peoples in Urban Centres* (cited in note 25), p. 17.

70. Gilchrist and Winchester, "Urban Perspectives", (cited in note 8).

71. Jason Thomas, All Nations Youth Council, RCAP transcripts, Prince George, British Columbia, 1 June 1993.

72. Linda Clarkson, "A Case Study of the Aboriginal Council of Winnipeg as an Inclusive Status-Blind Urban Political Representative Organization", research study prepared for RCAP (1994).

73. Statistics Canada, "1 - Disability, 2 - Housing", 1991 Aboriginal Peoples Survey, Catalogue No. 89-535 (Ottawa: 1994), and custom tabulations. 'Disability' is defined as any restriction or lack (resulting from impairment) of ability to perform an activity in the manner or within the range considered normal for a human being. See also Volume 3, Chapter 5.

74. Ted Harvey and Don McCaskill, *Evaluation of the Native Friendship Centre Program: Final Report* (Ottawa: Secretary of State, 1988).

75. Native Council of Canada, "The Urban Circle: Needs and Attitudes of Natives", brief submitted to RCAP (1993).

76. National Association of Friendship Centres, "Final Report to the Royal Commission on Aboriginal Peoples", Intervener Participation Program [IPP] report submitted to RCAP (1993).

77. National Association of Friendship Centres, "Final Report".

78. *1995-96 Estimates, Part III, Indian and Northern Affairs Canada and Canadian Polar Commission* (Ottawa: Minister of Supply and Services Canada, 1995), p. 2-57. See also SPR Associates, *An Evaluation of the Cultural/Education Centres Program* (Ottawa: DIAND, 1988).

79. Absolon and Winchester, "Cultural Identity" (cited in note 7) (Halifax).

80. RCAP, "Urban Workshop, Health and Wellness III", National Round Table on Aboriginal Urban Issues, Edmonton, June 21-23, 1992, unedited transcript.

81. Aboriginal Women's Council (B.C.), "Traditional Self-Government, Economic Development and Aboriginal Women", brief submitted to RCAP (1992), p. 43.

82. See Darlene Hall, Ikwe Widdjiitiwin, RCAP transcripts, Winnipeg, Manitoba, 23 April 1992.

83. See Jackie Adam, RCAP transcripts, Port Alberni, British Columbia, 20 May 1992.

84. See Vicki English-Currie, RCAP transcripts, Calgary, Alberta, 26 May, 1993; Melanie Omeniho, President, Women of the Metis Nation, RCAP transcripts, Edmonton, Alberta, 15 June 1993; and Indian Homemakers' Association of B.C. (IHABC), "A Quest for Self-Determination by First Nations Women", brief submitted to RCAP (1993).

85. IHABC, "Quest for Self-Determination", pp. 38-39.

86. See, for example, Jeanne Guillemin, *Urban Renegades: The Cultural Strategy of American Indians* (New York: Columbia University Press, 1975); Evelyn J. Peters, *Native Households in Winnipeg: Strategies of Co-Residence and Financial Support*, Research and Working Paper No. 5 (Winnipeg: Institute of Urban Studies, University of Winnipeg, 1984).

87. Obonsawin-Irwin Consulting, "Aboriginal Self-Determination: The Role of Aboriginal Housing Initiatives", research study prepared for RCAP (1994).

88. See Carol Croxon, Director, Ojibway Family Resource Centre, RCAP transcripts, North Bay, Ontario, 10 May 1993; Ronnie Leah, Sociology Professor, University of Lethbridge, RCAP transcripts, Lethbridge, Alberta, 24 May 1993; Luanna Dawn Harper, Youth Commissioner for the Day, RCAP transcripts, Toronto, Ontario, 3 November 1992; Doris Young, Founding President, Indigenous Women's Collective, RCAP transcripts, Winnipeg, Manitoba, 22 April 1992. See also RCAP, *Aboriginal Peoples in Urban Centres* (cited in note 25).

89. Margaret King, Saskatoon Urban Treaty Indians, RCAP transcripts, Saskatoon, Saskatchewan, 28 October 1992.

90. Vicki English-Currie, "Native Women's Issues", brief submitted to RCAP (1993), p. 4.

91. Louis Bordeleau, Centre d'entraide autochtone de Senneterre, RCAP transcripts, Val d'Or, Quebec, 1 December 1992 [translation].

92. Federation of Canadian Municipalities, "Municipalities and Aboriginal Peoples in Canada", IPP report to RCAP (1993), presented to the Commission in Montreal, 1 December 1993.

93. Federation of Canadian Municipalities, "Municipalities and Aboriginal Peoples", p. 43.

94. In its presentation to the Commission on 3 November 1993, the Native Council of Canada (since renamed the Congress of Aboriginal Peoples) put forward four suggestions for urban governance: (1) the creation of new bands in urban areas under the *Indian Act*; (2) Aboriginal neighbourhood communities; (3) pan-Aboriginal governments; and (4) autonomous Aboriginal agencies. The Commission suggests that developing an urban Aboriginal community of interest government would meet the needs these models were intended to address. See Native Council of Canada, "The First Peoples Urban Circle: Choices for Self-Determination", Book I: The National Perspective, brief submitted to RCAP (1993), p. 43.

95. Status-based urban organizations such as the Winnipeg First Nations Council and the Winnipeg Region of the Manitoba Metis Federation have so far chosen to associate themselves with provincial First Nation or Métis Nation organizations.

96. Some organizations have argued that this form of urban self-government is a logical development for the existing base of non-profit Aboriginal service agencies in urban areas. See, for example, Clarkson, "A Case Study" (cited in note 72) and Native Council of Canada, "The First Peoples Urban Circle" (cited in note 94), p. 26. At the same time, some urban Aboriginal organizations do not see themselves in such a role. See, for example, Larry Soldier, Ma-Mow-We-Tak Friendship Centre, RCAP transcripts, Thompson, Manitoba, 1 June 1993; and Thomas K. Dockstader, N'Amerind Friendship Centre, RCAP transcripts, London, Ontario, 11 May 1993.

97. Clarkson, "A Case Study".

98. Native Council of Canada, "The First Peoples Urban Circle" (cited in note 94).

99. Quoted in Native Council of Canada, "The First Peoples Urban Circle: Choices for Self-Determination", Book II, Legal and Juristictional Solutions, brief submitted to RCAP (1993), p. 46. See also National Association of Friendship Centres, "Final Report" (cited in note 76); and RCAP, *Aboriginal Peoples in Urban Centres* (cited in note 25).

100. This point was made in presentations by Sylvia Maracle and Wayne Helgason to a workshop on urban self-government. See Evelyn J. Peters, ed., *Aboriginal Self-Government in Urban Areas*, Proceedings of a Workshop, 25 and 26 May 1994 (Kingston: Institute of Intergovernmental Relations, Queen's University, 1994).

101. Terry Mountjoy, "Regina Perspectives on Aboriginal Government", in Peters, ed., *Aboriginal Self-Government in Urban Areas*, p. 150.

102. New Brunswick Aboriginal Peoples Council, "Aboriginal Self-Governance Within the Province of New Brunswick", research study prepared for RCAP (1994).

103. RCAP, *Aboriginal Peoples in Urban Centres* (cited in note 25), pp. 18-19. See also Margaret King, Saskatoon Urban Treaty Indians, RCAP transcripts, Saskatoon, Saskatchewan, 28 October 1992.

104. Andrew Bear Robe, "The Historical, Legal and Current Basis for Siksika Nation Governance, Including Its Future Possibilities Within Canada", research study prepared for RCAP (1995).

105. See, for example, Council for Yukon Indians, *Umbrella Final Agreement* (Ottawa: Supply and Services, 1993); Assembly of Manitoba Chiefs, "Planning Change, A Report to the Fifth Annual Assembly of Manitoba Chiefs and Submission to the Royal Commission on Aboriginal Peoples" (1993); and Federation of Saskatchewan Indian Nations, "First Nations Self-Government, A Special Research Report", research study prepared for RCAP (1993).

106. Marc LeClair, "Métis Self-Government Origins and Urban Institutions", research study prepared for RCAP (1993). See also Ernie Blais, President, Manitoba Metis Federation, RCAP transcripts, Winnipeg, Manitoba, 2 June 1993; Metis National Council, "The State of Research and Opinion of the Metis Nation of Canada", brief submitted to RCAP; Metis Family and Community Justice Services, "Metis Self-Government in Saskatchewan", research study prepared for RCAP (1995); and Manitoba Metis Federation (The Pas Region), "Metis Self-Governance in Urban Manitoba", research study prepared for RCAP (1995).

107. RCAP, *Aboriginal Peoples in Urban Centres* (cited in note 25), p. 57.

108. Instructions concerning definition of origin and particular directives for Aboriginal respondents have varied considerably over the years. See Gustave Goldmann, "The Aboriginal Population and the Census: 120 Years of Information – 1871 to 1991", paper presented at the 22nd General Population Conference of the International Union for Scientific Study of Population, Montreal, Quebec, 24 August 1993.

109. In contrast to the general census, the focus of the APS was on how individuals identified *themselves*. It sampled 135,000 individuals who had indicated on their general census forms either that they had Aboriginal origins or that they were a registered Indian under the *Indian Act*. The individuals selected for the APS were then asked whether they identified with an Aboriginal group or were a registered Indian. Those who answered in the affirmative were asked to respond to the rest of the questionnaire.

110. Patrick Falconer, "Urban Indian Needs: Federal Policy Responsibility and Options in the Context of the Talks on Aboriginal Self-Government", discussion paper (Winnipeg: 1985); and Peters, ed., *Aboriginal Self-Government in Urban Areas* (cited in note 100).

111. The data on and analysis of migrations patterns are drawn from a research study prepared for RCAP and CMHC by Stewart Clatworthy, "The Migration and Mobility Patterns of Canada's Aboriginal Population". Reserves located in urban areas were included with reserve areas. Urban non-CMAs are urban areas with a population of less than 100,000 that correspond to the definition of urban used for the census (population of 1,000 or more and a density of 400 persons per square kilometre).

112. Don Kerr, Andy Siggner, and Jean-Pierre Bourdeau, "Canada's Aboriginal Population, 1981-1991: A Summary Report", research study prepared for RCAP (1995).

113. Clatworthy, "Migration and Mobility Patterns" (cited in note 111).

114. Yngve Georg Lithman, *The Community Apart: A Case Study of a Canadian Reserve Community* (Winnipeg: University of Manitoba Press, 1984); Kathleen A. Mooney, "Urban and Reserve Coast Salish Employment: A Test of Two Approaches to the Indian's Niche in North America", *Journal of Anthropological Research* 32/4 (Winter 1976), pp. 390-410; and Stewart Clatworthy, "Patterns of Native Employment in the Winnipeg Labour Market", research study prepared for the Institute of Urban Studies, University of Winnipeg (Winnipeg: 1981).

115. Clatworthy, "Migration and Mobility Patterns" (cited in note 111), Table 35.

116. Ark Research Associates, "The Housing Conditions of Aboriginal People in Canada, 1991: Summary Report", prepared for Canada Mortgage and Housing Corporation (Ottawa: 1995).

117. Data on family status from Clatworthy, "Migration and Mobility Patterns" (cited in note 111).

118. Data on socio-economic characteristics from Clatworthy, "Migration and Mobility Patterns".

Appendix A

Summary of Recommendations in Volume 4

Chapter 2 Women's Perspectives

The Commission recommends that

Participation in
Nation Building
4.2.1

The government of Canada provide funding to Aboriginal women's organizations, including urban-based groups, to
  (a) improve their research capacity and facilitate their participation in all stages of discussion leading to the design and development of self-government processes; and
  (b) enable them to participate fully in all aspects of nation building, including developing criteria for citizenship and related appeal processes.

Participation in
Health Institutions
4.2.2

Aboriginal governments and organizations provide for the full and fair participation of Aboriginal women in the governing bodies of all Aboriginal health and healing institutions.

Inventory of
Aboriginal
Women's Groups
4.2.3

Aboriginal governments and planning bodies with a mandate to develop new structures for human services undertake, in collaboration with women's organizations, an inventory of existing services, organizations and networks with a view to building on existing strengths and ensuring continuity of effort.

Chapter 3 Elders' Perspectives

The Commission recommends that

Participation in
Nation Building
4.3.1

Aboriginal, federal, provincial and territorial governments acknowledge the essential role of Elders and the traditional knowledge that they have to contribute in rebuilding Aboriginal nations and reconstructing institutions to support Aboriginal self-determination and well-being. This acknowledgement should be expressed in practice by
  (a) involving Elders in conceptualizing, planning and monitoring nation-building activities and institutional development;

(b) ensuring that the knowledge of both male and female Elders, as appropriate, is engaged in such activities;

(c) compensating Elders in a manner that conforms to cultural practices and recognizes their expertise and contribution;

(d) supporting gatherings and networks of Elders to share knowledge and experience with each other and to explore applications of traditional knowledge to contemporary issues; and

(e) modifying regulations in non-Aboriginal institutions that have the effect of excluding the participation of Elders on the basis of age.

Protection of Sacred Sites **4.3.2**

Aboriginal Elders be involved in the formulation and implementation of policies for the preservation and protection of sacred sites. In co-management situations, Elders should be board members.

Access to Public Lands for Traditional Purposes **4.3.3**

Federal, provincial and territorial governments

(a) recognize Aboriginal people's right of access to public lands for the purpose of gathering traditional herbs, plants and other traditional medicines where the exercise of the right is not incompatible with existing use; and

(b) consult with Aboriginal governments on guidelines to govern the implementation of this right.

Chapter 4 The Search for Belonging: Perspectives of Youth

The Commission recommends that

Cultural Centres for Youth **4.4.1**

Youth centres be established on reserves and in communities, including urban communities, where there is a significant Aboriginal population. Where cultural centres exist they should develop a specific youth component, including cultural and recreational programs.

Cultural Camps for Youth **4.4.2**

Federal, provincial and territorial governments provide funding for community initiatives to establish Aboriginal youth camps that would

(a) pursue cultural activities linking youth with elders through the development of traditional skills and knowledge;

(b) promote a healthy lifestyle (counselling, fitness and nutrition); and

(c) encourage positive social interaction between Aboriginal youth of different nations and between Aboriginal and non-Aboriginal youth.

Aboriginal Sports and Recreation Advisory Council

4.4.3

The federal government, through the Minister of State for Fitness and Amateur Sport, establish and fund an Aboriginal sports and recreation advisory council to advise – in consultation with regional, provincial and territorial sports and recreation organizations – federal, provincial, territorial and Aboriginal governments on how best to meet the sports and recreation needs of Aboriginal people (including those living in urban areas).

Sports and Recreation Initiatives

4.4.4

The proposed Aboriginal sports and recreation advisory council promote programs and initiatives that are

(a) community-driven, based on needs identified by the community, with programming developed or modified by the community to meet the community's needs;

(b) sustainable, as opposed to one-time tournaments or events; and

(c) capacity builders aimed at providing instruction in recreation programming, leadership development and coaching skills.

Intergovernmental Forum within 1 Year of Report

4.4.5

A meeting of ministers responsible for sports and recreation be convened within one year of the publication of this report to discuss the form and structure of the proposed Aboriginal sports and recreation advisory council, and that Aboriginal youth and Aboriginal experts in the field – recreation and sports programmers, co-ordinators, administrators and researchers – be invited to take part in this discussion.

Co-operative Home Construction

4.4.6

Co-operative home construction, based on the Habitat for Humanity model, be initiated in Aboriginal communities to provide housing, employment and construction skills for Aboriginal youth.

Canada-Wide
Policy Framework

4.4.7

Federal, provincial and territorial governments develop and adopt, through the leadership of the Ministry of State for Youth, and in close consultation with Aboriginal youth and their representative organizations, a comprehensive Canada-wide policy framework to guide initiatives and programs directed to Aboriginal youth.

Key Program Areas

4.4.8

Key program areas for a Canada-wide Aboriginal youth policy be education, justice, health and healing, sports and recreation, and support programs for urban Aboriginal youth:

(a) Education in the broadest sense must be a priority, with greater efforts to develop a culturally appropriate curriculum that reinforces the value of Aboriginal culture. Transformative education – which uses students' personal experiences as a springboard for deeper analysis and understanding of the world around them – should be considered in developing initiatives in education.

(b) The justice and corrections system has a substantial impact on youth. New programs should be developed and existing programs modified to focus on reintegrating youth into the community through approaches that reflect Aboriginal culture.

(c) Health and healing must reflect the needs of Aboriginal youth, particularly in the areas of counselling and support.

(d) Sports and recreation must be treated as an integral part of Aboriginal youth policy. Increased resources for facilities and programming are needed, as are trained people to coordinate sports and recreation programs for Aboriginal youth. Also, the sports community – athletes and fans – must be seen as a way to build and strengthen relationships among Aboriginal and non-Aboriginal people.

(e) Aboriginal youth in urban areas need innovative programs to help them bridge the traditional and urban worlds and support their choices about where and how to live.

Developing and
Implementing
Youth Policy

4.4.9

All governments pursue the following goals in developing and implementing a Canada-wide Aboriginal youth policy: youth participation at all levels, leadership development, economic development and cultural rebirth, youth involvement in nation building, and cultural and spiritual development.

Monitoring Progress and Setting Priorities

4.4.10

The federal government provide funding for a biennial conference of Aboriginal youth delegates and invited representatives from government and non-government organizations, the purpose of which would be to

(a) review progress over the preceding 24 months on goals established under the Canada-wide Aboriginal youth policy; and

(b) set priorities for new policies and programs where a need is identified by delegates.

Chapter 5 Métis Perspectives

The Commission recommends that

Nation-to-Nation Approach

4.5.1

Political negotiation on a nation-to-nation or analogous basis be the primary method of resolving Métis issues.

Métis Identity

4.5.2

Every person who

(a) identifies himself or herself as Métis, and

(b) is accepted as such by the nation of Métis people with which that person wishes to be associated, on the basis of criteria and procedures determined by that nation,

be recognized as a member of that nation for purposes of nation-to-nation negotiations and as Métis for that purpose.

Section 91(24) Coverage

4.5.3

The government of Canada either

(a) acknowledge that section 91(24) of the *Constitution Act, 1867* applies to Métis people and base its legislation, policies and programs on that recognition; or

(b) collaborate with appropriate provincial governments and with Métis representatives in the formulation and enactment of a constitutional amendment specifying that section 91(24) applies to Métis people.

If it is unwilling to take either of these steps, the government of Canada make a constitutional reference to the Supreme Court of Canada, asking that court to decide whether section 91(24) of the *Constitution Act, 1867* applies to Métis people.

Constitutional **4.5.4**
Confirmation of The substance of the constitutional amendments relating to the
Alberta Metis Metis Settlements of Alberta, referred to in section 55 of the
Settlements Charlottetown Accord and contained in sections 12 and 23 of
the Draft Legal Text of 9 October 1992, be enacted as soon as
possible by joint action of the Parliament and government of
Canada and the legislature and government of Alberta.

Education **4.5.5**

When implementing this Commission's recommendations on
education affecting Aboriginal persons, great care be exercised
to ensure the preservation and propagation of distinct Métis cultures. Measures to achieve that goal might include, where
appropriate,

(a) consultation with Métis elders when educational programs
are being planned;

(b) establishment of and public funding support of separate
Métis schools where numbers warrant;

(c) assisted access to post-secondary education for Métis persons;

(d) creation of a college or faculty of Métis studies and professorships, scholarships and programs of Métis studies; and

(e) provision of residential facilities in post-secondary educational institutions that will be congenial to Métis students.

Culture and **4.5.6**
Language When implementing the recommendations made in Volume 3,
all governments and relevant agencies bear in mind the distinct
circumstances of Métis culture and languages.

Governments and private authorities and agencies should collaborate with authorized Métis representatives on measures to
preserve, cultivate and study elements of Métis culture, including the following:

(a) Aboriginal languages: to encourage and assist Métis people
to learn and use the Aboriginal languages with which their
Métis ancestors were historically associated;

(b) Michif language: to implement, with Métis collaboration
and public funding, special measures to save Michif from
extinction and to encourage and assist Michif research and
instruction;

(c) research and publications about Métis history and culture: to provide financial support for research and publi-

cations to disseminate information about Métis Nation history and culture by means of print, radio, television, film, theatre and other modes of expression;

(d) historical sites: to establish major Métis cultural history centres at historically significant sites such as Batoche and the Forks in Winnipeg, to be owned and operated by Métis representatives; and

(e) repatriation of artifacts: to repatriate major Métis artifacts from public and private collections to appropriate Métis-run locations.

Métis Land Bases **4.5.7**

The governments of Canada and the relevant provinces and territories be prepared to make available, through negotiations with each recognized nation of Métis people, land bases sufficient in number, size, location and quality to permit the fulfilment of the nation's legitimate social, cultural, political and economic aspirations.

Métis Right to Hunt and Fish for Food **4.5.8**

The governments of Manitoba, Saskatchewan and Alberta

(a) recognize immediately that the right, under the *Constitution Act, 1930*, of "Indians" of those provinces to hunt, trap and fish for food in all seasons on unoccupied Crown land and other land to which they have a right of access applies to all Métis persons in those provinces;

(b) consult with leaders of the Métis Nation when determining who qualifies as a Métis person for that purpose;

(c) give the same right to non-status Indians residing in the prairie provinces after they have demonstrated their Aboriginal ancestry by some prescribed and fair method; and

(d) give the same right to Aboriginal persons residing outside the prairie provinces unless it has been extinguished by a legally binding extinguishment measure, and extend the right, where appropriate, to public waters.

Interim and Permanent Land Use Agreements **4.5.9**

Federal, provincial and territorial governments

(a) be prepared to enter into temporary land use agreements with Métis nations while land claims negotiations are pending or continuing; and

(b) be prepared, where appropriate, to consider longer-term
       land use agreements with Métis nations, perhaps in asso-
       ciation with other interests, Aboriginal or private.

Negotiations on **4.5.10**
Métis Self-   The governments of Canada and of relevant provinces and ter-
Government   ritories

   (a) be prepared to negotiate immediately with appropriate
       Métis representatives (as well as, where appropriate, other
       Aboriginal governments) on the manner in which Métis
       self-government will be recognized by and integrated with
       other governments and assisted to become financially self-
       sufficient; and

   (b) pursue independently and swiftly those aspects of self-gov-
       ernment that are not dependent upon land base consider-
       ations, although it will be appropriate for part of these
       negotiations to take place in the context of negotiations
       concerning the nation's land base.

Chapter 6 The North

The Commission recommends that

Nations and Public **4.6.1**
Territorial   Dene of Denendeh (Northwest Territories) be given the oppor-
Government   tunity to come to future negotiations on new political arrange-
                    ments in Denendeh as a nation.

4.6.2
A treaty commission be established at the request of Dene
communities seeking a treaty process.

4.6.3
The treaty commission's deliberations be the means by which
the governing authorities for Dene are determined within the
new western territory in addition to the framework of public
government for that territory as a whole.

4.6.4
Those charged with developing institutions for Denendeh recognize the leading role Aboriginal nation government will play
across the territory and design a form of territorial government
that exercises lead responsibility in relatively few areas and plays

a co-ordinating role with other governments' activities where appropriate.

4.6.5

Communities that want to participate in a treaty implementation process rather than regional land claims be given the same range of flexibility in terms of subject matter and quantity of land as if they were participating in a land claims process.

High Cost of Government in the North

4.6.6

In Nunavut and in the remaining part of the Northwest Territories, future arrangements allocate clear responsibilities between Aboriginal nation governments and territorial institutions and be kept simple and focused, given the high cost of government across a widely dispersed population.

Public Education

4.6.7

Public education materials be developed in co-operation with Aboriginal communications groups to explain the institutional changes taking place in Nunavut and the remaining part of the Northwest Territories.

Aboriginal People in Environmental Stewardship

4.6.8

The government of Canada recognize the contribution of Aboriginal traditional knowledge to environmental stewardship and support its development.

4.6.9

The government of Canada make provisions for the participation of Aboriginal governments and organizations in future international agreements concerning environmental stewardship.

4.6.10

The federal department of health continue the close monitoring of contamination of northern country food by atmospheric and other pollution and, given the importance of these foods to northern people, communicate the results of this work quickly and effectively to users of these renewable northern resources.

4.6.11

All governments in Canada support the development of co-management regimes along the lines of those already established in the North.

Redesign of
Income Programs

4.6.12

Federal and territorial governments establish a task force with strong Aboriginal representation to review all social assistance and income supplement programs across the territorial North with the goal of restructuring these programs to make them effective instruments in promoting a mixed economy and sustain viable, largely self-reliant communities.

4.6.13

Based on the work of the task force recommended in 4.6.12 and recognizing the fundamental changes under way in the structure and administration of social assistance programs across Canada, territorial governments take the initiative, in consultation with federal and provincial governments, to create a northern social policy framework with sufficient flexibility to allow existing levels of social assistance spending to be used to fund community work creation and provide income supplements related to community employment or traditional production and harvesting.

4.6.14

Employment insurance and social assistance legislation be amended to take into account the specific differences in employment patterns, the high cost of living, the administrative delays that result from great distances between communities, and other factors unique to the northern economy.

Skilled
Management
Supports

4.6.15

Aboriginal, federal, provincial and territorial governments encourage innovative means of delivering skilled management support – including operations, financial and marketing expertise – to small enterprises through Aboriginal economic development corporations.

Research Program

4.6.16

Faculties of agriculture, forestry and business administration in Canadian universities, in collaboration with the proposed Aboriginal Peoples International University, develop a northern research program focused on the creation of employment and business opportunities through the use of the renewable resources sector, the exportation of traditional foods and food products, and the development of expertise to manage these resources at sustainable levels.

Hiring Criteria **4.6.17**

All governments hiring personnel for northern and remote communities take into account skills acquired through life experience and the demonstrated capacity to develop new skills along with, and at times in place of, formal educational credentials.

Accommodating the Traditional Economy **4.6.18**

Government employment policies accommodate the demands of traditional economic activities by increasing opportunities for job sharing, periodic leave and shift work.

Stable Funding for Education and Training **4.6.19**

Governments provide stable multi-year funding to northern educational institutions that have the capacity to deliver the education and training needed for self-government and a diversified economy.

Education and Institutional Development **4.6.20**

The education and training of Aboriginal adults and young people form an integral part of all plans for institutional development in the North.

Support for Traditional Knowledge **4.6.21**

Governments provide continuing support for the development of institutes that gather and research traditional knowledge and apply it to contemporary issues.

4.6.22

Traditional knowledge be incorporated in all appropriate institutions, including cultural and research institutes, regulatory boards and the education and training system.

Chapter 7 Urban Perspectives

The Commission recommends that

Cultural Identity **4.7.1**

Aboriginal cultural identity be supported and enhanced in urban areas by
(a) Aboriginal, municipal, territorial, provincial and federal governments initiating programs to increase opportunities to promote Aboriginal culture in urban communities, including means to increase access to Aboriginal elders;
(b) municipal governments and institutions and Aboriginal elders co-operating to find ways of facilitating Aboriginal spiritual practices in the urban environment; and

(c) all governments co-operating to set aside land in urban areas dedicated to Aboriginal cultural and spiritual needs.

Financing Social Programs   **4.7.2**

The federal government be responsible for

(a) the costs associated with developing, implementing and operating Aboriginal self-government initiatives on and off a land base through program funding and fiscal arrangements;

(b) programs, services and treaty entitlements for Aboriginal people living on reserves or extended Aboriginal territories;

(c) treaty entitlements or agreed upon social programs such as financial assistance for post-secondary education and uninsured health benefits for Indian people living off-reserve, to the extent that these exceed the programs or services provided to other residents by the province or territory in which they reside; and

(d) the cost of services for Métis people agreed to in treaty negotiations, once they have achieved self-government and a land base, including additional payments to Métis people living off their land base to cover benefits agreed to by treaty where those exceed benefits normally available to other provincial residents.

4.7.3

Provincial and territorial governments be responsible for

(a) providing and financing the programs and services that are available to residents in general, to all Aboriginal people residing in the province or territory, except those resident on-reserve, in Inuit communities or on extended Aboriginal territory; and

(b) providing programs and services for Aboriginal people that are culturally appropriate where numbers warrant.

Financing Affirmative Action Programs   **4.7.4**

The cost of affirmative action programs and services to address economic and social disadvantage affecting urban Aboriginal people be shared by the federal, provincial and territorial governments on the basis of a formula basis that reflects provincial/territorial fiscal capacity.

Aboriginal Service Institutions   **4.7.5**

Provincial, territorial and municipal governments give priority to making the existing Aboriginal service delivery system more comprehensive as the most effective means of meeting the immediate needs of urban Aboriginal people.

4.7.6
Federal, provincial and territorial governments ensure that existing and new Aboriginal service institutions have a stable and secure funding base by
(a) making contribution and grant agreements with Aboriginal service institutions for periods of at least five years; and
(b) adjusting funding for existing and new Aboriginal and non-Aboriginal agencies to reflect actual services provided and caseloads.

Non-Aboriginal Service Agencies

4.7.7
Aboriginal people and organizations be directly involved in the design, development, delivery and evaluation of all services provided to Aboriginal clients by non-Aboriginal agencies.

4.7.8
Staff of non-Aboriginal service agencies directly involved in Aboriginal service delivery be given cross-cultural training delivered by Aboriginal people and organizations and that government funding agreements reflect this obligation.

Status-Blind versus Separate Institutions

4.7.9
Services to Aboriginal people in urban areas generally be delivered without regard to legal or treaty status.

4.7.10
Government policies on service delivery take into account the history and tradition of separate institutional development for Métis and treaty people in Manitoba, Saskatchewan and Alberta as well as local cultural, political and economic conditions.

Youth Services

4.7.11
Aboriginal governments and organizations accord higher priority to youth programming, particularly leadership development, sport and recreation.

4.7.12
Municipal, provincial, territorial and federal governments support, fund and actively provide services and programs for urban Aboriginal youth.

4.7.13
Aboriginal youth be closely involved in the design, development and delivery of youth services.

Support for Disabilities Organization

4.7.14
The federal government provide funding for a national organization to represent and speak on behalf of Aboriginal people with disabilities.

National Friendship Centre Program

4.7.15
The federal government devolve the administration of the National Aboriginal Friendship Centre program to the National Association of Friendship Centres.

Urban Cultural Education Program

4.7.16
The federal government establish and fund a national urban Aboriginal cultural education program designed for Aboriginal and non-Aboriginal people in large urban centres across Canada, to be generally administered by friendship centres.

Aboriginal Women in Urban Areas

4.7.17
Aboriginal women give Aboriginal and non-Aboriginal service agencies direction and guidance in formulating policy and developing services that may be used by Aboriginal women and children and participate fully in the delivery of programs and services established specifically to meet the needs of urban Aboriginal women.

4.7.18
In addition to cross-cultural training, non-Aboriginal individuals and organizations whose work or responsibilities directly affect urban Aboriginal women's lives receive comprehensive information and education on the situation of urban Aboriginal women.

Representation of Urban Aboriginal People

4.7.19
Positions be designated for Aboriginal representatives on local boards and commissions responsible for services and the boards of institutions in which Aboriginal people have a significant interest.

4.7.20
Municipal councils and school boards in municipalities with a large Aboriginal population establish Aboriginal affairs committees to provide advice and guidance on Aboriginal issues.

4.7.21

Municipal, provincial, territorial and federal governments seek opportunities for co-management arrangements that would involve Aboriginal people in establishing, managing and operating urban institutions, programs and services in which they have an interest.

Urban
Community of
Interest
Approaches

4.7.22

Where urban Aboriginal residents wish to pursue self-government based on an urban community of interest, whether involved in multiple government functions or acting through a single institution,

(a) municipal, provincial and federal governments foster and support community building, including, where appropriate, developing the community of interest's governance initiative; and

(b) municipal, provincial and federal governments participate in negotiations to establish urban community of interest governments and assist them in operating institutions and services for members of the community of interest.

Nation-Based
Approaches

4.7.23

Nation-based urban governance initiatives be pursued by nations when they have sufficient capacity to assume governance responsibility for the needs and interests of urban Aboriginal citizens.

4.7.24

The urban citizens of Aboriginal nations be fully consulted and participate in decisions concerning urban governance initiatives pursued by nations.

4.7.25

Aboriginal nations ensure that their urban citizens' needs and interests are recognized and that mechanisms are instituted to ensure they are represented in the political structures and decision-making processes of the nation.

4.7.26

Federal, provincial, territorial and municipal governments give full support to Aboriginal nations when they develop and implement urban governance initiatives.

Appendix B

Abridged Tables of Contents Volumes 1-3 and Volume 5[*]

VOLUME I
Looking Forward, Looking Back

---

[*] Tables of contents in the volumes themselves may be slightly different, as a result of final editing.

VOLUME 2
RESTRUCTURING
THE RELATIONSHIP

PART ONE

VOLUME 3

GATHERING STRENGTH

6. Arts and Heritage